THE EVOLUTION OF
THE ENGLISH LANGUAGE

Geoffrey Chaucer (1340?-1400): first page of the "Prologue" to the *Canterbury Tales* from an illuminated manuscript of the first quarter of the fifteenth century. (Brit. Mus. Harleian Ms. 7334.)

THE EVOLUTION OF
THE ENGLISH LANGUAGE

from Chaucer to the Twentieth Century

FORMERLY TITLED MODERN ENGLISH IN THE MAKING

BY GEORGE H. McKNIGHT

with the assistance of Bert Emsley

DOVER PUBLICATIONS, INC., NEW YORK

This Dover edition, first published in 1968, is an
unabridged and unaltered republication of the work
originally published by D. Appleton and Company
in 1928 under the title *Modern English in the Making*. This edition is published by arrangement with
Appleton-Century-Crofts, a division of the Meredith
Publishing Company, New York City.

Library of Congress Catalog Card Number: 68-17396

Manufactured in the United States of America
Dover Publications, Inc.
180 Varick Street
New York, N. Y. 10014

PREFACE

The miracle of our land's speech—so known
And long received, none marvel when 'tis shown.

The modern world, Mr. Kipling believes, is too placid in its acceptance of its inherited wealth in language. In this view the present writer concurs. A traditional mode of speech is accepted with too little thought of the time required and the pains bestowed before it reached its present stage of development. The English language, it should be realized, is not a wayside tree that has grown up wild; it is, rather, a highly cultivated plant which has been crossbred with other languages, which has for centuries been grafted and pruned, and which has been forced in its growth in a soil fertilized by classical culture. Surely the stages in its growth and the processes employed in its development deserve to be more widely known.

In the present book attempt is made to show the principal changes that have taken place in the English language since the adoption in the fourteenth century of the East Midland dialect as the standard form of English. Effort is made to show the natural tendencies that have affected its growth and at the same time to exhibit the methods employed in its cultivation. An account is offered of its embellishment under the influence of classical rhetoric, its enrichment by borrowed elements, its molding under the influence of Latin spelling and Latin syntax, and later the more independent cultivation of its native qualities.

Of practical benefit should be a better understanding provided for the language of our own day. The natural speech of Chaucer and the plastic language which Shakespeare molded into artistic form have been succeeded by a more rigid language. Two and a half years of a modern child's school life, it has been estimated, are consumed in the effort, sometimes vain, to bring his language, his spelling, his pronunciation, his use of word and phrase, into conformity with the rigid form which is now accepted as standard. The freedom and naturalness associated with the phrase "the Mother Tongue" have yielded to a form of tyranny suggested by the phrase "the King's English." Only through a knowledge of earlier stages in the history of the language is one enabled to understand this modern government and to estimate properly the authority of its laws.

For the prevalent lack of knowledge concerning earlier stages in the history of English an explanation is easily found. In order to win the attention of the reader to productions in earlier literature, the modern editor has too often felt it necessary to modernize the form. In consequence the reader of our time not only has little idea of the sound of the language of Chaucer or of Shakespeare, but he is left in ignorance of earlier modes of spelling, of earlier grammatical forms, of earlier words and earlier meanings of words.

For this inadequate knowledge of the English of earlier periods it is hoped that the present work may provide a partial remedy. It is hoped that the teacher may obtain a more precise knowledge of the laws governing the modern form of English which he aims to interpret. It is hoped also that not only the teacher but the general reader may find matter for entertainment and even for amusement. In the history of the language one is able to observe progress in culture and the shaping power of genius. One may observe not only changing social ideals but exhibitions of amusing ignorance, of vain aspiration to culture, of snobbish pretention and pedantic folly. In fact, in the development of a medium for communication may be observed many of the most amusing elements of the human comedy.

There is, perhaps, one general impression deserving special emphasis. The standardization of modern English is not as nearly complete as is sometimes supposed. The language ideal of philosophers like Locke has never been realized. Idealistic efforts like those of Bishop Wilkins in the seventeenth century, of "Hermes" Harris in the eighteenth century, of Goold Brown and Richard Grant White in the nineteenth century, have been only partially successful. The English language has not been subjected to absolute rule like the Sanskrit language governed by the grammar of Panini. In other words, English is not yet a dead language. A distinguished student of jurisprudence has recently expressed a vital truth regarding political law by means of a striking paradox. "Law," says Roscoe Pound, "must be stable and yet cannot stand still." The statement applies with little modification to the case of language. Language, though regulated, is not fixed for all time but must change in company with changing conditions of life. Like human nature, of which it is a mirror, language has imperfections; and like human nature, its prospects of absolute perfection are distant and uncertain.

The debts incurred in the preparation of the present work have been numerous and heavy. Attempt is made in the footnotes to indicate the principal sources of borrowed information and borrowed ideas. The extent of the borrowing and the great amount of the debt are in part indicated by the number of citations registered in the index. A formal bibliography of earlier works on the English language it has seemed unnecessary to include on account of the recent appearance of the monumental Bibliography by Professor A. G. Kennedy, a work upon which all future workers in this field must rely.

There remains the pleasant duty of recording personal obligations to friends and colleagues. M. O. Percival has read with critical observation large sections both in manuscript and in the proof sheets. Other sections have been read by C. E. Andrews, E. H. McNeal, and J. W. Markland. The grateful acknowledgment here expressed, however, should not inculpate these friends in any of the sins of omission or commission which will doubtless be found in this book.

G. H. McK.

CONTENTS

PAGE

PREFACE v

CHAPTER

I. CHAOS 1

II. THE FIRSTE FYNDERE OF OUR FAIRE LANGAGE   17

III. CHAUCER'S SUCCESSORS AND THE AUREATE
        LANGUAGE 38

IV. CAXTON AND THE PRINTING PRESS . . . 56

V. TRANSITION FROM MIDDLE ENGLISH TO MOD-
        ERN ENGLISH 70

VI. HUMANISM 86

VII. PURISM 110

VIII. SIXTEENTH-CENTURY RHETORIC . . . 124

IX. SHAKESPEARE AND RHETORIC 151

X. SHAKESPEARE AND THE LANGUAGE OF HIS
        TIME 166

XI. CLASSICISM AND THE SCHOOLMASTER . . . 213

XII. THE RESTORATION PERIOD 264

XIII. THE AUGUSTAN AGE 296

XIV. JOHNSON'S DICTIONARY 351

XV. EIGHTEENTH-CENTURY GRAMMARIANS . . 377

XVI. ENGLISH PURISTS AND SCOTCH RHETORICIANS   400

XVII. THE ART OF POINTING, OR PUNCTUATION . 417

CONTENTS

CHAPTER   PAGE

XVIII. FIXING THE PRONUNCIATION 428

XIX. BEGINNINGS OF AMERICAN ENGLISH . . . 460

XX. THE NINETEENTH CENTURY 495

XXI. REVOLT 539

XXII. MODERN SPELLING AND PRONUNCIATION . . 559

APPENDICES

I. THE NEAR RELATIONS OF ENGLISH 577

II. DISTANT RELATIONS OF ENGLISH 580

INDEX 583

ILLUSTRATIONS

Geoffrey Chaucer (1340?-1400): first page of the "Prologue" to the *Canterbury Tales* from an illuminated manuscript of the first quarter of the fifteenth century
frontispiece

PAGE

A page from an illuminated manuscript of Lydgate's *Troy Book* . . . . *facing*   42

Page from the *Æsop* printed by Caxton, Westminster, 1483   59

King Henry VII (1457-1509): portion of a page of a signed document concerning the raising of funds wherewith to prosecute war against Scotland . *facing*   74

The House of Learning, from G. Reisch, *Margarita Philosophica,* 1503 . . . . *facing*   96

William Shakespeare (1564-1616): portion of the third of three pages in *The Booke of Sir Thomas More* which by many experts are believed to be in the handwriting of Shakespeare . . . . *facing*   192

Ben Jonson (1573-1637): dedicatory epistle to *The Masque of Queenes* (1609)   212

Antony and Cleopatra, Act I, Scene iv: First Folio (1623)   237

Antony and Cleopatra, Act I, Scene iv: Second Folio (1632)   238

Antony and Cleopatra, Act I, Scene iv: Third Folio (1664)   239

Antony and Cleopatra, Act I, Scene iv: Fourth Folio (1685)   240

John Milton (1608-1674): manuscript of the sonnet, "On His Having Arrived at the Age of Twenty-Three" *facing*   244

PAGE

John Dryden (1631-1700) : letter to Lawrence Hyde, Earl of Rochester, First Lord of the Treasury, on his necessities, etc.; without date, but probably written in 1682 or 1683 275

Joseph Addison (1672-1719) : conclusion of a letter written to J. Robethon, Secretary to George I, on the King's accession; dated Sept. 4, 1714 299

Daniel De Foe (1660-1731) : letter to Charles Montaigne, Lord Halifax, expressing gratitude for his favors, etc.; without date (1705?) 339

Charles Dickens (1812-1870) : a page of the manuscript of *Pickwick Papers* . . . . *facing* 422

Benjamin Franklin (1706-1790) : autograph letter showing among other things the use of capital letters favored by Franklin 425

Sir Walter Scott (1771-1832) : a page of the manuscript of *Kenilworth* . . . . *facing* 522

THE EVOLUTION OF
THE ENGLISH LANGUAGE

CHAPTER I

CHAOS

THERE has recently come from China a charming bit of comedy-romance turning on the language situation in that disorganized country. A young man from Canton and a young woman from Shanghai fell in love with each other. But a difficulty arose. They were confronted, not in this case by parental objections, but by an inability to communicate their sentiments owing to the difference between the language spoken in Canton and that in Shanghai. The situation was not an unusual one in China with its variant forms of local speech. Fortunately this story has a happy ending. These Chinese young people found a way out of their difficulty through use of a foreign language, English, which they had learned in the schools.

A parallel situation is inconceivable among educated English-speaking people of the modern world. A standardized form of English makes communication possible, not only between the millions of educated people in England or in the United States, but among English-speaking people in the most distant parts of the world. And yet there was a time when the language situation in England was not unlike that in modern China, when for communication between people of different parts of England resort must be had to a foreign language, either to French or to the universal learned language of that period, Latin. Going back about six centuries to the early fourteenth century, one finds the Midland writer, Robert Mannyng of Brunne, remarking that:

> Many hear good English rhymes
> Who their sense know not oft-times

and in another place, speaking of the English romance, *Sir Tristrem,* saying:

> 'Tis in such strange speech, I wis
> Many know not what it is.[1]

Later in the same century one learns from John de Trevisa that, "som useth straunge wlaffrynge chiterynge harrynge and garrynge grysbitinge." By these strange terms he expresses the uncouth effect produced by the sounds in dialects not familiar, much as in an earlier age the Greeks had expressed their feeling for the sounds in foreign speech by inventing for these sounds the imitative word *barbarous.* Trevisa in another place is more specific. He says that "Al the longage of the Northumbres and specialliche at York is so sharp slittynge and frotynge and vnschape, that we southern men may that longage vnnethe ['hardly'] vnderstonde."

From these words of a contemporary writer one may gain an impression of the diversity in the English used in different parts of England in the fourteenth century, a diversity which persists today in the dialectal speech of England. Not only were men from the North unintelligible to men of the South in oral speech, but literary works composed in one part of the country had to be translated in order to be understood in other parts. There is preserved

[1] Modern rendering by J. L. Weston.

one cycle of sacred poems, of the school of Richard Rolle of Hampole, which, according to one manuscript, is "translated out of northern tunge into southern, that it schulde the better be vnderstondyn of men of the selue ['same'] countreye." On the other hand, one version of the legend of the Assumption was translated from Southern to Northern English:

> In sotherin englis was it draun ['composed']
> And turnd ['translated'] it haue i till our aun
> Langage o northrin lede ['people']
> That can nan other englis rede.[2]

Only six centuries ago the English language was apparently in as chaotic a state as the oral language of China today. In the ensuing centuries, however, there has been developed a common form of English which education makes available in all parts of the English-speaking world. It is the development of this common standard of English speech which forms the subject of the present book.

For the purpose in mind we are not concerned with the remote origins of the English language. A search for origins would conduct one to the continent of Europe whence the Angles and Saxons brought the English language to Great Britain in the fifth century A.D. It would lead back to the common Teutonic language from which descended not only the language of the Angles and Saxons, but the modern languages of Holland and Germany and the Scandinavian countries. It would lead still farther back to the Indo-European language from which descended not only the Teutonic languages, but the language of the Romans, that of the Greeks, that of the Celtic races, that of the Slavic races, and the ancient languages of Persia and India. Such remote origins are not of present concern.

Nor are we immediately concerned with the earlier stages

[2] *Cursor Mundi,* 2061-64.

in the history of the English language in Great Britain. The development of the English language was considerable before the Norman Conquest. But during this period the cultivated form of speech was the Southern English of Alfred's kingdom of Wessex, the kingdom which had not London but Winchester for its capital, a form of English which was later degraded to use as the clown dialect of the Elizabethan dramatists and in our own time is confined to the use of rustics in Southern England. During this early period the form of English that has developed into the literary language of today was still a minor dialect.

The history of the cultivation of modern standard English has its beginning in the fourteenth century. In that century came the restoration of English to its natural place as the official and the literary language of England. In that century also came about the elevation of one of the English dialects to rank as a standard for cultivated use, and from that time begins the cultivation which has been continuous through the ensuing six centuries. The circumstances explaining these beginnings of modern standard English, however, are to be found in the chaotic language conditions prevailing during the Middle English period, that following the Norman Conquest.

The effect of the Norman Conquest on the English language had been shattering. A language which had belonged to official life and to the use of nobles and peasants alike, in which had been composed literary work of enduring worth, was reduced in station and limited to the domestic use of the lower classes. The French language became the language of the higher classes of whatever racial descent. "Vor bote a man conne Frenss, ne telth of him lute," ['For unless a man knows French, he is held of little account,'] says Robert of Gloucester writing in 1298. "Also gentil men ['noblemen's'] children beth Itaught forto speke

frensche from the tyme that they beeth Irokked in here
cradul and kunneth speke and play with a childs broche
and oplondisshe ['country'] men wil likne hem self to gentil
men and fondeth ['try'] for to speke frensche forto be
Itold of." Thus writes Ralph Higden about 1350. When
one recalls further that French was the language used in
the Parliament of the period and in the law courts and that
French was the language used in the instruction of the
grammar schools, one can readily realize the necessity of
a knowledge of French for anyone of consequence, for anyone who acquired learning, for anyone who had property
rights to defend, for anyone who cared to participate in
public affairs. The situation of the English language, for
the most part confined to the use of the uncultivated classes,
in its relation to French was in many ways like that of the
native Irish language in relation to English in the Ireland
of today. A parallel even closer perhaps is to be found in
the relation of Welsh to English in modern Wales. In the
relation of the native English to the foreign languages,
French and Latin, one is again reminded of the present-day
situation in China.

In this period in England, as in other countries of Europe,
Latin was the language of learning. In Latin were composed the works for the clerk, or scholar. But French was
the language used in the composition of works intended for
the entertainment of the chivalrous society of the period.
The literary use of English in the two centuries following
the Conquest was confined to compositions, few in number
and largely religious in nature, intended for the edification
of people of humble station.

For lewde ['uncultivated'] men y vndyrtoke ['undertook']
On englyssh tunge to make thys boke

writes Robert of Brunne in his *Handlyng Synne* (1303).

Is this romaunce of freyns ['French'] wrou3t
That mani lewed ['uneducated'] no knowe nou3t.

.   .   .   .

This lewed no can freyns non
Among an hundred vnneÞe on ['hardly one'].

Thus writes the English translator of a French romance of about the same period.

The gradual rise in importance of the English language, however, may be traced from about the middle of the thirteenth century on. In the struggle of the barons against the power of the king in the course of that century there grew up a popular hostility to the use of the foreign language. Matthew of Westminster, writing concerning the year 1263, says that "whoever was unable to speak the English language was considered a vile and contemptible person by the common people." It should be recalled that Edward I, who came to the throne in 1272, was the first king since the Conquest to bear a Saxon English name. During his reign, and particularly during the reign of his grandson Edward III, there was a remarkable rise in English national feeling associated with the wars against the French and the glorious victories of Edward III and his famous son, the Black Prince. This national feeling is reflected in a remarkable rise in the prestige of the native tongue. Its use was adopted even among the nobility.

Many noble ich haue ysei3e ['I have seen']
Þat no freynsche couÞe seye ['could speak']

writes the English translator of the romance of *Arthur and Merlin*. By the middle of the fourteenth century the English language had been in part restored to use even in royal circles. This may be inferred from the words of the English translator of the romance of *William of Palerne* (about 1350), who calls upon the reader to say a paternoster for the Earl of Hereford, Sir Humphrey of Bowne, grandson of Edward I, who

> First caused the fair tale to translate
> In ese of englysch men in englysch speche
>
> . . . . .
>
> He let make this mater in þis maner speche
> For hem that knowe no frensche ne neuer vnderston.

The restoration of the English language to its natural place was a slow and gradual process. The restoration, however, was practically completed in the decade 1360-70. In the year 1362 Parliament was opened by the Chancellor's address in the English language. In the same year it was decreed by royal statute that English should be the language used in English law courts. About the same time came a change of equal significance, the replacement of French by English in English schools. Ralph Higden in his Latin *Polychronicon,* written about 1350, speaks of the use of French in English school instruction. His English translator, John de Trevisa, writing in 1385, inserts in his translation an original note in which he informs the reader that the use of French in English grammar-school instruction continued down to the year of the first visitation of the Plague (1349), but that John Cornwaile introduced the use of English, a practice which was followed by Richard Pentrych, so that by 1385, the date of writing, "in all the grammar schools of England, children have abandoned French and construe and learn English." He recognizes in this change a loss, since, as a result, "children in grammar schools know no more French than does their left heel" and are in consequence at a disadvantage when they "cross the sea and travel in foreign countries."

Trevisa makes also the interesting remark that "gentil men ['noblemen'] have in great part given up the practice of teaching French to their children." The significance of this remark must not be lost sight of. Among the nobility the use of French was firmly intrenched. French literary fashions had persisted at the English court. The distinguished French poet Jean Froissart found a generous patron in the English queen Philippa, wife of Edward III, and spent a number of years at the English court serving as her secretary. Later in life, when he revisited England, he brought as a gift to the king, Richard II, a handsomely bound volume of French verse. The literary career of the English poet John Gower is also significant. In his earlier years he followed the contemporary fashion and wrote in French a number of *ballades* and a long work entitled *Mirour de l'Omme,* or *Speculum Meditantis.* Later in life he composed a second ambitious work, the *Vox Clamantis,* this time using the Latin language. Only in his later years did he conform to changed conditions and in his third long poem, the *Confessio Amantis,* use his native English.

That English was firmly established in royal circles in the last decades of the fourteenth century is certain. Gower in his English *Confessio Amantis* informs the reader that the work was undertaken by direct commission from King Richard II. Even more significant is the fact that Richard's young queen, the foreign-born Anne of Bohemia, acquired the English language. The Archbishop of Canterbury in preaching her funeral sermon said "that it was more joye of here than of any woman that ever he knewe. For she, an alien borne, hadde *in englisshe* all the IIII gospels with the doctours upon them "

John of Gaunt, too, uncle of the King and a dominant figure in the national life of his time, on one occasion of which there is record came to the defense of the English language. A bill had been introduced into Parliament to "adnulle" the Bible translated into English with other

English books in exposition of the Gospels. This anti-Wycliffite measure John of Gaunt violently opposed, and he declared: "We will not be refuse of all other nacions; for sythen they have Goddes law whiche is the lawe of oure belefe in there owne langage, we will have oures in Englishe whosoever say naye." And this, we are told, "he affermyd with a great othe."

By the end of the fourteenth century the position of the English language was assured. Henry IV, who came to the throne in 1399, was the first English king since the Conquest to whom English was the mother tongue. The opening of his reign was marked by the official use of English in Henry's formal challenge for the crown and his thanks to Parliament, also in the speech of the Chief Justice announcing the deposition of Richard II.

The relative positions of the three languages, Latin, French, and English, at the end of the fourteenth century is made clear in the words of Thomas Usk in his *Testament of Love* written about 1385. After discussing vain attempts of Englishmen to write French and of Frenchmen to write English, Usk concludes: "Let than clerkys endyten in Latin, for they have the propertee of science, and the knowinge in that facultee; and let Frenchmen in their Frenche also endyten their queynt termes, for it is kyndely to their mouthes; and let us shewe our fantasyes in suche wordes as we lerneden of our dames tonge."

But the task of reëstablishing the English mother tongue in cultivated use, of making it an effective medium for literary composition, was not a simple one. It must be held in mind that for three hundred years following the Norman Conquest there was no literary production in English by a literary artist of prominence or by a thinker of world influence. This does not mean that for three centuries England was entirely barren in culture. The noble

architecture that has come down from that period is sufficient to dispel any such idea. Nor does it mean that there
was no activity in literature. Names such as those of
Geoffrey of Monmouth, Gerald de Barry, Walter Map,
Roger Bacon, John of Salisbury, Duns Scotus, John of
Garland, and Robert Grosseteste, provide evidence to the
contrary. Such names lend distinction to the literature of
England but do not ordinarily appear on the honor roll
of English writers because the bearers wrote not in English but in Latin. In England, too, especially in the earlier
part of this period, were produced works which have an
honored place in the history of French literature. Such
writers as Wace, Benoit de Ste. More, Marie de France,
Robert de Boron, and Thomas, the Tristan poet, would
occupy distinguished places in the history of English literature if they had written in the language of the land whose
kings they served instead of in French.

But literature in English during this long period has no
such distinguished names to boast of. Lacking literary
cultivation and confined to the use of the "lewed" or uncultivated, English had become an impoverished language.
Much of its earlier wealth in word and phrase was lost.
Moreover, there was, as has already been pointed out, an
entire lack in uniformity. In the small number of English
writings that had been produced, each writer had been in
great part a law unto himself, making use of the form
of language current in the part of the country to which he
belonged. Furthermore, his works were copied by scribes
without any standard to conform to, each one disposed to
use forms of speech to which, largely through accident of
birthplace, he had become personally accustomed.

In the confusion of English dialects in use in the
fourteenth century it is possible to distinguish some general
lines of distinction. John de Trevisa, who has already been

quoted, speaks of three principal dialects of England, "Southorn, northorn & myddel speche in the myddel of the lond as thei come of thre manere peple of Germania," and he says further that the boundary lines of dialect run east and west, "for men of the Est with men of the West, as hit were vnder the same partye of heuen, accordeth more in sownynge of speche than men of the north with men of the south." But the difference in dialect was such as to make the language of one part of the country unintelligible in other parts.

Under such conditions, when English was once more adopted for use by literary artists in productions intended for cultivated readers, there was natural question which kind of English to use. The situation was in some respects parallel to that in Ireland today, where patriotic efforts are being made to restore the native Irish to cultivated use. There is no little perplexity regarding the standard literary form to be given the Irish language varying in the oral use of different parts of Ireland. So it was in England in the fourteenth century.

The decision was not reached all at once. Literary movements began in various parts of the country. In northern England, under conditions about which one would gladly have more certain information, there was a remarkable outburst of literary activity in the English language. There was activity in the creation of a body of independent romances, particularly of Arthurian romances with Gawain as the most prominent hero. These works not only were composed in a Northern, or Northwest Midland, form of English, but made use of an alliterative form of verse derived from native English tradition and differing conspicuously from the nonalliterative verse, influenced by Romance models, adopted by Chaucer and his followers.

The productions of this Northern group are, many of

them, of distinguished excellence. The *Morte Arthur* preserved in the Thornton Manuscript, and hence known as
the Thornton *Morte Arthur*, while difficult for the modern
reader, repays the effort required because of its genuine
artistic merit. Prominent among the productions in this
Northern movement is a group of four poems surviving in
a single manuscript of which the two best known have
been given the titles *The Pearl* and *Sir Gawain and the
Green Knight*. Late in gaining recognition on account of
the difficulty offered the modern reader by the peculiar
dialect in which his works are composed, the anonymous
author of these poems is now among the most highly honored of early English poets, excelling not only in a mastery
of a highly complicated form of verse, but in clearness of
pictures and refinement of feeling. No crude poet this, however strange may seem his language to one accustomed to
another form.

In order to observe the complexity of his verse form and
the artistic results achieved, and at the same time to observe the difference in versification and in language from
those used by Chaucer and his school and made the basis
for later English poetry, let us look at one specimen stanza
from the poem called *The Pearl:*

> The dubbemente of þo derworth depe
> Wern bonkeȝ bene of beryl bryȝt;
> Swangeande swete the water con swepe
> With a rownande rourde raykande aryȝt;
> In þe founce þer stonden stoneȝ stepe,
> As glente þurȝ glas that glowed & glyȝt,
> As stremande sterneȝ quen stroþe men slepe,
> Staren in welkyn in wynter nyȝt;
> For vche a pobbel in pole þer pyȝt
> Watȝ Emerad, saffer, oþer gemme gente
> Þat alle þe loȝe lemed of lyȝt,
> So dere watȝ hit adubbement.

The glamour of that glorious deep
Was banks beset with beryls bright,
Whereby the sweet waves swirl and sweep,
With gentle murmur flowing aright;
Down in the depths lay stones an heap,
As painted windows glow with light,
Or as twinkling stars, when the weary sleep,
Stare from the welkin on winter night;
For every pebble that met my sight
Was meet for royal ornament,
And all the water was alight
With this sweet sight that God me sent.[3]

The Northern form of English, the cultivation of which began in so promising a manner, has not played a very prominent part in the later history of English. Closely related to it, however, is the Northern English now called Scotch because of its association with another nationality. This form of Northern English, spoken from the Forth to the Tweed, was hardly to be distinguished from that spoken from the Tweed south to the Humber. In the hands of writers of Scotch nationality, such as King James I, Robert Henryson, and William Dunbar, this dialect of English was employed during the fifteenth and sixteenth centuries in a body of productions excelling in interest the productions of the contemporary Southern English poets.

Nearly contemporary with this literary activity beginning in northern England was another movement in the western part of central England. In this movement the best known production is the famous *Vision Concerning Piers the Plowman*. This work was an enormously popular one, as appears from the manuscripts, about fifty in number, in which it has survived. Differing in dialect from that of Chaucer, it differed also in verse form. Like the productions of the Northern writers, it is composed in an

[3] Modern English by G. C. Coulton.

alliterative form of verse, but a form different from that used by the Northern poets and differing in its rhythms both from the works of the Northern poets and from those of the Chaucer school. A few lines will serve to show the peculiarities of the dialect and of the metrical form, as well as the homespun coarseness of language of this poem.

And þanne cam couetyse ['covetousness'] ; can I hym nouƷte descryue ['not describe']
So hungriliche and holwe . sire Heruy hym loked ['he looked like'].
He was bitelbrowed ['with beetling brows'] . and baberlipped ['thick-lipped'] also,
With two blered eyghen . as a blynde hagge;
And as a letheren purs . lolled ['flapped'] his chekes,
Wel sydder ['even lower'] þan his chyn . þei chiueled for elde ['shivered for age'] ;
And as a bondman of his bacoun . his berde was bidraueled ['slobbered over']
And in a tawny tabarde . of twelue wynter age,
Al totorne ['torn to rags'] and baudy . and ful of lys ['lice'] crepynge;
But if þat a lous couthe ['could'] . haue lopen ['leaped'] þe bettre,
She sholde nouƷte haue walked on þat welche ['flannel'] . so was it thredebare.

This remarkable work does not stand alone. Possibly itself the work of a group of writers, it influenced other writers, and during the remainder of the fourteenth century it was imitated in a series of productions similar in dialect and in verse form. The group of writings here concerned represent a second movement toward developing a literary form of English, a movement whose influence, it remains to be seen, may be traced in the great literary activity of the sixteenth century.

The diversity in dialect appears not only in independent literary movements in different parts of England, but in variant forms of the same literary work. Among the numerous manuscripts of *The Travels of Sir John Mandeville* may be distinguished at least two independent versions, one the work of a Midland writer and one definitely Northern in character. In like manner the work of Trevisa, more than once quoted from, is preserved in manuscripts which show amazing variety not only in grammatical forms, but in words and phraseology. This independence in the scribes upon whom the author was dependent for the diffusion of his work demonstrates the prevailing diversity in language and the absence of controlling standard.

Over the other dialects, however, the Midland dialect had many advantages. Not only were "men of myddel engelond parteneres of the endes," but in the Midland were important centers of culture. In the Midland was situated Oxford. To Oxford flocked the youth from all parts of England, and unquestionably they must have experienced a leveling out of dialectal peculiarities in the cultured associations at this center of learning. John de Trevisa, himself a Cornishman by birth, came to Oxford at an early age and was keenly conscious of the harshness, as it seemed to him, of the Northern mode of speech. The influence of the Midland form of speech is even more apparent in the case of Wycliffe. Although a native of Yorkshire, he spent most of his active years at Oxford, and the language of his English writings is definitely Midland in character. The influence of Wycliffe, not only through the translation of the Bible associated with his name, but through the writings of his associates Hereford and Purvey and the preaching of his Lollard followers, was a powerful one in determining the standard form that the English language was to assume.

Supporting the influence of Oxford was that of an even

more important Midland center, London, the commercial metropolis and seat of government. In the nature of things the language of London was bound to exert wide influence. An East Midland dialect, though colored somewhat by Southern features, it enjoyed with the Midland speech used at Oxford the advantage mentioned by Trevisa of being something of a happy mean between the extremes of the North and the South. Its use, too, in governmental activities and its gradual adoption into use in the aristocratic circles of English court life lent to it prestige. To London even more generally than to Oxford were drawn people from different parts of the country, and the form of English there met with naturally became widely known. It may be asserted with reasonable certainty that even if Chaucer had never lived, the Midland dialect, especially the form in use in London, was destined to become the standard form of English.

CHAPTER II

THE FIRSTE FYNDERE OF OUR FAIRE LANGAGE

WITH the elevation of the East Midland dialect to the permanent rank of standard literary language must be closely associated the name of Geoffrey Chaucer. "The firste fyndere of our faire langage," he is called by his younger contemporary Occleve, and two centuries later to the Elizabethan poet Spenser he is still the "well of English undefiled." In the writings of Chaucer, therefore, are to be observed the first stages in the cultivation of modern standard English.

The choice of the East Midland dialect of English by Chaucer in his writings was determined by the place of his birth and residence. He wrote in his native dialect. He was born about 1340, the son of a London citizen of the merchant class. At an early age he became a page in the household of Elizabeth, wife of Lionel, Duke of Clarence, the third son of Edward III. Subsequent years were spent in the service of John of Gaunt and in the household of the King himself. He was repeatedly employed on important and delicate diplomatic missions. In the course of an active life Chaucer occupied a number of official positions—as comptroller of customs, as superintendent of construction work, as Forester of North Petherton Park, and in 1386 he was elected knight of the shire for Kent in Parliament. During most, if not all, of these years he was closely associated with courtly circles. The language of Chaucer, therefore, reflects the mode of speech current in

London, not only that of cultivated use in the aristocratic classes, but that of the everyday kind of man that his parental associations and his official employment brought him in contact with.

The date of the beginning of Chaucer's literary activities it is important to hold in mind. It should be recalled that 1362 is the date of the first use of English in the formal opening of Parliament and that in this same year English was restored to use in English courts of law. It should also be recalled that this was the time when English was being brought into use in English grammar-school instruction. In this same decade appeared the earliest literary productions of Chaucer. If in the same environment Chaucer had begun to write a generation, or even a decade, earlier, it is extremely probable that he would have written in the French language, for up to this time French was still the prevailing language in the courtly circles for the entertainment of which his writings were intended.

Courage was required to enable Chaucer at this critical point in English linguistic history to rest all his hopes for contemporary reputation and reward, and his possible hopes for future fame, in compositions in the English language as yet hardly elevated above the vulgar, as yet lacking the dignity of associations attached to a language long in cultivated use. The confidence, however, was not misplaced. Somewhat more tardy, doubtless encouraged by Chaucer's demonstrated success, John Gower ventured in his third long work to use the English language. The example set by Chaucer and followed by Gower was followed by other writers, forming a school of English writers, or perhaps one may better say, starting a movement in English writing, which, overshadowing the contemporary movements in the North and in the West, determined the direction of later English literature.

In many ways Chaucer's position as regards language was an enviable one. As his medium of expression he had a dialect of English which heretofore had not served the purposes of serious literary art, a comparatively rude form of speech with potentialities as yet quite unexploited. To be sure he had not the advantage, a questionable one perhaps, of a wealth of formed expressions upon a discriminating choice of which depends in great part the refinement of modern writing. In compensation, however, he had the distinct advantage of being unhampered in his movement, of being free to apply his own genius to invention of expression. He had the inestimable advantage of writing in a language not yet worn to triteness. Hence the freshness which so distinguishes the expression of Chaucer, a freshness in the search for which the modern writer is obliged to turn hither and thither in the desperate effort to find forms of speech not yet worn and faded.

The homeliness of Chaucer's expression is often startling. His Monk "yaf ['gave'] nat of that text a pulled ['plucked'] hen." His Pardoner had a voice "as smal as hath a goat." In making his lower characters "speke hir wordes properly" he puts in their mouths words and expressions of such naked frankness as to take one's breath away. Even the "gentils" at times use forms of expression so simple and so homely as to appear naïve. The "truly perfect noble Knight" that "never yet no vileinye ne sayde," uses words and similes of a simplicity that to modern taste seems crude. He speaks of Palamon as so violent in his expression of grief "that the grete tour Resouneth of his yowling and clamour." Of Arcite he says "that lene he wex and drye as is a shaft." When thrown from his horse, "as blak he lay as any cole or crowe."

To the writers of the classical period in English literature Chaucer was distinctly a primitive. Dryden found in

Chaucer's verse rudeness, "the rude sweetness of a Scotch tune—which is natural and pleasing, though not perfect." "We can only say," Dryden continues, "that he lived in the infancy of our poetry, and that nothing is brought to perfection at first." But it would be a mistake to attribute the seeming naturalness of Chaucer's language to want of art. The deepened appreciation which has followed the modern widening in knowledge of Chaucer's language and environment has revealed refinements of method hitherto unsuspected. The exact extent of Chaucer's art in the development of the language it is not easy to estimate. Contributions made in earlier periods, toward enrichment of vocabulary, expressive turns of meaning, and neat conciseness of phraseology, become so thoroughly assimilated, to such an extent common property, that it is not easy to conceive of the language without them.

Moreover, in estimating Chaucer's art, it must not be thought that he was without models. In earlier English, to be sure, there was little to provide for him a pattern. What was lacking in earlier English literature, however, Chaucer found elsewhere—in French, in Italian, or in Latin writings. Chaucer's literary antecedents, therefore, are to be sought in foreign literatures, which in turn lead back to classical civilization. In his early attempts at verse he did not use the alliterative form of verse with irregular rhythm native to England and employed by contemporary schools of writers in the West and the North. It seems to have come no more natural to him than it did to his Parson, another "Southren man," to "geste—rum, ram, ruf—by lettre." His earlier writings in verse were cast in the French forms of "ballades, roundels, virelays," and his first long composition was a translation of the French *Roman de la Rose,* and through his life, instead of the older traditional form of alliterative verse like that used in *Piers Plowman* or in *Sir Gawain and the Green Knight,* he used the rimed form of verse with regular rhythm, a form which had already found some use among his immediate predecessors in English, but which was recommended to him particularly by the practice of contemporary writers in the cultivated French and Latin. Upon Chaucer's choice of his form of verse depends to a great extent the later development of English versification.

In language, too, as in verse, Chaucer was much influenced by foreign patterns. From "olde bokes," out of which "cometh all this newe science that men lere," he drew material for his works. From "olde bokes" and contemporary ones in French, in Latin, and in Italian he gleaned not only subject matter but phrasal material as well. Chaucer, then, "the first fyndere of our faire langage," was not as entirely the pioneer as is sometimes supposed. The patterns lacking in earlier English were supplied by the literature in tongues which had earlier been brought under cultivation.

Nor did Chaucer lack the guidance of literary theory. In his time there were available numerous works bearing the class name *ars dictandi* or *ars dictaminis* which taught the forms of language to be used in letter writing and in official documents. Rhetoric, too, it must be held in mind, was a subject much cultivated in Chaucer's time. It was one of the three subjects forming the trivium of the medieval school. It covered the whole subject of composition, oral and written, prose and verse. Elocution, one of its five main divisions, applied to verse as well as to prose. For instruction in this subject there was available the *De Inventione* of Cicero and another classical work, the *Ad Herennium*, which was attributed to Cicero and appears frequently in manuscripts as a sequel to the *De Inventione*. The second work, called the *Rhetorica Nova* ['New

Rhetoric'], offered a remarkably elaborate classification of devices of style subdivided into thirty-five figures of words, ten tropes, and twenty figures of thought. Upon these classical works were based numerous medieval treatises employing a similar classification but offering rich supply of new illustrative examples. That these works were widely used appears from the number of manuscripts that still survive. The *Poetria,* for instance, of the English-born John of Garland is preserved in about eighty manuscripts and the *Poetria Nova* of Geoffrey de Vinsauf in nearly, if not quite, as many.

That Chaucer was familiar with the rhetorical doctrines current in his time there can be no doubt. Cicero, at least the Cicero of the Middle Ages, was familiar enough to him. Indeed Occleve remarks concerning Chaucer, "vnto Tullius was neuer man so lyk amonges vs." The Clerk of Oxford refers to "Fraunceys Petrark, the laureat poete— whos rethoryke swete Enlumined all Itaille of poetrye." The Squire quite appropriately shows familiarity with the art of rhetoric, as appears from his remark:

Accordant to his wordes was his chere ['countenance']
As techeth art of speche hem ['them'] that it lere ['learn'].

His modest disclaimer of mastery of the art is in keeping with his character:

Myn English eek ['also'] is insufficient;
It moste ben a rethor excellent,
That coude ['knew'] his colours longing for ['belonging to']
    that art
If he sholde hir discryven every part.

The Franklin could hardly be expected to be versed in the highly cultivated art. Hence the dramatic fitness of his apologetic remark:

> I lerned neuer rethoryk certyn;
> Thing that I speke, it mote be base and pleyn
> I sleep neuer on the Mount of Pernaso
> Ne lerned Marcus Tullius Cithero.
> Colours ne knowe I none, withouten drede
> But swiche colours as growen in the mede,
> Or elles swich as men dye or peynte
> Colours of rethoryk ben me to queynte.

In the earlier writings of Chaucer may be easily discerned traces of the influence of the artificial methods of composition prized in his day. In later years came emancipation from convention and from artifice. The schemes and colors of the rhetorician provide the materials for burlesque in the mock heroic tale of the Nun's Priest. Ironic appreciation of Geoffrey de Vinsauf, author of the *Poetria Nova*, appears in this tale in the rhetorical *exclamatio* used in expressing grief for the woeful plight of Chanticleer:

> O Gaufred, dere master souerayn,
>
> . . . . .
>
> Why ne hadde I now thy sentence and thy lore,
> The Friday for to chyde, as diden ye?
>
> . . . . .
>
> Than wolde I shewe yow how that I coude pleyne
> For Chauntecleres drede, and for his peyne.

Chaucer's small esteem in his later years for the ornate devices of the rhetorician appears clear enough. Host Bailly, whose sentiments we may feel sure were often Chaucer's own, admonishes the young Clerk:

> Your termes, your colours, and your figures,
> Kepe hem in stoor till so be ye endyte
> Heigh style, as whan that men to kinges wryte
> Sp-eketh so pleyn at this tyme, I yow preye,
> That we may vnderstonde what ye seye.

In his *House of Fame* (iii, 9, 10) Chaucer announces that "I do no diligence to shewe craft, but o sentence," that is to say, his concern is with the meaning alone. Earlier in the same work (ii, 346-54) the eagle who has just made to his helpless passenger an exposition of the nature of sound waves, gloats over his success with the words:

> Haue I not preved thus simply
> Withouten any subtiltee
> Of speche, or gret prolixitie
> Of termes of philosophye,
> Of figures of poetrye,
> Or colours of rethoryke?
> Pardee, hit oghte thee to lyke;
> For hard langage and hard matere
> Is encombrous for to here
> At ones;

These words, humorous enough as addressed in pedantic manner to the helpless poet passively suspended from the "grimme pawes stronge" of the eagle, nevertheless express a serious belief of Chaucer's. Prolixity is the vice to be shunned. Clear expression of thought in concise form is the ideal to be aimed at. "And for to maken shortly is the beste," he remarks in his legend of Cleopatra.

That this ideal was much in Chaucer's mind we may learn from a passage in his *Treatise on the Astrolabe.* In the Prologue to this work, addressed to "Litil Lowis," his son, he makes the following remarks, apologetic in nature: "Now wol I prey meekly every discreet persone that redeth or hereth this litel tretis, to have my rewde endyting ['literary composition'] for excused, and my superfluitee of wordes, for two causes. The firste cause is, for that curious endyting ['painstaking literary composition'] and hard sentence ['subject matter'] is ful hevy atones for swich a child to lerne. And the seconde cause is this, that sothly me semeth betre to wryten un-to a child twyes a good sentence, than he forgete it ones." To these apologetic remarks Chaucer adds the following sentence showing no little pride in his achievement in setting forth difficult matter in the un-cultivated English language instead of in Latin: "And Lowis, yif so be that I shewe thee in my lighte English as trewe conclusiouns touching this matere, and naught only as trewe but as subtil conclusiouns as ben shewed in Latin in any commune tretis of the Astrolabie, con me the more thank."

Avoidance of "prolixitie," that is to say, use of clean-cut, concise speech in place of the clumsy phrasing, the awkward circumlocutions, the twisted constructions of uncultivated speech—this seems to have been an ideal of Chaucer. This, rather than ornate phraseology, is his great contribution to the development of the language. Among the eulogistic passages not always discriminating in character to be found in the works of almost every British writer for more than a century following Chaucer's death, there are to be found a few which single out this distinctive virtue. Thus in the *Boke of Curtesye* published about 1478 appears the fol-lowing discerning praise:

Redith his [Chaucer's] werkis, ful of pleasaunce
Clere in sentence, in langage excellent.
Briefly to wryte such was his suffysance
Whateuer to saye he toke in his entente
His langage was so fayr and pertynente
It semeth vnto mannys heerynge
Not only the worde but verely the thynge ['the thing itself'].

John Skelton, also, writing about a century after Chau-cer's death, is discriminating in his praise. He says of Chaucer's language that "as it is employed, there is no English void," that is, there are no superfluous words. A little farther on he says:

> His terms were not dark
> But pleasant, easy, and plain;
> No word he wrote in vain.

Caxton, writing in 1484, passes the same judgment on Chaucer's language, emphasizing, it should be noted, Chaucer's avoidance of "prolyxyte." His "treatyces," says Caxton, he "so craftyly made that he comprehended hys maters in short, quyck and hye sentences, eschewyng prolyxyte, castyng away the chaf of superfluyte, and shewyng the pyked grayne of sentence . . ." This judgment of Caxton, it should be noted, is quoted from the prologue to his second edition of the *Canterbury Tales* (1484).

The same judgment could not so well be passed on Chaucer's prose. Concrete terms that served the needs of poetic expression were richly abundant in the simple English of uncultivated use; the more general terms, however, that carry the burden of prose, were lacking in the undeveloped language. Moreover, the pattern afforded by metrical design seems to have been necessary. Within the regulated measure of verse he attained an ease and grace and naturalness of manner which entitle his metrical compositions to the admiration of all ages. But without the guidance of metrical pattern the labored character of his expression in the uncultivated language, like that of his contemporaries and successors in the following century, is painfully evident.

The supreme achievement in the use of the English language by Chaucer is in the dramatic appropriateness of the language assigned to different characters. In this achievement he was not without the guidance of art. In the rhetorical treatises current in Chaucer's time different grades in speech were discussed. In the *Ad Herennium* are distinguished the grave style, the middle style, and the simple style. In medieval treatises the three styles are associated with three classes of men. John of Garland, for instance, who must have been known to Chaucer, distinguishes the speech of the shepherd, that of the agriculturalist, and that of persons of rank. That Chaucer was familiar with these distinctions he makes clear. He begs that it may not be attributed to "vileinye" though his characters speak "never so rudeliche and large." For, he says, each must speak "properly," that is, 'in character.' In support of his practice he cites the precept which he attributes to Plato:

The wordes mote be cosin to the dede.

In consequence of this dramatic appropriateness of language we have in the *Canterbury Tales* a range in dignity of language corresponding to the range in social station of the characters introduced, urbanity and courtliness in the language of the Knight, gentle dignity in that of the Prioress, a stiffness of professional dignity in that of the Man of Law, pompous dullness in that of the Monk, an eloquent vulgarity in the "cherles termes" of the Miller and the Reve, and finally a marvelous adaptability in the language used by Host Bailly in addressing the pilgrims so varied in social station.

As affording illustration of the range in Chaucer's language let us take two word-portraits from the *Canterbury Tales*. Let us first look at a picture painted by the Knight:

Til it fil ones, in a morwe of May,
That Emelye, that fairer was to sene
Than is the lilie upon his stalke grene,
And fresher than the May with floures newe—
For with the rose colour stroof hir hewe ['competed her complexion'],
I noot which was the fairer of hem two—
Er it were day, as was hir wone to do,
She was arisen, and al redy dight;
For May wol have no slogardye a-night.

> The sesoun priketh every gentil herte,
> And maketh him out of his sleep to sterte,
> And seith, "Arys, and do thyn observaunce."
> This maked Emelye have remembraunce
> To doon honour to May, and for to ryse.
> Y-clothed was she fresh, for to devyse;
> Hir yelow heer was broyded in a tresse,
> Bihinde hir bak, a yerde long, I gesse.
> And in the gardin, at the sonne up-riste,
> She walketh up and doun, and as hir liste
> She gadereth floures, party whyte and rede,
> To make a sotil gerland for hir hede,
> And as an aungel hevenly she song.[1]

The tone of the description is quite in keeping with the character of the "verray parfit gentil knight" who "never yet no vileinye ne sayde." With little of realistic detail he presents not so much a picture of a flesh and blood woman as a dream of ideal beauty. Small wonder that Palamon, the imprisoned knight, was uncertain whether it was woman or goddess that he was beholding.

Then let us look at a picture drawn by the Miller—that of the fair Alisoun:

> Fair was this yonge wyf, and there-with-al
> As any wesele hir body gent and smal.
> A ceynt she werede barred al of silk,
> A barmclooth ['apron'] eek as whyt as morne milk
> Up-on hir lendes ['loins'], ful of many a gore.
> Whyt was hir smok and brouded al bifore
> And eek bihinde, on hir coler aboute,
> Of col-blak silk, with-inne and eek with-oute.
> The tapes of hir whyte voluper
> Were of the same suyte of hir coler;
> Hir filet brood of silk, and set ful hye:
> And sikerly she hadde a likerous ye.

[1] "Knight's Tale," 176-197.

Ful smale y-pulled were hir browes two,
And tho were bent, and blake as any sloo.
She was ful more blisful on to see
Than is the newe pere-jonette tree;
And softer than the wolle is of a wether.
And by hir girdel heeng a purs of lether
Tasseld with silk, and perled with latoun.
In al this world, to seken up and doun,
There nis no man so wys, that coude thenche
So gay a popelote, or swich a wenche.
Ful brighter was the shyning of hir hewe
Than in the tour the noble y-forged newe.
But of hir song, it was as loude and yerne
As any swalwe sittinge on a berne.
Ther-to she coude skippe and make game,
As any kide or calf folwinge his dame.
Hir mouth was swete as bragot or the meeth ['two esteemed
    beverages'],
Or hord of apples leyd in hey or heeth.
Winsinge ['skittish'] she was, as is a joly colt,
Long as a mast, and upright as a bolt.
A brooch she baar up-on hir lowe coler,
As brood as is the bos of a bocler ['shield'].
Hir shoes were laced on hir legges hye;
She was a prymerole ['primrose'], a pigges-nye ['pig's eye'—
    'a peach'].[2]

No lack of charm here either. But the manner of description, how different! The garrulous Miller, utterly without restraint, pours forth the words, "cherles termes" perhaps, but forming a remarkably naturalistic picture of feminine beauty of the earthly kind.

In his *Troilus and Criseyde* Chaucer speaking of the language of earlier times says that words then "That hadden prys ['estimation'] now wonder nyce ['foolish'] and straunge vs thinketh hem ['they seem to us']." Much the

---

[2] "Miller's Tale," 47-82.

same remark applies now to the language as used by Chaucer. Many of his words seem "nyce and straunge."

The English language of Chaucer's time was in process of
reconstruction. Like an historic old building dilapidated
through neglect it needed to be restored, and in the restoration new material needed to be used. An English vocabulary shrunken through disuse among the cultivated classes,
had to be replenished through words borrowed from the more
cultivated French and Latin languages. In the years immediately following the Norman Conquest the borrowing of
French words had been relatively slight. But with the English language in the second half of the fourteenth century
fully restored at last to cultivated use, words were borrowed
at a rate unequaled in any half century before or since.

What was Chaucer's attitude toward the borrowing of
words? The impoverished English vocabulary did not af-
ford the forms of polished expression available in French.
It was not easy for a writer in English to compete with
French writers in possession of a more refined language.
That Chaucer was keenly alive to the difficulty of his task
appears in utterances here and there. In his *Compleynt of
Venus* appear the following lines:

> And eek to me hit is a greet penaunce
> Sith rym in English hath swich scarsitee.
> To folowe word by word the curiositee
> Of Graunson, flour of hem that make in Fraunce.

Not entirely to personal modesty are to be attributed the
following verses from the *Legend of Good Women:*

> Allas! that I ne had English ryme or prose
> Suffisant this flour to preyse aright.

The early part of Chaucer's career as a poet is a period of
apprenticeship. From foreign poets, French and Italian,
he adapted material and devices for his own works. Usually

he found English idiom for independent expression of adopted ideas. For example, take Chaucer's rendering,

> She is fals, and euer laughing
> With oon eye, and that other weping.

of the French of Guillaume de Machaut:

Elle est non seure;	She is not constant;
D'un oueil rit,	With one eye she laughs,
de l'autre larmie.	With the other she weeps.

Occasionally, however, though not frequently, and especially in his earlier writings, Chaucer adopts words as well as ideas. Machaut's "c'est l'envieuse charite" appears in Chaucer, "She is thenvyous charite." Machaut's "ydole de fausse pourtraiture" appears as "ydole of fals portraiture." "Planette en firmament" appears as "planete in firmament." It would be a mistake to assume that in all such instances Chaucer is introducing French words new to English. In many instances the French words were already in English use and belonged to idiomatic English expression. Moreover, when Chaucer introduced a French word into his writing, in later revisions he sometimes substituted a word more English in quality. In one version of the Prologue to his *Legend of Good Women* he used the word "florouns" taken from the French of Froissart. In another version and, if we may believe Professor Lowes, a later version, he uses "floures," a word already assimilated into English.

Chaucer's writings in prose are not as faithful to English idiom. These, four in number, deal with learned subjects. For handling such the cultivated colloquial English of the time did not afford a pattern. Furthermore, the learned forms of English expression in use before the Conquest were now obsolete. The labor required of one in Chaucer's situation in translating learned works into English it is now difficult to realize fully. The labor involved appears in the heaviness of Chaucer's style in these prose writings. Call to mind also Chaucer's apologetic manner and at the same time his pride in achievement in the passage already quoted from his *Treatise on the Astrolabe.*

Under such conditions simple and idiomatic English expression is more than could be expected. The adoption of forms of expression from the more cultivated French and Latin was inevitable. The adoption of foreign learned terms at this time was a general practice. How many of these are to be attributed to Chaucer it is not possible to say with certainty. But there are many of them, now thoroughly assimilated into English, such as *attention, diffusion, fraction, duration, position,* not cited from writings earlier than Chaucer, and not reappearing in English until the sixteenth century, which appear to be due to Chaucer.[3]

The changes that had come about in the English learned vocabulary since the Old English period are striking. Two translations of the *Consolation of Philosophy,* one in the West Saxon dialect of Old English by Alfred the Great about A.D. 900 and the one by Chaucer, afford excellent illustration of the change. A few phrases printed in parallel columns will show the difference:

ALFRED	CHAUCER
mid wordum arreccan	unpleyten with wordes
sio wiðerwearde wyrd	contrarious fortune
bið nytwyrðre	profiteth more
sio orsorge	fortune debonaire
mid þaere styringe	through exercise
hire agenre frecennesse	of hir adversitee
tihð from þaem soðum ges-aelðum	draweth fro the sovereyne good
mid hiere oliccunge	with hir flateringes

Many of the words used by Alfred seem like foreign words. In reality they are native words, and it is the words

[3] L. P. Smith, *The English Language.*

that have taken their place in Chaucer's English that are the foreign words.

Having considered briefly Chaucer's share in developing the potentialities for expression in the uncultivated Midland dialect which served his purpose, let us next center our attention on some of the mechanical features of the instrument. English of the fourteenth century belonged to what is called the Middle English period. The name Middle indicates a halfway stage. This halfway stage is best indicated by the nature of the inflections. Middle English inflections are spoken of as "leveled" inflections as distinguished from the "full" inflections of the earlier, Old English, or Anglo-Saxon period. The distinction may be illustrated by means of a few noun inflections:

OLD ENGLISH STRONG DECLENSION

	MASCULINE	FEMININE	NEUTER	
SINGULAR				
Nom.	stan ('stone')	lufu ('love')	scip ('ship')	word
Gen.	stanes	lufe	scipes	wordes
Dat.	stane	lufe	scipe	worde
Accus.	stan	lufe	scip	word
PLURAL				
Nom.	stanas	lufe, a	scipu	word
Gen.	stana	lufa, ena	scipa	worda
Dat.	stanum	lufum	scipum	wordum
Accus.	stanas	lufe, a	scipu	word

OLD ENGLISH WEAK DECLENSION

SINGULAR			
Nom.	guma ('man')	tunge ('tongue')	eage ('eye')
Gen.	guman	tungan	eagan
Dat.	guman	tungan	eagan
Accus.	guman	tungan	eage
PLURAL			
Nom.	guman	tungan	eagan
Gen.	gumena	tung(e)na	eag(e)na
Dat.	gumum	tungum	eagum
Accus.	guman	tungan	eagan

OLD ENGLISH MINOR DECLENSION

SINGULAR

Nom. Accus.	fot ('foot')	boc ('book')
Gen.	fotes	boca
Dat.	fet	bec
Instr.	fote, fet	bec

PLURAL

Nom. Accus.	fet	bec
Gen.	fota	boca
Instr. Dat.	fotum	bocum

The tables here given do not exhibit all but show the more usual modes of declension in the Old English period. There should be noted the distinctions in case and in gender and the independent types of inflection by no means fully demonstrated here.

The leveling which took place in Middle English affected the vowels of the endings. The distinct vowels were reduced to one indistinct sound, that of the final syllable in modern English *China,* but represented in writing by the letter *e.* Also the differences in gender and in type of inflection were in great part leveled out. The genitive singular form was preserved to indicate possession usually, but even here difference in gender and in inflectional type were for the most part lost, the masculine genitive form of the strong declension superseding the other forms. In the same way while difference between singular and plural continued to be indicated, the plural ending prevailing was that of the strong masculines. The typical form of inflection, therefore, in Chaucer's time was as follows:

	MASCULINE	FEMININE	NEUTER	FEMININE
SINGULAR				
Nom.	stoon	quene	word	tunge
Gen.	stoones	quenes	wordes	tunges
PLURAL				
	stoones	quenes	wordes	tunges

The principal difference from modern English, it will be noted, is in the survival, in many forms, of the ending with the indefinite sound already referred to, represented by the letter *e*.

This same leveling tendency affected words of all classes —nouns, adjectives, verbs, and, to a somewhat less extent, pronouns. There still survived traces of the older complexity of inflection, not only forms which survive in modern English such as *oxen,* but *asschen,* 'ashes'; *been,* 'bees'; *eyen,* 'eyes'; *fleen,* 'fleas'; *toon,* 'toes'; *schoon,* 'shoes.' There were also nouns which, like most neuter nouns in Old English, took no plural ending, not only such words as *deer, sheep,* and *swin,* 'swine,' which survive in modern English, but *folk, hors, thing, neet, yeer,* all plural forms.

In pronouns the older inflectional distinctions were longer retained. Indeed, many of them survive in modern English. In the Midland English of Chaucer's time the most striking forms, from a modern point of view, are those of the second person: NOM. SING. *thou, thow;* GEN. *thy, thyn;* ACCUS. *the, thee;* NOM. PLUR. *ye;* GEN. *your, youre;* ACCUS. *you, yow;* and in the third person the preservation of *his* for the neuter possessive (modern *its*) and the plural forms, NOM. *they, thei* (of Norse origin), but GEN. *hire, here,* ACCUS. *hem,* older forms still conspicuous in the seventeenth and eighteenth centuries and surviving in familiar speech today.

Another feature of the Middle English of Chaucer's time which must not be lost sight of is the difference between different dialects. It is hardly possible to make a grammar of Middle English because grammar in the modern sense of the word means regularity and system. This regularity and system was conspicuously absent in the English of the Middle English period. The difference in dialectal use appearing everywhere—in words, in pronunciation and in inflections—is nowhere so consistently maintained as in the personal endings of the verb in the present indicative. In the case of these endings standard modern use, as remains to be shown, was not permanently fixed until after the time of Shakespeare. The difference in the use of the three principal Middle English dialects may be shown by the following scheme:

	MIDLAND	SOUTHERN	NORTHERN
SINGULAR			
1.	-e	-e	-e
2.	-est	-est	-es
3.	-eth	-eth	-es
PLURAL			
1, 2, 3.	-en,-e	-eth	-es

The few details that it has been practicable to offer will suffice to convey an impression of the remarkable extent to which English inflections had been simplified before the time of Chaucer. This simplification, one must assume, came about in natural use in the course of a long period during which there was no cultivated use to give check to the natural processes of change. It should be noted that the simplified inflectional forms are still, almost without exception, native. Almost the only foreign forms to win a place in the English system of inflections are the pronoun forms, *they, their, them,* which seem to come from the Norse element assimilated into the English population, especially in the North, following the Danish invasions. The thoroughly English character of the surviving inflections appears in the way borrowed words from French and from Latin were anglicized in their forms. Strikingly hybrid in appearance are such words as *ybrouded* ('embroidered'), and *ycorouned* ('crowned'), where native prefix and native suffix have been attached to borrowed words.

Since Chaucer's writings mark a definite stage in the development of English, it will be well to learn something of the pronunciation of English at his time. It is not possible to make a statement concerning Chaucer's pronunciation that will be at the same time brief and accurate. The following brief account, however, will give an approximate idea.

In the first place, Chaucer's pronunciation, like that of Anglo-Saxon, was much more nearly phonetic than that of the present day. All syllables were pronounced. The final -e, which at this time was beginning to be dropped colloquially, still counted metrically, as it does in modern French, and was pronounced like *a* in *China* except before a following word with an initial vowel or *h*.

The great changes which later affected English vowels had not yet come about, and the vowels in general still had their continental values: ă as in *ăha;* ā as in *father;* ĕ as in *net;* ē as in *name;* ī nearly as in *bit;* î as in *weep;* ŏ as in English *not* (not American *nat*); ō as in *note;* ŭ as in *full;* ū as in *fool.* ŭ in words of French origin had the pronunciation of French *u*.

In the diphthongs the individual vowels were pronounced: *ai* as *a+i* as in modern *mile; ei* as *e+i* as in *veil; au* as *a+u* as in *now; oi* as *o+i* as in *toil; ou* as *o+u*.

The consonants in pronunciation did not differ so much from Modern English: *c* was pronounced before *e* and *i* as *s*, elsewhere as *k*; *i* was used as a consonant (*j*) as well as a vowel. The modern distinction between *u* and *v*, as vowel and consonant respectively, did not yet exist, the *v* appearing initially as a rule and the *u* medially; *ng* was always pronounced as in *linger*.

CHAPTER III

CHAUCER'S SUCCESSORS AND THE AUREATE LANGUAGE

ONE result of Chaucer's demonstrated success was that other literary artists adopted the English language as their medium of expression. That the practice was becoming general may be inferred from the words, already quoted, of Thomas Usk writing in 1387. Even Gower, who had produced earlier ambitious works both in French and in Latin, in his *Confessio Amantis* written about 1390 turned to the use of English, although he personally seems to regard this as a radical and patriotic step, as appears from the remark in his Prologue:

> And for that few men endite ['write literature']
> In oure englisch, I thenke make
> A bok for Engelondes sake.

In the new activity in English writing Chaucer gave not only an incentive but a pattern. There survive a number of anonymous poems, imitative of Chaucer, which at one time or another have been attributed to his authorship and which now form a Chaucerian Apocrypha. In the school of writers who were immediate followers of Chaucer the most prominent were Thomas Occleve, or Hoccleve, and John Lydgate. But in English poetry throughout the following century the influence of Chaucer appears everywhere. Its dominance is, to quote the words of Saintsbury in the *Cambridge History of English Literature,* "something to which there is hardly a parallel in literature." Even the faults of Chaucer were imitated, as, for instance, in the *Testament of Love* by Thomas Usk, in which are reproduced awkward features from Chaucer's prose translation of Boethius. From Occleve to Spenser there is a full chorus of praise. The tribute of Chaucer's disciple, Occleve, is personal and heartfelt:

But weylaway! so is myn herte wo,
That the honour of Englyssh tonge is deed,
Of which I wont was han ['was wont to have'] consail and
    reed ['advice'].

To Occleve Chaucer was not only "the firste fyndere of our faire langage," but his books of "ornat endyting" were "to al þis land enlumynyng." To Lydgate he was "the load-starre of our langage." He was:

Floure of Poetes thorghout al breteyne
Which sothly hadde most of excellence
In rethorike and in eloquence

                    . . . . .

To whom be 3oue pris ['given praise'], honure and glorye
Of wel seyinge ['phrasing well'] first in oure langage.[1]

To the author of the *Boke of Curtesye* he was "Fader and Founder of eternate eloquence."

Moreover, Chaucer's influence was not confined to England. The most distinguished poetry in Great Britain in the fifteenth century was produced by poets of Scotland. In their works Chaucer's influence appears in subject matter, in modes of treatment, in verse forms, even in words and phraseology. The Scotch poets add their voices to the general chorus of praise. To King James I Chaucer and Gower were "poetis laureate in moralitee and eloquence ornate" who sat on the "steppis of rethorike." Henryson

---

[1] *Siege of Thebes*, 40-42, 46, 47.

in his *Testament of Cresseid,* itself a sequel to Chaucer's *Troilus and Criseyde,* speaks of "worthie Chaucer glorius." William Dunbar, who a century after Chaucer occupied a place in Scotch courtly life somewhat analogous to that of Chaucer in England, addresses him:

> O reuerend Chaucer, rose of rethoris all.

Caxton, in the Proem to the second edition of the *Canterbury Tales* printed by him as early as 1484, says, "to-fore that he [Chaucer] by hys labour embelysshed, ornated, and made faire oure englisshe, in thys Royame was had rude speche & Incongrue, as yet it appiereth by olde bookes, whyche at thys day ought not to haue place ne be compared emongne to hys beauteuous volumes and aounate writynges—"

It should be noted that the royal Scotch poet James I divides his praise between Chaucer and Gower. In the later fifteenth and early sixteenth century Chaucer shares honor, not only with Gower, but with Lydgate. Skelton, already quoted in this connection, has praise for all three, but with discrimination. To him:

> Gower's English is old
> And of no value told;
> His matter is worth gold,
> And worthy to be enrolled.

Of Lydgate Skelton says that he:

> Writeth after an higher rate;
> It is diffuse to find
> The sentence of his mind.

Of Chaucer, however, he says:

> His matter is delectable
>
> . . . . .
>
> His English well allowed,

and in another place he addresses Chaucer:

> O noble Chaucer, whos pullisshed eloquence
> Oure Englysshe rude so fresshely hath set out.

Other fifteenth-century writers in their distribution of praise exalt Lydgate even above Chaucer. The author of the *Boke of Curtesye,* whose praise of Chaucer has already been quoted, reserves his superlative commendation for Lydgate:

> My maister whylome . . .
> Worthy to be renouned as poete laureate.

Stephen Hawes, also, in his *Pastime of Pleasure,* after eloquent tribute to "morall Gower" and to Chaucer and "all hys bokes so swete and profytable," launches forth in panegyric of Lydgate, "the most dulcet sprynge of famous rethoryke—the chefe orygynal of my lernyng."

In the later sixteenth century, however, there had come a reaction from the artificial style cultivated by Lydgate and the estimate of the relative merits of this trinity of early poets had come to be that of our own time. To Spenser it was Chaucer who was the "well of English undefyled." In Spenser's *Shepheardes Calender,* Tityrus, the god of shepherds, is Chaucer, comparable in "worthines" to the "Roman Tityrus, Virgile." Colin Clout, that is to say, Spenser, one reads, "of Tityrus his songs did lere." Spenser by his own wish, it is said, was buried near Chaucer in Westminster Abbey.

The position occupied by Chaucer in the minds of writers in the centuries following his death is clear enough. His claim to the title "Father of English Poetry" is soundly based. Either directly or indirectly through the works of his disciple Lydgate, his influence is all pervasive. To quote once more from the *Boke of Curtesye:*

. . . these faders anncyente
Repen ['reaped'] the feldes fresshe of fulsomnes ['luxuriance']
The flours fresh they gadred vp & hente ['took']
Of siluer langage, the grete riches,
Who will it haue, . . .
Must of hem begge, there is no more to seye
For of our tunge they were both lok & kaye.

From the last quoted words, words addressed in a book
of conduct to "litill John," a young boy of the fifteenth
century, it would appear that the English language was regarded as permanently fixed, that both lock and key were to
be found in the writings of the Chaucerian group. The
irony of life is here apparent. The very beginning is taken
for the end. The same exaggerated importance attached to
the form of language in contemporary use will be met with
later in judgments passed on the English in use at the end
of the sixteenth century and on that of the Augustan era at
the beginning of the eighteenth century. In our own day the
disposition to look on new forms in language as signs of decay arises from a similar want of historical perspective.

The influence of Chaucerian English, however, throughout the fifteenth century was a dominant one. It persisted
to some extent in the sixteenth century. Sir Thomas Wilson
in his Rhetoric published in 1553 remarks that "the courtier
will talke nothing but Chaucer," and later in that century
Spenser went so far in the use of Chaucerian English that
Ben Jonson said of him that he "writ no language." Again
either directly or through the medium of Spenser the influence of Chaucer appears in the archaic diction of poetry
in the eighteenth and nineteenth centuries, and in some of
the greatest narrative poetry of the twentieth century the
influence of Chaucer appears in the freshness and new
vitality gained from the use of homely and dialectal forms
of speech.

A page from an illuminated manuscript of Lydgate's *Troy Book*.

But in the fifteenth century the Chaucerian pattern was not exclusively dominant. Old garments will not continue to fit a growing body. Fifteenth-century English poets were not content to be merely followers of Chaucer. The ambition to compose in English, once enkindled, led to keen endeavor to beautify and adorn the language. In the course of the fifteenth century this endeavor led to an extravagance in artificiality not exceeded in any subsequent period. This extravagance reaches its height near the end of the century in the poetry of Stephen Hawes, whose efforts at "clokynge a trouthe with colour tenebrous" led him far from the simplicity of natural language which characterizes most of the work of Chaucer.

In the cultivation of this "aureate language" striven after by English poets of the fifteenth century guidance was provided by the Latin studies of the period. Effort is required in our time in order to realize the dominant place of Latin in the culture of medieval times. In the world of learning and culture it was the international, the universal language. In Latin books was to be found the learning of the time. Latin, therefore, was the central subject of study in the schools. Hence the name grammar school, in which the word *grammar* had, not its present-day meaning, but its original, etymological meaning, 'body of writings.' A grammar school, therefore, was one mainly concerned with Latin studies.

In the fifteenth century few English schools gave any attention to training in the use of the English language. There were a few conspicuous exceptions. In the College of Nether Acaster,[2] founded near the end of the fifteenth century, there were three masters, one to teach grammar, one to teach music and song, and a third "to teach to write and all such thing as belonged to Scrivener Craft." Another

[2] A. F. Leach, *The Schools of Medieval England*, pp. 274-5.

college founded at Rotherham in 1483, in order that certain youths "may be better fitted for the mechanical arts and other worldly matters," along with its grammar school and song school provided a third school with a master, "learned and skilled in the art of writing, and accounts." By "writing" is meant here, it seems, the mechanical side of writing, not the art of authorship for which the word *endyting*, it will have been observed in passages quoted earlier, was the name in current use. With occasional exceptions, as in these two colleges, public education was centered in the Latin of the grammar school.

The Latin which formed the principal subject for study in medieval schools, however, was not classical Latin. Its pronunciation was not that which later learning has revealed to have been that of the classical period. Its vocabulary included words unknown to Cicero or Virgil. Its accentual form of rimed verse differed strikingly from the quantitative verse of the classical Latin writers. But it was a living language. It was used not only in learned compositions but in personal letters and in familiar conversation among the learned. School discipline even required school boys to use it among themselves. For the enforcement of the rule in some schools, Eton for instance, special monitors were provided.[3] It was also a cultivated language. Indeed the concentration on grammar study, or Latin, permitted by the medieval curriculum, which lacked the bewildering variety of subjects now set before the modern scholar, permitted an intensity of cultivation for which there is no modern parallel. In the rhetoric, which was one of the principal subjects for study, the art of writing was made almost an exact science. Medieval fondness for minute analysis and for schematizing had free play. John of Garland with his fifty-seven figures of speech and eighteen

---

[3] *Ibid.*, p. 306.

figures of thought has already been alluded to. His schematism goes much farther. There are nine ways to begin a poem and nine to begin an epistle. Words and images are to be selected according to the persons addressed. For the court a grand style is appropriate; for the city, a middle style; for the country, a mean style.[4] In versification he distinguishes forty-four species of stanza forms. In another treatise, the *Exempla honestae vitae,* the same author "employs sixty-four rhetorical devices" including not only familiar figures such as antithesis, metaphor, hyperbole, and climax, but devices less familiar to the modern ear such as anaphora, epiphora, symploke, and polysyndeton.[5] The complexity of some of the *colores,* or 'devices,' to the modern mind is amazing. There are not only stanzas in which the opening letters in the lines serve to spell a name, but through the arrangement of medial letters intricate designs are wrought within the stanza.[6]

For the complex medieval Latin stanza forms a prime requisite was a rich riming vocabulary. To secure the needed wealth of riming words devices of all sorts were resorted to, and these devices are duly classified and listed in learned treatises. Classical rhetoricians had discussed methods of ornamenting style by varied words. For instance, Cicero[7] mentions the use for this purpose of unusual or archaic words, of new words, either new creations or new compounds, and of translated or transferred words, that is to say, words with shifts in meaning. Medieval treatises go much farther. A treatise by Nicolo Tibino[8] discusses no less than ten different ways of providing a needed riming word.

[4] D. L. Clark, *Rhetoric and Poetry in the Renaissance,* Chap. V.
[5] J. M. Berdan, *Early Tudor Poetry,* p. 125.
[6] *Ibid.,* p. 131.
[7] *De Oratore,* iii, 38.
[8] Berdan, *op. cit.,* pp. 136-8.

The elaborateness and the refinements of the modes of ornamentation employed by medieval Latin writers and set forth in medieval treatises have been dwelt on at some length because they enable one to understand the aims and methods of English writers of the fifteenth century in their strained efforts at embellishment of English style. It should be held in mind that *rhetoric* was the name then applied to the art of ornamentation in language and that the rhetorical term *eloquence* was the name applied to achievement in this form of art.

That Chaucer was not unacquainted with medieval rhetoric has already been pointed out. That his sound judgment saved him from the absurdities that this art might easily lead to has also been mentioned. His successors in the fifteenth century were not governed by the same moderation. To Lydgate the name *rhetoric* stood for the ideal of literary excellence. Affectedly modest in his own pretensions, to his admired Chaucer he attributes the "colours purperate of Rethoryke." His enthusiasm for this ideal is expressed with rhetorical eloquence in his *Court of Sapyence:*

Dame Rethoryke moder of eloquence
Moost elegaunt moost pure and gloryous

. . . . .

Within her parlour fresshe and precyous
Was set a quene, . . .

. . . . .

And many clerke had lust her for to here
Her speche to them was parfyte sustenance
Eche worde of her depured ['refined'] was so clere
And illumyned with so parfyte pleasaunce
That heuen it was to here her beauperlaunce ['fine language']
Her termes gay as facounde souerayne ['eloquence superior']
Catephaton in no poynt myght dystane ['surpass'].

> She taught them the crafte of endytynge
> Which vyces ben that sholde auoyded be
> Whiche ben the coulours gay of that counynge
> Theyr dyfference and eke theyr properte
> Eche thynge endyte how it sholde poynted be
> Dystynctyon she gan clare and dyscasse
> Whiche is coma colym perydus.[9]

The last three words mean respectively, 'comma,' 'colon,' and 'periods,' but the words are here applied to mean the rhythmical members of a sentence, the meaning borne by these words in Latin and in Greek.

The aureate style beginning to appear in Lydgate's writings is more fully developed about a century later in the writings of Hawes, who takes Lydgate as his model. To quote from Hawes:

> . . . my mayster Lydgate veryfyde
> The depured rethoryke in Englysh language;
> To make our tongue so clerely puryfyed
> That the vyle termes should nothing arage
> As like a pye ['magpie'] to chatter in a cage,
> But for to speke with rethoryke formally.[10]

The amount of artifice in the aureate style of fifteenth-century British poets is at once apparent. The precise nature, however, of the devices employed is not so easily recognizable to one untrained in medieval rhetoric. The modern reader, therefore, owes a debt of gratitude to an anonymous poet who near the end of the fifteenth century composed an *Epitaffe of—Jasper late Duke of Bedford*.[11] In this poem are employed more than twenty of the *colores* of rhetoric and their recognition is made easy because in the margin of the page is printed the name of the device em-

---

[9] Clark, *op. cit.*, pp. 48-9.
[10] *The Pastime of Pleasure*, quoted by Clark, *op. cit.*, p. 54.
[11] *Poetical Works of John Skelton*, ed. Dyce, II, p. 389.

ployed in the adjacent text. In the text, for instance, appears the line:

For thy might contrary to right thou dost gretly abuse,

in which the word *abuse* means 'to employ improperly,' a use of the word first cited in the Oxford Dictionary from about a hundred years later.[12]   In the margin appears the label *introductio* by which is meant, in the medieval treatises, the device named *aliene dictionis introductio* or 'borrowing of a foreign word.'   In another place appears the line:

Bydinge al alone, with sorowe sore encombred.

In the margin appears the annotation *ficcio*, referring to the *nove dictionis fictio* or 'making a new word' of the Latin treatises.   The new word in this case is *encombred* used with a meaning of which this is the first recorded instance. In another place appears the line:

Youre plesures been past vnto penalyte,

in which the word *penalyte* ['penalty'] appears for the first time, as far as the records of the Oxford Dictionary go, with the meaning 'suffering.'   In this instance the marginal label provided is *transsumpcio,* meaning 'new significance.'

The additional illustration afforded of the other *colores: recitatio simplex, narracio, discripsio, iteracio, exclamacio, reprobacio, newgacio, prosopopeya, onomotopeya, probacio, degressio, transuercio, excusacio, prolongacio,* and *conclusio,* make this poem an excellent key to the use of rhetorical devices so assiduously cultivated in the aureate style of writing.   The poem also demonstrates the deliberate pains taken in the cultivation of the aureate language, in "clokyng a trouthe with colour tenebrous."

[12] Berdan, *op. cit.,* p. 138.

The cultivation of prose in English lagged behind that of verse. In the first part of the fifteenth century prose continued, as with Chaucer, to play a comparatively humble rôle. Works of learned character on history or law, on philosophy or theology, in this period were normally composed in the language of learning, that is to say, Latin. For instance, Latin works made up the famous collection of books presented by Humphrey, Duke of Gloucester, to Oxford University and forming the nucleus of the Bodleian Library. In English were composed only a relatively small number of works, mainly of religious or controversial nature, and written in the vernacular language because intended to reach a popular audience.

In the development of English prose there was a lack of pattern corresponding to that provided by metrical forms. More serious still was the lack in English, in consequence of three centuries of neglect following the Norman Conquest, of general terms of the kind available in Latin. This lack goes far to explain the awkward circumlocutions and the lack of precision in the English writings of Wycliffe and of many other writers in the two following centuries. Under such conditions it is natural to expect to find the influence of cultivated Latin reflected in word and phrase and even in sentence structure.

In order to observe the language of English prose in the fifteenth century let us center attention on a single writer. For this purpose the writings of Reginald Pecock will serve. Pecock had been stirred by the attacks made by Wycliffe's followers, the Lollards, on ecclesiastical institutions. To counteract the influence of these Lollard attacks, he composed his *Repressour of ouer-much Blaming the Clergy.* The clumsiness of the English title is to be noted. Since Pecock's aim was to reach the popular audience of the Lollards, in this book he adopts, not Latin, the language of learning, but the vernacular tongue. He adopts the weapons of his opponents. His aim was not that of his poet contemporaries, to cloak the meaning in obscure terms, but to reveal the naked truth. "Whilis men accorden in the thing and in the treuthe in it silf," he says, "stryue thei not aboute wordis and namyng of the same thing." [13] And yet the word problem for him was one of practical importance. In order to reach his popular audience he had to find English equivalents for the Latin words familiar to him but not to his popular audience. At times he adapted Latin or French words into English, *e.g.*, *assumpt, excusatorye, explaying, defensory*. At times in order to make clear the meaning he joins native English words to learned borrowed terms, *e.g.*, *appetitis or lustys, accidentis or fallyngis, nextnesse or immediacioun*. At other times he turns English words to new uses in making them serve in place of Latin ones, *e.g.*, *ouerer*, 'superior'; *ouerte*, 'superiority'; *rennyngli*, 'cursim.' [14] In these three methods of providing needed words, it should be noted that he follows classical precept as laid down by Cicero.

In many instances the native expression favored by Pecock has later been superseded by a word of foreign origin, for example, *folewer* by *sequel*, *outdrau3t* by *extract*. Some of his native compounds fail to suit the genius of the language, in our day even seem monstrosities, *e.g.*, *vna3endressabli* and *vntobethou3tupon*. There are a considerable number of English words the earliest citations of which in the Oxford Dictionary are from Pecock, some of them now established in general use, *e.g.*, *accordingnes, avidiosely, charitative, corrupcioun, curraunt, insensible, noysum*.

Such were the heroic efforts required in order to provide expression in English for ideas heretofore associated with

[13] *The Folewer*, ed. Hitchcock, p. ix.
[14] *Ibid.*, pp. lx-lxi.

Latin forms. The prose of Pecock shows how undeveloped, how experimental, was the English available for use in plain prose in the century following Chaucer. It shows the methods used in the development of native resources for expression. It shows further how much English prose writers as well as poets drew materials and methods of expression from the highly cultivated Latin language.

In the hands of the successors of Chaucer literary English obviously drew farther and farther from the speech of everyday life. In poetry the natural graces of simple speech were replaced by affected manners. A fresh natural complexion was covered under colors of rhetoric. In prose writing a condensed mode of expressing general ideas was gained by the adoption, under Latin influence, of abstract words in place of concrete expressions with sharper edge. The native English tradition, however, was not completely supplanted. The popular form of speech which had provided the medium of expression for the *Piers Plowman* poet persisted throughout the following century. Jack Upland became the fifteenth-century spokesman for the class in the preceding century represented by *Piers Plowman*. In writings expressing the discontent of humbler classes there is reached a rude form of eloquence little related to the rhetoric cultivated in the schools.

In such writings words follow words in a tumbling rhythm in which fluidity is aided by the use of the native English device of alliteration. John de Trevisa in the fourteenth century in a dedicatory epistle to his patron, Lord Berkeley, adopts this popular English form of eloquence: "Therefore I will fond to take that travail . . . for blame of bakbiters will I not blinne; for envy of enemies, for evil spiting and speech of evil speakers." [15] The native vigor of this form of expression has always recommended it for use where

[15] Modernized spelling.

downright force was desired.   In the early days of the
Renaissance it served to express the reaction from medieval-
ism.   One will recognize a kinship between this mode of
English speech and the French of the contemporary
Rabelais.   Indeed this busteous mode of expression has
never become extinct.   It reappears again and again
throughout the fifteenth century and, as remains to be seen,
in the controversial writings of the sixteenth century.   In
the twentieth century it has been adopted anew as a weapon
for dealing heavy blows by American writers in belligerent
mood, and a well-known English woman poet of our own
day speaks with vehemence of the "lice upon the locks of
literature," an expression which in its vulgar plainness
polished by alliteration reproduces a quality cultivated by
homely writers in earlier stages in the development of English expression.

The stream of English literary expression which in the
course of the fifteenth century had been swollen through
the influence of Medieval Latin learning, was joined, near
the dawn of the sixteenth century, by a new tributary.   The
humanistic influence coming with the revival of classical
learning was the most potent force in shaping the course
of the English language in the centuries following the
Renaissance in England.   At the beginning of the sixteenth
century, however, the new influence was only beginning to
make itself felt.   For the time being it was not clearly
apparent what was to be the direction resulting from
the confluence of the classical stream with the native English and the Medieval Latin streams.

The uncertainty of direction appears in the writings of
John Skelton (born about 1460).   Among his writings the
modern student finds himself in a whirlpool of conflicting
currents rather than in a forward moving stream.   Skelton
was not unacquainted with the new Humanist movement

which was to determine the course of development in English literature and English language as the sixteenth century progressed. His attitude, however, toward the New Learning was not a friendly one. In his *Speke, Parrot,* he says sarcastically:

> But our Grekis theyr Greke so well haue applyed
> That they cannot say in Greke, rydynge by the way,
> "How, hosteler, fetche my hors a botell of hay."

The New Learning, he fears, is ruining the old. The schools, he says, are

> Settynge theyr myndys so moche of eloquens,
> That of theyr scole maters lost is the hole sentens.

For the earlier English writers he has words of praise, and he makes free use of the rime-royal, the stanza form invented by Chaucer and in general use among his followers. But he says, "Gower's English is old." Of Chaucer's English, he says:

> At those days much commended
> And now men would have amended
> His English, whereat they bark.

In the case of Lydgate, to commendation he joins censure. Concerning him, he says:

> It is diffuse to find
> The sentence of his mind.[16]

The earlier English tradition independent of the Chaucerian school, is also represented in Skelton. The alliterative form of verse with tumbling rhythm is frequently used. The rude strength of this kind of verse suited the fiery Skelton when in the mood for invective. In *Speke, Parrot,* at the end, he turns from the half serious vein of satirical

[16] *Philip Sparrow,* 784, 796-8, 806-7.

trifling to downright denunciation. He calls upon the Parrot to "Sette asyde all sophysms and speke now trew and playne." He then launches forth in torrential invective against his enemy, Wolsey, of which the following stanza will afford some impression:

> So myche raggyd ryghte of a rammes horne;
> So rygorous revelyng in a prelate specially;
> So bold and so braggyng, and was so baselye borne;
> So lordlye of hys lokes and so dysdayneslye;
> So fatte a magott, bred of a flesshe flye;
> Was nevyr suche a ffylty gorgon, nor suche an epycure,
> Syn(s) Dewcalyon's flodde, I make the faste and sure.

Diverse were the patterns followed by this versatile writer. He was not in sympathy with the classical movement getting well under way in his time. But earlier English models also were not altogether sufficing:

> Oure language is so rusty,
> So cankered, and so full
> Of frowards, and so dull
> That if I would apply
> To write ornately,
> I wot not where to find
> Terms to serve my mind.[17]

The literary guidance, therefore, not found in earlier English writers, Skelton sought in Medieval Latin. A short passage will serve to illustrate the form of verse with short lines, either in couplets or in a long series with single rime, which is associated with the name of Skelton:

> What can auayle
> To dryue forth a snayle
> Or to make a sayle
> Of an herynges tayle;

[17] *Ibid.*, 777-83.

> To ryme or to rayle,
> To wryte or to indyte
> Eyther for delyte
> Or elles for despyte;
> Or bokes to compyle
> Of dyuers maner style,
> Vyce to reuyle
> And synne to exyle.[18]

This seemingly original mode of writing, it has recently been demonstrated has its source in Medieval Latin.[19]

The new standards of taste that came to prevail in England in the sixteenth century as the result of the New Learning of the Renaissance, soon rendered Skelton's works out of fashion. Moreover, the conspicuous lack of dignity in his form of verse and in the kind of words employed by him made his mode of writing a medium for parody and satire. Under the dominance of new fashions his style of writing could seem nothing but absurd. The same revolt in taste which made the name of the learned Duns Scotus serve as the name for *dunce* caused the original and learned John Skelton to be thought of as a buffoon. In the later sixteenth century he was known as the hero of a jest book, the *Merry Tales of Skelton,* in a class with the German *Parson of Kalenborowe* and *Tyll Howleglas,* and with later English jesters and comedians such as Tarleton, Will Sommers, and George Peele. In the history of the English language, however, he deserves an important place because of his experiments in many modes of writing, but particularly because of his application in English writing of so many of the artifices of Medieval Latin. From his contemporaries Skelton won much praise, but his contribution to the development of literary expression in English was rendered abortive by the sudden and complete change of taste in the period immediately following his own.

[18] *Colin Clout,* 1-12.   [19] Berdan, *op. cit.,* Chap. III.

CHAPTER IV

CAXTON AND THE PRINTING PRESS

OBVIOUSLY at the end of the fifteenth century the English language in its progress had come to a parting of the ways. Before the writers of that time lay open three courses, that following the native tradition with its robustious form of eloquence, that guided by the art principles of Medieval Latin, or that directed by the New Learning, the product of the Renaissance. As has been seen Skelton ventured on each of these courses. His undoubted ability, however, was in great part wasted because of uncertainty of direction. Hawes, who lived until 1523, continued in the rhetorical road, but, as already mentioned, had a feeling of solitariness. He was obviously not in the main current of progress.

In the early lifetime of these two men, however, occurred an event which was destined eventually to do much in determining the subsequent course of English literature and which had greater influence than anything that preceded in fixing the form of Standard English. This event was the invention of the art of printing from moveable type. The honor of introducing this new art to England belongs to William Caxton. The personal history, therefore, of this distinguished man, and the circumstances leading to his famous achievement have their importance in the history of the English language.

Caxton was born and learned his English, he informs us, in Kent, "in the weeld where I doubte not is spoken as brode and rude englissh as in ony place of englond." Born about 1425, he was apprenticed in 1438 to one of the most prominent merchants of London. He remained in this service until 1441, when he went to the Low Countries, where he seems to have prospered. In 1469 he entered the personal service of the English Duchess of Burgundy, sister of King Edward IV, and there at Bruges found leisure to engage in literary pursuits. In the course of these years, associated with people of rank and under the correction of his Duchess patroness, he divested his language of features peculiar to his native Kentish dialect such as those which crop out occasionally in the language of the poet Gower, another native of Kent.

On a visit to Cologne in 1471 he presumably became acquainted with the printing press in operation there. In any event he was instrumental in having set up by Colard Mansion a printing press at Bruges. From this press about 1475 was issued the *Recuyell of the Histories of Troy,* the first book printed in the English language.

This book was a translation made by Caxton himself of a French compilation of stories of Troy made in 1464 by Raoul le Fevre, Chaplain of Philip, Duke of Burgundy. In his prologue Caxton tells of his enthusiasm in reading this French book and of his determination to translate it into "oure englyssh to thende that hyt myght be had as well in the royame of Englond as in other londes, and also to passe therwyth the tyme." He began the work, he tells us, on March 1, 1468, but after he "had made and wretyn a fyve or six quayers," he "fyll in dispayr," largely on account of his "vnperfightnes" both in French and in English, and laid the work aside. Later, encouraged by the Duchess of Burgundy, his patroness, who "ouersawe and corrected" his work, he resumed his task and brought the work to completion on September 19, 1471.

His book proved popular and Caxton was asked to make

copies. In this way probably he was led to the idea of a less laborious method of copying, and his translation was issued from the printing press at Bruges in 1475. In the same year he issued from his press another translation by himself, also from the French, his *Game and Playe of the Chesse*. The following year he brought the printing press to England and set it up at Westminster.

The importance of the printing press in molding a language is obvious. Even before the printing press it was the copying agent, the scribe, who had given to words their written forms, often forms not intended by the author. The author had needed to be continually on the alert to prevent his meaning from becoming distorted, his meter from being ruined, through the liberties taken by scribes. The methods of fifteenth-century scribes have made it difficult to determine the exact form of Chaucer's language, and they have made almost impossible the task of determining precisely the form of meter intended by Lydgate. The influence of the printer was greater even than that exercised by the scribe. The multiplication of copies of books made possible by the new mechanical means secured for books an incalculably wider circulation than had been possible in the days when literary works were reproduced by the laborious and expensive art of the scrivener. There was thus a gain in uniformity. Furthermore the products of literary art, before read aloud from precious manuscripts for the entertainment of a group of hearers, now became available for the individual reader in relatively inexpensive copies. Through individual reading English words became familiar to the eye as well as to the ear.

In the hands of the early printers the author was nearly as helpless as he had been in the days of the scribe as far as the written form of his words was concerned. This helplessness appears in the case of Sir Thomas Wyatt (1503-

no drede ne fere no thynge/ For I shalle not accuse the/ For I
shalle shewe to hym another way/ And as the hunter came/
he demaunded of the sheepherd yf he had sene the wulf pas¬
se/And the sheepherd both with the hede and of the eyen she¬
wed to the hunter the place where the wulf was / & with the
hand and the tongue shelwed alle the contrarye / And ins
contynent the hunter understood hym wel / But the wulf
whiche perceyued wel all the fayned maners of the sheepherd
fledd alwey/❡ And within a lytyll whyle after the sheepherd
encountred and mette with the wulf/to whome he sayd/paye
me of that I haue kepte the secrete/❡ And thenne the wulf
ansuerd to hym in this manere / I thanke thyn handes and
thy tongue/ and not thyn hede ne thyn eyen / For by them I
shold haue ben bytrayd/yf I had not fledde alwaye/❡ And
therfore men must not truste in hym that hath two faces and
two tongues/for suche folke is lyke and semblable to the scor
pion/the whiche enoynteth with his tongue/and prycketh so¬
re with his taylle

Page (reduced) from the *Æsop* printed by Caxton, Westminster, 1483.

1542). The various manuscripts in which Wyatt's poems are preserved depart in many instances from the text of the author's autograph manuscript, and the printed version in Tottel's *Miscellany* is far from an exact reproduction of the language of the author.[1] Indeed we are told that in the early sixteenth century, "aside from Latin works intended for an European public, there is no evidence that a single English author, with the exception of those engaged in controversies, ever prepared his manuscript for printing." [2]

The rule of the printer over the external form of the language, established at an early stage, has continued in later periods. In many instances, for instance in the case of Shakespeare, it is much to be deplored that the exact form of language used by the writer is so difficult to discover because of the intervention of the printer between author and reader. There has, however, been compensation. The printers contributed toward uniformity in the external form of language. The printed books of the sixteenth century, with all the irregularities that they offer to the eye of the modern reader, appear like order itself in comparison with the chaos still appearing in the epistolary correspondence of the time. In the following centuries, as remains to be seen, it was the printing establishments that exerted the most potent influence in giving to English words their modern forms. Nor has the influence of printing been confined to the surface, to the written forms of words. It has reached to the quick in language. In later periods the written forms of words, which should reflect the sounds of living speech, by a reversal of forces have come frequently to determine the pronunciation. That this form of retroaction, so much now in evidence, is early in making itself felt appears from a passage from Sir Thomas Elyot's *The*

[1] J. M. Berdan, *Early Tudor Poetry*, p. 505.
[2] *Ibid.*, p. 445, note.

Gouernour (1531) where in his recommendations for the education of a nobleman's son Elyot urges that "the nourishes ['nurses'] and other women aboute hym . . . speke none englisshe but that which is cleane, polite, perfectly and articulately pronounced, omitting no lettre or sillable, as folishe women oftentimes do of a wantonnesse ['lack of breeding'] whereby diuers noble men and gentlemennes chyldren, as I do at this daye knowe, haue attained corrupte and foule pronuntiation." It is evidently intended that the free and natural mode of speech like that reflected in many of the fifteenth-century *Paston Letters* should be governed by the written form.

In this connection it should be held in mind not only that Caxton's press was brought over from the continent, possibly with many of its operators, and that the Gothic type used by his press was like that used on the continent, but that Caxton and his successors, Wynkyn de Worde, Pynson, Copeland, and the others, had no monopoly in English printing. English books were issued from the presses of France, Germany, and the Netherlands. Books connected with the Reformation movement not as yet tolerated by the English government were issued from the presses on the Continent. Tyndale's New Testament, publicly burned in England, was printed, it will be remembered, at Worms. Occasionally, as in the case of the *Kalendayr of shyppars* ('Calendar of Shepherds') from the Parisian press of Antoine Vérard (1503), the English was transformed into a "corrupte englysshe" such as, in the opinion of the English printer Pynson, "no man coude vnderstonde."[3] In other instances, less extreme, the forms of words used by foreign printers appear to have had a permanent influence on English words. One cannot but suspect here the source of the *-gue* and *-que* endings, surviving in

[3] *Ibid.,* p. 500.

such words as *tongue, prologue,* (Chaucer, *tonge, prologe*) and in sixteenth-century use appearing also in *publique, musique,* and even in *dogue* ('dog').

But Caxton was more than a printer; he was himself a man of letters. His own writings reflect current literary tendencies and in their turn they exerted an influence on the language of his time and generation. He was a man of wealth and, therefore, able to follow his own taste to some extent. But the nature of his literary undertakings was necessarily influenced by his patrons, and these, like the patrons of Lydgate, were found among the nobility. In the prologue to his translation, *Charles the Great,* he says that "some persones of noble estate and degree haue desyred me to reduce thystorye and lyf of the noble and crysten prynce . . . to thende that thystoryes, actes & lyues may be had in our maternal tongue . . ." Who these "persones of noble estate" were, we know from his other works. His *History of Jason* (*ca.* 1477) was written "vnder the proteccion & suffraunce of" King Edward IV, but presented not to the King, "forasmoch as I doubte not his good grace hath it in French," but to "my moost redoubted yong lorde, My lord Prynce of Wales . . . to thentent he may begynne to lerne rede Englissh." His *Blanchardyn and Eglantine* (*ca.* 1489) was translated at the request of Margaret, Duchess of Somerset, from a manuscript she had bought from Caxton years before. His *Golden Legend* was translated under the patronage of William, Earl of Arundel. His *Mirrour of the World* (1480) was made "atte request and desyre, coste and dispence of the honourable and worshipful man, Hugh Bryce, Citezeyn and Alderman of London"— to be presented to Lord Hastings. *The Fayttes of Arms* was made at the express desire of Henry VII, who lent the manuscript.

It appears, therefore, that Caxton was a literary purveyor to the nobility and royalty of his time. His great task seems to have been to provide English versions of the literary works which a century earlier such patrons would have read in French. The conditions were not favorable for original production in English. About one-third of the works issued from Caxton's press were translations by himself. The other publications were for the most part new editions of earlier English works such as those of Chaucer and Lydgate, or works derived from translation, such as the *Morte d'Arthur* of Sir Thomas Malory, reflecting the medieval spirit still prevalent. The same trend may be observed in the works issued by Caxton's successors, Wynkyn de Worde and Pynson.

Caxton's first works were products of great travail of spirit. His *Recuyell,* begun in 1468, was not completed until 1471. For a time abandoned, it was resumed and completed only after the Duchess of Burgundy had "ouersawe and corrected" the first part. Obviously in his later works he must have developed greater facility, for his translation of the *Mirrour of the World,* which was begun on January 2, 1480, was finished on March 8 of the same year. His works, however, continue to be provided with apologetic remarks about his insufficiency. In his *Blanchardyn and Eglantine* he beseeches his "ladyes bountyous grace to pardoune me of the rude and comyn englysshe. . . . For I confesse me not lerned, ne knowynge the arte of rhetoryk ne of suche gaye termes as now be sayd in these dayes and vsed."

The humility of this remark must, of course, not be taken too literally. Such apologetic statements had become a form of commonplace in the works composed for noble patrons. In fact, Caxton in his writings was by no means without literary pretension. If he had little Latin learning and if he was not accomplished in the "arte of rhetoryk" that went to form the aureate style of his time, in the

French works which he translated he found a pattern. His most conspicuous artifice in writing was the use of synonyms in pairs, or triplets, or quadruplets. This feature of style, which he shared with many English writers of the period, he found firmly established in his French originals. In this respect as in others he is influenced by the language of his French originals. In fact his writings bristle with Gallicisms. Locutions such as *sixty and eleven* ('soizante onze'), *lo, here* ('voici'), *foreseen that* ('prevu que'), *the said* ('le dit'), *remembered myself* ('me souvenir'), *the which* ('le quel'), *all day* ('toujours') *brother germane,* patterned after French models, taken with French words adopted bodily such as, *gre, devoir, siege, bayned, debonnair,* and *taillage,* demonstrate conclusively his indebtedness to French.

Unfortunately for Caxton, imitable models of English prose were not at hand. Chaucer he worshiped only this side of idolatry. He is said to have placed a tablet in Chaucer's honor in Westminster Abbey. Some of his words of praise have already been quoted. The judgment is discriminating and just. What a pity that an ideal of style so clearly perceived could not have been put in practice in his own writings!

Unfortunately the changes which, as remains to be pointed out, were taking place in the English language of the fifteenth century had made much of the writing of Chaucer's time no longer available as a model. The language of Chaucer himself Caxton could reproduce with little change. But the rapidity of change had been such that the language of some of Chaucer's contemporaries was no longer intelligible. With this fact Caxton had to reckon. The policy adopted by Caxton appears in his printed edition of Trevisa's fourteenth-century translation of Higden's *Polychronicon.* Trevisa, a Cornishman by birth, had been educated at Oxford but had spent most of his life in Gloucester as chaplain to Lord Berkeley. His language, therefore, was not that of his contemporary, Chaucer, and in the late fifteenth century, although the influence of Chaucer was still a dominant one, the language of Trevisa seemed particularly "rude and incongrue." Caxton, therefore, in his edition found it advisable to change "the rude and old englyssh, that is to wete certayn wordes which in these days be neither vsyd ne vnderstandyn." The following list of words, with the substitutions made by Caxton, affords interesting illustration of the changing English vocabulary and the progress made toward a standard form.[4]

TREVISA	CAXTON
i-cleped	called
schulleþ fonge	shall resseyue
ich	I
to eche	encrece
lore	doctrine
to wone	dwell
byneme	take away
to welk	fade
eyren	eggs
buxom	obedient
hiꜩt	was named
as me troweþ	as men suppose
steihe	ascended
heleful	healthful
aꜩe	agayn
schrewednesse	ylle disposition
deel	part
ꜩede	went
swiþe good	right good
nesche	soft
chepinge	market

4 Collected by T. L. K. Oliphant, *The New English,* I.

But the most interesting passage in Caxton relating to the state of the language in his time is the oft-quoted passage from the preface to the *Eneydos*. In it Caxton makes clear the conflicting tendencies in literary circles of his time. He "stands abashed," he says, between patrons, "some gentylmen" who prefer the use of "olde and homely termes"—probably referring to the traditional form of language associated with the use of alliteration—and other patrons, "honest and grete clerkes" who desired him to write "the moste curyous termes that I coude fynde," that is to say, the aureate language of fifteenth-century rhetoric. In the preparation of this work Caxton had called Skelton into consultation, and it would be interesting to know what was the attitude in this matter of his counselor who showed himself an adept in both styles. Happily Caxton's conclusion was to use "a meane bytwene bothe." The passage further in most concrete fashion illustrates the conflict between dialects still alive in his time. The passage deserves to be reproduced in its entirety.

And whā I had aduysed me in ['made myself familiar with'] this sayd boke ['*Eneydos*']. I delyvered ['decided'] and concluded to translate it ['from French'] in to englysshe. And forthwyth toke a penne & ynke and wrote a leef or tweyne/ whyche I ouersawe agayn to corecte it/ And whā I sawe the fayr and straunge termes therein/ I doubted that it sholde not please some gentylmen which late blamed me, sayeing þᵗ in my translacyons I had ouer curyous termes which coude not be vnderstande of comyn peple/ and desired me to vse olde and homely termes in my translacyons. and fayn wolde I satisfye euery man/ and so to doo toke an olde booke and redde therin/ and certaynly the englysshe was so rude and brood that I coude not wele vnderstande it. And also my lorde abbot of westmynster ded do shewe to me late certayn euydences wryton in olde englysshe for to reduce it in to our englysshe now vsid/ And certaynly it was wreton in suche wyse that it was more lyke to dutche than englysshe I coude not reduce ne brynge it to be vnderstonden/ And certaynly our langage now vsed varyeth ferre from that which was vsed and spoken whan I was borne/ For we englysshe men/ ben borne vnder the domynacyon of the mone. whiche is neuer sted-faste/ but euer wauerynge/ wexynge one season/ and waneth & dycreaseth another season/ And that comyn englysshe that is spoken in one shyre varyeth from another. In so moche that in my dayes happened that certayn marchaūtes were in a ship in tamyse for to haue sayled ouer the see into zelande/ and for lacke of wynde thei taryed atte forlond. and wente to land for to refreshe them And one of thaym named sheffelde a mercer came in to an hows and axed for mete and specyally he axyd after eggys And the goode wyf answerde that she coude speke no frenshe. And the marchaūt was angry for he also coude speke no frenshe. but wolde haue hadde egges/ and she vnderstode hym not/ And thenne at laste a nother sayd that he wolde haue eyren/ then the good wyf sayd that she vnderstod hym wel/ Loo what sholde a man in thyse dayes now wryte. egges or eyren/ certynly it is harde to playse euery man/ by cause of dyuersitie & chaūge of langage. For in these dayes euery man that is in ony reputacyon in his coūtre. wyll vtter his comyncacyon and maters in such maners & termes/ that fewe men shall vnderstonde theym/ And som honest and grete clerkes haue ben wyth me and desired me to wryte the moste curyous termes that I coude fynde/ And thus bytwene playn rude & curyous I stande abasshed. but in my Iudgmente/ the comyn termes that be dayli vsed ben lyghter to be vnderstonde than the olde and aūcyend englysshe/ And for as moche as this present booke is not for a rude vplondyssh man to laboure therein/ ne rede it/ but onely for a clerke & a noble gentylman that feleth and vnderstondeth in faytes of armes in loue & in noble chyualrye/ Therefor in a meane bytwene bothe I haue reduced & translated this sayd booke in to our englysshe not ouer rude ne curyous but in such termes as shall be vnderstanden by goddys grace accordynge to my copye.

The printing press introduced by Caxton was one of the most important factors in fixing the English language in permanent form. From the consideration of Caxton's own literary activities, however, it does not appear that his example was a decisive force in determining the direction to be taken by English literature and the English language in their progress. On the contrary Caxton finds himself in uncertainty about the direction to be taken. Like Skelton, probably influenced by Skelton, whom he called into counsel, he pursues in general the medieval direction. The works issued from his press, in great part translations by himself or by others, made accessible in English form the products of medieval literature. These translations served to bring English literature abreast with the literature of other countries. But they did not serve the interests of the new humanistic movement then getting under way in other countries. Much the same may be said of the works published by Caxton's immediate successors, Wynkyn de Worde and Pynson.

The printing press, however, in other countries, especially in Italy, was turned to other uses. It provided a channel through which flowed the New Learning of the Renaissance. One should call to mind the labors of the Venetian printer Aldus Manutius in setting in circulation printed editions of the classical works newly brought to light by Renaissance scholarship. Through the agency of printing presses like that of Aldus Manutius, in the last twenty years of the fifteenth century all the principal works of classical Latin literature were made available in printed form, and in the first two decades of the sixteenth century the same was done for Greek literature. Without the instrumentality of the printing press the diffusion of the New Learning which so rapidly spread throughout Europe, could not have taken place. The printing press, therefore, was one of the most active agents in introducing a new age in the history of European culture, and a new period in the development of the English language.

CHAPTER V

TRANSITION FROM MIDDLE ENGLISH TO MODERN ENGLISH

THE efforts of literary men in the course of the fifteenth century unquestionably served to develop the expressive power of the English language. It should be noted, however, that the literary works that have been considered were composed for a cultured few. Lydgate's works were composed for an aristocratic audience. The list of his patrons includes men of the highest rank, such as the Earl of Salisbury, the Earl of Warwick, Humphrey, Duke of Gloucester, and the two kings, Henry V, and Henry VI. His choice of subjects and manner of treatment were largely determined by the taste of these distinguished patrons. The beautifully illuminated manuscripts in which many of his works survive were obviously not intended for general and popular use. Hawes, also, was a poet of the court, "somtyme grome of ye chambre of oure late souerayne lorde kynge Henry seventh," and Skelton served as tutor to Prince Henry, later King Henry VIII. Mention has also been made of the royal and noble patrons for whom Caxton labored. Obviously the artifices that embellished the productions of such writers do not reflect the nature of language in popular use.

In fact in this century is to be observed the beginning of an interplay of forces between literary language consciously cultivated on the one hand and, on the other hand, colloquial speech governed only by the natural laws of language, an interplay which in the course of five centuries shaped the standard English of our time. Let us now turn our attention to the language in popular daily use, which forms the main current in the progress of any language.

That the language in current popular use in the fifteenth century was unsettled and most irregular we know from many sources. Lydgate in his *Court of Sapyence* offers evidence:

> I knowe my selfe moost naked in all artes
> My comyn vulgare eke moost interupte;
> And I conuersaunte & borne in the partes
> Where my natyfe langage is moost corrupte
> And with moost sondry tonges myxte & rupte.[1]

The same kind of language difficulty is felt by Reginald Pecock. In his *Book of Feith*, written about 1454, he expresses his feeling as follows:

> Langagis, whos reulis ['rules'] ben not writen,
> as ben Englisch, Frensch, and manye othere,
> ben chaungid withynne ʒeeris ['years'] and countrees,
> that oon ['one'] man of the oon cuntre, and
> of the oon tyme, myʒte not, or schulde not
> kunne ['be able to'] vndirstonde a man of the othere
> kuntre, and of the othere tyme; and al
> for this, that the seid langagis ben not
> stabili and foundamentali writen.[2]

The situation before the days of printing should also be held in mind. With language so variable, individual scribes, for the most part trained craftsmen, and like publishers of later times with definite individual opinions, felt at liberty to use words and forms of words personally preferred. The consequence is great want of uniformity even among the different manuscripts of the same work, so that it is a matter of the greatest difficulty to determine

[1] *The Temple of Glass*, ed. Schick, p. ·lxiv.
[2] Ed. Hitchcock, p. lx.

the exact language used by the author. Chaucer's admonitions to Adam, his scrivener, because of his "negligence and rape (*i.e.*, haste)" are too well known to need quotation. His concern regarding the correct reproduction of his works is expressed in more serious tone in a remark introduced near the end of his ambitious work, the *Troilus and Criseyde*:

> And for ther is so greet diversitee
> In English and in wryting of our tonge,
> So preye I god that noon miswryte thee,
> Ne thee mismetre for defaute of tonge.
> And red ['read'] wher-so thou be, or elles songe,
> That thou be undirstonde I god beseche! [3]

If the manner of writing in manuscripts copied by trained scribes or scriveners, was careless and irregular, or capricious, in private correspondence it was not far from chaotic. How general was the ability to read and write in the fifteenth century it is not possible to say with certainty. That it was by no means universal even among the higher classes we must infer from the letter of Sir John Paston to Mrs. Anne Haute in 1468, in the postscript of which appears the following interesting remark: "Maitresse Annes, I am prowd that ye can reed inglyshe; wherfor I prey yow aqwent yow with thys my lewd ['untrained'] hand . . ." That writing was a matter of no small difficulty appears from a letter written by King Henry VII to his mother, which, he informs her, required three days to complete. Those who were able to read and write were not troubled by rules for spelling. That modern tyrant of language, the maker of the spelling-book, had not yet come into being. In consequence in the epistolary correspondence there appears a luxuriant variety of forms of words.

The voices of the fifteenth century are silent. Some

[3] Ed. Skeat, V, 1793-8.

records, however, of the sounds are left in the plastic spelling of the period. Of these speech records there is to be found an excellent supply in that remarkable collection of letters written by or to members of the Paston family in Norfolk during the reigns of Henry VI, Edward IV, and Richard III, and known as the Paston Letters. In these fifteenth-century letters one striking feature is the relatively small number of obsolete words. The words in everyday use at that time have for the most part remained permanently. It has been estimated [4] that "from 1290 to 1350 the proportion of Teutonic nouns, verbs, and adverbs that are now obsolete is 3 out of 50; from 1350 to 1400, 2 out of 50; from 1400 to 1450, 1 out of 50. After 1450 it is hardly worth counting." The modern words, however, appear in a variety of forms. The relative *which* appears in such varied forms as *wech, weche, wiche, quych, qwech, wheche*. In a single one of these letters the proper name *Worcester* appears as *Worsetyr, Wusseter, Wursseter*. Whereas the modern writer knows his words by sight and uses the written form which looks right, the fifteenth-century writer was in great part guided by sound, and, in consequence, his writing affords an idea of the mode of speaking in his time. The verb *have* is almost lost to view in such written phrases as *for to a spoke*, ('have spoken'), *shuld all abe* ('have been'), *he wold a be* ('have been'), *achamyd to a seyd* ('ashamed to have said'), but the sounds of fifteenth-century colloquial English are brought to our ears.

Dialectal difference in pronunciation appears in the case of certain words. The modern *give* in Northern speech of the time had the initial sound *g,* but in Southern speech the sound *y.* Hence in the Paston Letters the prevalent forms, *yeve, yeven, yoven,* or *ȝef, ȝovyn, ȝevyn,* with the *y* sound,

[4] T. L. K. Oliphant, *The New English*, I, p. 2.

and the less frequent forms, *geve, gevyng,* indicating the Northern pronunciation. In the same way along with *ayenst,* ('against'), *ayens, a3ens* appears the form *agens,* and along with *ayen* ('again'), *ayein, a3en,* appear *agayn, ageyn, agayne.* The Southern form *acsyd* ('axed') appears along with the more usual *asked* (or *haskyd*). The cockney *h*-occasionally makes its appearance, as in the forms *hoder* 'other'; *howyth,* 'oweth'; *honderstonde; haskyd,* 'asked.' The forms of words borrowed from French have an interest because in many instances they differ from later forms which have been modified in spelling, and sometimes in pronunciation as well, by the attempt made under Renaissance influence to bring these words into conformity with Latin patterns. Examples of such earlier forms are: *deffaut* (modern *default*), *defawt; assauted; savacion,* 'salvation'; *egallie,* 'equally'; *harrawd,* 'herald'; *reame,* 'realm'; *sowdyors,* 'soldiers'; *resceyte,* 'receipt'; *suget,* 'subject'; *leysir,* 'leisure'; *pleasir,* 'pleasure'; *displeaser.*

In Caxton's *Dialogues in French and English* are to be found scores of words of this kind whose spellings afford evidence of a popular mode of pronunciation little affected by the learned written forms, words such as: *auantage,* 'advantage'; *auctour,* 'author'; *briches; conduyte,* 'conduct'; *seeke,* 'sick'; *faucons,* 'falcons'; *feuerer,* 'February'; *Janiver,* 'January'; *Juyll,* 'July'; *kawdrons,* 'caldrons'; *leyzer,* 'leisure'; *recyte,* 'receipt'; *sawters,* 'psalters'; *samon,* 'salmon.' Many of these spellings, it will be observed, indicate a mode of pronunciation like that of French, from which the words are derived, rather than the later pronunciation affected by respelling under the influence of Latin learning. Occasionally appears a native word such as *eyrekakis* ('egg cakes') later superseded by the borrowed word, *omelette.* A popular pronunciation of proper names is recorded in such forms as: *Cecile,* 'Sicily'; *Coleyne,*

King Henry VII (1457-1509): portion of a page of a signed document concerning the raising of funds wherewith to prosecute war against Scotland. The language used is of the official kind taught in the *Ars Dictandi* of the period.

'Cologne'; *Reynes,* 'Rheims'; *Roen,* 'Rouen.' The same tendencies appear in the spelled forms of the popular drama. In the Towneley Plays, for example, appear: *vokettys,* 'advocates'; *sawgeoure,* 'soldier.'

One of the most remarkable features in the history of the English language was the sweeping change that affected the pronunciation of the long vowels. To this change has been applied the name the Great Vowel-Shift. The nature of this shift in pronunciation may be represented by pronunciations of representative words in parallel columns:

OLD ENGLISH	MODERN ENGLISH
ham (as in *ah*)	home
raedan (as in *am* prolonged)	read
bete (as in *ate*)	beet
ridan (as in *see*)	ride
sona (as in *bone*)	soon
hus (as in *goose*)	house

In all the words here represented the older pronunciation still survived, little changed, in Chaucer's time with the exception of words like *ham,* in which the earlier long *a* by Chaucer's time had developed to an open sound like that in modern *awe,* and possibly of words like *sona,* where the modern pronunciation seems to begin about Chaucer's time. With these exceptions the great changes in English vowel pronunciation have come about since 1400, and most of them are invisible in the written language since the spelling has not been changed to keep up with the change in sound.

The nature of this sweeping change has been summarized in the technical language of phonetics in a single sentence: "The great vowel-shift consists in a general raising of all long vowels with the exception of the two high vowels, *i* [as in *seed*] and *u* [as in *boot*] which could not be raised further without becoming consonants and which were first diphthongized" into sounds like those in *raid* and *hold*, later changed to the diphthongal sounds in *ride* (*ah* + *ee*) and *house* (*ah* + *oo*).[5]

But a satisfactory explanation of the causes producing this sweeping change has never been offered. Even the time of the change remains open to doubt. Certainly the shift in sounds was not completed even in the early eighteenth century, as remains to be seen. Some of the vowels retain their earlier sounds in local dialects of our own time, and in the form of Northern English used in Scotland, as everyone knows, the history of the vowel sounds has been different from that in Standard English.

There is even difference in opinion regarding the time when the change came about. The shift from long *a* to long *o,* as already pointed out, had advanced one stage before the time of Chaucer. Regarding the time of the other changes there exists great diversity of opinion. Recent opinion, however, tends to set these changes farther back in time than formerly supposed. According to Jespersen, the long *i* (*ee*) sound, as in *nice,* must have been diphthongized (*ay* + *ee*) about 1500, and the long *oo* sound in *thou* diphthongized to *o* + *oo* or *aw* + *oo* about the same time. Another eminent authority[6] sets these changes even farther back and asserts that "of fourteen vowel changes that differentiate Modern English from Middle English, all but one were completed, or at least begun before the end of the fifteenth century."

If this earlier period is accepted as the time of the great change in English vowel sounds, then the change in sound is synchronized with important changes in English syntax and in English inflections which in the fifteenth century

---

[5] Otto Jespersen, *A Modern English Grammar on Historical Principles,* I, 231. The bracketed expressions and the words following the quoted ones are additions made by the present writer.

[6] H. C. Wyld, *A History of Modern Colloquial English.*

were carried nearly to completion and which brought the language by the beginning of the sixteenth century in its general structure to the stage known as Modern English.

In the century preceding the dawn of the Modern English period, about 1500, the language was making striking progress in its capacity for linking word with word, clause with clause in precise relations by the development of those important elements in speech, the relative pronouns, the prepositions, and the conjunctions. The relative pronouns were enriched in variety. In the earlier Middle English period the prevalent relative form had been *that,* which had been shifted from its earlier function as a demonstrative. To this single form in the fourteenth century was added a new relative, *which,* developed from its earlier use as an interrogative. Somewhat later the forms, *who, whose,* and *whom,* in earlier English used as demonstrative and indefinite pronouns, became shifted in function to serve as relative pronouns. The latest of these forms to shift was *who,* which in Malory is still confined to use as an indefinite pronoun with the meaning 'whoever.' It will be recalled that in the language of the Lord's Prayer, which reflects the use of the early sixteenth century, *which* is used where modern usage requires *who.* In the fifteenth-century use these new relative forms, it is worth knowing, were not governed by modern restrictions. For instance, Malory speaks of *the lily in whome vyrgynyte is sygnefyed* and of *the Sancgreal thorow whoose grace. . . .* The use of *whom* applied to inanimate objects is not good Modern English use, and the similar use of *whose* has been frequently objected to by modern grammarians. That, however, through the adoption of these new relative forms there was gain in the indication of precise relations cannot be questioned.

Even more notable was the similar gain through the adoption of new prepositional and conjunctional words and phrases. For many of these a model was provided by Latin forms. *Notwithstanding,* which makes its first appearance in the fourteenth century, seems to be the equivalent of Latin *non obstante; by way of* translates the ablative form of Latin *via;* and the indispensable *because,* which in the fourteenth century makes its appearance in the forms *because of* and *because that,* seems to have its pattern in such Latin expressions as *honoris causa.* Probably in most cases based on Latin or French models, these words and phrases, along with others of their kind, such as, *on behalf of, for the sake of, during, concerning, except, in case of, provided that, considering,* and *meanwhile,* which in the later Middle English period begin to find adoption in English expression, unquestionably afford means of indicating relations more varied and more precise than could be indicated by the limited number of inflectional endings which in earlier stages had served to indicate distinctions in mood of verbs and case of nouns.

New flexibility and new precision in the indication of relations between ideas was provided by a more precise differentiation in the use of auxiliary verbs. The word *can* of which the earlier meaning had been 'know how to,' comes to its modern use in expressing ability or possibility. *May* which in earlier stages had meant 'to be able' comes to its modern use in expressing opportunity or permission.

Even more important are the new distinctions made possible in the indication of tense. In Old English the only tense distinction indicated by inflection was that between present and past. The present tense form served to indicate future as well as present. Later the verbs *shall,* originally meaning 'ought' or 'must,' and *will,* originally meaning 'want to,' 'intend to,' come to be used to indicate the simple future. In the fifteenth century both words are used in this way, also their preterit forms *should* and *would,* but as yet without a discrimination that can be formulated into definite rule.

It is interesting to note that in the fifteenth-century English of Malory the verb *to be* is regularly used as tense auxiliary with many verbs of motion such as: *come, go, enter, arrive,* and verbs of happening such as *become, fall,* and *befall,* a use the increasing disappearance of which is a feature of English in the nineteenth century.[7]

In the present state of knowledge regarding earlier English syntax it is not possible to make definite statements about the time when particular analytic or periphrastic forms of verbs first came into use. The fifteenth century, however, is certainly a time when such forms were generally adopted. In Malory the so-called progressive present and progressive past constructions, which in Modern English cause trouble to a foreigner learning English, are only beginning to come into use. Among the small number of instances are the following: *"this knyghte is goynge to the sege, an Heremyte . . . was goynge vnto masse."* [8]

The hortative subjunctive with the auxiliary *let,* now an established idiom in English, seems to have been establishing itself at this period. Compare the language of Wycliffe at the end of the fourteenth century with that of Malory a century later: *Hold we us appeased* (Wycliffe); *And bring ye a fat calf and eat we* (Wycliffe); *Now leue we of these knyghtes, and lete vs speke of the grete aray* (Malory).

The periphrastic forms with the auxiliary *do,* now established as regular modes of expression in negative statements and negative commands and in questions, were at this time beginning to come into use. Compare the following expressions: *I doubt not* (Caxton); *He saw you not* (Malory);

[7] C. S. Baldwin, *The Inflections and Syntax of the Morte d'Arthur of Sir Thomas Malory,* p. 84.
[8] *Ibid.,* p. 81.

And the three estates durst not come (Fortescue); *I trust I do not dysplese god* (Malory).

Double comparatives and superlatives were frequent in the fifteenth century and throughout the sixteenth century. In Malory appear: *more gladder, more leuer, more hardyer, moost royallest, moost shamefullest, moost lordlyest.*[9] In the language also of that distinguished exponent of the New Learning in the sixteenth century, Sir Thomas Elyot, one finds, *Aristotle, most sharpest witted . . . philosopher.* The use of the double negative was equally frequent: *ye shall never lose no blood* (Malory); *I know not in all my realm no knight more valiant than ye be* (Lord Berners).

These new analytical modes of expression which in the later years of the Middle English period were increasing in use, rendered more and more superfluous the older distinctions by means of inflectional endings. The absence of school instruction in the English language must be held in mind. There were as yet no English grammars, no English dictionaries, no spelling books. In everyday colloquial use natural tendencies were little controlled, and there was a strong natural tendency to abandon distinctions in form rendered superfluous by the analytical modes of speech rapidly finding adoption. A consequence was the loss, beginning as early as the thirteenth century in Northern English, and coming to completion everywhere in the course of the fifteenth century, of the final -e sound, nearly the last relic of the older English inflectional system. With the loss of the final -e, little was left, except in the case of pronouns, of the earlier modes of inflection. In great part verbs, nouns, adjectives, and many of the adverbs were left without endings and hence in form indistinguishable as parts of speech. The remains of English inflections were confined for the most part to the distinctive forms for

[9] *Ibid.,* p. 13.

the possessive case and for the plural number in nouns and to the personal endings and the distinction between present and past tenses in verbs.

Even in these forms the principle of analogy, the natural tendency toward uniformity, was in operation. The ending -*s* as the sign of the plural, in Old English confined to one class of masculine nouns, tended more and more to be used as the invariable sign of plural number in nouns of all classes and all genders, and the older genitive ending -*es,* in Old English distinctive of certain classes of masculine and neuter nouns, was becoming established as the sign of possession in nouns of all classes and all genders.

Of the older forms, there are, to be sure, exceptional survivals. Of the older plurals with the ending in -*en,* there survive in Chaucer: *yen,* 'eyes'; *oxen; pesen,* 'peas'; *fleen,* 'fleas'; *hosen,* and *foon* (along with *foos*), *asshen* (along with *asshes*), *been* (along with *bees*), *toon* (along with *toos*), *shoon* (along with *shoos*). In the writers of a century later there appear a diminishing number. In Malory there remain only *bretheren, children, eyen, oxen* and *kyen,* 'cows,' and the irregular forms *gamen* and *synnen,* possibly dialectic survivals.[10] Remains of the older genitive plural without -*s* used after numerals appear in Malory in expressions such as *twelve moneth, fourten nyght, seven ny3te, an hondred pound, thre hondred wynter, fourty yere, ten fadom, seven myle, two cast of brede, thyrtty coupel,* etc., contrasting with *monethes* (without numeral), *many wynters, many yeres agone,* etc.[11] Other plurals in Malory without -*s,* in part survivals of the earlier neuter plurals without -*s,* are; *folk* (along with *folkes* and *folke*), *good* (along with *goodes*), *thynge* (along with *thynges*). The plural form *hors* appearing in Chaucer, however, is in

[10] *Ibid.,* pp. 3-4.
[11] *Ibid.,* p. 2.

Malory always *horses*. Still other plurals without *-s*, most of them surviving to the present day, are the monosyllables of the Old English consonant declension, such as the following used by Caxton: *feet; men; gheet,* 'goats'; *ghees; lyce; kyen,* 'kine'; *myse.*

In the case of the pronouns the older distinctions were better preserved and have continued in great part down to the present. In the English of the end of the fifteenth century, however, there were a number of points of difference from the usage of the present day. One was the continued use of *his* as the neuter possessive, a use surviving to our own time in biblical language in expressions such as "every creature after his kind." Another was the declension of the personal pronoun in the second person: (Caxton) SINGULAR *thou, thy* or *thine, the;* PLURAL *ye, youre, you,* the singular forms, however, confined as in the continental languages of modern Europe, to familiar address. In general the pronoun forms were well preserved in the fifteenth century. "The confusion of cases that appears in Elizabethan writers, is barely apparent in Malory." [12]

In verbs the personal endings of the present indicative: *-e, -est, -eth* in the singular continue to be the regular forms throughout the fifteenth century. The influence of analogy, however, appears in the increasing tendency to shift many verbs from the strong to the weak conjugation, which was coming to be felt to be the "regular" mode of conjugation. The following verbs, strong in Chaucer, have in Malory changed to weak: *crepe, lepe, lete, sheete, slepe, weepe.* That the language in this respect, at the end of the fifteenth century, was in a transitional stage, is shown by the number of double forms in Malory such as: *clafe, cleft; brast, brest; grewe, growed; hewe, hewed; lough, laughed; sanke, synked; yolde, yelded.* The influence of analogy by the

[12] Baldwin, *op. cit.*

end of the fifteenth century is further illustrated by the fact that by the time of Malory's *Morte d'Arthur* the distinction in the preterit between singular and plural had been entirely levelled out.[13]

In addition to the changes in sounds and the leveling of forms through analogy in the Midland English of the fifteenth century, there is also to be reckoned with the influence of other dialects. The influence of Northern dialect appears in the plural of the pronoun of the third person. By the end of the fourteenth century *they* had made its way into the London English of Chaucer, but in Chaucer the possessive and objective forms are *her* and *hem,* the native English forms persisting in the South. In Caxton and Malory the prevalent forms are *they, their, them,* Norse forms which had made their way first into the speech of the North. In the present indicative of verbs the Chaucerian endings continue prevalent: SINGULAR *-e, -est, -eth;* PLURAL *-en (-n, -e)* ; but the influence of neighboring dialects appears, as in Shakespeare's English a century later, in the occasional use, in the plural, of the Southern ending *-th* or the Northern ending *-s,* which is fairly frequent in Lydgate. The Northern ending *-es* in the third singular, which is rare in Chaucer, continues to be rare in Malory and in Caxton. In the verb *to be,* however, the Northern form *are,* rare in Chaucer, in Caxton has become the prevalent one.

That the changes which were coming about in English syntax were unrelated to the changes in inflections seems inconceivable although there remains some doubt as to which was cause and which effect. Equally inconceivable is the contemporary change in English vowel sounds entirely independent of these changes in form and in syntax. It seems probable that the new distribution of stresses result-

[13] *Ibid.,* p. 47.

ing from the development of an analytical mode of speech was, not only contemporary with, but causally related to changes not only in the quantity but in the quality of vowel sounds.

In any event, amid all the welter and confusion of this transitional period there appears a general direction of change fundamental in character which made the language of the sixteenth century different from that of the four-teenth. Most obvious of these changes was the disappear-ance in pronunciation in the course of the fifteenth century of the final -e sound, the relic of the earlier inflectional endings. The loss of this final sound was attended with much confusion in the art of versification. To follow Chaucer in versification meant to count the final -e metri-cally as a syllable. To do so, however, was to use a form of speech which was coming to be more and more remote from the living speech. Hence, in great part, the irregu-larity and uncertainty prevalent in the verse making of the fifteenth century.

With the complete disappearance of the final -e sound the English language enters what is known as the Modern Eng-lish period. The language of the early sixteenth-century poet Henry Howard, Earl of Surrey (1516?-1547), exhibits the features of the new period. Presented in modern spell-ing and modern print his language offers little that could not pass for present-day English. The change, however, that had come about in the course of the fifteenth century appears from a comparison of Surrey's verse with that of Chaucer. The rhythm of Surrey is that of Chaucer; yet, in order to create this rhythm, changed forms of expression were necessary. The loss of the final -e in the meter re-quired the introduction of independent words in order to round out the meter. To Chaucer's *my grene yeres* corre-sponds Surrey's *my fresh green years ; soote floures* becomes *soot fresh flowers; smale foules* becomes *small fowls flocking.*[14]

The net result of the changes brought about in the course of the fifteenth century was a language markedly different from that of the fourteenth century. Middle English had changed to Modern English. In the beginning of the Modern English period obviously Chaucer's language could no longer serve as a pattern. "Now," says Skelton, "men would have amended his English, whereat they bark."

[14] Schick, Introd. to Lydgate's *Temple of Glass,* lxxiv.

CHAPTER VI

HUMANISM

LITERARY composition in English, so long neglected in the period preceding Chaucer, after his time had required a full century to come abreast with that in other languages. English writers, instead of devoting themselves to independent English composition, had more often turned their energies to adapting to English use the artifices borrowed from Medieval Latin and to preparing English versions of works earlier composed in Latin, or French, or Italian. To the service of such work was turned the printing press in the hands of Caxton and his immediate successors. But by the end of the fifteenth century a great part of the literary harvest of the medieval period had been garnered in English, and a standstill had been reached.

An impression of the intellectual torpor at the end of the century may be gained from the words of John Fisher, later Bishop of Winchester. At Cambridge in his day, he tells us, "there had stolen over well-nigh all of us a weariness of learning and study. There were few or no helpers of men of letters; the best of the nobility, the patrons of learning, had fallen on the battlefields or under the executioner's axe; little was taught even in the universities— save antiquated and artificial studies."[1] Such was the dark period before the dawn of the Renaissance in England. The prevalent lethargy is striking in contrast with the young enthusiasm which followed the introduction of the New Learning.

[1] E. M. G. Routh, *Lady Margaret*, p. 87. Modernized language.

Some effort is required for the modern mind to realize the interest aroused in the Renaissance world by the widened knowledge of classical literature. Revelations of the secrets of matter and of mind in our own time have been won from other sources and by other methods. The ideas of classical antiquity have in our day been in great part assimilated and absorbed. The merits of classical studies, much urged, are often urged in vain. The treasures of earlier times have become worn and tarnished through long use. How different was the situation in those earlier days! From the classical world came a knowledge of arts and sciences long hidden and a practical wisdom long forgotten, which possessed the liveliest interest not only for the scholar but for the man of affairs. Fostered by the patronage of Italian courts the New Learning became a fashionable pastime among the nobility of Italy, pursued by gentlemen and by ladies. The medieval knight, whose barbarism was often but thinly cloaked in Christian virtues and courtly etiquette, was succeeded by the courtier not only trained in arms but refined by learning in speech and in manners. Learned conversation was added to physical deeds of prowess among the diversions of courtly society.

In the medieval world the church had been the main channel through which the wisdom of ancient times had descended, and the church had neglected such parts of older literature as could not be made to serve the interests of Christian doctrine. In the classical literature preserved attempt was made to bring about harmony with the teachings of Christianity by means of allegorical interpretation. Even the book of nature was read allegorically. Marvelous ingenuity and subtlety were employed by the medieval mind in reading into it a symbolical meaning. The astrologer scanned the heavens for light on human destiny. In bestiary and lapidary the facts of animate and inanimate life, as recorded by classical writers, were interpreted with moral significance. The Homeric gods were converted into symbolic figures. Virgil and Ovid were allegorized, and older independent narratives were preserved in collections of *exempla* interpreted allegorically as lessons in Christian morality. The symbolical use of classical literature is strikingly exemplified in the medieval interpretation of the Fourth Eclogue of Virgil as prophetic of the Messiah.

With the Renaissance came a shift in the estimate of values. Human life in the present world came to share the importance that had before been attached to otherworld interests. A truce was declared in the age-long war against the World and the Flesh, and Titivullus and Belphegor and other manifestations of the personal Devil were relegated to mythology. Human aspirations took new direction. Sir Thomas More taught that "God's design was the happiness of men" and in his *Utopia* presented a conception of an idealized existence realized in this world. Such learning had its interest for laymen as well as for clergy. Its prosecution ceased to be the concern exclusively of churchmen and came to engage the attention of men of affairs, of statesmen, of kings. The name New Learning became synonymous with Humanism.

With the sixteenth century and the Renaissance came the conception of a world greater in extension as revealed by the discovery of another hemisphere in America, as well as greater in content and meaning than the fixed ideas governed by the authority of the medieval church had permitted men to realize. The change was comparable in many respects to that brought about by experimental science in later times. Then, as in our time, it was necessary to assimilate a set of new ideas and to reconcile them with inherited ideas fixed by long tradition. The difference between the two periods lies in the difference in source of the new ideas in the two cases. Whereas modern science lays bare the secrets of life by means of scientific observation and experiment, the Renaissance scholar opened to view the knowledge stored in neglected manuscripts from classical antiquity. The zeal of modern science in our day enables one to understand the zest with which in the period of the Renaissance the older manuscripts were sought for and the ardor with which their contents were studied.

The New Learning, relatively late in reaching England, when it did arrive, was welcomed with revolutionary enthusiasm. The spirit of the time is revealed in a scene from the Oxford life of the period. Such was the student enthusiasm in 1535 when lectures on the humanities were instituted by Henry VIII that the venerable volumes of Duns Scotus and other medieval logicians were seized and dispersed in triumph about the quadrangles.

A history of the English language obviously does not afford the space for a detailed account of the beginnings in England of the new movement which regenerated the thought and the literature, and eventually the language, of the nation. Mention, however, must be made of the names of the brilliant group of scholars that so much stirred the enthusiasm of Erasmus, the Apostle of the New Learning, when he first visited England in 1499. There was William Grocyn (1446ca.-1519), whom Erasmus refers to as "the friend and protector of us all," who brought to England a knowledge of Greek acquired in Italy and became the first English teacher of Greek at Oxford in 1491. There was Thomas Linacre (1460ca.-1524), who like Grocyn had absorbed the spirit of the Renaissance through a sojourn in Italy in the cultured circle at the court of the Medici in Florence. There was Sir Thomas More (1478-1535), whose rich personality radiated influence in so many directions. There was William Lily, whose name is attached to the Latin grammar of which he was one of the compilers and which superseding the earlier treatises by Donatus and by Priscian and their successors continued in use well down in the nineteenth century. He was headmaster at the famous Paul's School, the first to introduce the study of Greek. And there was John Colet, Dean of St. Paul's and founder of the Paul's School, a man whom Erasmus compared in wisdom to Plato himself.

The immediate contribution of this brilliant group of men toward the development of the English language and literature was not great. Their interest was centered in classical literature. Their direct ambition was to produce good Latinists rather than to promote the cultivation of English. From the pen of Grocyn practically nothing survives. Linacre was the author of a Latin Grammar and of a translation of Galen from Greek into Latin. The *Utopia* of Sir Thomas More was composed not in English but in Latin, and such was More's zeal for Latin studies that he required the children of his remarkable family to use Latin in their letters to him, permitting them only a preliminary draft in English.

And yet the permanent influence of this group of pioneers was far greater than that of the individualistic genius, Skelton (1460*ca.*-1529). While Skelton clung to the dying tradition of the medieval period, these men garnered from the classical world germinal ideas from which sprang the luxuriant growth in English expressive power later in the sixteenth century.

In the Tudor rulers the new movement found powerful supporters. Lady Margaret Beaufort, mother of Henry VII, was a promoter of learning and, guided by the advice of Bishop Fisher, was active in the endowment of colleges and lectureships at Cambridge and at Oxford. The King, her son, a less positive character, nevertheless lent support to his mother in her undertakings. In Henry VIII, however, appeared a ruler truly representative of the new spirit in learning. He has been called "the most highly educated person for his time who ever sat on the throne of England." It has recently been remarked that he was a Roosevelt without Roosevelt's domestic virtues. Under the most learned instruction available he was trained in Latin, dialectics, rhetoric, and music, and besides he knew French, Italian, and Spanish. The advent of his reign was greeted with enthusiasm by scholars. Attracted by the prospects for the encouragement of letters under the brilliant young ruler, Erasmus, in 1509, the year of the accession of the new King, left Italy for England as a place favorable for the furtherance of his ambitions. Many were the distracting interests in the reign of Henry VIII, but no other English king did more for the cause of learning and education in England. The results of the activities in the cause of education at this time appear in a recent computation which estimates that under Henry VIII there was one grammar school to every 5625 people, a state of affairs more favorable than that shown in the Schools Inquiry Report of 1864, which estimated one to every 23,750 people.[2]

The free spirit of inquiry of the Renaissance, with its revolt from authority, found an immense field for exploitation in the literatures of Greece and Rome. The new importance of the grammar ('literature') school in these circumstances is readily apparent. The famous Paul's School, founded, or at least reëndowed, by Dean Colet (1510-12), became a model for imitation.

The introduction of Greek studies at Paul's is alluded to in picturesque fashion in a letter to the founder from his friend Sir Thomas More in which the new school is compared to the "wooden horse in which armed Greeks were

[2] A. F. Leach, *The Schools of Medieval England*, p. 331.

hidden for the ruin of barbarous Troy." But Latin studies remained the chief element in the curriculum. Even here reforms of a most important nature were introduced. Characteristic of the English founder and significant regarding English ideals is the emphasis laid on the purpose to promote "good Cristen lyff and maners." More directly affecting language is the revolt from the form of Latin which had been the product of the Middle Ages, from the "Latin adulterate" produced by "ignorant blynde folis" which had poisoned the "varay ['true'] Roman tongue," and from "that fylthynesse and all such abusyon which the later blynde worlde brought in, which more ratheyr may be called blotterature thenne litterature," which Colet announces, "I utterly abbanysh and exclude oute of this scole." [3]

This school well exemplifies the new forces that assumed control of English education. William Lily, its first headmaster, was a layman, and the government of the newly endowed school was transferred from the Dean and Chapter of St. Paul's who had controlled the earlier Paul's School, into the hands of laymen, the London Company of Mercers. Freedom from church dogma in the unimpeded search of truth was thus promoted.

The revolt from Medieval Latin became general in English grammar schools. Uniformity in teaching was provided for by the grammar, the joint production of Colet, Erasmus, and Lily, though usually bearing the name of Lily, which came to have a legal monopoly not only during the reign of Henry VIII, but under his successors Edward VI and Elizabeth. The emphasis on pure Latin was general. In the foundation deed of Bruton School (1519) the founders announced their intention "to have the grammer of latyn tongue so sufficiently taught that the scolers— shall in tymes to come for ever be after their capacities

_____
[3] *Ibid.,* p. 280.

perfight Latyn-men." [4]   A similar emphasis on the importance of classical Latinity is to be observed in contemporary France. Francis I is said to have "abolished the Latin tongue from all public acts of justice, because the first president of the parliament had used a barbarous term in pronouncing sentence: and because the Latin code and judicial processes, hitherto adopted in France, familiarised the people to a base Latinity." [5]

In methods of study sound advice is offered by Colet. "Let the pupil above all busily learn and read good Latin authors—and note wisely how they wrote and spoke, and study always to follow them; desiring none other rules but their examples. For in the beginning men spoke not Latin because such rules were made, but contrariwise because men spoke such Latin; upon that followed the rules, not the rules before the Latin speech." [6]

Similar sound advice is offered by the famous Spanish scholar Vives, one of the active agents of Renaissance studies in England. In his "Plans for Boy's Studies" [7] he urges: "In all the authors you read notice how the grammatical forms are preserved and where they are neglected. . . . Now that which is constituted by actual use must be followed rather than the grammatical art, and not contrariwise. Yet that art on this account is not to be despised. Only do not follow it so closely as to be strangled by it. In our time we need rules, since we have not the Roman people to whom to talk, and all these rules have to be wrested out of their authors." On this subject the Renaissance scholars had absorbed the practical wisdom to be found in Cicero, in Horace, and in Quintilian. The counsel

---

[4] F. Watson, *The Beginnings of the Teaching of Modern Subjects in English,* p. 43.

[5] T. Warton, *History of English Poetry,* II, p. 414.

[6] F. Watson, *The Old Grammar Schools,* p. 14. Spelling and pronunciation are obviously modernized.

[7] Ed. Watson, p. 247.

of Vives is applicable in the use of the English language today, particularly among Americans.

Counsel practically identical in nature is offered by the famous French educational reformer Peter Ramus (1515-1572), whose methods were widely adopted in England as well as in France. "The material for grammar or language study he desires to have derived from actual usage—the ancient tongues from the classical writers, and the modern from the speech of the people." A main feature of his method is the substitution "in place of abstract rules, of illustrations from the works of classical authors and imitation of them in written and oral exercises." [8]

But the search for the "varay Roman tongue" in the practice of Latin writers rather than in the rules of the grammarian led to question regarding the models to be followed. The freedom in the use of modern constructions and in the adoption of new words which made of Medieval Latin at least a living speech, made it in the eyes of Renaissance scholars a "Latin adulterate." On the other hand the Renaissance idea that true Latin was to be learned only from the practice of Roman writers soon transformed it into a dead language. Here too is to be found a lesson for moderns engaged in the cultivation of modern tongues.

But who should be regarded as the proper model for true Latin? In the search for the perfect pattern Cicero came to hold the place of honor. Not only the amazing fineness of detail used by Cicero in the analysis of modes of speech to be found in his rhetorical treatises, but the practical illustration of effects to be gained by art afforded by his own writings, made of him a supreme master.

From Cicero was learned the possibilities of an artistic prose. Roger Ascham's method of teaching was based on a translation and retranslation of Cicero, a system which was

[8] F. P. Graves, *Peter Ramus*, pp. 110, 115.

like that recommended by Cicero for the cultivation of
Latin after a Greek pattern. Almost fanatical was the de-
votion to the cult of Cicero among the extremists of the
Renaissance period. The madness of Ciceronianism in its
extreme form provides a theme for the satire of Erasmus,
who in his *Ciceronianus* introduces a devotee who for seven
years has touched nothing save Ciceronian books. "I have
gathered," says Nosopomus, this devotee, "all the metrical
feet with which Cicero ever begins his periods and their
subdivisions, the rhythms which he uses in between, and
the cadences which he chooses for each kind of sentence,
so that no little point could escape. . . . It is not good to
speak like a grammarian, but it is divine to speak like
Cicero." The more sane attitude toward Cicero appearing
in this satirical exhibition by Erasmus appears also in Sir
Philip Sidney, who, in a letter to his brother Robert, advises: "So you can speak and write Latin not barbarously,
I never require great study in Ciceronianism, the chief
abuse of Oxford, *qui dum verba sectantur, res ipsas negli-
gunt* ['who while they choose words, neglect the things
themselves']." [9]   Sidney, as remains to be seen, here anticipates the judgment of Bacon.

From the language of Cicero, however, and from other
Latin writers Renaissance students learned their Latin. In
place of abstract rules, patterns were provided, and these
were imitated in written and oral exercises. The literary
productions of the classical world provided material to be
reworked by students in the Renaissance schools. As students of art of the school of Raphael gathered from the art
productions of the classical world the elements to be recombined in Raphaelesque designs, so students of classical
literature assembled the graceful forms of expression to be
recombined in literary design. Not only manner of ex-

[9] Sidney, *Defense of Poesy*, ed. A. S. Cook, p. xvii.

pression, but "sentence" or subject matter was derived from the literary productions of Greece and Rome. The pupil was expected to have his notebook at hand for use in transcribing ideas and phrases to be later used in conversation as well as in written exercises. To the culled passages from the classics which formed the contents of the *florilegia* of school students, it is to be suspected, more often than to a memory completely stored as prescribed by contemporary rhetoric, is to be attributed the wealth of classical illustration applied even in the English writing of the period. In any event the effect of this mode of study is everywhere discernible. John Lyly, for instance, in speaking of facial disfigurement is able to cite as classical parallels the scar on the chin of Helen, the mole on the cheek of Venus, the wart of Aristippus, the wen of Lycurgus.

Among the first promoters of the New Learning in England the subject of vernacular English was one of minor importance. In the schools of the period training in English had a subordinate place. The traditional stages in education are graphically represented in an illustration appearing in a Latin work, the *Margarita Philosophica*, published in 1504. In this picture appears the tower of knowledge, the two lower stages of which are devoted to grammar, or Latin, under the tutelage of Donatus or Priscian. The next two stages are occupied by the remaining six of the seven branches of learning comprised in the trivium and quadrivium. Above, the two forms of philosophy, natural and moral, find their places, and at the top of the tower is stationed Peter Lombard representing metaphysics and theology. To the door admitting to the lower stages of Latin study, the boy learner is conducted by a teacher, rod in hand and holding before the boy a horn-book. The primitive nature of the elementary instruction appears from the primitive character of the instrument used. This

The House of Learning, from G. Reisch, *Margarita Philosophica*, 1503.

horn-book consisted of a single leaf mounted in a frame in shape like a hand mirror, with the face covered by transparent horn. Across the top were written the nine digits and the letters of the alphabet in rows preceded by the cross +; hence the name *cross-row* or *Christcross-row*. The cross-row was followed by the Lord's Prayer. It is doubtful, in the opinion of one competent authority, "whether there were any systematic books for teaching of reading other than a crude form of Horn-book, till the time of the Renascence." [10]

Trained in reading through the horn-book, supplemented possibly by the "A B C," or Abecedarie, the pupil was ready to enter the grammar school. That elementary instruction concerned with the vernacular language was carefully excluded from the grammar school appears from a provision included in the foundation deed of Bruton School (1519) already quoted from, where it is definitely specified that the "maister shall not teche his scolers song nor other petite lernynge as the Cross Rewe, Reding of the mateyns, or of the psalter or such other small things [the elementary subjects of the horn-book and the medieval Primer], neither redyng of Englisshe butt such as shall concern lernynge of gramer." [11]

The neglect of training in English by the Latin teachers who dominated in grammar schools and in universities becomes the subject of frequent comment throughout the century. John Palsgrave, in his Dedication to Henry VIII of his translation of *Acolastus* (1540), speaks of the many men of high attainment in Latin studies who "be not able to express their conceit in their vulgar tongue. . . . In so much that for want of this sufficient perfection in our own tongue, I have known divers of them which—when they

---

[10] F. Watson, *The English Grammar Schools to 1660*, p. 173.
[11] Watson, *The Beginnings of the Teaching of Modern Subjects in English Schools*, p. 43.

have been called upon to do any service in your grace's commonwealth, either to preach in open audience or to have other administration—have been obliged to read over our English authors, by that means to provide a remedy unto their evident imperfection in that behalf." [12]   Concerning the faults of English schools and their neglect of English we have evidence later in the century from Shakespeare. We have not only his several allusions to schoolboy dislike of school [13] and to the boy product of the school who "did read by rote and could not spell" [14] but his exhibition of the Latin teacher, the parson and schoolmaster, Sir Hugh Evans, "identified by some critics with Thomas Jenkins, the master at Stratford School" who in his impatience at the boy's dullness in Latin, displays his own faulty English in the exclamation, "Thou art as foolish Christian creatures as I would desires."   Evidently the energy devoted to Latin studies was not at first accompanied by a like energy in the cultivation of the mother tongue or led to misdirected efforts like those exhibited in the pedantries of Holofernes.

English humanists, when they did adopt English as their medium of expression, greatly felt the lack of the rules and of the pattern that were available for their guidance in writing the classical language.   This feeling appears in the oft-quoted remark of Roger Ascham in the Dedication to Henry VIII of his *Toxophilus* (1545): "And althoughe to have vvritten this boke either in latin or in Greke (vvhich thing I vvold be verie glad yet to do, if I might surelie knovv your Grace's pleasure there in) had bene more easier and fit for mi trade in study—" [15]   The apologetic tone is striking and is further illustrated by Ascham's comment elsewhere: "And as for the *Latine* or *Greeke* tongue, everye

[12] *Ibid.*, pp. 3, 4.
[13] *R. and J.*, II, ii, 157-8; *As You Like It*, II, vii, 1-15.
[14] *R. and J.*, II, iii.
[15] Arber reprint.

thinge is so excellentlye done in them, that none can do better: In the *Englishe* tongue, contrary, everye thinge in a maner so meanlye both for the matter and the handelinge, that no man can do worse." In like vein Sir Thomas Elyot in 1531, speaking of the "good sentences," that is to say, good ideas, of the Latin poets, remarks on their ability to "express them incomparably with more grace and delectation than our englisshe tonge may yet comprehend."[16]

And yet the mother tongue was not without its champions. Perhaps the earliest in supporting the use of English was the brother-in-law of Sir Thomas More, the lawyer, printer, and playwright, John Rastell. This man of practical affairs, in his play, *The Nature of the Four Elements* (*ca.* 1520), courageously announces:

> Than yf connynge laten bokys were translate
> In to Englysshe wel correct and approbate,
> All subtell sciens in englyshe myght be lernyd.[17]

The importance, too, of cultivation of the vernacular was not entirely lost sight of among the earlier group of humanists in England. Vives, the Spanish scholar, friend of Erasmus, and educational adviser to Queen Catherine, was one of the most influential in the promotion of the New Learning in England. It was he who laid down the principles to govern instruction in England and was thus one of the fathers of English pedagogy. In his *De Tradendibus Disciplinas* (1523) Vives urges: "Let the teacher further keep in his memory the ancient forms of his mother tongue, and not only the knowledge of recent words, but also of the old words and those which now have passed out of common use, for unless this happens—books written a hundred years previously would not be understood by posterity."

English, however, to Vives was important mainly as an

---

[16] *The Gouernour*, ed. Croft, p. 129.
[17] C. R. Baskerville, *Modern Philology*, XIII, 192.

instrument in the great cause of Latin learning. The honor of shifting the emphasis and advocating the use of the New Learning in the promotion of learning in English belongs to a younger contemporary, Sir Thomas Elyot (1490ca.-1546). This remarkable man received his training in England, he tells us, under a "woorshipful physicion," perhaps Linacre, and was a friend of Sir Thomas More. To Elyot the "sure and honest rule of livynge" was to be found in the New Learning, and the fruits of this learning he aimed to make accessible in English form. In the Preface to his *Doctrinal of Princes* (1534), he says: "This little booke (whiche in mine opinion is to be compared in counsaile and short sentence with any booke, holy scripture excepted,) I haue translated out of greeke, not presumyng to contende with theim, whiche haue doone the same in Latine: but to thintent onely, that I wolde assaie, if our Englisshe tunge mought receiue the quicke and propre sentences pronounced by the greekes." The experiment, he decides, is successful; in fact, he finds that English idiom conforms to Greek more closely than Latin does. He, therefore, announces his purpose to devote "that little porcion of life whiche remaineth—in preparing for you such bookes in the readyng wherof, ye shall finde bothe honest passe tyme and also profitable counsaile and learnyng."

The plan thus announced Elyot carried into execution. In 1531 he published *The Boke named the Gouernour,* which deals with the education of statesmen. This work was followed by a series of didactic compositions including *Of the Knowleg whiche maketh a Wise Man* (1533), *Pasquil the Playne* (1533), *The Castel of Helth* (1534), a *Defence of Good Women* (1545), etc.

He went farther. He not only put in English form the lore which he had garnered from classical literature but, in order to enable his countrymen to read from the classical sources, he prepared a Latin-English dictionary which a century later Thomas Fuller pronounced to be "if not the first, the best of that kind in that age."

But this linguistic patriot did not stop with the effort by means of learning to augment the virtue and well being of his English countrymen. He aimed also at an enrichment of the English language. Let us take one concrete example illustrating his method. In his *Boke named the Gouernour* he discusses a virtue for which, he says, "we lacke a name in englishe." He finds himself, therefore, "constrained to vsurpe a latine worde, callyng it Maturitie, whiche worde though it be straunge and darke, yet—ones brought in custome, shall be as easye to vnderstande as other wordes late commen out of Italy and Fraunce, and made denisens among vs." This word *maturitie,* the Latin original of which he discusses at length, he adopts as the name for the virtue "whiche is the meane or mediocritie betweene slouthe and celeritie, commonly called spedynes."

This word, *maturitie,* is but a single instance of the many foreign words for whose use in English Elyot stood sponsor. Some of the transplanted words took root in the new soil, but many others failed to do so, or, as in the case of *maturitie,* in later English have developed meanings different from those intended by Elyot. In consequence the writings of Elyot contain many words and uses of words now obsolete. These obsolete words as assembled in lists by Croft, Elyot's nineteenth-century editor, now seem, to use the words of Chaucer, "wonder nyce and straunge." For instance, under the letter A appear: (1) from the Latin, *abhor* (from a thing), *abiecte, adminiculation, adolescencie, aggregate, allect, allectyue, amoue, annect, applicate, assentation, assentatour;* (2) from the French, *admonest, aduaunt, agreue* ('to aggravate'), *aigre, alay, appayse, approper, asprely, attemptate, auoutry, auoyd.*

Elyot was of course not the originator of this method of improving the language. Words of the kind adopted by him had been coming in in preceding centuries, and their increased use, as has been already pointed out, was a feature of the 'aureate' language of the fifteenth century. The striking feature in Elyot's case was the deliberate intent in the method.

Such conscious effort did not fail to meet with opposition as we learn from the "Proheme" to Elyot's *Of the Knowleg* [*sic*] *whiche maketh a Wise Man,* published two years later. Here Elyot informs his readers that "Diuers men rather scornyng my benefite than receyuing it thankfully doo shewe themselfes offended (as they say) with my strange termes." He then launches forth in an exposition of his ambition for increasing the resources of the English language. "His highnesse," he says, alluding to Henry VIII, to whom *The Gouernour* was dedicated, "benignely receyuynge my boke, whiche I named the Gouernour, in the redynge thereof sone perceyued that I intended to augment our Englyshe tonge, whereby men shulde as well expresse more abundantly the thynge that they conceyued in theyr hartis (wherfore language was ordeyned) hauynge wordes apte for the pourpose: as also interprete out of greke, latyn, or any other tonge into Englyshe, as sufficiently as out of any one of the said tonges into an other."

Perhaps no other man set out as deliberately as did Elyot to enrich the English vocabulary by foreign borrowing. But the method was more or less generally practiced. As a basis for this method, however, there was needed a familiar knowledge of Latin. One will recall the school regulation requiring the use of Latin by schoolboys in conversation with their fellows and the use of Latin required of the children of Sir Thomas More. On this subject Elyot offers suggestions in his recommendations concerning the rearing of a nobleman's son. "And if a childe," he says, "do begin therin at seuen yeres of age, he may continually lerne greke autours thre yeres, and in the meane tyme use the latin tonge as a familiar langage: whiche in a noble mannes sonne may well come to passe, hauynge none other persons to serue him or kepyng hym company, but such as can speake latine elegantly."[18]   A method like that suggested by Elyot was applied in France in the rearing of the young Montaigne (1533-1592). The young Frenchman was instructed by a tutor in a household where it was an inviolable rule that neither tutor nor servant nor mother even should speak in the boy's company except with such Latin words as each had learned in order to talk with the boy in training. Under such conditions of intensive training it is small wonder if familiar Latin words came to serve the needs of expression in the less developed vernacular language.

In any event, in the course of the sixteenth century, words of Latin derivation, either in their original Latin form, or recast in French form, came to be more and more familiarly used in English. The result was an immense enrichment of the language. Anyone who will take the pains to look up in the Oxford Dictionary the date of the earliest citations of words will be surprised to find how many words now familiar were first introduced at this period.

To discuss these new words in detail would be to discuss the cultural growth of the English nation. A few interesting sets of words, however, may be mentioned. In the world of learning a division of the broad general field of knowledge before covered by the word, *philosophy,* came to be indicated by the new word, *physicks* (1589) or 'nat-

[18] *The Gouernour,* ed. Croft, p. 54.

ural philosophy,' as distinguished from *ethicks* (1387) or 'moral philosophy.' From the broad field of geometry emerged a special form of study indicated by the name *geography* (1542). The word *physiology* was applied as a name for the study of natural objects as early as 1564; in its modern meaning, 'the science dealing with the function of living things,' in 1597. *Algebra,* derived through Italian from Arabic, appears in 1551. *Decimal* as an arithmetical term does not appear until 1585 or 1608. The comprehensive term *mathematics* first appears in 1581. *Analysis* (of things unmaterial) appears in 1581, of things material, not until 1667. The words *pernicious* (1521), *faction* (1509), *factious* (1535), *Puritan* (1572), *precise* (1526), *libertine,* 'free-thinker' (1563), *reprobate* (1545), were either newly borrowed or turned to special new uses in the controversial days of the Reformation.[19]

The influence of the New Learning naturally made itself felt in the terms of literature. There was a general revision of knowledge in this field, of which some indication is afforded by such words as: *poem* (1548), *ode* (1588), *drama* (1515), *stanza* (1588), *sonnet* (1557), *elegy* (1514), *lyric* (1586), *epic* (1589), *satire* (1509), *phrase,* 'group of words' (1530), *accent,* metrical (1588), *fiction,* a literary form (1599). Under the influence of a revived knowledge of classical rhetoric appeared the newer terms: *antithesis,* rhetorical (1529), *metonymy* (1547), *metaphor* (1533), replacing terms in earlier use.

From other languages the borrowing also was extensive. The debt to French it is impossible to measure since many of the Latin and Greek words entered English through French, often stamped in a French pattern. Italy, the source of the Renaissance movement, yielded a number of important words, many of which, such as *attitude,*

[19] L. P. Smith, *The English Language.*

cicerone, fiasco, influenza, isolate, motto, stanza, and *umbrella,* have held a permanent place in English. Spanish, too, in the sixteenth century more closely associated with English than in any other century, provided new word material for the absorbent English language of the sixteenth century. Some of the Spanish words which entered English at this time are: *brocade, ambuscade, desperado, disembogue, dispatch, grandee, negro, peccadillo, punctilio, renegade.*[20]

The widened English view of the world as a whole brought about by world exploration is indicated by such words as *caravan, caravanserai* (1599), *cannibal* (1553), *monsoon* (1584), *savannah* (1555), *hurricane* (1555). Of exceptional interest is the word *breeze,* first cited in 1564 (Fr. *brise;* Span. *brisa*).

The familiarity with Latin words promoted by the intensive cultivation of Latin led not only to the adoption of new words from Latin, but to the remodeling of words long established in English. To persons familiar with the classical Latin forms, *subtilis, advocatus, virtus, deceptus, aequalis, circumscribo,* forms such as *sotil* or *sutel, auocat, vertu, deceit, egal,* and *circumscrive* must have appeared incorrect if not barbarous. Hence there came about a refashioning of many words of classical derivation which in popular use, either in French or in English, had undergone change in pronunciation, which in turn was reflected in spelling. Under the influence of Latin learning earlier *auance, auenture, auyse, auocat,* were Latinized in spelling and in pronunciation to *advance,* etc. In like manner an *l* was inserted in such words as *salvation* (Chaucer, *sauacion*), *fault* (Mid. Engl., *faut;* Chaucer, *defaute*), *soldier* (Mid. Engl., *soudeour*), *psalm* (Mid. Engl., *saume*), *cauldron* (earlier *caudron*), *falcon* (Mid. Engl., *faucon*), *altar* (Chau-

20 H. Bradley, *The Making of English.*

cer, *auter*). Under similar Latin influence older *vertu* was changed to *virtue, ferme* to *firm,* and the full suffix *-ure* was given to such words as *leisure* and *pleasure.* After Latin models were respelled: *inscribe, describe, circumscribe* (Mid. Engl., *inscriue, descryue, circumscriue*); *receipt, conceipt* (Chaucer, *receit, conceite*); *debt, doubt* (Chaucer, *dette, doute*); *perfect, subject* (Chaucer, *perfit, subgit*); *equal* (Chaucer, *egal*).

Many of these Renaissance spellings did not permanently establish themselves, for example, such forms as *deceipt, counterfect, poinct, compt* ('count') used by Wilson in his *Arte of Rhetorique.* Furthermore, earlier modes of pronunciation established in popular use did not yield as readily as did the spelling to the Latin influence. The popular modes of pronunciation reflected in the fifteenth-century Paston letters should be recalled. In some words such as *debt* and *doubt, subtle* and *receipt* the older pronunciation has persisted in spite of a Latinized spelling. Many other older modes of pronunciation were slow in yielding to the learned influence and, as remains to be seen, persisted in popular use down into the eighteenth century and later. The resistance to the learned influence appears in the diaries and private correspondence of the sixteenth century. For instance in the diary of a London merchant, Henry Machyn, written in 1553-4, appear such forms as: *sawgyers,* 'soldiers'; *harodes,* 'heralds'; *sauden,* 'sultan'; *Raff,* 'Ralph'; *auter,* 'altar'; *Norfoke,* 'Norfolk'; *faucon,* 'falcon'; *sogettes,* 'subjects'; *amner* and *awmer,* 'almoner'; *pycter,* 'picture'; *pleasur,* 'pleasure'; *reme,* 'realm.' Even in literary composition the older forms make their appearance. For instance in Harman's *Caueat of Warening* appear such forms as: *faute,* 'fault'; *suttel* and *subtel,* 'subtle'; *caudren,* 'cauldron'; *vytellinge,* 'victualing'; *layser,* 'leisure.'

The assimilation of foreign elements into English offered difficulty of other kinds. Latin words and Latinized forms of words were readily assimilated into the language of those trained in the Latin schools of the period. With the speech of the unschooled the situation was different. The influence of the new classical learning appears to have penetrated but gradually to the speech of the unlearned. Indeed the popular assimilation of the borrowed terms was a slow and laborious process. To one grounded in Latin by the grammar-school training of the day, it came natural to adopt in his English speech words thoroughly familiar through Latin studies. But, to people entirely unacquainted with Latin, at an earlier period when words in *-osity* and *-ation* and *-ize* and *-ism* were not as familiar as they are today, these borrowed words must have offered difficulties hard now to appreciate fully. To them was applied the name "hard words," and the struggles on the part of the unlettered and the dull in handling these "hard words" are frequently exhibited in the writings of the period. On the one hand the pomposity arising from the excessive use of inkhorn terms, on the other hand the distortions produced in the vain struggles in their use, provide an inexhaustible source of humor. Mrs. Malaprop had sixteenth-century forbears.

In the early play, *The Prodigal Son* (printed about 1530) appears a boy who has not followed his father's counsel to apply himself to learning. Unable to understand what is said to him, he says: "I can vnderstande no laten, I was neuer at Oxynby. No, nor yet in Cambrydge nor other insteuynste." He is told, "Syr ye sholde say vniuersyte, not insteuynste" but replies, "I praye you good syr, holde me excused, for to such ropperype ['hanged'] termes I am not vsed." [21] Sir Thomas Wilson in his Rhetoric

[21] *Malone Society Publications*, I, p. 29.

introduces a number of amusing instances of the difficulties offered by the 'hard words' to the unschooled. A country-man asking a gentleman for money, gets himself involved in speech as follows: "We are so taken on with contrary Bishops ['contributions'] with reuiues ['relief'], and with Southsides ['subsidies'] to the King, that all our money is cleane gone." A man "out of the toune" coming to welcome the provost of King's College (presumably Sir John Cheke) lately come from court, in trying to elevate his language to the level of the learned, mingles the dialectal, the ungram-matical and the pseudo-learned as follows: "Cha good euen, my good Lord, and well might your Lordshippe vare . . . knowing that you are a worshipfull Pilate, and keepes abominable house, I thought it my duetie to come incan-tiuante ['incontinent,' 'at once']." In another instance cited by Wilson, an "officer and Maior of a toune" in re-buking a "runnegate fellowe" said in great heat: "Thou yngrame and vacation knaue, if I take thee any more within the circumcision of my dampnation: I will so corrup thee, that all other vacation knaues shall take ilsample by thee." The language, it will be noted, is of a kind with that assigned by Shakespeare to those distinguished officers of the law, Elbow and Dogberry.

The difficulties offered to the unlettered by these "ink-horn termes brought in by men of learning" and by the "straunge termes of other languages" it is not hard to un-derstand. In official documents appear frequently strange perversions of words. In a set of documents from Lin-colnshire [22] appear forms such as: *ffeber3er*, 'February'; *onormentes*, 'ornaments'; *suppowellorse*, 'supervisors'; *diademund*, 'diamond.' In Machyn's Diary appear forms such as: *sufferacan*, 'suffragan'; *crownenasyon*, 'coronation'; *experyng*, 'conspiring.'

[22] *Lincoln Documents,* Early English Text Society.

The learned themselves did not escape error. To mistaken explanations of the origin of words is to be attributed the form *abhominable* (supposed to be from *ab+homine*) and spellings that have remained permanently fixed such as *island* (with an *s* inserted in spelling from mistaken association of the word with *isle,* from Latin *insula*) and *rhyme* (mistakenly associated with *rhythm*). Even in the language of the most cultivated society appeared strange distortions. From the lips of Queen Elizabeth herself fell the words "shameful schandlers," 'slanders' + 'scandals.'[23]

The products of the new classical learning obviously were not absorbed all at once, nor were they absorbed without confusion. There were many instances of verbal indigestion, many pedantic exhibitions of false learning which afforded targets for the wit of the satirist. Time was required for complete assimilation. But the gains to the English language from the classical learning for which so great an enthusiasm was kindled in the early sixteenth century, though slowly absorbed, have been permanent. The words borrowed into the speech of the learned have slowly sunk to the popular level and have become essential elements in the common speech of later periods. Moreover from that day to the present the influence of classical models has been a continuous one. Only last year (1926) the British Premier paid his tribute to this influence. From "sin of speech or oratorical idolatry," he said he had been kept, "by the wonderful clarity and conciseness of the ancient languages" in which he had been disciplined from youth.

[23] F. Chamberlin, *Sayings of Queen Elizabeth.*

CHAPTER VII

PURISM

STRANGE to say the Renaissance movement and the restored knowledge of Greek, which awakened the desire to refashion the English language after a classical model, had a share also in a movement which served to counteract the classical influence. This movement was the Protestant Reformation. Already in the fourteenth century there had begun a revolt from the supreme authority assumed by the church in religious belief and indirectly in all forms of thinking. There was coming into being a belief that authority rested in the Word of God alone. The Wycliffite translation of the Bible had been a consequence. During the fifteenth century the circulation of the Wycliffe translation had been effectually controlled and the zeal for reform held in check. The fire, however, was still smoldering and the New Learning, fostering a sense of individualism, gave new life to the sense of personal responsibility in matters of religion, the sense of the necessity that each one should interpret for himself the Holy Book.

Serving the needs of the new situation came the revived study of Greek. In England, it must be recalled, the products of Renaissance learning were welcomed as means for advancing morality, for promoting "good cristen lyff." Under the influence of Colet in England Erasmus was led to the resolution to turn his interest to theological studies. In the search for theological truth he was led to search for knowledge at the sources themselves. In this way he was led to the search for the true text of the Scriptures and eventually in 1516 to the publication of the Greek text of the New Testament. Here at last was felt to be the authentic version of the Word of God. In his Preface Erasmus expressed the hope that the true text thus provided might be translated into all languages "so that not only the Scotch and Irish but even the Turks and Saracens might read it." The hope of Erasmus was not long in its accomplishment. In 1522 Luther published his German translation. In England the Church, fearing the sectarianism inevitable with freedom of individual interpretation of the Bible, was firm in its opposition. The spirit of the Reformation movement, however, was too strong. Tyndale in reply to one of his opponents, exclaimed: "If God spare my life, ere many years I will cause a boy that draweth the plowe shall know more of the scriptures than thou dost." Printed at Worms in 1525, publicly burned at St. Paul's Cross in England in 1530, and eventually leading to the burning of its author at the stake at Antwerp in 1536, Tyndale's translation of the New Testament was the means, nevertheless, of accomplishing his vow.

In the history of the German language the translation of the Bible by Luther was an event of the first importance, for the language of this translation became the standard for literary German from which comes the cultivated High German language of today. The work of Tyndale, while not so final in its effect on later English, has nevertheless been one of the dominant factors in shaping literary English, for upon Tyndale's work was founded the English Bible. Tyndale's translation was followed in 1535 by a complete English version by Coverdale. This was followed by the Matthew's Bible of 1537 which included Tyndale's translation of the first half of the Hebrew Old Testament. The Matthew's Bible in turn was followed by a further revision by Taverner and Coverdale in 1539, forming the edition which on account of its pulpit size was known as the Great Bible.

With the progress of the Reformation movement went continued activity in Bible revision. In the short reign of Edward VI (1547-1553), there appeared no less than thirty-five editions of the New Testament and thirteen of the whole Bible. Changes in printed form were brought about. The division into chapters brought about in an earlier period, about A.D. 1200, was followed, in the middle of the sixteenth century, by the division into verses made by the Parisian printer Robert Estienne for the sake of convenient reference in his concordance to the Greek Testament. This practice was adopted in later English revisions. In 1560 appeared an English version, the Geneva Bible, with verse divisions and with roman type succeeding the black letter hitherto used, a version which on account of its convenient size came into general household use. This in turn was followed by a revised version made by Archbishop Parker and known as the Bishop's Bible. Nearly the final stage in the formation of the English Bible was reached in 1611 with the completion of a revision made "by the best learned of the universities" appointed to the task by James I. The product of this revision was the Authorized Version, or King James Version, still in use. This version in the course of the two following centuries was revised in minor fashion. Many changes in spelling and in the use of italics were made in revisions of 1629 and 1638 under influences which remain to be discussed later. Other changes in text and in spelling were made in 1762, and in 1769, in a revision made by Dr. Blayney of Oxford, older words and forms of words were replaced by modern ones: *sith* was changed to *since, flixe* to *fluxe, fet* to *fetched*, etc., and the language of the Authorized Version was brought to its present form.

In the light of the facts here cited it appears that the language of the Authorized Version is not exactly representative of the English of any one period. Nevertheless, the dominant features of biblical English were determined early in the sixteenth century by William Tyndale. The New Testament, we are told by Professor Goodspeed, is "92 per cent as Tyndale wrote it 400 years ago." Hundreds of older words and forms of expression now survive exclusively in biblical language. How many words and expressions now in current use would have been lost but for the general knowledge of the Bible, it is impossible to estimate. While Tyndale's translation has not possessed the authority over standard English possessed by Luther's translation over literary German, its phraseology and its turns of expression have been woven into the texture of English and for centuries have pervaded the language of English-speaking people not only in all parts of the world but in all stations of life, serving the needs of simple speech and of formal eloquence. To the zeal of William Tyndale in bringing a knowledge of the Bible within the reach of the "boy that draweth the plowe" is to be attributed the simplicity of biblical language and the purity of its vocabulary. As remains to be seen, the simple language of the Bible has proved a shelter for native English against the foreign forces which at times have threatened to overpower it.

The spirit of Tyndale's translation and the principles which guided him in the choice of language are reflected in the tone of contemporary criticisms. To Sir Thomas More some of the words substituted by Tyndale for ones in traditional use were objectionable because lacking the dignity appropriate to the subject. The shock felt by More seems to have been of the kind created in our own time by a rendering of the Bible in modern colloquial idiom. Lan-

guage like Tyndale's, close to the popular idiom, seemed
to his contemporaries to be lacking in the reverence that
comes to attach to sacred language, the kind of reverence
which again in later times has come to cloud the naked
directness of Tyndale's simple phraseology. Bishop Gardner of Winchester objected to the style adopted by Tyndale
in translation because it was too clear. He brought forward
in 1542 a list of 102 Latin words which, he maintained,
should be retained in any English version "for the dignity
of the matter in them contained." [1] In this list appear such
words as: *idolatria, contritus, holocausta, sacramentum, ele-
menta, ceremonia, simulacrum, panis, peccator, zizania.*
The debt of the English language to Greek and Latin incurred through Bible translation is, as it is, a heavy one,
as appears from such words as *perdition, salvation, retribu-
tion, immortality, concupiscence, transfiguration.* But
from a more serious inundation the language was saved
through the preference given by Tyndale to simple language, through his rejection of such words as *peccator* in
favor of *sinner* and *panis* in favor of *bread.*

As a bulwark for native English the English Bible was
supported by the forces of popular preaching. Even in the
dark days for the English language after the Norman Conquest, when French and Latin prevailed in the use of the
courtly and the learned, the native tongue remained the
medium in the religious instruction of the common people.

In later periods, when English had been restored to general use, religious teaching continued to make use of a
simple form of native speech. Under the Tudors, even
before the Reformation, effort was made to supplant the
fatuities of scholasticism by a simple mode of popular
preaching. A main object in the endeavor of Bishop Fisher,
supported by his noble patroness, Lady Margaret Beau-

---

[1] T. L. K. Oliphant, *The New English,* I, 422.

fort, mother of Henry VII, was the abolishment from the pulpit of the medieval "cavillings about words and parade of sophistry" and the encouragement of men who should "preach the Word of God gravely and with an evangelical spirit, and recommend it to the minds of the learned by an efficacious eloquence." [2] How this "efficacious eloquence" was cultivated by Dean Colet, one may learn from Erasmus who has recorded how Colet "with a view to adorn and improve the style of his discourses and to acquire the graces of an elegant preacher, employed much time in reading Gower, Chaucer, and Lydgate, and other English poets, whose composition had embellished the popular diction." [3]

With the Reformation the importance of English preaching was vastly increased. With the introduction of the English Bible and the English Prayer Book in the Church service went a loss, to a certain extent, in the reverence felt for the Latin language. There arose also a new need of simple interpretation of the facts of religion. Such a need was not served by the artificial "eloquence" of the scholar trained in the rhetoric of the time. The utter sincerity of Tyndale led him to scorn the "oratory" of Fisher and the "painted poetry, babbling eloquence" of Sir Thomas More.

More directly serving the popular needs of the time was such a man as Hugh Latimer. This great preacher was of humble origin and the eloquence of his language is the eloquence native to the English language. "My father," he says in a sermon before King Edward VI, "was a Yoman, and had no landes of his owne, onlye he had a farme of .iii. or .iiii. pound by yere at the uttermost, and here upon he tilled so much as kepte halfe a dosen men. He had walke for a hundred shepe, and my mother mylked .xxx. kyne. . . .

---

[2] E. M. G. Routh, *Lady Margaret*, p. 90.
[3] T. Warton, *History of English Poetry*, II, p. 441.

He kept me to schole, or elles I had not bene able to have preached before the kinges majestie nowe." Ordinarily Latimer is simple and direct in his speech as in the passage cited. In plainness of speech he sometimes descends to homely, not to say vulgar, phrase. He inveighs against the Surveiers ('government officials'), "that gredyly gorge up their covetous guttes." The alliteration of the phrase is a traditional feature of English popular eloquence, it will be recalled. In this vein of popular eloquence Latimer declaims against the objects of his wrath, the unpreaching prelates, the bishops who enjoyed the emoluments and dignities of their rank without performing their duties as clergymen. He exclaims: "They are so troubled with lordly living, they be so placed in palaces, couched in courts, ruffling in their rents, dancing in their dominions, burdened with ambassages, pampering of their paunches like a monk that maketh his jubilee, munching in their mangers, and so moiling in their gay manors and mansions, and so troubled with loitering in their lordships, that they cannot attend it." [4]

In this rugged prose with its tumbling rhythm guided by alliteration reappears a native English manner of speech to be observed in homilies of the Old English period. The tradition has already been traced through the *Piers Plowman* poem down to the time of Skelton. Its influence may be traced throughout the sixteenth century. In competition with, sometimes in combination with, the cultivated graces derived from classical imitation or formed by rhetorical artifice, it contributed to form the artificial style cultivated by later speakers and writers, and, as remains to be seen, it provides a medium for the robustious eloquence of the pamphleteers in the last decades of the century.

Among the men associated with the learning of the six-

[4] Modernized spelling and punctuation.

teenth century a conservative force is represented by Bishop Gardner, the Chancellor at Cambridge, who "loved learning but hated novelties." His support of the adoption of Latin words in the English Bible has already been indicated. But at the same center of learning appeared an opposing force which lent active support to the native English element of the language in its resistance against foreign encroachment. Among the men active in the promotion of the New Learning at Cambridge was a group of men actively associated with the cause of the Reformation. In this group of Cambridge Protestants the cause of pure English found able supporters. Through them the language was defended from some of the extravagances to which it was exposed by the misdirected zeal in the classical movement. A central figure in this group at Cambridge was Sir John Cheke, first Regius Professor of Greek, Fellow at St. John's College, and later Provost of King's College. The clash between two contrasting modes of thought appears in the controversial letters which passed between Gardner and Cheke.

Closely associated with Cheke at Cambridge and reflecting his influence were a number of younger contemporaries, including Roger Ascham, Sir Thomas Smith, and Sir Thomas Wilson, all of whom became active in efforts toward improving the English language. These men, eminent for learning, were closely associated with royal education. Cheke was tutor to Prince Edward in 1544, Ascham was tutor to Lady Jane Grey and to the Princess Elizabeth (1548-50) and Wilson had under his instruction the two sons of the Duchess of Suffolk, nephews of Henry VIII. They were connected with government as well as with education; for instance, three of them, Cheke, Smith, and Wilson, served successively as Secretary of State. Their position, therefore, was such as to give weight to their opinions.

In this Cambridge group the most positive force seems to have been Cheke (1514-57). Both Ascham and Wilson came directly under his instruction and in their writings repeatedly refer to him in worshipful terms. "He had," says Wilson, "better skill in our English speache to iudge of the Phrases and properties of wordes and to diuide sentences: than any one else that I haue knowne." While one of the most active and effective promoters of classical learning, Cheke believed nevertheless most strongly that the English language must be kept pure. In carrying his idea into practical effect he began a translation of the New Testament, of which the Gospel of Matthew was printed about 1550. In this translation the preference of Cheke for native words led to many interesting substitutions, such as *outpeopling* (Tyndale *captivate*), *moored* (Tyndale *lunatyke*), *tollers* (*publicans*), *hunderder* (*centurion*), *crossed* (*crucified*).

But the most definite statement of Cheke's opinion regarding the English language is to be found in the famous letter written by him in 1557 to his friend Thomas Hoby regarding the translation of Castiglione's *Courtier* which Hoby had made and had submitted to the criticism of Cheke. In his letter Cheke refers to "changing certein wordes." These changes he explains in apologetic manner as having been made because "I am verie curious ['solicitous'] in my freendes matters." He then proceeds to explain his general attitude in a passage which for its importance deserves to be quoted entire:

I am of this opinion that our tung shold be written cleane and pure, vnmixt and vnmangeled with borrowing of other tunges, wherein if we take not heed bi tijm, euer borowing and neuer payeing, she shall be fain to keep her house as bankrupt. For then doth our tung naturallie and praisablie vtter her meaning, when she bouroweth no conterfeitness of

other tunges to attire herself withall, but vseth plainlie her
own with such shift, as nature craft, experiens, and folowing
of other excellent doth lead her vnto, and if she want at ani
tijm (as being vnperfight she must) yet let her borow with
suche bashfulness, that it mai appeer, that if either the mould
of our own tung could serue us to fascion a woord of our
own, or if the old denisoned ['admitted to citizenship'] wordes
could content and ease this neede we wold not boldly venture
of vnknowen wordes. This I say not for reproof of you, who
haue scarslie and necessarily vsed whear occasion serueth a
strange word so, as it seemeth to grow out of the matter and
not to be sought for: but for mijn own defens, who might be
counted ouerstraight a deemer of thinges, if I gaue not thys
accompt to you, mi freend and wijs ['wise'], of mi marring
this your handiwork. . . .

This passage from Cheke deserves attention because it
is the first formal statement of an opinion which in varied
form has been revoiced many times since Cheke's time.
The spelling also deserves to be examined closely because
Cheke was not only a purist in the use of words but a
practical advocate of spelling reform.

In 1530 Roger Ascham entered St. John's College, Cambridge, "that most famous and fortunate Nurse of all
learning" as it was called fifty-nine years later by Thomas
Nashe, in the same year that Cheke had been elected Fellow.
Although deeply devoted to classical learning Ascham in his
writings expresses opinions regarding English quite in accord with Cheke's. He did more; he carried his opinion
into practice. In 1545, while a Fellow at St. John's, he
wrote in pure English his *Toxophilus*, for "the pleasure and
commoditie of the gentlemen and yeomen of Englande."
In a famous passage in this book, already quoted, Ascham
speaks of the uncultivated state of the English language,
and in his dedication to the King he intimates that it would

have been "more easier" to have written in Latin or in Greek. Nevertheless he chooses to demonstrate by example (although modesty naturally prevents him from saying so) that it is possible to do good writing in English. His guiding principle in writing is in accord with the ideas of Cheke. Like Cheke he condemns the practice of many English writers who, "vsing straunge wordes as latin, french and italian, do make all thinges darke and harde." And where has this idea found expression more adequate than in Ascham's words: "He that wyll wryte well in any tongue, muste folowe thys councel of Aristotle, to speake as the common people do, to thinke as wise men do"?

The influence of Cheke, it appears, was exerted for the most part not through his own writings, but through the writings of those who had come within oral range of his teachings. His theory and practice in the matter of spelling have been alluded to. Among the students at King's College, Cambridge, while Cheke was there as provost, was Sir Thomas Smith, later Secretary of State. In 1568 Smith published his important treatise on English spelling, entitled *De recta et emendata linguæ anglicæ scriptione,* a work which, though published after Cheke's death, can hardly fail to have been influenced by the definite opinions of its author's close friend and associate.

More important still in the history of the English language was another of Cheke's disciples, Sir Thomas Wilson. Trained under Cheke in classical learning, Wilson seems to have absorbed many of Cheke's ideas regarding the English language. In 1551 he published *The Rule of Reason Conteyning the Arte of Logike,* a textbook "in the vulgar tongue," written, to quote the author's words, "because no Englishman vntill now hath gone through with this enterprise." This work, which was based on Aristotle, made no pretense at originality. Two years later, however, in 1553,

he published a more important work, his *Arte of Rhetorique*,
in which he assembled ideas on rhetoric from classical learning and applied them, with the addition of much original
illustrative material, to English use. In this work he joins
with Cheke and Ascham in the battle for pure English and
against the use of "inkhorne terms": "Emong all other
lessons this should first be learned, that we neuer affect any
straunge ynkehorne termes, but to speake as is commonly
receiued: neither seking to be ouer fine, nor yet liuyng
ouercarelesse, vsyng our speeche as moste men doe, and
ordering our wittes as the fewest haue doen." [5]   The precept of Aristotle quoted by Ascham is here reëchoed in
Wilson's paraphrase.

In the University of Cambridge, therefore, was formed
an influence which, radiating in various directions, reaching
the nobility and royalty through the work as tutors of
Cheke and Ascham and Wilson and a wider public through
the published works of Ascham and Wilson and Smith, was
a steadying force amid the tumultuous movements of a
seething period.

Indeed, a steadying influence was needed if the English
language was to remain English. "Some seeke so far for
an outlandische English," says Wilson, "that thei forget
altogether their mothers langage. And I dare sweare this,
if some of their mothers were aliue, thei were not able to
tell what thei say: and yet these fine English clerkes will
saie, thei speake in their mother tonge, if a man sholde
charge them with counterfeitying the kynges Englishe." [6]
Words and phrases from the more cultivated French and
Italian were much affected by the gallants of the time.
"Some far iourneyed gentlemen," says Wilson, "at their
retourne home, like as thei loue to goe in forraine apparell,

[5] Ed. 1580.
[6] *Ibid.*

so thei will pouder their talke with ouersea langage. He
that commeth lately out of Fraunce, will talke Frenche
English and neuer blushe at the matter. And other chops in
with Englishe Italianated, and applieth the Italian phrase to
our Englishe speakyng." Forms of English no longer current, or not in polite use, were commonly introduced.
Archaic expressions from Chaucer were revived. "The fine
courtier," says Wilson, "will talke nothing but Chaucer."
The language of the underworld, the original of modern
slang, was brought into use. "The Lawyer," says Wilson,
"will store his stomach with the pratyng of Pedlers."

But it is the dangers from the pedantry of classical
scholarship against which Wilson particularly directs his
satire. "I knowe them," he says, "that think *Rhetorique* to
stand wholie vpon darke woordes, and he that can catche an
ynke horne terme by the taile, hym thei coumpt to bee a
fine Englishman and a good *Rhetorician*." He then proceeds to caricature the pedantic tendencies of his time in a
letter supposed to have been written by a clergyman in
application for a "voide benefice." The burlesque letter
begins as follows:

"Ponderyng, expendyng, and reuolutyng, with my self,
youre ingent affabilitie and ingenious capacitie for mundane
affaires: I cannot but celebrate, and extoll your magnifical
dexteritie aboue all other. For how could you haue adepted
suche illustrate prerogative, and domesticall superioritie, if
the fecunditie of your ingenie had not been so fertile and
wonderfull pregnant. Now therefore beeyng accersited to
suche splendente renoume, and dignitee splendidous: I
doubte not but you will adiuuate suche poore adnichilate
orphanes, as whilome ware condisciples with you, and of
antique familiaritie in Lincolnshire. Emong whom I beyng
a Scholasticall panion, obtestate your sublimitie, to extoll
myne infirmitie . . . etc."

The danger to which the English language was exposed in the days of young enthusiasm for classical learning is exhibited in this letter. From this danger it fortunately was protected. From sins of excess in learning it was held through the need of a simple form of language to bring home to the plain Englishman the truths of the gospel. Through the sermons and religious writings addressed to a popular audience and through the English translations of the Bible continues to flow a stream of pure English. From learned extravagance, also, protection was afforded by a wisdom acquired through learning. The sound judgments passed by Wilson on the English of the sixteenth century are expressed in fresh and pungent phrase. But the doctrine conveyed is not of Wilson's invention. It is doctrine shared with Wilson by his associates in learning at Cambridge, and the precepts applied are classical precepts such as Cicero long before had applied to the Latin of his time.

CHAPTER VIII

SIXTEENTH-CENTURY RHETORIC

TO-DAY rhetoric is decried; in the Middle Ages it was called 'Madam Rhetoric.' . . . Ideas pass; but rhetoric is eternal." These words are attributed to Anatole France.[1] Certainly rhetoric was a potent force in shaping the English language in the period following the Renaissance. Along with the eager exploitation of the literatures of Greece and Rome in English grammar schools, there came a renewal in importance of this favorite subject with classical writers. In the medieval scheme of education dialectics had come to overshadow the other elements in the trivium, grammar, and rhetoric. To St. Thomas Aquinas logic, or dialectics, had been the art of arts because in action we are directed by reason.[2] With a fixed body of knowledge handed down by tradition, the most important task of the trained mind had been that of logical interpretation. With the widened outlook, however, of the Renaissance, the situation was changed. With the search for new knowledge and the application of knowledge to secular uses, the important thing came to be the well-stored memory and the ability to give to knowledge effective expression. Both these purposes were served by the study which in earlier times bore the name *rhetoric*.

The dramatic scene at Oxford when in 1535 lectures on the humanities were instituted will be recalled. The reign

[1] J. J. Brousson, *Anatole France Himself.*
[2] D. L. Clark, *Rhetoric and Poetry in the Renaissance.*

of dialectics was over. Duns Scotus was dethroned. The adherents of the older order came to be known as "dunse men," later 'dunces.' The dominant position formerly held by dialectics was assumed by rhetoric in the grammar schools of the Renaissance.

The prominent part played by rhetoric in the English poetry of the fifteenth century has already been considered. But medieval rhetoric was not identical with what is now called rhetoric. The name had become narrowed in meaning so as to apply mainly to features of style. Eloquence, the product of rhetoric, was the quality striven after even more by poets than by prose writers. "Grammar speaks; dialectics teaches the truth; rhetoric adorns" is the dictum of a medieval writer.[3] Nor was medieval rhetoric identical with classical rhetoric. In the Middle Ages the rhetorical writings of the classical world were known only in fragments. Quintilian was known through medieval abridgments, the original writings having been not available until newly brought to light by the Renaissance scholar Poggio in the monastery of St. Gall in 1418. The most widely known of Cicero's rhetorical writings was the youthful *De Inventione*. The inexact knowledge of classical rhetoric in the Middle Ages appears from the fact that the most widely influential work associated with the name of Cicero was the *Ad Herennium* which is now known not to have been written by Cicero.

With the Renaissance, however, came a restored knowledge of the classical rhetoricians. Not only was Quintilian rediscovered in his original form, but his work and the other classical treatises, Greek as well as Latin, were made accessible in printed editions. A work in general use in England as well as in France was the *Rhetoric* compiled by the French scholar Talon (Latin form, Talæus) in

[3] *Nicolaus de Orbellis,* 1455, quoted from Clark, *op. cit.*

1547, which contained most that had been written on the subject by Aristotle, Socrates, Cicero, and Quintilian. The scope of classical rhetoric was much broader than that of medieval times. Cicero in his *De Oratore* deplores the separation of training in manner of speech from training in philosophy, by which he means general knowledge. "The ancients," he says, "till the time of Socrates, united all knowledge . . . with the faculty of speaking, but afterwards, the eloquent being separated by Socrates from the learned, . . . the philosophers disregarded eloquence and the orators philosophy." The sophist came to be distinguished from the philosopher. A reunion of the two divisions of practical knowledge, that of subject matter and that of manner of expression, was sought for by the Roman rhetoricians. Rhetoric, which meant the training of the *rhetor,* or speaker, in days when the main use of language was oral, combined all the elements in the practical use of knowledge. Its five divisions were: (1) Inventio, which was concerned with the discovery or selection of material for use; (2) Dispositio, which dealt with effective arrangement of material; (3) Elocutio, which dealt with manner of expression; (4) Memoria, concerned with supporting or illustrative material; and (5) Pronuntiatio, concerned with the manner of vocal utterance. Rhetoric thus inclusive provided most of the elements of training for active public life.

There is an axiom that the aim of education is not knowledge but power. This idea was a guiding principle with Peter Ramus, the sixteenth-century French educational reformer, who held with Cicero that training in eloquence should be combined with training in philosophy. The philosophy which he had in mind covered the broad field of knowledge including not only metaphysics and moral philosophy, the field of the theologian, but natural philosophy or physics, the field of the physician, and political philosophy, the field of the lawyer or statesman. The division corresponds in general with that of Cicero who divides the province of philosophy into three parts; the obscurities of physics, the subtilties of logic, and knowledge of life and manners. It corresponds also with the three main directions of higher educational training in sixteenth-century England. The eloquence that Ramus had in mind was literary art or the effective expression of knowledge in speech. In brief, Ramus advocated a scheme of education which combined the principal elements of contemporary knowledge with means of effective expression.

In the period of the Renaissance the union was easily possible. The two sides of knowledge were gained from the same sources, from the works of classical literature. In the College of Presles in Paris presided over by Ramus, while the eminent teacher and author, Talon (or Talæus), in the morning lectured on philosophy, Ramus himself in the afternoon lectured on rhetoric, illustrating its principles through the poets, orators, and other authors. In this way Cicero's orations and his treatise *On Fate* served in teaching rhetoric or dialectics, the Dream of Scipio (in Cicero's *Republic*) in teaching astronomy, Pliny's *Natural History* and Virgil's *Georgics* in teaching science or 'natural philosophy,' Aristotle in teaching physics.

In our own day there has come about an unfortunate separation of the elements of study. The trained literary artist too often lacks the fundamental knowledge, the 'philosophy' of the time of Ramus. On the other hand the trained scientist in his eager pursuit of knowledge or 'philosophy,' notoriously, in many instances, fails to gain command of the literary art or 'eloquence.' The eternal importance of the first two divisions of earlier rhetoric, Invention and Disposition, finds modern expression in the reiterated statement that learning to write is learning to think. The fifth division of earlier rhetoric, the vocal utterance, in modern times is usually either entirely neglected or assigned to the attention of a distinct instructional force. The fourth division, Memory, having something to say, is left to be cared for in distinct departments of study. "Good English" is assumed to be merely English correct in spelling and grammatical form. Only of late has come a realization of the importance of making the study of English or literature, the means of teaching not only how to gain command of expression (*Elocutio*), but how to think (*Inventio* and *Dispositio*), how to enunciate (*Pronunciatio*), and how to stock the mind (*Memoria*) from literature.

In sixteenth-century Great Britain the educational method of Ramus was widely influential. Oxford was not hospitable to the method. At Cambridge, however, the influence of Ascham and Sidney led to its being largely adopted. Through this method the New Learning of the sixteenth century, unlike the scientific knowledge of modern times, came clothed in effective language. A sense of form was acquired along with a knowledge of subject matter. The double training thus afforded was unquestionably an important factor in the development of the capacities for literary expression in the Elizabethan period.

Not always sanely combined with philosophy after the manner of Ramus, the subject of rhetoric nevertheless had an important place in the education of the sixteenth-century England. In school use the works most widely used were in Latin. The pseudo-Ciceronian *Ad Herennium* was much in use. A second work even more popular was the compilation by Talon, which, says Brinsley (1612), "I take to be most used in schools." As early as 1524, however, there appeared an elementary manual in English by the schoolmaster Leonard Cox entitled *The Arte or Crafte of*

Rhetorique, and during the century appeared a considerable number of English works dealing with the subject; the *Treatise on Schemes and Tropes* by Richard Sherry (1550), the *Foundacion of Rhetoryke* by Richard Rainold (1563), the *Garden of Eloquence* by Henry Peacham (1577), the *Artes of Logike and Rethorike* by Dudley Fenner (1584), and the *Arcadian Rhetoric* by Abraham Fraunce (1588).

But the most important English writer to handle the subject was Sir Thomas Wilson. In his *Rule of Reason* (1551) Wilson speaks of rhetoric as making use of "gaie painted sentences" and "fresh colours and goodly ornaments," thereby exemplifying the meaning which through the medieval period down to his own times had usually been attached to the name rhetoric. In the year 1553, however, Wilson published his *Arte of Rhetorique.* In this work Wilson offers a broader view of the subject, a view more like that of the classical writers from whom he draws most of his general ideas.

After the manner of Quintilian he divides his subject into five parts: (1) Inuentio—"finding out of apt matter"; (2) Dispositio—"an apt bestowing and orderly placing of things"; (3) Elocutio—"an applying of apt words and sentences to the matter"; (4) Memorie—"a fast holding both of matter and words couched together"; (5) Vtterance—"a framing of the voice, countenance, and gesture after a comely manner."

He not only adopts the framework used by the Latin rhetoricians but he embodies in his work much of their sound counsel. With Aristotle, with Cicero, with Horace, and with Quintilian he agrees in recognizing that good language must be guided by common usage. He adopts the Ciceronian distinction of levels of speech. "There are," he says, "three maners of stiles of enditinges, the great or mightie kinde, when we vse greate wordes, or vehement figures. The small kinde, when wee moderate our heate by meaner wordes. . . . The lowe kinde, when we vse no *Metaphores* nor translated wordes, . . . but goe plainly to worke and speake altogether in common wordes." In this connection he gives expression, in clumsy fashion it must be admitted, to a related classical doctrine. "The oration," he says, "is muche commended . . . when we . . . vse suche wordes as serue for that kinde of writyng moste conuenient ['fitting']," an idea more neatly phrased by Chaucer and by Shakespeare.

This book of Wilson deserves to be read in its entirety by any one seeking to understand the underlying principles of Elizabethan literary art. In doing so one may find much entertainment as well as information. The classical rhetorician had given much attention to the art of raising laughter as a means of attuning an audience to persuasion. Erasmus in his *Praise of Folly* ranks the rhetorician among the devotees of Folly because of the emphasis laid by the classical rhetorician on the art of jesting. Quintilian, for instance, devotes a whole chapter to this important subject. Wilson does not overlook this means of persuasion. He not only expounds the principles involved, but contributes a number of amusing anecdotes in illustration of the use of the jest. To the importance attached by the rhetorician to the jest, and perhaps to school practice in this diverting feature of rhetoric, may in part be attributed the jest books which served the literary needs of the Elizabethans.

But the part of Wilson's book most directly related to the history of the language is Part III, that dealing with *Elocution,* a word, it must be noted, which had with Wilson a meaning quite distinct from *Vtterance.* By means of elocution, says Wilson, one "getteth words to set forth invention [Part I] and with such beautie commendeth the matter that reason semeth to be clad in Purple, walking afore both bare and naked. . . . Whom doe we most reuerence and compt half a God among men? Euen such a one assuredly that can plainly, distinctly, plentifully, and aptly vtter both words and matter." [4]   The extravagance of the claims for rhetoric is Ciceronian.

Under the head of *Composition,* or the "apte ioyning together of woordes," Wilson sets forth, though briefly, most of the Ciceronian ideals. Rhythm is to be secured by the use of "suche order that neither the eare shall espie any gerre ['jar'], nor yet any man shalbe dulled with ouerlong drawyng out of a sentence." At the same time Wilson objects to the "mingling of clauses suche as are needlesse, beyng heaped together without reason, and vsed together without number." Indeed, from Wilson, or more often directly from the classical rhetorics which were Wilson's sources, English writers learned the ideals of sentence structure. In the *Arte of Poesie* (1589) ascribed to Puttenham, Sir Nicholas Bacon, who was much praised for his "graue and naturall eloquence," is pictured "sitting in his gallery alone with the works of Quintilian before him." Latin writers certainly provided the patterns and Latin rhetoricians provided the rules for sixteenth-century English writers. From them were learned the methods by which elements of thought, instead of being strewn without system, were brought into symmetry by balanced structure or, by means of periodic structure, were thrown into perspective.

But it was the more showy, often the tawdry, features of composition that most captured the fancy of sixteenth-century writers. The rhetorical ideals of the time, the pursuit of "eloquence," led to an insistent demand for a manner of writing heightened by artifice. Lack of artifice was condemned as vulgar. In the Puttenham *Arte of Poesie*

[4] Ed. Mair, pp. 160-1.

appears an anecdote of an oration in Parliament made by a
speaker lacking this form of cultivated eloquence. This
oration is condemned with the comment: "I heerd not a
better alehouse tale told this seuen yeares." To the taste
of the period, authors of rhetorical works catered. Peacham
in his *Garden of Eloquence* (1577) offers his readers "all
manner of Flowers, colours, ornaments, Exornations,
Formes and Fashions of Speech." [5] In the Puttenham *Arte
of Poesie* 121 figures of speech are defined and illustrated,
of which 107 have been traced to Quintilian's *Rhetoric*.
This part of his subject Wilson treats under the head of
"Exornation by Colours of Rhetorique." These 'Colours'
were not to be "egally sparpled throughout" but "as starres
stande in the Firmament, or flowers in a garden or pretie
deuised antiques in a cloth of Arras." They are grouped
by Wilson under three heads: (1) tropes, (2) schemes in
words, (3) schemes in whole sentences.

Under tropes he groups metaphor or 'translation of
wordes'; word-making or 'onomatapoia'; intellection,
'synecdoche'; abusion or 'catachresis'; transmutation,
'metonymy'; transumption; change of name, 'antono-
masia'; circumlocution; and "tropes of a long continued
speeche," such as allegory, etc.

Under schemes in words he includes: Prosthesis, 'addition
at the beginning,' *e.g., berattle* for *rattle;* apheresis, 'abstraction from the first,' *e.g., gan* for *began;* epenthesis,
'interlacing in the middest,' *e.g., relligion* for *religion;*
syncope, 'cutting from the middest,' *e.g., idolatrie* for
idololatrie; proparalepsis, 'adding at the end,' *e.g., hasten*
for *hast your businesse;* apocope, 'cutting from the end,'
e.g., maie for *maide.*

Under schemes in whole sentences he includes a number
of devices such as Commoration, 'resting vpon a poinct';

5 G. P. Krapp, *Rise of English Literary Prose*, p. 309.

Discriptio 'vision'; rhetorical question; progressio, 'antithesis'; repetition, 'parallel construction'; doublettes, 'repetition of a word'; conuersion, 'repetition of last word'; egall numbers, 'balance'; like endyng and like fallyng, *e.g.*, "Thou liues wickedly; Thou speakest naughtely"; etc., etc.

This partial exhibition of Wilson's exposition of modes of exornation will serve to illustrate the diligence used in searching the classics, not only by individual writers looking for illustrative material and patterns in expression, but by rhetoricians looking for precepts and rules and systems.

The importance attached to exornation of style appears from frequent contemporary remarks. Leland, the student of English antiquities, writing in 1545, explains the popular neglect of antiquities as "because men of eloquence hath not enterprised to set them fourthe in a flourishinge ['florid'] style in some tymes past not commenly used in Englande of writers wele learned, and now in such estymacyon, that except truth be delycately clothed in purpure her written verytees can scant fynde a reader."[6] A little later, William Harrison, another antiquarian, is apologetic for his "foule frizeled Treatise" in which he has made no attempt at "rhetorical shew of eloquence" and modestly expresses the hope that his work may "prove a spur to others better learned."[7]

To excess in rhetoric, as to excess in Latinizing, objection was early raised. The attitude of Tyndale and his opposition to the rhetoric of Fisher and of More should be recalled. John Bale was of the opinion that the endeavor to satisfy "delycate eares and wyttes" with a more eloquent style "myghte wele be sparyd." Bishop Jewel in an *Oratio Contra rhetoricam* (about 1557) "declares the study of rhetoric to be useless, profitless, vain."[8] Three decades later Camden in his *Britannia* disclaims any intention "to

---

[6] *Ibid.*, p. 442.   [7] *Ibid.*, p. 405.   [8] *Ibid.*, p. 301.

pick flowers in the garden of eloquence." [9]   Such protests, however, but serve to show the strength of the general current of taste. Thomas Nashe in bringing to ridicule the pedantry of his learned opponent, Gabriel Harvey, says that Harvey's works will "shew a whole Talæus and Ad Herennium of figures." [10]

Wilson, it must be recalled, was one of the champions of pure English. He revolts not only from excess in the adoption of foreign words, but from excess in the use of the art which he expounds. As one might expect, therefore, he directs ridicule against much of the extravagance in the speech of his time. "Some," he says, "will speake Oracles, that a manne can not telle whiche waie to take them, some will be so fine and so Poeticall with all, that to their seemynge there shall not stande one haire a misse, and yet euery bodie els shall thinke theim meeter for a ladies chamber then for an earnest matter in any open assemblie." This warning, if observed, would have saved Elizabethan writers from many of the extravagances of later Arcadian style.

The favorite trick of repeating one word, tranlacing, he reduces to the absurd by means of example. "If a man knewe what a mannes life were, no man for any mannes sake woulde kil any man, but one man would rather helpe an other man, consideryng man is borne for man to helpe man, and not to hate man." "What man," continues Wilson, "woulde not be choked, if he chopt all these men at once into his mouthe and neuer dronke after it?"

'Hunting the letter' or use of alliteration, he holds likewise up to ridicule by exhibiting its extravagant use as follows: "Pitiful pouertie praieth for a penie, but puffed presumtion passeth not a poinct, pamperyng his panche

[9] *Ibid.*, p. 448.
[10] *Have with You to Saffron Walden*, p. 178.

with pestilent pleasure, procuryng his passe porte to poste it to hell pitt, there to be punished with paines perpetuall."

He objects not only to excessive Latinizing, but to an affectation for archaic English words. "Phanorimus the Philosopher," he says, "did hit a yong man ouer the Thumbes very handsomely, for vsing ouer old, and ouer straunge wordes." Wilson feelingly adds: "Ah, liue man, as they did before thee, and speake thy mind now as men doe at this day. And remember that which *Cæsar* saieth, beware as long as thou liuest of straunge wordes, as thou wouldest take heede and eschue great Rockes in the Sea."

The work of Wilson serves to illustrate the permeation of English learning in the sixteenth century by classical influences. But the same influences permeated the courtly life of the period, and in the environment provided by the courtly society of the sixteenth century are to be found conditions shaping the literature and the language. The change in social ideals that came with the Renaissance has already been spoken of. In the Middle Ages the young nobleman had been reared in the households of great princes and lords where, serving successively as page and as squire, he had been trained to knighthood. His training included hunting and horsemanship, courtesy and gallantry. He perhaps learned a little music. But in general he was trained to feats of strength and was little given to learning. With the new order of things under the Renaissance came a change. The sixteenth-century ideal nobleman became a man of learning as well as a man of arms. Under the centralized government of the Tudors came the need for councillors of state equipped in mind as well as in body, of men trained for government as well as trained for war. In *A Remedy for Sedition* we read, "It is small losse if a lorde shoote not well, or at least the losse hurteth but hym selfe. But gyue the gouernmente of common wealthes into their handes, that can not skyll thereof, how many must nedes goe to wracke?"[11]

The Tudor rulers were suited to the needs of a Renaissance state. They were themselves learned and were promoters of learning among their subjects. Henry VIII, with his energy and manifold accomplishments was, to use the words of Sir Thomas Elyot, "the chiefe author and setter foorth of an Introduction into grammer ['learning'] for the children of his lovyng subjectes."[12] "If kyng Edward had liued a litle longer," says Ascham, "his onely example had breed soch a rase of worthie learned ientlemen, as this Realme neuer yet did affourde." Queen Catherine was trained in the New Learning, and her daughter, Queen Mary, was carefully educated under the joint supervision of two of the most famous among the early Humanists, the English Linacre and the Spanish Vives.

Mary was succeeded by her younger sister Elizabeth, and "whatever the branch of art or literature in this epoch you wish to understand," it has been said, "you must first study Elizabeth." To the French Ambassador, Elizabeth once remarked, "When I came to the throne, I knewe six languages better than my own."[13] Concerning her, Roger Ascham her tutor says, "Yea I belieue that beside her perfit readines, in Latin, Italian, French, and Spanish, she readeth here now at Windsore more Greek euery day, than some Prebendarie of this Chirche doth read Latin in a whole weeke."

Learned rulers were served by learned statesmen. Most of the men thus far discussed in connection with literature, including More, Elyot, Ascham, Cheke, Smith, and Wilson, filled one post or another in the royal service. The same tastes that appear in the rulers appear in the courtiers,

[11] Quoted from Kelso, *J. E. G. Ph.*, July, 1925.
[12] *The Castel of Helth,* quoted from Krapp, *op. cit.,* p. 471.
[13] F. Chamberlin, *Sayings of Queen Elizabeth.*

among whom were included men famed for literary achievement from Wyatt and Surrey and Sackville down to Sidney and Raleigh.

The promotion of social culture was served by a series of literary productions from Elyot's *The Gouernour* to Lyly's *Euphues, the Anatomy of Wit,* and Peacham's *The Compleat Gentleman.* From other languages, from Italian, from Spanish, and from Latin, were translated works profitable for the promotion of good manners and good morals. The spirit in which these translations were made appears in the letter by Thomas Hoby to Sir John Cheke regarding the translation of the famous Italian epitome of courtly culture, Castiglione's *Il Cortegiano* ('The Courtier'). Hoby in his letter (1557) says, "As I therefore haue to my smal skil bestowed some labour about this piece of woorke, euen so coulde I wishe with al my hart, profounde learned men in the Greeke and Latin shoulde make the lyke proofe, and euerye manne store the tunge accordinge to hys knowledge and delite aboue other men, in some piece of learnynge, that we alone of the worlde may not bee styll counted barbarous in oure tunge, as in time out of minde we haue bene in our maners. And so shall we perchaunce in time become as famous in Englande, as the learned men of other nations haue ben and presently are." [14]

Interest in the new social refinements came to dominate even at the centers of learning. At the universities learning unrelated to practice passed out of fashion. "Schollars in ower age," says Gabriel Harvey in a letter to Spenser, "are . . . rather active than contemplative philosophers . . . most detestinge that spitefull malicious proverbe, of greatist Clarkes and not wisest men." They learned worldly wisdom from men in the school of life and they took "instructions and advertisements at your lawiers and courtiers

[14] Arber, Introd. to Ascham's *The Scholemaster,* p. 5.

hands, that ar continually better traynid and more lively experienced therein then we university men ar or possibely can be . . ." Since "Dunse and Thomas of Aquine . . . were . . . expellid the Universitye," new books have come into fashion. Among the books occupying the attention of men at Cambridge he mentions "Castiglione's fine Cortegiano, . . . Guatzoes newe Discourses of curteous behavior" and "a certayne parlous byoke callid . . . Il Principe di Niccolo Macchiavelli," . . . and "I know not how many owtelandish braveries besides of the same stampe." [15] With worldly wisdom combined with learning the 'University Wits' made their way to London to seek emoluments in life at court.

Another important feature in the new social refinement was the part played by women. In medieval times it had been feminine influences that had created the atmosphere in which thrived the courtesy and gallantry that distinguished the age of chivalry from the rudeness of the preceding time. So in the period of the Renaissance in England was created a form of courtly life reproducing that found in sixteenth-century Italy, a society dominated by learned and cultivated women like that at Urbino of which Castiglione offers so delightful a picture, gracefully presided over by the Duchess Elizabeth Gonzaga. Women provided inspiration for the poet. Women's eyes are for Biron "the books, the arts, the academes." In a more substantial way, by their patronage, women provided literary men with means of living. It was particularly to the ladies that Lyly dedicated his *Euphues*. "Euphues," he says, "had rather lye shut in a Ladyes casket, then open in a Schollers studie."

Another noteworthy fact regarding the English literature of the sixteenth century is that much of its poetry was the

[15] Camden Society, 1889, *Letter Book of G. H.*

production of men of rank and intended for private circulation in the courtly circles to which the authors belonged. This is true of the poems of Wyatt and Surrey early in the century and of the sonnet sequences of the last decade. The first English tragedy, the *Gorboduc* of Sackville and Norton, was not printed until its authors found it advisable in order to supplant an unauthorized earlier edition. Sidney's *Arcadia* was composed for the pleasure of his sister the Countess of Pembroke and, like Sidney's other principal works, was not published until after his death. Works composed under such conditions obviously reflect only the courtly speech of the authors and of the exclusive audience to which they were addressed.

In the refinement of courtly society, then, the English language found cultivation. "I have found," says Sidney, "in divers small-learned courtiers a more sound style than in some professors of learning . . . the courtier following that which by practice he findeth fittest to nature, therein, though he know it not, doth according to art though not by art." Of the same way of thinking was Ben Jonson, who says:

> The noblest way
> Of breeding up our youth in letters, arms,
> Fair men, discourses, civil exercises,
> And all the blazon of a gentleman—
> Where can he learn to vault, to ride, to fence,
> To move his body gracefuller, to speak
> His language purer, or to tune his mind
> Or manners more to the harmony of nature
> Than in these nurseries of nobility? [16]

The basis for the culture in courtly circles was of course provided by classical learning. This learning reached England not only directly in the literary products of the

[16] Quoted from F. Watson, *English Grammar Schools*, p. 100.

ancient world of which in the second half of the sixteenth century there was made a remarkable series of English translations, but indirectly through literary products of France, Italy, and Spain, countries in which classical culture had been assimilated earlier than in England.   The zeal for philosophy, or knowledge, and for eloquence, or heightened form of expression, demanded by the new sophistication led to a quality of style expressed by the word 'bravery,' a quality which, said Gabriel Harvey, "iointeth them bothe."   A representative product of this social environment with all its 'bravery' appears in the person of John Lyly.   Lyly was a grandson of William Lily, one of the pioneers in the English Renaissance.   He was educated at Magdalen College, Oxford, under the patronage of Burleigh, Lord Treasurer, a brother-in-law of Sir John Cheke and himself an active promoter of humanism.   In John Lyly, therefore, appears a representative of the third generation of English Humanists, and the 'bravery' of style which expresses the spirit of this generation appears in the writings of its representative.   In his two books, *Euphues, The Anatomy of Wit* and *Euphues and his England,* appears an artificial mode of writing which represents a culmination in the artificial tendencies of the time.   In these works Lyly assembles a wealth of material garnered from classical sources either derived from his own reading of Pliny and Plutarch and Ovid or appropriated from the storehouses of other Renaissance scholars such as the *Similia* and the *Adagia* of Erasmus.   This wealth of material is poured into language molds provided by the rhetorical studies of the period.

In the Euphuistic style, which takes its name from the books of Lyly, it is not difficult to recognize the schemes expounded by the rhetoricians; the *isocolon,* or equality of members, the *parison,* or equality of sound, the *para-*

moion, or similarity of sounds between words or syllables.[17] If one abandons these technical terms of the classical rhetorician in favor of terms more modern and more familiar, one still finds it not difficult to label the features of Euphuistic style, for they are definite in character.

First there is the use of balance usually for the sake of antithesis. This feature is omnipresent. One reads of "Counsailors, whose foresight in peace warranteth saftie in warre, whose provision in plentie, makes sufficient in dearth." The effect of balance is heightened by the use of alliteration, used particularly for pointing a contrast. The gentlewomen in Greece and Italy are said to "begin their morning at midnoone, and make their evening at midnight, using sonets for psalmes, and pastymes for prayers, reading ye Epistle of a Lover, when they should peruse the Gospell of our Lorde. . . ." This balanced structure is combined with the use of classical anecdote and classical allusion. "There hath alwayes beene *Achilles* at home to buckle with *Hector* abroad, *Nestors* gravitie to countervaile *Priams* counsail, *Ulisses* subtilties to match with *Antenors* policies." Along with classical allusion goes an even more striking feature, the element of natural philosophy in the form of a pseudo-natural history, or 'unnatural natural history' as it has been called. The error arising from following classical learning rather than independent observation of fact is nowhere better illustrated than in the Euphuistic comparisons drawn from the reputed habits of beasts, producing figures that to the modern mind have the grotesqueness of gargoyles. In eulogy of the queen we read: "This is that good Pelican that to feede hir people spareth not to rend hir owne personne: This is that mightie Eagle, that hath throwne dust into the eyes of the Hart, that went about to worke destruction to hir subjectes, into whose

[17] *Cf.* Croll, Introd. to edition of Lyly's *Euphues.*

winges although the blinde Beetle would have crept, and so being carryed into hir nest, destroyed hir young ones, yet hath she with the vertue of hir fethers, consumed that flye in his owne fraud.

"She hath exiled the Swallowe that sought to spoyle the Grashopper, and given bytter Almondes to the ravenous Wolves that endevored to devoure the silly Lambes, burning even with the breath of hir mouth like ye princely Stag, the serpents yat wer engendered by the breath of the huge Elephant, so that now all hir enimies are as whist as the bird *Attagen*, who never singeth any tune after she is taken, nor they beeing so overtaken." [18]

The elements that make up Euphuistic style, as has been indicated, are to be found in rhetorical writings in Latin and Greek. Many of them appear in Cicero, but they were particularly cultivated in the post-Augustan age, especially in the Asiatic eloquence of the church fathers. A good share of its features may be found listed and labeled among the schemes of rhetoric in English works like that of Wilson or the Puttenham *Arte of Poesie*. A more immediate stimulus is to be found, however, in the works of the Spanish writer Guevara. This writer in his works had absorbed much of the practical wisdom of the ancient world of such importance in the cultivation sought for in sixteenth-century England. English translations from Guevara's works had, therefore, been made by Berners, North, Bryan, Fenner, Hellowes, etc., and had been exceedingly popular as a source of Renaissance culture. But Guevara in his writings had not only absorbed the philosophy of the ancients, but had assimilated much of the eloquence and had organized the devices of the rhetoricians into a definite mode of writing. His writings, therefore,

---

[18] J. M. Garnett, *English Prose*, pp. 1-23. The text is unfortunately modernized in the use of the letters *u* and *v*, and *i* and *j*.

at first prized in England for their matter, came to be admired for their manner, and the artificial forms of sentence structure used by him afforded a pattern which, with alliteration as an added feature, provided the basis for the extravagant English style known as Euphuistic. The source of Euphuistic style further illustrates the variety of channels through which Renaissance culture reached England.

With its regular patterns for sentence structure Euphuism provided for prose a definiteness of pattern akin to that provided by meter and rime for poetry For about one decade its vogue prevailed. But its excessive artificiality caused it soon to pass out of fashion. The constant use of pointed antithesis, or *progressio,* had about it a cheapness now associated with another figure of speech once cherished by the rhetoricians, the figure of paronomasia, the modern estimate of which is expressed by its contemptuous name, *pun.*

Reaction from Euphuism was inevitable. In his *Defense of Poesie* Sidney condemns its excesses, its "courtesan-like painted affectation," the eloquence apparelled "one time with so far-fet words, that many seem monsters—but must seem strangers to any poor Englishman; another time with coursing of a letter, as if they were bound to follow the method of a dictionary; another time with figures and flowers extremely winter-starved." "For similitudes," he says, "I think all herbarists, all stories of beasts, fowls, and fishes are rifled up," having the effect of leading the mind from the central thought.

The reaction, however, from this particular mode of rhetorical writing did not mean the abandonment of rhetoric. The style of Sidney exhibits 'bravery' in many forms, not only a wealth of classical allusions, but rhetorical tricks of many kinds including various forms of plays on words, conspicuously the repetition of a single word, or tranlacing, for which the technical name was *traductio*. Among other contemporary writers forms of rhetorical artifice were used in profusion, and the wealth of the classics was squandered in comparisons and allusions. There was lacking, however, a uniformity of direction like that provided by Euphuism, and there was wide variance of opinion regarding modes of expression to be commended or to be condemned. There was a period of active fermentation before the appearance of the clear product.

For instance there persisted the old conflict regarding the use of foreign words. The purist side was represented by Gascoigne who preferred to have "faulted in keeping the olde English wordes" rather than "in borrowing of other such Epithetes and Adjectives as smell of the Inkhorne," and the author of the *Arte of Poesie* (1589) who offers admonitions regarding the "inkhorne termes" of preachers and schoolmasters and the "straunge termes" from other languages introduced by "Secretaries and Merchaunts and trauailours" and the many "darke wordes and not vsuall nor well sounding, though they be dayly spoken in Court." Yet this writer adopts for his own use a number of foreign words which he defends, and the practice of borrowing finds a zealous defender in George Pettie who in his *Ciuile Conversation* (1581) says: "I meruaile how oure English tongue hath crackt it [*sic*] credit, that it may not borrow of the Latine as well as other tongues; and if it haue broken, it is but of late, for it is not vnknowen to all men, how many words we haue fetcht from thence within these few yeares, which if they should be all counted inkpot tearmes, I know not how we should speak anie thing without blacking our mouths with inke." [19]

Still different was the attitude of Spenser who went back to earlier English for models in language. To him, it should

[19] Ed. 1588.

be recalled, Chaucer was the well of English undefiled. Spenser's point of view is expressed by E(dward) K(irke) in the Epistle Prefatory to the *Shepheardes Calender* (1579). In defending Spenser from blame for his "choyse of old and unwonted words" Kirke expresses the opinion that "it is one special prayse of many, whych are dew to this poete, that he hath laboured to restore, as to theyr rightfull heritage, such good and naturall English words, as have ben long time out of use, and almost cleane disherited. Which is the onely cause, that our Mother tonge, which truely of it self is both ful enough for prose, and stately enough for verse, hath long time ben counted both bare and barrein of both. Which default whenas some endevoured to salve and recure, they patched up the holes with peces and rags of other languages, borrowing here of the French, there of the Italian, everywhere of the Latine; not weighing how il those tongues accorde with themselves, but much worse with ours: So now they have made our English tongue a gallimaufry, or hodgepodge of al other speches."

In the form of purism that he advocated and put into practice Spenser did not have a large following among his contemporaries. A prevalent view was expressed in the dictum of Ben Jonson that "Spencer [*sic*] in affecting the Ancients writ no language." His influence, however, in a later period, as remains to be seen, in the Romantic movement of the eighteenth century, served to preserve, in poetic use at least, many a noble word which otherwise would have quite faded out of memory.

Regarding the use of words long and short, simple and compounded, there was similar difference in opinion. George Gascoigne in the advice to poets offered in his *Steele Glas* (1576) says:

"I thinke it not amisse to forewarne you that you thrust as few wordes of many sillables into your verse as may be:

and herevnto I might alledge many reasons: first the most
English wordes are of one sillable, so that the more mona-
syllables you vse, the truer Englishman you shall seeme,
and thelesse you shall smell of the Inkhorne." Thomas
Nashe, on the other hand, defends the practice of forming
compounds which from earliest times had been a feature
of English speech and by which in the Elizabethan period,
notably in the language of Shakespeare, richness in expression was contributed to the language. In his *Christs Teares
ouer Jerusalem* (1593), replying to his critics, the "rancke
of Reprehenders" that complained of his "boystrous compound wordes," Nashe says: "Our English tongue of all
languages most swarmeth with the single money of mono-
sillables, which are the onely scandall of it. Bookes written
in them and no other seeme like shop-keepers boxes, that
containe nothing else, saue halfe-pence, three-farthings and
tow-pences. Therefore what did me I, but hauing a huge
heape of those worthlesse shreds of small English in my *Pia
maters* purse to make the royaller shew with them to mens
eyes, had them to the compounders immediately and ex-
changed them foure into one and others into more, according to the Greek, French, Spanish, and Italian." [20]

Nashe in his various writings affords excellent illustration
of the native capacities of the English language at the end
of the sixteenth century. He defends the making of new
words by compounding, which suits the natural genius of
the language. But for the artificial eloquence of the schools
he expresses contempt. "Young students," he refers to,
"so besotted that they forsake sounder Artes, to followe
smoother eloquence." "Man is inclined," he says, "if to
vaine-glorie to eloquence: if to profounde knowledge to
Aristotle." In another place he says: "A man may baule
till his voice be hoarse, exhort with teares till his tongue

[20] Arber reprint.

ake,—and yet moue no more then if he had been all that while mute, if his speech be not seasoned with eloquence." [21]

And yet the language of Nashe is a product of studied method. In one place he says: "My Readers, whom loath to tyre with a home-spunne tale, that should dull them woorse than Holland Cheese, heere and there I welt and garde it with allusive exornations and comparisons." [22] The manner of writing, however, cultivated by rhetoric and classical reading is not that characteristic of Nashe. At times he fell into a simple and straightforward manner, to use his own more picturesque expression, "left descant and taskt me to plaine song." Following one such passage in his account of his arch-adversary, Gabriel Harvey, Nashe represents an interlocutor, impatient at the temporary mildness of manner, as exclaiming: "O peace, peace, exercise thy writing tongue, and let us have no more of this plaine English." [23]   Thus spurred, Nashe launches forth in a characteristic strain of invective.

The invective style employed by Nashe, and to a somewhat less extent by his contemporary Greene, exhibits anew the elements of native eloquence in the English language. Beneath the form of language cultivated under classical influence the current of popular speech had persisted. Its appearance and reappearance from the time of *Piers Plowman* has already been noted. With its torrent of words in tumultuous rhythm guided somewhat by the use of alliteration, it had served in the impassioned utterance of the popular preacher and in the violence of the pamphleteer. Near the end of the sixteenth century it appears in the heated religious controversy of the time. It is brought into service by Nashe in his violent controversy with that pedantic product of classical scholarship, the learned Gabriel Harvey.

[21] *Anatomie of Absurditie*, Grosart reprint, pp. 45, 67.
[22] *Terrors of the Night*, ed. Grosart, p. 275.
[23] *Have with You to Saffron Walden*, p. 48.

"Scoffing and girding," says Harvey, speaking of Greene and Nashe, "is their daily bread." "Noble, Reuerend, or whatsoever," continues Harvey, are to Nashe "al pesants and clownes: gowty Diuels and buckram Giants; Midasses and golden Asses; Cormorants and Drones, Dunces and hypocritical hot spurres, Earthworms and Pinchfart Penny-fathers; that feede not their hungry purses and eager stomacke." Now let Nashe speak for himself. In his language Harvey is referred to as: "Cowbaby," "Gorboduck Huddle-duddle," "Gabriel Scurueiers," "this Gogmagog," "Iewish Thalmud of absurdities," "this course Himpenhem-pen Slampant," "this stale Applesquire Cockledemoy," "Paraliticke Quacksaluer," "oure iracundious Stramutzen Gabriell." Harvey's handwriting is "that flourishing flanti-tanting goutie Omega fist." His language is made up of "rascally hedge rak't vp termes, familiar to roguish morts and doxes," "ridiculous senseless sentences, finical flaunting phrases, and termagant inkhorne termes."

The mode of expression is that of a Rabelais or an Are-tino. Such eloquence is not surpassed in the most virulent forms of modern American writing. Such "gunpowder-termes" employed by "that terrible Thundersmith of termes" serve to show the strong undercurrent of rugged speech that might not be suspected by one familiar only with the politer aspects of Elizabethan literature.

In the welter of conflicting tendencies then that made up the literary life of the sixteenth century may be dis-tinguished certain definite currents. There was the new courtly life refined under the influence of Renaissance learning, served by a language enriched by foreign elements and adorned by rhetorical artifice. There was the religious life profoundly stirred by the Reformation, with a sincerity served by simple language and a depth of feeling served by robustious eloquence. There was a cherishing of native tradition with an effort to revive the graces of Chaucer. Under all was a main stream of popular speech, receiving elements from the cultivated speech of the courtly and the learned, but in turn yielding rich store of popular words and phrases.

By the end of the century there had been reached a consciousness of the capacities of the English for artistic achievement. With the apologetic tone of fifteenth-century writers and the sense of the inferiority of English expressed in the earlier part of the sixteenth century by writers such as Elyot and Ascham is to be contrasted the proud proclamation in the later decades of the excellence of the English tongue. Pettie, in the preface to his translation of Guazzo's *Ciuile Conversation* (1581), says that critics place too low an estimate on the capacities of the English language. In schematic phrase he says: "They count it barren, they count it barbarous, they count it vnworthie to be accounted of." In disagreement, Pettie proclaims his ability to write in English "as copiouslye for varietie, as compendiously for brevitie, as choicely for words, as pithilie for sentences, as pleasantlie for figures, and everie waie as eloquentlie as anie writer should do in anie vulgar tongue whatsoever." [24] In like vein Sidney, in his *Defense of Poesie* (1581ca.) asserts that "for the uttering sweetly and properly the conceits of the mind, which is the end of speech, that hath it equally with any other tongue in the world." [25] Richard Mulcaster, in *The First Part of the Elementarie* (1582), says of the language "which we now vse, it semeth euen now to be at the best for substance, and the brauest for circumstance, and whatsoeuer shall becom of the English state, the English tung cannot proue fairer, then it is at this daie." The English language was in full leafage and ready to

---

[24] Krapp, *op. cit.*, p. 342. The use of the letters *v* and *u* is modernized.

[25] Ed. Cook, spelling modernized.

burst into brilliant bloom. That the flowers were not slow to open appears from the remarks only a few years later (1595-6) by R. Carew regarding the English writings of his time. Carew asserts that "whatsoever grace any other language carrieth, in verse or prose, in tropes or metaphors, in echoes and agnominations, they may be lively and exactly represented in ours." He then continues: "Will you have Plato's vein, read Sir Thomas Smith; the Ionic? Sir Thomas More; Cicero's? Ascham; Varro's? Chaucer; Demosthenes? Sir John Cheeke (who in his treatise on the rebels, hath comprised all the figures of rhetoric). Will you read Virgil? take the Earl of Surrey; Catullus? Shakespeare and Marlowe's fragment; Ovid? Daniel; Lucan? Spenser."[26] The pretensions are those of exalted feeling, of courage for great achievement.

[26] *The Excellencie of the English Tongue,* Camden's *Remaines,* 2d ed. Quoted by Adams, *Life of Shakespeare.* Modernized spelling and punctuation.

CHAPTER IX

SHAKESPEARE AND RHETORIC

THE intellectual ferment in sixteenth-century English reminds one of the effects attributed by Falstaff to a favorite beverage. Sherris-sack, if we may believe its eloquent votary, ascending into the brain, "makes it apprehensive, quick, forgetive ['inventive'], full of nimble, fiery, and delectable shapes; which deliver'd o'er to the voice (the tongue) which is the birth, becomes excellent wit." Like the potent beverage thus eloquently praised, the fumes of the Renaissance created in the spirits of English writers an exhilaration expressed in bravery of language, in extravagance and excess. The English thus quickened afforded a medium for some of the noblest expressions of the artistic genius of England. The galaxy of writers classed as Elizabethans provided a display of effects not afterwards surpassed in brilliancy. By Lyly the colors of rhetoric were wrought into elaborate and curious pattern; by Sidney elements of speech new and old were woven into "the embroidery of the finest Art and daintiest Witt"; by Nashe, the "thundersmith of termes," the boisterous elements of the language were made to serve in the expression of furibund passion; by Marlowe "the jigging veins of rhyming mother wits" were raised to the "high astounding terms" of Tamburlaine.

In this age the genius of Shakespeare found its outward habiliments. An "upstart crow beautified with our feathers," he is called by his envious contemporary, Robert

Greene. The language at his service was one little governed by rule. For discipline and restraint one must wait until later periods in English literature. For the time being the controlling force was usage. For cultivated language as for cultivated manners the pattern was given by the usage of courtly society. One should recall how, a century earlier, Caxton hesitated in his literary undertaking until his work was "ouersawe and corrected" by his royal patroness, the English Duchess of Burgundy. One should hold in mind also the already cited opinions of Sidney and of Ben Jonson regarding courtly speech as the source of good English. On this subject interesting information is to be found in the *Arte of Poesie* (1589). In this work the author, himself a man thoroughly bred in courtly customs, offers definite prescriptions to the courtly poets to whom his work is addressed. Their language, he says, shall not be that of "Piers Plowman, not Gower nor Lydgate nor yet Chaucer, for their language is now out of vse with vs." The writer evidently does not belong to the school of Spenser. The poet also shall not use the "termes of Northern-men, such as they vse in dayly talke, whether they be noble men or gentlemen, or of their best clarkes all is a matter." Nor shall he use the language spoken in the "marches and frontiers, or in port townes, wher straungers haunt for traffike sake," or in "any vplandish village or corner of a Realme, where is no resort but of poore rusticall or vnciuall people." Nor "shall he follow the speech of a craftes man or carter, or other of the inferiour sort . . . for such persons doe abuse good speaches by strange accents or ill shapen soundes, and false ortographie." The barbarism of foreigners is naturally to be avoided "as he that would say with vs in England, a dousand for a thousand, isterday for yesterday, as commonly the Dutch and French people do." (An interesting echo of older speech.) Nor shall he follow the use

in universities "where Schollers vse much peeuish affectation of words out of the primatiue languages." The stric-
ture on the language of the universities anticipates in a way
certain twentieth-century comments on Oxford speech. We
find finally the definite recommendation to the courtly
writers that "ye shall therefore take [as a pattern] the vsual
speach of the Court, and that of London and the shires
lying about London with lx. myles, and not much aboue."
In every shire of England, the writer goes on to say, "there
be gentlemen and others that speake but specially write as
good Southerne as we of Middlesex or Surrey do, but not
the common people of euery shire."

Here, then, in the usage of an aristocratic society centering in the English court, is to be found the form of English
prescribed for the use of the poets to whom this interesting
book is addressed. This form of language the well-bred
Elizabethan learned as he learned his manners. That it was
not without its affectation one may learn from Lyly.
Euphues while at the university, we are told, "gave himself
almost to nothing but practicing of those things commonly
which are incident to these sharp wits . . . fine phrases,
smooth quipping, merry taunting, using jesting without
mean, and abusing mirth without measure." [1] But that
training in more fundamental features was not entirely
neglected, one may learn from Lyly's prescriptions for the
training of children. "They are to be trained up in the
language of their country," he says, "to pronounce aptly and
distinctly without stammering every word and syllable of
their native speech, and to be kept from barbarous talk as
the ship from rocks; lest being affected with their barbarism, they be infected also with their unclean conversation." [2]

The problem, for which no final solution has yet been

[1] Ed. Croll, p. 10.
[2] Modernized spelling. *Euphues, Anatomy of Wit,* ed. Croll, p. 120.

offered, is how Shakespeare, the young provincial from Warwickshire, attained his command of the elegant form of
language the use of which was so closely associated with
courtly cultivation. The parentage and early surroundings
of Shakespeare make more conspicuous the miracle of his
achievement. Neither father nor mother, it appears, was
able to write; *burel* folk Chaucer would have called them.
Opportunity, however, for the attainment of the book-learn-
ing of the time was afforded by the excellent grammar
school of Stratford, an endowed school and one provided
with excellent masters. In this school Shakespeare acquired
a knowledge of the classical languages, "small Latin and
less Greek," Ben Jonson rated it, but doubtless more considerable in extent if rated by the standards of modern
times. The curriculum of the schools of the period included
not only a fairly wide range of reading of Latin writers,
but a drill in rhetoric of the inclusive kind taught in the
schools of the Renaissance period. The character of the
schoolmasters introduced in Shakespeare's plays and the
frequent allusions to schoolboy life do not indicate any enthusiasm on Shakespeare's part for the training afforded by
schools. There can be no doubt that he found "sermons
in stones, books in the running brooks." But that his writings contain only the "native woodnote wild," is certainly
open to question. The knowledge of classical authors and
of the art of rhetoric gained in school life unquestionably
contributed toward the mastery of expression in his writings.

School life, however, was interrupted at an early age,
probably at the age of about fourteen. Moreover an early
marriage at the age of eighteen and a rapidly expanding
family drew his energies into channels other than the mere
pursuit of learning. Unfortunately an almost impenetrable
obscurity surrounds the early manhood of Shakespeare.

About this formative period in his life little is known with certainty. In order to explain the secret of Shakespeare's mastery of the cultivated courtly speech theory has had to be brought into service. It has been conjectured that he served for a time as a lawyer's clerk, a theory which would explain his well-known familiarity with terms of law. Most recently (1926) attempt has been made to show that he lived for a time as page in the household of the erudite Sir Henry Goodere at Polesworth. It has also been suggested that his familiarity with courtly speech may have come from feminine associations. None of these theories has been established on certain evidence. More plausible is the theory based on fairly direct tradition that he served for a number of years as schoolmaster. Even if there were no confirmatory evidence, this supposition [3] provides an hypothesis that serves in explaining many features of Shakespeare's language, not only his facile use of the art and artifices of rhetoric, but his keen awareness of the Latin meanings of derivative words, his bilingual puns, and his sense of the absurdity in the malapropisms, or mishandlings of these "hard words," in the speech of the illiterate.

From the almost complete obscurity of these early years Shakespeare gradually emerges. About the year 1590 he came to London. There he was connected with a theatrical company in a double capacity as actor and playwright. His rise in the profession was rapid for by 1594 he had risen from the position of "hireling" to that of "full-sharer" in his company.

That Shakespeare from the first distinguished himself in the literary side of his profession appears not only from the spiteful words, already quoted, of the dying Greene, but from the evidence of Chettle, who in 1592 testifies that "diverse of worship have reported his [Shakespeare's] up-

[3] Sponsored by his recent biographer, J. Q. Adams.

rightness of dealing, which argues his honesty, and his facetious grace in writing, that approves his art.[4] Evidently Shakespeare, a member of the lowly esteemed actor's profession, had won from persons of rank ("diverse of worship") not only esteem for personal qualities but admiration for literary achievement. He had demonstrated that there was substantial ground for Greene's jealous remark about him being "as well able to bumbast out a blank verse as the best of you."

But not content with his achievement in the little regarded art of dramatic writing, the mercenary task of penning for actors lines not intended for print, Shakespeare comparatively early in his career boldly entered the literary preserves of the courtly poets. In 1593 there was issued from the press of Richard Field, a fellow townsman of Shakespeare settled in London, a thin quarto volume containing the *Venus and Adonis*. In this work, dedicated to the Earl of Southampton, a man from the provinces with no university associations and a member of a profession with no social standing, ventured into the most exclusive literary circles. Not only did he enter the lists in competition with the most cultivated wits of the time, but he early won from university men, and from the professional critic, recognition as the foremost living literary artist. Francis Meres, scholar and critic, writing in 1598, concludes a eulogy with the superlative assertion that "the Muses would speak with Shakespeare's fine filed phrase if they would speak English."[5]

Deep is the mystery that surrounds genius, and one cannot penetrate far into the obscurity that surrounds the forging by Shakespeare of his language instrument. Remarkable in itself was his ability to divest himself of his

---

[4] J. Q. Adams, *Life of Shakespeare,* pp. 141-2.
[5] F. Meres, *Palladis Tamia,* quoted from Adams, *op. cit.*

Warwickshire dialect. To adopt the words of Orlando addressed to Rosalind, his "accent was something finer than he could purchase in so removed a dwelling." Robert Burns, in a like situation, was not entirely successful. In Shakespeare's time cultivation of the mother tongue was not to be gained from grammars and schoolmasters; it must be gained, like manners, from social contact. "It is certain," says Falstaff, "that either wise bearing, or ignorant carriage, is caught, as men take diseases, one of another: therefore, let men take heed of their company." The influence of human pattern on Elizabethan speech may be learned from the remark of Lady Percy regarding the speech of Hotspur, her paragon husband:

> And speaking thick, which nature made his blemish,
> Became the accents of the valiant;
> For those that could speak low and tardily,
> Would turn their own perfection to abuse,
> To seem like him: So that in speech, in gait,
>
> .   .   .   .   .
>
> He was the mark and glass, copy and book
> That fashion'd others.

After what pattern was Shakespeare's language formed? The words of these Shakespearean characters doubtless reflect the experience of Shakespeare the writer. At tavern suppers such as the young gallants of the time were fond of providing for the players there was commerce in culture. The sharpened wit provided by the professional entertainers was paid for in coin of polished manners and polished speech. The very artificiality of the courtly modes of speech made them more easy of appropriation. More serious in purpose were gatherings like the famous ones at the Mermaid Tavern, said to have been inaugurated by Sir Walter Raleigh, where contact was established between the members of the acting profession and literary men of higher social rank.[6] That, in the case of Shakespeare, these convivial associations led to more intimate acquaintance, appears from the tone of his dedications and the sentiments expressed in his sonnets. In any event a familiar association with men of rank and fashion must have been a part of Shakespeare's schooling in language, a schooling in which he attained command of racy idiom "lacking the burden of lean and wasteful learning."

The profession followed by Shakespeare was itself a school for speech, also. The art of acting requires a cultivated pronunciation. It also affords training in the command of expression. The practice of translating foreign writings is held to be an excellent training because of the intimate relation established between the mind of the translator and that of the literary creator. The art of acting is that of translating in oral form the written words of another. The actor dons the language garb of the writer, and a fashion of language thus borrowed may later be appropriated to independent use. Small wonder that Greene, observing this form of appropriation on the part of the "puppet" actors, the "anticks garnisht in our colours," should warn his friends to provide no new patterns, not to "let those apes imitate your past excellence and never more acquaint them with your rare inventions." In this school of language Shakespeare soon surpassed his masters. Under his revision the often uninspired passages in versions by other playwrights were made to glow with the fire of genius.

But Shakespeare's language rises above mere imitation. Of him Dryden remarks that "he was naturally learn'd; he needed not the Spectacles of Books to read Nature; he look'd inwards, and found her there." With finer discernment, Ben Jonson says of him:

[6] Adams, *op. cit.*

> Yet must I not give Nature all; thy art,
> My gentle *Shakespeare*, must enjoy a part:
> For though the *Poet's* matter, Nature be,
> His Art does give the fashion.

The methods of art are apparent; the question again arises how they were learned. Adoption of the tradition that Shakespeare served as a schoolmaster would aid in explaining. Far be it from saying that Shakespeare shared the qualities which he held up to immortal ridicule in his character of Holofernes. Nevertheless, a few years spent in imparting to schoolboys an understanding of Latin grammar and an appreciation of the felicities of Latin writing would provide the master with principles of construction and patterns of expression for use in writing English. In all events the "small Latin" attributed to him by Ben Jonson formed an important part of his equipment for the use of the English language.

Of his acquaintance with Ovid there is abundant evidence. In the Bodleian Library there is preserved a copy of Ovid with Shakespeare's initials inscribed. Moreover the phraseology of Golding's translation of Ovid reappears in Shakespeare so frequently, says Sidney Lee,[7] "as almost to compel the conviction that Shakespeare knew much of Golding by heart." And have we not the significant remark, in punning vein, attributed by Shakespeare to one of his characters: "Ovidius Naso was the man: and why, indeed Naso, but for smelling out the odoriferous flowers of fancy, the jerks of invention?"[8] There is besides a scene in *Titus Andronicus* which, even if not written by Shakespeare himself, throws light on the formative influences on the literary art of his day. Lavinia is represented as seeking among the books of the young Roman boy Lucius the copy of Ovid's *Metamor-*

[7] *Quarterly Review*, April, 1909.
[8] *L. L. L.*, IV, ii.

phoses which had been given the boy by his mother. In picturing the Roman scene it seems probable that Shakespeare, here as elsewhere, has drawn from English experience, that to him an English boy, as to the Roman boy, Ovid was early familiar.

But Shakespeare's writings exhibit a knowledge not only of Latin writings, particularly those of Ovid, but of the formal art of rhetoric. On this subject the same scene from *Titus Andronicus* offers an interesting hint. Titus, addressing the boy, Livius, says:

> Ah, boy, Cornelia never with more care
> Read to her sons than she [Lavinia] hath read to thee
> Sweet poetry and Tully's Orator.

May we not interpret this also as evidence that the rhetoric of Cicero was familiar to the young Englishman?

Attempts have been made to show the influence of Wilson's *Rhetorique* on Shakespeare. The letter of Don Armado in *Love's Labour's Lost* is said to be modelled on one of Wilson's examples, and Sir Walter Raleigh recently pointed out that there is a similarity between the artful eloquence in some of Falstaff's speeches and some of those offered as models by Wilson.[9] Even more probable, however, as a source of Shakespeare's rhetoric is a direct knowledge of Cicero obtained either from the independent works of Cicero or from Cicero learned in the compendious work by Talæus already referred to, a work most used in grammar schools until superseded in the closing years of the century by the more abridged treatise by Charles Butler.[10] In any event there is little exaggeration in saying of Shakespeare what Nashe said of Harvey, that in his writings it would be possible to "shew you a whole Talaeus and Ad Herennium of figures."

[9] Wilson's *Arte of Rhetorique*, ed. Mair, p. xxxiii.
[10] *Rhetoricae, Libri Duo*, 1598.

In the earlier plays the influence of school methods is particularly apparent. The chop-logic methods of dialectics are turned to burlesque in the specious arguments of the witty pages with their use of equivocation. In the same way the lighter figures of rhetoric, especially the various forms of plays on words, the paronomasia, the prosonomasia, the atanaclasis, and the traductio or the tranlacer, which must have afforded glee to the English schoolboy, reappear in the quips and quirks and quibbles of the lively witted pages in the early plays. "Sweet smoke of rhetoric" they are called by the admiring Armado.

But rhetoric is turned to other uses. Not only are its colors applied in semi-serious fashion to form the eloquence of Falstaff, but in high seriousness they are applied in the embellishment of some of the noblest passages in Shakespeare. A close examination, for instance, of the oration delivered by Brutus over the body of Cæsar will reveal in striking fashion the dependence of English formal eloquence on the cultivated methods of rhetorical art.

The wisdom of the rhetorician, Shakespeare appropriates. The different levels of speech which writers on rhetoric from Cicero and the *Ad Herennium* to Sir Thomas Wilson had distinguished under three heads, are recognized by Shakespeare. His dramatic power in adapting speech to character is familiar enough. A low style varied in form, he uses with conspicuous success. A middle style he uses with ease, and in the grand style at times, as in the dialogue between King Henry IV and the repentant Prince, he soars on wings of eloquence. In some instances, as in some of the speeches of the Duke in *Measure for Measure,* the elevation of the grand style is reached by the use of stilted language. But in such instances the very obviousness of the attempt makes the more apparent the deliberateness of the effort to adapt the level of style to rank or to occasion.

It would be an exercise of interest and profit to select the artifices used by Shakespeare and label them with the names applied in sixteenth-century rhetorical treatises. To assume, however, that Shakespeare's language is solely a product of rhetorical art would be to exhibit not only insensibility, but ignorance. Like Chaucer two centuries earlier, he knew rhetoric and turned it to use, but was able to rise above it. In *Love's Labour's Lost* he turns its methods to ridicule, exhibiting excesses in learned artifice not only by the pedantries of Holofernes and Nathaniel who, in the language of Moth "have been at a great feast of language and stol'n the scraps," but in the braverie of the "braggart," Armado, and the cheaper rhetorical tricks, or "rope tricks," of the fool. To this satirical exhibition of forms of learned folly, he adds a judgment of the futility of learning in general, expressed in the well-known words of Biron:

> Small have continual plodders ever won
> Save base authority from others' books.
> These earthly godfathers of heaven's lights
> That give a name to every fixed star,
> Have no more profit of their shining nights
> Than those that walk, and wot not what they are.

The words assigned to Biron express the feeling of Shakespeare himself. Early in life he became aware of the limitations of learning. That nature, in his estimation, stood above art appears from ever-recurring observations such as: "Natural graces that extinguish art" and "Nature's above art in that respect."

The felicities of his language do not consist of "dainties that are bred in a book." He had not, like the pedants Holofernes and Nathaniel, "eat paper" and "drunk ink." From life rather than from learning he derived his inspiration. "For where is any author in the world," exclaims Biron, the lover, "teaches such learning as a woman's eyes?"

From woman's eyes this doctrine I derive.
They sparkle still the right Promethean fire;
They are the books, the arts, the academes.

"Lend me the flourish of all gentle tongues," says Biron
in another place in his praise of Rosaline, and then in complete reaction:

Fie, painted rhetoric! O, she needs it not:

Still later, in the final scene of the play, restored to sound
sense by the chastening wit of the ladies, Biron finally ab-
jures artifice of speech:

O! never will I trust to speeches penn'd,
Nor to the motion of a schoolboy's tongue;

· · · · ·

Taffeta phrases, silken terms precise,
Three-pil'd hyperboles, spruce affectation,
Figures pedantical; these summer flies
Have blown me full of maggot ostentation;
I do forswear them: and I here protest:

· · · · ·

Henceforth my wooing mind shall be express'd
In russet yeas, and honest kersey noes.

The contrast between the language of art and the language
of nature, so effectively presented in the language of Biron,
is turned to dramatic use by Shakespeare in his *Romeo and
Juliet*. The painted rhetoric of the first scene, in the love
paradoxes of the sentimental Romeo sinking "under love's
heavy burden," is succeeded in later scenes by the native
eloquence of Romeo's speech when fired by the consuming
passion for Juliet.

Obviously Shakespeare's relation to rhetoric was that of
master rather than of servant. The towering height which
gave him vision of the relative importance of rhetorical art

and natural eloquence enabled him also to perceive other forms of vanity in the language of his time. The cruder forms of popular verse he despises. His contempt for the scald rhymers of ballads is many times expressed, nowhere perhaps more eloquently than in the words of Hotspur:

> I had rather be a kitten and cry mew,
> Than one of these same metre ballad-mongers:
> I had rather hear a brazen canstick turn'd
> Or a dry wheel grate on an axle-tree;
> And that would set my teeth nothing on edge,
> Nothing so much as mincing poetry;
> 'Tis like the forc'd gait of a snuffling nag.

The ranting manner of speech of the popular stage he exhibits for ridicule in the famous scene where Falstaff speaks "in passion in king Cambyses' vein."

In writing *Hamlet* he had arrived at a stage of confidence and of well-defined opinions. Regarding forms of expression he is extremely critical. *Beautified,* a word which he had earlier used in the *Venus and Adonis,* is now in the opinion of Polonius "an ill phrase, a vile phrase." Instead of it he uses *beautied,* in the phrase, "beautied with plast'ring art." [11] The super-refined language with its "golden words" of the courtier, Osric, Hamlet affects not to understand until, to use the words of Horatio, he is "edified by the margent," that is to say, instructed by sidenotes. But if the "flourish" of Osric's courtly speech stirs Hamlet to ridicule, the high-astounding Marlovian manner of Laertes moves him to rage. In extravagance of grief Laertes, leaping into the grave of Ophelia, exclaims:

> Now pile your dust upon the quick and dead;
> Till of this flat a mountain you have made,
> To o'ertop old Pelion, or the skyish head
> Of blue Olympus.

[11] *Hamlet,* III, i.

Hamlet, who has leaped into the grave with Laertes, in exasperation breaks out in speech that out-Herods Herod. Taking his cue from Laertes, he exclaims:

> And if thou prate of mountains, let them throw
> Millions of acres on us; till our ground,
> Singeing his pate against the burning zone,
> Make Ossa like a wart! Nay, an thou'ld mouth,
> I'll rant as well as thou.

In modest appraisal of the art of rhetoric, which he is expounding, Sir Thomas Wilson declares: "I can not denie but that a right wise man vnlearned, shall doe more good by his Naturall witte, then twentie of these common wittes that want Nature to helpe Arte." Adapted to the vinous character of Falstaff, this thought finds parodied expression in the dictum: "Learning is a mere hoard of gold kept by a devil; till sack commences it, and sets it in act and use." Making allowance for the dramatic adaptation of expression to character, one may recognize in these words the judgment of Shakespeare himself. Learning must be set to use by nature. "The wordes mote be cosin to the dede" is Chaucer's manner of expressing a universal principle governing language, a principle which he professes to derive from Plato. This classical principle sounds anew in Hamlet's direction to the players to "suit the action to the word, the word to the action." A finality of critical judgment finds expression in the words, applicable to language as well as to acting, in which Hamlet admonishes the players that they "o'er-step not the modesty ['moderation'] of nature."

CHAPTER X

THE language of Shakespeare reflects the tendencies current in his time. Most of the rhetorical artifices he introduces at one place or another, in uses sometimes serious, sometimes satirical. From particular books such as Golding's translation of Ovid and Florio's translation of Montaigne he adopts not only matter but manner of expression. Placing, however, nature before art, as he does, he finds a principal source for his language in the manner of speech current in his day. In its fundamental features, in its spelling and its grammar and its use of words, the language of Shakespeare is that of the Elizabethan age in which he lived.

The difference of Elizabethan English from that of to-day is greater than is sometimes supposed. Not yet regulated by grammars and dictionaries, it was naturally subject to variation and change. The rapidity of change that had been going on in the late Middle English period, from the time of Chaucer to that of Caxton, had become somewhat reduced in the sixteenth century. There was somewhat less ground than in the days of Caxton for complaint that English men "ben borne vnder the domynacyon ['control'] of the mone ['moon'] whiche is neuer stedfaste but euer wauerynge." In fact the language of Henry Howard, Earl of Surrey (1516ca.-1547), in appearance is not unlike that of the Elizabethan poets a generation later. That change, however, was not at an end appears from differences in language in successive editions of the romance of *Huon of Bordeaux* translated by Lord Berners. The original edition appeared about 1540. In a third edition, "corrected and amended," published in 1601, appear changes comparable to those which Caxton, a century earlier, had found it necessary to make in his new edition of the *Polychronicon* translated by Chaucer's contemporary, Trevisa. Older grammatical forms are replaced: *eyen* by *eyes,* *yere* by *yeares,* *ye* by *you,* *tho* by *those,* *moo* by *more,* the endings -*yd,* -*yde* in the preterit and past participle by -*ed.* The expression *these thynges hath* becomes *these thynges haue;* *I se them aproche that desyryth my deth* becomes *I se them aproche that desire my death.* Double negatives are simplified: *none other shall haue no profyght* becomes *none other shall haue any honour;* *nor neuer none of hys lynage* becomes *nor euer any of his lynage.* In the use of words a similar revision was made: *to her warde* becomes *toward her;* *to the host ward* becomes *towardes the Hooste;* *ween, went* become *think, thought;* *chere* becomes *countenance;* *clypped* becomes *embraced;* *fordo* becomes *vndoe;* *leuer* becomes *rather;* *scot* becomes *shotte;* *wanhope* becomes *false hope.* French words and word forms are replaced: *bayngned* by *bathed,* *bountye* by *goodness,* *condute* by *conduct,* *defend* by *forbid,* *mastres* by *mistress,* *dolour* by *ill hap.*[1]

In the Elizabethan age not only was change still in progress, but there persisted the dialectal variation of earlier periods. Caxton's merchant named Sheffield, who in the fifteenth century had trouble in expressing to the countrywoman his desire for eggs, in the sixteenth century would have met with like difficulty. The older regional dialects maintained their existence among people not influenced by courtly usage. They found a place in literary use. The

[1] The examples cited are quoted from the list by the modern editor, S. L. Lee.

Southern dialect provided a form of speech for the clown scenes in the drama, and Northern dialect aided in the creation of the pastoral atmosphere in Spenser's *Shepheardes Calender*. Even in the polite use of courtly life differences of regional dialect persisted. The rivalry between the Northern pronoun form *them* and the Southern form *'em,* and between the Northern verbal ending *-es* in the third singular and the Midland and Southern *-eth,* persisted through the century and later. In pronunciation there was variation comparatively wide. Spellings such as *tafeta, taveta, tafta* ('taffeta') in the diary of King Edward VI reflect an uncertainty in pronunciation, and the variant spellings *wight* and *whit* ('white'), exhibit the struggle for supremacy, to this day not finally settled, between Northern and Southern modes of pronouncing words beginning with *wh.* The prevalence of the spelling *wich* ('which'), however, indicates a preference for the Southern mode in the speech of the young king. The evidence regarding Sir Walter Raleigh is even more striking. From a contemporary authority we learn that Raleigh, "notwithstanding his so great mastership in style, and his conversation with the learnedst and politest persons, yet spoke broad Devonshire to his dyeing [*sic*] day." [2]

Compared with the language of earlier periods, the language of the Elizabethan period, at least the cultivated form of speech, had gained in uniformity. But there were still no definite rules for guidance. There was only a local class dialect to which conformity was necessary. The looseness of the rules governing this dialect may be learned from the directions, already quoted, concerning the form of language to be used, offered to young poets in the Puttenham *Arte of Poesie.*

This form of speech, little regulated except by custom,

[2] H. C. Wyld, *A History of Modern Colloquial English,* p. 109.

was the language available for Shakespeare's use. It was still many stages removed from the language of today. To adopt the Elizabethan mode of speech in modern colloquial use would create as great consternation as would be created by the adoption of Elizabethan garb for modern street wear. Indeed the sad consequences of such an experiment provide the material for a story, supposedly true, recently widely circulated in English newspapers. A young Syrian in his native land had acquired a fluent command of English through the study of England's greatest literary artist. Equipped with a command of Shakespearean English, he came to London. The misunderstandings arising from the use of sixteenth-century English in twentieth-century England brought the young man from misadventure to misadventure culminating in confinement in a madhouse. This tragic story perhaps leaves an exaggerated impression of perils associated with the use of Shakespearean English. But it serves to make more vivid an appreciation of the difference that exists between the English of our day and that of three centuries ago.

Let us now examine more in detail the nature of this difference. First of all let us consider the use of words in the Elizabethan period. Probably the greatest single achievement of the English language in the sixteenth century was the assimilation of the flood of words that came in following the Renaissance. This assimilation was not accomplished without difficulty, without occasional throes of verbal indigestion. The adoption of foreign words, as has been pointed out, met with opposition from purists such as Cheke and Ascham and Wilson. The epithet 'inkhorn terms' so frequently applied to them, expresses the feeling of hostility. In their use there was frequent display of pedantry. Marston's use of the learned terms is turned to burlesque by Ben Jonson as follows: "Now, sir, whereas the ingenuity of the time, and the soul's synderisis are but embrious in nature, added to the paunch of the Esquiline, and the intervallum of the zodiac," etc., etc. Such a manner of expression plainly merits the names "fustian" language and "gallimaufrey of words" bestowed by Jonson. In the Puttenham *Arte of Poesie* the author says that "Young schollers . . . from the Universitie or schooles . . . will seeme to coyne fine words out of the Latin . . . thereby to shew themselves among the ignorant the better learned." For this vice of style he provides the Greek label, *cacozelia*, with its English equivalent, 'fonde ['foolish'] affectation.'

At the same time the value of the words borrowed from the classical languages cannot be denied. Their usefulness and at the same time the wealth in power of expression contributed by them is shown by Puttenham's defense of his own use of these "vsurped words." *Scientificke*, for example, referring to knowledge (Lat. *scientia*, 'knowledge') he defends as necessary to balance with the word *mechanicall* referring to physical action. Other such words from Greek, Latin, or French, regarded by him as essential are: *maior-domo, politien, conduict, idiome, significatiue, methode, methodicall, placation, function, assubtiling, refining, compendious, prolixe, figuratiue, inueigle, impression* ("borrowed of our common Lawyers"), *numerous, numerositee, metricall, harmonicall, penetrate, penetrable, indignitie, declination, delineation, dimention* (the last three "scholastical termes"), *audacious, facunditie, egregious, implete, attemptat, compatible.*

The name "hard words" applied to these products of classical learning affords an impression of the difficulties created by them particularly among people unacquainted with Latin. Characteristic of the freedom in Elizabethan speech is the way in which these hard words were modified in the process of assimilation. Like the changes in form undergone by Latin words in the Vulgar Latin from which sprang the modern Romance languages are some of the English transformations. In Shakespeare's language appear such forms as *ignomy*, 'ignominy'; *allycholly*, 'melancholy'; *parlous*, 'perilous'; *charact*, 'character'; *phisnomy*, 'physiognomy'; *inter'gatory*, 'interrogatory'; and numerous aphetic forms such as *greed*, 'agreed'; *cerns*, 'concerns'; *'casion*, 'occasion'; *fray*, 'affray'; *spite*, 'despite'; *pointed*, 'appointed'; *scapes*, 'escapes.' In the letters of Queen Elizabeth appear not infrequently similar modifications of the original forms such as *attemps*, 'attempts'; *decerue*, 'deserve'; *acceptable*, 'acceptable'; *perswations*, 'persuasions.' These transformations in some instances betray confusion in the royal mind, as in the case of *except*, 'accept,' and *victorar*, 'victor,' found in her autograph letters.

If such transformations occur in the cultivated speech, in the uncultivated dialects and among the illiterate distortion runs riot in forms which at times reach the grotesque. Christopher Sly, in *The Taming of the Shrew*, converts the, to him, unfamiliar *comedy* into *commonty*. In a pre-Shakespearean form of this play the same word appears as *commodity*. The Vice in the play of *Sir Thomas More* converts *extemporaneously* into *extemprically*. The Clown in *Antony and Cleopatra* turns *infallible* into *falliable*. In fact the difficulties experienced by the uncultivated in the use of the 'hard words' is an inexhaustible source of humor in the plays of Shakespeare, reaching a climax perhaps in the immortal expressions of Dame Quickly with her "alligant termes," her *canaries* for *quandaries*, her *honeysuckle* for *homicidal*, and *honeyseed* for *homicide*.

For all this confusion the knowledge of Latin provided by the grammar schools afforded a partial remedy. The word *orthography* makes its appearance in English about 1450, and guidance in orthography was afforded by classical patterns. The word *orthography* Shakespeare evidently associates with affectation and pedantry. Benedick, speaking of Claudio in love says, "he was wont to speake plaine, and to the purpose (like an honest man and a souldier) and now is he turned orthography, his words are a very fantasticall banquet, iust so many strange dishes."[3] The pedantry of the schoolmaster in this matter Shakespeare exposes to ridicule in the classic passage where Holofernes passes judgment on the language of Armado:

"I abhor such fanatical fantasms, such insociable and point-devise companions; such rackers of orthography, as to speak, dout, fine, when he should say doubt; det, when he should pronounce debt;—d, e, b, t; not d, e, t:—he clepeth a calf, cauf; half, hauf; neighbour, *vocatur*, nebour; neigh abbreviated, ne. This is abhhominable (which he would call abominable)."

The guiding principle of Holofernes, the pedant, is obviously English spelling after Latin pattern, and pronunciation governed by spelling. The written language is made by the pedant to govern the spoken. The last word cited is particularly instructive, illustrating how the pedant in his zeal for correctness is led into error through his false etymology of the word *abominable* as if derived from the Latin *ab*+*homine*.

The words *debt* and *doubt,* cited by Holofernes, are good examples of a large class of words, already mentioned in an earlier chapter, which under the influence of Latin learning were restored, in part at least, to their Latin spelling. Words long in use and modified in form through popular use either in English or in French were refinished and, like pieces of furniture, made into genuine antiques. Earlier forms, some of them already cited, such as Chaucer's *avantage, aventure, avys,* are restored in the forms

[3] *Much Ado,* II, iii.

advantage, adventure, advice. Earlier *vertu* and *ferme* and *enquire* become *virtue* and *firm* and *inquire.* *Receit* becomes *receipt; perfit* and *verdit* become *perfect* and *verdict.* Earlier *faute* and *cawdron* and *sowdyer* and *savacion* become *fault* and *cauldron* and *soldier* and *salvation.* Earlier *foren,* or *foreyne,* and *soverayn,* in this case through mistaken etymology, become *foreign* and *sovereign. Descryve* and *inscrive* become *describe* and *inscribe. Monark* becomes *monarch, stomack* becomes *stomach, egal* becomes *equal, saint* becomes *sainct.* Among respelled words of this kind in Wilson's *Rhetorique* appear such forms as *deceipt, counterfect,* and *poinct.*

In the letters of Queen Elizabeth, which survive in autograph form, appear many spellings of this kind such as: *parfaict, traictment, accompt,* and *seubdain,* 'sudden.' The effort to conform to classical pattern was of course not confined to English. The French language was exposed to the same tendencies in the time of the Renaissance, and many of the spellings of Queen Elizabeth betray a classical influence coming indirectly through the French. Thus are to be explained her spelling of *parfaict* and *seubdain,* already cited, and such other forms as *reciproke,* 'reciprocal,' and *desaing,* 'design.'

Not infrequently, as in the case of the spelling *abhominable* favored by Holofernes, the effort to make words conform to Latin spelling led to error. *Fang* is thus mistakenly converted to *phang, curfew* to *curphew, crystal* to *chrystal, triumvirate* to *triumpherate, sentinel* to *centinel.* Most of these spellings, products of false learning, have later been rectified. But *centinel* persisted down to the nineteenth century, and such spellings as *scythe* (earlier *sithe*), *rhyme* (earlier *rime*) and *island* (earlier *iland*) persist to our day.

In the use of words and the meanings to which they were

applied in the time of Shakespeare are to be recognized tendencies like those affecting the forms of words. There is a freedom in the use and the misuse of words, controlled, however, in part by the classical learning of the time. Bardolph, conversing with Justice Shallow, remarks: "Sir, pardon; a soldier is better accommodated than with a wife," using *accommodated* in the sense 'furnish' or 'equip,' a meaning earliest cited from 1597. Upon this Justice Shallow comments: "It is well said, in faith, sir; and it is well said in deed too. Better accommodated—it is good; yea, indeed it is: good phrases are surely, and ever were, very commendable. Accommodated! it comes of *accommodo;* very good; a good phrase." Pedantry thus airs its learning, in doing so making use of the word *phrase,* a classical derivative not yet assimilated in the language of the soldier Bardolph, who rejoins: "Pardon me, sir, I have heard the word. Phrase call you it? By this day, I know not the phrase; but I will maintain the word with my sword to be a soldier-like word."

This scrap of dialogue affords interesting suggestion regarding the conditions under which the classical words were adapted to English use. There appears the application, in the speech of the unlearned, of borrowed words to new meanings, and there appears the application of learning in testing their use. To people of modern times familiar with these words adapted in form and in meaning to English use, it is not easy to appreciate the feeling toward these words when they were new to English. For people who were unable to read and who, therefore, learned these words not from the printed page but through the ear, there were provided many pitfalls. Small wonder that in illiterate use they were misapplied in most amusing fashion and were transformed into the strange and the grotesque. For the sophisticated, as has already been pointed out, the awkward efforts at their use, especially on the part of the uneducated making pretension to knowledge, provided constant subject for jest. From this source Shakespeare derives entertainment in most of his plays, in all but eight it has recently been pointed out. The Nurse in *Romeo and Juliet* with her *confidence* for *conference,* and Dame Quickly with her "alligant termes," her *speciously* for *especially,* her *conceal* for *reveal,* her *infection* for *affection,* are worthy forerunners of the eighteenth-century Mrs. Malaprop. Costard, the clown, provides *contempts* for *contents* and an unintentional paradox in his remark that "Affliction may one day smile again." Shakespeare's opinion of agents of the law, at least of some of them, he conveys in the forms of speech assigned to the constables, in Dull's use of *reprehend* for *apprehend* and in Dogberry's eloquent flow of words twisted in meaning, his *salvation* for *damnation, aspicious* for *suspicious, vigitant* for *vigilant, desartless* for *deserving,* reaching pure paradox in; *most senseless and fit men, most tolerable and not to be endured.* "Do you hear how he misplaces?" exclaims Escalus after listening to Elbow's talk about *profanation* for *reverence,* and about *notorious benefactors.* Further illustration would be superfluous. "Comparisons are odorous," says Dogberry, and odious if not odorous might become too rich an assemblage of these products of vanity in the feeble mind, removed as they are from the life of the context.

Controlling to some extent the use of these words, and the meanings to which they were applied, was the classical learning diffused by the grammar-school training of the time. Distortions in meaning, like distortions in form, were thus held in check. A knowledge of Latin, like that paraded by Justice Shallow, served to hold newly introduced words to their Latin meanings and even to restore earlier borrowed words to their original meanings. Many of these words in later periods, in their complete assimilation into English have been turned to new uses. In consequence the Elizabethan manner of expression has for the modern reader a quality of strangeness, of formal dignity, which finds explanation only through a realization of the control still exerted in this period by the original meanings over the words derived from classical sources.

In the language of Shakespeare illustrative examples are everywhere at hand. One finds *deliberate* with its original meaning 'weighed,' *inquisition* meaning 'questioning,' and countless other instances such as invest, 'clothe,' 'cover'; *pernicious*, 'destructive,' *rage; vexed*, 'shaken' or 'agitated'; *plant*, 'sole of the foot'; *character*, 'imprint'; *anatomized*, 'laid open minutely' or 'analyzed'; *carnation*, 'flesh color'; *prouokes*, 'calls for'; *aspersion*, 'sprinkling'; *desperate*, 'without hope'; *dissolve*, 'loosen'; *improuident iealousie*, 'unforeseeing' or 'blind'; *regiment*, 'rule'; *pedant*, 'schoolmaster'; *impudent*, 'shameless'; etc., etc. To fail to recognize these earlier meanings is of course to fail to appreciate the shades of meaning conveyed by an Elizabethan writer.

The use of words with the original Latin meaning appears especially in the speech of persons of dignity to whom the 'grand' style of the rhetorician is appropriate. For example, take five lines from a speech by Prospero:

> The direful spectacle of the wreck, which touch'd
> The very virtue of compassion in thee,
> I have with such provision in mine art
> So safely ordered, that there is no soul—
> No, not so much perdition as an hair [4]

In these five lines an original Latin meaning changed in later English, appears in *virtue*, 'strength'; *compassion*, 'sympathy'; *provision*, 'foresight'; and *perdition*, 'loss.'

[4] *Tempest,* I. ii.

The awareness, on the part of Elizabethan writers, of the original Latin meaning provides the possibility for bilingual puns. In Shakespeare one meets with puerile exhibitions of this form of artifice as in the one already cited where *Naso* in the name of Ovidius Naso is associated with the nasal function of smelling. One meets with other exhibitions which for the modern reader need to be "explained by the margent." For instance, Touchstone says: "I am here with thee and thy goats, as the most capricious poet, honest Ovid was, among the Goths." The play on the words *goat* and *Goth* is apparent, but the relation between *goat* and *capricious* is lost to one who is not aware of the connection between the adjective *capricious* and the Latin word *caper,* 'goat.'

That the preservation not only of the original form but of the original meanings in the borrowed words was consciously striven for is apparent. There were books provided as aids to this end, the earliest of purely English dictionaries. An interesting work of this kind is the book the third edition of which was published in 1613, with the significant title: *A Table Alphabeticall, containing and teaching the true writing and vnderstanding of hard vsual English words.* The nature of the "true understanding" recorded for these "hard words" may be illustrated by means of a few words listed under the letter A:

> *abject,* base, cast away in disdaine
> *absonant,* vntuneable, absurd
> *accommodate,* to make fit to, or conuenient to the purpose
> *accumulate,* to heape together
> *accurate,* curious, cunning, diligent
> *acertaine,* make sure, certiffe
> *admire,* maruell at, or be in love with
> *aduertise,* give knowledge, aduice, counsell
> *anatomie,* cutting vp of the body.

In English use, however, these borrowed words were early brought into new associations which affected their use. In the language of Shakespeare one finds already signs of the influences which, in the course of a few generations, turned many of the borrowed words to new meanings or limited them to specialized uses. The causes producing specialization appear in the case of the word *occupy*. This word, in the opinion of Doll Tearsheet, was "an excellent word before it was ill sorted." The associations, however, of this word in Shakespeare's time were so disreputable, it was so "ill sorted," that it was held from respectable use for two centuries. Somewhat similar was the history of other words such as *luxurious* and *companion*.

But changes in the meanings of these words were not entirely dependent on chance associations. Already in the classical languages, by means of tropes, or 'translations' of various kinds, words had been turned to varied uses. Let us take a single instance. The Latin *intendere* applied originally to the physical meaning 'stretch out,' or 'extend,' a meaning surviving in the English derivative, *tension*. From connection with the use of the spear or the bow the word became specialized so as to mean the stretching of the arm or of the bowstring in aiming. It was next transferred in meaning from physical aim to mental aim, or purpose. In the rhetorics of the Renaissance in France and in England such shifts in meaning were classified and labelled with such names as: *translation* or *metaphor, intellection* or *synecdoche, abusion* or *catachresis, transmutation* or *metonymy*. The shifts in meaning, thus provided with learned names, were consciously resorted to by writers seeking new effects. But they appear even more frequently in the simple processes everywhere to be observed in natural, popular speech. The words borrowed from the classical languages, in English use were brought anew to life and were subjected to the many tendencies toward change on all sides to be found in living speech.

To return to the word already discussed, *intend* in English use has been applied to many meanings, twenty of which are listed in the Oxford Dictionary, as varied as: to direct one's eye or mind, to direct one's course, to start on a journey, to give auditory attention, to pretend. The centrifugal force producing variety in the meanings of a single word is evidently strong. Controlling this tendency to some extent, however, is an opposing, centripetal force, particularly strong in the Elizabethan period, pulling the word back to its meaning in the classical language from which it sprang. In this way is to be explained the Elizabethan use of *intend* with the earlier Latin meaning, 'to stretch out,' or 'extend,' of which the earliest citation is from the year 1601.

It is evident that the classical training of Elizabethan grammar schools had a share in the cultivation of the Elizabethan literary language. Not only did the schemes and colors of rhetoric provide means for exornation, but the classical word hoard yielded rich treasure and, after the pattern of the original Latin and Greek, English borrowed words were refashioned in form and restored in meaning. Even Shakespeare with all the emphasis laid by him on nature as the source of art is clearly influenced by classical example.

But granting this pervading classical influence, one can not fail to recognize the admirable freedom which distinguishes Elizabethan English. This freedom is defended by the Elizabethan grammarian. Richard Mulcaster, a pioneer in the undertaking to determine the "right writing" of the English tongue, writing in 1582, professes to plant his rules upon "ordinarie custom." In support of his method he cites the authority of Quintilian, who said that it was one thing to speak like a grammarian and another to speak like a Latinist. In accordance with this doctrine Mulcaster, in his efforts at "fining" the English language, aims to teach not a grammarian's English but the English of Englishmen. The "prerogatiue and libertie, which the peple hath to vse both speche and pen at will," he says, "is the cause, and yet not blamed therefor, why the English writers be now finer, then theie were som hondreth yeares ago." This "prerogatiue," or freedom in natural usage, is apparent in most Elizabethan writers. It appears in the liberty taken in the use of one part of speech for another and in the interchange of transitive and intransitive forms of verbs. The language of Shakespeare everywhere provides illustrative examples:

Borrowing only *lingers* and *lingers* it out	(2 *Henry IV*, I, ii)
repeat and *history* his loss	(*Ibid.*, IV, i)
To *ripe* his growing fortunes	(*Ibid.*)
and *violenteth* in a sense as strong	(*T. and C.*, IV, iv)
Andromache *shrills* her dolours forth	(*Ibid.*, V, iii)
i' the ooze is *bedded*	(*Tempest*, III, iii)
there lie mudded	(*Ibid.*)
I hold you as a thing *enskied*	(*M. for M.*, I, iv)
the business he hath *helmed*	(*Ibid.*, III, ii)
Lord Angelo *dukes* it well	(*Ibid.*)
Let him be but *testimonied*	(*Ibid.*)
A *forted* residence	(*Ibid.*, V, i)
That *brain'd* my purpose	(*Ibid.*)
Spaniell'd me at heels	(*A. and C.*, IV, xii)
beautied with plast'ring art	(*Hamlet*, III, i)
whilst you do *climate* ['dwell'] here	(*Winter's Tale*, V, i)

The native capacity of Elizabethan English to provide varied needs of expression is further illustrated by the number of native words and phrases which are the equivalents of words provided by borrowing. In Shakespeare one finds the meaning 'perplexed' expressed by the native word combination, *knit up*. It will be noted that the English words are nearly the exact equivalent of the word derived in Latin from *per+plectere,* to 'weave' or 'plait.' The modern *balled up* naturally comes to mind. One meets also with the phrase *reputation gnawn at,* in which *gnawn at* bears a relation to the borrowed word *corroded,* like that of *knit up* to *perplexed.* This phenomenon, frequent in the language of Shakespeare, may be illustrated by citations such as:

be *in eye of* ['inoculated in'] every Exercise
(*Two Gent. of Verona,* I, iii)
reckoning ['estimation'], (*R. and J.,* I, ii)
ghostly ['spiritual'] father (*Ibid.,* II, iii)
breather ['living or animate being'] (*A. and C.,* III, iii)
feeders ['parasites'] (*Ibid.,* III, xiii)
fellowly ['companionable'] (*Tempest,* V, i)
our dull *workings* ['operations'] (*2 Henry IV,* IV, ii)
with scorn *shov'd* ['expelled'] from the court (*Ibid.*)
such *limbs* ['members'] of noble counsel (*Ibid.,* V, ii)
you have *put* him *down* ['depressed him'] (*Much Ado,* II, i)
fatherly and *kindly* ['natural'] power (*Ibid.,* IV, i)
testimonied in his own *bringings forth* ['productions']
(*M. for M.,* III, ii)
it is not the *wear* ['fashion'] (*Ibid.*)

One would be glad to know whether these English uses of words originate in the translation of foreign words or if they are independent in origin. In any event they give to a meaning a direct force not given by the words of foreign derivation. The effect produced is like that of the renewed metaphors to be heard in modern times in the speech of the frontier where, free from the blighting influence of learning, forms of language are created afresh.

The freedom in Elizabethan speech appears further in the way words were joined together. Juggled in various

combinations simple words were made to express varied
meanings. A form of language magic appears in the variety of ideas the word *come* is made to evoke. Joined to
about in the combination *come about,* it meant (1) to veer
around, (2) to turn out to be true. In *come behind* there
was associated the idea of hostile intent. In *come by* the
meaning was to get possession of. In *come forth* the meaning was to become publicly known. In *come in* the meaning
was to get within an opponent's guard. To *come off* was to
escape; to *come over* was to surpass; to *come up* was to
come into fashion; to *come upon* was to approach.

Somewhat similar to the freedom in phrasal combinations
with varied meanings was the freedom in forming compound words. The word *deep* will serve to illustrate. This
word forms an element in combinations, most of them
strange to modern English, such as *deep-contemplative,*
deep-divorcing, deep-drawing, deep-drenched, deep-green,
deep-premeditated, deep-revolving, deep-searched, deep-sore,
deep-sweet, deep-wounded, deep-fet, deep-sworn, deep-
brain'd.

Facility in the expression of varied meaning was promoted not only by this freedom in combining words, but
by a freedom in shifting words to new meanings. Shifts
or 'translations' in meaning, as has been pointed out, were
recognized and labelled by classical rhetoricians. In Elizabethan language they are a conspicuous feature. The
word *ecstasy* is used meaning (1) frenzy, (the etymological
meaning); (2) swoon; (3) rapture, delight (the present
meaning). The simple word *close* has meanings bewildering
in variety. As adjective, or adverb, it appears in: *keeping*
close, 'enclosed,' 'confined'; *close intent,* 'secret'; *close vil-*
lain, 'secretive.' The verb *close* has even greater variety
of meanings; *chest to close so pure a mind* ('enclose'); *Do*
thou but close our hands ('join'); *many lines close in the*

dial's centre ('meet,' 'are united') ; *If I can close with him* ('grapple') ; *He closes with you in this consequence* ('comes to terms').

The formation of word compounds and the shifting of word meanings appear of course in all periods in the history of English as of other languages. The peculiarity of the Elizabethan period was that, whereas today the forms of words and the various meanings attached are fixed and recorded in dictionaries and little freedom is left for departure from a standard thus fixed, in the Elizabethan period shifts of meaning were little controlled and word compounds were still in the making. The difference between the two periods is that between a rigid medium of expression and a plastic one easily molded.

The native resources of Elizabethan English appear also in the modes adopted for giving intensive force. The fading quality of words of this kind is a familiar feature of language. Words of intensive force in one generation, in a succeeding generation sink to the level of plain expression. Hence it is that the speech of each period is distinguished by its peculiar intensive words. In the Elizabethan age some of the intensive words most familiar in later periods had not yet come into use. The words *awfully, bloody, jolly, mighty, precious, prodigiously, tremendously* and *vastly,* for instance, are conspicuously absent.[5] The active freedom in the language of the period, however, appears in the variety of words brought into service in the expression of lively feeling.

The word *all,* as an intensive now little familiar except in phrases such as "all too soon," appears in Shakespeare in such uses as "all as mad as he," "all aloud the wind doth blow," "all-disgraced friend," "all-praised knight," "all-licensed fool."

[5] W. Franz, *Shakespeare-Grammatik,* 2d ed., secs. 370-396.

Clean, now colloquial in quality, appears not infrequently in Shakespearean use in expressions such as "clean starved," "clean past your youth."

Clear, now associated with the speech of childhood, as in the phrase "gone clear away," in its adverbial form, *clearly,* is used by Shakespeare in expressions such as "wound our tottering colours clearly up," "from my remembrance clearly banish'd his."

Cruelly is turned to intensive use in the expression, "I love thee cruelly."

The variety in the Elizabethan manner of intensive expression further appears in Shakespeare's language in expressions such as "grieve thee *dearer* than my death"; "*exceeding* well read"; "*excellent* well"; "*far* unfit to be a sovereign"; "cut the clouds *full* fast"; "but I will punish *home*"; "*hugely* politic"; "a *monstrous* little voice"; "*monstrous* delicate"; "I am *mainly* ['entirely'] ignorant"; "a *marvellous* witty fellow"; "*wondrous* strange snow"; "give up yourself *merely* ['entirely'] to chance"; "began to be *much* sea-sick"; "a *passing* valiant man"; "he is so *plaguy* proud"; "I am *right* loath"; "he's *shrewdly* vexed"; "*sore* hurt and bruised"; "let the supposed fairies pinch him *sound*"; "he's *vengeance* proud" (solitary instance); "will be *well* welcome." In the Elizabethan use of intensives the striking feature is not only the variety in words of intensive force, but the way this variety is attained through the freedom in the shifting of words to varied uses.

The flexibility of Shakespearean English as compared with that of today is nowhere more apparent than in the use of prepositions. In Shakespeare's language one finds not only different prepositions used to express the same relation, but one preposition used in the expression of different relations. In the English of today there is uncertainty of usage between *averse to* and *averse from,* between *different to, different from* and occasionally, *different than.* In the language of Shakespeare this kind of confusion is worse confounded. Corresponding to the present-day *repent of* anything, in Shakespeare may be found; *repent at, repent for, repent in, repent over, repent of.* In the centuries before Shakespeare a sharper distinctness in the expression of relations had been developing through new prepositional phrases. The process was not complete in Shakespeare's time for, as has already been pointed out, many of these newer forms, such as *in default of, in addition to, in comparison to* or *with, in proportion to, in compliance with, in consequence of, in front of, in opposition to, with regard to, upwards of,* are not used by Shakespeare. Other such phrases, such as *in accordance with, on account of, owing to, in advance of, ahead of,* had not in his time been brought into use.[6] The use of these definite phrases of relation produces a more fixed, a more rigid union between the principal words in expression. Their non-use, on the other hand, goes with a looser jointed, more flexible, form of speech. For instance, notice the Shakespearean use of *by.* In present-day English we *say, speak, think, know,* etc., *concerning* or *about* or *of* or *against* or *with regard* to a person or thing. In contrast notice the Shakespearean expressions: "How say you *by* the French lord?" "How think you *by* that?" "*By* him and *by* ['against'] this woman here what know you?" "In any thing that I do know *by* her" ['in regard to'].[7]

The plasticity of Elizabethan English as a medium of expression springs not only from the natural ease with which words might be turned to new meanings or joined to form phrase or compound but from the variety in word material. It has been said that no other man has ever

---

[6] *Cf.* Franz, *op. cit.,* sec. 458.
[7] Franz, *op. cit.,* sec. 473.

employed a vocabulary as rich as that used by Shakespeare. By means of a vocabulary test it has been attempted to demonstrate the superiority of Shakespeare's genius to that of Milton. It has been said that Shakespeare made use of 15,000 words while Milton used only 8,000. The validity of these claims is open to question. The comparatively narrow range of Milton's vocabulary is to be explained by the comparatively narrow range of subjects in his poetry upon which the statistics are based. The number of words in the rapidly expanding vocabulary of modern times also probably exceeds that in sixteenth century use. A vocabulary test made at Princeton University in 1916 showed that the upperclassman at that institution had at his command 16,500 words, and a similar test ten years later in 1926 showed that the same class of students had a vocabulary of 17,500. In other words in the course of ten years the English vocabulary in upperclassman use at Princeton had expanded by 1,000 words. The maximum number of words ever accredited to Shakespeare is 25,000 words, and the usual estimate is much below that figure. It thus appears that the vocabulary of Shakespeare was not remarkably large if compared with that in modern use.

With every abatement, however, the vocabulary of Shakespeare must be rated as one remarkably rich. In it are exhibited most of the language resources of his time. In general in his writings the injunction of Puttenham to courtly poets is followed. The words usually are those belonging to the cultivated dialect of the district centering in London. There are, however, indications of influence from other dialects. There are a number of words or meanings of words which now survive only in local dialects, words perhaps derived from Shakespeare's native Warwickshire dialect. To this class belong such words as *ballow*, 'cudgel'; blood-*boltered*, 'matted'; *bum-baily*, 'sheriff's officer'; *chop,* 'thrust with force'; *elder-gun,* 'pop-gun'; *father,* 'relative that gives away bride'; *gallow,* 'frighten'; *geck,* 'fool'; *honey-stalks,* 'stalks of clover'; *mobled,* 'muffled'; *muss,* 'scrambling game'; *old,* 'abundant'; *pash,* 'head'; *potch,* 'thrust at'; *sight,* 'pupil of eye'; *soiled,* 'high-fed'; *tarre,* 'provoke'; *vails,* 'perquisites.'[8] Among these words are a number which have been abandoned in standard British use but survive in American use, such as: *jolly,* 'merry'; *sick,* 'ill'; *mad,* 'angry'; *candy* and *sugar candy.* The spelling *butt* (for *'boat'*) in the *Tempest* suggests an American pronunciation surviving in eastern New England. In the expression *here comes himself,* appears a construction now associated with Anglo-Irish idiom.

The influence of local dialect, however, is not a conspicuous feature in the language of Shakespeare. His language, in general, is that provided by his London environment. Upon this instrument provided for him he plays with the hands of a master. The different levels of style, the grand, the mean, and the low, distinguished by the rhetorician, appear in his writings. The dignity of the grand style is served by full-toned words such as *circummured, perdurable, vasticity, prolixious, cold obstruction,* and *multitudinous seas incarnadine.* For such effects, however, he does not confine himself to the classical elements in the language. Native and classical elements are joined to produce the euphony of such a line as:

O polished perturbation! golden care!

As already pointed out, he brings the native resources of the language into use in freshening the color of faded metaphors. In the phrase *glassy essence* he reverses the use of classical and native that appears in the modern equivalent expression *fragile being.*

[8] C. T. Onions, *The Oxford Shakespeare Glossary.*

From the level of the grand style Shakespeare sinks with ease to the low style exhibited in the red-lattice phrases of Doll Tearsheet, in the ale-house language of Falstaff, or in the robustious raillery of Thersites. From the canting terms of his times he appropriates words such as *bully-rooke, shuffle, hedge, lurch,* and *cog,* which have the quality of modern slang. Of similar quality are other colloquial words such as: *drie,* 'thirsty'; *ken; bobbed; pash; buss; frush; fills,* for 'thills'; *chinks,* 'money.' Some of these words and phrases seem to have passed rapidly out of fashion. Others such as *dumps* ('low spirits'), *smoked* ('discovered'), *in this pickle, to this tune* remained in vogue in the colloquial speech of a century later and are not unknown today.

One cannot always be sure, however, regarding the extent of his original contribution. The language of Shakespeare has been more carefully studied than that of his contemporaries, and it is always possible that features first recorded in Shakespeare's use may have had their origin elsewhere. There are, however, many words or applications of words which make their earliest recorded appearance in his writings. Among words first appearing in his use may be mentioned: *bump, dwindle, credent, illume, orb, inauspicious, baseless, multitudinous, cerements, courtship, dickens, lonely.*

His creative power as exhibited in forms of language, however, appears not so much in the creation of new elements as in molding of the plastic language of his time into new forms. The prefix *en-,* which was actively alive in his time, he applies in the combinations *enmesh, enrank, enridged, enscheduled, ensear, ensteeped, entame, entreasured,* which are not recorded in writings antedating his. Independent words he joins in compounds such as *eye-beam, eye-drop, eye-wink, fire-eyed, after-eye* ('to look after'), *fire-new, fire-robed, fire-work, dog-weary, arm-gaunt* ('weary from army service'), none of which are found earlier than his time.

More striking still is his use of the Elizabethan freedom in applying words to new meanings. First recorded in Shakespeare are word uses such as: *capable,* 'having ability,' 'gifted'; *censure,* 'adverse judgment'; *cheap,* 'costing little effort,' 'accounted of little value'; *cloud,* v., 'overspread with gloom'; *cog,* v., 'wheedle a thing from a person'; *common,* 'vulgar tongue'; *condolement,* 'tangible expression of sympathy'; *converse,* sb., 'intercourse,' 'conversation'; *conveyance,* 'vehicle'; *crop,* v., 'yield a crop'; *dateless,* 'endless'; *description,* 'kind,' 'class'; *despite,* prep., 'in defiance of another's wish'; *directly,* 'at once'; *discharge,* sb., (1) 'emission,' (2) 'payment,' (3) 'performance'; *distemper,* (1) 'illness,' (2) 'intoxication'; *drown,* 'to make completely drunk'; *dull,* 'tedious.'

Many of the word forms molded by Shakespeare failed to harden into fixity. Among words formed by him but later fallen out of use may be mentioned: *congree,* 'to agree'; *congreet,* 'to agree mutually'; *congrue,* 'to agree'; *definement,* 'description'; *disliken,* 'disguise'; *disproperty,* 'to alienate a possession.' A similar fate awaited some of his applications of words to new meanings, such as: *ceremony,* 'portent,' 'omen'; *channel,* v., 'to furrow'; *citizen,* adj., 'city-bred'; *crack,* 'pert little boy'; *distaste,* 'to render distasteful.'

In other instances the stamp of his genius is permanently impressed on the language. If, in the case of single words, there always lingers a shade of doubt whether Shakespeare gave new direction or merely followed in a path already made, in the grouping of words in expressive phrases there can be no doubt of his original contribution. Many of his phrases, such as "public haunt of men," "fortune's fool," "custom stale her infinite variety," "moated grange," and "pomp and circumstance," like the forms of classical art, or shall we say Gothic art, have become permanent elements in the architecture of the English language. To enumerate them all would be obviously impossible in limited space. An impression, however, of the wealth of expression contributed to the English language by a single artist in a period of language plasticity may be conveyed by the following list: "mind's eye," "primrose path," "to the manner born," "making night hideous," "a tale unfold," "shadow of a dream," "caviare to the general," "flesh is heir to," "mortal coil," "sicklied o'er," "glass of fashion," "out-herod Herod," "mirror up to nature," "counterfeit presentment," "flaming youth," "whet thy blunted purpose," "hoist with his own petard," "fellow of infinite jest," "ribband in the cap of youth,"—all from one play, *Hamlet*.

The lack of government which appears in the forms and the meanings of words as used by Shakespeare appears also in his grammatical forms and constructions. In the last two decades of the century, as remains to be seen, the English schoolmaster appears on the scene. That his efforts were not without result appears in the nature of the revisions made in the 1601 edition of the Berners translation of *Huon of Bordeaux*. The new methods of the schoolmaster, however, were too late to affect the men of Shakespeare's generation who had been schooled under an earlier régime. Shakespeare's little respect for the pedant schoolmaster has appeared in the citations already introduced. Shakespeare's attitude toward English grammar seems to have been that of Sidney who, it will be recalled, held that "grammar it might have, but it needs it not." The "fining," therefore, of the English language, attributed by Meres to Shakespeare, consisted more in phrasal enrichment or in rhetorical 'exornation' than in reduction to grammatical correctness. In the more mechanical features of language appears an irregularity and a freedom like that in his use of words.

Modern editors have done much to disguise the real nature of Shakespeare's language. Not only the spelling but, in many instances, the syntax, have been reformed to make his language conform to the modern standard. A single glance, however, at a page of Shakespeare in one of the original Quarto editions or in the first collected edition, the First Folio of 1623, will reveal striking points of difference. In the First Folio the Roman type is used, but the forms of some of the letters are different. Most striking at first glance is the peculiar form of the letter *s,* easily confused with *f.*

Next one will observe the irregular spelling. Classical scholarship, as has been seen, was trying to make English words of classical derivation conform in spelling to their classical originals. But in the case of native English words there was no original pattern word. In consequence in the spelling of these words the greatest uncertainty prevailed. Attempts at improvement were made. Sir John Cheke in his translation of the Gospels, as has already been pointed out, made such an attempt. More systematic was the attempt made by Sir Thomas Smith who in 1568 published a treatise in Latin, *De recta et emendata linguæ anglicæ scriptione.* In this work Smith offers a system of spelling with thirty-four letters supported by the use of diacritical signs. One year later, in 1569, John Hart published a book on spelling which he had composed some years earlier. The nature of this book is indicated by its title, *An Orthographie Conteyning the due order and reason howe to write or painte thimage of mannes voise most like to the life or nature.* In 1580 still another new system of orthography was offered in a book by William Bullokar.

These writers have a place near the head of a long line of men who have attempted to improve English spelling.

But their efforts, like those of their successors, had little result, and in Shakespeare's time English spelling was most irregular. One will at once notice the irregular use of the final -e. Even more striking is the use of the letters u and v, i and j. The later use of these pairs of letters to distinguish between vowel and consonant was adopted about 1625 and appears in the Second Folio edition published in 1632.

A closer examination of Shakespeare's language reveals not only many strange uses of words and words in strange spellings, but many constructions which are archaic in character and, here and there, a construction which, judged by modern standards, is ungrammatical. There is an obvious fallacy in the remark occasionally made, especially in opposing some modern innovation, some so-called corruption of modern language, that the language of Shakespeare is good enough. Shakespeare's language is not "good enough" for present-day use. If judged by modern standards the greatest of all English writers would have to be rated as illiterate.

The explanation of this striking paradox has, it is hoped, been provided in the preceding pages. The language of Shakespeare was that of cultivated Elizabethan use. It had not, however, been subjected to the discipline of the schoolmaster. Its remarkable flexibility and plasticity are explained in part by the freedom in the use of words, but in part also by an absence of formal control, which permitted, often, a closer fitting of language to meaning than would be possible with more rigid forms.

The larger freedom of Shakespearean language is everywhere apparent. Double negatives not tolerated by Latin use, though freely used in Greek, are to be found through-

William Shakespeare (1564-1616): portion of the third of three manuscript pages in *The Booke of Sir Thomas More* which by many experts are believed to be in the handwriting of Shakespeare.

out earlier English and survive in frequent use in Shakespeare, in expressions such as: "say nothing neither," "nor hath not" (*Tempest*, III, ii), "nor nature neuer lends" (*M. for M.*, I, i). "I will not budge for no man's pleasure" (*R. and J.*, III, i).

Double comparatives and double superlatives, which were objected to by the critical taste of the following century, and which Rowe and Pope tried to eliminate in their editions of Shakespeare, are frequent in the original language of Shakespeare. No objection apparently was felt to "worser" (*R. and J.*, III, ii); "more brauer" (*Tempest*, I, ii); "more hotter" (*All's Well*, IV, v); "more larger" (*A. and C.*, III, vi); "more mightier" (*M. for M.*, V, i); nor to "most unkindest," "most heauiest." Words already superlative in meaning were given added intensity by redundant comparative or superlative endings, as in *chiefest, extremest, perfecter, perfectest*. The hyperbole involved is obviously at the expense of the logic.

In the case of adverbs in place of the modern uniform use of the ending *-ly*, there survived an earlier variety of method, among others the use of the adverb without ending and, therefore, indistinguishable in form from the adjective. These "flat adverbs" are far more frequent than in present-day English, *e.g.*, "to speake *plaine*" (*Much Ado*, II, iii); "knauery cannot *sure* hide himself" (*Ibid.*); "she is *exceeding* wise" (*Ibid.*); "*Sure* I thinke so" (*Ibid.*, III, i); "an *excellent* good name" (*Ibid.*, III, i); "how *pittifull* I deserue" (*Ibid.*, V, ii).

In the case of the personal pronoun of the second person, in Elizabethan speech there was a choice to be made between the *thou, thee* forms and the *ye, you* forms. At the end of the sixteenth century *you*, the old plural form, was the prevalent form in the natural speech of the higher and middle classes; but *thou* persisted in the use of the lower

classes with no pretension to culture.[9] The choice between
the two forms continued, however, to serve in expressing
differences in attitude of speaker to listener, shades of
distinction which do not admit of precise definition. The
nature of this distinction, however, may be seen in the
dialogues between Benedick, on the one side, and Claudio
and the Prince on the other, between Shylock on the one
hand, and Bassanio and his friends on the other, between
Prospero and his daughter Miranda. The abandonment in
present-day English of the old discrimination has unquestionably afforded relief from a choice which in many instances must have been embarrassing.

In the use of the personal pronouns in Shakespeare's
English, as in the colloquial English of today, there is a
noticeable confusion, as appears in expressions like the
following:

Is she as tall as me	(*A. and C.*, III, iii)
with the hand of she here	(*Ibid.*, III, xiii)
This is he I spoke of	(*M. for M.*, V, i)
betweene my goodman, and he	(*Merry Wives*, III, ii)
nobody should be sad but I	(*King John*, IV, i)
my father hath no child but I	(*As You Like It*, I, ii)
nothing this wide universe I call, save thou	(*Sonnets*, 109)

In use with *than, such as*, and *like*, the confusion is
striking.

Patience is for poltroons, such as he	(*3 Henry VI*, I, i)
hates nothing more than he	(*As You Like It*, I, i)
and yet no man like he doth grieve my heart	(*R. and J.*, III, v)

Joined to a preceding noun or pronoun with *and,* the
nominative form replaces the objective in instances like
the following:

[9] Franz, *op. cit.*, sec. 289a.

I never saw a woman,
But only Sycorax my dam and she   (*Tempest,* III, ii)
a league between my goodman and he (*Merry Wives,* III, ii)
all debts are cleared between you and I
                                    (*Merchant of Venice,* III, ii)

The use of oblique case for nominative also appears not infrequently:

and yet I would not be thee   (*Lear,* I, iv)
if this should be thee   (*Twelfth Night,* II, v)
when him we serve's away   (*A. and C.,* III, i)
And damn'd be him that first cries   (*Macbeth,* V, viii)
our parents and us twain   (*Cymbeline,* V, iv)

In *Twelfth Night,* Malvolio reproving Sir Toby says, "Besides you waste the treasure of your time with a foolish knight," a remark which draws from Sir Andrew the comment, "That's me, I warrant you." The idiom sounds modern and natural, but in reality is rare in Elizabethan use. Contrary to what one might expect, in Elizabethan speech, even in popular use, the modern form was not yet the one in current use. One will recall the biblical "It is I, be not afraid." In sixteenth-century French the phrase *c'est moi* had established itself. Ramus, in the first edition of his grammar, objected to it. In later editions, however, he warmly championed the expression because it was established in customary use. In Elizabethan English, however, the prevalent grammatically regular use is exemplified by such expressions as:

The fairest here, . . . am I
                    (George Peele, *Arraignment of Paris,* II, i)
The only she that wins this prize am I   (*Ibid.*)
I knew't was I   (*Twelfth Night,* II, v)
That's I   (*M. for M.,* V, i)

The construction, *it is me,* is said to appear eight times in Shakespeare, two times in Marlowe.[10]

In the use of *who* and *whom* the confusion in Shakespearean English was like that surviving in present-day colloquial English. The natural position of this pronoun, whether used as relative or as interrogative, is at the beginning of the sentence or clause. This position is also the natural one for the nominative case. Hence a natural advantage of the nominative form *who* over *whom*. In present-day English the form *whom* could hardly maintain its existence without the support of the grammarian. In the dialects of England it has practically disappeared. In Shakespearean English the use of *who* for *whom* is already frequent:

Who t'aduance and who to trash	(*Tempest*, I, ii)
Who does he accuse?	(*A. and C.*, III, vi)

It even appears following prepositions:

IAGO. He's married.	
CASSIO. To who?	(*Othello*, I, ii)
. . . He is in love? With who?	(*Much Ado*, I, i)
CLOTEN. . . . yield thee, thief.	
GUIDERIUS. To who?	(*Cymbeline*, IV, ii)

The lack of regularization in Elizabethan English appears, however, in Shakespeare's occasional use of *whom* for *who:*

whom—would here haue kill'd your King	(*Tempest*, V, i)
whom—were wrackt	(*Ibid.*)

In the inflection of nouns a tendency in present-day English, especially in provincial speech, to use a collective singular form in place of the plural, is even more active in the Elizabethan English of Shakespeare:

[10] C. A. Smith, *Studies in Syntax,* p. 81.

A teeme of horse	(*Two Gent. of Verona*, III, i)
twelue yeere	(*Tempest*, I, ii)
We kill the fowle [plural]	(*M. for M.*, II, ii)
subject [for subjects]	(*Ibid.*, III, ii, *et passim*)
twentie mile	(*Merry Wives*, III, ii)
twelue score	(*Ibid.*)

The treatment of word groups as units and the application of the plural sign or the possessive sign at the end of the group, appears in expressions such as *paile-fuls* (*Tempest*, II, ii) and *the Dutchesse of Millaines gowne* (*Much Ado*, III, iv). It should also be noted that the use of the apostrophe as a distinctively possessive sign had not yet established itself.

Closely akin to the use of collective singular nouns is the type of expression represented by, *These kind of knaues* (*Lear*, II, ii) and *these set kind of fools* (*Twelfth Night*, I, v). This form of expression, still in popular use, and not unknown to cultivated use in England today, in Elizabethan times was frequent. The demonstrative pronoun is made to agree in number with the plural idea of the following word group rather than with the singular form of the noun it precedes.

In a similar way in the case of indefinite pronouns singular in form, such as *each, everyone, nobody, everybody*, etc., the plurality in meaning often leads to the use of the plural verb or plural pronoun:

God send *euery one their* hearts desire   (*Much Ado*, III, iv)
And *euery one* to rest *themselves* betake   (*Lucrece*, 125)
Each leaning on *their* elbows and *their* hips   (*V. and A.*, 43)
Haue *euery* pelting riuer made so proud, that *they*

                              (*Mid N. Dream*, II, i)

In a similar way verbs are used in singular or plural forms not infrequently corresponding with singular or plural meaning, rather than with singular or plural form, in the subject:

heuen and fortune still *rewards*   (*Two Gent. of Verona*, IV, iii)
My old bones *akes*   (*Tempest*, III, iii)
Art and practise *hath* inriched   (*M. for M.*, I, i)
To death of Fulvia, with more vrgent touches, *do*—speake
                                         (*A. and C.*, I, ii)
The Silken Tackle *swell*   (*A. and C.*, II, ii)
The merchandise which . . .
Are all to dear   (*A. and C.*, II, v)
. . .   both our remedies
Within thy helpe and holy physicke *lies*   (*R. and J.*, II, iii)
All disquiet, horrour, and perturbation *followes* her
                                         (*Much Ado*, II, i)
that which simplenesse and merite *purchaseth*   (*Ibid.*, III, i)
the watch that *are* their accusers   (*Ibid.*, IV, ii)
My education *beene* in Arts and Armes   (*Pericles*, II, iii)
Bee one of those that *thinkes*   (*Ibid.*, IV, iii)
While Sommer dayes *doth* last   (*Ibid.*, IV, i)
Where our scenes *seemes* to liue   (*Ibid.*, IV, iv)
Then *is* Cæsar and he   (*A. and C.*, II, vi)

In the interpretation of the verb forms in the phrases cited, there is another complicating element in the variation in form of the personal endings in Elizabethan verbal conjugation. In the third plural, along with the usual forms with no personal endings, appear in Shakespeare forms ending in -s due to Northern influence, and occasional forms with the -*th* ending, and rare instances of the older ending -*en* ("All *perishen* of man"—*Pericles*, II, i, Quarto 2, and "Where when men *been*" . . . (*Ibid.*). With these four variant forms in use, one cannot always be sure whether a plural or a singular meaning is intended. The uncertainty appears, for example, in: "The Heuens . . . encrease . . . and *sets* vp your fame" (*Pericles*, III, ii, Quarto 2).

In the third singular of the present also there are two endings in use, providing a choice which is useful, at least to the poet, because of the freedom provided in versification. Along with the older forms in -*eth* appear forms in -*s* or -*es*, thus affording the poet a choice in the third singular between a dissyllable and a monosyllable. The -*s* forms, of Northern origin, appear earlier in verse. Lyly has only four per cent of the -*s* forms in *Euphues* as compared with 85 per cent in the metrical *Woman of the Moone*. In the prose of the first half of the sixteenth century the -*eth* forms prevail; in the verse of Marlowe (d. 1593), however, the -*s* forms are 92 per cent of those used.[11] The lack of any definite rule guiding Shakespeare's use, appears from passages like the following:

The King *riseth* from his state, *takes* her up, *kisses* and *placeth*
 her by him (*Henry VIII*, I, ii, stage dir. ed. Gollancz)
Has Page any braines? *Hath* he any eies?
                                        (*Merry Wives*, III, ii)
Who *wanteth* food and will not say he *wants* it?
                                        (*Pericles*, I, iv)

The use of the subjunctive had already in Shakespeare's time become much limited through the use of modal auxiliary verbs and through the intrusion of indicative forms. The subjunctive was not yet, however, as much restricted as in present-day English. In concessive clauses and in temporal clauses introduced by *ere* and *before*, its use was more general than today.[12] The confusion characteristic of the period, however, appears in such passages:

Wish chastly . . . that your Dian
Was both her selfe and loue   (*All's Well*, I, iii)

[11] *Cf.* Franz, *op. cit.*, sec. 154.
[12] Franz, *op. cit.*, sec. 636.

With the use of the subjunctive are associated two idioms which play a large part in English expression, and the use of which has been much debated, the expressions *had rather* and *had better*. In the evolution of these idioms the language of Shakespeare represents a half-way stage. The earliest stage is represented by the form *me were lever* (to me [it] would be preferable), which was in common use in the fourteenth and fifteenth centuries. Along with this impersonal construction developed the personal construction, *I had lever* (I should regard [it] preferable). About the year 1530 the archaic word *lever* or *liefer* was superseded by *rather*, making the phrase *I had rather*. Shakespeare does not use *I had liefer*, although he quite frequently uses *had as lief*, but *had rather* he uses frequently. Parallel with *had rather* comes into use the form *would rather* in which *would* is the preterit subjunctive of *will*. This form, which in present-day English is on about equal standing with *had rather*, appears in the First Folio eight times.[13]

Corresponding, however, to present-day *had better* the prevailing Elizabethan form of expression is with the preterit subjunctive of the verb *to be*, appearing in such Shakespearean expressions as: "You *were best* meddle" (*Merry Wives*, III, iii) ; and "You *were best* take" (*Lear*, I, iv).

The progressive form of the present tense active represented by the expression, *is coming*, is comparatively rare in Shakespeare, and the passive form, the *is being built* construction, does not appear at all, in fact, makes its earliest appearance in English in the second half of the eighteenth century.[14]

In the preterit and pluperfect forms of intransitive verbs the use of the auxiliary *be* instead of *have* is frequent in

[13] W. Van der Gaaf, *Transition from Impersonal to Personal Construction*, p. 50, quoted from Franz, *op. cit.*, sec. 627.

[14] Franz, *op. cit.*, sec. 622.

Shakespeare, for example: Don Pedro *is* approacht (*Much Ado*, I, i) *are* you come (*Ibid*.); now I *am* returnde (*Ibid*.).[15]

In the history of the future tense also the language of Shakespeare represents a half-way stage in development. It should be held in mind that earliest English had no special form for the future. Future meaning was conveyed by the use of the present tense form. In the German language a compound tense form was created by the use of the auxiliary verb *werden*, whose meaning was 'become.' In English, use was made of two verbs originally independent in meaning, the verbs *shall* and *will*. Of these *shall* was first to be made to serve and down to the age of Elizabeth it was the prevalent form. In the Wycliffe-Purvey translation of Matthew it is used almost exclusively, and the same is true in the later translation by Tyndale. Competing with the use of *shall* began that of *will* late in the Middle English period, and in the Elizabethan period the use of these two future auxiliaries began to differentiate. As late as Ben Jonson's *Grammar*, however, published in 1640, no distinction of person between *shall* and *will* is formulated. In Shakespeare's language there are many instances of the use of *shall* and *will* quite at variance with the rule formulated in the seventeenth century which governs the usage of today. Such statements as, "They [the Gods] *shall* assist" (*A. and C.*, II, i); "Cæsar, I *shall*" (*Ibid*., III, xii); "I *will* be horribly in loue" (*Much Ado*, II, iii) are disturbing to one accustomed to the modern distinction. A remarkable phenomenon in language, however, is the extent to which unregulated Elizabethan usage, as represented by Shakespeare, had naturally fallen into the use of the distinction prescribed by the later formulated rule, which for the simple future prescribes *shall* for the first person, *will*

[15] *Ibid*., secs. 608 *ff.*

for the second and third; and for promises and threats, *shall* in the first person, *will* in the second and third. An investigation of Shakespeare's use yields the following statistics:

SIMPLE FUTURE [16]

1st person *shall* 16 times, *will*   3 times
2d   person *shall*   5 times, *will*   2 times
3d   person *shall* 15 times, *will* 16 times

PROMISES AND THREATS

1st person *shall*   0 times, *will* 72 times
2d   person *shall* 12 times, *will*   0 times
3d   person *shall* 12 times, *will*   0 times

Obviously natural usage had advanced far in the direction of the distinction which was later formulated into rule.

The difference between Elizabethan English and that of today appears in the analytical forms of the verb, with the auxiliary *do*. This verb, originally a word with independent meaning, has been brought to service in a number of ways. In present-day use it is used for emphasis in affirmation and in denial of inactivity, *e.g., I do think*. Its principal uses, however, are in negative statements (*I do not think* in place of *I think not*), in negative commands (*Don't think*), and in questions (*Do you think?* in place of *Think you?*) and as a substitute for a principal verb, like a pronoun as a substitute for a noun. Shakespearean use is much less settled. *Do* is used more generally for emphasis: "I *do* believe thee" (*Winter's Tale*, I, ii); "I *do* entreat you" (*Julius Cæsar*, III, ii); "I *do* confess my fault" (*Henry V*, II, ii). The use of *do* in negative commands had become universal by the year 1700; in Shakespeare the simple form is the more usual one. Such forms of command as: "answer

[16] F. A. Blackburn, *The English Future*, 1892.

not" (*Two Gent. of Verona*, II, ii) ; "pursue me not" (*Mid. N. Dream*, II, i) ; "wish not a man from England" (*Henry V*, IV, iii), obviously do not belong to the English of to-day. In negative assertions the present-day use had been reached by about 1700; but in Shakespeare still appear more usually forms of expression such as: "a nun . . . kisses not more religiously" (*As You Like It*, III, iv) ; "they perceiue not" (*Ibid.*, III, ii) ; "you salute not at the court" (*Ibid.*).[17]

The infinitive in earlier English was used more frequently than at present without *to* as its distinctive sign. The earlier stage of the language is represented by such forms of expression in Shakespeare as: "Behoves me keep at utterance" (*Cymbeline*, III, i) ; "commands me name myself" (*Coriolanus*, IV, v) ; "Constrains them weep" (*Coriolanus*, V, iii) ; "desire her call wisdom to her" (*Lear*, IV, v) ; "it is best put finger in the eye" (*Taming of the Shrew*, I, i). The much disputed 'split infinitive' is recorded by Fitzedward Hall from as far back as the fourteenth century. But he offers no citations of its use in Shakespeare.

The forms of the strong verbs have been sources of confusion in all stages of English. Many of them have settled into fixed form only within the present generation. Some of them such as *eat* are still subject to debate, and in the speech of the uncultivated there persists hopeless confusion. In the less settled usage of Shakespeare's time one is not surprised, therefore, to meet with forms such as *broke*, for 'broken'; *spoke*, for 'spoken'; *loaden*, for 'laden' or 'loaded'; *took*, for 'taken'; *eate*, for 'eaten'; *droven*, for 'driven.'

Worthy of notice in this connection is the number of Latin preterit participles adopted without the addition of the English ending *-ed*, words such as: *contract*, for 'con-

---

[17] Franz, *op. cit.*, secs. 594-601.

tracted'; *confiscate,* for 'confiscated'; and other like forms such as *consecrate, create, fatigate, felicitate, incorporate.* It should be noted that forms such as these have yielded a number of important adjectives still in standard use, such as: *compact, deliberate, intricate, desperate, consummate.*

The general impression gained from a survey of the grammar of Shakespeare is that of an intermediate stage in a course of development, of a language little governed as yet by rules, but on account of its very irregularity, flexible, and, therefore, adaptable to the expression of varied meaning. The irregularities in Shakespeare's language are of course not to be looked on as signs of lack of cultivation. Quite the contrary, his language in its general features fairly well represents the courtly and cultivated speech of his time. It is important to observe that irregularities of the same kind appear in the language of Queen Elizabeth herself. In the letters written by the Queen to James VI of Scotland, her successor on the English throne,[18] appear the same popularized forms of words, such as *complices* (for 'accomplices'), *misconstred* (for 'misconstrued'), *attemps* (for 'attempts'); the same use of double superlatives as in *the most gladlist* ('gladliest'), *the most gridiest* ('greediest'); the same want of concord between verb form and grammatical subject, frequent in expressions such as "what seasons . . . *moues* me," "that all our subjectes *takes* after," "some wordes and fourme *was* suche—," "smal flies *stiks* fast," "sirenes tongues! wiche . . . in ende, *ruines* and *destroies*," "many my deere subiectz *liues*," "that so disorderd coursis *makes*," "the offending lordz *hopes* . . . I suche practisis *hathe* passed . . ." "one whos yeres *teacheth* more"; the same use of double negative as in *"nor neuer did," "nor neuer* shall," *"nor* do *not"*; the same use of the collective singular as "I trust shall receaue your *thanke.*"

18 *Camden Society Publications,* 1849.

The spelling shows the same kind of irregularities tending, however, toward the phonetic method. All in all, it appears that the unregulated form of language used by Shakespeare did not represent lack of cultivation but was, to borrow a nineteenth-century phrase, the Queen's English.

The fifth division of rhetoric, it should be recalled, dealt with Utterance, that is to say, the vocal side of language. That this feature of English did not escape attention we have evidence as early as the reign of Henry VIII. Henry Dowes, the tutor of Gregory Cromwell, in reporting concerning his pupil's progress refers to a certain Mr. South-well "dailie heringe hime to reade sumwhatt in thenglishe tongue, and advertisinge hime of the naturell and true kynde of pronunciacion thereof." [19] We have also the evidence of Lyly, already cited, regarding this side of a young man's training. We have also interesting evidence provided by Nashe in his satirical account of Gabriel Harvey. Queen Elizabeth on meeting Harvey had commented on Harvey's appearance. Puffed with pride, Harvey, we are told, "quite renounst his naturall accents and gestures & wrested himself wholy to the Italian puntilios, speaking our homely Iland tongue strangely, and but ten daies before had entertained a schoole-master to teache him to pronounce it." [20] Evidently guidance was needed in courtly pronunciation as in courtly behavior. Evidently also, then as now, there was affectation in manner of speaking.

But while a cultivated pronunciation was an element in courtly breeding in Elizabethan times, there was then even more than at present a lack of uniformity. Members of courtly society, coming as they did from different parts of the country, brought with them, as in the case of Sir Walter Raleigh, provincial modes of speech. Older modes

[19] Wyld, *op. cit.*, p. 103
[20] *Have with You to Saffron Walden*, p. 112.

of pronunciation survived along with newer fashions. The old jostled with the new then as it does today in the pronunciation of words such as *wound, again, either*. In fact throughout the sixteenth century there prevailed the greatest uncertainty not only in the written forms of words, but in their manner of pronunciation. If we go back to the period before the dominance of the New Learning, we find in the translation of Froissart by the courtly writer, Lord Berners (1467-1532), such variant spellings as *stirr, sterr* ('stir'), *businesse, besynes* ('business'), *herte, harte* ('heart'), *ferre, farre* ('far'), spellings which plainly indicate varying pronunciation.[21] If we leave courtly society and turn our attention to the middle-class Londoner, we find variety even more bewildering in the irregular spellings already cited from the diary of Henry Machyn.

These variant spellings clearly reflect a varying pronunciation. The number of instances may easily be expanded. Some of the modes of pronunciation indicated by the irregular spelling of this sixteenth-century London merchant, with the rising importance in succeeding centuries of the middle classes, have made their way into standard English. Others which persist in the use of the uncultivated, with the sharpened definition of the modern standard of cultivated English, have become branded as vulgarisms. The struggle for supremacy between the -*er* forms and the -*ar* forms just cited, in many instances persisted through the succeeding centuries and in some instances has not yet reached a final decision or serves to differentiate American usage from British usage. In the use of initial *h*- there appears in Machyn's diary the same kind of uncertainty that marks the cockney speech of today, as in the forms: *hoathe, hoythe*, 'oath'; *olles*, 'holes'; *orbese*, 'herbs'; *have be hat*, 'have been at'; *Amtun courte; alff fulle*, 'half full'; *arolds*,

21 Wyld, *op. cit.*, pp. 117-8.

'heralds'; *elmet, elmett,* 'helmet.' There is to be noted a prevalent use of the letter *e* in words which before and since have been spelled with *i; reches,* 'riches'; *vetell,* 'victual'; *wedow,* 'widow'; *Necolas,* along with 'Nicholas,' etc.

There is represented in spelling the tendency in popular speech to abbreviate longer words as in: *raynyd,* 'arraigned'; *prentes,* 'apprentice'; *spital,* 'hospital'; *longes,* 'belongs'; *contenentt,* 'incontinent'; *secturs, sekturs,* 'executors'; *salt,* 'assault'; *sosyatt,* 'associate'; *envetore,* 'inventory;' etc.

In proper names, particularly, there is much uncertainty. Sweden is referred to as *Sweythland, Swatheland, Swaythland, Swaythen, Sweythen, Swaynland.* Popular modes of pronunciation appear in: *Masselsay,* 'Marshalsea'; *Syssel, Sysselle,* 'Sicily'; *sant Towlys,* 'St. Olave's'; *Damanes,* 'Dame Agnes'; *Semer,* 'Seymour'; *Chamley,* 'Cholmondeley'; *sant Bathelmuw,* 'St. Bartholomew'; *Cornelle,* 'Cornhill'; *Hatford,* 'Hertford'; *Crumwelle,* 'Cromwell'; *Wosetur, Vossetur,* 'Worcester'; *Callys, Calys,* 'Calais.'

The speech of Henry Machyn, the London citizen, does not represent courtly usage. In the courtly circles of the sixteenth century distinction was striven for not less in language than in dress. In I *Henry IV,* Hotspur admonishes his wife to swear "like a lady" and to leave such mild forms of oath as "in sooth" to "velvet-guards and Sunday-citizens." And yet in pronunciation courtly language was hardly more uniform than that of the citizen. The varying pronunciation indicated by the spelling of the young king Edward VI has already been cited. We have also the testimony of Gabriel Harvey regarding words that might "indifferently be vsed eyther wayes." "For you shall," he says, "as well, and as ordinarily heare *fayer* as *faire, Aier* as *Aire.*" Other such words with varied pronunciation mentioned by Harvey are *died* or *dyde, spied* or *spide, tryed* or *tride, fyer* or *fire, myer* or *myre,* "with an infinyte companye of the same sorte" often in the speech of the same person.

The unsettled state of pronunciation appears in the language of Queen Elizabeth. The remarkable attainments of the queen in foreign languages, classical and modern, did not provide her with a uniform manner of speaking the vernacular language of her own country. The *-ar* forms that were making their way into London speech found their way into the language of the Queen, as shown by such spellings as *discrued, desarue, desart, sarued, marcy,* etc. The forms with *e* for *i* are represented in her writings by *bellowes,* 'billows'; *sence,* 'since'; *rechis,* 'riches.' Many other forms of the kind which in modern times would be associated with illiteracy appear in her writings, such as: *attemps,* 'attempts'; *behavor,* 'behaviour'; *nimlest,* 'nimblest'; *brinkinge* of me up, 'bringing'; the *chawes,* 'jaws,' of death. Nor does her spelling indicate consistency in her speech. In her writings appear *bisy* and *busy, disarued* and *deserued, hard* ('heard') and *herde, sarued* and *serues, styrring* and *sturred.*[22]

The exact quality of the sounds in Shakespeare's speech we shall never be able to know. If he had lived in the twentieth century there would be many records of his appearance and of his voice. Living as he did three centuries ago, we know of his appearance only from portraits of somewhat doubtful authenticity and of his voice only what is revealed by his writings. Even here evidence is scant. The evidence of his published works is uncertain because of the intervention of the printer. There has recently been brought to notice in the manuscript of the play entitled *Sir Thomas More* a passage which, in the opinion of many experts, was not only composed by Shakespeare, but is in his own handwriting. Only few and uncertain,

[22] Wyld, *op. cit.,* pp. 136, 216.

however, are the inferences that are to be drawn from this fragmentary and somewhat doubtful record. The sum of the matter is that we know concerning the sounds of Shakespeare's language little beyond what is revealed in his published works, in his puns and rimes and occasional spellings, and what is known concerning the pronunciation of his time revealed by comments made by grammarians and orthoëpists and by the spelled forms of words.

In the little regulated language of Shakespeare's time, in a language controlled by human pattern rather than by bookish rule, it is natural to expect much variation in pronunciation. There were many who, like Hotspur, provided a "mould of form" for speech, and variety in patterns produced variety in copies. Affectations, also, like those appearing in Elizabethan style of writing would certainly appear in mode of pronunciation. One should recall Nashe's satirical account of Harvey's affected speech. Pedantry, too, which belongs to all periods, played its part in the Elizabethan age. Its effect on pronunciation is satirically represented by Shakespeare in the precepts attributed by him to Holofernes. The pronunciation of Shakespeare, therefore, even if controlled by the "modesty of nature," we may be sure shared the qualities of the language of his time.

Regarding the position of the accent in polysyllabic words, usage in present-day English has in many instances not settled into uniformity. The variation in Shakespeare's language, however, was much wider. Borrowed words were exposed to two opposing forces, one favoring the preservation of the original accentuation, the other favoring a more complete anglicization by accenting the first syllable of the root in accordance with the principle of Germanic accentuation prevailing elsewhere in English. The consequence was in many cases possible choice in the position of the accent in such words, a choice lending flexibility in versification.

Hence in Shakespeare's verse appear such dual modes of pronunciation as: *cháracter* vb. (*charácters*—once); *cómmune*, vb. (*commúne*—once); *cómplete*, adj., *compléte;* *cómplots, complóts; cómrade, comráde; cónfessor, conféssor; cónfines, confínes; cónfiscate, confiscáte* ('confiscated'); *cóntract*, sb., *contráct; exíle*, sb., *éxile* (*exíle*, vb.); *perfúme, pérfume;* etc. In many instances the Shakespearean accentuation of such words is now obsolete or survives only in dialectal use. Examples are: *advértised, ántique, aspéct, authórized, charácters, chástise, commérce, cómplete, córrosive, détestable, intér'gatories, Júly's, oppórtune, perséver, perséverance,* etc., etc.[23] A prevalent tendency, however, to place the accent on syllables after the first is indicated by the frequency in colloquial use of the aphetic forms already mentioned such as *cerns* for *concerns, scuses* for *excuses, 'noynted* for *anointed, point for appoint.*

More fundamental than the difference in the position of the accent was the difference between Elizabethan English and present-day English in the quality of the vowel sounds. The Great Vowel-Shift has been referred to in an earlier chapter. In this remarkable shift in vowel pronunciation there is much difference of opinion regarding the stage reached in Shakespeare's time. Professor Wyld, as has been seen, finds evidence that most of the important changes had at least begun by the beginning of the sixteenth century. These changes, however, had not become universal. A general idea of the stage in development reached in Shakespeare's time may be gained from a brief summary of conclusions on the subject, reached by Jespersen.[24]

In the shift from Chaucerian long *i* (-'ee') to present-day long *i* (-'ah' + 'ee') in the time of Shakespeare the intermediate pronunciation 'ay' + 'ee' (phonetic sign, *ei*) had

[23] Franz, *op. cit.*, sec. 74.
[24] *A Modern English Grammar on Historical Principles*, I, Chap. viii.

been reached. Hence modern *bite* ('*bah*' + '*eet*') was represented by a sound something like '*bay*' + '*eet.*'

The parallel changes in the case of other long vowels
may be exhibited by the following table:

PRESENT ENGLISH	PHONETIC SPELLING	SHAKESPEARE	PHONETIC SPELLING
bite ('ah' + 'ee')	bait	'ay' + 'ee'	ei
beet ('ee')	bît	'ee'	bît
beat ('ee')	bît	'ay'	bêt
('ay')	abeit	*a* in *man* prolonged	abất
foul ('ah' + 'oo')	faul	'oh' + 'oo'	foul
fool ('oo')	fûl	'oo'	fûl
foal ('oh')	foul	'oh'	fôl

We may reach certain general conclusions regarding the
language of Shakespeare. It was little controlled except
by the cultivated usage of the time and by the classical
influence only beginning to make itself felt in the mother
tongue. In consequence, it was uncertain in its spelling and
constructions and free in its use of words, its combinations
of them into new compounds, and its application of them
to new meanings. In pronunciation it had advanced somewhat beyond the half-way stage in the shift of vowel pronunciation. But its pronunciation was still unstable and
uncertain, as appears from the unstable and uncertain forms
of spelling which conformed more closely to pronunciation
then than does our modern rigid mode of spelling.

The irregular language available for Shakespeare's use
had its advantages over more rigid modern language. It
was a flexible instrument easily turned in the varying directions of thought. It was a plastic medium ready for the
molding hand of genius.

Humanitye, is not the least honor of y^o Wreath. For, if once the Worthy Professors of those learnings shall come (as heretofore they were) to be the care of Princes, the Crownes theyr Soueraignes weare will not more adorne theyr Temples; nor theyr stamps liue longer in theyr Medalls, than in such Subiects labors. Poetry, my Lord, is not borne wth euery man; nor euery day: And, in her generall right, it is now my minute to thanke y^{or} Highnesse, who not only do honor her wth y^{or} eare, but are curious to exa= mine her wth y^{or} eye, & inquire into her beauties, and strengths. Where, though it hath proud a Worke of some difficulty to mee to retriue the particular authorities (according to y^{or} gracious command, and a desire borne out of iudgment) to those things, wch I writt out of fulnesse, and memory of my former readings; yet, now I haue ouercome it, the reward that meetes mee is double to one act: wch is, that thereby, y^{or} excellent Vnderstanding will not only iusti= fie mee to y^{or} owne knowledge, but decline the stiffnesse of others originall Ignorance, already armd to censure. For wch singular bounty, if my Fate (most excellent Prince, and only Delicacy of mankind) shall reserue mee to the Age of y^{or} Actions, whether in the Campe, or the Councell=Chamber, y^t I may write, at nights, the deedes of y^{or} dayes; I will then labor to bring forth some Workes as wor= thy of y^{or} fame, as my Ambition therein is of y^{or} pardon.

By the most trew admirer of y^{or} Highnesse Vertues,

And most hearty Celebrater of them
Ben: Jonson.

Ben Jonson (1573-1637): dedicatory epistle to *The Masque of Queenes*, 1609. (Brit. Mus. Royal MS. 18A, xlv.)

CHAPTER XI

THE uncurbed enthusiasm of the Elizabethan period, with its unregulated freedom in language, was followed by a period of restraint. The change coming over the ideals of English culture in the period following the reign of Elizabeth may be traced by the history of the English word *classical*. This word comes of course from the Latin adjective *classicus*, the primary meaning of which was 'belonging to the first or principal class of citizens,' but which had also the figurative secondary meaning, 'of first rank,' somewhat like the modern vulgarism *classy*. Borrowed into English this word is first cited in the Oxford Dictionary from the year 1599, with the meaning 'of the first rank of authority; constituting a standard or model; especially in literature.' From the year 1607 it is cited with the meaning, 'Of the standard Greek and Latin writers.' This word served to express a newly arisen sense of the existence of a standard by which to measure human achievement, including language, and at the same time to associate this standard with the productions of Greek and Latin antiquity.

Nature is no longer to be the sole guiding principle; over nature is to be imposed the rule of art. From books rather than from running brooks this art is to be acquired. In other words the romantic freedom of Shakespeare is succeeded by the neo-classic art of Ben Jonson.

First is to be noted the recoil from the rhetorical extravagance of the last decades of the sixteenth century. The Euphuism of Lyly and his imitators was obviously too extreme in its artificiality to have a lasting vogue. Drayton (d.1631) credits Sidney with the rescue of the language from this form of rhetorical excess. The extravagance of Marlovian eloquence also becomes a subject for satire. Marston exposes it to ridicule in the character of Matzagente [1] "a modern Bragadoch," a "Rampun, scrampun, mount tuftie Tamburlaine."

The robustious freedom exemplified by Nashe also is held in leash by a growing refinement. Puritan objection to blasphemy and ribaldry had its influence. Thomas Heywood [2] condemns the use by the dramatist of "lascivious shewes, scurrelous jeasts, or scandalous invectives." [3] An Act of Parliament in 1606 "forbade the jesting and profane use of the names of God, Christ, or the Holy Ghost or the Trinity in any stage play or show," [4] a law somewhat relaxed by King Charles I in 1633, who ruled that *faith, death* and *slight* should be regarded as "asseverations and no oaths." [5] Even with this modification in the interpretation of the law, it is obvious that there had come a marked change in manner of speech from the time when Hotspur recommended to his wife a good mouth-filling oath as a mark of breeding, when the wonted oath of Queen Elizabeth was "God's-death," a sharp contrast between the "russet yeas and honest kersey noes" that Biron resolved to use, the plain speech of "an honest man and a soldier that Benedick approved," and the "perfumed terms," such as *accommodation, complement, spirit* referred to by Ben Jonson as current in his time. Rhetorical extravagance was objected to

---

[1] *Antonio and Mellida,* 1602.
[2] *An Apology for Actors.*
[3] M. P. Tilley, *Publications Modern Language Association,* XXXI, 66.
[4] H. Bradley, *Shakespeare's England,* II, 569.
[5] J. Q. Adams, *Life of Shakespeare,* p. 509.

by Bacon, who alludes with disapprobation to "this im-
modest and deformed manner of writing lately entertained,
whereby matters of religion are handled in the manner of
the stage." [6]   Changes in words such as that of *ear-bussing*
in the Quarto edition of *King Lear* to *ear-kissing* in the
Folios, are symptomatic of a growing nicety in the use of
words.

Affectations in the use of newfangled words, to be sure,
persisted. Words were quarried from the two-language dictionaries of the time (for as yet purely English dictionaries
had not come into use) and provided a theme for satire.
"Ods my life, how he does all-to-bequalify her! *ingenious,
acute, polite*," says Philautia in Jonson's *Cynthia's Revels*.
To which Hedon rejoins, "Yes, but you must know, lady,
he cannot speak out of a dictionary method." [7]   But this
use of newfangled words formed one of the subjects for
ridicule in the famous War of the Theatres in which the
protagonists were Marston and Jonson. Marston ridicules
Jonson for his "new-minted Epithets (as *Reall, Intrinsicate,
Delphicke*), when in my conscience hee vnderstands not the
least part of it." Jonson replies with heavier artillery in
ridicule of Marston's use of words such as *incubus, mag-
nificate, turgidious, prorumped, obstufact,* and concludes
with the words, assigned to Vergil, a character in the play
(*Cynthia's Revels*):

> You must not hunt for wild, outlandish termes,
> To stuffe out a peculiar dialect:
> But let your Matter runne before your Words,

Satire, the most effective of remedies, in this instance
evidently had a salutary effect. Early in the new century
the reaction from the excessive use of the newfangled terms,
the 'hard words' of the time, and from the excessive em-

[6] G. P. Krapp, *Rise of English Literary Prose*, p. 129.
[7] J. L. Moore, *Tudor-Stuart Views*, p. 58.

ployment of the artifices of rhetoric was well under way. There was closer approach to the "modesty of nature" prescribed by Shakespeare. The extremes of manner and of method which had been features of the bravery of style were sweepingly condemned by Bacon in one of the most famous passages in his works. Bacon speaks of the "affectionate study of eloquence and copie ['wealth' or 'richness'] of speech, which then [following the Renaissance] began to flourish." "This," he continues, "grew speedily to an excess; for men began to hunt more after words than matter; and more after the choiceness of the phrase, and the round and clear composition of the sentence, and the sweet falling of the clauses, and the varying and illustration of their works with tropes and figures, than after the weight of matter, worth of subject, soundness of argument, life of invention, or depth of judgment." In this disapproval of excess in artifice Ben Jonson concurred. He quotes with approval the remark of Aulus Gellius that he "would rather have a plaine downright wisdome, then a foolish affected eloquence." [8] With this sane appraisal of the situation a stage had been reached from which, with the ancient languages as patterns, an orderly progress was possible in the development of literary expression in English. In Falstaffian metaphor, the language after a rhetorical spree was by these sedative judgments restored to sobriety.

But the freedom characteristic of Elizabethan speech had manifested itself not only in riotous excesses in the use of the schemes and colors of rhetoric, but in a more elemental form of lawlessness in its spelling and even in its grammatical forms and constructions. Of this anarchic state, which strikes the attention of the modern reader, contemporary writers were not unaware. The language

---

[8] *Discoveries,* ed. Castelain, quoted by Krapp, *op. cit.*

with all its merits was felt to lack the polish that belonged to English manners. This feeling is expressed by Lyly, who in *Euphues and his England* comments on "the English tongue (which as I have heard is almost barbarous) but the English manners which as I think are most precise." [9]

For this form of irregularity the learned treatises of the time offered little remedy. One should not fail to realize that works on rhetoric, like that by Sir Thomas Wilson, were composed for people advanced beyond the stage of instruction in the elementary forms of speech. The Puttenham *Arte of Poesie* was composed for the use of courtly poets. One should notice the nature of such a work as Abraham Fraunce's *Arcadian Rhetoric*. In this work the subject matter is divided into two parts, "congruitie" and "brauerie." The second part, dealing with bravery, is developed in detail with an elaborate discussion of rhetorical tropes and figures; the first part, however, that dealing with congruity, or grammatical concord, is passed over as too elementary for prolonged consideration. The treatises on spelling by Hart and Smith and Bullokar, which have been mentioned, were learned works with elaborate schemes for systematic modes of spelling, but remained on the level of theory rather than descending to the more humble task of offering practical guidance. Nor did the grammar schools afford much aid in learning the elementary features of the mother tongue. As already pointed out, they were Latin schools. The word *grammar* applied to Latin studies. Not before the seventeenth century, says the Oxford Dictionary, "had the word grammar become so completely a generic term that there was any need to speak explicitly of Latin grammar." The training in Latin and Greek, which was the principal aim of grammar-school instruction, provided little direct guidance in the use of English. Queen

[9] Ed. Croll, modernized spelling.

Elizabeth with all her amazing attainment in foreign languages would obviously not provide a pattern for English writing. Henry Peacham in his *Compleat Gentleman* says: "I have known even excellent scholars so defective this way that when they have been beating their brains twenty or four and twenty years about Greek etymologies . . . could neither write true English nor true orthography." [10]

The dominance of classical studies over English culture persisted through most of the seventeenth century. The learned Queen Elizabeth was succeeded in 1603 by the learned King James in whom, however, learning sank to the level of pedantry. He is said to have exhibited his fondness for Latin by his delight in teaching it to his favorites. His pedantry afforded opportunity for the use of diplomatic guile. Gondemar, the Spanish ambassador, it is said, made a practice of speaking false Latin, in order to give the King the pleasure of correcting him. The glories of this reign are ironically praised in the *Dunciad*:

> Oh (cried the goddess) for some pedant reign!
> Some gentle James to bless the land again;
> To stick the doctor's chair into the throne,
> Give law to words, or war with words alone,
> Senates and courts with Greek and Latin rule,
> And turn the council to a grammar school. . . .

In the grammar-school instruction of the period knowledge of grammar continued to be gained from the study of the Latin grammar of William Lily, the "Royal Grammar" as it came to be called. This famous book, which adopted from Quintilian the definition *Grammatica est recte scribendi et loquendi ars,* continued throughout the century the principal guide book in the art of writing and speaking English. It was translated into English in 1641 and near the end of the century, in 1695, in order to make it more

[10] F. Watson, *The Beginnings of the Teaching of Modern Subjects in English*, p. 12.

available in the teaching of English, which at that time had at last·come to be recognized as a main purpose in education, it was reissued with the title, *Royal Grammar reformed into a more easie method, for the better understanding of the English, and more speedy attainment of the Latin tongue.*

In Latin studies were grounded the styles of the most famous writers. The study of Latin authors and the collection of noble passages in *florilegia* continued, as in the sixteenth century, to provide pattern and material, and the analysis of Latin sentences provided a knowledge of syntactical relations and of the mechanical structure of the sentence. A later writer, Margaret Cavendish, Duchess of Newcastle, enviously remarks:

> The Latin phrases I could never tell,
> Ben Jonson could, which makes him write so well.

In the cultivated eloquence of the great Latin writers are to be found the patterns for the rhythms and cadences and for the stately periods so much to be admired in such seventeenth-century writers as Burton and Taylor and Browne and Milton. Remarkable testimony regarding the dependence of English writers on classical patterns is offered by Dryden in the preface to his *Troilus and Cressida.* Speaking of his occasional perplexities regarding English syntax, Dryden says that "I have [at times] no other way to clear my doubts but by translating my English into Latin, and thereby trying what sense my words will bear in a more stable language." [11]

The lack of more specific guidance in the use of the native English was widely felt. Joshua Sylvester in his translation of *Du Bartas his Divine Week* (1606) laments that:

[11] Otto Jespersen, *Growth and Structure of the English Language,* p. 128.

> Our language hath no law but use; and still
> Runs blinde, unbridled at the vulgars will.

So irregular was the English spelling that many writers in the early seventeenth century gave up in despair. Middleton, the playwright, in the "Address to the Reader" prefatory to his *Father Hubbards Tale* (1604), says: "I never wished this book better fortune than to fall into the hands of a true-spelling printer and an honest-minded bookseller," and Humphrey King in the Preface to his *Halfe Penny-worth of Wit* (1613) says of himself: "I am a very bad writer of orthography, and can scarce spell my a, b, c, i, e, if it were laid before me. The printer may helpe me to deliver to you true English; but as I am a true man to my God and my King, he finds it not in my coppy." [12]

Throughout the first half of the seventeenth century grammarians continue to deplore the lack of regularity in English. Charles Butler in his *English Grammar,* published in 1634, after extravagant praise of the "Excellenci of our Moother-tung," asserts that what is lacking is "a tru' and constant writing ther' of." Simeon Daines, in his *Orthoepia Anglicana,* published in 1640, speaks of "divers, otherwise great Schollers, who so much vary in their manner of speaking and writing English, for want of one uniforme and certaine method." In the commendatory verses prefixed to this volume of Daines appear statements similar in their purport. M. Timperley, Esquire, asserts that:

> England has had so many tongues as men,
> And every one his way of speaking, and
> Thus many spake, that could not understand.

A second set of verses by T. B. Esquire is in similar strain:

> How many have I heard chat French as fast
> As Parrats! that, being put to write in hast

---

[12] Spelling in part modernized.

An English Letter, would perhaps incline
To make an act to pardon for each line
A solecisme!   And this chiefly is
Because for practice they instructions misse.

The tardiness in providing a remedy for the obvious defects in the vernacular language is remarkable.   The explanation is of course to be found in the concentration of
interest in the assimilation of the classical learning that
inspired the Renaissance.   The ideas and the new words
provided by classical learning were appropriated, but little
thought was given to applying its methods of grammatical
study to the cultivation of the native tongue.   In the sixteenth century, however, a beginning had been made.   The
country to take the lead in this respect was Italy.   France,
however, was not far behind and the second half of the
sixteenth century saw great achievement in the effort to
bring French up to the level of Latin as a language of
learning.   These efforts of the sixteenth-century French
grammarians, preceding, as they did, similar efforts in
England and offering, as they did, suggestion to English
grammarians, deserve attention in the study of the English
language.

In 1559 Jean Bodin, a French jurist, proclaimed the
opinion, novel for the time, that an enormous gain in labor
and in time would be achieved by the use of the mother
tongue in learning.   One should be trained, he held, to
speak and write in French as in Greek and in Latin.   What
was needed in French, it was felt, was rules for good speech,
"la loi de bien parler."   To supply this need grammars
were composed by Meigret (1550), Estienne (1557), Ramus
(1562), and others.   In the search for the law of good
speech both Meigret and Ramus were guided by principles
somewhat conflicting.   Meigret, writing in 1550, cites the
precept learned from classical writers, that "il n'y a point

d'autre regle du language que l'usage." In his treatises on logic, however, he holds that usage must be "joint a la rezon." Anything without order and logic, "c'est l'abus." Ramus follows Meigret in basing his laws of syntax on usage. In the edition of 1572 he indicates where usage is to be learned. "According to the judgment of Plato, Aristotle, Varro, Cicero," he says, "the people is sovereign lord in language—one owes recognition to no other master." He is even more explicit. He says that good French is to be learned, not from teachers of Hebrew, Greek, or Latin, but "au Louvre, au Palais, aux Halles, en Greue, a la place Maubert." In his first edition (1562) Ramus objected to the expression *c'est moi*. In a later edition, however, published in 1572, he reverses his judgment. "To rob our language of such expressions," he says, "would be like drawing the sword alone against all France." A conflict in principles is apparent. There was a desire for classical regularity and uniformity; there was the characteristic French love of logic and order, but there was also a recognition of the soundness of the classical precept that language is governed by natural usage. The situation reached may be summarized in the words of Brunot, the modern historian of the French language: "One had not yet arrived at a feeling for an inviolable rule governing the writer, but one had the feeling for a rule exterior to oneself, which on occasion one might violate, but which in general one must obey."

The movement begun in Italy and taken up by France, in turn was taken up by England though more tardily. Learning to read in horn-book and Abecedarie and primer had been associated with religious instruction and, since Latin was the language in church use, it was natural that learning to read Latin should come early. It was a question whether to learn to read English or Latin first. With the Reformation came a change. The English language was introduced in church services. That the change was felt to be a distinct novelty appears from the Diary of Henry Machyn, the London merchant. Among the entries in this diary for the year 1561 mention is made of "xxx chylderyn syngyng the Pater Noster in Englys" and in another place of the "prestes . . . syngyng the Englys prossessyon." The use of English in sixteenth-century religious services seems to have created a sensation of novelty like that produced in the twentieth century by the use of English in grand opera. The effect on the English language was soon appreciable. Richard Mulcaster in his *Positions* [13] writing concerning the effects of the Reformation, remarks that "while our religion was restrained to Latin, it was either the onely, or the onelyest principle in learning to learne to read Latin:— But now that we are returned home to our English a, b, c, e, as most natural to our soil, and most propter [*sic*] to our faith . . . we are to be directed . . . to read that first, which we speake first. . . ."

Under such conditions the English language had been restored to its natural place of prime importance among the subjects for elementary instruction. There remained, however, the neglected task of regulating its forms and establishing logic and order in its constructions, of doing what had been attempted for French, that is to say, applying to it the rules of grammar.

In accomplishing this task there were encountered the same conflicting opinions that the French grammarians had tried to reconcile. There was conflict between the authority of natural usage with all its irregularities and inconsistencies and that of logic and of conformity to the standards provided by the cultivated classical languages, in other words between native idiom and artificial rule.

[13] Chap. 5.

On the part of the proletariat there was resistance to discipline in language as to other forms of discipline. Shakespeare in facetious vein sets forth the views of the proletariat in the words of the rebel leader Jack Cade. Lord Say has been taken prisoner by the rebels, and Jack Cade, in his arraignment of the prisoner, brings against him the heavy charge: "Thou hast most traitorously corrupted the youth of the realm, in erecting a grammar-school: and whereas, before, our forefathers had no other books but the score and the tally, thou hast caused printing to be used; and, contrary to the king, his crown, and dignity, thou hast built a paper mill. It will be proved to thy face, that thou hast men about thee, that talk of a noun, and a verb; and such abominable words, as no Christian ear can endure to hear."

But the grammarless tongue had defenders higher in station, sounder in judgment than Jack Cade. Some will say, remarks Sir Philip Sidney, that the language "wanteth grammar." "Nay truly," he continues, "it hath that praise that it wanteth not grammar. For grammar it might have, but it needs it not; being so easy in itself, and so void of those cumbersome differences of cases, genders, moods, and tenses, which I think, was a piece of the Tower of Babylon's curse, that he should be put to school to learn his mother tongue." [14] Good English Sidney found in cultivated courtly use. He professed to find "in divers small-learned courtiers a more sound style than in some professors of learning."

Of the same way of thinking with Sidney was his learned friend Gabriel Harvey. "We are not to goe a little farther—," says Harvey, "then we are licensed and authorised by the ordinarie vse and custome, and proprietie, and Idiome, and, as it were, Maiestie of our speach; which I

[14] Modernized spelling.

accounte the only infallible and soueraine Rule of all Rules."

There was, however, another view of the matter. Arthur Golding, in verses prefixed to Baret's *Alvearie* (1573), expresses a hope for a "sound Orthographye set out by learning and aduysed skill." Without it he fears that "blynd and cankered custome" will "wilfully maynteyne his former errors." [15] The revolt, here expressed, from custom as the sole source of authority in language found an active promoter in the person of Richard Mulcaster. In agreement with Sidney, Mulcaster holds that the English tongue "semeth euen now to be at the best for substance, and the brauest for circumstance, and whatsoeuer shall becom of the English state, the English tung cannot proue fairer then it is at this daie. . . ." But in disagreement with Sidney, Mulcaster believes in "the fining of our own English tung" by the study of grammar, which, he holds, will serve to "reduce our English tung to som certain rule, for writing and reading, for words and speaking, for sentence and ornament, that men maie know, when theie write or speak right." The clash in opinion is sharp. On the one hand Sidney, the courtier, believes that the best English is to be learned only from the practice of cultivated society; on the other hand, Mulcaster, the schoolmaster, advocates the plan, as yet novel, of applying grammar to the mother tongue in determining how to "write or speak right."

The conflicting opinions have never been completely reconciled. Indeed to our own time persists the controversy between the supporters of native idiom as the supreme authority and the supporters of the authority of formal grammar. In the sixteenth century, however, the irregularities in English were manifestly in need of control. A new attitude toward the native language finds expression

[15] Moore, *op. cit.*, p. 97.

in the phrase "the King's English," first applied by Wilson in his *Rhetorique*. The phrase "Mother Tongue" implied a product of nature; the phrase "the King's English" implied something subject to government. The King's English required government, and government was administered through the schoolmaster.

Hence the importance of Richard Mulcaster, a man whose name deserves prominence in the history of the English language. Mulcaster was a prominent figure in his time. Trained in part at King's College, Cambridge, which he left in 1555, he seems to have absorbed much of the sound doctrine of Sir John Cheke and may be regarded as one of the channels through which the influence of that remarkable man came to bear on the life of his time. The life work of Mulcaster was that of education. He was for twenty-five years headmaster at the famous Merchant Taylor's school and later served as surmaster and headmaster at St. Paul's School for an additional twelve years. Of commanding nature, harsh in personal methods of instruction, not without pedantry, he has been thought by some to be the original of Shakespeare's famous pedant, Holofernes. But Mulcaster was far more than a pedant. In a first book, his *Positions*, published in 1581, he set forth certain sound principles of education, emphasizing notably the importance of physical training in relation to mental development. The nature of his second work, published in 1582, is indicated by its title, *The First Part of the Elementarie which Entreateth Chefelie of the right writing of our English tung*. In this work Mulcaster sets forth his ideas regarding the neglected early stages in education, the stages preliminary to the grammar school with its study of Latin. This "elementarie" education occupied the years up to the age of twelve and included five subjects, reading, writing, drawing, singing, and playing. The "pettee schole

of spelling and writinge Englishe" licensed to Butter in
1580 seems to represent the humble kind of institution that
was devoted to this elementary instruction. This stage in
education, in the opinion of Mulcaster, should have the
services of the best-trained and the best-paid teachers. One
should not fail to notice the independence shown by a headmaster successively in two of the most famous Latin schools
of the period in thus elevating the part of education dealing
with training in English to the rank of first importance.

In his discussion of the art of writing, Mulcaster champions the cause of the English tongue. "For our naturall
tung being as beneficiall vnto vs for our nedefull deliuerie,
as anie other is to the peple which vse it; . . . and being
readie to yeild to anie rule of Art, as anie other is; why
should I not take som pains, to find out the right writing
of ours, as other cuntrimen haue don . . . ? & so much the
rather, bycause it is pretended, that the writing thereof is
meruellous vncertain, . . . I mean therefor so to deall in
it, as I maie wipe awaie that opinion of either vncertaintie
for confusion, or impossibilitie for direction, that both the
naturall English maie haue wherein to rest, and the desirous
stranger maie haue whereby to learn."

Unlike Sir John Cheke, he is not rigidly opposed to the
use of foreign words. "For mine own words," he says, "and
the terms, that I vse, theie be generallie English. And if
anie be either an incorporate stranger, or quite coind anew,
I haue shaped it as fit for the place, where I vse it, as my
cunning will giue me."   Indeed a whole section of his work
is devoted to borrowed words treated under the heading
"Enfranchisement" which "directeth the right writing of all
incorporat foren words."

In general, however, he holds the English language to be
self-sufficing. Chapter XII of his work bears the heading,
"That the English tung hath in it self sufficient matter to

work her own artificiall direction, for the right writing thereof." He defends the language in use from those who "rate at custom as a vile corrupter," and holds that writing should be under the "regiment," or rule, of "sound, reason and custom ionytlie togither." Among the seven "precepts" to be followed he gives a prominent place to "prerogatiue," and this he defines as the "secret mystery, or rather quickening spirit that dwells in every spoken tongue." The modern equivalent would be 'genius of the language.' "This prerogative," he says, "and liberty which the nation has, to use both speech and pen at will, is the cause why English writers are finer now than they were some hundred years ago." Obviously the genius of the language should be the guiding force.

That learning penmanship in Mulcaster's time was not easy of achievement, we must infer from his directions from which we learn that two modes of writing had to be learned at the same time. The double system of writing taught in sixteenth-century English schools, the Roman and the English or 'black letter,' was like the double system imposed on the German pupil of today. Mulcaster expounds the "ortografie" for "both the English and the latin letter." "I ioyn the latin letter with the English," he says, "because the time to learn the latin tung is next in order after the Elementarie, and the childes hand is then to be acquainted with the latin character, which is nothing so combersom as the English character is, if it be not far from easie."

The eminence of Mulcaster in the school life of his time, as well as the weight of his style and the solidity of his reasoning, served to win attention for his ideas. But in his opinions he by no means stood alone. Rather he seems to have been spokesman for ideas already becoming prevalent. In any event there were others who were active in promoting the same cause. A name worthy of memory is that of William Bullokar, who has already been mentioned as the author of a *Booke at large for the Amendment of Orthographie for English speech* (1580). In this work Bullokar was less conservative than Mulcaster, the practical schoolmaster. Like John Hart and Sir Thomas Smith before him, instead of basing his system of spelling on custom, as Mulcaster did, he devised an artificial system of representing English sounds by means of thirty-seven letters, and his radical scheme, like the two others of its kind before and like the many similar schemes in succeeding centuries, exercised little influence on actual practice. But Bullokar also claims our attention as the author of a *Bref grammar for English* published in 1586. This work is small in size, consisting of only sixty-eight pages. But in an autograph note by the author in one of the surviving copies appears the interesting entry, "the first grammar for Englishe that euer waz, except my grammar at large" [apparently referring to his earlier work on Orthographie]. The author's ambitious designs for regulating the language appear in his preface in verse, in which he promises, as a third work, a dictionary of the English language.

In the following decade appeared several works aiming to promote the cause of regularity in English. One of the most interesting of these was the book published in 1594 by a writer who gives only his initials P. Gr. This work is in Latin and bears the Latin title *Grammatica Anglicana* with the sub-title, *praicipue quatenus à Latina Differt, ad vnicam* P. Rami *methodum concinnata.* The author evidently is endeavoring to apply to English the methods of the French educator and grammarian Ramus. That the book is composed in Latin indicates that it was not intended for elementary instruction. But most striking is the evident aim to measure the English language by Latin

standards. The author aims to assign English constructions to their places in the scheme provided by Latin grammar. In this respect the author anticipates the classicizing
tendencies of the following century and offers what is perhaps the first instance of the type of English grammar to
which has been applied the suggestive epithet 'make-believe
grammar.'

Underlying this work is a keen sense of the faults of
English in current use. The author extols the literary
achievements of his contemporaries, "by whose labors the
language has been so polished that nothing could be added
to the felicity of expression." "And yet," he continues,
"scarcely one in thousands has used as much purity in
language, as all have used eloquence and rhetorical skill."
He speaks of "numerous Englishmen who in other languages write with entire accuracy but in their native language are disgracefully irregular." As specific instances of
deviation from regularity, he cites the expressions, *more
better, such works was finished, He spake to shee whose
fountaines is dried up*. He adds the comment that it is
"little to be wondered at if common people speak in a
manner entirely barbarous when the learned write with
such impurity."

But works of a more elementary and more practical type
began to make their appearance. In 1590 appeared an
English Accidence by J. Stockwood and in 1596 appeared
a work which continued in service for nearly a century, *The
English Schoolmaster* by Edmund Coote. The author of
this book was a practical teacher, "Master of the Freeschoole in Bury St. Edmond." His aim was to teach "all
his schollers, of what age soeuer, the most easie, short,
and perfect order of distinct Reading, and true Writing
our English-Tongue." That the "true writing" was not
yet governed by a definite standard may be learned from

his preface in which he informs the reader: "Also where I vndertake to make thee to write the true Orthography of any word truely pronounced, I must meane it of those words whose writing is determined; for there are many, wherein the best English men in this land are not agreed, as some with *malicious* deriving it from malice, others write *malitious*, as from the Latin *malitiosus*. So some with *German* from the Latin, some with *Germaine* from the French . . ." That this work of a practical schoolmaster was a powerful influence appears from the number of successive reissues in the following century, thirty-three editions before 1665 and forty-two editions before 1684.[16]

"To be a well-favored man is the gift of fortune," says Dogberry, "but to write and read comes by nature." This distorted remark, whatever it may have meant to the speaker, ceases to apply to the English of the seventeenth century. The schoolmaster had definitely made his appearance on the scene of English studies and henceforth was to exert an increasing influence. For the time being, however, his influence was limited to the elementary schools. Down to 1660 there is no evidence that the study of English had any place in the curriculum of the grammar schools.

The influence, however, of grammar-school Latin training reached the English language. Not only were English writers dominated by a sense of Latin form, but works were composed in which the methods of Latin instruction were applied to the study of English.

This mode of procedure had been approved by Mulcaster who, speaking of Latin learning, says: "Doth it not I praie you shew vs Englishmen a verie great pleasur, if it help to the fining of our own English tung, & thereby to make it to be of such account, as other tungs be, which be therefor of best account, bycause they be so fined? whereby we our

16 J. Vodoz, *An Essay on the Prose of John Milton.*

selues also shall seme not to be barbarous—." P. Gr., the author of the *Grammatica Anglicana* (1594), adopts the method, applying Latin learning in the teaching of "whatever is needed for the understanding of English." The method is continued in the book published by Io. Hewes in 1624, the nature of which is indicated by its title, *A Perfect Survey of the English Tongue Taken according to the Use and Analogie of the Latine.*

Confined as it was to the elementary schools, the training in English was of an elementary kind, and the writers composing books for English study confined their attention to the first stages in grammar, to the spelling and pronunciation. Charles Butler in his *English Grammar* (1633) says that in the mother tongue "there wanteth nothing to perfection, but that which in the learned languages, as a special grace and ornament, is precisely observed," that is to say, "a true and constant writing thereof." This defect he aims to remove and thus bring English up to the level of the classical languages, and for this purpose devises a new system of English spelling. In like manner Simeon Daines in his *Orthoepia Anglicana* (1640) deplores the English neglect of the mother tongue, and speaks of "otherwise great schollers, who so much vary in their manner of speaking and writing English, for want of one uniforme and certaine method." Daines, therefore, in his book devoted to training in English, takes up the subjects of pronunciation and spelling, subjects which he claims to have "reduced to a classical method."

The effort of writers such as Butler and Daines was to bring to a "classicall method" those features of English for which Latin grammar afforded no guidance, namely the spelling and the pronunciation. The influence of this "classicall method" survives to this day in the terminology of English grammar. It has recently been pointed out that the designation of the personal pronouns as first, second, and third persons rests on the typical Latin and Greek order, *I* and *you* and *he,* where the English order would be *you* and *he* and *I.* To English grammatical error still clings the name *solecism* used in Latin teaching, which has outlived the more popular school expression, 'breaking Priscian's head.'

Instruction in these elementary features of English was provided in several other books produced by schoolmasters during the first half of the seventeenth century. Of these one of the most important was the *Logonomia Anglica* by Alexander Gill, successor to Mulcaster as headmaster at St. Paul's. This work has an interest because its author was the teacher of Milton. It also is the source of much information concerning the pronunciation of the time, particularly of prevalent modes of pronunciation disapproved of by Gill, for which he coined the picturesque epithet *fictitiæ Mopsarum.* It is highly significant regarding the lack of culture among the women of the period that, among the Mopsas whose pronunciation he scorns, are included the mothers of the boys at St. Paul's.

Significant of the importance that had come to be attached to the idea of "bringing the language into Arte" (the expression is Gabriel Harvey's) was an English *Grammar* composed by no less a person than Ben Jonson. The commanding influence of the author in his own age makes his work one of importance. It was not published until 1640, three years after Jonson's death. As a sub-title appears the comment, "Made by Ben Jonson for the benefit of all strangers out of his observation of the English Language now spoken and in use." There appears a natural hesitation on Jonson's part, perhaps a sense of presumption, in venturing to teach the English tongue to Englishmen. One must recall the opinion of Sidney. In defense of his work Jonson sets forth the benefits to be derived. "We free our language from the opinion ['reputation'] of rudeness and barbarism, wherewith it is mistaken to be diseased: we show the copy ['richness'] of it, and matchableness with other tongues; we ripen the wits of our own children and youth sooner by it, and advance their knowledge." The ideas advanced, it will be noticed, are the ones already urged by Mulcaster.

For the motto on his title page Jonson adopts from Quintilian the oft-quoted dictum of which an English translation, provided elsewhere by Jonson, is: "Custome is the most certaine Mistress of Language, as the publicke stampe makes the current money." Upon English custom Jonson bases his work, the material for which he professes to derive "out of his observation of the English language now spoken and in use." One should recall the opinion of Jonson, already quoted, in agreement with Sidney, about where the best English was to be learned.

The influence of classical learning, however, is everywhere apparent. The material drawn from his own observation Jonson casts in forms provided by Latin grammar, and the opinions advanced are supported by principles quoted from classical authorities, Varro, Cicero, and Quintilian, and from Renaissance expounders of classical doctrine, such as Scaliger, Ramus, and Sir Thomas Smith.

Jonson's work is to be regarded as a symptom of the new attitude toward the mother tongue rather than as one of the great forces in shaping it. There is little evidence of its influence. Certainly it was not adopted in grammar-school use. Nor did any work of this nature find adoption in general use. As late as 1685 Charles Cooper in his *Grammatica Linguæ Anglicanæ* speaks of the difficulty in learning English due to the lack of any generally adopted English grammar.

The growing sense of the need of correctness in the writing of English not only called forth the earliest grammars for English, but led to revisions in the language of English books when issued in new editions. Changes made in the 1601 edition of Berners' *Huon of Bordeaux* have already been cited. Changes similar in nature may be observed in successive editions of the plays of Shakespeare. In 1600 was published a Quarto edition of *Much Ado about Nothing* supposedly based on the prompt book of the actors and therefore authentic. In the First Folio edition of 1623 appear changes in language which seem to represent the current striving after correctness.

QUARTO EDITION (1600)	FOLIO EDITION (1623)
ere a be cured	ere he be cured
what a will say	what he will say
pleases	pleaseth
brings	bringeth
she has bin	hath beene
this vij yeare	yeares
ha tane	haue
not to be spoke of	spoken
whose wrongs doe sute	doth
all things sorts	sort

In the Folio edition of *Hamlet* appear changes of another kind, in the weakening of the oaths in the earlier quartos.[17]

QUARTO EDITIONS	FOLIO I
God (I, ii, 150; II, i, 76)	Heauen
Gods	Heauens
By heauen	It seemes
s'wounds	Why
s'bloud	Why
God a mercy	Gramercy
O God	you Gods
s'wounds	come

[17] B. A. P. Van Dam, *The Text of Hamlet*, 1924.

As the seventeenth century advances, the movement toward regularity in language accelerates. An examination of the four Folio editions of Shakespeare published in 1623, 1632, 1664, and 1685 will afford an exhibition of the stages through which in the course of the century the language is brought more and more to mechanical regularity. Already in the revisions made in the Second Folio, the influence of the regularizing tendency appears.[18] In the text of *Hamlet,* for example, besides general changes in spelling and occasional changes in words, there appear grammatical changes in the interests of conformity to rule such as:

Folio I		Folio II
I, iv.	Reuisits thus	Revisitst thus
II, i.	Betweene who?	Betweene whom
III, ii.	more richer	more rich
III, iv.	To who do you speake this?	To whom . . . ?
V, i.	nine yeare	nine yeares
V, i.	Whose phrase of sorrow coniure the wandring starres	Conjures the wandring starres

Similar revised forms in *The Tempest* are:

Folio I		Folios II, III, and IV
I, ii, 439.	more brauer	braver
III, iii, 2.	My old bones akes	ake

The progress made in the seventeenth century toward the modern method of spelling is particularly well illustrated in these successive Folio editions of Shakespeare. In Folio II appear many changes in the spelled forms of words. The most striking of these changes, perhaps, and

18 C. A. Smith, *The Chief Difference between the First and Second Folios of Shakespeare, Englische Studien,* xxx.

Mef. Cæfar I bring thee word,
Menacrates and *Menas* famous Pyrates
Makes the Sea ferue them, which they eare and wound
With keeles of euery kinde. Many hot inrodes
They make in Italy, the Borders Maritime
Lacke blood to thinke on't, and flufh youth reuolt,
No Veffell can peepe forth : but 'tis as foone
Taken as feene : for *Pompeyes* name ftrikes more
Then could his Warre refifted.

   Cæfar. *Anthony*,
Leaue thy lafciuious Vaffailes. When thou once
Was beaten from *Medena*, where thou flew'ft
Hirfius, and *Paufa* Confuls, at thy heele
Did Famine follow, whom thou fought'ft againft,
(Though daintily brought vp) with patience more
Then Sauages could fuffer. Thou did'ft drinke
The ftale of Horfes, and the gilded Puddle
Which Beafts would cough at. Thy pallat thé did daine
The rougheft Berry, on the rudeft Hedge.
Yea, like the Stagge, when Snow the Pafture fheets,
The barkes of Trees thou brows'd. On the Alpes,
It is reported thou did'ft eate ftrange flefh,
Which fome did dye to looke on : And all this
(It wounds thine Honor that I fpeake it now)
Was borne fo like a Soldiour, that thy cheeke
So much as lank'd not.

   Lep. 'Tis pitty of him.

   Cæf. Let his fhames quickely
Driue him to Rome, 'tis time we twaine
Did fhew our felues i'th'Field, and to that end
Affemble me immediate counfell, *Pompey*
Thriues in our Idlenefe.

   Lep. To morrow *Cæfar*,
I fhall be furnifht to informe you rightly
Both what by Sea and Land I can be able
To front this prefent time.

Antony and Cleopatra, Act I, Scene iv: First Folio (1623).

Mef. *Cæfar* I bring thee word,
Menacrates and *Menas* famous Pyrates
Makes the Sea ferve them, which they eare and wound
With keeles of every kind. Many hot inrodes
They make in Italy, the borders Maritime
Lacke blood to thinke on't, and flefh youth revolt,
No Veffell can peepe forth, hut tis as foone
Taken as feene : for *Pompeyes* name ftrikes more
Then could his Warre refifted.

   Cæfar. *Anthony*,
Leave thy lafcivious Vaffailes. When thou once
Wert beaten from *Medena*, where thou flewft
Hirfius, and *Panfa* Confuls, at thy heele
Did famine follow, whom thou foughtft againft,
(Though daintily brought up) with patience more
Then Savages could fuffer. Thou didft drinke
The ftale of horfes, and the gilded Puddle
Which Beafts would coughat. Thy pallat then did daine
The rougheft Berry, on the rudeft Hedge.
Yea, like the Stagge, when Snow the Pafture fheets,
The barkes of Trees thou browfedft. On the Alpes,
It is reported thou didft eate ftrange flefh,
Which fome did dye to looke on. And all this
(It wounds thine honor that I fpeake it now)
Was borne folike a Souldiour, that thy cheeke
So much as lank'd not.

   Lep. Tis pitty of him.

   Cæf. Let his fhames quickely,
Drive him to Rome, tis time we twaine
Did fhew our felves ith Field, and to that end
Affemble we immediate counfell, *Pompey*
Thrives in our Idleneffe.

   Lep. To morrow *Cæfar*,
I fhall be furnifht to informe you rightly
Both what by Sea and Land I can be able
To front this prefent time.

Antony and Cleopatra, Act I, Scene iv: Second Folio (1632).

Mef. Cæsar I bring thee word,
Menacrates and *Menas*, famous Pyrates
Makes the Sea ferve them, which they ear and wound
With kneels of every kind. Many hot inrodes
They make in *Italy*, the borders Maritime
Lack bloud to think on't, and flefh youth to revolt,
No Veffel can peep forth, but 'tis as foon
Taken as feen: for *Pompeyes* name ftrikes more
Then could his War refifted.
   Cæfar. Anthony.
Leave thy lafcivious Vaffails. When thou once
Wert beaten from *Medena*, where thou flew'ft
   Hirfius, and *Panfa* Confuls, at thy heel
Did famine follow, whom thou faught'ft againft,
(Though daintily brought up) with patience more
Then Savages could fuffer. Thou didft drink
The ftale of horfes, and the gilded Puddle
Which Beafts would cough at. Thy pallat then did dain
The rougheft Berry, on the rudeft Hedge.
Yea, like the Stag, when Snow the Pafture fheets,
The barks of trees thou browfed'ft. On the Alpes,
It is repoted thou did'ft eat ftrange flefh,
Which fome did die to look on: and all this
(It wounds thine honor that I fpeak it now)
Was born fo like a Souldier, that thy cheek
So much as lank'd not.
   Lep. 'Tis pitty of him.
   Cæf. Let his fhames quickly
Drive him to *Rome*, 'tis time we twain
Did fhew our felves ith' Field, and to that end
Affemble we immediately councel, *Pompey*
Thrives in our Idleneffe.
   Lep. To morrow *Cæfar*,
I fhall be furnifh'd to informe you rightly
Both what by Sea and Land I can be able
To front this prefent time.

Antony and Cleopatra, Act I, Scene iv: Third Folio (1664).

239

Mes. Cæsar, I bring thee word,
Menecrates and *Menas*, famous Pyrates,
Make the Sea ferve them, which they ear and wound
VVith knells of every kind. Many hot inrodes
They make in *Italy*, the borders Maritime
Lack bloud to think on't, and flefh youth to revolt,
No Veffel can peep forth, but 'tis as foon
Taken as feen: for *Pompeyes* name ftrikes more
Than could his VVar refifted.
 Cæfar. Anthony.
Leave thy lafcivious Vaffals.   VVhen thou once
VVert beaten from *Medena*, where thou flew'ft
Hirtius and *Panfa* Confuls, at thy heel
Did famine follow, whom thou fought'ft againft,
(Though daintily brought up) with patience more
Than Savages could fuffer. Thou didft drink
The ftale of horfes, and the gilded Puddle
VVhich Beafts would cough at. Thy pallat then did dain
The roughest Berry on the rudeft Hedge.
Yea, like the Stag, when Snow the Pafture fheets,
The barks of trees thou browfed'ft. On the Alps,
It is reported thou did'ft eat ftrange flefh,
VVhich fome did die to look on : and all this
(It wounds thine honour that I fpeak it now)
VVas born fo like a Souldiers, that thy cheek
So much as I lank'd not.
 Lep. 'Tis pitty of him.
 Cæf. Let his fhames quickly
Drive him to *Rome*, 'tis time we twain
Did fhew our felves ith'Field, and to that end
Affemble we immediatly councel, *Pompey*
Thrives in our Idlenefs.
 Lep. To morrow, *Cæfar*,
I fhall be furnifh'd to inform you rightly
Both what by Sea and Land I can be able
To front this prefent time.

  Antony and Cleopatra, Act I, Scene iv: Fourth Folio (1685).

certainly the most systematic is in the distinction at length made between *i* and *j,* and between *u* and *v.* In the First Folio will be observed the use of *v* at the beginning of words and *u* in the medial positions, of *j* in various positions, particularly as the last in a series of two or more *i's.* As early as 1559 Ramus had recommended the use of *j* and *v* as distinctive consonant signs in French, but not until about 1625 was the formal distinction between *i* and *u* as vowel signs and *j* and *v* as consonant signs regularly established in English use. In this connection may be pointed out the interesting phenomenon that the modern letter named double *u* is formed by combining two *v's.*

The spelling in the Third Folio, it will be observed, is much more modern in appearance than that in the second. The most striking point of difference is in the more regularized use of final -*e.* This ending throughout the sixteenth century and the first half of the seventeenth was used apparently without any governing law. Its use seems to have been determined largely by the needs of the printer in filling spaces in the line and to have little, if any, relation to pronunciation. By the middle of the seventeenth century its modern strange and peculiarly English use as a means of indicating the length of the vowel in the preceding syllable was reached. In the *New English Grammar* by J. Wharton, published in 1655, the third chapter bears the title, "Of e final, and the uses thereof," and the new method appears in use in the Third Folio.

The spelling in the Fourth Folio marks some advance. The most striking single feature to be noted is the use of the apostrophe in the possessive forms of nouns. The use of the apostrophe in earlier stages had been as a sign of elision in phrases such a *'t was* and *too 't* (for *to it*) and particularly in forms of verbs indicating the elision of the *e* in final syllables, as in *disclos'd.* Later in the seventeenth century it came to be associated with the possessive sign. This use appears in the Third Folio but is more consistently applied in the Fourth Folio. For instance, in *Julius Cæsar*, Act III, Folio III has *Enter Octavio's Servant, but Enter Mark Antony, with Cæsars body;* while Folio IV more consistently prints, *Enter Octavio's Servant* and *Enter Mark Antony with Cæsar's Body*.

The development of modern regular method appears in the case of the possessive form of the neuter personal pronoun. In earlier English the form *his* had served both for masculine and for neuter. This earlier use survives in the biblical phrase, *Every creature after his kind*. This form was later superseded in the neuter by *it*, indistinguishable from the nominative, which in turn yielded to the modern *its*. In *Hamlet*, Act I, modern use appears in the Third Folio, *It lifted up its head, and did addresse* where, in the First and Second Folios as well as in the Second Quarto, the form *it head* is used.

By the end of the century there had been reached a regular mode of forming the possessive, nearly but not quite identical with that in use today, and this mode was formulated into rule. In the *Nouvelle Methode pour apprendre l'Anglois*—an English grammar for French use, by Guy Miege, published in 1685, appear directions for forming the genitive singular of nouns, which translated into English are as follows: "Observe that here one adds an apostrophe and an *s;* the apostrophe here is not a mark of elision, but rather a number distinction—The apostrophe is superfluous in nouns whose plural does not end in *s*. The *s* is used in the singular even in nouns already ending in *s, e.g., S. James's*. But in the plural one elides the *s* as plural sign, *e.g., the two souldier's arms*."

It will be observed that the formation of grammatical rule is nearly contemporaneous with the formation of a new practice in printing. In the adoption of new forms, however, it is the printer, rather than the grammarian or the author, that is the innovator in most cases. The grammarian records rather than initiates in language. The grammarians who, like Smith and Hart and Bullokar in the sixteenth century, and Gill and Butler in the seventeenth century, tried to establish new modes of spelling, had little influence. Nor does the printed form represent the written form used by the author. Of this dominance of the printer convincing evidence may be found by comparing the spelling and punctuation in the first printed editions of Milton's poetry with the manuscript texts provided by the author. The accompanying facsimile page will afford illustration. The conclusion to be reached, therefore, is that the growing regularity in English spelling in the course of the seventeenth century had its origin in the printer's need of uniformity in method. The achievement of the printer was later consolidated and formulated into rule by the grammarian.

But with all the gain in regularity in the external form of the language, there persisted many of the forms of irregularity that are features of Shakespeare's language. Ben Jonson, it will be recalled, based his grammar on the observation of current usage. Among the irregular forms of speech recorded by him are double plural forms of nouns; *eyes* and *eyen, shooes* and *shooen,* and double comparatives and superlatives of adjectives such as *more readier* and *most basest.* These adjective forms he supports on the authority not only of English but of Greek usage. He lends his support likewise to certain deviations from grammatical concord between noun and verb. "Nouns signifying a multitude, though they be of the singular number, require a verb plural." On the other hand "the verb sometime agreeth not with the governing noun of the plural number—

as *Riches is a thing more hurtful. . . ."* The use of the
preposition at the end of the sentence finds support in the
citation, *direct them in the way they have to walk in.*

An impression of the irregularities persisting in the cultivated language of the seventeenth century may be gained
from an examination of the prose of Milton.[19] For the
neuter possessive Milton occasionally uses the newly developed form *its.* The preferred form with him, however,
is the older *his* identical with the masculine, *e.g.,* "That
other clause which we thought had died with *his* brother."
Milton does not use the apostrophe $+ s$ (*'s*) as the sign of
the possessive singular to distinguish it from the plural
sign. Like Ben Jonson he uses the apostrophe as a sign of
elision, rarely failing to indicate by this means the elision
of a weak vowel at the end of a word. In this respect his
practice is that of the earlier Shakespeare Folios and that
recorded in Ben Jonson's *Grammar.* The modern possessive form, which begins to appear in the Third Folio and is
regularly established in the Fourth Folio, owes its origin
to a mistaken theory that the *'s* ending originates in an
elision of the first part of *his,* that *prince's* was an elided
form of *prince his.* This idea appears in the *Grammar* of
Butler (1633), who explains the genitive ending *s* as a

---

[19] See Vodoz, *op. cit.*

How soon hath Time the suttle theef of youth,
    Stoln on his wing my three and twentith yeer!
    My hasting dayes flie on with full career,
    But my late spring no bud or blossom shew'th.
Perhaps my semblance might deceive the truth,
    That I to manhood am arriv'd so near,
    And inward ripenes doth much less appear,
    That som more timely-happy spirits indu'th.
Yet be it less or more, or soon or slow,
    It shall be still in strictest measure eev'n,
    To that same lot, however mean, or high,
Toward which Time leads me, and the will of Heav'n;
    All is, if I have grace to use it so,
    As ever in my great task Masters eye.

John Milton (1608-1674): manuscript of the sonnet, "On His Having Arrived at the Age of Twenty-three." The form in which it appeared in the first printed edition of 1645 is reproduced on the opposite page.

shortening of *his*. The theory was finally exploded by Samuel Johnson. Indeed the fallacy, as has been pointed out, was recognized by Miege (1685), who, however, formulates the rule for the use of the modern form.

Adverbs of manner are usually formed by Milton with the ending *-ly*. But the use of adverb forms without this suffix, "flat-adverbs," continued to be not infrequent, *e.g.*, "in a hand *scarce* legible," "I cannot set so *light* by," "he determines *plain* enough."

Among the uses of verbs a striking feature is the frequent use of *be* in affirmative statements, "These they *be* which——," "Many there *be* that——," "There *be* also books——."

In the use of *do* in negative statements, which seems to have had its origin in popular use and which was regularly established in cultivated use by the time of Pope, Milton follows the earlier practice, that prevalent in Shakespeare, of using the simple verb form. For instance, notice the following expressions from the *Areopagitica:* "I stay not"; "He flatters not"; "He who fears not"; "I know not." Occasional instances of the use of *do* occur: "I *did* not flatter"; "We *doe* not see"; but in general Milton, like his contemporaries, Herbert, Taylor, Hobbes, Bacon, and Browne, favors the earlier form of expression.

In the use of *shall* and *will, should* and *would,* it is interesting to notice that the modern distinction appears in the language of Milton. Indeed the earliest formulation of the modern rule governing this distinction appears in Milton's time in the Latin *Grammatica Linguæ Anglicanæ* by J. Wallis, the first edition of which appeared in 1653, and it is to be assumed that the rule here formulated is based, not on theory, but on observation of current use.

Among Elizabethan writers the original distinction between *ye* the nominative form and *you* the oblique case form had largely broken down. Alexander Gill, Milton's master, in his *Logonomia Anglica* (1619) had formulated a rule prescribing the use of *ye* and *you* in the nominative and vocative cases and of *you* alone in the accusative case. But the impotence of the grammarian and schoolmaster in controlling prevailing natural use here appears. With Milton, as with most of his contemporaries, much confusion prevails. For instance, in the *Areopagitica* appear frequently such forms of expression as *"Ye* must reform." But, less frequently, appear such irregular uses as, *"You* must then become . . ."* and "them that praise *yee* are known by *ye,"* "many who honour *yee,"* etc.

The absence of the control of formal grammar, however, appears most conspicuously in the relations between the subject and predicate of sentences. One should recall Ben Jonson's observations on this point. Quite in accord with Jonson's observations was the practice of contemporary writers. In Bacon's *Of True Greatness* one finds, "No nation which doth not directly professe armes, may looke to have greatness fall in *their* mouths." In Sir Thomas Browne one finds, "Whilst the mercies of God *doth* promise us heaven" and "Civill society *carrieth* out *their* dead and *hath* exequies." The usage of Milton is of the same kind. The grammatical number in pronoun or verb is determined by the number, plural or singular, of the idea rather than by the grammatical number of the subject. Thus Milton uses the plural verb after collective nouns, such as *clergy, nation, state,* etc. More striking is his use of a singular verb following a subject made up of two or more nouns connected by *and.* The use by Kipling of the singular form, *dies,* in the line, "The tumult and the shouting *dies,"* which has attracted much modern comment, finds parallel in the language of Milton. There may be cited not only the familiar lines:

> Bitter constraint and sad occasion dear
> Compels me to disturb your reason due,

but frequent instances of the same use in the prose such as: "Our faith and knowledge *thrives* by exercise"; "Zwinglius and Calvin *hath* beaconed up . . ."; "Where one mind and person *pleases* aptly"; "The Rabbins and Marmonides *tells* us"; "Both love and peace, both nature and religion *mourns* to be separated." Obviously the earlier Elizabethan freedom had not yet been reduced to formal grammatical regularity.[20]

If the state of spelling and pronunciation and syntax in the age immediately following the Elizabethan was confused, the state of the vocabulary was not less so. The flood of foreign words had by no means receded. The "hard words" which had proved so baffling to Dame Quickly and her kind in the sixteenth century still offered pitfalls for the unwary. In addition there was added to the English vocabulary a new stock of words in the form of 'terms of art' or technical terms. This subject must be reserved for discussion in a later chapter. Besides these classes of words there were to be reckoned with the "old words" of the kind revived by Spenser. A less prominent, but interesting class of words, was the set of "canting terms" originating in the underworld.

So variegated had become the language that John Selden (1584-1654) says it is "as if a man had a Cloak that he wore plain in Queen *Elizabeth's* days, and since, here has put in a piece of Red, and there a piece of Blew, and here a piece of Green, and there a piece of Orange-tawny. We borrow words from the *French, Italian, Latine,* as every Pedantick Man pleases." Thomas Blount, writing in 1656, speaks of the "foraign Words, providently brought home

---

[20] The illustrations of Milton's language have been derived from the monograph by Vodoz, already cited.

from the *Greek, Roman,* and *French Oratories,* which though in the untravel'd ears of our Fathers, would have sounded harsh, yet a few late years have rendered them familiar even to vulgar capacities." He refers to these words as appearing in the "learned Works of *Lord Bacon,* Mr. *Montague, Sir Kenelm Digby, Sir Henry Wotton,* Mr. *Selden,* Mr. *Sands,* Dr. *Brown,* Dr. *Charlton,* etc." Though he had "gained a considerable knowledge in the Latine and French tongues" and had "a smattering both of Greek and other Languages," Blount confesses that he is "often gravelled in English Books." [21]

In these days of uncertainty and doubt, counsel and guidance was afforded by classical precepts of moderation. Ben Jonson's adoption of Quintilian's dictum that "custome is the most certaine Mistresse of Language," has already been cited. To this aphorism, however, Jonson adds the warning, "But wee must not be too frequent with the mint, every day coyning. Nor fetch words from the extreme and utmost ages; since the chiefe vertue of style is perspicuitie, and nothing so vicious in it, as to need an Interpreter." He warns particularly against the use of archaic words in the manner of Spenser. In fact, throughout this period the condemnation of Chaucerisms of the kind sponsored by Spenser is usual. But excess in borrowing words was likewise held reprehensible. This form of excess is labelled in the Puttenham *Arte of Poesie* with the Greek name *Soraismus,* a name to which for the sake of sharper distinctness is added its etymological equivalent, the English word *mingle mangle,* a name applied originally to the contents of the hog trough. The objection to compound words formed of elements from different languages is expressed in similar crass fashion. The meaning veiled in the name *hybrid* is brought to a naked plainness by the use of an

[21] Moore, *op. cit.,* pp. 141-4.

English etymological equivalent, the name *mule-word* which Edward Phillips in his *New World of English Words* (1658) applies to the kind of words "propagated by a Latin Sire, and a Greek Dam." Not only were classical principles applied in the control of words, but the effect of classical criticism was reinforced by the use of plain English words in bringing its meaning into clear light.

The sounding of classical precept and the satirical exhibition of faults aided in forming taste, a taste needed in the selection of words at this period. But more practical guidance through the jungle of newfangled words, 'hard words' and 'terms of art,' was provided by means of English dictionaries that began to appear early in the seventeenth century. Two-language dictionaries had been in use during the fifteenth century and sixteenth century from the time of the *Promptuarium Parvulorum* (1440) on, lexicons with words usually arranged according to subject and evidently used as aids in the Latin studies of the grammar school. Important among these was the *Dictionary* made by Sir Thomas Elyot, which appeared in six successively enlarged editions. In this work the words were arranged in alphabetical order. This book also bore the name *Dictionary*, "the first work, so far as I know," says Sir James Murray, "to take this name in English." Later in the century appeared a number of two-language dictionaries, French and English, Spanish and English, Italian and English. These works, as has already been suggested, had a part in supplying new words for the use of English writers who deliberately aimed to enrich their native language.

Apparently not until the end of the sixteenth century was there felt a need for books to explain the meaning of words in the mother tongue. The appearance of such books follows closely the dawn of appreciation of the literary capacity of the native language. The first English dictionaries therefore follow close after the first English grammars. In fact at the end of the *Grammatica Anglicana* (1594) there appears a short list of about 120 English words with definitions consisting of a "Dictionariolum" of English words used with Latin meanings and a section containing "Vocabula Chauceriana." This work, it must be held in mind, is in Latin. More intended for the ordinary layman was the book published by the schoolmaster, Robert Cawdrey, in 1604, the purpose of which is indicated by its title, *A Table Alphabeticall, containing and teaching the true writing and vnderstanding of hard vsual English words borrowed from the Hebrew, Greeke, Latine, or French, &c.* —"gathered for the benefit of all vnskilfull persons, Whereby they may more easily and better vnderstand many hard English words . . ." This book of 120 pages contains about 3,000 of the new learned terms. Some of them have been quoted above in illustration of the conscious effort on the part of the learned, to hold English words derived from the Latin to their original Latin meanings. But the book includes also many of the archaic words such as Spenser strove to keep alive. For example under W appear such words as:

warish,	ease, deliuer
welde,	moue
walter,	wallow
wean,	refrain one from anything
wene,	thinke
wend,	goe
wote,	know
wonne,	dwell
wist,	knowne
wood,	madde
wreke,	revenge

This book affords an excellent idea of the perplexity that must have been felt by Englishmen of Shakespeare's time in making their choice of words from the unsifted vocabulary of the period in which older words came into competition with new.

Cawdrey's work was followed by one of like nature published by Dr. John Bullokar in 1616 with the title *An English Expositor*. This in turn was followed in 1623 by *The English Dictionarie* by H. C., Gent. (Henry Cockeram). The title, Gent., indicates that the lexicographer's task has passed from the hands of the schoolmaster. This work passed through many editions down to 1659. The arrangement of words is alphabetical, but the author makes use of an ingenious plan suited to the times and illustrating the distinction then existing between the learned and the vulgar vocabulary. "The first Booke," the author informs the reader, "hath the choicest words themselves now in vse, wherewith our language is inriched and become so copious, to which words the common sense is annexed." "The second Booke," on the other hand, "containes the vulgar words, which whensoeuer any desirous of a more curious explanation by a more refined and elegant speech shall looke into, he shall there receive the exact and ample word to expresse the same." [22]

Apparently superseding the work of Cockeram came the *Glossographia* published by Thomas Blount in 1656, a work which appeared in successive editions down to 1707. This work in turn was followed in 1658 by *The New World of English Words* by Edward Phillips, nephew of John Milton. A distinguishing feature of the book by Phillips is the guidance offered in the choice of words by means of a mark of disapproval set upon many words in order "that he that studies a natural and unaffected stile, may take notice of

[22] *Ibid., p.* 134.

them and beware of them. . . ." The sifting process is evidently under way.

One other dictionary of the seventeenth century may be mentioned, the *English Dictionary* published by E. Coles in 1676. This work which, the author boasts, contains "some thousands more than are in Mr. Blunts [*sic*] *Glossographia* or Mr. Philips [*sic*] *World of Words*," includes a respectable total of about 30,000 words. It explains terms of art, "the difficult terms that are used in Divinity, Husbandry, Physick, Phylosophy, Law, Navigation, Mathematicks, and other Arts and Sciences." It contains also "Many Thousands of Hard Words—more than are in any other English Dictionary or Expositor." It contains also "Canting Terms," words from the underworld, the prototypes of modern slang, of which earlier lists are to be found in the works of Greene and Harman composed in the sixteenth century. The use of such terms was a fashionable affectation on the part of some. To justify their inclusion in his dictionary, the author remarks: "Tis no disparagement to understand the Canting Terms. It may chance to save your throat from being cut, or (at least) your Pocket from being pickt."

It is worthy of note concerning these seventeenth-century dictionaries that they make no pretension to all-inclusiveness. The earliest dictionary aiming to include all the words of the language was that of Bailey which made its appearance in the following century, in 1721. The purpose of seventeenth-century dictionary makers was quite different. Their task was to aid in the assimilation of the flood of new words that had come into English use. A "Dictionary for the Explanation of Hard Words" is included by Addison, along with a "Spelling Book" and a number of fashionable romances, in the list he gives of the books composing the library of Leonora, "a lady of learning," and this seems to indicate the use made of these early English dictionaries. They could make no pretension to the authority held by modern dictionaries. But they aided in the use of the learned words and helped to fix their meanings. In the sifting of words, the abandonment of archaic words and the condemnation of new words, aspirants for a place in the language, they also had a share as has been pointed out in the case of the *New World of Words* by Edward Phillips.

Another feature worthy of remark in these seventeenth-century dictionaries is their relation to the culture of women. Both Cawdrey's and Bullokar's works are dedicated to women, and Cockeram proclaims the purpose of "Enabling as well Ladies and Gentlewomen . . . as also Strangers of any Nation to the vnderstanding of the more difficult Authors. . . ." A change appears in the attitude of Blount whose work is "chiefly intended for the more-knowing women and less-knowing men." He had evidently learned the secret of "what every woman knows." As Sir James Murray has pointed out, "all these references to the needs of women disappear from later editions and are wanting in dictionaries after 1660." In language as in behavior, both of which are governed by social conventions, feminine influence promotes cultivation. It is remarkable how soon men removed from feminine influence relapse into barbarism. Was the making of dictionaries, then, at first promoted by feminine preciosity following the days of Elizabeth? The general purposes proclaimed by the dictionary makers hardly support this explanation. A more likely explanation is to be found in the nature of education provided for women. "There is no gown nor garment," said Martin Luther, "that becomes a woman worse than when she will be wise." The opinion is that of a German, but a similar way of thinking prevailed in sixteenth-century England.

Woman was given the inferior place. Sir Thomas Wilson in his rhetoric, in discussing the subject of order, says that "Order is of two sorts, the one is when the worthier is preferred and set before. As a man is set before a woman." The same assumption of man's superior importance appears elsewhere in Wilson's book. In discussing faults in composition, he says: "Some will set the cart before the horse, as thus, My mother and my father are both at home, as though the good man of the house did weare no breches." Under the reign of Elizabeth there was a change in the position of women. There were still no schools provided for their instruction except of the most elementary kind. Under private instruction, however, not only the Queen, but many of the women of her court became paragons in natural wit and in learning. They provided inspiration for the poet; they provided financial patronage for literary endeavor of all kinds. Under Elizabeth's successor there was a return to the earlier order of things. King James called upon the Church to support him in a campaign to make women obey their husbands. When a "learned maid" who could write pure Latin and Greek and Hebrew was presented to him, his question was, "But can she spin?" [23]   There was an outcry against the pretensions of women who cropped their hair, wore men's beaver hats, and wore daggers at their hips. The slogan was that man wanted to "wear the breeches."

In such a social environment learning for women ceased to be fashionable. The instruction provided for them in schools was in feminine accomplishments. In a Girls' School at Hackney (1643) the principal subject in the curriculum was music, instrumental and vocal, along with which went dancing and "whatever curious works of the needle or otherwise can be named which females are wont to be

[23] V. Wilson, *Society Women in Shakespeare's Time.*

conversant in." [24] The language used by women naturally reflected the instruction, or lack of instruction, provided for them. Their mode of pronunciation, as has already been pointed out, was a subject for scorn on the part of the schoolmaster Gill expressed by his phrase, *fictitiæ Mopsarum*. In manner of speech they are classed by Gill with country-people and the uneducated people of the towns.

The manner of writing of women was of a kind with their pronunciation. It is Cicero that remarked that "women more easily keep the pure tradition." A traditional rather than a schooled form of language appears in the letters of women of the seventeenth century. Among the *Verney Letters* appears a letter from Mrs. Margaret Pulteney, an heiress whose hand was much sued for, who clothes her sentiments in expressions such as: "all ouer natewers is to apte to set ouer hartes on that which is worse for us; but I hope I shall neuer put my trust in unsartin richis."

Such language, we may assume, was fairly typical of the true mother tongue, the language of women. The irregularities were the traditional ones. They were of the kind observed in the Elizabethan period. This form of language, that of home life was, therefore, that current among men apart from the as yet comparatively small number who had received school training in English.

The vocal speech of the seventeenth century is no more to be heard, but in the letters written during the period may be observed the lack, so much deplored, of a method of 'true writing,' and in the irregular forms of spelling may be found definite indication of modes of pronunciation. From the *Verney Memoirs,* the *Correspondence of Dr. Basire,* and the *Wentworth Papers* which belong to the seventeenth and early eighteenth centuries, Professor Wyld has been

[24] Watson, *op. cit.,* p. xlviii.

able to create a remarkably clear impression of the language in current use in this period.[25]   In these personal letters appear spellings such as: *sartinly, sarvint, divartion,* and *larne* 'learn'; *byled* 'boiled' *implyment* and *gine* 'join'; *misfortin, venter* 'venture'; *futur* 'future'; *seein* 'seeing'; *comin* and *shillins; quater* 'quarter'; *father* 'farther'; and *dorset* 'Dorset'; *respeck* 'respect'; *nex* 'next', and *Wensday; stell* 'still'; *spertis* 'spirits'; *fefty* 'fifty'; etc.   The modes of pronunciation indicated are to be regarded, not as perversions of a standard speech, but as survivals by direct tradition of earlier modes of pronunciation.   Most of them survive here or there in dialectal use of modern times, and some of them, such as *Wensday* and *Crismus,* persist in modern cultivated use, in words whose sounds have not yielded to the influence of spelling.

Such evidence affords invaluable information regarding the main current of English speech, that in daily colloquial use, as yet only beginning to be controlled by confining rules.   But if the older traditions continued in everyday speech, there were beginning also to form traditions in the language of literature.   Traditions that were rapidly forming in modes of spelling and in indicating the possessive relation have already been pointed out.   Modes of writing thus brought into use were later given fixity through the influence of lexicographers in the following century.   The native tradition initiated by Chaucer, the well of English undefiled, which Spenser tried to revive, was for the time allowed to languish.   The dictum of Ben Jonson regarding Spenser's language expressed the sentiment which continued to prevail throughout the seventeenth century.

A stream of pure English tradition, however, came down through another channel, through the English Bible.   The edition of the King James Version, the Authorized Version

[25] H. C. Wyld, *A History of Modern Colloquial English.*

of 1611, aimed to avoid extremes—that of too great simplification of the kind favored by the Puritans on the one
hand, that of the obscurity cultivated by the Papists on
the other. A policy expressed in the Preface was that of
using "different English words to represent the same Greek
or Hebrew word, lest they should seem to wrong the
copious English tongue." [26] In the 1611 version, however,
survives much of the simplicity of language, much of the
racy quality that had been imparted by Tyndale and his
fellow translators of a century earlier. The Bible was one
of the principal sources of seventeenth-century culture.
Under the Puritan régime there were many statutes requiring its study or its public reading.[27] The richness of
the tradition thus provided appears from the fact that the
English Bible sufficed in itself to provide language material
and patterns for one of the masterpieces of English literature, the *Pilgrim's Progress,* which is a veritable mosaic of
biblical forms of expression. In fact the English Bible
has served to keep alive English words and to fix their
meanings, and it has provided language material and pattern
in word, in phrase, in rhythm, not only to Bunyan, but to
English writers and speakers of all subsequent time.

Other writings, however, were contributing to the formation of an English tradition in literary language. The attempt on the part of Abraham Fraunce in his *Arcadian
Rhetoric* to give permanency to the graces of Sidney's style
proved ineffectual because of the passing fashion for this
form of preciosity. But among the great writers of the
period there was forming a tradition that has remained
permanent. The cruder elements of the language were
wrought into polished forms which have been handed
down. Most notable, of course, is the case of Shakespeare

---

[26] Moore, *op. cit.,* p. 32.
[27] Watson, *op. cit.*

in whose words and phrases and images so many fugitive impressions have found a permanent habitation and a name.

The rapid formation of a literary tradition in this period was favored by the nature of the rhetorical training still in use. It should be held in mind that one of the five divisions of classical rhetoric was Memory. A well-stored memory provided the material for the copiousness of expression striven for. The ideal of individualism had not yet become all dominant. That Shakespeare's own memory was remarkably stocked is clear. Only recently has been exhibited the wealth of words and phrases and images assimilated by him from Ovid and from Montaigne. Shakespeare's plays were published in collective form in the Folio edition of 1623. The successive Folio editions and separate Quarto editions made his works readily accessible to the reader, and the forms of expression into which the cruder elements had been crystallized by his genius provide rich store for the memory of subsequent writers.

How English literary tradition was forming in this period has recently been shown by means of an impressive demonstration of Milton's debt to Shakespeare.[28] A few of the hundreds of passages in which parallelism appears, may be quoted here:

The grey eye'd *morn smiles* on the *frowning night*. (*R. and J.*, II, iii, 1)	When fair *morning* first *smiles* on the world. (*Paradise Lost*, V, 124)
	Dark, waste, and wild, under the *frown of night*. (*Ibid.*, III, 424)
Graves have *yawned* and yielded up their dead. (*Julius Cæsar*, II. ii, 18)	Sin and Death and *yawning grave*. (*Ibid.*, X, 635)

[28] A. Thaler, *Publications Modern Language Association*, XL, 645-91.

The dreadful *thunder* doth *rend* the region.	*Thunder* mixed with hail must *rend* the Egyptian sky.
(*Hamlet*, II, ii, 508)	(*Ibid.*, XII, 181)
Wicked dreams abuse The *curtain'd sleep*.	The litter of close-*curtained sleep*.
(*Macbeth*, II, i, 51)	(*Comus*, 554)
The most forward bud Is eaten by *the canker* ere it blow.	As killing as *the canker* to the rose.
(*Two Gent. of Verona* I, i, 45)	(*Lycidas*, 45)
I know *a bank* . . . Quite over-*canopi'd* with luscious woodbine. . . .	*A bank* With ivy *canopied* and interwove With flaunting honeysuckle.
(*Mid. N. Dream*, II, i, 249)	(*Comus*, 543-5)

The few examples here quoted do not adequately represent
the amount of parallelism that has been revealed as existing
between the earlier and the later poet of the seventeenth
century. They may suffice, however, to show the richness
of Milton's memory and his ability to turn to new service
this store of phrases and of images. More important for
the present purpose, they reveal the rapidity in the development
of a literary tradition distinctively English.

But, throughout the seventeenth century, classical sources
continued to supply an important element in the stream
of literary tradition that was forming. In the short sentence
units that serve in the sententious style of Thomas Fuller
will be found tricks of expression of the kind classified and
labelled in the classical Latin works on rhetoric. To take
but one instance, in his "Jerusalem once well compacted . . .
but now distracted from itself" appears a rhetorical scheme,
a play on words for which the rhetorical name is *adnominatio*. On the other hand, in the redundant phrases which

provide the musical cadences in the longer sentences of Sir Thomas Browne will be found exemplified the forms of rhythm and modes of ending sentences analytically discussed by Cicero. In like manner the majesty of Miltonic verse is the product of one whose natural ear for music has been trained through familiarity with the cultivated rhythms of Latin style.

The influence of Latin in forming an English literary language is most clearly apparent in the use of words. The use of words freshly introduced from the Latin or controlled by the original Latin meaning is apparent in most of the great writers of the period. This influence is everywhere apparent in Fuller, for instance in the use of *compacted* and *distracted* already cited. The writings of Milton afford abundant illustration. The well remembered "confusion worse confounded" is the creation of one to whom the common Latin origin of *confusion* and *confound* was familiar. "There are several words of Latin origin, *e.g., horrent, impassive, irresponsible,* which," according to Henry Bradley, "so far as known, occur first in Milton's works." "In the middle of the seventeenth century words of this kind were,—*potentially* English; that is to say, the right of forming them at will, by anglicizing the form of Latin words or by attaching a Latin prefix or suffix to a word derived from that language was in practice generally assumed and conceded." [29]

In *Paradise Lost* appear countless instances of words from Latin [30] used in English but with the original Latin meaning:

> *Abject* and lost lay there (I, 312)
> Heav'ns *afflicting* Thunder (II, 166)

[29] H. Bradley, *The Making of English*, pp. 234, 235.
[30] E. Holmes, *Essays and Studies*, x.

th' *amaz'd* Night-wanderer (IX, 640)
Apparent Queen unvail'd (IV, 608)
The sun in Western *Cadence* low (X, 92)
exact of taste, and *elegant* (IX, 1017-18)
With Serpent *errour* wandring (VII, 302)
frizl'd hair *implicit* (VII, 323)
liquid *lapse* of murmuring Streams (VIII, 263)
Reluctance against God (X, 1045)

In considering the development of English in this period
one must not lose sight of the fact that this was the great
age of Puritanism. Puritan influence appears in the regulation of profane language already spoken of. It appears
in the prominence given to the use of the Bible with its
fructifying influence on the language. The Puritans, too,
with their sense of authority were disposed to subject themselves to discipline in language as in conduct. Schools and
learning were fostered by them. But their zeal in language
as in conduct was little curbed by the moderation which
should have been learned from the classical languages to
the study of which they devoted so much zeal. In language
as in conduct their enthusiasm, in the seventeenth-century
meaning of that word, led to an extravagance which was a
potent cause of the reaction which set in so promptly following the Restoration.

The violence of the reaction from the Puritan manner of
speech appears in the caricature by Samuel Butler of the
Presbyterian knight, Sir Hudibras, in which the pedantries
of the Puritan are held up to immortal ridicule:

> Beside, 'tis known he could speak Greek
> As naturally as pigs squeek:
> That Latine was no more difficile
> Than to a Black-bird 'tis to whistle

> •   •   •   •   •

> For Rhetorick he cou'd not ope
> His mouth, but out there flew a Trope;
>
> . . . . .
>
> But, when he pleas'd to shew't, his speech
> In Loftiness of Sound was rich;
> A *Babylonish* Dialect,
> Which learned Pedants much affect;
> It was a party-colour'd Dress
> Of patch'd and py-ball'd Languages:
> 'Twas *English* cut on *Greek* and *Latin,*
> Like Fustian heretofore on Sattin.
> It had an odd promiscuous Tone,
> As if h' had talk'd three Parts in one;
> Which made some think, when he did gabble,
> Th' had heard three Labourers of Babel;
> Or *Cerberus* himself pronounce
> A Leash of Languages at once.[31]

Evidently there was need of the sobering influence of classical taste.

That Puritan manner of speech provided abundant material for this ludicrous picture there can be no doubt. Fortunately there is another side to the case. The age that produced the qualities which were combined to form the fictitious character of Hudibras also produced a living man whose use of English in many respects has never been surpassed. This age produced John Milton. In Milton's English appear most of the features that characterize the language of this period. In it, as already pointed out, may be observed uncertainty in spelling, irregularities in syntax, the use of classical words not yet completely assimilated into English. The defects are those of a language which had as yet only classical learning to guide it. From this incompletely regulated English, however, the Puritan Mil-

---

[31] London, 1772, ed.

ton, with the methods of classical art and the guidance of classical taste, was able to frame a mode of expression which, to use the words of Addison, "carried our language to greater Heights than any of the English Poets have ever done before him."

CHAPTER XII

THE RESTORATION PERIOD

THE influence of classicism in the first part of the seventeenth century is easily apparent. An examination of the successive folio editions of Shakespeare shows that a long stride had been taken in the effort to give to English a regularity in its written forms comparable to that in the classical languages. Moreover there was under way a movement toward a refinement of English expression. It is worthy of note that the earliest citation of the word *refine* with the meaning 'to polish or improve language' is from the year 1617, although the verb *fine* had earlier been used with a similar meaning. Puritan regulation of the use of profanity early in the century has already been mentioned. Puritan influence also had imposed restrictions on the English downrightness of speech of earlier periods. Malheureux, a character in Marston's *Dutch Courtezan*, is reminded by his friend that " 'Tis not in fashion to call things by their right names," and Chapman, defending language used in his *Widow's Tears*, protests that since the "holy reformation has fallen to the skirts of the city, honesty is stripped out of his true substance into verbal nicety." [1] There was not only a Puritan squeamishness and a pedantry favoring the use of magniloquent 'newfangled' words, but an incipient form of preciosity revealed in the use of 'perfumed terms' referred to by Ben Jonson. The tendencies manifesting themselves continued through-

[1] M. P. Tilley, *Publications Modern Language Association*, XXXI, 72-3.

out the century and beyond. But the changed social conditions and changed social ideals that came with the restoration of royalty in the person of Charles II had their effect on the English language. In England were introduced ideals like those which had earlier developed in France. The efforts of the sixteenth century in France to enrich the French vocabulary had been succeeded by efforts at refinement and regulation. One should recall the efforts of Malherbe (1555-1628), "the tyrant of words and syllables," to refine the language of the court. One should recall also the artificiality of sentiment and the excessive refinement of speech cultivated in the salons of France and appearing in the courtly romances of the early seventeenth century. There came into being the theory of good usage, propagated particularly by Vaugelas, the belief that true French was that used in courtly society. This critical position was consolidated by the formation of the Academy about 1635 which had the triple purpose in language, to frame definite rules, to observe and pass critical judgment on words and phrases and finally to make a dictionary, a grammar, a rhetoric, and a treatise on versification.

Ideals of refinement in language similar to those that had earlier come to dominate in France came to prevail in England following the Restoration. The pedantries of the Puritan were laughed to scorn by Butler in his *Hudibras*. Over-refinement was warned against by Blount, who in his "Instructions for writing and addressing letters" in his *Academy of Eloquence* (1664) says: "You are not to cast a ring for the perfumed moding terms of the time; as *to acquiesce, to espouse an interest, to incommode, to have a pique against one*, &c., but use them properly in their places as others." [2] The stilted form of language used in the heroic plays of the time was ridiculed out of use by the

[2] J. L. Moore, *Tudor-Stuart Views*, p. 57, note 2.

satire of Buckingham's *Rehearsal*. In the place of a bookish standard was substituted a conversational standard.
Words instead of being derived by a dictionary method
from the two-language dictionaries, as earlier ridiculed by
Ben Jonson, came to be drawn from living use. In English,
as earlier in French, the learned words with which the
language had been enriched through the zeal of the Renaissance were now filtered through living speech, yielding a
product of clear English.

As spokesman for this new age in English literature who
can better serve than John Dryden, who in 1670 was made
historiographer-royal and poet laureate? With parents
whose families had been distinguished for Puritanism, Dryden had served as secretary to his cousin, Sir Gilbert Pick-
erington, a member of Cromwell's Council of State. Following the Restoration, however, he quickly adapted
himself to the new order of things. With young enthusiasm
he entered into the spirit of the new social order and, with
the zeal of a convert, in his writings he voices the ideals
of the new age. Ben Jonson, the dominant literary figure
in the preceding age, he praises, yet finds reason to criticize.
"If there was any fault in his [Jonson's] Language, 'twas
that he weav'd it too closely and laboriously, . . . perhaps
too, he did a little too much Romanize our Tongue, leaving
the words which he translated almost as much Latine as he
found them: wherein though he learnedly followed their
Language, he did not enough comply with the Idiom of
ours." [3] The wit of his own age Dryden maintains "is
much more courtly." True-wit in *The Silent Woman*, Dryden asserts, is Jonson's masterpiece, "and True-Wit was a
scholar-like kind of man, a gentleman with an allay of
pedantry, a man who seems mortified to the world by much
reading. The best of his knowledge is drawn, not from

[3] *Of Dramatick Poesie*, ed. 1684.

the knowledge of the town, but books; and, in short, he would be a fine gentleman in an university." For the 'grave gentleman' of his time, the surviving admirers and followers of Jonson who had enjoyed the distinguished honor of entertaining Jonson at supper in the Apollo and who bore with pride the title of "Son," which Jonson had bestowed upon them, Dryden had little praise. "Learning I never saw in any of them; and wit no more than they could remember. In short, they were unlucky to have been bred in an unpolished age, and more unlucky to live to a refined one. They have lasted beyond their own, and are cast behind ours. . . ." "I have always acknowledged the wit of our predecessors," says Dryden, "with all the veneration which becomes me, but, I am sure, their wit was not that of gentlemen: there was somewhat that was ill-bred and clownish in it, and which confessed the conversation of the authors."

In the courtly society in England following the Restoration there was substituted an easy colloquial form of language in place of the more artificial and formal manner produced by reading and Latin schooling. To the pattern set by the king, Dryden, in adulating manner, attributes the superior refinement of the age in which he lives. "At his return," says Dryden, "he found a nation lost as much in barbarism as in rebellion. And as the excellency of his nature forgave the one, so the excellency of his manners forgave the other. The desire of imitating so great a pattern first awakened the dull and heavy spirits of the English from their natural reservedness; loosened them from their stiff forms of conversation, and made them easy and pliant to each other in discourse. Thus, insensibly our way of living became more free; and the fire of the English wit, which was before stifled under a constrained melancholy way of breeding, began to display its force by mixing the solidity of our nation with the air and gayety of our neighbours." [4]

As a symptom of change in taste may be cited the changed attitude toward the pun. This trick of language, beloved of the Elizabethans, and in its various forms worthy the attention of the classical rhetoricians, under such names as *paronomasia, prosonomasia, adnominatio,* could not stand the test imposed by Restoration refinement. Dryden cites it in illustration of Ben Jonson's occasional "meanness of expression." "Nay," says Dryden, "he was not free from the most grovelling kind of wit, which we call clenches, of which *Every Man in his Humour* is infinitely full."

More direct in their bearing on the cultivation of the English language as an instrument of expression are Dryden's comments on the syntax and the words in the language of his predecessors. "It is therefore my part," he says, "to make it clear that the language, wit and conversation of our age, are improved and refined above the last; . . . I may safely conclude that our improprieties are less frequent, and less gross than theirs. One testimony of this is undeniable, that we are the first who have observed them; and, certainly to observe errors is a great step to the correcting of them." [5]   Shakespeare and Fletcher he dismisses with slight comment, since less can be expected of those "who wanted the learning and care which Jonson had." He turns his attention, instead, to Jonson, who is "a most judicious writer," and casting his eyes over the "four last" pages of *Catiline,* finds convincing evidence that "Jonson writ not correctly." Of Dryden's standards of criticism an impression may be gained from a few of the dozen passages from Jonson cited by him in illustration of faults:

[4] *Defence of the Epilogue;* spelling modernized, etc., 1672.   [5] *Ibid.*

> . . . to make empty way
> For thy last wicked nuptials, worse than they
> That blazed that act of thy incestuous life.

"The sense is here extremely perplexed," says Dryden, "and I doubt the word *they* is false grammar."

> What all the several ills that visit earth,
> Plague, famine, fire could reach unto,
> The sword, nor surfeits, let thy fury do.

Against this passage Dryden brings the objection of the use of the preposition at the end, the redundancy of *unto* and the *synchysis* "or ill-placing of words, of which Tully so much complains," in the words *the sword, nor surfeits*.

> Go on upon the Gods, kiss lightning, wrest
> The engine from the Cyclops, and give fire
> At face of a full cloud, and stand his ire.

Go on upon Dryden criticizes for redundancy; *give fire at face of a full cloud,* he says, was not understood in Jonson's own time; the word *ire* is antiquated; and "the article *his* makes false construction."

> Cæsar and Crassus, if they be ill men,
> Are mighty ones.
> Such men, They do not succour more the cause, &c.
>
>   . . . . .
>
> Though heaven should speak with all *his* wrath at once,
> We should stand upright and *unfear'd*.

Here objection is brought by Dryden to the use of *ones* in the plural number, to the use of *his* as "ill syntax with heaven," and to *unfear'd* for *unafraid*.

In *The ports are open* Dryden objects to the use of *ports* for *gates*—"an affected error in him, to introduce Latin by the loss of English idiom."

> Contain your spirit in more stricter bounds.

Dryden's comment is that "few of our present writers would have left behind them such a line—but that gross way of two comparatives was then ordinary; and, therefore, more pardonable in Jonson."

By way of apology for criticism of this kind Dryden says that "I live in an age where my least faults are severely censured." His critical attitude toward his own language appears in his comment on Jonson's use of "the preposition in the end of the sentence." This he says is "a common fault with him, and which I have but lately observed in my own writings." In the second edition of the *Essay of Dramatick Poesie,* Dryden is said to have made revisions eliminating this "fault." More open to criticism according to modern standards is Dryden's own use of the locution *four last* and of the *and which* construction, in the use of which he apparently has no hesitation.

Dryden and his contemporaries, it is evident, were by no means blind to the excellencies of their predecessors. Shakespeare, says Dryden, "many times has written better than any poet in any language."

> Shakespeare's magic could not copied be;
> Within that circle none durst walk but he.

And yet Shakespeare's plays in their original form did not always suit the new age. Pepys in his *Diary* (September 21, 1662) pronounces *Midsummer Night's Dream* "the most insipid, ridiculous play that ever I saw in my life," and Evelyn in his *Diary* (November 26, 1661) records: "I saw Hamlet Prince of Denmark played, but now the old plays begin to disgust this refined age." Revision and adaptation were felt to be necessary. Dryden collaborated with Sir William Davenant in an adaptation of *The Tempest,* in which symmetry was provided by the addition of a male counterpart for Miranda and a sister for Caliban and

another, and feminine, Ariel. And Dryden's own best beloved play was his *All for Love* in which the classical
unities were applied in a newly constructed version of
Antony and Cleopatra.

But it is language that is of present concern, and the
changes in Shakespeare's language made in the revised
version of his plays admirably exhibit the change in language standards. Let us take as a source of illustration the
Davenant version of *Hamlet* printed in 1676.[6] The supposed superiority in refinement appears in the elimination
or modification of oaths so conspicuous in Shakespearean
language. In the Davenant version, "Pray let me hear"
takes the place of "For Gods love let me hear." "Peace be
with his soul" succeeds "God a mercy on my soul";
"Heavens creatures" replaces "Gods creatures." Older
words are replaced; *"meet* Ophelia here" takes the place of
"here *affront* Ophelia." *"Incorporeal* air" succeeds *"in-
corporall* air." "A very *Feather* in the cap of Youth"
succeeds "A very *riband";* corresponding to changes in
fashion for hats, Shakespeare's lines are modified to make
them conform to the Restoration meter. More to our
present purpose are the grammatical changes in conformity
with the new standards: "How *prodigally* the soul" where
earlier editions used the flat adverb *prodigall; richer* for
earlier *more richer;* "he *who* hath" succeeding "he *which*
hath." In general the desire for greater elegance leads to
substitutions of words, as in *"groan* and sweat" for *"grunt*
and sweat"; "wants not *whispers"* for "wants not *buzzers";*
"stept in between" for *"popt* in between"; "gentle *Maid"*
for "poore *wench."* "And froward liberty does justice
strike" succeeds "And libertie, plucks justice by the nose."

In the "refinement" of English manners and speech fol-

[6] H. Spencer, *Publications Modern Language Association,* December,
1923.

lowing the Restoration the influence of French example is manifest. The trend of cultivation was that followed in contemporary French life. There was borrowing not only of French ideas, but of French words. The extent of this influence, however, has often been exaggerated. Some of the insular English prejudices of earlier periods were in part overcome, but the character and the speech of Englishmen in general remained sturdily English. Dryden with all his awareness of earlier English defects, nevertheless wrote his *Essay of Dramatick Poesie* "chiefly to vindicate the Honour of our English Writers, from the censure of those who unjustly prefer the French before them." The borrowing of French words also was not as extensive as sometimes supposed. Of a thousand English words borrowed from the French, the first hundred listed under each of the first ten letters in the Oxford Dictionary, Jespersen finds only 34 borrowed in the half century, 1650-1700, fewer than in the preceding half century, 1600-50, where the corresponding number is 69, and much fewer than between 1550 and 1600, where the number is 91, or the period of most active borrowing, 1350-1400, where the number reaches 180. Relatively, then, the borrowing was not extensive. The critical taste of the time checked excess in this as in other features of language. Dryden's opinions expressed in his *Defence of the Epilogue* (1672) may be taken as fairly representative of his period. He takes as a guide the rule of Horace "not to be too hasty in receiving of Words: but rather to stay till Custome has made them familiar to us, *Quem penes, arbitrium est, et jus et norma loquendi.* For I cannot approve of their way of refining, who corrupt our *English* idiom by mixing it too much with *French:* that is a Sophistication of Language, not an improvement of it: a turning English into French, rather than a refining of English by French. We meet daily with those Fopps, who value themselves on their Travelling, and pretend they cannot express their meaning in English, because they would put off on us some *French* Phrase of the last Edition. . . ." That the fops of whom Dryden speaks were not all male in sex he shows in another place, in a satirical scene in his play *Marriage à la Mode*.[7] In this scene he offers a conversation between Melantha, "an affected lady," and Philotis, "woman to Melantha." [8]

Mel. O, are you there, minion? And, well, are not you a most precious damsel, to retard all my visits for want of language, when you know you are paid so well for furnishing me with new words for my daily conversation? Let me die, if I have not run the risk already to speak like one of the vulgar, and if I have one phrase left in all my store, that is not threadbare *et usé,* and fit for nothing but to be thrown to peasants.

Phil. Indeed, madam, I have been very diligent in my vocation; but you have so drained all the French plays and romances, that they are not able to supply you with words for your daily expense.

Mel. Drained? What a word's there! *Epuisée,* you sot you. Come, produce your morning's work.

Phil. 'Tis here, madam. (*Shows the paper.*)

Mel. O, my Venus! fourteen or fifteen words to serve me a whole day! Let me die, at this rate I cannot last till night. Come, read your works! Twenty to one, half of them will not pass muster neither.

Phil. Sottises.

Mel. Sottises! bon. That's an excellent word to begin withal; as, for example, he or she said a thousand *sottises* to me. Proceed.

Phil. Figure! As, what a *figure* of a man is there! *Naïve,* and *naïveté.*

[7] Act III, sc. i.
[8] Modern edition, ed. Saintsbury.

Mel. Naïve! as how?

Phil. Speaking of a thing that was naturally said, it was so *naïve,* or, such an innocent piece of simplicity, 'twas such a *naïveté.*

Mel. Truce with your interpretations. Make haste.

Phil. Foible, chagrin, grimace, embarrassé, double entendre, équivoque, éclaircissement, suite, bévue, façon, penchant, coup d'étourdi', and *ridicule.*

The scene offers a caricatured exhibition of this form of affectation. It affords also an idea of the kind of French words borrowed at this time. It should of course be held in mind that the affectation was by no means peculiar to this period. The distinguishing feature of the words borrowed at this time is that instead of being completely anglicized as for the most part earlier borrowed words had been, these words retain French features in spelling or pronunciation or both. French accent as well as French use of words was affected, a striving regrettably persisted in in later times.

In setting forth his conception of refinement in language Dryden adopts the precept of Quintilian that refinement consists "either in rejecting such old words or phrases which are ill sounding, or improper, or in admitting new, which are more proper, more sounding and more significant." The emphasis is on the choice of words. In the regulation of spelling and of grammatical forms and constructions a beginning had been made. Latin pattern and the efforts of the printer had had their effect. But there remained in the language of Dryden, as has already been observed in the language of Milton, a number of forms of ·expressions which have been rejected, or at least challenged, in the more rigidly regulated language of later periods.

As a source for illustrative examples let us take the *Essay on Dramatick Poesie* (2d ed., 1684). In this work,

My Lord

I know not whether my lord Sunderland has interceded with your Lord:
=ship, for halfe a yeare of my salary: But I have two other Advocates;
my extreame wants, even almost to arresting, & my ill health which
cannot be repaird without, immediate retireing into the Country.
A quarters allowance is but the Jesuites powder to my disease;
the fitt will return a fortnight hence. If I durst I would
plead a little merit, & some hazards of my life from the Common
Enemyes, my refuseing advantages offerd by them, & neglecting my
beneficiall studyes for the Kings Service: But I onely thinke I
meritt not to sterve. I never applyd my selfe to any Interest contra:
-ry to your Lordships; and on some occasions, perhaps not known to
you, have not been unserviceable to the memory & reputation of
My Lord your father. After this, My Lord, my conscience assures me
I may write boldly though I cannot speake to you. I have three
Sonns growing to mans estate, I breed them all up to learning beyond
my fortune; but they are too hopefull to be neglected though I want.
Be pleasd to looke on me with an eye of compassion; some small
Employment would render my condition easy. The King is not un=
satisfyed of me, the Duke has often promisd me his assistance; &
your Lordship is the Conduit through which their favours passe.
Either in the Customes, or the Appeales of the Excise, or some other
way; meanes cannot be wanting if you please to have the will.
Tis enough for one Age to have neglected Mr Cowley, and starved
Mr Butler: but neither of them had the happiness to live till your
Lordships Ministry. In the meane time be pleasd to give me a gracious
and speedy answer to my present request of halfe a yeares pension
for my necessityes. I am goeing to write somewhat by his Majestyes
command, & cannot stirr into the Country for my health and studies,
till I secure my family from want. You have many petitions of
this nature, & cannot satisfy all, But I hope from your goodness
to be made an Exception to your generall rules; because I am, with
all sincerity, Your Lordships most obedient
Humble Servant

John Dryden.

John Dryden (1631-1700): letter to Lawrence Hyde, Earl of Rochester,
First Lord of the Treasury, on his necessities, etc.; without date, but
probably written in 1682 or 1683, since he was made Collector of
Customs in the port of London on December 17, 1683. (Brit. Mus.
Add. MS. 17,017, F. 49.)

even in its revised form, appear frequent uses of verb forms later abandoned: *chose,* for 'chosen'; *writ,* for 'written'; *spoke,* for 'spoken'; *sung,* for 'sang.' Adverb forms without the ending *-ly* ('flat adverbs') are still not uncommon: *exceeding* vain; *extream* elaborate; *sure,* for 'surely.' Clauses are occasionally introduced by *and who* when no relative clause has preceded, a construction of which an instance has already been cited. The use of collective noun with plural verb or pronoun is at times striking: *e.g.,* "the *world have* mistaken"; "the *audience* can never recover *themselves"*; "the *audience are* satisfied"; "the *company were* all sorry." Two nouns connected by *and,* as with Milton, when representing a single idea, may be followed by a singular predicate; *e.g.,* "the great *eagerness* and *precipitation . . . makes* us. . . ." Similar in nature is the use of the locution, *"these kind of* thoughts," of which the correctness is now challenged. The alternative construction, however, appears in *"this sort of* narrations." The expressions, *"the two first"* and *"the three last"* are of a kind later challenged as illogical. In the expression, "the event which they knew *was then deciding"* appears the older construction which was still favored by nineteenth-century conservative grammarians but which has been gradually superseded by the construction evolved in the late eighteenth century, *being decided.*

Most striking, however, is the use of prepositions. These particles which in later stages in language have taken over the function of declensional endings in indicating the relations between words, were used in Elizabethan English, as already pointed out, with remarkable freedom and lack of precision. The increased precision, but at the same time increased rigidity, in present-day English has been brought about by a stiffening in these joints of language. The contrast between seventeenth-century English and present-day

English appears in expressions by Dryden such as: "we may cry out *of* the writers of this time"; "will not pass *upon* those who" (mod. 'with') ; "prefer'd the English Plays *above* . . ."; "tax'd us . . . *in* some irregularities"; "it suited not *with* . . ."; "preferr'd *before* him"; "diversions *to* the main design"; "I have a great quarrel *to* you."

If now one parts company with the extremely cultivated speech of Dryden and looks at the language of writers of this period who were less self-conscious in speech, one finds reflected much of the earlier irregularity and freedom. In the plays of Aphra Behn, for instance, one meets with the double negative: "not so joyful neither"; "not so happy neither"; "No, Sir, nor don't care." One meets with confusion in the pronoun forms. "*Who* mean you, Woman?"; "*Whom* shou'd I mean but *thou*"; "My Sister, Sir, *who* I disguised"; "between you and I" (frequent). Contrary to what one might expect, is the relative infrequency of the objective forms of the personal pronouns following the verb *to be.* Guy Miege in his *Nouvelle Methode pour apprendre l'Anglois* (London, 1685) says that "after verbs and prepositions (except the impersonal verb, *it is*) I is changed to me." The exception is to be noted. In an edition of the same work nearly a century later (Paris, 1777) the directions are even more definite. "The English," according to the directions in this book, "say *It is I,* equivalent to French *C'est je,* instead of following the French practice of using the objective form as in *C'est moi."* The directions given by the French writer seem to represent current English usage. In four plays by Aphra Behn (Vol. IV, 3d ed.) appear such expressions as: "that was *I*"; "that must be *I*"; "that I was not *he*"; "pray Heaven it be *he*"; "that's *he* you see." The solitary exception to the prevailing practice, observed by the present writer in a volume of four plays, occurs in the Prologue contributed by Dryden to Mrs. Behn's *The Widow*

Ranter in which occurs the expression, "when none would cry that Oaf was *me,*" where the *me* rimes with *pedigree* in the following line. In the case of this particular construction, it appears, seventeenth-century colloquial usage conformed more closely to grammatical regularity than does the colloquial use of today.

If in the language of literature there persisted many features of the irregular form of English of earlier centuries, in the colloquial manner of speech reflected in the familiar letters of people outside literary circles, the irregularity, judged by modern standards, amounted to illiteracy. It must be held in mind that training in the refinements of English was still confined to a minority. The amazing consequences of lack of training are revealed in detail by Professor Wyld in his analysis of the language of the *Verney Memoirs* and the *Correspondence of Dr. Basire,* which belong to this period. It remains for a later chapter to show the relation of this unregulated form of seventeenth-century English to the beginnings of American English.

But even refinement in the choice of words still remained a matter of individual judgment and of individual taste formed through reading or through social relations. In his *New World of Words,* as has been pointed out, Edward Phillips attempted to indicate certain distinctions in propriety in words, but for final judgment on a subject of such general concern as the rejection of old words and the adoption of new it is obvious that no one man had competence. Greater authority was needed. The minds of the time, under such circumstances, naturally turned to the idea of an Academy like the Accademia della Crusca, formed in Italy in the sixteenth century, and the French Academy founded by Richelieu about 1635.

Let us turn to Dryden once more for an expression of

the current feeling on this subject. In the Dedication to *The Rival Ladies* (1664) he says: "I have endeavour'd to write English, as near as I could distinguish it from the Tongue of Pedants, and that of affected Travellours. Only I am Sorry, that (Speaking so noble a Language as we do) we have not a more certain Measure of it, as they have in France, where they have an Academy erected for that purpose, and Indow'd with large Privileges by the present King." The idea here expressed is one to which Dryden comes back frequently in his later writings. In 1679 he calls upon the Earl of Sunderland to serve as the English Richelieu. "I am desirous," he says, "if it were possible, that we might all write with the same certainty of words, and purity of phrase, to which the Italians first arrived, and after them the French." Later, in 1693, in despairing tone, he speaks of the English language as "in a manner barbarous." "What government," he says, "will encourage any one, or more, who are capable of refining it, I know not: but nothing under a public expense can go through with it." [9]

This idea of an English Academy was by no means original with Dryden. The need of official control in language had been felt by Gabriel Harvey, who felt that the only way to arrive at uniformity in English spelling was to have the orthography "publickely and autentically established, as it were by a general Counsel, or acte of Parliament." Elaborate plans for a literary "Corporation Royal" to bear the title "King James his Academe or College of Honour," proposed by Edmund Bolton in 1617, met with royal favor, but came to naught on account of the death of King James in 1625. An English Academy was proposed by Sir F. Kynaston in 1635 and, in the ideal commonwealth described in the *New Atlantis* (1660) by R. H. Esquire,

[9] B. S. Monroe, *Modern Philology*, VIII, 7-8.

there is pictured an "Emminent *Academy* of selected wits" one of whose duties it was "to purifie our Native Language from Barbarism or Solecism, to the height of Eloquence, by regulating the termes and phrases thereof. . . ." [10]

The plan, which was so much cherished and which was urged with renewed force in the Augustan Age of Addison and Swift, was never carried into effect. It came probably most near to realization as one of the activities of the Royal Society established in 1662. But that is a new matter. It leads one to another side of seventeenth-century intellectual activity, to the movement from which sprang the beginnings of modern science, which had a profound influence on the development of the English language.

The earlier history of the scientific movement leads one back again to the first part of the seventeenth century. At this time there were in English intellectual life two currents of ideas. On the one hand was the stream of ideas from antiquity the authenticity of which must be vouched for by classical authority. On the other hand was the new stream of ideas springing from freshly observed fact and supported by reason. From Descartes came an attitude of mind, "to accept nothing as true which I do not clearly recognize to be so." From Bacon came the inductive method in the search for knowledge. The natural powers of observation were infinitely multiplied by mechanical means, by the telescope and the microscope. The voyages of the sixteenth century had brought geographical knowledge, a conception of the world, its shape, its size, and its variety. Far wider was the extension of knowledge made possible by the new mechanical instruments. The telescope opened to view something of the infinity of the outer universe, and the microscope revealed some of the secrets of

[10] E. Freeman, *Modern Language Review,* XIX, 291*ff.*

the elements of which the universe is composed. The spirit
of research and of progress was kindled, a spirit which is
indicated by new words brought into use. *Progress* with
the meaning 'going on to a higher stage,' is first cited in
the Oxford Dictionary from the year 1603; *improve* meaning 'raise to a better quality' from 1617, *amelioration* from
1659.

The energy in geographical discovery of the sixteenth
century was in the seventeenth century turned into exploration of the field of knowledge. Furthermore the
commercial success of the merchants of one century provided the means of leisure for the men of science of the
following. Frowned upon by the orthodox believers, the
promoters of the new scientific spirit worked in semi-secrecy.
In 1645 Robert Boyle founded the "Invisible College," a
group of men meeting at Gresham College. The discussions were limited to the "New Philosophy," and it was
explicitly agreed not to "meddle with Divinity, Meta-
physicks, Moralls, Politicks, Grammar, Rhetoric, or Logic."
The revolt from the methods of the grammar school was a
sharp one. The shift from the older intellectual interests
was rapid. The transition is to be observed in the writings
of Sir Thomas Browne. In the *Religio Medici* (1635-6)
Browne adheres to the "ancient faith," and to the end
Browne clung to the Ptolemaic system and did not "reject
a sober regulated astrology." "We do not," he says in his
Vulgar Errors (1646), "deny the influence of the stars."
But in the same work he asserts that "the mortalest enemy
unto knowledge, and that which hath done the greatest
execution unto truth, hath been the peremptory adhesion
unto Authority, and more especially of our belief upon
the dictates of Antiquity." [11] In Milton's writings appears
a similar conflict between the old ideas and the new. In

[11] C. S. Duncan, *The New Science and English Literature,* pp. 30-4.

the background of *The Hymn to the Nativity, the Arcades,*
and *Comus* are the old beliefs, which also provide the cosmology for *Paradise Lost.* But to Adam, Milton "gave the
inquisitive mind of the new philosopher." [12]

The New Philosophy came rapidly into fashion. The
little group of men who had met at Gresham College formed
the nucleus of a larger organization for the most part composed of men of rank. King Charles II was enrolled as a
member and he granted the society a Royal Charter and the
privilege of using the Royal arms. He gave to it a silver
mace still used at its meetings. Thus in 1662 was formed
the Royal Society. Royal interest in the New Philosophy
appears from the laboratory equipped by the King at White-
hall. The interests of the King became those of courtly
society. "It was almost necessary to the character of a
fine gentleman," says Macaulay, "to have something to say
about airpumps and telescopes." The effect of this new
fashion on classical learning appears from the feeling remark of Dr. Barrow, Professor of Greek at Cambridge:
"I sit lonesome as an Attic owl who has been thrust out
of the companionship of other birds; while classes in
Natural Science are full." [13]

The achievements of the New Science of the seventeenth
century one must contemplate with wonder. The revelations of the telescope and microscope supplemented by
habits of observation and classification of natural phenomena led eventually to the illuminating discoveries of Newton. A new conception was reached of natural phenomena,
of human life, of the world, of the universe. The pretensions of the new scientists, or *virtuosi,* were in many instances extravagant, and there were not wanting defenders
of the older form of culture. An interesting episode in

[12] *Ibid.,* p. 39.
[13] *Ibid.,* p. 20.

English literary history was the celebrated controversy over the merits of "ancient and modern learning," the heat of which was cooled by the ridicule of Swift in his *Battle of the Books*. The practical result, however, of the scientific activity of the seventeenth century, was a firm foundation provided for the achievements of modern science.

On the English language the effect of the New Philosophy was most important. To begin with there was the revolt from artifice in style. With Bacon, it has been said "the English language first became the vehicle for scientific expression." [14] "First then," says Bacon, "away with antiquities and citations or testimonies of authors . . . and for all that concerns ornaments of speech, such like emptiness let it be utterly dismissed." [15] *Nullius in Verba* was adopted as the motto of the Royal Society, and the language ideal of the society was more explicitly worded in the formula of its historian, Sprat, a "clear and naked style approaching mathematical plainness." The influence of science, it will be observed, supported the taste of Restoration society for a style based on natural colloquial use rather than upon the patterns provided by Latin rhetorical art. The new influence appears not only in subject matter, but in style in such works as Wilkins's *New World in the Moon* (1638), Walton's *Compleat Angler* (1655), and Evelyn's *Sylva* (1664). It appears also in the style of the pulpit oratory in the later seventeenth century.

Somewhat later arose the distinction between the manner of writing in science and that in mere literature. On the one hand there arose the fashion on the part of courtly writers with shallow scientific knowledge to ridicule the extravagant pretensions of the *virtuosi* scientists. On the other hand there arose a disposition among the scientists

[14] *Ibid.*, p. 147.
[15] *Novum Organum*, quoted by Krapp, *Rise of English Literary Prose*, p. 526.

to neglect the cultivated graces of refined style. In this way came into being a difference in manner which has been a misfortune to the English language, a difference which early in the nineteenth century gave rise to De Quincey's famous distinction between the "literature of knowledge" and the "literature of power."

The expanding knowledge, however, of the seventeenth century promoted not only a change in English style, but a more precise knowledge of the nature of the language. Antiquarian research took up, among other studies, that of earlier church history. In the interests of this study there was cultivated a knowledge of the earlier English language. Sir Henry Spelman in 1639 founded a Saxon (Anglo-Saxon) Lecture at Cambridge, and in a letter to Abraham Whellock he refers to the preparation for a grammar and dictionary of that tongue.[16] In this period were carried on the etymological studies of Junius and of Skinner which, although not final in their results, nevertheless provided most of the material for the etymologies in the *Dictionary* of Samuel Johnson in the following century.

Still more significant of the new spirit is the *Grammatica Linguæ Anglicanæ* published by John Wallis in 1653. The author of this work was one of the small group of men that formed the nucleus of the Royal Society. He was a scientist, later Savilian Professor of Geometry at Oxford. But the subject of language evidently early engaged the attention of the group of scientists, and one of the earliest products of this interest was this remarkable book. The method followed by Wallis is indicated in his preface where he criticizes the methods of earlier English grammarians, including Alexander Gill and Ben Jonson, because "no one of them, in my opinion, has followed the method best suited to this task; for all, by reducing our English language too

[16] *Camden Society Publications*, 1843.

much to the Latin norm, have given too many rules concerning cases of nouns, genders and declensions, tenses of verbs, moods and conjugations." Wallis, although writing in Latin, abandoned in great part the method of Latin grammar, and in the spirit of the New Science recorded the results of his own observation of actual English usage. He offers an account of English pronunciation actually heard, and by purely inductive method he arrived at a statement of the distinction between *shall* and *will, should* and *would,* as observed in actual English use. His work passed through numerous editions, the fifth edition appearing in 1674, and the conclusions reached are quoted again and again by the better informed grammarians of the later seventeenth and the eighteenth centuries.

From another member of the group of men associated with Wallis, from John Wilkins, Dean of Ripon, came a book which further illustrates the interest on the part of the scientists in the subject of language. This work, which was presented at a meeting of the Royal Society in 1668, was entitled *An Essay Towards a Real Character, and a Philosophical Language.* It consists of three parts. A first part offers a discussion of the origin of languages, alphabets and other like matters. A second part deals with "Universal Philosophy" and attempts to arrange and classify things so that they may be scientifically or logically named. It offers a method of nomenclature for sciences such as botany and zoölogy. A third part deals with "Natural Grammar," with logical terms in great part replacing the terms of Latin grammar and offers an elaborate method of classifying the elements of language itself. The work was regarded by the author as representing an ideal to be aspired to rather than as a scheme capable of immediate realization. It reflects, however, the spirit of the time, the revolt from Latin pattern and an attempt to provide an independent and scientific basis for the analysis of language.

The importance attached by the Royal Society at large to the English language is indicated by the appointment in the year 1664, of a committee, "for improving the English tongue." This committee included Evelyn, Waller, Sprat, Dryden, Sir John Berkenhead and Sir Peter Wyche. No definite action was ever taken by the committee, but an idea of the subjects under consideration may be gained from a letter written by Evelyn to Sir Peter Wyche, the chairman, in which he outlined his ideas regarding the objectives to be attained. Briefly summarized these objectives were: "a Gram'ar for the Præcepts"; "a more certaine Orthography"; "some new Periods and Accents . . . to assist, inspirit, and modifie the Pronunciation of Sentences" (The purpose of punctuation is to be noted) "a Lexicon or Collection of all the pure English Words by themselves"; "a collection of technical words"; "a better interpretation of difficult things than afforded by existing dictionaries"; "a full Catalogue of exotic Words"; a collection of dialectal "Idiomes and Proverbs"; "a collection of the most quaint ['ornate'] and Courtly expressions, by way of Florilegium"; a reduction in number of the "old layd-aside words," translations from Greek, Latin and even from modern languages; an art of Rhetoric based on the selected compositions of members of the Royal Society. An ambitious set of undertakings, this; one which, if carried out, would have more than equalled the actual achievement of the contemporary French Academy.

It is highly significant that the scientists of the seventeenth century keenly realized the close relation between knowledge and the instrument for its expression, language. In the study of the natural sciences variation in the names of natural objects stands in the way of precision of statement and accuracy of knowledge. Let us cite an instance from the language of twentieth-century America. A fisherman who catches in Massachusetts a *horn pout* and a *kiver*, in New York State may catch the same kinds of fish but with the names *bullhead* and *sunfish*, and the same kinds of fish again in Ohio but with the names *catfish* and *blue gills*. The local variation in names which exists in the standardized language of modern America cannot be compared in extent with that in the various dialects of seventeenth-century England. One of the earliest tasks, therefore, confronting the seventeenth-century student of natural history was that of providing a uniform system of nomenclature. Hence we find one of the important works of John Ray, Fellow of the Royal Society, the celebrated botanist of the period, was a book devoted to language, entitled, *A Collection of English Words not Generally used . . . with Catalogues of English Birds and Fishes; and an Account of the preparing and refining such Metals and Minerals as are gotten in England*. This work, published in 1674, contains two interesting lists of dialect words: (1) North Countrey Words, (2) South and East Countrey Words. This work apparently the author regarded as preliminary to a more ambitious *Method and History of Plants* which he feared he might not "live so long as to perfect." The scientist evidently had his task in standardizing that part of the English language which served his uses.

More important, however, than the direct share of the scientist in shaping the English language was the influence exerted by him in turning general interest from ancient to modern forms of learning and in giving to English, the natural instrument of modern learning, its natural place in the curricula of schools. Before taking up this subject, however, let us turn back briefly to the earlier stages in the development of the study of modern subjects including the English language. The dominance of the grammar school in English education of the sixteenth and early seventeenth centuries has already been pointed out. Modern and practical studies, however, had been not entirely neglected. In the sixteenth century the education of the nobility had been broader in scope including subjects not provided for in the grammar schools. The expanded culture of the time had caused the abandonment in great part of the medieval system of fosterage in the households of princes. Besides the physical accomplishments distinctive of rank, the young nobleman was trained in mathematics and the natural sciences of the time and in modern foreign languages. As men of affairs they received training much like that of the lawyer; in fact they were often trained at the Inns of Court.[17] The foundation of Gresham College in London, at which lectures began in 1597, is significant as indicating the beginnings of a modern trend in education. The instruction there offered was practical in its nature and was intended for "merchants and other citizens." Moreover the instruction was in the English language. There should also be recalled the admonition of Mulcaster that now, when English has replaced Latin as the language of church, one should learn "to read that first which we speak first." The *Ludus Literarius,* or *The Grammar School,* published by John Brinsley in 1612, in the words of Foster Watson, "marks an epoch in the development of the teaching of English." The author complains of the "want of care in our schools for growth in our language as in Latin" and maintains that "our chief endeavor should be for our own tongue." This voice crying in the wilderness presages a change in attitude toward English which becomes apparent soon after the Restoration in 1660.

Significant of the diminished prestige of Latin was its

[17] *Cf.* F. Watson, *The Beginnings of the Teaching of Modern Subjects in English,* pp. xxix*ff.*

replacement by French as the language of diplomacy. The royal favor, also, lent to the new scientific studies added greatly to their prestige and to that of their propagators. The undue amount of time devoted to Latin studies had been complained of by Milton, who asserted that a "tenth part of man's life, ordinarily extended, is taken up in learning, and that very scarcely, the Latin Tongue." After the Restoration, attention came to be centered more on the elementary subjects of reading and writing, which the grammar schools had stubbornly refused to admit into their curricula. The more modern and the more practical subjects of study came to be provided for in mathematical schools, navigation schools and commercial schools and by the endowment of 'Charity schools' which in the early eighteenth century became, in the words of Addison, "the glory of the age." In Hoole's *New Discovery of the Old Art of Teaching School,* published in 1660, there are prescribed for reading not only books on religion and manners, and on history, but Herbert's *Poems* and Quarles's *Emblems,* "apparently," says Foster Watson, "the first instance of the recommendation of English literature for school teaching." [18] The suggestion seems to have met with approval. Later in the century, in 1690, John Locke in *Some Thoughts Concerning Education,* recommends, in place of the customary declamation and verses in Latin, the production of themes in English and the reading of "those things that are well writ in English." As a reason he urges that "no care is taken anywhere to improve young Men in their own Language."

A feature of English education following the Restoration was the creation of the Dissenting Academies. Thrust out of church and out of the schools by the conformity legislation of 1662, the Puritans were forced to establish schools

[18] F. Watson, *The Old Grammar Schools,* p. 101.

of their own. Throughout most of the seventeenth century, in the Dissenting Academies, as in the grammar schools, the older classical education continued to dominate, and De Foe complained that students "come away masters of Science, critics in Greek and Hebrew, perfect in language, and perfectly ignorant of their mother tongue." There were, however, exceptions. There was the Academy at Newington Green of which the master was Charles Norton, later, it is of interest to know, vice-president of Harvard College. This Academy was attended by De Foe, who reports concerning the training received there: "We were not destitute of language, but we were made masters of English; and more of us excelled in that particular than of any school at that time."

The influence of the training received at this excellent school appears in many of the ideas offered by De Foe in his *Essay upon Projects*. In this work De Foe offers in detail a scheme for the establishment of an English Academy in its essential features like that earlier favored by Dryden and others. More original are his recommendations regarding provision for the neglected education of women. He recommends the usual studies of French and Italian, but he adds, "They should, as a particular study, be taught all the graces of speech, and all the necessary air of conversation, which our common education is so defective in that I need not expose." He recommends particularly the study of history, but a main purpose is that they should "be capable of all sorts of conversation." "I would have men," he continues, "take women for companions and educate them to be fit for it." The ideas of De Foe represent a new feeling becoming prevalent, not only in favor of modern studies, but in favor of general education. In this general education it had come to be felt that the study of English deserved a prominent place.

The consequences of the continued agitation in favor of English studies appear at the beginning of the following century. In the year 1700 appeared an interesting work on English grammar by A. Lane, M.A., entitled, *A Key to the Art of Letters: or, English a Learned Language, Full of Art, Elegancy and Variety.* This work, because it illustrates the stage reached in the cultivation of the English language, deserves to be lingered over.

The author was a schoolmaster, "late Master of the Free-School of Leominster in Herefordshire, now Teacher of a private School at Mile-end green." An introductory note of commendation is signed by masters of several of the most prominent schools of England, of the famous Merchant-Taylors School, of Charterhouse, of the Grammar School in Christ's Hospital, and of the Free School of St. Martins, Westminster.

"To write an English Grammar for English Youth," says the author, "may seem to many, at first view, a very superfluous and ridiculous thing." The point of view of Sidney should be recalled. The modest attitude of earlier writers on the grammar of the mother tongue also should be recalled—of Ben Jonson, whose *Grammar* was avowedly made "for the benefit of strangers," and of Wallis, who wrote his grammar because 'he had seen many foreigners desirous of learning English.' The assignment of the special needs of the fair sex as the occasion for early dictionary-making should also be recalled. Lane, in his book, drops all of this apologetic pretence and announces his work as "an Essay to enable both Foreiners, and the English Youth of either Sex, to speak and write the *English* Tongue well and learnedly, according to the exactest Rules of *Grammar*." He assails the mistake common among European nations of looking upon grammar as "nothing else but an Instrument to acquire some unknown Tongue" and asserts that "the true End and Use of *Grammar* is to teach how to speak and write well and learnedly in a language already known, according to the unalterable Rules of right Reason." The abandonment of usage as the sole guide is to be noted. The reason, he asserts, that "Scholars can speak and write with more sense and understanding than others" is "not for having Greek or Latin, or any other Forein Language, but because they have learned the Art of *Grammar* with those Languages which yet they might have learned far better, and with much less expence of Mony, Time, and Pains, in their Mother-Tongue, as the *Greeks* and *Romans* did." "Must we still," he asks, "grace their dead Languages with the Title of *Literae humaniores,* and leave our own out, by which we tacitly seem to acknowledge ourselves *Gentem barbarem, aut saltem minus humanam?*" He vigorously assails the current methods of Latin schools where "both Masters and Scholars" are "so miserably toyl'd and perplexed in teaching and learning Grammar that almost all learned and ingenious Persons shun to be Schoolmasters, but whom necessity drives to those Workhouses—and generally all Children are utterly averse to go to the Schools." "To conclude," he says, "if no children were to learn Latin, or any other Forein Language, till they had first learn'd the Art of *Gramma*r in their Mother-Tongue, I doubt not but our Latin Schools would soon become much more successful and Useful to the Nation than ever yet they have been."

The views of this teacher and grammarian are much the same as those of John Locke and are so much in accord with modern opinion that it is not easy to realize their radical character at the end of the seventeenth century. The seventeenth-century point of view appears, however, in the aspiring patriotic sentiment in the belief expressed that "the cultivating and enriching our Mother Tongue with all manner of good Literature, would soon make our happy Island famous for all kind of Learning and Virtue. . . ." Even more characteristic of the period is the emphasis laid on moral value. This cultivation of the mother tongue, Lane asserts, "would be a more effectual means to reform the corruption of Manners, so much complained of among us . . . ; for, as Learning and Virtue generally go together, so Ignorance and Vice are inseparable Twins. . . ."

In method of presenting his subject matter this author introduces some new features. His efforts toward logical system appear in his transference to grammar of the logical terms, *subject, object, predicate,* "not usual in Grammar," he remarks. In fact the earliest instances cited in the Oxford Dictionary of the application of these terms to grammatical use are: *subject* (1638), *object* (1727), *predicate* (1638). "If I have borrowed these Terms from Logick," says Lane by way of apology, "I am persuaded that Aristotle borrowed them first from *Grammar,* which was in being long before his Logic. . . ."

In general he follows the conventional order of presentation of subject matter. First comes a brief consideration of letters and sounds. Here one noteworthy feature is the rule governing the use of capital letters in his day. Not only the "first word of every new Period, of every Verse, all proper Names" and so on, as in present-day use, but "all Emphatical or Remarkable Words begin with Capitals." There follow a brief consideration of syllables and of accent and then a more detailed exposition of the uses of words. Here the influence of Wilkins appears. Words are classified into:

Substantives,	signifying things
Adjectives,	signifying manners of things
Verbs,	signifying actions
Particles,	signifying manners of actions

Noteworthy is his account of 'S servile,' "so called because it serves for several uses in the Variation of *Nouns* and *Verbs* in English." This 'S servile' is distinguished into "S Plural, S Possessive and S Personal."

But the inevitable influence of Latin grammar appears in his recognition of six cases of nouns and three modes and five tenses of verbs. The well-informed character of the author, however, appears in his adoption of the distinction, first formulated by Wallis, between *shall* and *will*. "*Shall*, in the first Persons *barely foretells*, in the second and third Persons it *promises*, or *threatens*. *Will*, in the first Person *promises* or *threatens*, in the second and third Persons it *barely foretells*."

Striking to the modern reader is the special attention given by this human grammarian to the needs of the fair sex. Even young gentlewomen, "their more nice and tender constitutions not being able to endure those rugged and thorny Difficulties in the Methods hitherto practiced, may attain to a perfect knowledg [*sic*] of the Art of Grammar in the method here proposed. . . . And if the Author has found out the true Secret of an easy and rational Education that may prove to the advantage of the fair Sex, who have so many Slights and Affronts put upon them for want of Learning, he thinks all his Pains and Labour happily bestow'd."

For the propagation of his plan the energetic author of this book brought all available forces to bear. He not only presented his ideas in a vigorous style, but he won the commendation of eminent contemporary schoolmasters. He also secured commendatory verses from prominent poets of his time. Facetious in tone certainly, and one suspects not without irony, was the extravagant praise offered. Verses by J. Ovington reach the superlative in the following concluding lines:

Such *Miracles* of *Knowledge* we'l acquire,
Before this *new born Century* expire;
Which shall proclaim, if they this Book peruse,
Each Town an *Athens,* and each *Maid* a *Muse.*

Nahum Tate, the poet laureate, is inspired to three pages of verse, of the real or assumed enthusiasm in which, the following selected lines will afford an impression:

To *Grecian* Hills our Youth no more shall roam,
Supply'd with your Castalian Spring at Home.

· · · · ·

Ah! had my tender Years been thus supply'd
With such a skilful *Moses* for my Guide

· · · · ·

Wondrous Discov'ry!   Comprehensive Art,
That do's, with *English,* Forreign Tongues impart.

· · · · ·

This Tribute from the *Muse* you justly claim,
For teaching Youths the Path to early Fame;
She next must thank you in the Ladies Name,
For whose fair sake your gen'rous Pen you draw,

· · · · ·

By Nature taught, with Beauty's single Charm,
They did, long since, our Sex's Hearts disarm.
Our very Souls, you teach 'em to surprize
With Learning's Charms more bright and dazzling than their Eyes.

In this grammar by Lane one sees the English language at last given the position of prominence that is its natural place in the scheme of English education.   The classics which, since the days of the Renaissance, had been so assiduously studied, had yielded a great share of their store of knowledge and had provided material and pattern for the cultivation of English.   The time was now arrived for the cultivation of more modern fields of knowledge and for the general study of the mother tongue.

CHAPTER XIII

THE AUGUSTAN AGE

IN the Age of Queen Elizabeth earlier tendencies had reached a culmination. The human forces released by the Renaissance found play in exuberance of spirit and extravagance of manner. A similar culmination of earlier forces came in the reign of Queen Anne. The classicizing tendencies which had been gathering force throughout the seventeenth century and the newly developed sense of law and order associated with the cultivation of Natural Philosophy, united to create a sense for regularity and a feeling for a classical perfection to be striven for.

In the progress toward a new ideal a first stage had been reached in the period of the Restoration. There had been a revolt from the pedantry of the age preceding. A cultivated language based on conversational usage had superseded the cultivated language based on Latin pattern and rhetorical precept. Gilbert Burnet in the Preface to his translation of More's *Utopia* remarks that "the English Language has wrought itself out both of the fulsome Pedantry, . . . and the trifling way of dark and unintelligible Wit, that came after that, and out of the coarse Extravagance of *Canting* that succeeded this." The change in fashion of language is more concretely exhibited by Durfey in his play *The Fool turn'd Critick.*. Old Winelove, whose character is indicated by his name, is speaking to Smallwit, also appropriately named, concerning Winelove's son, of whom Smallwit is the tutor: "He sends me word," says Winelove, "you have your

Tropes and Figures, your Syllogisms, Epithetes and Phrases,
I could have nam'd 'em right in my young days." That the
form of language thus learned is no longer in fashion appears in another place in the words addressed by Lucia to
the young man:

> Pray spare your Rhetorick—
>
> . . . . .
>
> I hate a man that flatters worse than death
>
> . . . . .
>
> No, 'tis a careless blunt and
> Manly carriage that likes me best— Besides
> Sir, I think 'tis newer, and more modish.

But there remained need for improvement in the colloquial manner of speech and, in the period following the
dawn of the eighteenth century, effort was made to refine
its coarser elements and particularly to curb its license.
In this direction, as remains to be pointed out, were turned
the critical energies of the Age of Queen Anne. There resulted a prevalent feeling that the language had been
brought near to perfection. "The English Language," says
Leonard Welsted (1724), "does at this Day possess all the
Advantages and Excellencies, which are very many, that its
Nature will admit of. . . ."[1] Freed from pedantry, the
language became elegant rather than ostentatious and, subjected to refinement, it became familiar rather than coarse.
This was the age that produced Addison.

The new age with its classical ideals naturally had much
in common with the Restoration period preceding. A spirit
common to the two periods finds expression in words which
were in vogue. The phrase *common sense*, used not with
its modern meaning, but with its philosophical meaning,
referring to the unified perception based on the use of the

[1] W. H. Durham, *Critical Essays of the Eighteenth Century,* 1915.

five individual senses, served to express the test of truth that supplanted the earlier test by authority. Opposed to *common sense* in this meaning of the expression, was the quality expressed by the word *romantic*. *Romantic*, referring to the supernatural elements of earlier romances, was used as practically synonymous with *absurd*. "Can anything," asks Bishop South (1633-1716), "be imagined more profane and impious, absurd and indeed romantic?"[2] Similar was the hostility felt for a quality associated with the Puritan and expressed by the word *enthusiasm* meaning "divinely inspired." "Enthusiasm," says John Locke (1632-1709), "takes away both reason and revelation, and substitutes in the room of it the ungrounded fancies of a man's own brain, and assumes them for a foundation both of opinion and conduct." "Inspiration," says Shaftesbury (1671-1713), "is a real feeling of the Divine Presence, and enthusiasm is a false one."

The adoption of neoclassic standards of taste is illustrated by the word *Gothic*. The classical forms of architecture which had begun to appear in England in the sixteenth century by 1675, with the beginning of the new St. Paul's Cathedral, had become dominant. The name *Gothic* belonging to earlier forms of English architecture became synonymous with 'barbarous,' 'rude,' 'uncouth.' It is thus first used by Dryden in 1695, and there are citations in the Oxford Dictionary of the word used with this meaning, from Shaftesbury (1710), Burnet (1715), etc., down to Miss Burney (1782) and J. T. Hewlett (1841). The words *attic, piazza,* and *porch,* all associated with a classical type of architecture, it is to be noted, first come into use in this period. The same standard of taste, it is to be noted, appears in the 'colonial style' of architecture introduced into America.

[2] L. P. Smith, *Society for Pure English,* Tract XVII.

liberty to send you Enclosed a poeme written on this occasion by one of our most Eminent hands which is indeed a Masterpiece in its kind and tho very short has touched upon all the topics which are most popular among us. I have likewise transmitted to you a Copy of the preamble to the prince of Wales's Patent which was a very gratefull task imposed on me by the Lords Justices Their Ex^{ies}. have ordered that the Lords and others who meet His Matie. be out of mourning that day, as also their Coaches, but all serv^d except those of the City-magistrates to be in mourning. The shortness of the time which would not be sufficien for the making of new Liveries occasioned this last Order. The Removal of the Lord Bolingbroke has put a seasonable check to an Interest that was making in many places for Members in the next Parliament and was very much relished by the people who ascribed to him in a great measure the Decay of Trade and publick Credit. you will do me a very great honour if you can find terms submissive enough to make the humble Offers of my Duty acceptable to His Majesty. May God Almighty preserve his person and continue him for many years the Blessing of these Kingdomes!

I am with great Esteem and Respect

Sir

your most Obedient and
most Humble Servant

J. Addison.

Joseph Addison (1672-1719): conclusion of a letter written, to J. Robethon, Secretary to George I, on the King's accession; dated Sept. 4, 1714. (Brit. Mus. Stowe MS. 227, F. 419.)

The nature of the culture in the new age is suggested by the word *mob*. This word, one of the fashionable clipped forms of the time, comes from the Latin *mobile vulgus*, the expression adopted in university life to express the contempt of a superior class for the outsider in culture. Shortened to *mobile* and, more frequently, to *mob*, the word came to apply to those outside the select social circles. Anyone who had not the good fortune of association with the cultivated wits of the Town was, in the words of Dryden, "known by his Clown-Accent and his Country-Tone." The word *prude* (1704), a term originally applied to general human excellence, was imported from the French to express a rigid correctness in conduct, which was not in keeping with the free and easy manner cultivated at this period. "One may now know a Man that has never conversed in the World," says Addison (*Spectator*, No. 119), "by his Excess of Good Breeding."

One more word may be cited in illustration of the reformed taste of the Augustan Age. The word *pun*, first cited from the year 1662, apparently a clipped form like *mob*, expresses the changed attitude toward the plays on words once in fashion. One will recall Dryden's opinion of this rhetorical artifice. In this judgment Addison concurs. He concedes (*Spectator*, No. 61) that three forms of this trick of style are admitted by Aristotle under the name of *paragrams* "among the Beauties of good Writing." He alludes to Mr. Swan, "the famous Punster" skilled in the use of the *paronomasia*, the *ploce*, and the *atanaclasis*. He refers to "a famous University of this land formerly very much infested with Punns" and to the reign of King James I "in which the Punn chiefly flourished, a reign in which the learned Monarch was himself a tolerable Punnster and made very few Bishops or Privy Counsellors that had not some time or other signalized themselves by a Clinch, or a

Conundrum." And yet Addison expresses the chastened spirit of his age by classing the pun among the forms of 'false wit.'

With the words *mob* and *pun,* clipped forms provided by academic slang for the expression of contempt, may be joined *fop* (1672) and *prig* (1676), words expressing special aversions, and like *doodle* (1628) and *noodle* (1753) and *humbug* (*ca.* 1750), apparently lifted into polite use from the cant language of the time. Such words provide a kind of index to the taste of the time. They indicate a cultivated keenness of social perception and a critical distinction striven for in manners and in language. For the man of letters at least, as distinguished from the *virtuosi,* or men of science, the "proper study of mankind was man."

The nicety and precision in language demanded by the classical taste of this period was not reached without painstaking effort. Bishop Burnet (1645-1715), in the preface to *The History of My Own Time,* informs the reader that he intends to employ himself in polishing it every "day of his life," a vow apparently kept since the book was not published until 1724-1734, more than ten years after its author's death. Striking is the contrast between this careful method and that of Shakespeare, who, if we may believe Ben Jonson, "never blotted out a line."

The apparent lack of care in Shakespeare's language as preserved in seventeenth-century editions naturally offended the taste of the new age. The adaptation of Shakespeare's plays to the taste of the Restoration period has already been discussed. The new age went farther. The reading of Shakespeare was fairly general. Theobald, writing in 1726, states that "there is scarce a Poet, that our *English* Tongue boasts of, who is more the subject of the Ladies Reading." The works of Shakespeare, however, had been accessible only in the four collected Folio editions, the latest one printed in 1685, and in Quarto editions of individual plays. For the reading public of the Augustan Age a new edition was desirable. This need Jacob Tonson the publisher undertook to supply and enlisted the services of Nicholas Rowe the poet and playwright. The new edition was published in 1709. In it Shakespeare was offered to the reader in modern dress. The editor divides the plays into acts and scenes throughout and indicates the nature of the staging for each scene. The Fourth Folio, according to Lounsbury, is made the basis for the text, but there are frequent emendations and additions based on the Quarto editions. In the external features of spelling and capitalization and punctuation the text is made to conform to the mode of the new period, and the ironing out of grammatical irregularities, which had begun as early as the Second Folio, was more completely carried through. A few examples from the first act of *Hamlet* will illustrate the freedom with which changes were made in spelling, etc. *Hast* in Folio IV becomes *haste* in Rowe; *fantasie* becomes *Phantasie; bin* becomes *been; week* becomes *Week*. Changes in grammatical forms are made. *Some sayes* of Folios I and IV becomes *Some say* in Rowe; *Dos't not divide* of Folio IV becomes *Does not divide*. Occasional verbal changes are made: *To business with the King* in Folio IV (*busines,* Folio I, and Quarto II; *businesse,* Quarto I) becomes *Of Treaty with the King* in Rowe. *That he might not between the winds of Heaven* in Folio IV (*beteene,* Folio I; *beteeme,* Quarto II; not in Quarto I) becomes in Rowe, *That he permitted not. . . .* In general, however, the changes in words are not arbitrary ones made to suit the taste of a new age, but are based on readings from one or the other of the earlier folios and quartos. In fact, Rowe's edition is the first critical edition of Shakespeare's works.

In 1723 Tonson published a second critical edition of

Shakespeare, this time edited by no less a person than Alexander Pope. In this edition besides some changes in external features, spelling, and so on, the principal ones were in reducing the verse here and there to the regularity demanded by the new age. *What we have two nights seen* in Pope succeeds *What we two Nights haue seene* of Folio I, with which Quartos I and II agree. *Yet here, Laertes: get aboard for shame* in Pope succeeds *Yet heere Laertes: Aboord for shame* of Folio I (the reading also of Quartos I and II). *That father his, and the surviver bound* succeeds *That father lost, lost his, and the Suruiuer bound* of Folio I (a repetition of words appearing in Quartos I and II). By changes such as these Shakespeare's language was brought into conformity not only in spelling and in grammatical forms, as in Rowe's edition, but in meter, with the new standards of taste.

Pope, however, was relatively conservative. He expressed a "religious Abhorrence of Innovation." Less reverent toward earlier editions was the next editor of Shakespeare. To Theobald (1733) Shakespeare's works were an "unweeded Garden grown to Seed." He proposes "to restore Sense to Passages in which no Sense has hitherto been found." The faults of early editions are such that the critic is reduced to the "necessity of guessing, in order to amend him." The confident spirit of the new age appears, however, in the assertion that "these guesses change into Something of a more substantial Nature, when they are tolerably supported by Reason and Authorities." The pretensions of the editor are extravagant, but his systematic comparison of the earlier texts, in many instances, brought out the true reading, and some of his emendations have been generally adopted by succeeding Shakespearean scholars.

Before the middle of the century there were printed two

additional critical editions, both by men of rank who lent to their critical opinions an authority derived from their social or official prominence. Sir Thomas Hanmer, earlier Speaker of the House of Commons, published a sumptuous edition. The critical attitude of the Augustan Age appears in the contempt expressed by this editor for the "low stuff which disgraces the works of this great Author," which, however, he explains as "foisted in by the Players after his death," and for the witticisms and conceits, for which, however, "the vicious taste of the age must stand condemned." The textual changes appearing in this amateurish work reflect the spirit of the age. Hanmer's "principal Object" if we may adopt the words of Warburton, a rival editor, "was to reform his Author's Numbers; and this, which he has done, on every Occasion, by the Insertion or omission of a set of harmless unconcerning Expletives, makes up the gross Body of his innocent corrections. And so, . . . he hath tricked up the old Bard, from Head to Foot, in all the finical Exactness of a modern Measurer of Syllables."

Bishop Warburton, "the most impudent man alive" he was called by Samuel Johnson, in his edition of Shakespeare, which appeared in 1747, lent to his criticisms the full weight of his episcopal dignity. It is dedicated to Mrs. Allen of Prior-Park, near Bath, the wife of Fielding's Squire Alworthy, "one who reads few books besides those of Piety and Morals." Shakespeare's language in his opinion is "licentious," a word which he explains by the remark that "to common terms he hath affixed Meanings of his own, unauthorised by Use, and not to be justified by Analogy." The contrast between this flexibility and the stiffness of the classical standards prevailing in Warburton's time is to be noted. Furthermore Shakespeare's works have been "left to the Care of Door-keepers and Prompters" and consequently are "so disguised and travested (*sic*) that no classic Author . . . ever came out in half so maimed and crippled a condition." Warburton set about the task of "amending the corrupted Text where the printed Books afford no Assistance" (surely a presumptuous undertaking!), of "explaining his licentious Phraseology"—and of "illustrating the Beauties of his Poetry."

The liberties taken by Warburton may be judged by one or two examples of his emendations:

FOLIO I	WARBURTON
Why thy Canoniz'd bones Hearsed in death.	Why thy bones hears'd in canonized earth.
Niggard of question, but of our demands Most free in his reply.	Most free of question, but to our demands Niggard in his reply.
Which might depriue your Souereignty of Reason.	Which might deprave your sov'regnty of reason.

Surely upon "Nature and Common-Sense," assumed by Warburton as the basis of his judgments, is imposed a heavy weight of responsibility.

The attitude toward Shakespeare well reveals the spirit of the classical age in English literature. The sifting to which the earlier English vocabulary was subjected, the loss of words and the changes in meaning, are shown in the glossaries appended to the editions of Rowe and of Hanmer. Only a few illustrative examples may be cited here. Among "words still obsolete" Rowe lists: *ballow,* 'pole'; *cautless,* 'uncautious'; *foyzon,* 'plenty'; *to fatigate,* 'to tire'; *gasted,* 'frighted'; *to gleek,* 'to jeer'; *hent,* 'took hold of'; *hight,* 'called'; *maund,* 'a basket'; *orts,* 'scraps'; *riggish,* 'rampant'; *soilure,* 'a blot'; *teen,* 'pain.' The loss in the case of most of these words has proved to be permanent. Hammer gives a longer list of "obsolete and difficult words" occupying twenty-four pages.   Listed as "obsolete" appear: *aiery*, 'nest of hawk or brood of hawks'; *to bandy*, 'to dispute' or 'to canvass'; *base court*, 'back yard'; *to besmirch; to bewray; to bold* or *boult*, 'to sift'; *to budge*, 'to give away'; *a broch*, or *brooch*, or *brouch; dank*, 'moist' or 'damp'; *a deck of cards.* Hanmer's list might be further studied with profit. It affords illustrations of a kind of words later rescued from the inquisitorial spirit of this critical age.

Further examples of this kind of words are offered by Rowe's second list of "Old Words" labelled "Words now used."   In his second list appear: *besmirched*, 'daub'd'; *broch*, 'a buckle'; *to carol*, 'to sing'; *dank*, 'moist,' 'raw'; (listed by Hanmer as "obsolete";) *dulcet*, 'sweet'; *dumps*, 'melancholy'; *foemen*, 'enemies'; *garish*, 'gay,' 'glaring'; *guerdon'd*, 'pay'd'; *gleeful*, 'merry'; *meed*, 'reward'; *murky*, 'obscure'; *ribald*, 'noisy,' 'impudent'; *saws*, 'maxims'; *scath*, 'mischief,' 'harm'; *shrift*, 'confession'; *thewes*, 'sinews,' or 'manners'; *welkin*, 'the heaven,' 'sky.'

Under "words changed in meaning" Rowe lists among others: *moody*, 'angry'; *mood*, 'anger'; *to palter*, 'to trifle,' 'banter'; *paragon*, 'peer' or 'equal'; *to renege*, 'to deny.' In these lists one finds vindication of the judgment of Horace:

> Full many a word, now lost, again shall rise,
> And many a word shall droop which now we prize.
> As shifting fashion stamps the doom of each,
> Sole umpire, arbitress, and guide of speech.

The treatment of Shakespeare's works in the first half of the eighteenth century finds a partial parallel in the treatment of Milton's *Paradise Lost*. The admiration felt for this work came to be almost universal. Addison devotes nearly a score of numbers of the *Spectator* to its criticism and particularly to an analysis of its beauties. Milton he alludes to as the "greatest Poet which our Nation or perhaps any other nation has produced." And yet the blindness of Milton gave ground for doubts about the authenticity of the text of *Paradise Lost* like those felt concerning the text of Shakespeare. In reality two editions of *Paradise Lost* had been issued during Milton's lifetime, the first edition of 1667 and a second edition in the year of his death. There survive three impressions of the first edition with slight modifications such as the change of *fal'n* in the first and second impression to *fall'n* in the third (I, 92). In the second edition of 1674 changes in spelling and capitalization are numerous, including *Illumine* to *Illumin* (I, 23), *fowl* to *foul* (I, 33), *assert th' Eternal Providence* to *assert Eternal Providence* (I, 25), and a consistent change of *their* to *thir*. A number of verbal changes seem to represent revision by the author, such as *Yielded thir Matrons to prevent worse rape,* changed to *Expos'd a Matron to avoid worse rape* (I, 504). In general, however, the changes seem to be printers' changes and afford further illustration of the kind afforded by a comparison of Milton's manuscript and the first printed edition of his sonnet, of the dominance of the printer over the printed text.

Editions followed each other in fairly rapid succession, the ninth edition being printed for Jacob Tonson in 1711. These editions reproduced, with minor variations, the corrected text of the second edition. In 1732, however, there was printed for Jacob Tonson and others a new edition by the distinguished scholar Richard Bentley. In this edition not only the faults "in Orthography, Distinction by Points, and Capital Letters, all which swarm in the prior Editions, are here very carefully, and it's hop'd judiciously corrected" but in the notes and the margin are offered emendations that "attempt a Restoration of the Genuine Milton." "The Friend or Acquaintance," Bentley asserts, "whoever he was, to whom Milton committed his Copy and the Overseeing of the Press, did so vilely execute that Trust that Paradise . . . may be said to be twice lost."

Among the emendations proposed by Bentley are some that fill one with amusement and amazement. On Milton's *To be weak is miserable,* Bentley's comment is that "the Printer here has bestowed upon our Poet absolute Nonsense. . . . The Author gave it *To be Here is miserable."* For *On the secret top,* Bentley suggests *sacred top.* The verse, he says, was "dictated by Milton." Of Milton's *Which tempted our attempt* Bentley says, "lay it at the Editor's Door; and let's believe Milton gave it, *That tempted our revolt."*

Fortunately the authority of Bentley's learning did not win for Bentley's emendations general adoption. Pope laughed to scorn in the *Dunciad* the "mighty scholiast whose unwearied pains Made Horace dull, and humbled Milton's strains." Thomas Newton, in his edition of *Paradise Lost* published in 1754, rejects the emendations as the "dotages of Dr. Bentley." But the attempt of this Olympian scholar is but an extreme instance of the prevalent tendency of the age to reduce even the products of the imagination to the level of the so much esteemed 'common sense.'

Cultivated colloquial English from Elizabethan times on had been a class dialect. In the Restoration period and the Augustan Age that followed, it was a distinction marking the "Man of the Town." The manners of the tradesman-citizen and of the countryman aspiring to courtly elegance had, from before the days of Ben Jonson, been the subject of jest and satire. The countryman as distinguished from the "Man of the Town" was, to use once more the words of Dryden, to be "known by his Clown-Accent and his Country-Tone." Even the "People of Mode in the Country" were old-fashioned, says Addison, in their "Excess of Good Breeding." "The Fashionable world," on the contrary, he says, "is grown free and easie"; "our manners sit more loose upon us." The "free and easie" manner went to shocking extremes in frankness. The "call a spade a spade" ideal of Swift, should once more be called to mind. In the expression of the obscene there was an abandonment of the "modest terms and distant Phrases" and a relapse from Puritan prudishness to a primitive directness. "So that," continues Addison, "at present several of the Men of the Town, and particularly those who have been polished in France, make use of the most coarse uncivilized Words in our Language and utter themselves in such a manner as a Clown would blush to hear." The language used in the social circles of country life was less affected by the fashionable license. "If a man but rap out an oath the people start as if a Gun went off." [3]

The elegant ease of manner which was assiduously cultivated in the Age of Queen Anne belonged to the elect few as distinguished from the many, or the *mob*. John Hughes, in his essay *Of Style* (1695), prescribes for guidance in the "proprieties of words" not etymologies, "for general Acceptation, which is the only Standard of Speech, has given many Words a quite different Sense from their Original," but a "careful Perusal of the most correct Writers" and familiarity with the "Conversation of People of Fashion, that speak well and without Affectation." Unfortunately good models of the kind suggested were not universally accessible. Moreover, people of fashion were limited in their language attainments. They revolted from pedantry,

[3] Etherege, *She Would if She Could*, I, i, p. 83.

but "What is a greater pedant," asks Addison, "than a meer Man of the Town? Barr him the Play-houses, a catalogue of the reigning Beauties, and an Account of a few fashionable Distempers that have befallen him, and you strike him Dumb." (*Spectator*, No. 105.) The same limitations Addison finds in the conversation of the military man, the lawyer, and the statesman. Even Will Honeycomb, so accomplished in gallantry, was less proficient in the art of written speech. In some of his letters to a "Coquet Lady," which he exhibited to his associates with pride, it was found that "several of the Words were wrong spelt." Thrown on the defensive by the raillery of his friends, "he told us, with a little passion, that he never liked Pedantry in Spelling, and that he spelt like a Gentleman, and not like a Scholar."

Evidently there still survived something of the medieval distinction between the courtly knight with no pretension to learning and the clerk whose profession was scholarship. If learning was not highly esteemed by courtly gallants such as Will Honeycomb, with men outside of courtly circles it was rare indeed. The prevalent illiteracy in prominent families like the Verneys and Wentworths, as recently revealed by Professor Wyld, has already been referred to. Made the subject of gentle satire by Addison, the deficiencies in the language of gentlemen are bluntly proclaimed by De Foe. In his *Compleat English Gentleman* (1728 or 1729) he expresses astonishment at "how few gentlemen in England are masters even of the English tongue itself." He speaks of "gentlemen of fortunes and families,—that can hardly write their own names, at least that can't write legibly. . . . When they do write, and supposing they could write a tolerable hand, they can neither write stile nor English; in a word, they can't spell their mother tongue." In support of his assertions he cites the example of "a gentleman of sence and of tollerable good discourse too," who in writing of a servant's drowning says that "there was a mollinkolli accidence be happen'd in his house."

If among men there prevailed a contempt for learning, an association of learning with pedantry, among the fair sex there prevailed what Sir James Murray has called an "elegant illiteracy." The education of girls, beyond the most elementary stages, consisted largely in training the tongue in singing or speaking French, the hands in the arts of sewing and cookery, and, more than all, the feet in dancing. The eighteenth-century attitude toward the education of girls appears in the advice of Lord Lyttleton to his daughter for which Mary Wortley Montagu provides the metrical version:

> Be chaste in dress and frugal in your diet
> In fact, my dearie, kiss me and be quiet.[4]

Among women the revolt from pedantry was more marked than among men. An extreme appeared in the French society which provided in so many ways the pattern in English manners. Addison quotes a French author who "tells us that the Ladies of the Court of France in his time, thought it ill Breeding, and a kind of Female Pedantry to pronounce an hard Word right; for which Reason they took frequent occasion to use hard Words that they might show a Politeness in murdering them." (*Spectator*, No. 37.) "In the female world," says Samuel Johnson in his *Life of Addison*, "any acquaintance with books was distinguished only to be censured." The writers of an English grammar (1711) admonish their "Female correspondents to Buy, Read, and Study this *Grammar*, that their letters may be something less Enigmatic." The most that could be said of women's language was that it was not worse than that

---

[4] Quoted by J. St. Loe Strachey, *New York Times*, August 15, 1926.

of men. Swift in his ironical *Treatise on Polite Conversation* refers to the need he felt at a social gathering, in the search for current conversational bromides, "wherewith to fill his Pocket-Book," to leave the company of the men "over a Bottle of Wine" where there was lack of material worth transcribing, for the discourse was "all degenerated into smart Sayings of their own Invention, and not of the true old Standard" and in despair to "attend the Ladies at their Tea" in his search for the conversational *cliché*. But in quite serious vein he writes in another place that "if the Choice had been left to me, I would rather have trusted the Refinement of our Language, as far as it relates to Sound, to the Judgment of the Women, than of illiterate Court Fops, half-witted Poets, and University Boys. For, it is plain that Women in their manner of corrupting Words, do naturally discard the Consonants, as we do the vowels." Faint praise this but in tone like that of Addison, who says that "my fair Readers are already deeper Scholars than the Beaux" and, in comparing the letters of "fine ladies" and "pretty fellows," asserts that the Ladies are superior "not only in the Sense but in the Spelling," and says further that he "could name some of them who talk much better than several Gentlemen that make a figure at Will's." (*Spectator*, No. 92.)

It is obvious that if cultivated language were to be based on the usage observed in the "Conversation of People of Fashion" it would have a narrow foundation. The foundation, moreover, would be not only narrow but, based as it was on a form of language controlled by fashion, unstable. The revolt from pedantry was like the revolt from the bookish, or high-brow, form of language in our own time, and it produced results quite like the slangy language of today.

From the license in current fashionable speech a counter

revolt was led by Swift. Thomas Pope Blount in 1694 [5] had remarked, "I question whether in Charles the Second's Reign, English did not come to its full Perfection." From this opinion Swift dissents, and in his *Proposal for Correcting, Improving and Ascertaining the English Language* (1712), expresses the opinion: "The Period wherein the English Tongue received most Improvement, I take to commence with the beginning of Queen Elizabeth's Reign and to conclude with the Great Rebellion in Forty Two." He then proceeds to criticize the colloquial tendencies following the Restoration. "From the Civil War to this present Time," he says, "I am apt to doubt whether the corruptions in our Language have not at least equalled the Refinements of it; and these Corruptions very few of the best Authors in our Age have wholly escaped. During the Usurpation such an infusion of Enthusiastick Jargon prevailed in every Writing, as was not shaken off in many Years after. To this succeeded that Licentiousness which entered with the Restoration, and from infecting our Religion and Morals, fell to corrupt our Language, which last was not like to be much improved by those who at that time made up the Court . . . so that the Court, which used to be the Standard of Propriety and Correctness of Speech, was then, and, I think, hath ever since continued the worst School in England for that Accomplishment; and so will remain till better Care be taken in the Education of our young Nobility . . ."

Two years earlier in the *Tatler*, September 26-28, 1710, Swift had said: "I would engage to furnish you with a catalogue of English books, published within the compass of seven years past . . . wherein you shall not be able to find ten lines together of common grammar or common sense. . . . These two evils, ignorance and want of taste, have produced a third; I mean the continual corruption of

[5] *Characters and Censures*, p. 243.

the English tongue, which without some timely remedy, will suffer more by the false refinements of twenty years past, than it hath been improved in the foregoing hundred."

In this same number of the *Tatler* Swift offers a fictitious letter by means of which he exhibits in concentrated form the affectations to which he objects:

SIR,

I cou'd n't get the things you sent for all *about Town* . . . I thôt to *ha'* come down my self, and then *I'd ha' brôut 'um;* but I *han't don't,* and I believe I *can't do't,* that's *Pozz* . . . *Tom* begins to *gi'mself Airs* because *he's* going with the *Plenipo's* . . . 'Tis said, the *French* King will *bamboozl' us agen,* which *causes many Speculations.* The *Jacks,* and others of that *Kidney,* are very *uppish,* and *alert upon't,* as you may see by their *Phizz's* . . . *Will Hazzard* has got the *Hipps,* having lost *to the Tune of* Five hundr'd Pound, *thô* he understands Play very well, *no body better.* He has promis't me upon *Rep,* to leave off Play; but you know 'tis a Weakness *he's* too apt to *give into, thô* he has as much Wit as any Man, *no body more.* He has lain *incog* ever since. . . . The *Mobb's* very quiet with us now . . . I believe you *thôt* I *banter'd* you in my Last like a *Country Put.* . . . I *shan't* leave Town this Month, &c.

This letter is followed by an enlightening commentary:[6]

"This letter," says Swift, "is in every point, an admirable pattern of the present polite way of writing; nor is it of less authority for being an epistle; you may gather every flower of it, with a thousand more of equal sweetness, from the books, pamphlets, and single papers, offered us every day in the coffee houses. And these are the beauties introduced to supply the want of wit, sense, humour, and learn-

[6] From this point on the text is no longer based on the text of the original edition but upon that of a later edition of Swift's Works, London, 1803.

ing, which formerly were looked upon as qualifications for a writer. If a man of wit, who died forty years ago, were to rise from the grave on purpose, how would he be able to read this letter? and after he had gone through that difficulty, how would he be able to understand it? The first thing that strikes your eye, is the break at the end of almost every sentence; of which I know not the use, only that it is a refinement, and very frequently practised. Then you will observe the abbreviations and elisions, by which consonants of most obdurate sounds are joined together without one softening vowel to intervene; and all this only to make one syllable of two, directly contrary to the example of the Greeks and Romans; altogether of the Gothick strain, and of a natural tendency towards relapsing into barbarity which delights in monosyllables, and uniting of mute consonants, as it is observable in all the Northern languages. And this is still more visible in the next refinement, which consists in pronouncing the first syllable in a word that has many, and dismissing the rest; such as *phizz, hipps, mobb, pozz, rep,* and many more; when we are already overloaded with monosyllables, which are the disgrace of our language. Thus we cram one syllable, and cut off the rest; as the owl fattened her mice after she had bit off their legs, to prevent them from running away; and if ours be the same reason for maiming words, it will certainly answer the end; for I am sure no other will desire to borrow them. Some words are hitherto but fairly split, and therefore only in their way to perfection as *incog* and *plenipo;* but in a short time, it is to be hoped, they will be further docked to *inc* and *plen*. This reflection has made me of late years very impatient for a peace, which I believe would save the lives of many brave words as well as men. The war has introduced abundance of polysyllables, which will never be able to live many more campaigns. *Specula-*

tions, operations, preliminaries, ambassadors, palisadoes, communications, circumvallations, battalions, as numerous as they are, if they attack us too frequently in our coffee-houses, we shall certainly put them to flight, and cut off their rear.

"The third refinement observable in the letter I send you, consists in the choice of certain words invented by some pretty fellows, such as *banter, bamboozle, country put,* and *kidney,* as it is there applied; some of which are now struggling for the vogue, and others are in possession of it. I have done my utmost for some years past to stop the progress of *mob* and *banter,* but have been plainly borne down by numbers, and betrayed by those who promised to assist me.

"In the last place you are to take notice of certain choice phrases, scattered through the letter, some of them tolerable enough, till they were worn to rags by servile imitators. You might easily find them, although they were not in a different print, and therefore I need not disturb them.

"These are the false refinements in our style, which you ought to correct: first by arguments and fair means; but if those fail, I think you are to make use of your authority as censor, and by an annual *index expurgatorius* expunge all words and phrases that are offensive to good sense, and condemn those barbarous mutilations of vowels and syllables. In this last point the usual pretence is that, they spell as they speak: a noble standard for language! to depend upon the caprice of every coxcomb, who, because words are the clothing of our thoughts, cuts them up and shapes them as he pleases, and changes them oftener than his dress. I believe all reasonable people would be content, that such refiners were more sparing of their words, and liberal in their syllables. On this head I should be glad you would bestow some advice upon several young readers in our churches, who, coming up from the university full fraught with admiration of our town politeness will needs correct the style of our prayer books. In reading the absolution, they are very careful to say '*Pardons* and *absolve's*'; and in the prayer for the royal family it must be *endue'um, enrich'um, prosper'um* and *bring'um;* then in their sermons they use all the modern terms of art, *sham, banter, mob, bubble, bully, cutting, shuffling* and *palming;* all which, and many more of the like stamp, as I have heard them often in the pulpit from some young sophisters, so I have read them in some of those sermons that have made a great noise of late. The design, it seems, is to avoid the dreadful imputation of pedantry; to show us that they know the town, understand men and manners, and have not been poring upon old unfashionable books in the university."

The shafts of ridicule were directed by Steele and Addison and Swift not only against the prevalent illiteracy among fine ladies and pretty fellows but against stale and vulgar forms of expression. In his *Treatise on Polite Conversation* Swift ironically proposes "an appendix to deal with Oaths (to be sold for Six-pence stitched, and with a Marble cover) because a just collection of Oaths, repeated as often as the Fashion requires, must have enlarged this Volume, at least to double the Bulk." For, to use the words of "an ancient Poet":

> . . . now adays, Men change their Oaths
> As often as they change their Cloaths.

He also gives ironic praise to the fashion of "refining the Orthography, by spelling the Words in the same manner as they are pronounced." As examples of this practice he gives: *can't; ha'n't; sha'n't; didn't; coodn't; woodn't; isn't; e'n't; jommetry,* 'geometry'; *verdi,* 'verdict'; *lard,* 'lord';

larnin', 'learning'; and *pozz*, 'positive'; *mobb*, 'mobile vulgus'; *phizz*, 'physiognomy'; *rep*, 'reputation'; *plenipo*, 'plenipotentiary'; *incog*, 'incognito'; *hipps* or *hippo*, 'hypochondria'; *bam*, 'bamboozle'; and (a crowning instance) *insickly pay-day*, 'encyclopedia.'

The contraction of words and the consequent heaping up of consonants and multiplication of monosyllables is a pet aversion with Swift. In this feeling he had been anticipated by Dryden who in 1685 finds "in the preponderance of monosyllables 'encumbred with consonants' the cause of the inferiority of English to French," and asserts that "poetry requires adornment, and that is not to be had from our old Teuton monosyllables."[7] Similar ideas, apparently borrowed from Swift or developed in discussion with Swift, form the material for the number of the *Spectator* dated August 11, 1711 (the date is to be noted). Addison objects to converting longer words to monosyllables by rapidity of pronunciation, to contracting the length of syllables in long words from the Latin, such as *liberty, conspiracy, theatre, orator*, etc., to "Closing in one syllable the Termination of our Præterperfect Tense, as in the Words *drown'd, walk'd, arriv'd* . . . which has very much disfigured the Tongue, and turned a tenth part of our smoothest Words into so many Clusters of Consonants." To "this reflection" derived "from one of the greatest Genius's this Age has produced" (evidently Swift), Addison adds an observation on the substitution of *-es* for *-eth* in verbs, a change which "has multiplied a Letter which was before too frequent in our English Tongue, and added to the hissing in our Language, which is taken so much Notice of by Foreigners." He comments further, in ignorance of the true history of the form, on another use of the letter *s* which "on many occasions does the Office of a whole Word, and represents the *His* and *Her*

---

[7] J. L. Moore, *Tudor-Stuart Views*, p. 11.

of her Forefathers." With Swift he deplores the use of contracted forms such as *mayn't, can't, shan't,* and *won't* and the curtailing in such words as *mob, rep, pos,* and *incog.* He also points out the perplexity arising from the frequent suppression of several particles, such as the relatives *whom* and *which,* an idiomatic English practice prevalent already in Elizabethan times. The tone of Addison is much milder than that of Swift but is interesting as showing a remarkable lack of true knowledge of the history of the forms of speech discussed.

Addison comes back to the discussion of the English language in the *Spectator* of September 8 in the same year. This time he satirizes the adulteration of English through French words introduced as a result of the war with France. The tendency he illustrates by means of a letter from a young gentleman in the army to his father written in the year of the battle of Blenheim. This letter, in which are introduced such words as *reconnoiter, hauteur, marauding, corps, gensd'armes, corps de reserve, gasconade, posse, commandant, cartel, carte blanche,* was unintelligible to the English father who, therefore, turned for assistance to the curate of the parish, who in turn pronounced the letter "neither fish, flesh, nor good red-herring." The father thereupon produced an earlier letter with the remark, "You see here when he writes for money he knows how to speak intelligibly enough, there is no man in England can express himself clearer, when he wants a new furniture for his horse." The old man was "so puzzled . . . that it might have fared ill with his son, had he not seen all the prints about three days after filled with the same terms of art, and that Charles only wrote like other men."

Another source of deep concern with Swift and Addison and their contemporaries was the instability of the language. The change in English from the time of Chaucer, even

from the time of Shakespeare, was noted. A century earlier
Bacon had expressed the fear that "these modern languages
will at one time or other play the bank-rowtes with books"
and, later in the seventeenth century, Waller had expressed
like forebodings:

> But who can hope his Lines should long
> Last, in a daily changing Tongue,
>
> . . . . .
>
> Time, if we use ill Chosen Stone,
> Soon brings a well-built Palace down.
>
> Poets that Lasting Marble seek,
> Must carve in Latin or in Greek,
> We write in Sand, our Language grows,
> And like our Tide, Ours overflows.

The fears of the seventeenth century in the Augustan Age
find renewed expression in the lines of Pope:

> Our sons their father's failing language see,
> And such as Chaucer is shall Dryden be.

In search for a remedy for the instability of the language
and the ills affecting it Augustan writers recurred to the
scheme which had been long and ardently advocated by
Dryden and for which De Foe in his *Essay on Projects*
(1692-3) had elaborated a detailed plan. Addison, in the
first paper discussed above, arrived at the conclusion that
the debatable points in English language would "never be
decided till we have something like an Academy, that by
the best authorities and Rules drawn from the Analogy of
Languages shall settle all Controversies between Grammar
and Idiom." To this idea he comes back in the second
paper. "I have often wished," he says, "that as in our
constitution there are several Persons whose Business it is
to watch over our Laws, our Liberties and Commerce, cer-

tain Men might be set apart, as Super-intendants of our Language."

The plan thus suggested, was favored by Swift who, the following year, 1712, addressed to the Lord High Treasurer, his friend, Robert, Earl of Oxford, a formal "Proposal for Correcting, Improving and Ascertaining the English Tongue." One should of course note the early meaning as here used of the word *ascertaining*, 'making certain' or 'fixing.' This open letter issued in booklet form begins with a formal statement: "What I had the Honour of mentioning to Your Lordship sometime ago in Conversation, was not a new thought, just then started by Accident or Occasion, but the Result of long Reflection; and I have been confirmed in my Sentiments by the Opinion of some very judicious Persons, with whom I consulted. They all agreed, That nothing would be of greater Use towards the Improvement of Knowledge and Politeness, than some effectual Method for *Correcting, Enlarging* and *Ascertaining* our Language; and they think it a Work very possible to be compassed, under the Protection of a Prince, the Countenance and Encouragement of a Ministry, and the Care of proper Persons chosen for such an Undertaking . . ."

Swift proceeds to offer a remarkably well-informed account of the changes that had come about in the language since the Elizabethan period and the corruptions that had affected it. He deplores especially its instability and asks how a writer of history, even if endowed with genius, could undertake a work on history "with Spirit and chearfulness when he considers, that he will be read with Pleasure but a very few Years, and in an Age or two shall hardly be understood without an Interpreter."

He then makes to the Lord Treasurer the formal suggestion: "In order to reform our Language, I conceive, My Lord, that a free judicious Choice should be made of such

Persons, as are generally allowed to be qualified for such a Work, without any regard to Quality, Party, or Profession. These, to a certain Number at least, should assemble at some appointed Time and Place, and fix on Rules by which they design to proceed. What Methods they will take, is not for me to prescribe."

Swift's plan for an Academy came near to success. David Mallet in the dedication to Lord Chesterfield of his *Amyntor and Theodora* (1747) says that the plan "was agreed to by the late Treasurer Oxford: and a certain annual sum, for the support of it, was certainly promised . . ." Mallet renews the suggestion to Lord Chesterfield. "May we not hope," he writes, "that some such scheme, or one yet more extensively useful, will take• place, so as to be rendered effectual, under your Lordship's influence?" But neither the suggestion by Swift nor the later one by Mallet gained final adoption. Other ideas prevailed and other ideals have been created. The Royal Society of Literature which was granted a royal charter early in the nineteenth century has undertaken tasks quite different from those undertaken by the French Academy and those had in mind by Swift. Lord Balfour, the vice-president of 1926, in a recent address expressed the opinion that "it would be folly for them to set themselves up as in any sense the guardians of their language." He did not think that "any member of the society would seriously propose that they should set to work to make a dictionary of the English language at all corresponding to the task undertaken in France, and he was sure that if they did undertake the task they would perform it without any success, or any advantage to the cause they had at heart." The bond of union in the twentieth-century Royal Society, in the opinion of Lord Balfour, is simply "the love of literature."

The features of language decried by Swift are not extinct

today, and somewhat akin to the organization proposed by Swift is the recently formed voluntary body, the Society for Pure English. But the general situation today is not that of the early eighteenth century because the objectives that Swift had in mind have in great part been attained through other agencies.

The agencies thus involved have been the English grammars and English dictionaries applied in great part through the school and the schoolmaster. The eighteenth century saw a remarkable falling off in the prestige of the old grammar schools. By the end of the eighteenth century the old endowed grammar schools had so sunk in importance that, to quote the words of Lord Chief Justice Kenyon (1795), they were become "empty walls without scholars, and everything neglected but the receipts of the salaries and emoluments." [8]   The educational task formerly accomplished by the grammar schools came to be accomplished by schools different in kind. There were the Charity Schools which provided popular elementary instruction, and there grew up "English" schools, founded either in conjunction with the Latin schools or independently, and private schools, a development from the earlier elementary "writing" and "arithmetic" schools. [9]   Methods earlier applied to the teaching of Latin came to be applied in the teaching of English. Both in England and in America the English language came to be "taught grammatically."

The *English Grammar* published by Lane in 1700 should be recalled. The ideas there expressed, ten years later had become widely current, and stirred by the discussions by Steele and Addison in the *Tatler* and the *Spectator* and the various utterances by Swift, interest in English grammar came to rival the heated interest in the contemporary

[8] F. Watson, *The Old Grammar Schools,* pp. 131*ff.*
[9] *Ibid.*

struggles between Whigs and Tories. The subject of grammar was in the air. The general interest led to the composition of grammatical treatises, and in the years 1711-2 three important books on English grammar made their appearance.

The earliest of these new works was *A Grammar of the English Tongue . . . adapted to the use of Gentlemen and Ladies, as well as of the Schools of Great Britain,* published in 1711. Facing the title page was printed "The Approbation of Isaac Bickerstaff, Esq.," which concludes with the admonition for "all my Female Correspondents to Buy, Read, and Study this *Grammar,* that their letters may be something less Enigmatic; And on all my Male Correspondents likewise, who make no Conscience of False-spelling and False-English, I lay the same Instruction, on Pain of having their Epistles expos'd in their own proper Dress, in my *Lucubrations.* Isaac Bickerstaff, Censor." It should be recalled that the last number of Steele's *Tatler* had appeared as recently as January of this year.

The Dedication, addressed to the Queen, concludes as follows: "A *Grammar* of the *French Language* was the First Labour of that Learned Body the *French Academy.* That being the foundation of all Writing; And as YOUR MAJESTIES Arms have been Superiour to those of France, so we hope that, by *Your Royal Influence,* You will give the same superiority to *Our Arts* and *Sciences,* which are all built on *This* that is now Presented to YOUR SACRED MAJESTY, by MADAM, *Your Majesties most Obedient and Dutiful Subjects.* The Authors."

In the Preface the "Authors" assert that the dignity and importance of the English language make it worthy of "a Grammar proper to it self." This, however, they say, "has never yet been brought to any tolerable Perfection, but was left so helpless, that to write it Purely and Correctly, it was necessary to study other Languages, in which the Art of Grammar was fixt. But this was encumbred with so many Difficulties, that few Natives know how to write their own Mother Tongue." The "Authors" have been "commissioned by Mr. Brightland to undertake this task" so that "furnish'd with all the Helps, that either ancient or modern Writers cou'd supply us withal, and the Assistance of all our Learned Acquaintance, we have ventur'd to Suffer our Endeavours to see the Public." Obviously here is an independent attempt to accomplish one of the most important tasks of an Academy.

Worthy of attention in the Preface is the remark that: "We still call our Animals by Names of German Original, whose Flesh turn'd into Food we call by Gallic Names, as an Ox, a Cow, a Calf, a Sheep, a Hogg, a Boar, a Deer, &c., but call their Flesh Beef, Veal, Mutton, Pork, Brawn, Venison, &c . . ." The idea here expressed which is derived from the grammar by John Wallis, has been made classic through its adoption by Sir Walter Scott in his *Ivanhoe*.

The plan proposed in this work is "not to forge a New Language, nor to alter the Orthography now in Use and settled by Custom, the *Jus* & *Norma Loquendi* . . ." The "Authors" also "wou'd have nothing to do with the Whimsical Invention; in which those err very wide who wou'd Spell all Words deriv'd from the Latin or Greek according to those languages. . . . On the contrary we ought to lay down the certain Rules of Reading and Writing the Language, as it is establish'd by the general Use of the Learned themselves, and the Nature of the Tongue." The "Authors" hold that radical attempt at improvement would be in vain, that "to hope to reform the Errors of a Nation without the Supream Authority, or ev'n with it, but by degrees, and a Combination of the Learned, is a jest." English conservatism supported by classical precept here appears.

There is lurking in the minds of the "Authors" the idea of
an Academy. They proceed, however, to proclaim that:
"we are to have no manner of Regard to the Properties of
other Tongues, either Ancient or Modern, and this in the
construction of Sentences, as well as in Letters, Syllables or
Words, the Rules of English being only to be drawn from
the English it self." Here the grammar of Lane, "the best
English Grammar, except Dr. Wallis," is held at fault, because "he has done as Ben Johnson [*sic*], and most others
who have attempted English Grammars, that is, he has
extended and tortur'd our Tongue to confess the Latin
Declensions, Conjugations, and ev'n Construction, whereas
there is nothing so different." Wallis is found fault with
because "he wrote in Latin, and for the use of Foreigners,
whom he supposes masters of the Latin Grammar, and
makes use of Terms accordingly. All which are in this
thrown aside, and we may say that it is *Entirely* English."

This work, sound in general plan, is well executed.
Earlier authorities were judiciously used. "There was no
Spelling-book or Grammar," the reader is informed, "in
English, Latin, French, &c., that we have not consulted,
and in our own Tongue alone there are about Thirty." The
general division of the subject is the usual four-fold one
into Letters, Syllables, Words, Sentences.

The discussion of sounds under the division of Letters
follows closely that of Wallis, whose table with the double
classification of vowel sounds is offered in English translation. One or two of the pronunciations indicated have an
interest to the modern reader because unlike the pronunciation established in later use. The letter *a* has the broad
sound not only in *all* but in *shall*, not only in *war, ward,
warm*, and in *wash* and *water*, but in *wrath*. "The sound of
e is shortened when it is expressed by *ea* in the middle of
several Words," not only in *already, bearn* ('child'),

weather, treasure, etc., but in *beard* and *earth.* The pronunciation of *o* in *folly* and *fond* is "the same sound with *a*
in *fall* and *aw* in *fawn,* only the last is long and the former
short." . . . "The proper Double Vowel *oi* . . . is written
by *oi* . . . in *Oister, oil, etc.,* and in *poise, noise, voice, re-
joice, etc.*" But "this Double Vowel in many words has the
sound of *i* long, as in *Point, anoint, jointure,* etc." The
vowel *i* besides its long and short sounds has a third in some
few words . . . like double *ee, magazine, machine, shire.*

A second ambitious treatise appearing in the year 1711
was *An Essay towards a Practical English Grammar* by
James Greenwood. The author adopts as his motto the
Latin sentence, *Extera quid quærat, sua qui Vernacula
nescit?* He announces three definite aims: (1) "to excite
Persons to the Study of the Mother Tongue;" (2) to make
study of grammar "easy and delightful to our *English*
Youth, who have for a long time esteemed the Study of this
Useful Art very irksome, obscure and difficult"; (3) "to
oblige the *Fair Sex* whose *Education* perhaps, is too much
neglected in this Particular."

With zeal he defends the English language from certain
criticisms. That English has too many monosyllables, the
objection urged by Swift and Addison, he attempts to dis-
prove. Languages made up of monosyllables, he informs
the reader, "are ancienter than the others; the Greek
Tongue abounded in Monosyllables" and "tho Monosyllables are not so fit for *Numbers,* yet that Happiness of
Composition, which is peculiar to our Language with the
Greek, makes our Poetry as musical and harmonious as that
of any Nation in the World." He emphasizes the copiousness of English and supports his contention by showing the
number of synonyms and points out that there are forty-
two English words associated with the meaning 'anger.'

He finds fault, however, with the "unfixed Sense of

Words, by reason of *Metaphor* and *Phraseology.*" The remarkable freedom of the Elizabethan period, exemplified by the language of Shakespeare, in turning words to new uses should be called to mind. The resulting confusion in days when authoritative dictionaries were not at hand may be easily appreciated. Greenwood urges that: "Varieties in Language may seem to contribute to the Elegance and Ornament of Speech; yet like other affected ornaments, they prejudice the native Simplicity of it, and contribute to the disguising of it with false Appearances." But it is the tendencies of his own time that he has particularly in mind, the tendencies condemned by Swift. "Witness the present Age," he says, "especially the late Times, wherein the grand Imposture of phrases hath almost eaten out solid Knowledge in all Professions; such Men being of most esteem who are skilled in these canting Forms of Speech, tho' in nothing else."

Greenwood makes the usual division of his subject into four parts. For practical effectiveness he presents his matter in the catechism form of questions and answers. Like the authors of the other grammar of 1711, he uses an English method. "I have been obliged," he says, "to pursue a quite different Method, neglecting the Latin Way, and keeping close to what the particular Nature of our Tongue required."

In the following year, 1712, appeared a third ambitious work, *The English Grammar: or, an Essay in the Art of Grammar, Applied to and Exemplified in the English Tongue* by Michael Mattaire. This work, it will be observed from the title, is less modern than the two just discussed. The author does not use a purely English plan but goes back to the earlier Latin method of Ben Jonson. He speaks of his "attempt upon Grammar; wherein i [*sic*] exemplify in English the Rules and Terms of that Art, and draw a Parallel between that Language and the Learned ones; to the end that the English may be an Introduction to them . . ." This book, somewhat reactionary in spirit, aims to teach grammar through English, rather than English through grammar. It aims, however, at an improvement in method, for "it is now the miserable Fate of Grammar to be more Whip't than Taught; . . . Youths . . . are forced to learn what they can't understand; being hurried into Latin, before they are well able to read English." Like his contemporaries this writer is solicitous for the fair sex. "As for that tender Sex," he asks, "which to set off we take so much care and use such variety of breeding, some for the feet, some for the hands, others for the voice; what shall i call it, cruelty or ignorance, to debar them from the accomplishments of Speech and Understanding . . . ?"

In this work grammar is regarded as governed by authority and logic rather than by the facts of actual usage. In passages printed in finer type are cited authoritative remarks from Dr. Busby the Latin grammarian, from Apollonius the Alexandrian, from Aristotle and Quintilian and Priscian. Of greater significance is the emphasis thrown on "Analogy," the principle made prominent in later eighteenth-century works on the English language, and upon "Anomaly" the logical opposite of analogy. Regularity and uniformity spring from analogy. Irregularity goes with anomaly. Under the head of anomaly of parts of speech this author considers the following classes:

Heterostoichy: a vowel for another, *e.g., older, elder, oldest, eldest.*

Heterology: the same word signifying person or thing, the age of youth; *the youth, young man.*

Heteroclisy: words redundant; *folly, foolishness.*

Heterogeny: different genders applied to neuter things.

This treatise is complex and difficult. With the emphasis on authority and upon logic went a neglect of the results already achieved by the codification of actual usage. For instance, he fails to make the distinction between *shall* and *will* which Wallis had formulated and which was adopted by the two other grammarians of the years 1711-2.

The age was one of satire, the age that had produced the *Battle of the Books* and was later to produce the *Dunciad*. Representing the spirit of the age and at the same time reflecting the prevalent interest in the subject of grammar, was an anonymous book published in 1712 with the title, *Bellum Grammaticale: or, the Grammatical Battel Royal, in Reflections on the Three English Grammars, Publish'd in about a year last past* . . . In "a Word to the Reader" the anonymous author informs the "Courteous Reader" that: "The Town having been so long teiz'd with Party Squabbles of political Whig and Tory, I did not know but that a new Sort of Warfare might be welcome; and that is betwixt Professors of Arts about their own Provinces . . . There has been lately a mighty Bent, in the Buyers of Books, to Grammatical Essays; and particularly those which treat of the Nature of our own Language; for which I congratulate the Genius of our Time. 'Tis a Sort of Promise of its being weary, or asham'd of that general Barbarism which has spread through our Writers in all the politer Arts; and that we may hope, if Emperio do not intrude with their empty Pretences, in a few Years to see our Nation as polite, as brave."

This work sinks to abuse of Greenwood in the hope expressed that: "By showing how unfit thou ar't to write any Book at all, thou might'st, if it were possible, come to know thy self and learn Modesty; and so, *Scindapsus, Blictri, Lirum, Larum, Screlum, Scraulum in Æternum valeto*, heartily farewell." The work is feeble in wit and sounds like a puerile attack by a former pupil on a not well-beloved master. It has an interest, however, as showing that grammar was for a time "the talk of the town."

Most of the grammatical works of this period exhibit a knowledge broadened beyond the limits of mere classical learning. This broadened knowledge appears in the increase of knowledge regarding earlier English. The study of Saxon English, or Anglo-Saxon, which had begun in the seventeenth century, was continued and in 1689 Dr. George Hickes published an Anglo-Saxon grammar, *Institutiones Grammaticæ Anglo-Saxonicæ* and in 1703-5 an important collection of Old English texts in his *Linguarum veterum septentrionalium Thesaurus.* Not long after, in 1715, appeared *The Rudiments of Grammar for the English Saxon Tongue* by Elizabeth Elstob, said to be the "first given in English." Attention to the interests of the fair sex was beginning to yield fruit. On the title page of this book appears an interesting commendation from a bishop: "Our English possessions are truly enough called a patrimony, as derived to us by the industry of our fathers: but the language that we speak is our mother-tongue; and who so proper to play the critics in this as the females?"

The widening knowledge of the period is further shown by the new attention given, beginning with Wallis in 1653, to the earlier history of languages in general. Greenwood speaks of eleven mother tongues; four "Noble," seven "of less dignity." The four chief mother tongues are: Greek, Latin, Teutonick, and Sclavonick. The seven minor ones are: Albanese, European Tartar or Scythian, Hungarian, Finnish, Cantabrian (border of France and Spain), Irish, Old Gaulish or British. An interesting partial anticipation of the doctrine of modern comparative philology appears in the statement by Greenwood that it is the "opinion of some that the Scythian tongue was the common mother tongue from which both the Greek, Latin, German, and Persian are derived."

The English grammars of 1711-2 were important shaping forces in the early eighteenth century. The first of them, the one published anonymously, was issued in new editions, and the third edition, which appeared in 1714, was signed by the name of John Brightland. To the work were appended the "Arts of Logick, Rhetorick, Poetry, &c.," and the book in its enlarged form makes pretension to be "a compleat System of English Education. For the use of the Schools of Great Britain and Ireland." One must not fail to notice the completeness of the shift from Latin, the basis of instruction in the old grammar schools, to English which now affords a "Compleat System" of education. The grammar by Greenwood also appeared in new editions throughout the century and, as remains to be seen, the grammars by Brightland and by Greenwood served in the self-education of the American, Benjamin Franklin.

But these books by no means had the field to themselves. In the first half of the seventeenth century there were produced not only dictionaries, of which a discussion must be deferred until the following chapter, but numerous grammatical works. Among these works may be mentioned: *A Compleat Guide to the English Tongue* (no date or author indicated); *A Guide to the English Tongue, In two Parts*, by Tho. Dyche, Schoolmaster in London, 2d ed., 1710; *A Spelling Dictionary*, by the same author, 3d ed., 1731; *The Protestant Tutor*, London, 1716; *A New Guide to the English Tongue*, by Dilworth, 13th ed., London, 1751; *The Art of Reading and Writing English* by Isaac Watts, London, 1721. The works by Dyche and Dilworth, both of them practical schoolmen, were long influential. Dilworth's grammar was one that Noah Webster aimed to supersede, and Dyche's *Guide*, dealing with writing and pronunciation, appeared in revised form as late as 1816. Addressed not exclusively to persons of quality, but, as expressed by the *Compleat Guide,* to "all Young People that are designed for any Thing of good Education," these books laid special emphasis on the elementary features of spelling and pronunciation. "By daily experience it is found," says Dilworth, "that even many, who have attained to the Art of writing a good Hand, are so unfortunate in Spelling, that neither themselves, nor the more knowing, can guess at their Meaning, couched under such a preposterous jumble of Letters set for Words." In the practical works by Dyche and by Dilworth and their kind, words were arranged in groups, first monosyllables, then words of two syllables, and so on to the lists of words with six or seven syllables. The position of the accent was indicated and "Praxes" for pronunciation provided. The centuries-long struggle to teach English spelling was begun. To the work of Dyche were contributed commendatory verses. Nahum Tate, the poet laureate, declares

> These Rules are well design'd, to take away
> The *Scandal* that upon our Nation lay;
> Where *Elegance* a stranger was, and few
> The Beauties of their Mother-Language knew,
> These Rules must rectify both *Tongue* and Pen,
> If Youth wou'd speak and write like *learned* Men:

and John Williams in his rimed tribute asserts that:

> This just Essay you have performed so well,
> Records will shew 'twas *Dyche* first taught to Spell.

In the publications of this period it will be observed that the use of capital letters does not follow modern rules. Nor were the grammarians of this period in agreement. Dilworth prescribes the modern uses but in addition the use of capitals "for all Words put for proper Names, or that have any great *Emphasis* in a Sentence." Dr. Watts gives nine rules governing the use of capitals, the last of which is the remark: "It has also been the growing Custom of this Age in printing of everything, . . . to begin every Name of a thing . . . with a Great Letter; tho I cannot approve it so universally as it is practiced."

Regarding the indication of the possessive relation also there was difference of opinion among the grammarians of this period. Greenwood rules that the "genitive case ends in Singular and Plural in *s* or *es*," *e.g., Man's Nature*. "If the Substantive be of the Plural Number, the first *s* is cut off," *e.g., the Warrior's Arms*. "But when the Singular Number ends in *s*, both *s's* are for the most part expressed," *e.g., Charles's Horse, St. James's Park*. His rule, it will be observed, agrees with that of Miege which has already been quoted. Greenwood adds a rule governing what is in modern times called the 'group genitive.' When three substantives come together, he says that the "genitive case is made by adding *s* to the second," *e.g.*, the Queen of England's Crown.

The author of the *Compleat Guide* revolts from Latin grammar. Latin, he says, has six cases arising from variable termination of Latin nouns, but this is "a thing incident to the Latine Tongue, but not to our Vulgar Speeches. . . . Only the English may be said to have a *Genitive* in the Latine Sense;—in which case the Substantive assumes an *s* with an Apostroph. In the Plural Number, the Apostroph, for Distinctions' sake, is left out; as, *both Kings Armies* . . ."

Among the grammarians the distinction established by Wallis between *shall* and *will, should* and *would* is frequently adopted but by no means universally, and some of the independent attempts at distinction are too confusing for the modern reader as they must have been to the contemporary generation. The distinction between the relatives *who, which,* and *that* provoked discussion and provided Steele with material for the amusing "Humble Petition of Who and Which" (*Spectator,* No. 78) in which the use of *which* (for *who*) in the Lord's Prayer and in the invocation, "Spare Thou them, O God, which confess . . ." of the General Confession, is objected to. The allusion in this "Petition" to "the Jacksprat *That*" provokes in a later number of the *Spectator* (No. 80) "the just remonstrance of affronted That." The entertaining discussion affords illustration of the current social interest in questions of speech as in questions of manners and morals.

That in this period the singular form *thou* of the personal pronoun had been in general superseded by *you* appears from Greenwood's statement: "And it is counted ungentile and rude to say, *Thou dost so and so.*"

Let us turn our attention now from the recommendation of the grammarians to the actual usage of the time. In the language of the cultivated there continued to appear occasional forms of expression which in later age, subjected to grammars and dictionaries, have been condemned or at least challenged. Let us look at the language of the *Spectator.* The collective noun, singular in form, is followed by a plural verb, *e.g.,* "Tho' the dull Part of Mankind are harmless" (No. 43, Steele). The indicative form is used where the subjunctive would now be required; *e.g.,* "told her, That if he was in Mr. Truelove's Place" (No. 57, Addison). *Who* is used for *whom; e.g.,* "but who should I see there but . . . ?" (No. 266, Steele). The much debated "it is me" construction appears; *e.g.,* "It is not me you are in love with" (No. 290, Steele).

That the language even of the ultra-critical writers of this age was regulated by a different standard of correctness from that of today appears even more clearly in the writings of Swift. In *Gulliver's Travels*,[10] for instance, words are frequently employed in uses later abandoned; *e.g.,* "all my Friends and *Relations";* "Custom soon *reconciled* the want of it"; "nothing . . . to which I could *resemble* them"; "They *admired* to hear me answer them"; "so *impudently* abused"; "I *enlarged* myself much on these . . . Particulars"; *"abhorring* to cover myself"; "a great *Disgust against";* *"missive* weapons" ('missiles') ; "bring away *a Couple* more" ('a few,' a use now objected to by some). Earlier grammatical forms are used; *e.g., foot* for *feet* (regularly used after numerals), and verb forms such as *eat* for *ate* (used consistently), *drank* for *drunk, loaden* for *loaded* or *laden, writ* for *wrote.* Constructions later abandoned or at least challenged are frequent; *e.g.,* "A crew of Pyrates *are* driven"; "the wisest part of the Ministry *were";* "till the Family *were* asleep"; *"these kind* of Feasts"; "where neither of them *pretend";* "There *are* likewise another kind of Princes"; "The Numerousness of those that dedicated themselves . . . *were* such that . . ."; "such that the . . . Advantage and Income of the Profession *was* not sufficient to . . ."; "since the Maintenance of so many *depend* on . . ."; "this Society hath a peculiar Cant and Jargon of *their* own"; "each Nation priding itself upon the Antiquity . . . of *their* own Tongue"; "The Enemy *was* so frighted when *they* saw me." The modern distinction between the indicative *was* and the subjunctive *were* is not always observed: "I could heartily wish a law *was* enacted"; "I durst not . . . until I *were* sufficiently aired." Redundancy appears in the language of this arch-foe of redundancy; *e.g., but however* (frequent) and *from whence* (regularly used).

Turning from the language cultivated in courtly use to that of the scholar one finds in the writings of Richard

[10] Ed. H. Morley. "Exactly reprinted from the First Edition."

Bentley (1662-1742) forms of expression such as "a ripening," "those kind of requests," "no goat had been there neither," as well as a frequent use of words and expressions later branded as Americanisms. Regarding the use of words one finds Bentley in controversial writings objecting to the use of *ignore* and *recognosce* by his opponent Boyle, and Boyle objecting to Bentley's use of *concede, commentitious, idiom, negoce, putid, repudiate, timid, vernacular.* The arbitration later provided by authoritative grammars and dictionaries was not yet available.[11]

If one descends one stage in the social ladder to the level of De Foe, one finds the difference from modern accepted good usage even more apparent. Original editions of De Foe's writings are not generally available to the modern reader, and editors of De Foe, even editors of facsimile editions, have not always faithfully reproduced the original form of the language. But in a recent edition of *Robinson Crusoe* such as that by J. W. Clark, which makes pretension to adherence to the original form, one will find forms of expression to be explained in part by De Foe's aim to make language dramatically appropriate to characters lacking school training, but in any event not tolerated in modern correct writing. One will find the survival of the double negative frequent in such expressions as: "lost no time, nor abated no Diligence," "I did not act so hastily neither," "was not true neither," "no need . . . nor no room," and, on the other hand, the use of *or* correlative with *neither, e.g.,* "neither man or beast," "I neither saw, or desir'd to see." The frequent survival of the flat adverb will catch the attention: *e.g.,* "nothing near so anxious," "a tolerable good Taylor," "an exceeding nourishing food," "it was scarce safe," "dreadful high," "excessive dear," "excessive hot." Irregular uses of the personal pronoun ap-

[11] *Cf.* H. E. Shepherd, *American Journal of Philology,* II, 20-30.

pear: *e.g.*, "Why does not God kill you and I . . . ?" "between Friday and I." *Who* is used for *whom: e.g.*, "the bearded Men, who he had told me of," "Friday also, who I had made an excellent Marks-Man," "The old goat who I found expiring," "some Turks, who I saw," "prisoners . . . who we had trusted with Arms." In the use of verbs there are many forms of expression either not in accordance with modern usage or subject to challenge. There is the debated use of *had best* in "what I had best to do" and "what I had best do." There is the use of indicative form for subjunctive in "as if he was bound for. . . ." There are many tense forms since abandoned; *Awak'd,* for 'awoke'; *eat,* for 'ate'; *took,* for 'taken'; *situate,* for 'situated'; *run,* for 'ran'; *laid* down, for 'laid himself'; had *drank,* for 'had drunk'; *sunk,* for 'sank'; "while this *was doing.*" There survive the use of the plural without *s, e.g.*, "eight year"; the use of the collective followed by the plural pronoun, *e.g.*, "every thing at large in their Places"; and uses of words later condemned, *e.g.*, "a more *healthy* . . . Spot of Ground." In general De Foe's language in *Robinson Crusoe* represents a stage before the discipline of the English grammarian had been applied.

If now one descends lower, near the bottom of the social ladder, one finds irregularities even more striking. It must not be lost sight of that the cultivated form of language concerning which Swift and Addison were so solicitous was the language of the few, the people of quality as distinguished from that of the vulgar many, the mob. Country speech and country manners even among the gentry are charitably described by Addison as old-fashioned and are less charitably exposed to ridicule by satirical playwrights. The boorishness of the fox-hunting squire and the absurdities in speech as in manners of the Country Put provide inexhaustible matter for comedy. The language of the Citizen Man of Business was even farther removed from the

Pardon me My L: to believe yo Lordships favour to me has at Least So much share in y Conduct of it; if Not in y Subtance, that I am Perswaded I can not be more Obliged to y Donor, than to your Lordships Singular goodness, which tho' I can not Deserve, yet I shall always Sencibly reflect on & Improve, And Should be Doubly blest if Providence would put it into my hands, to tender yo Lordship Some Service Suited to y Sence I have of yo Lordships Extra ordinary Favour.

And yet I am yo Lordships most Humble Petitioner, That if Possible I may kno' the Originalls of This Munificence, Since That hand That can Suppose me to Merit So much Regard, Must believ me Fitt to be Trusted wth The knowlege of my benefactor, and Uncapable of Discovering any Part of it, That Should be Conceal'd: But I Submitt This to yo Lordship and the Pesons Concern'd.

I Frankly Acknowlege to yo Lordship, and to y Unknown Rewarders of my Mean Performances, That I do Not See y Merit They are Thus Pleas'd to Vallue, The most I wish and wth I hope I can Answer for is, That I Shall Allwayes Preserv the Homely Despicable Title of an Honest Man If This Will Recomend me, yo Lordship Shall Never be Asham'd of giving me that Title, Nor my Enemys be able by Fear Or Reward to Make me other wise

In all other things I justly Apprehend yo Lordships Disappointment and That yo LShip will find little Else in Me worth yo Notice.

I am
May it Please yo Lordship
yo LShips Highly Oblig'd
Most Humble and Most Obed Serv
Daniel De Foe

Daniel De Foe (1660-1731): letter to Charles Montaigne, Lord Halifax, expressing gratitude for his favors and anxiety to know the name of the unknown benefactor who had sent him money, and protesting that he would always preserve the title of "an honest man"; without date (1705?). (Brit. Mus. Add. MS. 7,121, F. 27.)

courtly manner. Social distinction in speech is indicated by the sources from which metaphors and comparisons are drawn. "Your Men of Business," says Addison, "usually have recourse to such Instances as are too mean and familiar. They are for drawing the Reader into a Game of Chess or Tennis, or for leading him from Shop to Shop in the Cant of particular Trades and Employments." If for chess and tennis, as sources of figurative expression, more modern forms of recreation, such as baseball, horse racing, card games, pugilism, and motoring, are substituted, it will be found that Addison's comment on the speech of men of business in his day will apply to the speech of the modern Babbitt. In general it may be said that where the cultivated speech of the Augustan Age is on the plane of an aristocratic social class, that of the present time is on a plane to which under later democratizing influences the great middle class has been raised by the training of books and schools.

The earlier modes of speech of the illiterate peasant of the eighteenth century are to a considerable extent preserved in the conservative provincial dialects of today. The forms of speech of the older fashion of the eighteenth-century country gentleman, as well as many belonging to the illiterate, are richly preserved in American speech which in earlier times was little disturbed by the shifting fashions of courtly life. The speech of the London citizen is, on the whole, less well preserved. With the spread of English education the speech of the Londoner has been in great part brought to conformity with a common standard of correctness, and the earlier peculiarities survive only as the vulgarisms belonging to the submerged class of people whose speech has not been ironed out by educational processes to the level standard. For this reason the information afforded by some of the grammars of the early eighteenth century has a special interest. The modes of pronunciation, for instance, recorded in the grammar of Dilworth and particularly in that of Isaac Watts, introduce one to the speech atmosphere of Dickens' London as it was a century and a half before the time of Dickens.

Let us then examine at some length *The Art of Reading and Writing English* published by Dr. Isaac Watts in 1721. Isaac Watts is better known as a hymn writer than as a grammarian. There are few children—at least there were few children a generation ago—unfamiliar with his admonitions to "improve each shining hour." Watts received his early education at a Dissenting Academy. He was a nonconformist theologian and pastor of an Independent church in London. His grammatical work was originally composed for three daughters of Sir Thomas Abney at whose house he had been cared for during a long illness. For his book he borrows from Greenwood the motto, *Extera quid quærat, sua qui vernacula nescit,* for which he provides the translation:

> Let all the Foreign Tongues alone
> Till you can spell and read your own.

Watts commends the "Custom of common Spelling-Books, in the first part of them, after the Letters, to join Consonants and Vowels together in various Forms; then to make Tables of common Words, of one, two, three, and more Syllables." But significant regarding the purpose which, in his opinion, should be served by English grammar are his recommendations regarding the second Part which, he believes, "would be much better composed of Lessons for children of various Kinds: Wherein there should be not only such Praxes on the Words of different Syllables, . . . but several easy Portions of Scripture . . . Sentences to discourage the Vices . . . Proverbs, . . . short and useful Stories, . . . a short

Account of England . . . : And the World will forgive me, if I should say, let a few Pieces of Poesy be added."

But this book by Watts is principally important to modern times because of the clear light it throws on popular modes of pronunciation prevailing in the early eighteenth century. "Custom," says Watts, "is and will be, Sovereign over all the Forms of Writing and Speaking." Since he recognizes only custom as authority and since he was a resident of London, his book may safely be taken to indicate the London spelling and pronunciation of his day.

The information with which the modern reader is chiefly concerned, appears in the series of tables by means of which Watts shows what is current custom in language. Table I offers a list of words with the position of the accent varying, *e.g., Academy, Acádemy; Avenue, Avénue,* etc. The author adds the comment that in such words both pronunciations "are used among Persons of Education and Learning in different parts of the Nation; and Custom is the great Rule of Pronouncing as well as of Spelling, so that every one should usually speak according to Custom."

Table II illustrates the principle already long established, that English words of more than one syllable are accented on the first syllable when they signify the *name of a thing,* but are accented on the later syllable when they signify an action. Examples are given: *"ábsent, to absént"; "áccent, to accént,"* etc.

Table III gives a list of words the "same in Sound, or nearly alike, but different in Signification and Spelling," a feature of most English grammars and spelling books since the grammar by Charles Butler (1633). The list by Watts affords hints rather than precise information, but is of interest as revealing the indistinctness in pronunciation prevalent at this time when, it should be held in mind, words were still known by ear rather than by eye.

Acts
Axe

Achor, a Valley
Acorn, of Oak
Acre, of Land

Arras, hangings
Harrass, to trouble

Beacon, give notice
Beckon, to wink

Cornhill, London
Cornwall, County

Cittern, instrument
Citron, a Fruit

Comet, blazing Star
Commit, to do

Creek, of the Sea
Crick, in the Neck

Dear, of value
Deer, in Park

Deep, low in Earth
Dieppe, in France

Earth
Hearth

File, a Tool
Foil, to overcome

Floor, Ground
Flour, for Bread

Genteel, graceful
Gentile, Heathen
Gentle, quiet

Gesture, Carriage
Jester, merry Fellow

Haven, Harbour
Heaven, on high

Herd, of Cattle,
Heard, did hear
Hard, difficult

Home, House
Whom, What man
Holm, Holly

I'll
Ile, in Church
Isle, Island
Oil, of olives

Imploy, work
Imply, signify

Ketch, a Ship
Catch, to lay hold

Kind
Coin'd

Knave
Nave, of wheel

Knight
Night

Lattice, of Window
Lettice, A Woman's Name
Lettuce, an Herb

Liquorish, dainty
Liquorice, a sweet Root (sur-
    vives)

Line
Loyn, of Veal

Marsh, watery ground
Mesh, or Mash, the hole of a
  Net

Mile
Moil, labor

More
Mower
Moor, or marsh

No
Know

Neal, harden Glass
Kneel

Nell, Elenor
Knell, for Funeral

Not
Knot, etc.

Pint
Point

Porcelain
Purslain, an Herb

Pour, water
Power, Might

Raisin, dry'd Grape
Reason, Argument

Reddish, red
Rhadish, a root

Rice, Corn
Rise, Advancement

Rome
Rheum
Room

Rough
Ruff, a band
Roof, of House

Sea, Water
Say, to speak

Seam
Seem

Seas, great Waters
Seize
Cease

Soon, quickly
Swoon, to faint

Tare, Weight allow'd
Tear, to rend
Tare, did tear

Tile
Toil

Wail
Whale
Wale, mark of whip

Wear
Were, was
Ware, Merchandize

Wen
When

Wet	Wist
Whet	Whist
While	Woe, misery
Wile	Who, which
Wight	Yarn, Woolen
White	Earn, to get; *cf.* herb
	Yern, to compassionate
Which	Early, betimes
Witch	Yearly, every year

The Tables IV and V are not of present concern. But Table VI gives a list of "Words that may be spell'd in different Ways," of which the following will afford an idea: *Accrue, Accrew; Abricot, Apricock; Accompt, Account; Ambassadour, Embassadour; Alembick, Limbeck; Alarm, Alarum; Balk, Baulk; Bedlem, Bethlehem, Bethlem; Biscuit, Bisket; Briar, Brier;* etc.

Table VII gives a list of "Proper Names different in the Old from the New Testament."

Table VIII gives a highly important list of "Words written very different from their Pronunciation." The list affords interesting illustration of the struggle for supremacy between popular forms of words and the written forms. The list is a long one of about 238 words, and the words here selected are, in most instances, ones in which the written form has eventually determined the pronunciation.

Apparitor, *Paritur*	Atchievement, *Hatchment*
Apprentice, *Prentis*	Atheist, *Athist*
Artichoke, *Hartichoke*	Asthma, *Asma*
Apothecary, *Potticary*	Aukward, *Awkurd*, or *Unkurd*
Alchymy, *Occamy*	Balast, *Ballas*
Anemone, *Emmeny*	Ballad, *Ballet*
Apron, *Apurn*	Carrion, *Carren*

Chariot, *Charrut*

Colonel, *Curnel*

Construe, *Constur*

Courtesy, *Curchee*

Coyn, *Quine*

Cuckow, *Coocoo*

Cucumber, *Cowcumber*

Cupboard, *Cubburd*

Dictionary, *Dixnery*

First, *Fust*

Handkerchief, *Hankechur*

Jaundise, *Janders*

Knowledge, *Hnollege*

Knop, *Hnob*

Knuckle, *Hnukk'l*

Knight, *Hnite*

Leopard, *Leppurd*

Lieutenant, *Liftenant*

Liquor, *Likkur*

Mastiff, *Mastee*

Medicine, *Mets'n*

Nurse, *Nus*

Oatmeal, *Otmell*

Postcript, *Poscrip*

Perfect, *Parfet*

Purse, *Pus*

Psalm, *Saam*

Saffron, *Saffurn*

Scent, *Sent*

Schedule, *Sedule*

Schism, *Sism*

Sheriff, *Shreeve*

Sallad, *Sallet*

Sword, *Soard*

Swoon, *Sound*

Thirsty, *Thustee*

Toilet, *Twaylet*, or *Twilight*

Vault, *Vawt*

Verdict, *Vardit*

Waistcoat, *Wescote*

Wrist-band, *Risban*

Yacht, *Yot*

To this list Watts appends the following remarks: "There are many other Words that are pronounced in a very different Manner from what they are written, according to the Dialect or corrupt Speech that obtains in the several counties of England; . . . I have therefore chosen chiefly those Words which are written different from their common and frequent Pronunciation in the City of *London*, especially among the Vulgar." He adds that: "There are some other corruptions in the pronouncing of several Words by many of the Citizens themselves . . . which I have not thought worthy of a place in this Catalogue . . . *yourn* for *yours*, *ourn* for *ours*, *gould* for *gold*, *ould* for *old*, *squench* for *quench*, *squeedge* for *squeeze*, *scroudge* for *crowd*, *yerb* for *herb*."

Table IX is a list of "Proper Names written very different from their Pronunciation." The list gives interesting instances of a kind of words which in popular speech has more than any other resisted the influence of written forms. A few selected examples follow:

Augustin, Austin	Katharine or Catharine, Catturn
St. Albans, St. Awbans	
Abraham, Abrum	Lincoln, Lincon
Bartholomew, Bartlemy	London, Lunnun
Birmingham, Brummijum	Marlborough, Marlburro
Berwick, Barrick	Okehampton, Okkinton
Cirencester, Sisseter	Ralph, Rafe
Cologn, Cullen	Rotherhith, Redriff
Deptford, Dedfurd	Sevenoak, Sennuck
Egypt, Eegip	Sarah, Sarey
Guild-hall, Eeld-hall	Ursula, Usley
Holborn, Hoburn	Walter, Water

The pronunciation of *Sarah*, it will be noted, introduces one to the social atmosphere in which in nineteenth-century London Sairey Gamp was a typical figure.

Table X, which follows offers a list of contracted phrases current in the early eighteenth century: *'tis; 'twas; can't; mayn't; shan't; coodn't; shoodn't; woodn't; won't; 'tisn't; ha'done; ha'n't; gi'mmee; gee't'er,* 'give it her'; *gi'ne ye,* 'given you'; *gaffer; gammer; goodee,* 'good wife'; *wi'mmee,* 'with me'; *wee'ye,* 'with you'; *Goodbw'y,* 'God be with you'; *ben't you; won't ye; cumt'ee,* 'come to you'; *howd'ee,* 'how do you'; *de'e no,* 'do you know'; *y'a' been,* 'you have been'; *tak'n,* take him; *gee't'n,* 'give it him'; *gee'nsum,* 'give him some'; etc. To this list Watts appends the following comments: "I have given these few only as a Pattern, that the Child may learn to spell others of the like nature, by pronouncing each Word distinct and apart." "There are also some other corrupt Pronunciations of Latin

Words, or Terms of Art in use among the Vulgar, as *Icipri-zys* for Nisi prius, *Sessarero* for Certiorari, *Suppiney* for Sub-Pænâ, *Hippo* for Hypocondriacal, *Pozz* for positively, *Plenipo* for Plenipotentiary," etc., "which I cannot much approve, tho (*sic*) some polite Persons have used them . . ."

Dilworth in his *New Guide to the English Tongue* (13th ed., London, 1751) offers a considerable amount of similar information. The accentuation indicated in general does not differ from that of today. A few striking exceptions, however, are the words: *Eu-ró-pe-an, Ce-sá-re-a, Ca-ná-da, Ca-ra-ván*. The list of homonyms, or words the same in sound but different in meaning, supplements the lists by Watts. In part the pronunciations indicated are corrobora-tive of Watts; in part, however, they differ from those indi-cated by Watts and afford illustration of the unsettled usage of the time in the pronunciation of words. The difference is to be noted in the pronunciation of *creek* and of words beginning with *kn*, where Watts indicates a dis-appearing stage reached in the pronunciation of the initial *k* while Dilworth indicates a complete disappearance. A few examples from Dilworth's lists of homonyms may be given:

Air, one of elements
Are, they are
Heir, to an Estate

Bean, pulse
Been, was in a place

Beat, strike
Beet, Herb

Bile, a Swelling
Boil, Water in Fire

Boar, beast
Boor, country Fellow
Bore, make a hole

Brake, an Herb
Break, part asunder

Calais
Chalice

Cart, to carry things in
Chart, A Description of a Place

Clark, a Book-keeper
Clerk, A Clergyman

Creek, of the Sea
Creak, make a noise

File, of Metal
Foil, to overcome

Flea, Insect
Flee, to run

Grate, for coals
Great, large

I'll
Ile ('aisle')
Isle ('island')
Oyl, of olives

Knave, dishonest man
Nave, of a wheel

Knight
Night

Know
No

Known
None

Meat, to eat
Meet, together
Mete, to measure

Of, belonging to
Off, at a distance

Pear
Pair
Pare

Pint
Point

Rice, corn
Rise, advancement

Rome
Room
Rheum

Salary, wages
Selery, an Herb

Saver, that saveth
Savor, taste
Saviour, J. C.

Starling, a bird
Sterling, Engl. money

Tour, a journey
Tower, fortif. place

Wale, mark of a whip
Whale, a Sea Fish

Way
Weigh
Wey
Whey

Weal, good
Veal, Calf's Flesh
Wheale, a Pimple
Wheel, of a Cart

Weather
Whether
Whither

White, Colour	Vile, base
Wight, Island	Wile, a Trick
	While, in mean Time
Wither	Ye, yourselves
Whither	Yea, yes

In such works as the grammars by Dilworth and by Watts, is revealed something of the irregularity that prevailed in the colloquial speech of the early eighteenth century and of the wide gulf that then separated the oral from the written forms. They suggest also the different levels of speech in the Age of Queen Anne. There was the refined mode of speech based on classical training to which was imparted ease and elegance by conversation in the cultivated society of the period. Such was the language of Addison. Such also was the natural and concise mode of expression used by Swift which may be characterized in his own words as "like a Shrewsbury cake short and sweet upon the palate." Quite different was the manner of speech of the country squire and that of the London citizen, neither of them as yet greatly affected by courtly refinement or by literary standards. There remained for succeeding periods the task of bringing the speech of different classes to a common level, of producing uniformity by means of dictionaries and grammars and school training.

CHAPTER XIV

JOHNSON'S DICTIONARY

IN the later eighteenth century there was variety in opinion regarding the English language of the Age of Queen Anne. There were many who shared the opinion frequently expressed early in the century that the language had reached perfection. This opinion, as far as pronunciation was concerned, was that of Thomas Sheridan, father of the more famous Richard Brinsley Sheridan, but himself famous throughout the eighteenth century as a teacher of elocution. In 1780 Sheridan published *A Complete Dictionary of the English Language* in which he attempted to register what Johnson had not ventured to indicate, beyond the accentuation, the true pronunciation of English words. In support of his pretensions to competence for this task, Sheridan in his Preface offered the following interesting statements:

"There was a time, and that at no distant period, which may be called the Augustan Age of England. I mean during the reign of Queen Anne, when English was the language spoken at Court; and when the same attention was paid to propriety of pronunciation, as that of French at the Court of Versailles. This produced a uniformity in that article in all the polite circles; and a gentleman or lady would have been as much ashamed of a wrong pronunciation then, as persons of a liberal education would now be of mis-spelling words. But on the accession of a foreign family to the throne, amid the many blessings conferred by that happy event, the English language suffered much by being banished the Court, to make room for the French. From that time the regard formerly paid to pronunciation has been gradually declining; so that now the greatest improprieties in that point are to be found among people of fashion; many pronunciations, which thirty or forty years ago were confined to the vulgar, are now gaining ground; and if something be not done to stop this growing evil, and fix a general standard at present, the English is likely to become a mere jargon, which every one may pronounce as he pleases. It is to be wished, that such a standard had been established at the period before mentioned, as it is probable, that English was then spoken in its highest state of perfection."

With these views of Sheridan regarding the superiority of the English of the Augustan Age those of Samuel Johnson seem at first to clash. Commenting on *An Account of Scotland* published in 1702, Johnson's remark (1778), quoted by Boswell, was: "It is sad stuff, Sir, miserably written, as books in general then were. There is now an elegance of style universally diffused. No man now writes as ill as Martin's *Account of the Hebrides* is written. A man could not write so ill if he should try. Set a merchant's clerk now, to write, and he'll do it better."

But the clash in opinion between Johnson and Sheridan is in this case more apparent than real. Sheridan has in mind pronunciation, and the pronunciation of a fastidious few. He obviously has not in mind the popular modes of pronunciation recorded in the grammars by Dilworth and Watts. Johnson, on the other hand, has in mind the general level of literary English in the earlier eighteenth century. He obviously does not refer to writers like Addison whose style he extolled in words that have become classic. It must also be held in mind that Johnson's remark was made late in his life when he could look with some compl6placency on a general cultivation in English writing, an achievement in which he had no inconsiderable share.

There can be no doubt that the level of literary excellence was lower in the early eighteenth century than in the second half. Swift, in his essay on the *Education of Women,* estimates the number of "males with reading and good sense" in England, including Wales, at about two thousand and the number of females at one thousand. The estimate is exaggeratedly low. Of this one may be sure when one thinks of the larger public that greeted the numbers of the *Spectator* as they appeared. The *mob,* however, greatly outnumbered the select few. The writers eminent for refinement and taste were outnumbered by a host of scribblers. In the army of the moderns engaged in Swift's *Battle of the Books* the rear was occupied by "infinite swarms of Calones, a disorderly rout led by L'Estrange; rogues and ragamuffins, that follow the camp for nothing but the plunder, all without coats to cover them." Under the figurative language may be recognized the allusion to the countless number of unbound pamphlets composed by men willing to serve any side for profit. There was abundance of material for the *Dunciad.*

With the accession of the Hanoverian line to the English throne came not only a profound change in the political situation, but a change in the position of the language. There came the adoption of French referred to by Sheridan, and the consequent loss of a courtly center of refinement for the cultivation of English. The Tory ministry headed by Harley and Bolingbroke, cultivated men and personal friends of Swift, was succeeded by a cabinet having at its head Sir Robert Walpole, who according to Samuel Johnson, quoted by Boswell, "always talked bawdy at his table, because in that all could join." Following the death of

Queen Anne in 1714 Swift is described by his friend, Dr. Arbuthnot, as "like a man knocked down." His political and cultural plans as well as his personal aspirations, were annihilated.

Apparent loss of ground, however, as far as the cultivation of the language was concerned proved to be an eventual gain. The aristocratic control of language through the agency of an Academy was doomed. But under the new order of things there was laid a broader foundation for culture. In government rule by king was succeeded by rule by Parliament. It should be recalled that since the death of Queen Anne no English king has ever appeared at a cabinet council or ventured to veto an Act of Parliament. Government by Parliament is based on public opinion, and in the molding of public opinion Walpole and his successors at the head of the cabinet, as well as their political opponents, made use of all available means of propaganda. Not only were political ballads set in circulation, but the prose pamphleteering of the preceding century was developed to an unprecedented extent, and the newspaper, in earlier times merely a register of current events, particularly of foreign news, was developed into a powerful organ of public opinion. Public responsibility in government created public interest in general affairs and this interest naturally broadened into an interest in matters outside the field of politics.

Even more important than the political change was the change in the ideals of education. The shift in interest from classical learning to modern subjects has already been dwelt upon. In the numbers of the *Tatler* and the *Spectator* ridicule is lavished upon the earlier misapplication of classical learning. In the *Tatler* (No. 173) Addison writes of a pastry cook who "is going to apprentice his son to a soapboiler as soon as he has a smattering of Greek."

The revolt was general. The Quaker, William Penn (1644-1718), complains of children burdened with rules, grammar, and rhetoric, the subjects involved in Latin education, and "leaving their natural Genius to Mechanical and Physical, or Natural Knowledge uncultivated and neglected." Mary Wortley Montagu (1689-1762), speaking of the study of Latin and Greek, refers to "many schoolmasters, who, though perhaps critics in grammar, are the most ignorant fellows upon earth." One should recall Partridge in Fielding's *Tom Jones.* In the new type of schools which came to overshadow the older grammar schools, the more modern subjects, and with them the English language, came to receive a more adequate share of attention. In the *Guardian* (No. 105) Addison, writing of the Charity Schools recently established says: "There will be few in the next generation who will not at least be able to write and read, and have not had an early tincture of religion." The cultural education of women, which it had been the fashion to neglect, more perhaps than any other subject, engages the attention of Addison and Swift and particularly of Steele in their social satires. Women, says Addison (*Guardian,* No. 155) have the "natural gift of speech in greater perfection" than men. And yet, he says: "I am concerned, when I go into a great house, where there is not a single person that can spell, unless it be by chance the butler, or one of the footmen." The pungent satire and the continued admonitions of these reformers of manners had their effect. Throughout the eighteenth century writers of grammars and dictionaries and spelling books continue to address their works to the supposed needs of the fair sex, but the progress made by women in the course of the century appears in a striking alteration of tone at its close. The anonymous author of a *Dictionary of the English Language,* published in 1794, addresses his feminine public in the following gallant terms: "The unaffected grace which animates the conversation of a lady, cannot fail to charm on paper, and as the fair sex have hitherto maintained the prize of epistolary ease, it may happen that in the unpremeditated flow of style a word may be improperly spelled, . . . the purer the snow the more conspicuous the speck; . . . the slightest reference to this Dictionary will remove the defect."

The change in the political order and the change in the aims and methods of education serve in part at least to explain the expanded reading public of the eighteenth century, a matter of prime importance in the development of literary art and of language, its medium. The needs of the English reading public in the seventeenth century had been supplied, as far as Shakespeare was concerned, by a few quarto editions of separate plays and the four Folio editions, about 500 copies in all, it has been estimated, of Shakespeare's collected works. In the early eighteenth century new editions appeared in rapid succession and, by the end of the century, there had been distributed, it is estimated, about 30,000 copies of Shakespeare's works. The seventeenth-century neglect of Milton's *Paradise Lost* is in part explained by the uncongenial relation of the poet to his times, but that does not suffice to explain entirely the contrast between the £20 called for in Milton's contract with his printer and the £10 personally received by Milton, and the £9,000 gained by Pope from his translation of the *Iliad* in 1715. For this neglect of Milton the eighteenth century compensated. In the course of that century there were published 70 complete editions of Milton and more than 100 editions of *Paradise Lost*. That the reading public of the eighteenth century had greatly expanded appears not only from the earlier literary productions absorbed by it, but from the new literary works for which it provided a market. The *Spectator*, by the time of the appearance of the tenth number, had reached a circulation of 3,000 and a reading public of 60,000. Of some numbers as many as 20,000 were sold, and the first collected edition was of 9,000 copies. The *Gentleman's Magazine*, which began in 1731, attained a circulation of 15,000. Between 1731 and 1780, 60 magazines were published in England, 10 in Scotland, and 11 in Ireland. From 1740 dates the institution of circulating libraries, which had an important part in the creation of a unified reading public.[1]

Regarding the cultivation of the language there were two schools of opinion. One should recall the opposing attitudes represented in the sixteenth century by the courtly Sidney on the one side and the schoolmaster Mulcaster on the other. In the seventeenth century this opposition, the well-bred versus the learned, continued to exist and persisted in the eighteenth century. Steele (*Guardian*, 24), in discussing good conversation, concludes that "there is something that can never be learned but from the company of the polite," and in another place (*Guardian*, 94) contrasts the "accomplishments which make up the character of a well-bred man" with "what is called deep learning." The spirit was one of revolt from pedantry and found classical support in the oft-quoted dicta of Horace and Quintilian regarding usage as the mistress of language.

The limitations of learning as a source of culture were widely felt. Even the accomplished Addison was held up to gentle ridicule by Lord Chesterfield. He was, says Chesterfield (*Letters to his Godson*, cxxxviii), "the most timid and awkward man in good company I ever saw, and no wonder, for he had been wholly cloystered up in the cells at Oxford till he was five and twenty years old."

There was, however, an opposing view. In an anonymous

---

[1] A. S. Collins, *Review of English Studies*, II, pp. 284-294, 428-439.

work published in 1724, *The Many Advantages of a Good Language to Any Nation,* the authors protest. Schools, the clergy and scholars, these authors complain, hold that "Living Languages do best by themselves; Help spoils them, and care and Pains make them worse, nor hath any Patron of Learning provided one single Professor who should turn his Thoughts and Care towards that." For this protest there was ground. Illiteracy among the higher classes, which De Foe exhibited in his *Compleat Gentleman,* continued to be prevalent. "I think he spells pretty well, for a Lord" is a remark appearing in *Sir Charles Grandison* (IV, 61). More important than the inability to spell was the fashionable illiteracy in the use of words of low origin often from the canting language of thieves. Words of this kind, as has been seen, were strenuously objected to by Swift. But their use persisted, not only in fashionable jargon, but in the popular form of language adopted by the pamphleteers. Berkeley (*Guardian,* 62) enumerates among the corrupters of language "the Law-Latin, the Lucubrations of our paltry newsmongers, and that swarm of vile pamphlets which corrupt our taste, and infest the public." This form of language is deliberately adopted by Dr. Arbuthnot, the friend of Swift and of Pope, in his *History of John Bull.* In this pamphlet the cultured author produces a popular effect by the use of many of these words from the vocabulary of a lower social stratum. Many of them make their earliest cited literary appearance in this famous work. Among these expressions appear such words as *chopped; nebused,* 'deceived'; *bubble,* 'cheat'; *flush in ready,* 'money'; *tuned up,* 'started talking'; *yellowboys,* 'coins'; *went to pot; a swinging sum; to cabbage,* 'steal'; *a clod-pated numskulled ninnyhammer; huffs and dings; rantipole; honey,* 'dear one'; a rare *tweague; run a tick* at the market; *squirters; old boy,* familiar salutation.

What were the later eighteenth-century tendencies in colloquial use uncontrolled by learning, one may learn from an essay on conversation which appeared in number 138 of *The Connoisseur* (1754-6). The English genteel, we are told, afford little material for discussion because they "scarce ever meet but to game." But there are many objectionable types of talkers. Among these are enumerated the wits, the whistlers, the time-hummers, the bawlers and the swearers. The excessive use of oaths had been satirized by the promoters of refinement from the beginning of the seventeenth century. In this essay is exhibited a new class, of half-swearers, "who split, and mince, and fritter their oaths into gad's bud, ad's fish and demme." The word *humbug* was a creation of this period and its use was frowned on as a barbarism. The earliest citation in the Oxford Dictionary is from about 1750. The word provided a name for one of the objectionable types of speakers enumerated in this essay, the "Gothick humbuggers." Another class of objectionable speakers is made up of those who "nickname God's creatures, and call a man a cabbage, a crab, a queer cub, an odd fish, an unaccountable muskin."

The faults of current colloquial English are further set forth in another number of *The Connoisseur* (No. 42). The excellencies of the English language are emphasized; it is said to be "preferable to most, if not all others now in being." But it is said to be treated with neglect, a neglect due to false pride of men of learning and fine gentlemen, and wit pretenders. Gentlemen use French, and wits, "when they talk of Humbug, etc., seem to be jabbering in the uncouth dialect of the Huns, or the rude gabble of the Hottentots or the strange cant said to be in use among housebreakers and highwaymen. . . . Their jargon may be found in the Scoundrel's Dictionary." To the kind of words here referred to as in use among the wits of the eighteenth century applies the word *slang* in its original meaning. The wits of that century, in their revolt from refinement, turned to the language of the underworld, which in our own time continues to be one of the sources of the words disreputable in tone expressing modern revolt from propriety, and forming a main element in modern slang.

Such were some of the tendencies in eighteenth-century colloquial speech. Cultivated forms of speech were distorted in the use of the London citizen. Refinement in language was despised by the fox-hunting squire. Even in courtly circles in the days following the reign of Queen Anne propriety in speech was in low esteem. The efforts of Swift seemed to have been in vain. Usage, the mistress of language, seemed to be conducting the speech toward anarchy.

But the spirit favoring cultivation in language was not extinct. Lord Chesterfield in the new age leads the forces of refinement. He admonishes his godson to avoid "a stiff and formal accuracy, especially what the women call hard words, when plain ones as expressive are at hand." On the other hand he warns him that "few things are more disagreeable than to hear a Gentleman talk the barbarisms, the solecisms, and the Vulgarisms of Porters" (Letter cxlii). In another place he instructs his godson that: "Two things are absolutely necessary for every young Man who has a laudable ambition to make a figure in the world. They are *learning* and *politeness*, and they should always go together; for learning without politeness makes a disagreeable Pedant, and politeness without learning makes a superficial frivolous Puppy."

In the mode of cultivation recommended by Chesterfield, courtly usage, the guiding principle of Sidney, was joined with school training, the method advocated by Mulcaster. The adoption of learning as a guide was favored by the

mode of thought dominant in the Age of Enlightenment.
License in speech was not in harmony with the intellectual
mood of the age. The qualities of language most highly
prized in the age of reason were the logical qualities, correctness and regularity. In the seventeenth century the
word *analogy* had been taken over from the language of
logic and mathematics to express a quality of uniformity
sought for in language. More and more, as the eighteenth
century progressed, it was sought to make analogy supersede anomaly.

The works on grammar by Brightland and by Greenwood
were influential and were produced in new editions. They
were highly commended and frequently cited. But, to
quote the words of Gough, a grammarian of 1760, they
were adapted "for men, but not for children." The needs
for school instruction were mainly served during the first
half of the century by "Guides to the English Tongue" of
the kind already mentioned, elementary works concerned
mainly with spelling and pronunciation and the forms of
the parts of speech.

Guidance in the use of English words and their spelling
was also provided by numerous dictionaries. In 1702 appeared *A New English Dictionary* by J. K., "Chiefly designed for the benefit of young Scholars, Tradesmen, Artificers, Foreigners, and the Female Sex, who would learn
to spell truly." Of far greater importance was the *Universal Etymological English Dictionary* by Nathaniel Bailey
first published in 1721. This work, as its title indicates,
was more inclusive than any preceding; in fact, it was the
first dictionary that aimed to include all English words.
Another added feature was the etymologies. The edition
of 1731 also was the first to indicate the position of the
accent in words. Its influence was great. "Will you never
learn a proper use of words?" exclaims Mrs. Western in

Tom Jones. "Indeed, Child, you should consult Bailey's Dictionary." This work was issued in edition after edition throughout the century, the twenty-fourth edition appearing in 1782. The edition of 1731 provided the basis for the greater work by Samuel Johnson. That such books were in demand appears from the rival works that were produced. The *Spelling Dictionary* of the schoolmaster Thomas Dyche was issued in expanded form by William Pardon in 1735 with the title, *"A New General English Dictionary;* Peculiarly calculated for the Use and Improvement of such as are unacquainted with the Learned Languages. Wherein the difficult Words, and Technical Terms made use of in Anatomy, Architecture, . . . Sculpture, Surgery, *etc.,* are not only fully explain'd, but accented on their proper Syllables, to prevent a vicious Pronunciation." To this work is prefixed a *Compendious English Grammar.* This grammar pretends to enable "such as understand English only . . . to write as correctly and elegantly, as those who have been some Years conversant in the *Latin, Greek,* &c., Languages." That the pretensions of this "Compendious" work could hardly be realized appears evident, since all this grammatical information is comprised within the space of ten pages.

Still other dictionaries of this period were those by B. N. Defoe, by Ephraim Chambers, and by Benjamin Martin. Samuel Johnson, it may be recalled, told Boswell that he had "formed his style upon that of Sir William Temple and upon Chambers's Proposal for his Dictionary."

The cultivation of good English was promoted also by the formation of clubs. *The Connoisseur* (No. 42) gives an account of an English club which met to "cultivate their mother tongue." This club offered prizes for words available for replacing "any exotic terms, that have been smuggled into our language, by homespun British words, equally significant and expressive." It also imposed fines for "modish barbarism" and for "any cant terms coined by the Town, for the service of the current year." From the activities of a club devoted to the cultivation of English sprang the anonymous book already referred to, entitled *The Many Advantages of a Good Language* (1724). The authors dedicate their work to Thomas, Earl of Macclesfield, Lord High Chancellor of Great Britain. They say that several have agreed to spend "spare hours" upon this subject and hope for help from others, "both Single and in Societies." They aim "to examine the present State of the Language, to fix what is right by Grammars and Dictionaries, to fill up what is wanting, straighten what is crooked, and make it easy to be learnt and remembered by Youth and Strangers." Surely an ambitious undertaking. We have here to do with an Academy of a volunteer type.

In support of their plan these authors set forth what was needed for the cultivation of the language. "Its very Alphabet is only what Chance has made it, and is much out of Order. We have no Grammar of it that is taught in any School that we ever heard of [This statement is to be noted]; We have no good Dictionary to bring it into method, with an account of the Derivations, and Senses and Uses of Words: We have no Collection of its Idioms, Phrases, and right use of its Particles."

Practically identical is the feeling expressed by Bishop Warburton in the introduction to his edition of Shakespeare published in 1747. The English language, says Warburton, in somewhat lofty tone, is "destitute of a Test or Standard to apply to, in cases of doubt or difficulty. . . . For we have neither Grammar nor Dictionary, neither Chart nor Compass, to guide us through this wide sea of Words."

From expressions of opinion like the two just cited, one may gain a fairly clear insight into the mind of the early eighteenth century in regard to language. There persisted an insistent demand that means be provided for fixing or standardizing the language. With this knowledge one is in a position to appreciate the importance attached to the creation of an authoritative dictionary and the honor and applause that attended its achievement.

The final achievement of this work long desired and much planned for fell not to an official body of eminent men such as Swift had in mind, a body like the French Academy, nor to a volunteer organization like that which had formulated the ideals set forth in 1724 in the book entitled *The Many Advantages*, but to a single individual. If the story of the English language has one leading character, a single hero, that hero is Samuel Johnson. Son of an obscure Lichfield bookseller, this one man, ungainly in appearance, conspicuously lacking in social graces, and unsupported by wealth or influence, accomplished what literary eminence and official dignity had been unable to accomplish.

Johnson's life was one of struggle. He was obliged to abandon Oxford on account of lack of financial support. He found teaching uncongenial and in 1737, at the age of twenty-eight, went up to London to win a precarious livelihood by literary pursuits. The struggle was a severe one. By translations of various kinds and by original contributions, principally to the *Gentleman's Magazine* published by Edward Cave, he was able to keep alive and to gain a reputation for ability, but he was obliged to be on the watch for any opportunity that might offer. The suggestion of the dictionary, according to Boswell, came from a chance remark made by Robert Dodsley, the bookseller, to Johnson, who was sitting in his shop, "that a Dictionary of the English Language would be a work that would be well received by the public." The suggestion, apparently unheeded at the time, seems nevertheless to have taken root, and eventually Johnson entered into a contract with a group of booksellers for the production of such a work.

A "Plan" for the work was published in 1747 and was addressed to the Earl of Chesterfield, then one of the principal Secretaries of State and a general arbiter of elegance of the period. The "Plan" was admirably composed. It won much commendation and created a wide interest in the undertaking. From it one learns that many of the writers who were to be cited as authorities had been selected by Pope. It appears, therefore, that Johnson fell heir to an earlier undertaking which had been abandoned but of which some of the preparatory material remained in the hands of Dodsley and was now turned over to the new editor.

The undertaking was carried through with the aid of six amanuenses to do the mechanical part of the work. Concerning these aids a fact worthy of note is that five of the six were Scotch. Boswell gloats somewhat over this fact. There was in reality reason for Scotch pride, for here is evidence of the love of culture which had long been prevalent in the North. De Foe alludes to it in his *Compleat Gentleman.* Deploring the lack of education among the English higher classes, he says that this condition does not exist in other countries, "and even to go no farther than the northern part of our island . . . You find very few of the gentry, and I may say, none at all of the higher rank of them, either ignorant or unlearn'd; nay, you cannot ordinarily find a servant in Scotland but he can read and write." To the same effect may be cited the testimony of Swift in his *Essay on Modern Education.* Expatiating on the want of respect for learning among the nobility, he says that some nations are "to be excepted, and particularly Scotland." Boswell also does not fail to mention that Mr. Strahan and Mr. Andrew Millar, the booksellers most active in bringing out Johnson's *Dictionary,* were Scotchmen. It appears, therefore, that Scotchmen in the eighteenth century were as active in directing the cultivation of the English language as they have since been in directing the course of British politics.

There is a close analogy between the government of the English language and the government of the English state. Both are based on common law, and it is a striking fact that the codification of the government of the language in Johnson's *Dictionary* should have been followed only a decade later by Blackstone's *Commentaries on the Laws of England.* The common law of the English language Johnson found in the usage of great English writers. In fact, a feature distinguishing Johnson's work from earlier dictionaries was the wealth of citations with which he illustrated the different uses of words. In the assemblage of this material he was aided by a wide range of reading supported by a remarkable memory. In the cited passages the writers before the Restoration are well represented because their works he regarded as "the wells of English undefiled," that is to say, as yet uncorrupted by French influence or later modish affectations. Sidney's works, however, he "fixed as the boundary beyond which he made few excursions," a time limit to which exception was taken by many critics and which has been extended by later lexicographers.

The method followed by Johnson led to the omission of many technical words, "terms of art and manufacture." He was unable, he declares in his Preface, "to visit caverns to learn the miner's language, nor take a voyage to perfect my skill in the dialect of navigation, nor visit the warehouses of merchants, and shops of artificers, to gain the names of wares, tools and operations, of which no mention is found in books . . ." From books, rather than from life, is drawn the material of his *Dictionary*, and the use of his work as a guide and authority gave to the language of the later eighteenth century, and to a considerable extent that of the nineteenth century, a bookish quality which is a distinguishing feature.

Johnson's work could not have gained the authority it came to possess if it had not expressed the spirit of the nation. Johnson was in politics a staunch Tory and in general attitude of mind conservative. The conservative spirit of the British people, who alone among the great peoples of Europe have not adopted the decimal system but have preserved the older systems of pounds, shillings and pence, of feet, yards, and miles, was expressed in this conservative work governing its language. Johnson cites with approbation the dictum of Hooker that "change is not made without inconvenience, even from worse to better." "There is in constancy and stability," he says, "a general and lasting advantage." In his treatment of spelling, he asserts, "where caprice has long wantoned without controul (*sic*), and vanity sought praise by petty reformation, I have endeavoured to proceed with a scholar's reverence for antiquity, and a grammarian's regard for the genius of the language." It should be recalled that in the French Academy dictionary published in 1762, nearly contemporaneous with Johnson's work, there are new spellings for about five thousand words, about twenty-eight per cent of all the words in this dictionary. In contrast with this spirit of reform may be cited the words of Johnson, "I have attempted few alterations, and among those few, perhaps the greater part is from the modern to the ancient practice; and I hope I may be allowed to recommend to those whose thoughts have been, perhaps, employed too anxiously on verbal singularities, not to disturb, upon narrow views, or for minute propriety, the orthography of their fathers. It has been asserted, that for the law to be *known,* is of more importance than to be *right."* The spirit of extreme conservatism here expressed was a racial one, not one peculiar to Johnson, but Johnson's influence had an important share in its perpetuation. To Johnson, therefore, may be attributed, to no little extent, the firm hold on the English language possessed down to our time by the traditional modes of spelling.

Among the gains achieved in Johnson's *Dictionary* may perhaps be mentioned the etymologies. From a modern point of view these etymologies are unsatisfactory indeed. But Johnson made use of the authorities available in his day. Anglo-Saxon study of the seventeenth century had yielded the *Etymologicon Linguæ Anglicanæ* published by Skinner in 1671, and the *Etymologicum Anglicanum* by Junius (d.1677), published posthumously by Edward Lye in 1743. These works as aids were supplemented in amateurish fashion by a collection of Welsh proverbs which, Johnson assured a visitor, "will help me with my Welsh." An inadequate equipment indeed, and one which led him many times into absurdities, as when he explained the word *peacock* as derived from the peak, or tuft of pointed feathers, on its head.

More important was his achievement in fixing English spellings. In his *Dictionary* the forms of words gradually reached through the practice of English printers, as has been pointed out, in the seventeenth century were recorded in a work which might be referred to as an authority. Of the anomalies involved, Johnson was fully aware. He treated them as inconveniences which "in themselves once unnecessary, must be tolerated among the imperfections of human things, and which require only to be registered, that they may not be increased, and ascertained, that they may not be

confounded." There are a number of remarkable inconsistencies such as those pointed out by Lindley Murray:
*immovable, moveable; chastely, chastness; fertileness, fer-
tily; sliness, slyly; fearlessly, fearlesness; needlessness,
needlesly.* There are one or two general classes of words
which have changed in spelling in later times, notably the
words ending in *-ick* and *-ie,* later spelled with the endings
-ic and *-y,* and there are a number of individual words such
as Johnson's *catcal, downfal, downhil, bethral, miscal, over-
fal, unrol, forestal, reconcileable, fulness, etc.,* which have
later been changed. There are also to be mentioned the
changes in spelling later made by Noah Webster which have
in great part become distinctive of American usage. In
general, however, the spelling fixed upon in Johnson's *Dictionary* has remained permanent.

In Johnson's *Dictionary* the first meaning assigned to the
word *ascertain* is "to make certain; to fix; to establish."
The most important part of Johnson's task was that of
"ascertaining the signification" of English words. The
earlier freedom in shifting words to various meanings, especially prevalent with the Elizabethans, resulted in much
uncertainty and confusion regarding meanings. For this
remedies had been suggested. Wilkins had framed an ideal
system of language in which there should be an exact relation between words and things, and John Locke in his *Essay
upon Human Understanding* discoursed at great length on
the uncertain relation between words and ideas. In illustration he tells of a "meeting of very learned and ingenius
physicians where a discussion was quite diverted from its
original direction by a debate concerning the meaning of
the word *liquor."* A series of chapters in this work by
Locke is devoted to the consideration of the imperfection
of words, the abuse of words, and the remedies proposed.
Not only among the ignorant but among the learned, con-

fusion prevailed on account of uncertainty about meanings.

On this subject Johnson had no illusions. He well realized that a mathematical exactness and fixedness of relation between words and meanings was not attainable even if desirable. "With justice," he says, "may the lexicographer be derided, who, being able to produce no example of a nation that has preserved their words and phrases from mutability, shall imagine that his dictionary can embalm his language, and secure it from corruption and decay." With this realization, however, of the necessary limits to the functions of the lexicographer, Johnson went far ahead of his predecessors. His dictionary is not merely a spelling book or a lexicon with synonyms, apologetically addressed, like so many earlier works, to foreigners or to the fair sex, but one in which sharpness of distinction in meaning is attempted. Special attention is given to those joints in articulate speech, the particles, which in earlier writers, such as Shakespeare, were so vague in their meanings and consequently so loosely used. The variant meanings of individual words also are carefully distinguished. "Such is the exuberance of signification," says Johnson, "which many words have obtained that it was clearly impossible to collect all the senses." But for the single word *carry* he lists no less than thirty-two distinct meanings.

In this work, in which Johnson was to so great an extent a pioneer, there were faults. There were inaccuracies early pointed out, such as the words *windward* and *leeward* with identical definitions. There was awkwardness, of which Johnson was painfully aware, in the definitions provided for many of the simple, elemental words. Contemporary criticism was not slow to point out obscurity rather than clarity provided by such definitions as: 'sepulture' or 'interment,' for *burial;* 'paroxysm,' for *fit;* 'desiccative,' for *dry.* This feature of Johnson's work provided the theme for "malicious drollery" in a satirical Lucianic Dialogue entitled *Lexiphanes* published in 1767 by Archibald Campbell. Indeed burlesque could hardly surpass the famous definition provided by Johnson for *network* as "any thing reticulated or decussated, at equal distances, with interstices between the intersections." The accuracy of such definition is painful. Upon this part of his work Johnson expected "malignity most frequently to fasten." In spite, however, of obvious faults, Johnson's work in this respect was a remarkable achievement. "With little assistance from the learned, and without any patronage of the great," by dint of clear thinking supported by wide range of knowledge, he was able to frame a series of definitions which gave to English words the much needed quality of precision.

The subject of purity and propriety in English words Johnson approached with much diffidence. There should be recalled the dictum of Lord Chesterfield on this subject: "It is with language as with manners; they are both established by people of fashion." In his dedication addressed in 1747 to Lord Chesterfield, Johnson, speaking of purity and propriety, says: "I was once in doubt whether I should not attribute to myself too much in attempting to decide them, and whether my province was to extend beyond the proposition of the question, and the display of the suffrages on each side; but I have since been determined by your Lordship's opinion, to interpose my own judgment, and shall therefore endeavour to support what appears to be most consonant to grammar and reason. Ausonius thought that modesty forbade him to plead inability for a task to which Cæsar had judged him equal:—And I may hope, my Lord, that since you, whose authority in our language is so generally acknowledged, have commissioned me to declare my own opinion, I shall be considered as exercising a kind of vicarious jurisdiction; and that the power which might have been denied to my own claim, will be readily allowed me as the delegate of your Lordship." Thus provided with authority, Johnson ventured to offer his judgment of words. In this respect, however, his work is colored by his natural conservatism. For new words, he felt an aversion. Boswell writes, "he assured me that he had not taken upon himself to add more than four or five words to the English language, of his own information; and he was very much offended at the general licence by no means 'modestly taken' in his time, not only to coin new words, but to use many words in senses quite different from their established meaning . . ." Words with well-established etymologies he was disposed to accept with little hesitation. But toward words not thus established, especially new words, the products of modish affectation, he was not hospitable. *Sherbet* he allowed to be a good word because of its known derivation from Arabic, but *punch* he branded "a cant word" because without etymology. Among words labelled by him as "low" or "cant" or "low cant" or "barbarous" appear not only such words as *cabbage* ('to steal in cutting clothes'), *flip* ('a liquor'), *bubble* ('to cheat'), *bamboozle,* but *budge, fib, banter, swimmingly, clever, stingy, fun. Fop* is "a word probably made by Chance, and, therefore, without etymology." *Flippant* is "a word of no great authority." *Excepting* as a preposition is "not proper"; *smoothen* is "bad"; *womanize* is "not used" but "proper." The idiom *have rather,* which he himself uses in Rasselas, in his dictionary he condemns as "a barbarous expression of late intrusion into our language, for which it is better to say *will rather."*

That an authoritative work was needed to determine not only the meanings but the choice of words appears from a paper contributed by Lord Chesterfield to *The World* in 1754, the year before the publication of Johnson's

Dictionary. "It must be owned," says Chesterfield, "that our language is, at present, in a state of anarchy, and hitherto, perhaps, it may not have been the worse for it. During our free and open trade, many words and expressions have been imported, adopted, and naturalized from other languages, which have greatly enriched our own. . . . The time for discrimination seems to be now come. Toleration, adoption, and naturalization, have run their lengths. Good order and authority are now necessary. But where shall we find them, and at the same time, the obedience due to them? We must have recourse to the old Roman expedient in times of confusion, and choose a dictator. Upon this principle, I give my vote for Mr. Johnson to fill that great and arduous post. And I hereby declare, that I make a total surrender of all my rights and privileges in the English language, as a free-born British subject to the said Mr. Johnson during the term of his dictatorship. Nay, more, I will not only obey him like an old Roman, as my dictator, but, like a modern Roman, I will implicitly believe in him as my Pope, and hold him to be infallible while in the chair, but no longer." This passage was written by Chesterfield in the hope that the complete dictionary would be dedicated to him, a hope in which he was disappointed, as is well known. But the attitude is significant. The little controlled English language of the time of Sidney and Shakespeare, the elegant freedom of expression of the Restoration period, was to be subjected to authority. Both learning represented by Johnson and fashionable breeding represented by Chesterfield came together in a common form of language, reduced to regularity and uniformity.

The two ponderous volumes in which Johnson's work finally appeared still offer much of interest to one who has opportunity to peruse them. In them one will find not only quaintly learned definitions of familiar words and labels of disapproval attached to words now regarded as wholly reputable, but evidence of earlier meanings and earlier modes of accentuation in many words, and above all one will come to feel the presence of an interesting personality. The rugged honesty of Johnson appeared in his reply to a lady who had asked how he came to define *pastern* as "the knee of a horse." "Ignorance, Madam, pure ignorance," was Johnson's reply. Many of his definitions attracted the attention of his contemporaries and have remained classical material in the literature of anecdote. Most famous is his half-assumed contempt for the Scotch expressed in the definition of *oats*, "a grain, which in England is generally given to horses, but in Scotland supports the people," and his stern sense of wrong in the definition of *pension*, "an allowance made to any one without an equivalent. In England it is generally understood to mean pay given to a state hireling for treason to his country."

Johnson's dictionary had many successors before the end of the century, three of which have already been mentioned. These works, however, were mainly concerned with the attempt to go farther than Johnson had ventured and to fix not only the spelling and signification of words, but their pronunciation. A detailed discussion of these works must be reserved for later. In this direction Johnson did not go farther than his predecessor Bailey had gone. He contented himself with the indication of the position of the stress accent. His wisdom here is apparent. In the unsettled state of pronunciation of the time no work attempting to prescribe uniformity could have won general acceptance, as indeed appears from the rivalry among the works that attempted the task from which he had refrained. To the end of his life Johnson doubted the possibility of success in this attempt. In discussing Sheridan's dictionary with Boswell in 1772 he says that it is impossible to fix the pronunciation "after the example of the best company because they differ among themselves." In support of this assertion he relates his own experience, how Lord Chesterfield "told me that the word *great* should be pronounced so as to rhyme to *state;* and Sir William Yonge sent me word that none but an Irishman would pronounce it *grait.* Now here were two men of the highest rank, the one the best speaker in the House of Lords, the other the best speaker in the House of Commons, differing entirely." Significant not only of Johnson's attitude toward language but of a general tendency prevalent since his day is the dictum to be found in his *Grammar:* "For pronunciation the best rule is, to consider those as the most elegant speakers who deviate least from the written words." Quite consistent with this position is his attitude toward reforms in orthography. The arguments against a purely phonetic spelling have never been more effectively expressed than in Johnson's words: "Some have endeavoured to accommodate orthography better to pronunciation, without considering that this is to measure by a shadow, to take that for a model which is changing while they apply it." The literary products of the best writers, according to Johnson's principles, form the standards not only for written but for spoken English. The contrast between this position and that of Dryden is to be noted. In fact during the remainder of the eighteenth century and continuing down to our own times, this attitude of mind has been a prevalent one.

The long cherished plan for an English Academy never came to fruition. To it Johnson was opposed because, to quote his own words: "If an academy should be established for the cultivation of our style, which I, who can never wish to see dependence multiplied, hope the spirit of English liberty will hinder or destroy, let them. . . ." His own work, however, it will be observed, accomplished much that it had been intended an Academy should accomplish. Toward the accomplishment of Swift's plan for "correcting, improving, and ascertaining the English tongue," it made a long stride. Later lexicographers based their works on Johnson. Walker in his *Pronouncing Dictionary* (1791) says: "His Dictionary has been deemed lawful plunder by every subsequent Lexicographer, and so servilely has it been copied that . . . words omitted merely by mistake . . . as *Predilection, Respectable, Descriptive, Sulky, Inimical, Interference,* are not in Mr. Sheridan's, Dr. Kenrick's, nor several other dictionaries." Sheridan, who cherished a personal resentment toward Johnson, in his *Plan of Education* (1769) generously says of him: "If our language should ever be fixed, he must be considered by all posterity as the founder, and his dictionary as the cornerstone." Nares in his *Elements of Orthoëpy* (1784) says that "Dr. Johnson's Dictionary has nearly fixed the external form of our language. Indeed so convenient is it to have one acknowledged standard to recur to, . . . that it is earnestly to be hoped, that no author will henceforth, on light grounds, be tempted to innovate."

CHAPTER XV

EIGHTEENTH-CENTURY GRAMMARIANS

TO his *Dictionary* Johnson prefixed *A Grammar of the English Language.* This work was done in a perfunctory way and offers little that is original beyond certain observations, some of which have been just quoted. Having indicated the spelling and the signification of words, he contents himself with certain general rules for pronunciation and a classification of the principal forms of declension and conjugation. To the consideration of how the words with their inflected forms are to be combined into sentences he gives almost no attention. The reason assigned by Johnson for his scant attention to syntax was that "our Language has so little inflection, that its Construction neither requires nor admits many rules." This scant treatment is criticized by Bishop Lowth who, in his *English Grammar* (1762), remarks that: "The English Grammar that hath last been presented to the public, and by the Person best qualified to have given us a complete one, comprises the whole Syntax in ten lines."

An examination of the cultivated speech of the earlier eighteenth century, as recorded in the works of the great novelists of the period, will provide support for the contention of Lowth that English syntax needed further regulation. In the cultivated colloquial speech recorded in the writings of Smollett and Richardson and Sterne, for instance, appear numerous forms of speech that could not bear the test of grammatical correctness. For instance may be mentioned the prevalent use of *you* with the singular form of the verb: *What was you afraid of?* (*Roderick Random*); *You was too eager* (*Ibid.*); *Where was you born?* (*Ibid.*); *If I thought you was able* (*Tristram Shandy*); *You was led* (*Ibid.*); *Was you angry?* (*Sir Charles Grandison*); *But you . . . was an adept* (*Ibid.*). The double negative is not infrequent: *Nor never will* (*Roderick Random*); *nor none that ever came* (*Ibid.*); *not quite came to neither* (*Sir Charles Grandison*); *But that won't do neither* (*Ibid.*). Further locutions ungrammatical according to later standards are: *it don't signify* (*Roderick Random*); *asked who he called a fool* (*Ibid.*); *Who have we got here?* (*Ibid.*); *if he was in my place* (*Ibid.*); *scarce ever* (*Ibid.*); *had smote* (*Ibid.*); *had wrote* (*Ibid.*); *if I was not morally sure* (*Ibid.*); *if a man was to sit down* (*Tristram Shandy*); *if I was a prince* (*Ibid.*); *if it was not for the aids* (*Ibid.*); *more imperfect* (*Ibid.*); *more perfect* (*Ibid.*); *Why don't he speak louder* (*Sir Charles Grandison*); *extreme bad terms* (*Ibid.*); *Every one in their way* (*Ibid.*); *Mr. Orme . . . don't look so ill* (*Ibid.*); *to know if I have written tolerable* (*Ibid.*); *he applied to every one for their interest* (*Ibid.*). Such forms of expression taken with the irregular forms of strong verbs such as *had drank, have rode, having stole away, who had broke, sunk* (for 'sank'), *spoke* (for 'spoken'), *sprung* (for 'sprang'), etc., and the use of words in ways later objected to, such as *the loan of a shirt, implicitly* ('without question), *aggravating* ('irritating'), create the impression of an unregulated language. There should be noted also the frequency of the expressions, *had better,* and *had rather,* later challenged by the more extreme supporters of regularity.

Such features, which are to be met with on nearly every page in the works of the great group of English novelists, afford ample evidence of the neglected regulation of English syntax. Against this neglect John Locke had raised his voice in protest. And now again following the success of Johnson's *Dictionary,* the complaint is renewed. Joseph Priestley (1761) says of his contemporaries that most of them are "sensible that their knowledge of the grammar of their mother tongue hath been acquired by their own study and observation since they have passed the rudiments of the schools." To the same effect is the remark by Lowth (1762) that: "A Grammatical Study of our own Language makes no part of the ordinary method which we pass through in our childhood; and it is very seldom that we apply ourselves to it afterward." Is it, Lowth asks, because the English language is "in its nature irregular and capricious; not hitherto reducible to a system of rules?" This idea, which seems to have been that of Johnson, Lowth rejects with vehemence. Moreover, French opinion on this subject found its way into England. The four-volume French work by M. Rollin on *The Method of Teaching and Studying the Belles-Lettres* had long been familiarly known in English translation, and a fifth edition of the translation had appeared in 1759. Rollin emphasizes four things: knowledge of rules, reading French books, translation, composition. Priestley, proposing a remedy for the faults in English, makes prescriptions similar to those made by Rollin for French. He says: "We must introduce into our schools English Grammar, English Compositions, and frequent English translations from authors in other languages."

Both Priestley and Lowth went beyond admonition and published grammars of the English language, Priestley in 1761 and Lowth in 1762. The *Short Introduction to English Grammar* by Robert Lowth, later Bishop of London, is in many ways an epoch-making book. In the standard Latin grammar by William Lily, in use for more than three centuries, one finds the definition, *Grammatica est recte scribendi et loquendi ars.* Lowth attempts this kind of a grammar for English. He aims to provide rules for distinguishing what is right from what is wrong in English syntax. He makes the law of universal grammar like the law of logic or the moral law, and in his application of these laws to English is largely responsible for belief in an absoluteness in grammatical rule which since his day has become widely prevalent.

The fame of Joseph Priestley the grammarian is much overshadowed by that of Priestley the scientist, the celebrated discoverer of oxygen. In his earlier life a schoolmaster, he prepared his *Rudiments of English Grammar* for practical service. It is of American interest to know that in this and other grammatical treatises Priestley was influenced by the counsels of a kindred spirit, also a distinguished contributor to physical science, the American Benjamin Franklin. With the names of Priestley and Lowth among the pioneers should be joined that of James Buchanan, of whom Samuel Johnson in semi-jocular humor once said that "he was the only man of genius his country ever produced." Buchanan was one of the class of Scotchmen of whom Smollett in his *Roderick Random* offers a picture, or a caricature—North Britons who made a career through teaching Englishmen the use of their own language. As early as 1753 Buchanan published an ambitious work entitled *The Complete English Scholar* in which Part III was devoted to English grammar. He was editor of a revised edition of Bailey's dictionary, published in 1759, and later produced a pronouncing dictionary, one of the earliest of its kind. His name deserves a place with those of Lowth and Priestley because of the *British Grammar*, published without date, probably 1762, now generally attributed to him. Buchanan vigorously attacks the idea of learning English through Latin, and the *British Grammar* had important influence through the direction it gave to later grammatical treatises, particularly in America.

The works of Priestley and Lowth and Buchanan were followed by a long line of English grammars, by William Ward, by Anselm Bayley, by Gough (Ireland), by Corbet, by Burn (Scotland), by Ash, by Smetham, by Fell, by Elphinston, by Norman, by Coote, by Harrison, by Walker, by Crombie, by G. Wright, by Alexander, not to mention a number of anonymous works, all leading up to that remarkable compendium of earlier achievement, the *English Grammar* by the American Lindley Murray which was published at York in 1795.

In this eighteenth-century "better English" movement were involved men varying in social station and in intellectual bent. Practical schoolmen like Buchanan were joined by gentlemen scholars like Dr. John Ward, by churchmen of rank such as Lowth and Anselm Bayley, and by men of science such as Priestley. With so many points of view represented there could hardly be expected any unanimity of opinion or uniformity of method. Varied modes of exposition were used. In many of the books, in Priestley's for example, the traditional question and answer method was preserved. As an aid in the memorizing process resort also was had to the mnemonic device of riming verse. In the grammar, for instance, by J. W., the distinction between the definite and the indefinite article is expressed in jingles:

> The Article stands with a Noun
> And shows us its extent;
> A, is indefinite; A Town;
> The, definite; The Rent.

In the grammar by William Ward the distinction between *shall* and *will* is taught in verses beginning:

The Verb by *shall,* states of fix'd order shows;
Or States which Chance directs, as we suppose.
And *shall* those verbal Future States declares
Which *for itself,* an Object hopes or fears . . .

But these earlier methods relying solely on the memory came more and more to be superseded by methods more concrete. Illustrative examples were offered, and there were introduced praxes for parsing. Most effective among these new methods was that by examples of false syntax. Lowth in the preface to his grammar says: "I will not take upon me to say, whether we have any Grammar that sufficiently instructs us by rule and example; but I am sure that we have none, that, in the manner here attempted teaches us what is right by shewing what is wrong." In his notes Lowth illustrates the faults to be avoided by means of expressions from the most esteemed of earlier writers. The method of "false syntax" is also used in the *British Grammar* supposed to be by James Buchanan. Neither Lowth nor Buchanan, however, can claim the credit, or discredit, of this innovation. Its earliest use may be claimed by the anonymous author of a work entitled *A Practical New Grammar, with Exercises of Bad English,* which, judged by number of editions, must have had a wide and long continued popularity. The third edition appeared in 1753, and a nineteenth edition, edited by A. Fisher, was published at Newcastle in 1780. The exercises in bad English, the reader is informed, are made "after the manner of Clark's or Bailey's Examples for the Latin tongue." In fact the method can be traced back as far as Quintilian. The author takes pride in his application of this method to English teaching, but says that "never anything of the same Nature appearing in an English Grammar before, I run the risk of singularity." Although this method is now all but universally condemned, there are many things to be said in its favor. In the eighteenth century it gave a degree of popularity to a subject hitherto generally unpopular. In English instruction then as now, a main end achieved is unfortunately less a constructive than a corrective one. In the accomplishment of this task, negative in character, no method is more direct than that by concrete exhibition of error. In place of more or less general principles to be applied, there is offered definiteness of task.

But in the grammars of this period, as in those of subsequent times, there was inability to reach general agreement due to the lack of a uniform guiding principle. There was still to be reckoned with the overshadowing influence of Latin training. The well-paved Roman road was easier to follow than were newly blazed trails. This Roman road had been followed by earlier English writers. James Buchanan in his grammar (1762), speaking of the "grammatical improprieties" to be found in the writings of Swift, Addison, and Pope, remarks: "Should it be urged, that in the time of these Writers, English was but little subjected to Grammar, that they had scarcely a single Rule to direct them; a question naturally occurs: Had they not the Rules of Latin Syntax?" In the second half of the century the old Roman road was much in use. Lord Monboddo in his six-volume work *Of the Origin and Progress of Language* (1773-92), is chiefly concerned with the classical languages. The Latin language, he remarks, deterioriated after the Augustan Age of Virgil and Horace; the English language likewise, he believed, was in process of deterioration after its Augustan Age. In illustration of this decay Lord Monboddo cites the word *ingenuity* "which is now used even by the best writers, to signify that which is clever or acute in the operations of the mind; a sense which has no connection with the signification of the Latin word, *ingenuitas*, from which it is derived." In the determination not only of meaning but of spelling resort was had to Latin etymology. In Dr. John Ward's *Four Essays upon the English Language,* for instance, on etymological grounds *horizon* is preferred to *horison, mystery* to *mistery, proclame* and *reclame* to *proclaim* and *reclaim.* In many of the English grammars of this period, not only Latin nomenclature, but Latin systems of inflection are retained. William Ward, for instance, and Anselm Bayley still distinguish six cases in English nouns.

Even where the attempt was abandoned to teach English through Latin, a reversed procedure was used and the system and nomenclature of Latin grammar were retained in order that English study might prepare for Latin learning. William Ward in his *Grammar of the English Tongue* (1767) defends the retention of the older method on the ground that: "as no Man knows but he may have Occasion to learn some other Language, why should he not be taught the English Rudiments in such a Manner as may be of Service towards his learning any other Language?"

It was not easy all at once to gain complete independence of English grammar from the Latin learning which had dominated for so many centuries. Since the middle of the seventeenth century, however, there had been forming a new school of opinion which sought a more universal basis for English grammar. One should recall Bishop Wilkins's *Essay towards a Real Character, and a Philosophical Language* (1668), in which is made the idealistic attempt to arrange and classify things so that they might be scientifically or logically named, in other words, to bring words into precise relations with things, and thus provide the basis for a natural grammar. One should recall also the ideas of John Locke concerning the relation between words and ideas. A natural sequel to these works by Wilkins and Locke is the work published in 1751 by James Harris, Esq., entitled, *Hermes, a Philosophical Inquiry Concerning Universal Language.* This work attracted much attention and exerted no little influence. Harris is referred to as the "Prince of modern Grammarians." His book appeared in new editions in 1765 and 1771. "All speech or discourse," declares Harris, "is a publishing or exhibiting some part of the soul." In an analysis of the operations of the soul, therefore, is to be found the basis for the analysis of the elements in language.

The impractical, if not fallacious, nature of Harris's reasoning was exposed by Horne Tooke in his *Diversions of Purley* (1785) in which is shown the indirectness of the relation existing between words and things and between words and ideas. In the meantime, however, the ideas of Harris were widely prevalent. Lowth intended his grammar to be a companion volume to that of Harris. He bestows high praise on Harris. "Those," he says, "who would enter more deeply into this subject, will find it fully and accurately handled, with the greatest acuteness of investigation, and elegance of method, in a treatise entitled *Hermes,* by James Harris, Esq., the most beautiful and perfect example of Analysis that has been exhibited since the days of Aristotle."

The principles of universal grammar Lowth aims to apply to the English language. "The English language," he says, "hath been much cultivated during the last two hundred years . . . considerably enlarged . . . its energy, variety, richness, and elegance, have been abundantly proved . . . but . . . it hath made no advances in Grammatical accuracy." The remedy, in his opinion, is not to be found in cultivated usage alone. "Much practice in the polite world," he asserts, "and a general acquaintance with the best authors, are good helps, but alone will be hardly sufficient." In fact, in discussing Swift's attacks on prevailing faults of speech, Lowth asks: "Does it mean that the English as it is spoken by the politest part of the nation, and as it stands in the writings of our most approved authors, often offends against every part of grammar?" "Thus far," he says, "I am afraid the charge is true." Lowth, therefore, abandons usage as the mistress of language. In fact the examples of "false syntax" cited for correction in Lowth's grammar are garnered from the most admired of earlier English writers. Nor, in Lowth's opinion, is the guidance which is not provided by polite usage, to be found in Latin learning. "Much less," he says, "will what is commonly called Learning serve the purpose: . . . The greatest critic and most capable grammarian of the last age [1] was frequently at a loss in matters of ordinary use and construction in his own vernacular idiom." The basis for English grammar not found in polite usage or in classical learning, Lowth, like Harris, found in principles of universal grammar. "The Grammar of any particular language," he says, "applies those common principles to that particular language, according to the established usage and custom of it."

Applying principles of universal grammar, Lowth subjects to criticism many modes of expression long current in English use. He objects to the use of the double negative. He challenges the expression *a means,* which he suggests should be *a mean.* He objects to the use of *whose* in reference to inanimate things, and finds both Dryden and Addison at fault in this. He objects to *lesser* and *worser,* which he finds to be used by Dryden and Addison. *You was,* which he finds in the language of Addison, Bolingbroke, and Pope, he rates as a fault. He condemns the use of the past participle for the preterit, such as *begun* for *began,* a kind of fault which he finds in the language of Milton, Dryden, Atterbury, Addison, Pope, Clarendon, and

---

[1] Evidently Richard Bentley, the famous classical scholar, is meant.

Gay. He condemns further the confusion of *who* and *whom*, the misuse of prepositions, the use of flat adverbs and of the locutions *It is me* and *These kind of*. To many of Lowth's judgments later assent has been given. His assertion that "two negatives . . . are equivalent to an Affirmative" has been generally adopted as a guiding principle. The earlier use of the double negative, persisting to some extent, as has been pointed out, through the first half of the eighteenth century, has disappeared from cultivated English language since his day. To other rigid rules as formulated by Lowth assent has not been as freely accorded. *"Whose,"* says Lowth, "is by some writers made the possessive case of *which* and applied to things as well as persons; I think, improperly." Lowth's objection in this instance has not been sustained. Lindley Murray (1795) cites ample authority for this condemned use among standard English writers. "Adjectives," says Lowth, "are sometimes employed as adverbs improperly, and not agreeably to the genius of the English language." To this Anselm Bayley (1772) retorts that "What the custom and usage of a language may be, it is easy to determine, but not what is the genius of the language," and Bayley proceeds to defend the use of what would today be termed 'flat adverbs,' such as *very, mighty, right, excessive, exceeding,* joined with adjectives in expressions such as *prodigious cold* and *exceeding fair*.

The judgments of Lowth, however, and his mode of criticism, found wide adoption. In 1765 William Ward, Master of the Grammar School at Beverley in the county of York, published *An Essay on Grammar, as it may be applied to the English Language,* a voluminous work of 554 large pages; and two years later, in 1767: *A Grammar of the English Tongue, In Two Treatises. The First, containing Rules for every Part of its Construction; with a Praxis both of True and False English . . . The second, shewing the Nature of the Several Parts of Speech, and the Reasons of every Part of Construction.* Ward expresses approbation of the grammar by "the learned Dr. Lowth, now Lord Bishop of Oxford," and particularly commends the notes by Lowth, in which "are shown the grammatic Inaccuracies that have escaped the Pens of our most distinguished Writers." This practical schoolmaster, "Head of a public school above thirty Years," found the new method extremely helpful, "For my Profession as a School-Master obliged me to explain the Principles of Grammar to my Scholars; and I found the Grammars made use of in our Schools gave but a very imperfect Account of them. . . . This determined me many Years ago, to attempt a Discovery of the Reason of every Part of its Construction." Here we have perhaps the earliest instance of the practice much decried in the nineteenth century, of "schoolmastering" the English language. Reason is enthroned. Custom in language, says Ward, is not the "Effect of Chance," but is "a consistent Plan of communicating the Conceptions and rational discursive Operations of one Man to another. . . . And it is the Business of Speculative or Rational Grammar to explain the Nature of the means. . . . The most simple of the Elements of Logic will become familiar to those who engage in a Course of Grammar, and Reason will go hand in Hand with Practice."

The same abandonment of natural usage in favor of precise rules appears in the grammar by Charles Coote (1788). Language in actual use may not safely be taken as a pattern, says Coote, because "Among the middling ranks of life grammar appears to be much discarded. . . . The members of the three learned professions are confessedly superior to the generality in the accurate use of their native language. But even among them there is some deficiency in this respect. . . . Persons of rank and fashion, though they generally speak with ease and elegance, are not remarkable for being models of accurate expression. . . . Authors are, without controversy, the persons on whom it is more particularly incumbent both in speaking and writing, to observe a strict adherence to grammatical propriety. . . . But this is a point to which the greater part of our most esteemed writers have not sufficiently attended." [2]

But the assumption of the existence of a universal grammar governing language and of an absolute distinction between right and wrong ran counter to long-established belief and to traditions based on classical authority supported by the wisdom of antiquity. The judgments of Horace and Quintilian regarding the rule of nature in language could not be lightly dismissed. And there was the dictum of Seneca (*Epistle* 95) that "Grammarians are the guardians, not the authors of language." This wisdom had been expressed in the lines by Pope:

> The rules of old discovered, not devis'd
> Are Nature still, but Nature methodiz'd.

And there was the critical opinion of Goldsmith, that "Rules will never make a work or discourse eloquent." [3] This attitude toward the critic and his rules had been that of Fielding. In *Tom Jones* (1749) he declares: "The critic, rightly considered, is no more than the clerk, whose office it is to transcribe the rules and laws laid down by those great judges whose vast strength of genius hath placed them in the light of legislators, in the several sciences over which they presided. This office was all which the critics of old aspired to; nor did they ever dare to advance

[2] Quoted from C. C. Fries, *Publications Modern Language Association*, XL, 980-1.
[3] *On Eloquence*, 1759.

a sentence, without supporting it by the authority of the judge from whence it was borrowed.

"But in process of time, and in ages of ignorance, the clerk began to invade the power and assume the dignity of the master. The laws of writing were no longer founded on the practice of the author, but on the dictates of the critic. The clerk became the legislator, and those very peremptorily gave laws whose business it was, first, only to transcribe them."

The classical view of the function of the critic and grammarian which had gained the support of earlier English writers, is the one adopted by Joseph Priestley, whose grammar was contemporary with that by Lowth. In his *Course of Lectures on the English Language* (1762) he proclaims that "the general prevailing custom, where ever it happen to be, can be the only standard for the time that it prevails." To the same effect John Fell, in his *Essay towards an English Grammar* (1784), declares: "It is certainly the business of a grammarian to find out, and not to make, the laws of a language. In this work the Author does not assume the character of a legislator, but appears as a faithful compiler of the scattered laws. . . . It matters not what causes these customs and fashions owe their birth to; the moment they become general, they are laws of the language; and a grammarian can only remonstrate, how much so ever he disapprove." The most radical of present-day supporters of usage as a guide could hardly go farther in a statement of the humble function of the grammarian. Fell modestly disclaims any intention "to supersede or controvert those ingenious tracts on the subject which the Public has been favored with of late years . . . and would more especially bear his testimony to the taste and learning of Dr. Lowth's introduction." The deferential attitude toward rank and position is to be noted. And yet Fell has

a quite different conception of the function of the grammarian. "Our critics," he says, "are allowed to petition,
but not to command: and why should their power be enlarged? The laws of our speech, like the laws of our
country, should breathe a spirit of liberty; they should
check licentiousness, without restraining freedom." He
disapproves of an institution like the French Academy, for,
he asserts, "the republic of letters is a true republic, in its
disregard to the arbitrary decrees of usurped authority."
Moreover, he disapproves of the effects of rigid rules appearing in the style of writers of his time who "give the
phraseology a disgusting air of study and formation."
They "may perhaps have given our language a higher polish;
but have they not also curtailed and impoverished it? . . .
Have they not reduced all kinds of writing to an insipid
uniformity?" He has words of praise for Swift, Pope, Addison, Dryden, for the prose of Cowley and for Shakespeare's
"immortal wit." "Let the writings of these great men be
compared with those of more modern date, and I am persuaded we shall not find them excelled, perhaps not equalled,
by their successors."

The view of Priestley and of Fell is also that of the
Scotch rhetoricians, Campbell and Blair. In his *Lectures
on Rhetoric and Belles Lettres* (1783), Blair says: "I admit
that no grammatical rules have sufficient authority to controul (*sic*) the firm and established usage of Language.
Established custom, in speaking and writing, is the standard
to which we must at last resort for determining every con-
troverted point in Language and Style." Like Fell, Blair
is not disposed to attach great importance to mere mechanical regularity. "My other observation," he says,
"which applies equally to Dean Swift and Mr. Addison, is,
that there may be writers much freer of such inaccuracies,
as I have had occasion to point out in these two, whose

Style however, upon the whole, may not have half their merit. Refinement in Language has, of late years, begun to be much attended to. In several modern productions of very small value, I should find it difficult to point out many errors in Language . . . ; whilst yet the Style, upon the whole, might deserve no praise."

But, though they denied the absolute authority of grammatical rule, even the supporters of the authority of usage recognized the need of control, at least of a curbing of license. This control was found in the principle of analogy already mentioned. In the seventeenth century the promoters of the new science had substituted for classical authority as a guide, the methods of observation and reason. These sources of knowledge in their application to language, became observed usage and analogy. These, as has been seen, were the guiding principles of Samuel Johnson. To them the grammarians also had resort. "The chief thing to be attended to in the improvement of a language," says Priestley, "is the analogy of it." In another place Priestley says that "were the language of man as uniform as the works of nature, the *grammar of language* would be as indisputable in its principles as the *grammar of nature;* but since good authors have adopted different forms of speech, and in a case that admits of no standard but that of *custom,* one authority may be of as much weight as another; the *analogy of language* is the only thing to which we can have recourse, to adjust these differences. . . ."

The task before the grammarian in fixing the language was that of doing with English constructions what Johnson had done with English words, to record the established practices and to adjust differences by the principle of analogy. In this adjustment, however, general agreement was almost impossible to reach. It proved impossible to register the usage in grammatical constructions as Johnson had done that of words in his *Dictionary*. "It is not the authority of any one person, or of a few, . . . that can establish one form of speech in preference to another. Nothing but the general practice of good writers and good speakers can do it." By way of illustration Priestley takes the construction exemplified in the phrase *it is me*. "All our grammarians," he says, "say, that the nominative cases of pronouns ought to follow the verb substantive as well as precede it, and the example of some of our best writers would lead us to make a contrary rule; or at least, would leave us at liberty to adopt which we liked best." From standard English writers he cites the following expressions: *Yes, they are them, It is me, It is him, It is not me you are in love with* (Addison); *It cannot be me* (Swift); *To that which once was thee* (*Prior*); *There is but one man . . . and that is me* (Richardson's *Clarissa Harlowe*). He cites other constructions similarly irregular: *more interest at court than him; understand poetry better than him; was far more happy than him* (Smollett's *Voltaire*). Concerning such expressions Priestley remarks: "The custom of speaking draws one way, and an attention to arbitrary and artificial rules another. Which will prevail at last, it is impossible to say."

A culmination in the grammatical and rhetorical labors of the eighteenth century was reached with the appearance of Lindley Murray's *English Grammar* published at York in 1795. The name Lindley Murray is one that today excites varied feelings. To some Murray is a demi-god, a second founder of the English language, the "father of English grammar." To others he is the betrayer of the liberties of the English language. To neither of these titles is he entitled. He was not the father of English grammar. A long line of predecessors deprives him of that claim to honor. His work, as he modestly announces, was that of a compiler. Nor is he solely responsible, as sometimes supposed, for the betrayal of the language into the fettered bondage of grammatical rules. His theory was liberal. He quotes with approval the familiar dicta of Quintilian and of Horace that usage is the mistress of language. "The practice of the best and most correct writers, or a great majority of them, corroborated by general usage," he asserts, "forms, during its continuance, the standard of language. . . . Every connexion and application of words and phrases, must therefore be proper, and entitled to respect." There is one striking exception, it must be noted, indicated by the qualifying phrase, "if not exceptionable in a moral point of view." In fact, Murray relaxes to a certain extent some of the more rigid rules of his predecessors. He defends the treatment of the word *means* as singular in number, a use objected to by Lowth. He permits the use of *whose* as the possessive form of *which*, another use to which Lowth was opposed. He joins with Priestley in objection to the requirement that in the case of compound words such as *averse* and *abhorrence*, the following preposition should correspond with the prefix in the adjective or noun. Such expressions, therefore, as *averse from, abhorrence from*, and *depend from* insisted on by some, he objects to because "general practice, and the idiom of the English tongue, seem to oppose the innovation."

But with all his lip service to the doctrine of freedom in usage, Murray was a child of the eighteenth century. Order and regularity were the qualities esteemed. Admitting that in some respects the classic tongues may be more regular than the modern, he nevertheless asserts that "every polite tongue has its own rules; and the English that is according to rule, is not less regular than the Greek that is according to rule; and a deviation from the established use of the language, is as much an irregularity in the one as in the other. . . ."

With Murray, as with his eighteenth-century predecessors, analogy was the principle to be applied in the overcoming of anomaly. Guided largely by this principle, Murray compiled from the works of his predecessors a system to include the forms of speech in English and a series of rules governing their combination into phrases and sentences. Following a middle course, he trimmed down the extravagance of some of the extremists among his predecessors and at the same time preserved most of the features in systems of classification already established. For instance, in the analysis of English words into parts of speech, some earlier grammarians had distinguished ten sorts of words, others had reduced the number to two kinds, nouns and verbs. Murray, following "those authors who appear to have given them the most natural and intelligible distribution," distinguishes nine kinds. In the analysis of verb-forms Harris had enumerated no fewer than twelve tenses. Other grammarians, recognizing only the distinctions of tense indicated by distinction of form, reduced English tenses to two, "the present and the past in the active verb, and in the passive no tenses at all." Murray presents an English verbal system after the pattern of the classical languages, on the ground that "though the learned languages, with respect to voices, moods, and tenses, are, in general differently constructed from the English tongue, yet, in some respects, they are so similar to it, as to warrant the principle which he has adopted." In handling the cases of nouns, some earlier grammarians had recognized only two, those distinguished by difference in form, the nominative and the possessive or genitive. Murray after "a renewed, critical examination of the subject," concludes that "the nouns of our language are entitled to" an objective case, a conclusion in which he was guided by the analogy of Latin, which distinguishes between nominative and accusative in many cases where, as in English, the two cases have no difference in form. By such methods, following established practice, usually following classical pattern rather than radical attempts toward the formation of a system more closely fitting the peculiar structure of the English language, Murray arrived at a system now familiar because adopted by a long succession of grammarians in the nineteenth century.

He not only established a system generally followed by later grammarians in the classification of the elements of the language, but he compiled a series of definite rules governing syntactical arrangement. Earlier forms of expression such as "Tranquillity and peace *dwells* here," "Ignorance and negligence *has* produced the effect," "the discomfiture and slaughter *was* very great," though used by reputable writers, are condemned as "evidently contrary to the first principles of grammar," a judgment supported by the opinion of Dr. Blair. "These kind of sufferings" and "those set of books," forms of expression found in reputable English use to some extent from the sixteenth to the twentieth century, are definitely proscribed. "The distributive adjective pronouns, *each, every, either,* agree with the nouns, pronouns, and verbs, of the singular number only." The earlier freedom which had tolerated expressions such as "Let each esteem others better than *themselves,*" "Every freeman, and every citizen, have a right to *their* votes," is now definitely curbed by rule. The use of 'flat adverbs,' as in the expressions, *indifferent honest, excellent well,* Murray joins Lowth in condemning. One exception, however, he makes, when the adverb is joined to an adjective or adverb ending in -*ly,* in which case the termination is omitted in the first word. For example, "Some men think exceeding clearly." Adjectives having a superlative signification, "do not properly admit of the comparative or superlative superadded." Under this rule are condemned such forms as *chiefest, extremest, perfectest, most universal, most supreme.* Governing the form of construction represented by the phrase, *it is me,* a construction concerning which Priestley hesitated in his judgment, Murray offers the rule that, "The verb *to be,* through all its variations, has the same case after it, expressed or understood, as that which next precedes it." As instances of deviations from rule, exhibiting the pronoun in a wrong case, are cited such forms of expression as: "it could not have been me." He also condemns the confusion between *who* and *whom* appearing in expressions such as "Who do you think me to be?" "Whom do men say that I am?" The confusion of the preterit form with that of the perfect participle, a form of irregularity conspicuous in eighteenth-century English and only gradually disappearing in the nineteenth century, Murray warns against. As examples of uses to be avoided he cites the expressions: *he begun, he run, he drunk, I had wrote, I was chose, he would have spoke, verses wrote on glass, too strong to be shook by such causes.*

In the original introduction to his grammar Murray speaks of "the number and variety of English Grammars already published" and expresses his feeling that "little can be expected from a new compilation, besides a careful selection of the most useful matter, and some degree of improvement in the mode of adapting it to the understanding, and the gradual progress of learners." The modesty in Murray's pretension here apparent gives little suggestion of the magnitude of his achievement. He obviously was not the "father of English grammar," nor was he the originator of the idea that the language should be reduced to system and governed by rules. Nevertheless, he produced a work which was for many years the most widely used textbook on grammar, and which provided the pattern for later works produced in succeeding generations. The book in its original form passed through 50 editions. In 1816 it was published in revised form in two volumes octavo, and an abridgment of this revised edition went through more than 120 editions of 10,000 each.

The achievement of Murray was a remarkable one. With all abatement of credit due to lack of originality, the work had distinguished merits. Worthy of the highest admiration is the skill shown in trimming a course through the conflicting currents of opinion in the works of eighteenth-century grammarians, shunning the Scylla of arbitrary rule on the one hand and the Charybdis of uncontrolled freedom on the other. Furthermore, the pedagogic skill in presenting the material is remarkable. Murray, in his Introduction, speaks of the "sentiment generally admitted, that a proper selection of faulty composition is more instructive to the young grammarian, than any rules and examples of propriety that can be given," and accordingly provides ample supply of "instances of false grammar." Following an approved method, therefore, he arranged exercises to accompany the rules. Exercises in parsing were also included, and the whole set of language problems was combined with a key. The system, involving, as it did, the active coöperation of the learner, gave to the subject an interest absent in earlier works which had called solely on the memorizing process in the absorption of grammatical rules.

The circumstances under which this work was composed have their interest. It was not a Scotchman, strange to say, but an American, though with a Scotch name, who produced this important English grammar. A man naturally drawn to learned pursuits, Murray after a short but successful career in the practice of law in America, had at the early age of thirty-one settled at Holgate near York in 1784. While there leading a life of cultured leisure, he was requested to prepare an English grammar for use in a Friends' school for girls at York. The manuscript of the petition signed by the teachers asking Murray to undertake this work is still preserved. Thus it was that by an interesting chance the interests of the fair sex, whose use of English for two centuries had been the subject of so much solicitude, at last called into being the book which more than any preceding book brought the forms and constructions of the English language to uniformity and system, and provided guidance for those whose command of language is gained from books and schools rather than from social environment.

CHAPTER XVI

ENGLISH PURISTS AND SCOTCH RHETORICIANS

SAMUEL JOHNSON, it will be recalled, undertook only hesitatingly the task of passing judgment on the propriety of words. It will be recalled also that his criteria in this important matter were lacking in definiteness. This shortcoming in Johnson's work was felt and numerous volunteer attempts were made to remedy the defect. In 1770 appeared a work published anonymously with the title *Reflections on the English Language.* This work, "A Detection of many Improper Expressions used in Conversation and of many others to be found in Authors," is referred to by Richard Grant White [1] as the "first work of avowed English verbal criticism" known to him and is attributed by him to Robert Baker. The aim of the author is to do for English something like what Vaugelas had done for French. The judgments offered in this book, like those offered in many later works of its kind, are based largely on personal taste. They have an interest, however, as reflecting some of the prevailing tendencies of the period and the attitude of those striving after correctness in language. Among the hundred and more words and locutions objected to appear: *chay,* for 'chaise'; *pre-sentiment* (felt to be an undesirable importation from French); *demean* (with the meaning *debase* or *lessen*) said to be "used by all the lower People, as well as by great Numbers of their Betters"; *mutual* (in expressions such as *Our mutual benefactor,* and *our mutual friend*) which properly should be used only to

[1] *Every-Day English,* p. 394.

"signify that there is an interchange"; *left off,* for 'ceased';
different to and *different than.*

Among ungrammatical uses objected to may be mentioned: the confusion of *sit* and *set,* which are said to be
misemployed even by "People of very good Education"; and
of *lie* and *lay,* which "are as often confounded as *set";* of
him, her, me, them, "frequently used in the nominative case
even among the better Sort of People" in expressions such
as *'tis him, 'tis me* (examples of misuse are cited from Congreve); *every one* used with plural verb or pronoun.

Similar is the tone of another work published anonymously and without date, but evidently belonging to this
period, entitled *Observations upon the English Language.*
The author of this work favors changes in spelling to bring
conformity with etymology, such as dropping the *g* in such
words as *sovereign* and *foreign,* and the *u* in such words as
honour and *splendour,* the substitution of *t* for *c* in such
words as *spatious, gratious, pretious,* and *in-* for *un-* in
words such as *incertain* and *instable.* Further he asserts
that "we ought to make it an invariable rule, never to abbreviate any word in our prose Writings by the Omission
even of a single Letter, altho *(sic)* the Place of it is supplied by an Apostrophe." He, therefore, condemns forms
of words appearing in "the works of our most approved
Prose Writers," such forms as *lov'd, 'tis, it's, shant* and
hant. The use of such forms, he asserts, is so prevalent
that "I shall not be surprized *(sic)* at seeing in a short
Time such mutilated Words as *genral* for *general, natral* for
natural, lengthning for *lengthening, solly* for *solely,* with
many other Monstrosities of the like Stamp."

But it is the remarks on the use of words that are of
present concern. This writer condemns the use of *that* as a
relative and lays down the rule that "Who is the only proper
Word to be used in Relation to Persons and Animals;

WHICH in Relation to Things. . . ." Furthermore, like
Lowth, he condemns the use of the possessive form *whose*
in relation to things. The word *One,* he asserts, "ought
seldom to be used but when it answers to the Use of the
Latin Word *unus."* Such expressions as: *One told me so,
Virtue* is *One's* great *Concern, These* books are excellent
Ones, he brands as incorrect.

Like, he asserts, ought never to be used, when it cannot
be translated into Latin by the word *similis.*

Constituents, he holds, can never properly signify persons
appointed, but ought only to denote persons *appointing.*

*Now a days, as how, withal, whereof, hereof, wherewith,
howsoever, whatsoever, etc.,* he asserts, are "obsolete, vulgar, and ungrammatical, and not one of them is wanted."

"Relation and *Council* are improperly used to denote
Persons. . . . *Acquisition, Donation,* &c., should never be
used to denote Things acquired, or things given; for with
Propriety such words can only signify the Act of giving
or acquiring."

"ADO is an abbreviation of *to do,* and ought never to be
used by any Man, who has the least regard for the English
Language or his own Credit."

"The Particle *a* should never be prefixed to the Word
few: a always denoted the singular Number, and *few* is of
the plural."

"The letter *s,"* he says, "frequently stands for *his:* for
Example we say *The KING'S Majesty,* instead of *the King
his Majesty* . . . I need not tell you," he continues, "that
the *s* displeases me, as an Abbreviation; but this is not now
my only Objection, for the very Mode of Expression, when
wrote (*sic*) at Length, is ungrammatical and cannot be
translated. . . ." "In short *of* ought always to be expressed,
for it is the only true Sign of the Genitive Case in English
Words; and may our Authors for the future not suffer the

specious Name of Anglicism to deceive them." "I had almost forgot (*sic*) to mention another instance in which *s* is used as an Abbreviation, without the least Pretense for it: *The Doctrine of a future* STATE'S *being universally taught*— for *a future State being. . . .*"

Still another book of this kind is the anonymous work published later in the century, in 1798, with the title *The Structure of the English Language*. In this work one finds not only condemnation of current forms of expression, irregular in their grammatical construction, such as *Who will you give this to?* and *an extraordinary fine horse*, but an attempt to limit precisely the meanings of the prepositions. Attempt is made to limit *of* to use as sign of the possessive case. *Of whom did you buy this* is corrected to *From whom*. "*By*," one is told, "is generally understood to signify near one side or part of a place. To say, then, that a man goes *by* himself is absurd."

Works of this kind are indicative of a mode of thought prevalent in the later eighteenth century. As in similar works in the nineteenth century there is a lack of sweet reasonableness. Personal opinion is elevated to a position of general authority. Learning leads less in the direction of wisdom than in that of pedantry. That they did not command universal respect appears from the complaint of one of them concerning the "opprobrious titles" such as *word-catchers* and *point-setters* applied to the authors by "illiterate witlings and half-learned poets." Indeed, the autobiographical information offered by the author of the *Reflections* is not such as to create confidence in the judgments he offers. He is, the reader is informed, "entirely ignorant of the Greek and but indifferently skilled in the Latin." He "quitted the School at fifteen." "Such as my Work is," he continues, "it is entirely my own. Not being acquainted with any Man of Letters, I have consulted

Nobody. . . . I have never yet seen the folio edition of Mr. *Johnson's* Dictionary; but, knowing Nobody that has it, I have never been able to borrow it, and I have myself no Books; at least not many more than a Church-going Woman may be supposed to have of Devotional Ones upon her Mantle-piece. . . . Nor did I ever see even the Abridgment of this Dictionary till a few Days ago, when, observing it inserted in the Catalogue of a Circulating Library where I subscribe, I sent for it." Satire could hardly go farther in picturing incompetence. This judge of language, judged by his own account, deserves a place with the justices at law made immortal by Shakespeare. Is the species quite extinct in our own day?

More effective in the cause of purism than the efforts of these English free-lances were the more concerted efforts of Scotch scholars. The earlier attention in Scotland to refinement in speech, referred to by Swift and by De Foe, has already been mentioned. The Scotch share in the production of Johnson's *Dictionary* has also been mentioned. In the eighteenth century Scotch schoolmasters made a living in England by teaching the English language. The valiant efforts made by one of them, James Buchanan, in English grammar and in English lexicography, are mentioned elsewhere.

To the North Briton the standard form of English was an acquired language. There are innumerable stories of the difficulties experienced by him in acquiring an English pronunciation. Boswell cultivated his English, he informs us, "by the aid of the late Mr. Love of Drury-lane Theatre, and also of old Mr. Sheridan." The solicitude of the Scotchman for the purity of his English naturally gave to his language a formal correctness. The situation was in many ways parallel to that in North Germany today where the acquired High German is spoken with a formal precision which distinguishes it from the High German of Southern Germany where it is the indigenous mode of speech. Boswell was alive to the danger of pedantic formality and warns his countrymen against "High English . . . which is by no means *good English,* and makes the fools who use it truly ridiculous." The vocabulary of the acquired English, however, gave to the Scotchman no end of trouble. Constant vigilance was required on his part if he were to give to his thought an expression purely English. Hume was much concerned with this matter and was constantly subjecting his works to revision in the effort to eliminate any element that.was Scottish rather than standard English. Collections of Scotticisms with their English equivalent were made. Such a collection made by James Elphinston was appended to the *Political Discourses* of Hume in the edition of 1752. The collection was omitted in subsequent editions presumably because Hume's revision made it no longer necessary. Another collection of Scotticisms was published by Elphinston in the *Scots Magazine,* XXVI (March 31, 1764). Still another collection of this kind was published in 1779 by the Scotch philosopher-poet James Beattie.

Scotch learning was also much turned to the general subject of language. In 1762 Henry Home, Lord Kames, published a classic work entitled *The Elements of Criticism* in which the art of English writing receives much attention, and in 1773-92 the Scotch judge, Lord Monboddo, published the six volumes of his work entitled *Of the Origin and Progress of Language.* Scotch universities also laid stress on general cultivation in language and literature. To this subject no less a person than Adam Smith, author of *The Wealth of Nations,* in his earlier years turned his attention. From 1748 to 1750 he lectured on logic and rhetoric at Edinburgh, and an essay entitled *Considerations Concerning the First Formation of Languages* was appended to his work on *Moral Sentiments* published in 1759. At the University of Edinburgh in the twenty-four years ending in 1783 were read the lectures by Dr. Hugh Blair published in 1783 with the title *Lectures on Rhetoric and Belles Lettres.* In a footnote (p. 3) the reader is informed that "The Author was the first who read Lectures on this subject at the University of Edinburgh." This statement is of real significance when one recalls how much later was the first establishment of a Chair of English Literature at the English University of Cambridge. A center even more active in this form of study was Aberdeen. James Beattie, already referred to as the author of a collection of Scotticisms, and the author also of a treatise on *The Theorie of Language* was Professor of Moral Philosophy at Marischal College, Aberdeen. Occupying the post of Principal at Marischal College was Dr. George Campbell, who in 1776 published his classic work, the *Philosophy of Rhetoric.*

Of these learned works on language by eighteenth-century Scotchmen probably the most enduring influence was exerted by the works by Blair and by Campbell. Some of the criteria set up by Campbell for the judgment of language have become classical. Adopting the doctrine of Horace and Quintilian that usage is the mistress of language, he proceeded to ask what kind of usage. In the answer that he provided for this question, he made what has been called the first formulation of the principles of propriety.[2] Good usage must be *national* and *reputable* and *present.*

These three tests as applied by Campbell to eighteenth-century English afford an excellent means of exhibiting the attitude then toward certain words and the difference from the attitude of today.

[2] W. F. Bryan, *Studies in Philology,* July, 1926.

National use in the opinion of Campbell excluded not only local dialect forms such as the Scotticisms, concerning which his fellow countrymen were unduly sensitive, but forms belonging to class dialect. Among words not national in use for this reason, he included: *advice,* meaning 'information' or 'intelligence,' which he classed as commercial idiom; *nervous,* meaning 'having weak nerves,' a meaning surviving in American use, which, following Johnson, he attributed to medical cant; and *turtle,* properly meaning 'dove,' but "employed by sailors and gluttons to signify a tortoise."

The use of French words in English has ever been a subject for debate. When have such words a claim to be called national? In the eighteenth century, as in earlier and in later periods, there was variety of opinion. Many of these words, newly borrowed, are classed by Campbell as barbarisms. The established words, *pleasure, opinionative* and *sally* he holds to be as expressive as *volupty, opinionatre,* and *sortie. Last resort, liberal arts* and *polite literature* he holds not inferior to *dernier resort, beaux arts,* and *belles lettres.* Words such as *connoisseur, reconnoitre, agrémens,* and a thousand others which may be "very emphatical" in their native language environment, he asserts, "with us look rather like strays than like any part of our own property." Words such as *opine, ignore, fraicheur, adroitness, opinionatry,* and *opinionatrety,* in Campbell's opinion, appear as "spots in the work" of some ingenious writers. Some of the words objected to by Campbell, may now be regarded as national in use; others are no longer in English use of any kind. The criterion by which such words are to be tested is evidently not so much national use as present use.

The second of the classical tests provided by Campbell for the use of words was that of *reputability.* Campbell speaks of the current vulgarisms fallen into in conversation but carefully avoided in writing or "in solemn speech on any important occasion." "Their currency, therefore," he says, "is without authority and weight." But the English language of the eighteenth century was not as uniformly precise and solemn as might be supposed by one who had based his judgment solely on Johnson's *Dictionary,* on the reading of such writers as Gibbon and Burke, or on the judgments passed by Scotch rhetoricians such as Blair and Beattie and Campbell. There is to be taken into account not only the speech of the illiterate, the true vulgarism, but the affectation of vulgarisms on the part of fashionable society. In earlier periods effective use had been made of the coarser elements of the language by men such as Nashe in controversial writings, by Butler in his *Hudibras* and by pamphleteers like L'Estrange. Dr. Arbuthnot had adopted the weapons of the pamphleteer in his *History of John Bull.* The famous "Orator" Henley, who died about 1756, is said to have "prayed in Slang, and first charmed and then swayed the dirty mobs in Lincoln's Inn Fields by vulgarisms." [3] Such forms of speech had their fascination then as now. Samuel Johnson himself is said, though on questionable authority, "when young and rakish" to have "contributed to an early volume of the *Gentleman's Magazine* a few pages, by way of specimen of a Slang dictionary, the result of his midnight ramblings." [4] Johnson, if he ever had contemplated making a slang dictionary, never carried out his plan, but such a work was made somewhat later by the jovial and convivial Captain Grose, the favorite of Robert Burns, for whom, it is said, *Tam O' Shanter* was composed. Grose's *Classical Dictionary of the Vulgar Tongue,* which was published in 1785, is a rich assemblage of vulgar word material and offers the first

---

[3] J. C. Hotten, *Dictionary of Slang,* p. 35.
[4] *Sportsman's Dictionary,* 1825, quoted by Hotten, *op. cit.*

written record of the word *slang* with its modern meaning, "Cant or vulgar language."

That the robust elements of popular speech were taken up in fashionable use there is ample evidence. The *cant* of the streets became the slang of the drawing room. "Slang has superseded language," complains Lady Louisa Stuart in a letter written about 1800. Satirical allusions to the "Gothick humbuggers" and to affectation of the "uncouth dialect of the Huns" and the "gabble of Hottentots" have already been cited. Campbell speaks of terms of "vile and despicable origin," words associated with "disagreeable and unsuitable ideas," such as *bellytimber, thorowstitch* and *dumbfound,* and words "betraying some frivolous humour in the formation of them," such as *transmogrify, bamboozle, topsyturvy, pellmell, helterskelter,* and *hurlyburly.*

Mrs. Piozzi, better known by her earlier name, Mrs. Thrale, the friend and hostess of Samuel Johnson, in her later life, it is interesting to know, turned her hand to the production of a book on words. In her *British Synonymy,* published in 1794, she makes "an attempt at regulating the choice of words in familiar conversation." She quotes her distinguished friend, Dr. Johnson, as saying that "there was such a thing as a city voice—a city laugh there is, that's certain, different from that of the people who inhabit, and have from their youth inhabited, the court end of the town." In illustration of the vulgar, or citified, mode of speech as distinguished from the courtly, she cites as synonyms for money the words: *cash, cole, assets, ready rino, chink,* and *corianders.* Evidently the eighteenth century could vie with the twentieth in facetious coinage of names for money. These words Mrs. Piozzi characterizes as "a string of hateful words . . . in the vulgar and despicable dialect of coarse traders in the hour of merriment." *Cash* she characterizes as "pert and pedantic, unless used in its native soil, the banker's shop, where it means coin, opposed to notes"; *assets,* she says, "belongs rather to the cant of lawyers than of merchants." The other words, in her judgment, "are nothing better than a mere jargon of school-boys, 'prentices, &c." She feels confident that no nobleman would introduce into the society of the diplomatic world even the son of a best friend should the youth be heard to say that he "took care not to set out from home without having touched the *Cole,* provided the *Ready Rino,* and tipt Old Squaretoes for the *Corianders.*" A youth of today might offer expressions of this kind richer in variety and even more defiant of propriety. But the spirit of youth now and then was evidently the same, differing in degree of boldness and defiance rather than in kind. Mrs. Piozzi's remarks of disapproval betray that this form of language, though disapproved, was not unfamiliar even in her own circle.

From excess in refinement there was revolt. Goldsmith objected to the application of the word *low* to forms of language lacking in formal dignity. Fielding had been of the same way of thinking. The monosyllable *low,* he asserted, is "a word which becomes the mouth of no critic who is not *Right* Honorable." He complained that: "In the theatre especially, a single expression which doth not coincide with the taste of the audience, or with any individual critic of that audience, is sure to be hissed." He ridiculed the false refinement of the age which favored the reform even of the Punch and Judy show by "throwing out Punch and his wife Joan, and such idle trumpery." He insisted that books give a very imperfect idea of an age, that the "fine gentleman formed upon reading the former [books] will almost always turn out a pedant, and he who forms himself upon the latter [the stage], a coxcomb." For language as for manners, in the opinion of Fielding, the only true pattern is that provided by Nature.

That the fashionable world of the eighteenth century was not without its vulgarities in speech as well as in conduct is clear enough. Lord Chesterfield writes from Bath of the "strange mixture of company" there. He warns his godson particularly against the *bucks* and the *bloods,* the sons of riot and ill manners. "The choicest figures of their rhetorick are oaths and curses, and their favorite curse is *Damn* you." The rich soil of underworld speech yielded a store of word material for the polite world. Even the wits of the time, we are told, used a "jargon found in the scoundrels' dictionary."

In cultivated circles of society each set had its own form of cant. In the university world arose such terms as *mob* and *chum* and *lounger.* The world of fashion in turn had its own special lingo. "Indeed," says Mrs. Piozzi, "the pedantry of a drawing room is no less offensive than that of a college, or an army coffee-house, or a merchant's comptinghouse; . . . all are tedious and should be swept away." Satire had its influence. In the preceding century, she reports, the Duke of Buckingham's *Rehearsal* drove the phrase *Egad and all that* from fashionable use. Dryden's *Sir Martin* is said to have cleared the language of the phrase, *in fine, Sir.* And yet fashionable life was one of bondage to certain set forms of expression. Collins speaks of living under the dominion of a word, whether *sentiment,* or *rage,* or *bore,* or *pledge one's self* and refers to this fashion in language as a "despicable mode of proving our good breeding."

And yet in all this activity in language is to be seen evidence that the language had not been embalmed by the grammarian and the lexicographer. The language was actively alive. Fashion is short-lived and words raised to the height in fashionable use in one period, in many instances have later sunk into the abyss of oblivion. But in many other instances words rose from lower levels to the level of reputability. Words like *banter* and *fun* and *fop* and *flippant*, condemned by Johnson, have found a permanent place in good use. Campbell speaks of the "words of low or dubious extraction; such, for instance, as have arisen, nobody knows how, like *fig, banter, bigot, fop, flippant,* among the rabble, or, like *flimsy,* sprung from the cant of manufacturers, in illustration of the power of good use to ennoble words like the power of an absolute monarch to nobilitate a person of obscure birth." Lord Chesterfield in a paper contributed to *The World,* December 5, 1754, praises *flirtation* and *fuzz* and *vastly* (in extended meanings) and advises Johnson to publish a "genteel Neological dictionary, containing those polite, though perhaps not strictly grammatical words and phrases, commonly used, and sometimes understood by the beau monde." Certain it is that the list of words raised in the course of the eighteenth century from low or obscure origin to reputable use is an impressive one. Among words branded at one time or another by eighteenth-century purists either as cant or as slang or as "low" are: *banter, cocksure, dumbfound, doodle, enthusiasm, extra, flimsy, flippant, flirtation, fun, gambling, hanker, helter-skelter, humbug, jilt, kidney, mob, nervous, noodle, palming, pell-mell, prig, quandary, shabby, sham, shuffle, topsy-turvy, touchy, turtle, twang.*

Words, however, in order to be certified by a critic such as Campbell, as in good use, must stand a third test. They must be in *present* use. The application of this third test of good use affords interesting information regarding eighteenth-century language. When were new words to be regarded as established in *present* use? Barbarism often resulted from the introduction of not needed words from the French of the kind already cited under the head of *national* use. Barbarism also resulted from the formation of new words from words already established. Such new coinages, in the opinion of Campbell, must be in response to a need, and to be acceptable, they must be "not disagreeable to the ear" and must be "so analogically formed that a reader, without the help of the context, may easily discover the meaning." As examples of words to be barred from use by this test, Campbell cites: *incumberment,* for 'encumbrance'; *martyrized,* 'martyr'd'; *eucharisty,* 'eucharist'; *analyze,* 'analysis'; *connexity,* 'connexion'; *fictious,* 'fictitious'; *acception,* 'acceptation,' etc. These words, with the exception of *martyrized,* seem to have been effectually excluded from later use by the critical bar set up. Other words mentioned by Campbell as of "recent introduction" which in his opinion it "might be accounted too fastidious in the critic entirely to reject" have not been effectually barred. Among words condemned under this third test by Campbell are *continental, sentimental, originality, criminality, capability, to originate, to figure, to adduce*—words which afford striking evidence of the living activity in the language of the period.

But the test of present use in the eighteenth century was applied particularly in the exclusion of obsolete words. The loss of older English words in use in Elizabethan times has already been illustrated by means of the glossaries which earlier eighteenth-century editors felt it necessary to append to their editions of Shakespeare. The seventeenth-century aversion to the archaic language of Spenser has also been mentioned. The classical taste of the eighteenth century was hostile to the archaic English vocabulary. Campbell objects to the use, not only of "words no longer understood by any but critics and antiquaries," such as *hight, cleped, uneath, erst,* and *whilom,* but to terms which "though not unintelligible, all writers of any name have now ceased to use," such as *behest, fantasy, tribulation, erewhile, whenas, peradventure, selfsame, anon.* Even old words embedded in fixed phrases, such as *lief* in *had as lief, dint* in *by dint of,* *whit* in *not a whit,* *moot* in *moot point,* he would root out by avoidance of locutions which give to style "an air of vulgarity and cant." For like reason he recommends the discarding of the "idiomatical" expression, *I had rather.*

The same spirit, the desire for refinement in language, appears in the eighteenth-century attitude toward Milton's "quaint Uncouthness of Speech." L. Welsted (1742) speaks of the "Phrase and Stile of Milton" as "a second Babel, or confusion of all languages." Some further interesting instances of this critical attitude toward words have recently been pointed out.[5] "In 1742 Gray mentions *beverage, mood, array, smouldring,* as obsolete words in Dryden. About the same time Peck names among Milton's 'old' words, *minstrelsy, murky, carol, chaunt,* and among his 'naturalized' Latin words, *humid, orient, hostil, facil, fervid, jubilant, ire, bland, reluctant, palpable, fragil, ornate.* James Beattie with his Scotch fear of being not correct, in 1778 declares *bridal, gleam, hurl, plod, ruthless, wail, wayward, woo,* to be 'now almost peculiar to poetry' though 'once no doubt in Common use.'"

But the example of Milton had its effect in counteracting the curbing influence of classical taste on the English vocabulary. Addison, it will be recalled, said that Milton "by the choice of the noblest words and phrases . . . carried our language to a greater height than any of our English Poets have done before him." In fact the poetry of Milton provided for the eighteenth century a quarry of poetic diction. The revival of the cult for Spenser also had its effect

[5] R. D. Havens, *The Influence of Milton,* 1922.

in restoring old words at least in poetic diction.[6] **Prior, in** the introduction to his *Ode* (1706), "Written in imitation of Spenser's Style," remarks that he has "avoided such of his words as I found too obsolete"; but he retained "some few of them": *behest, band* ('army'), *prowess, I weet, I ween, whilom.* Shenstone in his *Schoolmistress* uses 40 Spenserian words in 35 stanzas and William Thompson in *An Hymn to May* (1746) uses 51 Spenserian archaisms in 75 stanzas. James Thompson followed the practice of his fellow-Spenserians in his *Castle of Indolence* and influenced Byron, who in the early stanzas of *Childe Harold* uses Spenserian diction in burlesque.[7] The effect of the Romantic movement on the English vocabulary is manifest. Not only the influence of Spenser, but the aroused interest in the popular ballad and the general interest awakened in things medieval, contributed toward the restoration of English words banned by prevalent standards of taste and well on the road to obsoleteness and oblivion.

The discussion of good use offered by Campbell fairly well represents the taste of the later eighteenth century. Moreover, his ideas were potent in forming the taste of the nineteenth century. The threefold test became classical. Not only did Campbell's own book continue in circulation, but his discussion of good use was incorporated in large part in a work of much wider circulation and much more extensive influence, Lindley Murray's grammar.

The stamp given to cultivated English was a permanent one. The formality and dignity which characterize the English prose and to a great extent the cultivated speech of the nineteenth century, as distinguished from the ease and sprightliness in French of the same period, is in great part to be explained by the differing standards of good use

[6] H. G. De Maar, *History of Modern English Romanticism.*
[7] *Ibid.*

in the two countries. Accepting the classical dictum that language is to be determined by usage, the question arises who determines good usage. For this question the answer for French was provided by Vaugelas in the preface to his classic work *Remarques sur la Langue Française.* The judges of good use, according to Vaugelas, were "the soundest part of the court, and the soundest part of the authors of the age." This conclusion Campbell is unwilling to accept as applicable to English. He distinguishes between the monarchical France with the exaggerated respect of inferior for superior, and the English government which is more republican than monarchical. In France, says Campbell, the humble respect of inferior to superior seems, from an English point of view, "to border even upon adoration." The usage of the British court, therefore, which Dryden, following Vaugelas, had accepted as a standard, Campbell declines to accept. "The British Court is commonly too fluctuating an object. Use in language requires firmer ground to stand upon." This firmer ground, in his opinion, is to be found only in the usage of authors of reputation. For the dual standard of Vaugelas, therefore, colloquial use of the court and literary usage of authors, Campbell substitutes a single, a literary standard. The bookish characteristics which for so long prevailed in English writing and in English formal speech are in great part determined by the conclusion reached by Campbell and given wider currency by Lindley Murray, that good use in language consists of "whatever modes of speech are authorized as good by a great number, if not the majority, of celebrated authors."

CHAPTER XVII

THE ART OF POINTING, OR PUNCTUATION

THE matter of punctuation is sometimes regarded as about on the level of importance with crossing one's *t*'s or dotting one's *i*'s. In reality, of course, these two forms of finishing detail are on quite different levels of importance. Whereas in one case there is improvement only in the legibility, in the other case there is clarification of the meaning. Scores of instances might be cited where a crucial decision depended on a matter of punctuation. In a recent American land grant case argued before a congressional commission, the decision turned on expert testimony from members of the Yale English Department regarding the use of the comma. In earlier English literature one will recall that the fate of Edward II in Marlowe's tragedy hung on the position of a comma. One will recall in *Midsummer Night's Dream,* the distortions in meaning in the Prologue read by Quince before Theseus. "This fellow," remarks Theseus, with *double entendre,* "does not stand upon points." One will recall the effect produced in the play of *Ralph Roister Doister* by the wrong "pointing" in the hero's love letter, a means adopted by the schoolmaster author of this play to bring home to his schoolboy actors the importance of punctuation.

In English writing the punctuation cannot be said to have been reduced to a definite system until near the end of the eighteenth century. With the method of "teaching English grammatically" firmly established, a method in earlier centuries applied only in Latin study, a firm basis was at last provided for a system of pronunciation based on syntactical system. In earlier periods punctuation, like spelling, had been largely controlled by the printer. In the eighteenth century one will recall that Benjamin Franklin gained his knowledge of these two features of language from early experience in his brother's printing establishment. Even at a later period Sir Walter Scott, in this feature of language, seems to have depended on his printer, since in his manuscripts he contents himself usually with the use of the dash for the indication of pauses. In earlier periods the control of the printer over punctuation is everywhere discernible. The *Interpungendi Ratio* (1566) of Aldus Manutius, the celebrated Venetian printer, was the principal authority on the subject in the sixteenth century and continued to be influential in later centuries. In fact, in earlier periods the precise application of principles of pronunciation was hardly possible except to Latin, since only Latin was subjected to the syntactical analysis which must be the basis of systematic punctuation. The authority of the printer appears in eighteenth-century editions of Milton. In the edition by Thomas Newton printed by the Tonsons in 1754, the text is based on the two editions printed in Milton's life, but with "some alterations . . . necessary . . . in consequence of the late improvements in printing, with regard to the use of capital letters, italic characters, and the spelling of some words; but to Milton's own spelling . . . we pay all proper regard. . . . His pointing too we generally observe." But in the edition by Capel Lofft in 1792 the punctuation is corrected and extended, and it is remarked that "the great and elegant utility of Punctuation has, in this century, added much to the extent, certainty, and precision" of the art of orthography.

Luckombe in his *History of the Art of Printing* (1771) offers some significant remarks regarding the relation of printer to author in the eighteenth century. He admits that "the expectation of a settled Punctuation is in vain, since no rules of prevailing authority have yet been established for that purpose; which is the reason that so many take the liberty of criticizing upon that head; . . ." But much of the responsibility in pronunciation rested with the printer. The liberties taken with an author's text appear from the advice that "where a corrector understands the language and characters of a work, he often finds occasion to alter and to mend things that he can maintain to be either wrong or ill digested. If therefore a Corrector suspects Copy to want revising, he is not to postpone it, but to make his emendations in the Manuscript before it is wanted by the Compositor." Some concession, to be sure, is made to the rights of the author. Compositors, one is told, who "are dubious whether they can maintain their notion of Pointing, ought to submit to the method, or even humour, of Authors, . . . rather than give them room to exclaim about spoiling the sense of the subject, because the Points are not put their right way. . . ."

The methods of printers were evidently often not less high-handed, or shall we say free-handed, than those of the copyist scribes complained of in the thirteenth century by Orm and in the following century by Chaucer. The intervention of earlier printers, like that of still earlier scribes, prevents the modern reader from a distinct view of the actual forms of language used by earlier English writers. In this way has recently arisen a controversy of real moment regarding the significance of the punctuation in the Quarto editions and the First Folio edition of Shakespeare. Editors and printers have long made free with Shakespearean punctuation. Within recent years, however, has come a changed attitude, an abandonment of the idea that the punctuation in the earlier editions is chaotic and therefore negligible. In fact, among English scholars there has been developed a conception of earlier punctuation quite the reverse of the one prevailing for more than two centuries. The punctuation in the earlier editions, these modern English scholars maintain, was not logical in character, but rhythmical. The copy for the earlier texts, they assert, consisted for the most part of theatrical prompt copy and in many instances was in the author's autograph. The punctuation in the earlier editions was close to, if not identical with, the author's own punctuation. The earlier marks of punctuation, therefore, according to the view of Wilson, one of the editors of the new Cambridge edition of Shakespeare, far from being negligible, are invaluable. On account of the rhythmical effects thereby indicated by the author, they are almost equivalent to stage directions since "the pause, especially with the semicolon, the colon, or the period, often needs filling by a sob, a kiss, or by other lengthier 'business.'"

These extravagant claims have been opposed in recent articles.[1] But with all abatement of credit due to extravagance of claims in the new interpretation alluded to, there remains an element of truth. The basis for English punctuation in Shakespeare's time was not entirely syntactical. "For, whereas our breath is by nature so short," says Ben Jonson, "that we can not continue without a stay to speak long together; it was thought necessary as well for the speaker's ease, as for the plainer deliverance of the things spoken, to invent this means, whereby men pausing a pretty while, the whole speech might never the worse be understood."

Ease in breathing in oral speech, therefore, is a main

R. Alden, *Publications Modern Language Association,* XXXIX, 557-580.
C. C. Fries, *Studies in Shakespeare, Milton and Donne,* pp. 67-86.

use for the "distinction of sentences" (Latin meaning, 'separation' or 'punctuation') according to Ben Jonson. Mulcaster likewise in writing "Of Distinction" ('Punctuation') refers to these "characts . . . signifying but not sounding . . . which helpe verie much, naie all in all to the right and tunable uttering of our words and sentences." The same use was in the minds of later grammarians. Simeon Daines in his grammar (1640) adopts the singing-master's method of counting one to four in measuring the relative length of the pauses indicated by comma, semi-colon, colon, and period, and the method persists down to the nineteenth century if not later. According to Lindley Murray: "the Comma represents the shortest pause; the Semicolon, a pause double that of the comma; the Colon, double that of the semicolon; and the Period, double that of the colon." Noah Webster (1828) adopts the geometrical ratio of Murray, with slight modification, and asserts that the four pauses may bear to each other the proportion of one, two, four, and six.

In thus bringing the rules of punctuation into relation to the speaker rather than the writer, English grammarians were following a Latin precedent, since Latin rhetorical treatises, in days before printing, were intended for the rhetor, or speaker, rather than for the reader. The influence of Latin authorities was felt in other ways. The names *comma, colon,* and *period* were derived by the Romans from the Greek, and in Latin use in general retained their original Greek meanings: *comma,* 'section' (of a period); *colon,* 'member'; and *period,* 'circuit' or 'complete sentence.' In later times, both in Latin and in English, these words were shifted to their present meanings as signs respectively of a section of a sentence, a member of a sentence, a complete sentence. But to English scholars conscious of the original meanings, the words were

sources of great confusion and led to much ambiguity in
statement.   The fact, however, that the earlier meanings
were not lost sight of had the result of holding the signs of
punctuation somewhat to their original use in indicating
different degrees of thought division.   The earlier English
discussions of English punctuation, like those of other
features of English, closely followed Latin authorities.
"The marks of punctuation," says Alexander Gill (1619),
"are the same in English as in Latin, and the use is the
same" (*Eædem sunt nobis quæ Latinus, et usus idem*).
And later English discussions of the subject draw from
learned Latin works by Aldus and Cellarius, and particularly from those of the Dutch classical scholar, Ger. J.
Vossius, which appeared in English editions.

The application of Latin rules to English use, however,
was not altogether simple, and it was not until English
syntax had been more precisely analyzed in the later
eighteenth century that exact syntactical rules for English
punctuation became applicable.   Lowth in his grammar
elaborates considerably on the subject but asserts that:
"Few precise rules can be given, which will hold without
exception in all cases; but much must be left to the judgment and taste of the writer."   Lowth's judgment in
Lowth's own words is adopted by Lindley Murray, who,
however, offers more detailed directions, twenty precise
rules, for instance, for the use of the comma.   The subject
of punctuation in the later years of the eighteenth century
was receiving more and more attention.   The remarks,
already quoted, of the editor of Milton (1792) must be recalled.   The new interest appears from the succession of
books on the subject issued in numerous editions.   In
1771 appeared a work entitled *De Usu et Ratione Interpungendi: an Essay on the Use of Pointing* by James Barrow, Esq., F.R.S. and F.A.S.   The author professes agree-

Charles Dickens (1812-1870); a page of the manuscript of *Pickwick Papers*.

ment with Lowth and modestly says, "I do not pretend to lay down certain and indisputable rules for it." He speaks of "SOME *Persons* who affect to *despise* it, and treat the whole subject with the utmost *contempt,* as a Trifle far below *their* Notice, and a formality unworthy of *their* Regard:" "Yet," he continues, "it would surely be very desirable to fix some general *RULES,* if they can be agreed upon . . . And though it is hardly to be expected, that *all* men will agree in *one Opinion* about such *best* and *properest* Method; yet there can be no Harm in throwing out a few Hints upon a subject so little regarded." The author emphasizes *"THE CONVENIENCE,* I may say *THE NECESSITY* of Interpunctuation, in order to prevent Ambiguity and assist Perspicuity." There are to be noted the following significant points regarding this work: the rank of the writer, the Latin title chosen, the purpose of punctuation, and the moderateness in pretension.

The subject cautiously broached soon won more general attention. In 1785 appeared *An Essay on Punctuation* by Joseph Robertson, which was reissued in numerous editions in England and in America down to 1806. In 1786 appeared the *Elements of Punctuation* by David Steel, which appeared in new editions down to 1810. In 1800 appeared a work by Thomas Stackhouse with the title, *A New Essay on Punctuation,* with the significant sub-title, "being an attempt to reduce the practice of pointing to the government of distinct and explicit rules, by which every point may be accounted for after the manner of parsing."

The dawn of the new century is thus marked by the appearance of the point of view which has persisted to our own time. Careful attention to punctuation as well as to the spelling is to be observed in the works of most writers of the nineteenth century and later, the writings of Scott forming a striking exception. That Scott, however, is not the only modern writer who has surrendered to his printer his prerogative in punctuation may be seen by a comparison of many an author's manuscript with the printed edition. A comparison, for instance, of punctuation of the manuscript of the *Pickwick Papers* with the text of the printed edition will show that the printer ruled the punctuation in Dickens's books much as he ruled the spelling in Milton's.

There remains a word to be said regarding some of the external forms of writing, the use of italics, of capital letters and the like. In the sixteenth century, following the introduction of printing, there were in use different forms of letters. In a sixteenth-century book on the art of writing there are described a score and more of forms of handwriting that belonged to the craft of the professional scrivener. In printing the variety in forms was less. The forms of letters cast in Caxton's type were based on forms of letters used by scribes at Bruges, where Caxton began his work as printer. In the sixteenth century there were in use two principal forms of printed letters, the Gothic, or Old English type, and the Roman type brought into use by Italian printers. The situation was much like that in Germany today. English schoolboys, as one may learn from Mulcaster's account, learned the two modes of writing, a double task like that imposed on German children today. The Old English type persisted particularly in works of popular character. It is of significance that most of the English Bible translations, those of Tyndale and Coverdale, and the King James Bible in 1611, were printed in the native black letter type. Along with these two forms of printed characters was used to some extent the italic form devised for the Venetian printer Aldus for the sake of economy of space. The use of italics as a means of singling out words for the reader's attention has persisted to our day. Some interesting differences from the modern use of

Dear Sir,

Passy, April 14. 1782

The Bearer having been detain'd here, I add this Line to suggest, that if the new Ministry are dispos'd to enter into a General Treaty of Peace, Mr. Laurens being set intirely at Liberty may receive such Propositions as they shall think fit to make relative to Time, Place, or any other Particulars, and come hither with them. He is acquainted that we have full Powers to treat & conclude, and that the Congress promise in our Commission to ratify and confirm, &c. — I am ever,

Yours most affectionately

Franklin

Benjamin Franklin (1706-1790): autograph letter showing among other things the use of capital letters favored by Franklin. (Brit. Mus. Add. MS. 23,206, F. 77.)

italics may be observed in the books of earlier days in which the italic forms were applied to various uses later abandoned, among others to that of giving distinction to proper names.

The use of capital letters was a feature in English which was long in settling into uniformity. The divergent use today of capital letters in German and in English is to be noted. In preceding chapters allusions have been made to earlier uses of capital letters. The difference between earlier and modern use is at once apparent to anyone reading books in editions of seventeenth and early eighteenth centuries. That a change to something like modern use was reached by the middle of the eighteenth century appears from the remarks of the Milton editor already quoted. The change from the use of the form of the letter *s* elevated above the line like an *f* came not long after. Such changes, in which the æsthetic taste of the printer played an important part, were accepted with regret by many sentimentally attached to the older forms. In the sixteenth century in France there had been a change in the forms of letters in the interests of a more level line. The older forms of letters were defended by some because they were thought to add attractiveness to the printed page. On this æsthetic judgment the comment of the French grammarian Meigret was that the use of such forms was like "a painter putting scars or other marks on a portrait." In the eighteenth century, changes of this kind were opposed by Benjamin Franklin, who, it will be recalled, was a printer by profession. He remarks that in "English books printed between the Restoration and the Accession of George II, all Substantives were begun with a capital." This method, which Franklin believed was useful to those not well acquainted with English, he says "has by the Fancy of Printers, of late Years, been laid aside; from an idea that suppressing the capitals shows the Character to greater Advantage." He remarks further that "From the same Fondness for an even and uniform Appearance of Characters in the Line the Printers have of late banished also the Italic types." "Another Fancy," he continues, "has induced some printers to use the short round *s* instead of the long one" a practice which, says Franklin in facetious vein, "makes the Line appear more even . . . but less immediately legible; as the paring all Men's noses might smoothe & level their Faces, but would render their Physiognomies less distinguishable."

CHAPTER XVIII

FIXING THE PRONUNCIATION

THE feature of language in all stages least subject to regulation is the pronunciation. To some extent the lack of uniformity in pronunciation in earlier periods of English is reflected in the irregular spelling. But even the written forms of words under the influence of scribal habit or of printer's system fell more naturally into uniformity than did the spoken. In other words, the variation in pronunciation in earlier periods was even greater than appears in the varied modes of spelling. In the eighteenth century the earlier variation in pronunciation persisted. Samuel Johnson's cautious attitude in his dictionary will be recalled. He recognized the prevailing lack of uniformity. In pronunciation, as in the use of words, he fell back on literary authority. "The most elegant speakers," he asserted "deviate least from the written words." He tried, however, in pronunciation as in spelling, to control anomaly by the application of the principle of analogy. He pronounced "*heard* with double *e*, *heerd*," says Boswell, "instead of sounding it *herd*, as is most usually done." In support of this pronunciation, he said, "that if it were pronounced *herd*, there would be a single exception from the English pronunciation of the syllable *ear*, and he thought it better not to have that exception." The arbitrary judgment of Johnson in this instance, a judgment unsupported by the other eighteenth-century writers on pronunciation, causes one to feel that it was a guardian angel that led him to refrain from the attempt to regulate English sounds.

Another dictum of Johnson's on pronunciation should be recalled. "Most of the writers on English grammar," he asserts in his *Grammar*, "seem not sufficiently to have considered that of English, as of all living tongues, there is a double pronunciation, one cursory, the other regular and solemn." The possible variation in formality of utterance may be illustrated from earlier in the century, from Congreve's *Way of the World* in different scenes of which the maid Mincing, in her pronunciation of the word *Madam*, runs the whole gamut of sounds, *madam, ma'am, mæm, mem*.

But more in Johnson's mind probably was the contrast between the irregular modes of pronunciation in popular use and in familiar cultivated use on the one hand and that in more formal cultivated use on the other. In this connection the London pronunciation recorded by Watts and by Dyche should be recalled. That these forms of pronunciation in living speech little controlled by written forms, persisted later in the century there is abundant evidence. Interesting information is afforded by a work published anonymously in 1767 with the title *A Short Treatise on the English Tongue*, a work intended for the guidance of foreigners. The author of this work, recently identified as Granville Sharp,[1] in his Introduction offers criticism of some of the contemporary spelling books. He particularly criticizes the "Table of Words written very different from their Pronunciation" offered by Gignoux in his *Child's best Instructor in Spelling and Reading*. Gignoux, in the opinion of Sharp, "has too much followed the common London pronunciation; which tho' perhaps in general the best, yet has some very exceptionable peculiarities." Sharp then proceeds to enumerate some of these words, among which will be recognized many of the words earlier listed by Watts

[1] K. Malone, *Philological Quarterly,* III, 208-27.

or by Dilworth; *Potticary*, 'Apothecary'; *Athist*, 'Atheist'; *Awkurd*, 'Aukward,' (*sic!*); *Belcony*, 'Balcony'; *Carrin*, 'carrion'; *Sirket*, 'Circuit'; *Crowner*, 'Coroner'; *Gorjus*, 'Gorgeous'; *Hankerchur*, 'Handkerchief'; *I'urn*, 'Iron'; *Ilan*, 'island'; *Spanel*, 'Spaniel'; *Stummuch*, 'Stomach'; *Sound*, 'Swoon'; *Thusty*, 'Thirsty'; *Vawt*, 'Vault'; *Venzun*, 'Venison'; *Verdit*, 'Verdict,' &c.

Gignoux also, says Sharp, "signifies that the terminations *-tial, -cial, -cian, -tious, -cious, -tient, -cient* make each of them 'but one sound or syllable.'" To the approval of such modes of popular pronunciation, to be found also in the works of Buchanan, Sharp takes exception. "However common," he says, "such pronunciation may be, it ought not by any means to be taught, or laid down as a rule."

That pronunciation was less brought into conformity with spelling than in present-day English appears from some of the directions offered by Sharp. "In *Pretty, Yes*, and *Yet*," he asserts, "*e* is pronounced like short *i*, and in *Yellow* like a short *a*." "*O*," he asserts, "has the sound of *u* in *Bomb, Conduit, Coney, Mongrel*, along with a score of other words such as *Af-front, Attorney*, etc." Evidence of a similar kind is provided in *The English Grammar, by Question and Answer* (2d ed., London, 1760). From this elementary work one learns that single *o* is pronounced like *oo* in *do* ... *gold, Rome, smoke*, like *u* in *colour, come, conjure, coney, London, Monmouth, Worcester, glove novice, novel;* that *h* is silent in *Anthony, Dorothy;* that *l* is silent in *Bristol, Holborn, Lincoln, yolk, dolphin, almond, chauldron, Walter, calf, balm, psalm*, etc.; that *c* is silent in *verdict, perfect*.

Further information regarding prevalent popular modes of pronunciation is afforded by the list of "words with pronunciation differing from the spelling" in the *Practical Grammar* published in 1774 by the London schoolmaster, Thomas Smetham. The information is corroborative of that already offered, since many of the forms cited by Sharp, and earlier by Watts, here reappear. In Smetham's list appear the words: *hartichoke, potticary, athist, awkurd, querrister* ('chorister'), *constur, cowcumber, frenship, henkerchar, farden, quooshin* ('cushion'), *dixnery, anuff* ('enough'), *ilan* ('island'), *parfit, likkur, vawt, Wensday, sedule, saffurn, vittels, stummuck, westcote, yat* ('yacht'), *risban.*

That there might be variation in the pronunciation even of individual speakers appears from remarks in the *New Dictionary of the English Language* published by William Kenrick in 1773. Kenrick makes pretension to a record of pronunciation "according to the present Practice of polished Speakers in the Metropolis." He says of the vowel sounds that "some of them are so nearly allied as to be interchangeably made use of, and that by the best speakers, without any sensible impropriety." In illustration he says that *"shoe, do, rue, rule, tune,* and many others may be pronounced in either manner [as *oo* in *Pool,* or as *ew* in *New* or *eau* in *Beauty*] without any sensible impropriety," and that the words *door, floor, gold,* may be pronounced either with the *oo* of *Pool* or the *o* of *No* "without any imputation of a foreign or even a provincial accent."

That pronunciation varied somewhat with social station appears from the varying recommendations of writers. In 1772 a *Plain and Complete Grammar of the English Language* was published by Anselm Bayley, LL.D., Sub-Dean of his Majesty's Chapel-Royal, and was dedicated to H.R.H. George, Prince of Wales. Kenrick, whom Lounsbury refers to as "a sort of Ishmaelite man of letters," in the *Rhetorical Grammar* prefixed to his dictionary published the following year, 1773, violently disagrees with Dr. Bayley regarding certain sounds. "The native sound of *A,*" says Bayley, "is broad, deep, and long in *all, aw, war, daub;* but it hath generally a mixed sound, as in *man, Bath, Mary, fair*, which are sounded as if written *maen, baeth,* &c." "But who," asks Kenrick, "except flirting females and affected fops pronounce *man* and *Bath,* as if they were written *maen, baeth* or like *Mary, fair,* &c.?" Kenrick records the pronunciation of *hand, barr'd* short, and *hard, guard, laugh* long, as "a sound common to most languages," like "Italian *padre, madre* long and short in *ma, la, allegro.*" Dr. Bayley says *make* and *take* are to be pronounced as in *eat, break, speak.* Kenrick's comment is: "I can hardly conceive that this learned writer meant . . . that *make* and *take* have the same quality of sound as *eat, break, speak.* *Break* is generally pronounced like *make, take,* etc., but few except natives of Ireland or the provinces say *ate, spake!*"

To the varying modes of pronunciation thus far mentioned must be added the variation due to regional dialect. To Sir Alexander Macdonald, who had expressed doubt "if any Scotchman ever attains to perfect pronunciation," Johnson made the reply: "Sir, when people watch me narrowly, and I do not watch myself, they will find me out to be of a particular county. In the same manner, Dunning may be found out to be a Devonshire man." Standardized pronunciation evidently had not pervaded provincial England.

Small wonder, in the circumstances, that the sagacious Johnson refrained from the attempt to "ascertain" pronunciation as he had done spelling and word meanings. The need, however, at least of guidance, if not of uniformity, was evident. The foreigner in whose interest, if we may take the authors' avowals as literally true, so many books were composed, from the time of Ben Jonson's *Grammar* on, was still in need of guidance in English pronunciation, and in the matter of pronunciation the Scotchman was much in the same position as the foreigner. In the use of words

English speech gave him difficulty, but in diction literature was available as a guide, and the usage in literature was now registered in dictionaries. For pronunciation, however, no such written guidance had been hitherto available. Hence it is not surprising that the first dictionary devoted to pronunciation should have been the production of a Scotchman. To James Buchanan belongs this honor. His *Linguæ Britannicæ Vera Pronunciatio* or *New English Dictionary* was published in 1757. In this work he marked the long and short vowels, distinguished the silent letters and "ascertained" the various sounds of the vowels and diphthongs and of the single and double consonants. The primitive method of indicating sounds makes the meaning of Buchanan often ambiguous to the modern reader, but this first work was an important achievement. The nature of his pretension and the need for his work may be expressed in his own words: "Thus was I the first who endeavored to make the proper Pronunciation of our language of easy acquisition to foreigners and to introduce a uniform one for the sake of natives; amongst whom it is still so notoriously vague and unstable."

In 1764 the province of pronunciation was entered by another Scotchman, William Johnston, who in that year published *A Spelling and Pronouncing Dictionary* following the plan adopted by Buchanan. Apparently stimulated by rivalry, Buchanan in 1766 published a more ambitious work entitled *"An Essay Towards Establishing a Standard for an Elegant and Uniform Pronunciation of the English Language* . . . Designed for the Use of Schools, and of Foreigners as well as Natives." In this work, devoted solely to pronunciation, Buchanan printed lists of English words in double columns, one in the "true orthography," one with spelling indicating the pronunciation.

Buchanan's work is the earliest of a long series of works

dealing with this most disputed of all features of language. He was not able to hold undisputed possession of this im· portant field. He met with competition from his fellow countrymen. Not only did Johnston publish a *Dictionary* in 1764, but Elphinston in his *Principles of the English Language,* a two-volume work published in 1765, devoted the first 217 pages to the subjects of Alphabet and Pronunciation. Also English rivals were not lacking. There were spelling books, the *Complete English Spelling Dictionary* by John Carter (1764), and the *New Spelling Book* by John Entick (1765), the *Child's best Instructor in Spelling and Reading* by John Gignoux, and the *Short Treatise on the English Tongue,* already cited from, by Granville Sharp (1767). There may be mentioned also the work by Benjamin Franklin on the closely related subject of phonetic spelling, the *Scheme for a New Alphabet* published in 1768. Franklin's aim, it is to be noted, was not to make the pronunciation conform with the spelling, but to make the spelling fit the pronunciation.

More influential than the printed works mentioned was the activity of another man not native to England, the Irish-born Thomas Sheridan already referred to. This famous teacher of elocution devoted an active life to the cultivation of spoken English. Boswell, it will be recalled, was instructed by him in English pronunciation. From one end of the island to the other he journeyed lecturing on cultivation in speech. In his *Lecture on Elocution* published in 1762 he proclaims that "Spoken language is the gift of God, written the invention of men." "We have," he says, "many flagrant instances in our methodist preachers, of the power which words acquire, even the words of fools and madmen, when forcibly uttered by the living voice." In his *Plan of Education for the Young Nobility and Gentry of Great Britain* (1769) dedicated "to the King" he indicates the need of assistance in bringing to realization a long cherished plan to "establish a uniformity of pronunciation, in the rising and all future generations, not only throughout your Majesty's British dominions, but in all quarters of the globe, where English shall be taught by this method, and to remain immutably so, whilst that language shall be spoken in any part of the earth." A grandiose scheme surely!

English submission of the native language, not only in the eighteenth but in the nineteenth centuries, to regulation at the hands of the foreign born is an interesting phenomenon. Native jealousy of foreign influence, however, was not wanting in the eighteenth century. In 1773 *A New Dictionary of the English Language,* a work already referred to, was published by the Londoner, William Kenrick. A principal feature of this work was "Orthoëpia or Pronunciation in Speech." The authority was found in the "present Practice of polished Speakers in the Metropolis." In his Introduction Kenrick points out as "a phænomenon in the literary world, that, while our learned fellow subjects of Scotland and Ireland are making frequent attempts to ascertain and fix a standard to the pronunciation of the English tongue, the natives of England themselves seem to be little anxious either for the honour or improvement of their own language." "There seems indeed," he continues, "a most ridiculous absurdity in the pretensions of a native of Aberdeen or Tipperary, to teach the natives of London to speak and to read."

Regarding the competence of Kenrick for his undertaking, there is ground for doubt. Indeed his variance in opinion with the learned Dr. Bayley in regard to certain sounds has already been pointed out. For the student of today, however, his work affords much information regarding prevailing tendencies in the London pronunciation of his day, for instance the interchangeable pronunciations, already mentioned, of one and the same word.

To some prevailing tendencies Kenrick objects. In regard to the vowel sound in *joy, boy, oil* he speaks of the "vicious custom" of converting it into the sound of *why* and *nigh*. For instance *oil, toil* are frequently pronounced "exactly like *isle, tile*." And yet, he says, some of these words, "by long use, have almost lost their true sound." For instance in the case of *boil, join*, "it would now appear affectation to pronounce other than *bile, jine*." Many of the other recommendations made by Kenrick have their interest, for instance: *European,* accent on second syllable; *cucumber,* vowel of first syllable that of *town; China,* sound of *why,* but "vulgarly called Cheyney"; *balcony,* accent on second syllable; *merchant,* as in *cur,* but "vulgarly" as in *hard; yes,* as in *fit; yet,* as in *met* or as in *fit; what* and *was,* as in *war.*

The growing concern felt in this period regarding correct oral speech appears from the number of books produced dealing with the subject. In the two years following the publication of Kenrick's dictionary appeared dictionaries by Barclay, by Ash, and by Perry. Somewhat later were the *Elements of Orthoëpy* published in 1784 by Robert Nares, the two-volume work by James Elphinston (1786) setting forth a system of phonetic spelling and offering the "propper immage ov propper sound" and the *Dictionary* published by Enfield in 1790. Evidently the subject of pronunciation in this period had come to be regarded as one of prime importance.

But the most prominent figures in this field were Thomas Sheridan, already referred to, and John Walker. The long continued activity of Sheridan, already referred to, in the cultivation of spoken English culminated in the publication in 1780 of his long planned *Dictionary of the English Lan-*

guage. In this two-volume work Sheridan "implicitly followed" the spelling of Dr. Johnson. For guidance in pronunciation, however, he adopted an independent method. He looks back with reverence at a supposed uniformity of pronunciation that prevailed at the court of Queen Anne. This mode of pronunciation, he asserts, is still "the customary one among the descendants of the politer part of the world bred in that reign." He laments the later decadence in polite pronunciation, asserting that "many pronunciations, which thirty or forty years ago were confined to the vulgar, are gradually gaining ground." To a knowledge of the cultivated pronunciation of the earlier period this Irish-born authority makes pretensions because he had been carefully trained by his father who had been closely associated with Swift. An investigation on the part of Sheridan of the principles underlying the earlier cultivated pronunciation revealed to him that "though there were no rules laid down for its regulation, yet there was a secret influence of analogy constantly operating, which attracted the different words according to their several classes, to itself as a center. And where there were any deviations from that analogy, the anomalies were founded upon the best principle by which speech can be regulated, that of preferring the pronunciation which was the most easy to the organs of speech, and consequently most agreeable to the ear." Sheridan bases his claims to authority upon a knowledge of the custom and fashion upon which pronunciation depends. But he adds further that he is "the first who ever laid open the principles upon which our pronunciation is founded and the rules by which it is regulated," and, therefore, he "hopes that the claim he has laid in to the office he has undertaken will not be considered as either vain or presumptuous."

Sheridan was under one great disadvantage. He was an Irishman. There was published a pamphlet which ran through several editions, bearing the title *A Caution to Gentlemen Who Use Sheridan's Dictionary*. Sheridan, objected this critic, was "an Irishman; and to the last period of his life his origin was obvious in his pronunciation." [2]

This racial flaw in Sheridan gave a decided advantage to his great rival, John Walker. Like Sheridan, Walker was an actor and a lecturer on elocution. He had been associated with Garrick and had carefully noted the pronunciation of this most renowned of English actors. But, unlike Sheridan, he was English born. "To a man born," he says, "as I was, within a few miles of the Capital, living in the Capital almost my whole life, and exercising myself there in publick speaking for many years; to such a person, if to any one, the true pronunciation of the language must be familiar." With these pretensions Walker published in 1774 *A General Idea of a Pronouncing Dictionary of the English Language,* a work which he dedicated to David Garrick. Like Johnson's plan for his dictionary, this preliminary essay by Walker is an admirable exposition of principles to be followed. Walker says that "foreigners have ranked the English among the most barbarous speakers of Europe." He speaks, however, of progress recently made toward uniformity. But he says that Johnson and Lowth have narrowed their attention to orthography and phraseology, and the pronunciation, "as if too insignificant has been little noticed by any author except Mr. Elphinston." Elphinston, he says, "has attempted to reform our pronunciation on the most rational principles." This radical method of phonetic spelling, however, he rejects because, in his opinion, language is governed less by reason and logic than by usage. "Language is no more than the totality of such usages as form a relation between signs and ideas, these relations can only be understood as usage or custom

---

[2] T. R. Lounsbury, *The Standard of Pronunciation,* p. 66.

has explained them. So that custom is not only the law of language, but strictly speaking it is language itself." Yet he says that while everyone assents to the well-known dictum regarding usage the mistress of language, "we hardly ever find a person so thoroughly satisfied with it, as not to think an appeal from the tyrant custom lawful when the obvious rights of language are violated." To the principle of analogy, therefore, he turns, as "the standard to which the mind ultimately recurs when confounded by the contrarieties of custom." But he cites the words *orthography, advertisement, satiety, conversant, knowledge, academy, authority* as variously pronounced in polite use by the best speakers and says there are "a thousand others without the least prospect of being fixed either by custom or analogy." Walker found himself in the position in which many a teacher of today finds himself. "Being engaged in the instruction of youth," he says, "I could not content myself with answering their questions on pronunciation by a constant repetition of the word custom, and this put me on tracing the analogies of this part of our language." His hopes were not extravagant. Like Johnson he was conservative. He had no ambition "to alter fixed and settled modes of speaking." All that he aimed to accomplish was "preventing that vicious change which we see daily creeping in upon us; . . . and inclining any future alterations . . . to the genius and general turn of the language." It is to be noted, however, that Walker quotes with commendation the dictum of Johnson that "for pronunciation the best general rule is to consider those the most elegant who deviate least from written words."

The *Pronouncing Dictionary,* thus planned in 1774, did not make its appearance until seventeen years later, in 1791. In the preface to the work finally completed Walker defines the "good usage" which he attempts to record. This good usage is not that of the multitude of speakers. Nor is it necessarily the usage of the "studious in schools and colleges, with those of the learned professions," although he admits such persons "appear to have a natural right to have a share, at least, in the legislation of language, if not the absolute sovereignty." Nor is it necessarily court use, the usage of "those who, from their elevated birth or station, give laws to the refinements and elegancies of a court. . . . The polished attendants on a throne are as apt to depart from simplicity in language as in dress and manners; and novelty, instead of custom, is too often *jus et norma loquendi* of a court." "A majority of two of these states," he concludes, "ought always to concur, in order to establish what is called good usage." Based on the authority of good usage thus broadly defined, Walker's work won immediate popularity, and exerted strong influence not only in the last decade of the eighteenth century but well down into the nineteenth century. Edition after edition appeared. Either in its earlier form or in the form later revised by Smart, his work may still be found in the older private libraries of England and of America.

Complete uniformity in English pronunciation has never been attained. Nor, with the widely separate English speaking peoples of today, is it likely to be attained. Certainly it was not attained in the eighteenth century. An interesting exhibition of the varying modes of pronunciation at the close of the eighteenth century is afforded by a book published in 1797 with the title, *A Vocabulary of such words in the English Language as are of dubious or Unsettled accentuation; in which the Pronunciation of Sheridan, Walker, and other Orthoëpists is compared.* The writer in his preface speaks of the progress toward uniformity, though still not complete, in orthography resulting from Johnson's *Dictionary.* In pronunciation he aims to record the varying opinions of the principal authorities, including Bailey, Johnson, Ash, Entick, Kenrick, Nares, Perry, Sheridan and Walker. He has praise for Sheridan and expresses the opinion that "it would have been fortunate had the publick (*sic*) determined to elect him dictator." Unfortunately, he points out, Sheridan was an Irishman and, moreover, had aroused the antagonism of the clergy by "his indiscriminate abuse of the clergy in his lectures." Walker's *Dictionary* he calls "a valuable work," although he has "the misfortune sometimes to differ from him." Disagreement, however, he says, "generally proceeds from his sacrificing custom to analogy."

As a key to his recommended pronunciation this anonymous writer gives a number of key words each with its number. These key words are: $\overset{1}{\text{H}}$at, $\overset{2}{\text{h}}$ate, $\overset{3}{\text{h}}$all; $\overset{1}{\text{B}}$et, $\overset{2}{\text{b}}$ear, $\overset{3}{\text{b}}$eer; $\overset{1}{\text{F}}$it, $\overset{2}{\text{f}}$ight, $\overset{3}{\text{f}}$ield; $\overset{1}{\text{N}}$ot, $\overset{2}{\text{n}}$ote, $\overset{3}{\text{n}}$oose; $\overset{1}{\text{B}}$ut, $\overset{2}{\text{b}}$ush, $\overset{3}{\text{b}}$lue; $\overset{1}{\text{L}}$ovely, $\overset{2}{\text{l}}$ye; $\overset{1}{\text{T}}$hin, $\overset{2}{\text{T}}$his.

Varying opinions regarding the pronunciation may be illustrated by words selected from this interesting list:

$\overset{1}{\text{A}}\overset{1}{\text{C}}\overset{3}{\text{A}}\overset{1}{\text{D}}$EMY: **Accent** first syllable (Johnson, Ash); second (Sheridan, Walker, Bailey, Entick).

ACORN: $\overset{2}{\text{a}}$'korn (Walker); $\overset{1}{\text{a}}$'korn (Sheridan).

ADVERTISEMENT: Second syllable, Bailey; first syllable, Entick, Ash; either, Sheridan, Walker.

BALM: $\overset{1}{\text{b}}$am. *l* audible in *bal-my, pal-my, psal-mist, psal-mody* but not in *calmer*.

BEARD: Properly pronounced as if *d* added to *bear*.

BEEN (bin), Mr. Pope rimes with *between*, but later shortened. Sheridan and Walker agree, but "a few people persist in lengthening the Sound."

BEYOND: be-$\overset{3}{\text{y}}$ond$\overset{1}{}$'. Johnson, Sheridan, Walker agree, "but the Cockneys, and many provincials, are apt to give the *o*, in the last syllable, the sound *a*, as if the word were written *beyand*."

CELERY: sĕl'-e-ry. Walker and Sheridan; "yet it is full as often pronounced *Sallery*, and by people of good education."

CHAMBER: tschāme-bŭr (Walker). Sheridan and Kenrick give tschăm-bŭr. "About thirty years ago," Mr. Walker remarks, "the first syllable of *chamber* was universally pronounced so as to rhyme with *palm, psalm*, etc. However, since that time, it has been gradually narrowing to the slender sound above mentioned, and seems now to be fully established therein."

CHEW: tshō. Sheridan and Walker prefer this but give both ways. "Mr. Walker observes upon the second, tshā, that it is grown vulgar." Johnson remarks, "it is very frequently pronounced *chaw*, and perhaps properly."

CLERK: *klărk*. This word is, by some, pronounced as it is written, sounding the *e* like *e* in bet; but "these are few as in comparison of those who pronounce it as above." So Sheridan and Walker. Walker remarks: "There is a remarkable exception to the common sound of this letter in the words *clerk, serjeant*, and a few others, where the *e* is pronounced like *a* in *dark* and *margin*." Formerly it had been the general practice. "Thirty years ago," says Walker, "everyone pronounced the first syllable of *merchant* like the monosyllable *march*. . . . *Service* and *servant* were still heard among the lower order of speakers as if written *sarvice, sarvant*. *Derby* and *Berkeley* still retain their old sound; but even these, in polite usage, are getting into the common sound, nearly as if written *Durby* and *Burkeley*." This tendency, in the opinion of our anonymous writer, was to be encouraged.

COMMODORE. Accent first syllable, Ash, Entick; last syllable, Bailey, Johnson, Sheridan, Walker. Our anonymous writer says the "accent will be found placed on the last syllable by most gentlemen of the navy."

CONSTRUE: kŏn'-stur. Accent on first syllable. Thus Sheridan; Walker favors cŏnstrū.

CUCUMBER: kŏu-kŭm-ur. Accent invariably on first. "In some counties of England," says Walker, "especially in the west, this word is pronounced as if written *coocumber;* this though rather nearer to the orthography than *cowcumber,* is yet faulty" . . . "It seems too firmly fixed in its sound of *cowcumber* to be altered."

DAUNT: dănt. Thus Walker, who thus pronounces *paunch, gaunt, taunt, saunter,* in this supported by Dr. Kenrick; while Sheridan preserves the broad sound, as if written *pawnch,* etc.

DICTIONARY: dĭk'-shun-a-ry. Authorities all favor this practice, but, says Walker, "a few years ago this word was universally pronounced as if written *Dixnary,* and a person would have been thought a pedant if he had pronounced it according to its orthography; but such has been the taste for improvement in speaking, that now a person would risk the imputation of vulgarity should he pronounce it otherwise than it is written."

DUKE: dūke. All authorities support this pronunciation, but Walker says, "There is a slight deviation often heard in the pronunciation of this word, as if written *Dook;* but this borders on vulgarity. . . . There is another impropriety in pronouncing this word, as if written *Jook;* this is not so vulgar as the former, and arises from an ignorance of the influence of the accent."

EARTH: $\overset{1}{e}$rth. This pronunciation is supported by all authorities, yet it is very often liable to a coarse vulgar sound, as if written *urth*. "There is," says Walker, "but a delicate difference . . . but quite sufficient to distinguish a common from a polite speaker."

FAULT: f$\overset{3}{a}$t. Thus Sheridan. Walker sounds the *l*.

FIERCE: f$\overset{1}{e}$rse. Thus Sheridan. Walker gives f$\overset{3}{e}\overset{3}{e}$rse.

GOLD: g$\overset{2}{o}$ld. Sheridan gives g$\overset{3}{o}$ld; Walker gives both; he prefers g$\overset{2}{o}$ld but thinks g$\overset{3}{o}$ld most in use.

HAUNT: h$\overset{1}{a}$nt. Sheridan gives h$\overset{1}{a}$nt or h$\overset{3}{a}$nt, preferring h$\overset{1}{a}$nt. Walker prefers h$\overset{1}{a}$nt and says: "This word was in quiet possession of its true sound till a late dramatick piece made its appearance, which, to the surprise of those who had heard the word spoken half a century, was, by some speakers, the *Hawnted* Tower. This was certainly the improvement of some critick in the language; for a plain common speaker would undoubtedly have pronounced the *au* as in *aunt, jaunt,* &c., and as it had always been pronounced in the *Drummer,* or the *Haunted House.*"

HEINOUS: h$\overset{3}{a}$n'-$\overset{1}{u}$s. So Walker. Sheridan gives h$\overset{3}{e}$-n$\overset{1}{u}$s.

HOSPITAL: $\overset{3}{a}$s'-p$\overset{1}{i}$-t$\overset{1}{a}$l. Sheridan and Walker also suppressed the *h* although they sounded it in *hospitable, hospitably, hospitality.*

HOUSEWIFE: h$\overset{1}{u}$z'-w$\overset{1}{i}$f. So Sheridan and Walker; some affected speakers pronounced it house-wife.

IMBECILE: $\overset{1}{i}$m-b$\overset{1}{e}$s'-s$\overset{1}{i}$l. Accent on second syllable (Johnson, Ash, Kenrick, Entick); on last (Scott, Sheridan). Walker gives $\overset{1}{i}$m-b$\overset{1}{e}$s'-s$\overset{1}{i}$l and $\overset{1}{i}$m-b$\overset{3}{e}$-s$\overset{3}{e}$el'; prefers former, but, like Sheridan, regards latter as most fashionable.

LIEUTENANT: l$\overset{1}{i}$f-t$\overset{1}{e}$n'-n$\overset{1}{a}$nt. So Sheridan. Walker gives lĕv-tĕn'-nant and says, "but the regular sound, as if written Lewtenant, seems not so remote—as to make us lose all hope that it will in time be the actual pronunciation."

MANKIND: mǎn-kȳind'. Accent on first syllable (Ash, Bailey); second (Johnson, Sheridan, Entick, Walker).

MEMOIR: mē-moir'. Accent first syllable (Ash, Bailey, Scott, Entick); second (Johnson, Kenrick, W. Johnston, Buchanan, Perry).

NATURE: nā-tshur. So Sheridan. Walker pronounced it nǎt'-shure; Walker remarks, "there is a vulgar pronunciation of this word as if written *nater*, which cannot be too carefully avoided."

OBLIGE: ō-blī'-dzh. Sheridan, Walker give precedence to this form but also recognize the pronunciation with short *i*. Walker remarks that "when Lord Chesterfield wrote letters to his son, it was, by many polite speakers, pronounced as if written *obleege* to give a hint of their knowledge of French; but it was so far from having generally obtained that Lord Chesterfield strictly enjoins his son to avoid this pronunciation as vulgar . . . His [Lord Chesterfield's] authority had such weight with the polite world, that a change was soon perceptible; and we not infrequently hear the word pronounced with the open sound of *i* in *fight* in the very circles where, a few years ago, it would have been an infallible mark of vulgarity."

PRINCESS: prin'-ses. So all orthoëpists. Our writer refers to an "affectation which prevails in some of the higher circles of laying the stress on the last syllable."

RATHER: rath'-ur. So Sheridan and Walker. Nares gives the first syllable the sound of that in rā-ven. "In familiar conversation," says Walker, "when *rather* signifies just preferably, we lengthen the first vowel, and pronounce it long and slender, as if written *rayther*."

ROME: ro͞om. So Walker, who remarks: "The *o*, in this word, is irrevocably fixed in the English sound of that letter in *move, prove,* &c." "There are many, however," says our anonymous writer, "who sound it rhyming with *dome*."

SAUCY: saw'-se. So Sheridan and Walker. Walker remarks: "The regular sound of this diphthong must be carefully preserved, as the Italian sound of *a* given to it in this word, and in *saucer, daughter,* &c., is only heard among the vulgar."

SAUSAGE: sau'-sidge. Sheridan uses the pronunciation sas'-sidge. Walker gives the pronunciation as here marked and then adds: "This word is pronounced in the first manner [sau'-sidge] by the correct and in the second by the vulgar."

SEA: se. So all orthoëpists. "But there is a vulgar pronunciation which prevails in some counties of sounding it *say*, rhyming with *day,* which should be carefully avoided."

SOOT: sut. So Sheridan. Walker sounds soot after the analogy of *sooty*.

TASSEL: tosl. So Sheridan. Walker pronounces tas'-sel.

TEA: te. So all orthoëpists, "but in many counties it is improperly pronounced as if written *tay*."

TOWARDS: to'rds. So Sheridan, Walker, Ash, Bailey. The last syllable is stressed by Dr. Johnson and by Entick.

TRAIT: tra. So Sheridan. Walker pronounces tra or trate, "and says that the *t* begins to be pronounced."

TURKOIS: tur-keeze'. So Walker. Sheridan gives the

French sound tur-ke̊-ze. Kenrick pronounces it *turkiz* when spelled *turcois,* and gives the *oi* the broad sound, as in *boys,* when written *turkois.* He accents on the first syllable, as do Dr. Johnson, Ash, and Entick.

VASE: vå'se. Rimes with *case.* "That is the pronunciation I have always heard." So Sheridan. Walker gives våze and adds, "I have uniformly heard it pronounced with the *s* like *z,* and sometimes, by people of refinement, with the *a* like *aw;* but this being too refined for the general ear, is now but seldom heard."

VAULT: våt. So Sheridan, who leaves out *l* also in its compounds, "which," says our writer, "I take to be the most fashionable pronunciation." Scott, Perry, and Walker, retain the *l,* and Walker, though he marks the word våwlt, or våwt, thinks the *l* should never be dropped, unless in the sense of a *cellar for wine.*

WRAP: råp. So Sheridan and Walker. But Walker observes it is "often pronounced *rop* rhyming with *top,* even by speakers much above the vulgar."

YET: ye̊t. Walker says: "The *e* in this word is frequently changed by incorrect speakers into *i;* but *though this change is agreeable to the best and most established usage in the word yes,* in *yet* it is the mark of incorrectness and vulgarity."

The record of varying judgments of late eighteenth-century orthoëpists regarding the pronunciation of individual words will afford some idea of the degree of success that attended efforts at fixing the pronunciation. There had been progress. The lists of "words with pronunciation differing from the spelling" which had been features of the elementary grammars and spelling books throughout the seventeenth and eighteenth centuries, beginning as early as the Grammar of Charles Butler in 1639, had kept alive the sense of an irregularity in language needing to be smoothed out. The irregular modes of popular speech such as appear in the list quoted from Dilworth and Dr. Watts find little place in the pronunciations recognized as correct in the dictionaries by Sheridan and by Walker. A few words such as *clerk, towards, Christmas, heart, hearth, sergeant, iron, Wednesday, wristband, colonel,* have retained to our day their traditional popular pronunciation more or less independent of the spelled form, and many more of the older modes of pronunciation persist in dialect and the language of old-fashioned speakers. In the case of English proper names, known better to the ear than to the eye, these forms also have persisted in great numbers so that English family names and geographical names provide fascinating puzzles in pronunciation for the foreigner who knows only the written forms. Most other words, however, in the second half of the eighteenth century were rapidly being brought under the domination of the written form and, controlled by the principle of analogy, were being brought into conformity and system.

Indirectly, then, Johnson's *Dictionary* aided in fixing the pronunciation. In this way the influence of Latin learning again makes itself felt. For instance, a pronunciation indicated by spellings such as *sartinly, desarve, sarvant, sarve, presarve, divartion, vartus* ('virtues'), *marcy* which appear in the letters of the seventeenth century people represented in the *Verney Memoirs*,[3] was brought under the influence of a spelling determined largely by Latin pattern and thus brought to its present mode as recommended by Walker. The final syllable in such words as *jointure, venture, future, pasture, adventure, gesture, nature,* which in the seventeenth

[3] H. C. Wyld, *A History of Modern Colloquial English,* p. 165.

and early eighteenth century was commonly sounded -*er*,[4] was similarly affected. Latin pattern, either directly, or through the influence of analogy, was responsible for the present spelling of the ending, which in turn served to fix the pronunciation, the earlier popular pronunciation surviving to our day only in such vulgar or dialectal pronunciations as *figger* and *critter*.

The same control by spelling appears in the prescriptions by Walker for the pronunciation of words ending in -*ward*. From the *Practical Phonographer* (1701) by Jones we know that the prevalent pronunciation earlier in the century of such words as *athwart, backward, eastward, Edward, forward, inward, Northward, Windward,* had been with silent *w*. Such pronunciation today survives only in a few words such as *toward* and in proper names such as *Harwich, Greenwich* and in such vulgarisms as *innard*. In Walker the pronunciation in such words is usually made to conform to the spelling. An exception is *towards,* for which Walker indicates the pronunciation *to-urdz*.

In the case of the ending -*ing* the domination of the written form by the end of the eighteenth century was not quite so absolute. Of the earlier pronunciation with -*n* instead of -*ng* there is abundant evidence. It is to be found in rimes such as those quoted from Butler's *Hudibras*. It is attested in the early eighteenth century by spellings of Lady Wentworth such as: *dynin-room; levin,* 'living'; *takin,* 'taking'; *approachin; divertin; fardin,* 'farthing'; *mornin*.[5] The popular pronunciation persisted in good use throughout the eighteenth century and persists today to some extent in cultivated use in England and in parts of the United States, particularly in the South. Walker found himself in difficulty in this case. He could not condemn a mode

4 *Ibid.,* pp. 173, 175.
5 *Ibid.,* p. 290.

of pronunciation so well established. He admitted that "our best speakers universally pronounce *singin, bringin, flingin.*" And yet his deference to the authority of the written form led him to assert that "*Writing, reading, speaking* are certainly preferable to *writin, readin, speakin,* wherever the language has the least degree of solemnity." Some eighteenth-century orthoëpists attempted a compromise, asserting that when *ing* is preceded by *ing,* as in *singing, bringing,* it should be pronounced *in.* This compromise Lindley Murray rejects in agreement with Johnson, asserting that "it is a good rule, with respect to pronunciation, to adhere to the written words, unless custom has clearly decided otherwise."

Other words which by the end of the century had been made to conform in pronunciation to their spelling, were the words with the diphthong *oi.* As shown in the case of several words already mentioned, the resistance of the popular mode of pronunciation was a stiff one, but by the end of the century Walker felt justified in prescribing the pronunciation according to the spelling. One word, *choir,* which retained the earlier popular pronunciation, probably did so under the influence of the variant spelling *quire.*

In great part to a standardized written form is to be attributed the gradual disappearance in the pronouncing dictionaries, of pronunciations such as *jine* ('join'), *bile* ('boil'), *creater* ('creature'), *sarvice* ('service'), *nater* ('nature'), *figger* ('figure'), *aukerd* ('awkward'), *fortin* ('fortune') and the marks of disapproval attached to others such as *sarvant, marchant* ('merchant'), *cowcumber* ('cucumber'), *sparrowgrass* ('asparagus'). Pronunciations of this kind, as is well known, did not become extinct, but they were henceforth more and more excluded from cultivated use, more and more relegated to the class of vulgarisms.

There were, however, a number of sounds for which the

written forms provided but uncertain guidance. This lack of guidance appears particularly in the case of the sounds represented by the letter *a*. On account of the several sounds for which this one letter was the regular sign, the written form of a word often leaves one in uncertainty regarding the sound intended. In fact there seems to have been a lack of uniformity in the pronunciation of the vowel sounds represented by this letter, particularly in the case of the two sounds represented in the words *cat* and *cart*. It is to be noted that the distinction between these two sounds has not been used in distinctions of case or number in nouns, or in distinction of tense in the principal parts of the strong verbs. Nor has it been used in distinguishing words one from another. Other distinctions in vowel sounds have been made to serve as means of distinguishing from one another words such as *rack, reck, rick, rock, ruck*. But the two sounds of *a* have not thus been brought into service, if we except comparatively recent times when the unrounding of the short *o* prevalent in American speech has brought words like *rock* into the vacant place left unoccupied by the so-called broad sound of short *a*. Precise distinction in sounds is in great part determined by the need of distinction in meaning. Little used for such distinction, the two sounds of *a* have been subject to interchange and uncertainty.

Uncertainty regarding the sound in the eighteenth century represented by the letter *a* is increased by the lengthening of the vowel that occurred before certain continuant consonants such as *f, n, r, s,* and *th*. The statements made by eighteenth-century orthoëpists regarding the pronunciation of *a* are for the most part ambiguous, and modern conclusions drawn from these statements are varied. Grandgent [6] makes the sweeping assertion that "until 1780, or

[6] *Old and New*, p. 27.

thereabouts, the standard language had no broad *a*. People said not only *'fast,'* but *'father,' 'far,' 'hard.'"* Krapp,[7] speaking of the lengthened sound, says that "Critical opinion through the eighteenth century certainly favored the sound [æ:]," that is to say, the narrow or fronted sound. Jespersen,[8] however, expresses the opinion that long *a*, that is to say, the broad or "continental" sound, "is considerably older than has been commonly supposed" and traces the sound back to the seventeenth century. An independent examination on the part of the present writer leads to the opinion that then as now the two modes of pronunciation co-existed and that the distinction between the two was not made a sharp one because it was not a distinction associated with difference in spelling or difference in meaning. Throughout the seventeenth century the use of the narrow or fronted sound (as in modern *cat*) as already explained is attested by Wallis and Cooper and Miege. Even earlier in the century the Scotch grammarian Hume (1611), discussing Latin pronunciation, speaks of the English pronunciation of *a* in the first two syllables of the Latin *amabant* as "not far unlyke the sheeps *bae.*" He is making use of the comparison used by the Romans in describing the sound of the Greek *eta*. There exists some evidence of an attempt to propagate the broad sound. The broader sound was better suited to musical tone, and it was the sound prevalent in continental languages. The remark of Simeon Daines (1640) should be recalled. He thought it "farre more tolerable to incline to too full a sound after the manner of a Forreigne Calfe, than with some that nicely mince it, to make it resemble the bleat of an English Lamb." The situation in the eighteenth century with relation to these two sounds seems to have been unsettled

---

[7] *The English Language in America*, II, p. 40.
[8] *A Modern English Grammar on Historical Principles*, I, pp. 305, 307.

as it is today in American speech. One should recall the varying pronunciations of the word *madam* by Mincing in Congreve's *Way of the World*. There was dialectal difference. There was also a difference corresponding with difference in social class. The differing judgments of Kenrick and Bayley should be recalled. The broad sound is often associated with the "rustical." The narrow or fronted sound, on the other hand, is referred to as "mincing" and is often regarded as affected.

Let us examine the comments of some of the leading eighteenth-century authorities. Johnson (1755) leaves one much in doubt. He says that "*A* has three sounds: *A* slender in *face, mane* and in words ending in *-ation; A* open, the *a* of the Italian or nearly resembling it, as *father, rather, congratulate, fancy, glass; A* broad like the *a* of German as *all, wall, call*. This last sound, anciently written *au* is retained in the northern dialects and in the rustick pronunciation, *mawn* for *man, haund* for *hand*." Buchanan (1766) distinguishes four sounds in stressed syllables: (1) the long sound of *same, male*, etc.; (2) the short sound of *man, hat, band*, etc.; (3) the broad sound of *bald, ward, walk*, etc.; (4) the acute sound, which seems to approach to *au* but is really short *a* twice, but rapidly pronounced, as *father, rather, arm*, etc. Kenrick distinguishes between (1) *call, hawl*, etc.; (2) *hard, part, carve*, etc.; and (3) *and, hat, crag, bar*. The second sound is identified with that in Italian *padre, madre* and the third with that in Italian *ma, la, allegro*. Ash distinguishes: (1) broad *a* in most words before *ld, ll, lt;* (2) narrow *a* in all words or syllables lengthened by final *-e;* (3) a middle sound which prevails in most words. William Ward (1765) distinguishes three sounds: (1) *a* slender as in *place, waste* and in *-ation, -ageous, -arious;* (2) *a* open, like the *a* of the Italian, as in *father, languish, grass;* (3)· *a* broad, which is the open sound pronounced long, as in *call, wall,* etc., but which when pronounced short, as in *sally, valley,* is the same as *a* open. Ward's judgment coincides with that of Johnson and indicates a preference for the broad sound. By the end of the century four sounds are usually associated with the letter *a*. G. Wright in a grammar published in 1794 at Sunderland and, therefore, possibly indicating Northern pronunciation, distinguishes four sounds appearing in (1) *ago, lady, same,* (2) *man,* (3) *art,* (4) *hall.* The third sound is usual before *r, s, n, f, th,* or silent *l.* Lindley Murray also distinguishes four sounds appearing in (1) *ale, pale,* (2) *at, bat, barrel, fancy, glass,* (3) *arm, farm,* (4) *all, call.* But he remarks that "in the opinion of some grammarians the *a* in *arm* is the same specific sound as *a* in *at.*" Perry in his dictionary (1775) criticizes Sheridan for failing to distinguish "the sound *à,* as heard in the words, *part, dart,* etc." This sound Perry, practically in agreement with Wright, records as usual before *r, f, s, st, nce* in words such as *chaff, grass, mast, dance.* He records the same sound for *au* in words such as *daunt, haunch, haunt.*

In the later eighteenth century there seems to have been a growing fashionable affectation for the narrow fronted sound. Kenrick, it will be recalled, contemptuously attributes the use of the fronted sound to "flirting females and affected fops." Batchelor in his *Orthoëpical Analysis* (1809) speaks of "what Mr. Jones terms 'a mincing, modern affectation,' by which *lass, palm, part, dance,* etc., are passed over as hastily as *pan, mat, lack,* and *fan.*" [9] George Mason in a *Supplement to Johnson's Dictionary,* London, 1801, questions Johnson's accuracy in assigning the same Italian value to the *a* in *father, rather, congratulate, fancy, glass.* He asks, "Is it not something of a rustical accent to pronounce *a* in *rather* the same way as in *father?* Should it

[9] Jespersen, *op. cit.,* I, p. 305.

not be sounded as in *fancy?*" Leigh Hunt speaks of the "dandy watchman" who "had a mincing way with it, pronouncing the *a* in the word *past* as it is in *hat,* making a little preparatory hem before he spoke, and then bringing out his 'past ten' in a style of genteel indifference." [10] Walker in his dictionary is definite in his remarks about this prevailing tendency in the cultivated pronunciation of his time. Speaking of "the long sound of the middle or Italian *a,*" he says: "This sound of *a* was formerly more than at present found before the liquid nasal *n,* especially when succeeded by *t* or *c,* as *grant, dance, glance, lance, France, prance,* etc. The hissing consonant *s* was likewise a sign of this sound of the *a* . . . *glass, grass* . . . *last, fast,* etc., but this pronunciation of *a* seems to have been for some years advancing to a short sound of the letter, as heard in *hand, land, grand,* etc., and pronouncing the *a* in *after, answer, basket, plant, mast,* etc., as long as in *half, calf,* etc., . . . borders very closely on vulgarity . . . though the termination *mand* in *command, demand,* etc., . . . still retains the long sound inviolably." [11]

In the speech of the vulgar Londoner the, for that period, unfashionable modes of pronunciation persisted. The anonymous author of *Vulgarities of Speech* (1826) speaks of the vulgar pronunciation in London of *a* long as in *far* for short *a* as in *man,* indicating the pronunciation objected to by the spellings, *chawnce, dawnce, pawrt, bawnket, awfter, glawss.* In provincial speech also unfashionable modes of speech were in vogue.

In an Irish edition of Johnson's *Dictionary* (1798) the Irish are taken to task because they pronounce words ending in *-lm* as if they were written *bawm, sawm, quawm, cawm,* etc. A hint regarding Northern English pronuncia-

---

[10] G. P. Krapp, *Modern English,* p. 132.
[11] Quoted from Jespersen, *op. cit.,* I, p. 306.

tion of *a* is offered by the well-known rimes of the Scotch
Marjorie Fleming:

> She was more than usual calm,
> She did not give a single dam.

The sounds represented by the letter *a* are by no means
the only ones concerning which the spelling affords uncertain information. An interesting set of words in which the
written signs represented a pronunciation different from
that represented by the same signs today, is the series of
words with a final syllable beginning with the letter *d*.
From Walker one learns that "polite speakers" not only
used the pronunciations *edjucate, verchew, verdjure,* but
ought also to say *ojeous, insidjeous, Injean.*[12]

Another set of words in which the spelling leaves one in
doubt regarding the pronunciation is made up of words in
which *k* or *g* is followed by one of the front vowels *a, e,* or *i.*
In such words a glide vowel developed before the *a, e,* or *i.*
That this mode of pronunciation had begun as early as the
seventeenth century one knows on the authority of Wallis
(1653), who records the pronunciation of *can, get* and
begin by the spellings *cyan, gyet, begyin.* By the end of
the eighteenth century this mode of pronunciation was a
prevalent one. Nares (1784) rejects it, but Sheridan
(1780) recognizes it in *guide* and *guile,* pronounced "as if
written *gyide, gyile,*" and Elphinston not only recognizes
kyind and *gyide* but asserts that a *y* before the vowel in
sky, can, skirt, guard, etc., is essential in polite pronunciation. The same mode of pronunciation is recognized by
Walker (1791) who prescribes it in the words *sky, kind,
guide, gird, girl, cart, cap, carpenter, guard, regard,* etc.

Somewhat less widely prevalent and less frankly recog-

[12] Wyld, *op. cit.,* p. 294.

nized by the orthoëpists was the pronunciation without aspiration of *wh-* at the beginning of words, a mode of pronunciation today prevalent in Southern England, and in parts of the United States, *e.g., white* pronounced like *Wight*. This mode of pronunciation, which was not unknown as early as the fifteenth century, was spreading somewhat rapidly in the seventeenth century, although grammarians are slow to recognize it and Walker (1785) notes it only to condemn it as one of the "faults in the pronunciation of the younger class of pupils."

This departure from the written form, condemned by Walker in his *Rhetorical Grammar* (1795), is one of a series of faults of the same nature. One of the most interesting of these from a modern point of view is the fault of not sounding the *h* where it ought to be sounded, and inversely, "chiefly among the people of London." Elphinston (1787) notes that "many Ladies, Gentelmen and others have wholly discarded" initial *h-* in places where it ought to be used.[13] This feature of language, now perhaps above all others associated with English vulgarism, is regarded by Jespersen as recent at the end of the eighteenth century, and Wyld believes it not to have been "widespread much before the end of the eighteenth century."

A second fault among those listed by Walker is the "use of *v* for *w* and more frequently of *w* for *v,* among inhabitants of London, and those not always of the low order." This manner of pronunciation, so Pickwickian in its associations today, Jespersen believes to have been of late eighteenth-century origin. The earlier instances cited by Wyld are not convincing because explainable as due to orthographical confusion. Almost as striking as its sudden appearance not only in London but in transatlantic Boston and Philadelphia was its later complete disap-

[13] *Ibid.,* p. 295.

pearance. Wyld asserts (1920) that it "is now apparently extinct in the Cockney dialect."

Another set of words whose pronunciation it was difficult to bring into agreement with English spelling was the set of words of recent importation from French. The uncertainty regarding such words appears in the variant pronunciations of the words *envelope, environs* and *trait* cited by eighteenth-century orthoëpists, and the uncertainty persists to the present day, in the case of the word *trait* forming a mark of distinction between British pronunciation and American.

The subject of eighteenth-century pronunciation is one of vast complexity of which the few details here given can give no perfect conception. Many new influences were at work. One would gladly know more of the influences of the cultivated pronunciation of the stage. It is not practicable here to attempt to disentangle the different strains of influence. There may be clearly recognized, however, two sharply different tendencies, one the conservative tendency to preserve forms established by popular usage of the kind already discussed, the other the rationalizing tendency, so strong from the time of Johnson on, to bring pronunciation into conformity with the written form. The strength of the first tendency in the early nineteenth century it is not easy to determine because the sounds may be concealed by the written forms. But the conservative Englishman who clings so tenaciously to ancient customs, one may be sure would not be quick to abandon old modes of pronunciation. When representatives of the two tendencies came together, there was naturally a sharp contrast. An illustration of this contrast is afforded by the comments of Leigh Hunt (1784-1859) on the pronunciation of the famous actor John Philip Kemble (1757-1823). In his *Autobiography* Hunt discusses the matter at some length and calls to attention Kemble's affectation of older pronunciations strange to the nineteeenth century ear, such as: *aitches,* 'for aches'; *marchant; innocint; conshince; varchue,* 'virtue'; *furse,* 'fierce'; *bird,* 'beard'; *ojus,* 'odious'; *hijjus,* 'hideous'; *perfijjus,* 'perfidious'; *furful,* 'fearful'; *airth,* 'earth'; *etairnally; maircy; quality* (*a* of universality). The pronunciation of Kemble, whose style was stilted and declamatory and whose pronunciation was presumably governed by tradition rather than by the precepts of the orthoëpist, Hunt regarded as "vicious."

CHAPTER XIX

BOSWELL in his *Life of Johnson,* under the year 1772, tells of the Scotch Earl of Marchmont who had tried to cultivate an English pronunciation. That he had not been successful appears from his experience with "a master of a shop in London." "I suppose, Sir," remarked the shopkeeper, "you are an American." "Why so, Sir?" said his Lordship. "Because, Sir," replied the shopkeeper, "you speak neither English nor Scotch, but something different from both, which I conclude is the language of America." This incident, recorded by Boswell to illustrate the vain attempt of a Scotchman to master English pronunciation, also may serve to illustrate an English feeling in the eighteenth century regarding the English of America. From that day to this a subject constantly discussed, and one to-day of extremely practical importance, has been the relation of the transplanted language to that of the mother country.

It has repeatedly been pointed out that the English carried to America was English in its seventeenth-century stage of development. How was the language affected by its change of environment? Let us consider first the situation in New England, where the conditions are best known. The first English settlers reached New England in 1620. For ten years there were few followers. But in the years 1630-40 came ships thronged with new settlers. Then with the establishment of a Puritan régime in England, Puritan migration to America practically ceased. The consequence is that from the 21,000 inhabitants settled by 1640 has sprung the great share of the New England stock, a population said to be as pure and unmixed as that of any English county. The Puritan colonists were not lacking in learning. It is said that about the year 1650 "there were in New England as many graduates of Cambridge and Oxford as could be found in any population of similar size in the mother country." [1] Coming, however, as they did, not only from London, but from the eastern and southern counties of England, they did not represent any single speech community in England, but brought with them not only the standard forms of seventeenth-century English, but dialectal forms as well. In the speech of the rural New Englander, therefore, many seventeenth-century forms of English, abandoned in the cultivated speech of the mother country, still survive. It is to this archaic manner of speech of rural New England that James Russell Lowell turned in his *Biglow Papers* in his attempt to create a homely intimacy of expression. To Lowell's Prefaces to the two series of *Biglow Papers* one may still turn for an exposition of the nature of this Yankee form of speech. The modes of pronunciation appearing in such words as *nater, critter, figger, sartin, varmint, narves, varses, larnin, vartu, ile, jine, pizen, spile, ketch, git, obleeged, hanted, jant, Sheby, soffies,* Lowell points out, are not Yankee perversions of the English of England, but modes of speech, some of them dialectal, but most of them current in the cultivated use of the seventeenth-century England. The contracted forms of speech which feature the language of Shakespeare and of the Restoration period and were so vigorously objected to later by Swift and Addison, are conspicuous features of the Yankee speech recorded by Lowell. In the *Biglow Papers* appear such forms as *ath'ism, curus* and *cur'ous, Dannill, experunce, Gabr'el, illustrous, intellectle, Ishmel, materil, notorous, pecooler,*

[1] M. C. Tyler, *History of American Literature,* I, p. 98.

prem'um, promiscu'sly, spiritoolism, varus and *var'ous, victor'ous.*[2] One should compare the forms of words in the early eighteenth century listed in the grammar by Isaac Watts. The same relation to seventeenth-century language appears in the vocabulary of rural New England speech. Nearly all of the distinctive words, such as *guess, sick* (for 'ill'), *bug* ('insect'), *afeard, fall* ('autumn'), *loan* ('lend'), *fleshy, chore, creek* (for 'brook'), *poor* ('lean'), *dry* ('thirsty'), *allow* ('affirm'), Lowell traces to English originals, since become obsolete, or surviving only in local English dialect.

The conclusions reached by Lowell regarding the relation of New England dialect to the earlier or the dialectal English of England have been in great part confirmed by later studies.[3] A recent examination of "occasional spellings" appearing in diaries, journals, and local records of New England in the seventeenth and eighteenth centuries affords much supporting evidence.[4] Seventeenth-century records afford such significant spellings as *sarge, marchantable, sarvice, clark, parsons* (for 'persons'), *sarch, Marcy,* and eighteenth-century works provide *reharsth, sarmoun, desarted.* From the same centuries is recorded evidence of a fluctuation between the short vowels *e* and *i* in such forms as *assest, sperit, shellings, smeth* along with *chists, kittle, divell, git* from Essex County, Massachusetts, and *tell* (for 'till'), *sence* ('since'), *fitched* ('fetched'), from the records of the Salem Trials, a fluctuation attested in English use by "occasional spellings" from the sixteenth century on.

The records of the Southern colonies are less abundant than those for New England, and have been less thoroughly examined, but there too one finds the development of an

---

[2] B. A. P. Van Dam, *Angl. Forsch.* 9.
[3] C. H. Grandgent, "A Century of New England Pronunciation," *Publications Modern Language Association,* 1899.
[4] H. Alexander, *American Speech,* I, pp. 141-148.

archaic form of English speech. The early Southern colonists were somewhat different in social type and were governed by purposes different from those that led to New England colonization. In the new country they set up a mode of life different from that set up in New England. They were impelled, not by the desire to establish an idealized mode of existence, but by the desire to profit by the rich abundance of a new country. In consequence they reproduced in the new land many of the conditions of English country life. There is available an excellent contemporary account of the mode of life in Virginia a century after the arrival of the first English colonists in that state.[5] In this account one learns of an English mode of life in America much like that surviving in the South to the time of the Civil War. In the new land there was necessary a certain amount of adaptation to environment. The abundance of wood in the new country led to the use of wood in the structure of houses. English thatch and tile as covering of houses were superseded by the wooden shingle, which this eighteenth-century writer feels it necessary to define for his English readers as "an Oblong Square of Cypress or Pine-Wood." New kinds of food were brought into use of which this writer mentions *pone,* "which is Bread made of Indian Meal . . . so-called . . . from the Indian Name *Oppone.*" But many of the distinctive features of English life reappear in the new land. There is much social intercourse among families distributed over the country. "Here," says our early eighteenth-century authority, "is the most Good-nature and Hospitality practis'd in the World, both towards Friends and Strangers: but the worst of it is, this Generosity is attended now and then, with a little too much Intemperance. The Neighborhood is at

[5] R. Beverley, *The History and Present State of Virginia,* London, 1705.

much the same distance, as in the Country in England: but with this Advantage, that all the better sort of People have been abroad, and seen the World, by which means they are free from that stiffness and formality, which discover more civility, than Kindness: And besides the goodness of the Roads, and the fairness of the Weather, bring People oftener together." Our authority mentions also the various forms of hunting, not only the hunting of deer and hares familiar in England but the more distinctive form of "Vermine hunting," by which is meant the hunting by night of raccoons, opossums, and foxes. Altogether the mode of life described is one in which the contemporary English Squire Western would have found himself at home and one in which we may suppose the language was of the undisciplined form determined by social usage like that in the nearly contemporary Wentworth letters in England recently brought to notice [6] rather than a language regulated by school training.

Not only were English modes of life recreated in the Virginia colony, but close relations with the mother country were maintained. Furthermore in a country with softer climate and with a soil less resistant to cultivation, the Virginian was less drilled than his Yankee contemporary in resourcefulness. Already in 1705 Beverley says, "I must at the same time reproach my Country-Men with a Laziness that is unpardonable." The natural products of the soil were made easily available through the labor of slaves and bond servants, and manufactured articles, the "Improvements," were imported. "All their Wooden Ware, their cabinets, chairs, tables, chests, stools, boxes, cart-wheels," says Beverley, "were brought from England."

Under such conditions the speech of the Southern colonists might be expected, even more than that of New

---

[6] H. C. Wyld, *A History of Modern Colloquial English*, pp. 162*ff.*

England, to retain earlier features of the English of the mother country. Indeed, the rustic speech of Virginia to-day shares many features with the rustic speech of New England, features which are a common heritage from the earlier language of England. This likeness appears from an examination recently made of the peculiarities in speech today in Scott county, a secluded district in Virginia. A summary of these peculiarities includes: the pronunciation of *Sarah* as *Sairy;* of *kettle, get, stead,* as *kittle, git, stid;* of *empty* and *general* as *impty* and *gineral,* of *potato, widow, fellow, tobacco* with the ending pronounced as if spelled *-er;* of *haunt* and *jaundice* with the narrow sound of *a* (*æ*); of *boil, hoist, pennyroyal* as if spelled *hist,* etc.; of *Baptist* as if spelled *Babtis;* of *land* and *wild* with silent final *-d;* of *morning, nothing, running,* etc., as if spelled *mornin,* etc.; of *burst, parcel, curse* and sometimes *horse* with the *r* not pronounced; and of *post* and *toast* with silent final *t.* Professor Krapp asserts that all of these details "might have been taken from a description of New England speech in the seventeenth and eighteenth centuries." [7]

Perhaps enough evidence from the American side has been offered to demonstrate the seventeenth-century source of American English, particularly of dialectal forms, whether of the South or of New England. An impression even more vivid is to be gained by reversing the process and examining the current pronunciation and the colloquial vocabulary of seventeenth-century England. An examination, for instance, of the rimes of Butler's *Hudibras* will show the currency of modes of pronunciation now associated with American dialect. The weak pronunciation of final syllables appears in the rimes: *nature-water* (I, 21-2); *question-quest on* (I, 605-6); *for it-chariot* (II, 327-8); *talent-valiant* (II, 449-50); *palace-gallows* ([*Cf.* Amer. *galluses*] II,

[7] G. P. Krapp, *English Language in America,* II, p. 35.

531-2). The Yankee dialectal modification of the long *o* sound appears in: *skull-whole* (II, 733-4); *once-stones* (I, 115-6); *once-dunce* (I, 153-4); *bone-one* (II, 915-6); *spoke 'em-took 'em* (I, 113-4). The New England dialectal pronunciation of final *-a* appears in *India-gay* (II, 283-4); the silent *w* in the ending *-ward* in *accouter'd-outward* (I, 237-8); the pronunciation of *e* before *r* in *part-desert* (II, 39-40); the *e* sound for *i* in *spirit-bear it* (505-6; II, 875-6); *inherit-spirit* (II, 25-6); *spirit-merit* (II, 1035-6); the pronunciation of final *-ng* as *-n* in *sodden-pudden* (II, 121-2); *sin-thing* (I, 809-10); *something-Bumkin* (I, 421-2); *discoursing-Orsin* (II, 199-200).

In the colloquial language, also, of the plays of Mrs. Aphra Behn (1640-89) appear words and expressions such as *bag and baggage, bluff, sick, sickness, on the square, smart fellow, O Geminy! cagg of syder,* which if not now confined to American use, have been included in earlier lists of Americanisms. Even the supposedly New England habit of talking through the nose is one of the features of the seventeenth-century English "canting" manner of speech adopted by Lady Fancy [8] in mimicking her Puritan husband.

With these American modes of speech, falsely assigned to American origin, may be listed the Southern use of *reckon* meaning 'conjecture,' 'be of the opinion,' which Beattie (1784) lists as a Scotticism, and the modern American use of *nervous* meaning 'having weak nerves' which, in the eighteenth century, Samuel Johnson labels as "medical cant."

But the colonization of New England and of Virginia forms only the first stage in the settlement of America. Later English colonies were planted from New Jersey on the north to Georgia on the south as well as a Dutch colony in New York, and earlier colonists were reinforced by set-

[8] In Mrs. Behn's play *Sir Patient Fancy*.

tlers from other countries in Europe, by Huguenot French in New Jersey and Virginia and by Germans particularly in Pennsylvania. James Fenimore Cooper, writing in 1828, says that one-third the population of Pennsylvania is of German descent, and a German mode of speech has to this day continued to give local color to much of the rural speech of that state.

What may be called a third wave in the settlement of America by English-speaking people was one broader in its sweep and less sharply to be defined. By it different forms of English were carried into the Central and Western states, forms of Northern English along with Southern, and these mingled with the colonial American forms which had been carried westward. There are communities in Western states, such as the Western Reserve district in Ohio, which are practically New England colonies. There are sections in states west of Virginia, such as that about Lexington, Kentucky, where the conditions and the manner of speech of Virginia have been transplanted. But the settlement of most of the United States west of the seaboard has been accomplished by later comers from Europe. Among these later arrivals from the British Isles there is a greater representation from Northern England and from Ireland, and the Scotch-Irish or Presbyterian-Irish element in the settlement of the Central and Western states is a most considerable one and explains many of the features of language in this part of the United States.

The general conclusion to be reached is that the United States west of the seaboard has been settled by people of diverse origin, earlier colonists from New England and Virginia in the western regions mingling with later colonists from Northern Britain and Ireland and from other European countries, particularly from Germany and from Scandinavia. The thoroughness of this mingling is perhaps its most remarkable feature, and the result has been the formation of a mode of speech with only comparatively minor variations, common to the United States outside the areas of the New England and the Southern dialects. The remarkable uniformity in American speech west of the Atlantic seaboard is something that has always caught the attention of the foreigner. The older modes of speech preserved in the dialects of New England and the South came to be remarked as exceptional. As early as 1783 Noah Webster, who did so much to promote the pretensions of the New England form of speech, says that "the inhabitants of New England and Virginia have a peculiar pronunciation which affords much diversion to their neighbors." The influence of the manner of speech developed in the Central and Western states, with time, has more and more penetrated the Eastern and Southern districts and bids fair to become eventually the basis for a general standard of American speech.

It remains to consider the nature of the development of this mingled form of English on a new soil. It must be held in mind that every language has its frontier. There is the intellectual frontier where the language confronts new territory of knowledge won by progressing science. Language must continually advance into this new territory and consolidate intellectual conquests by means of new words and expressions for newly won ideas. But language also has its physical frontiers, and one of the most important frontiers of the English-speaking world in the seventeenth and eighteenth centuries was that occupied by the American colonists.

On the American frontier the pioneer, provided with a language adapted only to the needs of a long settled mode of existence, found himself at a loss for words suited to the new conditions that confronted him. In consequence his creative energies in speech were called into active service. In many instances he turned old words to new uses. In the wooden structure that formed his home a name was needed for the weatherboard that covered its sides. For this purpose the earlier English name for a thin board used by a barrel maker was brought into use, and the weatherboard was called a *clapboard*. In the same way in harvesting the Indian corn a new use was made of the English word *husk*. To small American streams was applied the name *creek* which in England continues to mean an estuary. The English name *hemlock* for a ground plant or shrub was applied to an American tree with similar leafage. The plural of the English *gallows,* with its popular English pronunciation *gallus*, was humorously adopted as the name for the device that supported his breeches. The English names *robin* and *blackbird* and *lark* were applied to American birds somewhat resembling the English birds.

As frequently the American colonist combined English elements into names for American phenomena. In this way he formed names for such American birds as the *catbird,* the *meadow lark,* and the *mudhen,* for American trees such as the *basswood* and the *buttonwood,* for American beasts such as the *ground hog* and the *rattlesnake,* and scores of other words many of which gained only local circulation. Some of these new words and new uses of words, such as *backwoods* and *backwoodsman, clearing, landslide, cold snap, barrens, underbrush, snow plow, frame house* and *log house,* offer vivid suggestion of harsh conditions in a new land. Such a word as *breadstuffs* indicates the function of the American colonies to supply raw material to the mother country. In a relatively small number of instances there was creation of new names such as the imitative names *bobolink* and *bob white.* But more frequently, older English elements were made use of, in many instances, as already indicated, of words neglected or abandoned in the standard language of England.

Perhaps more important than the independent activity of Americans in word creation are to be reckoned the new foreign influences to which Americans were exposed. On the American frontier contacts were established with other languages. Most obvious was the contact with the languages of the original inhabitants of the country. The relations between the English colonists and the American Indians were not exclusively those associated with such words as *tomahawk* and *massacre*. Jonathan Edwards gives an account of his boyhood spent on the colonial frontier, at Stockbridge, Massachusetts. The place was at that time inhabited almost solely by Indians. Indians were the nearest neighbors. Indian boys were his daily schoolmates and playfellows. Outside his father's house he seldom heard any language spoken except the Indian. Small wonder that under such conditions Indian names were adopted for new physical features, for newly learned customs and for new forms of animal and plant life. Many of the Indian names in their English transformation might possibly be unrecognizable to the Indian, but such words as *squaw, papoose, chinkapin, paw-paw, wigwam, toboggan, chipmunk, woodchuck,* and *skunk,* rich in their associations with frontier life, were important contributions to the English language.

In New York there was close contact with the earlier Dutch colonists. Noah Webster writes of a visit at Albany in 1786 and of the tenacity of the Dutch inhabitants in preserving their own speech. The Dutch language was used by their preachers in sermons of which Webster says he could not understand a word. Such conditions explain how such Dutch words as *boss, cold-slaw, cookie, waffle, sleigh, pit* (of a cherry), and *stoop* made their way into American speech.

The French language is today an official language in one of the most populous provinces of Canada. At one time French colonization had carried the French language across the continent from Acadia (or Nova Scotia) to Mobile and New Orleans. To contact between English-speaking and French-speaking colonists on the American frontier the English language owes such words as *prairie, seep, portage, chowder, caribou, crevasse, shanty, bayou,* and *levee.*

Extended still farther west the American frontier brought contact between speakers of English and speakers of Spanish. To this new contact established in America between the two European languages, the English language owes words rich in association with a romantic mode of life, such as *adobe, broncho, burro, bonanza, loco, canyon, chapparal, corral, coyote, lariat, ranch, peon, fandango,* and *sombrero.*

On their plantations and within their own households Americans have lived in intimate contact with still another people of alien race. The American negro adopted the language of his masters, and traces of his original African speech are not easily distinguished. That there are surviving elements, however, can hardly be doubted, and to African influence through the American negro are probably to be attributed words such as *voodoo,* and its variant, *hoodoo; goober,* a synonym for *peanut; pickaninny, Gullah, tote,* and probably, *jazz.*

Noah Webster informed the English traveler, Basil Hall (1827-8), that "there were not more than fifty words in all which were used in America and not in England" and that "all these apparent novelties are merely old English words." The prevailingly English character of the American vocabulary is further attested by another English observer, Captain Marryat (1838), who remarks that "you may travel through all the United States and find less difficulty in understanding, or in being understood than in some counties in England." Such testimony, however, is to be taken as evidence of the prevalence of American education and of the persistent effort of cultivated Americans to conform to a standard of correct speech common to England and America. That a difference existed, however, one may learn from some of Captain Marryat's further observations. He mentions words such as *snags* and *sawyers* as "coined for local uses on the Mississippi" and words such as *stoup* (*sic*) from the Dutch. He singles out also a number of American uses of English words with meanings strange to an Englishman. The words commented on include not only the American uses of *reckon, calculate, guess* (colloquial synonyms for 'think' or 'believe'); but *clever* (for 'good-natured'), *smart* (for 'clever'), *fix* (for 'repair), *mean* (for 'ashamed'), *great* (for 'fine,' 'splendid'), *how?* (for 'what?'), to feel *bad*, he *dissipates,* he *stimulates,* I *suspicion,* intend to write *considerable, right away, absquatalized.* Obviously by the third decade of the nineteenth century American use of words in colloquial speech had come to deviate to an appreciable extent from the use current in England.

An impression of the way new words were making their way into American speech is afforded by a list of words submitted to Noah Webster for inclusion in his dictionary. The list included the "Aboriginal" words: *esquaa* ('woman'), *pappoos, terrapin, thiskitama* ('nut'), and a number of other words including: *clevice, stall* ('balk'), *swivel-tree, glut, journey-cake, wilt, yellow-fever, clape, catbird, sheerwater, canvass-back, oldwife* ('alewife') *Boblincoln, weakfish* ('salt-water perch').

It is extremely difficult to measure accurately the amount

of the American contribution to the English language. Not only have many supposed Americanisms been found to be English survivals, but in many instances American words have been adopted into English and are not easily distinguished from words belonging to the original stock. In consequence earlier lists of Americanisms have been subject to constant revision. Only in our own time has been begun the long needed systematic collection and sifting of this interesting mass of word material.[9]

In America, however, as in the mother country, the fundamentals of speech were cultivated in schools. In this respect there was marked difference among the separate colonies. In Virginia the population was widely scattered in the plantation mode of life. Hence there was a lack of common schools. The well-to-do planters educated their sons by means of private tutors or sent them to England for education. But for the education of ones less fortunately situated there was little provision. Indeed the royal governors were not friendly in their attitude toward popular education. The words of Governor Berkeley have often been cited in this connection. In his report to the English government in 1670 he exclaims: "But, I thank God, there are no free schools nor printing, and I hope we shall not have these hundred years; for learning has brought disobedience and heresy and sects into the world, and printing has divulged them, and libels against the best government. God keep us from both!" The results of the unfriendly attitude appear in the following century. Governor Spottiswood, in dissolving the colonial assembly in 1715, made the striking comment: "I observe that the grand ruling party in your house has not furnished chairmen of two of your standing committees who can spell English or write com-

---

[9] The work is in the hands of Dr..W. A. Craigie, who is working under the auspices of the University of Chicago.

mon sense as the grievances under their own handwriting will manifest."

The lack of interest in learning in Virginia appears from the neglect of printing. There is no record of a printing press in Virginia before 1681. In fact in 1683 the printing press was prohibited, and from that date to 1729 no printing was done in Virginia.[10] Later in the eighteenth century Noah Webster remarks with contempt that "Gentlemen [of Norfolk] are obliged to send their children Northward for education," and remarks, "A shame for Virginia." In another place Webster speaks of the prevalence of illiteracy in the South. He says that "Virginians have little money & great pride, contempt of Northern men & great fondness for dissipated life. They do not understand Grammar." He says further: "An eminent merchant in Alexandria informed me that of fifty planters in Virginia who sold him tobacco, four or five only could write their names." There was evidently some ground for Webster's complacency in his exclamation: "O New England! how superior are thy inhabitants, in morals, literature, civility & industry!"

In parts of the North also general education was much neglected. William Smith, writing in 1757 regarding New York, says that for a long time his father and James De Lancey were the only academics in the province and that as late as 1745 there were only thirteen more. "What a contrast," he exclaims, "in everything respecting the cultivation of science, between this and the colonies settled by the English! . . . Our schools are of the lowest order . . . our common speech is extremely corrupt; and the evidences of bad taste, both as to thought and language are visible in all our proceedings, public and private."[11]

In educational activity New England was the leader.

[10] Tyler, *op. cit.*, I, p. 88.
[11] *Ibid.*, II, p. 207.

From the time of Tyndale and the early Reformers Protestantism was vitally interested in popular education. Especially was this true with the nonconformists who in revolt from state control in England, for the sake of freedom of worship, made a home in a new land. Hence it was natural that provision should be made by the New England Puritans for general education. In 1647 in Massachusetts it was provided by law that every township, "after the Lord hath increased them to the number of fifty householders, shall then forthwith appoint one within their town to teach all such children as shall resort to him to write and read" and further that "where any town shall increase to the number of one hundred families or householders, they shall set up a grammar school." [12] Similar provisions were made in the other New England colonies, and by the year 1649 in every one of them except Rhode Island public instruction was compulsory.[13] With the passing of the schools from church to secular control at the end of the seventeenth century the schools languished somewhat, but, with the establishment of peace following the Revolution, their revival was rapid, and a high general level of culture was reached, particularly in urban centers. "Boston in 1762 was a city of 30,000 inhabitants provided with many booksellers' shops which found employment for five printing-presses." [14] But education was not confined to cities. Timothy Dwight in his *Travels* (1796-1815) offers an attractive view of the New England country scene with its numerous villages and every one of them with its church and "suit of schools," [15] and James Fenimore Cooper, a New Yorker, somewhat later, is flattering in his account of New England intelligence and declares that beyond a doubt nowhere is to be found a popu-

[12] Krapp, *op. cit.*, I, 27.
[13] Tyler, *op. cit.*, I, 98.
[14] *The American Gazetteer,* London, 1762.
[15] Krapp, *op. cit.*, I, 23.

lation as well instructed, in elementary knowledge, as the people of these six states.

New England influence affected the neighboring states. Writing in 1828, Cooper estimates that one-third of the population of New York is made up of natives of New England or of New England extraction. Writing of common schools, he records: "The policy of New York and Ohio differs but little from that of New England in this particular. Unhappily that of Pennsylvania is less enlightened." Farther west this influence extended. Whole New England communities, shifting westward, carried with them their New England church organization and their New England school system, and individual Yankee schoolmasters bore Yankee methods of elementary education into the most distant parts of the scattered American territory. Between 1690 and 1840 the sales of the *New England Primer* have been estimated at 3,000,000 copies.

Perhaps enough has been said in demonstration of the thesis, for which a recent writer has provided ironical expression, "how civilization came into America by way of New England." In many ways other parts of the country took the lead in the cultivation of the English language. This is true particularly in case of the private schools. The application to English teaching of the grammatical methods formerly applied only to Latin teaching, was first made in a private school of South Carolina. This system was adopted in the Academy founded in 1750 by Benjamin Franklin in Philadelphia, and spread rapidly thereafter in American schools. Between 1725 and 1775, it has been estimated from the information derived from school advertisements, that ten per cent of all private schools taught "English grammatically." [16] In other ways the lead was taken by other parts of the country. The first English

[16] R. L. Lyman, *English Grammar in American Schools before 1850.*

grammar by an American was one by Hugh Jones, Professor of Mathematics at William and Mary College, published in London in 1724. The Middle Colonies, led by Pennsylvania, were two generations ahead of New England in giving prominence to English grammar in private schools, and North Carolina in 1795 was the first college to prescribe for admission an examination in the English language "taught grammatically."

In the schooling provided in colonial America there had to be taken into consideration the hard facts of life in a new country, conditions different from those in a mode of life settled into permanent grooves. There was constant need of resourcefulness in meeting new conditions. Hence the emphasis on practical forms of instruction, the eternal drill in 'the three R's,' which along with the elements of grammar and a little geography so long persisted as the main feature of American education.

It must not, however, be forgotten that during three-fourths of the eighteenth century the position of America was that of an English colony, and American schools were subject to the influence of English schools. The newer forces which in eighteenth-century England were affecting education were in harmony with the spirit of the American colonies. In England, as has been pointed out, added emphasis was given to the study of modern subjects including the mother tongue, and books for English instruction produced in England found use in American schools. Books were imported, and American editions were issued. Among the books recommended by Benjamin Franklin for the Philadelphia Public Library, of which he was one of the founders, were the English grammars by Brightland and by Greenwood. The grammar by Greenwood Franklin mentions in his *Autobiography* as one of the important books serving in his self-education. Of the English elementary works on grammar the most influential in America appears to have been that by Dilworth. When Noah Webster produced his spelling book it was intended to supersede the spelling book by Dilworth which in the year 1783 was said to have a circulation of 10,000 annually. For more advanced instruction the grammar by Lowth was most widely used. It was used at Harvard as early as 1774 and as late as 1841.[17] Moreover, the critical tests applied to the use of English words, the attention to propriety prevalent in the second half of the eighteenth-century England, reached across the Atlantic. Franklin advised Webster in his dictionary to set a "discountenancing mark" on unauthorized words. Among the earliest list of words subjected to this form of criticism in America is that submitted by Franklin in a letter to Noah Webster in 1789. The list includes: *improved* meaning 'employed,' *e.g.*, "*improved* as a tavern"; *notice* as a verb; *advocate* as a verb; *progress* as a verb ("most objectionable of the three"). He also objects to *opposed* ("tho' not a new word") as in "*opposed* to this measure."

More important still in its effect on the development of American English from its beginnings in the seventeenth century was the influence of English writers. In America, as in England, the influence of the Augustan writers remained a dominating one. The story of how Franklin cultivated a literary style by the systematic imitation of the language of the *Spectator* is a classic one. Moreover, the case of Franklin is in many ways typical. Literary models for American use, like models in other forms of art, were provided mainly by England. For manner of expression an English standard was accepted. Like their eighteenth-century Scotch contemporaries, Americans assumed that deviation from English use was faulty. President Wither-

[17] Lyman, *op. cit.*

spoon of Princeton, a Scotchman by birth it is to be noted, in 1781 published a series of essays entitled *The Druid,* of which three, about twenty-five pages in all, were devoted to peculiarities in American speech. In these essays appears for the first time the word *Americanism* coined by Wither-spoon and, to quote his words, "exactly similar in its formation and signification to the word Scotticism." The same deference to English literary authority appears somewhat later in the comments made by the Boston *Review* on Webster's efforts at improving the language. "He must remember," is the comment, "that a volume of the Augustan Age of our literature is of more value than all the play-things of etymology."

The changing fashions of language in English social use also were not without their influence in America. Concerning these ephemeral fashions Cooper remarked somewhat later (1828) : "There is also a slang of society in England, which forms no part of the true language. Most of those who escape the patois, adopt something of the slang of the day. There is also a fashion of intonation in the mother country which it is thought vulgar to omit." An impression of the tendencies in American speech in the decade following the Revolution, and of the conflict between English refinements and affectations and plain American manners may be gained from the plays of that period. In Royall Tyler's *The Contrast* (1787) is exhibited the contrast between the Chesterfieldian manners and mode of speech of Dimple and the honesty and downrightness of the plain American, Manly. At the same time there is exhibited the difference between the American countrified mode of speech and the refinements of speech in American urban life. In the language of the urban characters appear forms of speech such as *the vapours, in the dumps, tiptop, an't* which reflect English colloquial forms familiar in the author's English models, and grammatical forms since rejected but still current in eighteenth-century English use, such as "he looks as if he *was* married." But the principal source of humor is in the manners and the speech of the rustic Jonathan. "Must I buss her?" asks Jonathan. "I told you you must kiss her," he is corrected. "Stretch his legs," Jonathan's phrase, calls forth the exclamation, "What an indelicacy of diction!" Regarding a play at the theater Jenny's remark is, "he [Jonathan] thinks it was a show, as he calls it." The language of Jonathan is interlarded with vulgarisms, most of them older forms of English speech abandoned in cultivated use, American as well as English, but preserved in the conservative environment of country life. There are not only the word *buss,* already mentioned, a Shakespearean word which Davenant had replaced in his Restoration version of *Hamlet,* but *tarnation, such a tarnal rate, topping folks, think on't, by the living jingo, rantipole, chock-full, a sly tike, cute,* all of them in earlier English use. Possibly American in origin are such expressions as *to spark it* (for 'to court'), *shooting irons, dang'd,* and *dumb rich.* The countryman's attempts at urban modes of expression lead him into malapropisms; *hysterics* on his tongue becomes *hystrikes,* and *gallantry* is converted into the plausible form *girl huntry.*

Similar features of language appear in the play *The Politician Out-witted* by Samuel Low published one year later, in 1788. American efforts at cultivation of language are represented by one of the leading characters, Trueman, who is "a professor of Orthography, Analogy, Syntax, and Prosody." The influence of the father appears in the daughter Harriet, in one of whose speeches appears the remark that "in this enlighten'd age, when words are so curiously refin'd and defin'd, modern critics and word-mongers have, in the abundance of their wisdom, made a very nice distinction between them." That Americans of this period, however, or at least the writer of this play, were sensible of the dangers of pedantry in a schoolmastered language appears from the burlesque of learned speech assigned by the playwright to Trueman when he speaks of the "old constitution . . . as superannuated, embecilitated, valetudinarianated, invalidated, enervated and dislocated." The language of the sophisticated characters in the play exhibits many of the features of eighteenth-century language not yet subjected to grammatical rule. The following expressions will illustrate this feature: *You was going to; Who have you here?; Was you not a little nettled?; If there was only one more; If he was here, he wou'dn't deny it; I wou'd not have wrote to him; I have wrote for him; I wish Charles was here now; Was you not?; tell him who it is from; Have who, sir?; No sooner had I began; Ay, that's me; Ah, that's me . . . that's me; She don't love you; of which our sex are . . . susceptible.* An affected manner of speech appears in the pronunciation of the fop Worthnought, represented by spellings such as: *'pan hanor* ('upon honor'), *apportunity, Canquest, prepasterously, Gathic, addity, palitics, canstitutions, astanishing.* One would gladly know precisely the sound represented by this spelling.

But in this play, as in Tyler's *The Contrast*, the principal source of humor is in the language of the countryman, this time named Humphrey. That the language of the country and that cultivated in American city life had grown so far apart is highly significant regarding the sources of language change. Humphrey remarks, "your city folks calls it constitushon; they've got such a queer pronunciation." In the speech of Humphrey appear many of the older forms now surviving only in dialectal use. There appear the pronunciations: *backards and forards, larnt, sartin, desarves, larning, vartuous, ax* ('ask'), *axing, clark, marchant.* Double comparatives and superlatives such as were frequent in Elizabethan times survive in Humphrey's speech, such as *worser and worser, the most carefullest, the most un-luckyest, most largest, most grandest, the more freer the more welcomer.* The new words of cultivated speech offer difficulties to Humphrey as to Jonathan and lead to remarkable malapropisms such as *vandue option,* for 'vendue auction'; *mackinarony,* 'macaroni'; *pollikichens,* 'politicians'; *scratchetary,* 'secretary.'

Eighteenth-century American plays like the two considered, afford interesting evidence of the attention paid to cultivation of language in American urban society and of the wide chasm that was being formed between this cultivated language reduced to something like standard form and the conservative form of speech maintained in rural life unaffected by the new cultural influences. They exhibit also some of the foppish affectations associated with the Chesterfieldian manners of eighteenth-century England and hold up for admiration a plain, downright manner of speech.

American plays of the kind discussed afford a concrete impression of American cultural conditions in the first decade of political independence. They aid one to understand some of the extravagance in the assertions of American independence in language which are heard at this time, when Benjamin Franklin, sent to France in 1778 as diplomatic representative, was instructed to use "the language of the United States." Of this spirit of independence in language probably the best exponent was Noah Webster. In *The American Spelling Book,* published in 1783, which formed "The First part of a Grammatical Institute of the English Language," Webster gives expression to the intense spirit of American nationalism at that time prevalent. "For America," he says, "in her infancy to adopt the present maxims of the old world, would be to stamp the wrinkle of decrepit age upon the bloom of youth, and to plant the seed of decay in a vigorous constitution." In 1785 he dissuaded General Washington from his plan to bring from Great Britain a suitable person to serve as his secretary and as instructor to the Custis children, grandchildren of Mrs. Washington. "What," he asks, "would be thought of this country by European nations, if, after . . . the achievements in the War of Independence . . . we should send to Europe for secretaries, and for men to teach the rudiments of learning?" In a letter written in 1783 he maintains that "America must be as independent in literature as she is in politics, as famous for arts as for arms. . . ." In series of lectures delivered in the principal cities of the country, and in his *Dissertations on the English Language* written in the South, where he was obliged to spend much time in the tedious process of securing copyright for his *Grammatical Institute,* he set forth his ideas regarding language. In the *Dissertations,* published in 1789, and dedicated to Benjamin Franklin, he vigorously denounced methods of teaching in practice, based on the books of English origin by Dilworth, Lowth, and Sheridan. "Young gentlemen," he says, "who have gone through a course of academical studies, and received the usual honors of a university, are apt to contract a singular stiffness in their conversation. . . . Thus they enter the world with such phrases as, *a mean, averse from, if he have, he has gotten,* and others which they deem correct. . . ." "After ten years of study," he says, "I have been able to unlearn a considerable part of what I learnt in early life ; and at thirty years of age, can, with confidence, affirm, that our modern grammars have done more harm than good. The authors have labored to prove, what is obviously absurd, *viz.,* that our language is not made right ; and in pursuance of this idea have tried to make it over again, and persuade the English to speak by Latin rules, or arbitrary rules of their own." In another place he remarks that "it would have been fortunate for the language had the stile [*sic*] of writing and the pronunciation of words been fixed, as they stood in the reign of Queen Ann [*sic*] and her successor." There have been, he thinks, few improvements since; but innumerable corruptions, in pronunciation, introduced by Garrick, and in style by Johnson, Gibbon and their imitators. Characteristic is the following opinion: "Gibbon is one of the *first*, it is hoped he may be the *last*, to attempt the gratification of our *ears*, at the expense of our understanding."

In a course of six lectures delivered in Boston in 1786, the subject for the third, as announced in the *Massachusetts Centinel*, is, "Some differences between the English and Americans considered. Corruption of language in England. Reasons why the English should not be our standard, either in Language or Manners." What were the "corruptions of language" that Webster had in mind, may be learned from a letter to Pickering in the same year, in which he says: "I shall make one General effort to deliver literature and my countrymen from the errors that fashion and ignorance are palming upon Englishmen. The question will then be, whether the Americans will give their opinions and principles as well as their purses to foreigners, and be the dupes of a strolling party of players, who, educated in the school of corruption, have no profession, but to make people laugh, and who, dependent on opinion, for subsistence, must conform to caprice, at the expense of every principle of propriety." Webster, it will be observed, shares the feeling expressed by Tyler in *The Contrast*. The nature, however, and the strength of the forces opposed to Webster's ideals appear in the same letter from his remark: "Two circumstances will operate against me. I am not a *foreigner;*

I am a *New Englandman*. A foreigner ushered in with titles and letters, with half my abilities, would have the whole city in his train."

Webster's ardent support of America's linguistic independence was lifelong. His great masterpiece, the *American Dictionary of the English Language*, published in 1828, the crowning achievement in an active career of nearly a half century, while recognizing that "the body of the language is the same as in England," a sameness which "it is desirable to perpetuate," yet takes into account important differences. In spelling, while abandoning some of the radical changes which, supported by Benjamin Franklin, he had earlier favored, he nevertheless makes a number of well known important modifications, such as: the endings *-or* in *honor, favor,* etc., *-er* in *center, meter,* etc.; a single final consonant in derivatives of *travel, worship,* etc., the forms *mold* and *molt* without *u,* etc., some of which remain distinctively American, some of which have even been adopted in British use. The pronunciation recommended was based in great part on American practice, and new words of American formation were admitted on a parity with words of British origin. Moreover, in his Preface he proclaims his "pride and satisfaction" in placing the names of American writers from Franklin to Irving "as authorities on the same page" with the most distinguished of British writers.

Webster is controlled by the sense of a classical standard to be found in the language prevailing in the Augustan Age of English literature. He resists the changes which, originating "in the English world of fashion," he with others felt to be corrupting the purity of the language. At the same time he aimed to reduce the number of "anomalies," to give to the language greater regularity. In accomplishing this purpose he brought into service the eighteenth-century "principle of analogy" which, along with "universal undisputed practice," in his opinion, formed "the basis of a standard in speaking." He favors the short vowel in the pronunciation of the first syllable in *leisure,* because *pleasure* and *measure* are so pronounced. He disapproves of the "modern fashionable" pronunciation of *European* with the penultimate accent because contrary to the analogy of the pronunciation in *Mediterranean, Pyrenean, Herculean,* and *subterranean.* He objects to the current pronunciation of *Rome* with the *oo* sound because inconsistent with the *o* sound in *Romish* and *Roman.* This disposition to introduce regularity based on analogy, while by no means exclusively American, has nevertheless remained a peculiarly dominating influence in later American speech.

Webster, however, was not able single-handed to establish an entirely independent American standard. That he was unpleasantly aware of the prestige associated with foreign culture appears plainly in the passage from the letter already quoted. That he did not entirely neglect to take it into account is to be seen in the letter from American correspondents in England containing information, solicited by Webster, concerning the pronunciation of the final syllable in such words as *nature.* W. S. Johnson, writing to Webster in 1807, says: "At the time I went to England in 1766 we pronounced in this country the word you mention as if it was spelled *nater.* When I arrived in England I found it was universally pronounced *nature* with the full sound of the *u,* & I heard nothing of the *ch* pronunciation until the latter part of my residence in that country, when I first heard it at the theatre . . . : and I perceived that it was adopted by some of the younger Barristers & Members of Parliament, but had not become common." A letter from another correspondent, O. Ellsworth, written the same year, reports: "I can only say that the standard sound of *u* as practiced in the Universities & by the best informed in London & Bath is *yu;* but that *chu* prevails among other classes . . . as also upon the Stage, of which I believe it to be an affectation." Such letters show that Webster was not entirely independent of English influence. They also show some of the tendencies in the speech of English fashionable society, and in that used on the English stage, which in Webster's opinion were corrupting the language.

Webster met with much opposition from his contemporaries, among whom a colonial attitude of mind persisted. The remarks of the Boston *Review* (1809) have already been quoted. John Quincy Adams in a letter to Webster, in commenting on Webster's treatment of spelling and pronunciation in his *Compendious Dictionary* (1806), says: "I have always considered them as under the absolute dominion of fashion, and as we are in the habit of receiving all our fashions from England, this has regularly been imported with the rest. . . . I do not think it your wish to engage national prejudices or passions in the cause." When Webster adopted the more fashionable mode of pronunciation which he associated with the influence of the stage, he met with criticism. In picturesque phrase Judge Thomas Dames objects to Webster's pronunciation of *Tuesday* as *Chooseday* and *kind* as *keind* which, he says, "sits worse on my stomach than Indian root." But in the face of opposition Webster stood by his guns with admirable fortitude. In a letter written to Joel Barlow in 1807 he maintains his contention that it is desirable "to detach this country as much as possible from its dependence on the mother country." A dependence on England, in his opinion, had the effect of "checking improvement," of putting "an end to inquiry." Such dependence had already been injurious. "Our gentlemen, even in the colleges and professions, rarely question facts and opinions that come from English authors of reputation; hence we have no *spirit of investigation.*"

Opinions regarding American language became more sharply accentuated in the period of the War of 1812. Americans, although politically independent, had continued to look upon England as the mother country. A change in attitude appears in Silliman's *Journal* published in 1810, which is said to be "the first book of travels by an American which attempted to describe and discuss England as though she were actually a foreign land." [18] The change reflects the feeling of the period. As long as Americans were content with the position of colonial dependence, the English were disposed to assume a natural superiority. English revulsion from the ideas of the French Revolution led to contempt for things American associated with these ideas of liberty. Cooper in 1828 [19] says that "a deep settled aversion to America grew in the minds of that portion of the English community who possessed sufficient knowledge to be aware of our existence." In the journals of England, "whenever it was thought necessary to mention America, it was invariably done in terms of disparagement and disgust." The aversion naturally extended to American forms of speech. Americanism to the Englishman became a synonym for vulgarism. "Some itinerant," says Cooper, "hears a gross expression from the lips of a vulgar man in New York, or a horrid oath in the mouth of some blasphemous boatman of the Mississippi, and they are instantly transferred to the pages of works like the Quarterly." Such an attitude was naturally not one to promote a spirit of docility in America. One can readily understand the popular state of feeling that supported the War of 1812. "The War of 1776," says Cooper, "is called the war of the revolution, that of '12 is emphatically termed the war of independence." With the

[18] R. E. Spiller, *The American in England.*
[19] *Notions,* p. 422.

second decade of the nineteenth century, therefore, is to be observed a growing spirit of American independence in language.

The difference that had come to exist between the English of America and that of England was made the subject of a book by John Pickering. While living in London in the years 1799-1801 Pickering had begun observing American peculiarities in expression. Noting that no one had "undertaken the task of making a general collection of them," he engaged in this task. The results of his labors he published in 1816 with the title, *A Vocabulary, or Collection of Words and Phrases which have been supposed to be peculiar to the United States of America.* Of the 500 specimens here exhibited it has since been demonstrated that only 70 are expressions of American origin. Like earlier collectors of Scotticisms, Pickering mistakenly assigned to American origin many forms of expression because he had not met with them in English use. The work, whatever its faults, served to bring out with sharp distinctness the differences in the current speech of the two countries.

What should be done? William Ellery Channing, in the first volume of the *North American Review,* championed the cause of "the American language and literature." But the general trend of opinion favored conformity to English use. Even Webster in later years became less radical. In the half century of his activity he had himself abandoned one radical position after another, notably in the matter of spelling, and his *American Dictionary* of 1828, his final achievement, it is to be noted, was suited not only for American but for English use. The first American edition of 2500 copies was speedily followed by an English edition of 3000 copies. Even the few departures, however, from English use, made his work the subject for attack. Spelling books by Cobb, and a dictionary by Worcester, gained the support of the language Tories. As late as the last decade of the nineteenth century Harvard University, in its English entrance requirements, specified Worcester's dictionary as the authority in spelling. The experience of Webster demonstrated that daring and independence in matters of language found little support in American critical opinion.

American dependence upon England was particularly apparent in the literary language. In colloquial speech often daringly inventive, in writing, Americans have been singularly lacking in independence. There were few literary models of American origin. Pickering, writing in 1816, remarks, "In this country we can hardly be said to have any authors by profession." In 1820, it has been estimated, "not quite one-third of the publications issued in the United States came from American writers." [20]   Under such conditions it was natural for the earlier nineteenth-century American writers to follow the earlier practice of Benjamin Franklin and adopt English models. Hence the lack of independence so strikingly apparent in earlier American literature. Washington Irving in the *Sketch Book,* speaks of "England . . . the fountain head from which the literature of the language flows." Of Americans he says: "We are a young people, necessarily an imitative one, and must take our examples and models, in a great degree, from the existing nations of Europe. . . . There is no country more worthy of our study than England." To English contempt for things American he repeatedly alludes. In his "Advertisement to the First English edition," he says, "The author is aware of the austerity with which the writings of his countrymen have hitherto been treated by British critics." Less seriously, in the "Author's Account of Himself," he remarks, "I had read in the works of various philosophers,

[20] C. A. and M. R. Beard, *The Rise of American Civilization,* I, p. 164.

that all animals degenerated in America, and man among the number." And where can one find a better exhibition of the colonial spirit than in "L'Envoy"? Irving almost cringingly says that he "finds himself writing in a strange land . . . appearing before a public which he had been accustomed, from childhood, to regard with the highest feelings of awe and reverence. He is full of solicitude to deserve their approbation, yet finds that solicitude continually embarrassing his powers and depriving him of that ease and confidence which are necessary to successful exertion."

From the original genius of Poe one might expect daring and independence in language as well as originality in conception. In fact, one finds in Poe the same following of pattern. In so doing he, like Irving, is thus two stages removed from living idiom, that in cultivated colloquial discourse. Poe, to be sure, shows some disposition to rebel. He gives a satirical recipe for the production of "A Blackwood Article" and writes in burlesque an article produced by following his recipe. He complains of the prestige of foreign books. "One might suppose," he says, "that books, like authors, improve by travel . . . their having crossed the sea is, with us, so great a distinction." Yet the deference to a literary standard is apparent in Poe. Note his apology for colloquial use in the following sentence: "It is this latter, in especial, which imparts to a work of art so much of that *richness* (to borrow from colloquy a forcible term) which we are too fond of compounding with the ideal." A colonial attitude toward Wordsworth and Coleridge appears in his remark concerning them: "The diffidence, then, with which I venture to dispute their authority would be overwhelming did I not feel, . . . that learning has little to do with imagination."

James Fenimore Cooper, in theory, was a defender of American independence in language. He speaks of the "extraordinary mental bondage" of Americans during the first ten years of the nineteenth century. Other remarks of his have already been cited. Yet in his own writings he is governed by eighteenth-century English literary standards. He introduced occasional single words or pronunciations to suit particular American characters, but in general employed language as far from natural as are the manners and sentiments of his characters. In *The Prairie* Cooper presents a fine contrast between Doctor Obed Battius, a pedantic scientist vainly trying to reconcile the facts of experience with the doctrines and the nomenclature of his science and, on the other hand, the Trapper, eighty-six years old, whose time had "been mainly passed looking natur' steadily in the face and in reasoning on what I have seen rather than what I've heard in tradition." If Cooper had followed the principles he advocated in language, he would have been guided by the practice of his hero, the old trapper; in reality in the use of language, his principles are more those of the pedantic character whom he holds up to ridicule.

William Cullen Bryant belonged to the Tory school in language. In reprinting in the *Evening Post* the attack made on Webster by Edward S. Gould in 1856, he said that "the English language had been undergoing a process of corruption for the last quarter of a century." [21]   In his editorial capacity he aided the forces of conservatism in a practical way by preparing his well known list of words, many of them Americanisms, which represented the corrupting forces of the time and which were not to be used by writers for the *Evening Post*. Bryant's transatlantic sources of inspiration are illustrated by the remark made by Richard H. Dana to his editorial colleagues in the *North American Review* when the manuscript of poems (including *Thanatopsis*) by the youthful Bryant was under editorial

[21] H. L. Mencken, *The American Language,* p. 253.

consideration. "Ah! Phillips," remarked Dana, "you have been imposed upon; no one on this side of the Atlantic is capable of writing such verses." [22]

The dependence on foreign inspiration, the indirect relation to American life, in the great New England writers, is too much a matter of common knowledge to need further rehearsal here. "Refinement of temper, conscientious sense of form, and instinctive neglect of actual fact, remained the most characteristic traits, if not of American life, at least of American letters," says Barrett Wendell. A consequence has been that, to quote further from the same critic, "despite our superficial modernity, America has lagged behind that older world [as Noah Webster had predicted] with which it has not been at one for more than two hundred years."

But after all, why repeat what has long ago been so well said? The voice of Noah Webster sounds anew in 1848 in Lowell's *Fable for Critics*, the jingling verse of which carries the tune of America's literary slavery.

The most of you (this is what strikes the beholders)
Have a mental and physical stoop in the shoulders;
Though you ought to be free as the wind and the waves,
You've the gait and the manners of runaway slaves;
Though you brag of your New World, you don't half believe
        in it;
And as much of the Old as is possible weave in it;
Your goddess of freedom, a tight, buxom girl,
With lips like a cherry and teeth like a pearl,
With eyes bold as Here's, and hair floating free,
And full of the sun as the spray of the sea,
Who can sing at a husking or romp at a shearing,
Who can trip through the forests alone without fearing,
Who can drive home the cows with a song through the grass,
Keeps glancing aside into Europe's cracked glass,

[22] B. Wendell, *A Literary History of America*, p. 218.

Hides her red hands in gloves, pinches up her lithe waist,
And makes herself wretched with transmarine taste;
She loses her fresh country charm when she takes
Any mirror except her own rivers and lakes.
You steal Englishmen's books and think Englishmen's thought,
With their salt on her tail your wild eagle is caught;
Your literature suits its each whisper and motion
To what will be thought of it over the ocean.

CHAPTER XX

THE NINETEENTH CENTURY

Sacred Interpreter of human thought,
How few respect or use thee as they ought!

F OR the kind of sentimental regret here expressed by
Cowper, in the England and America of the early
nineteenth century there remained little substantial ground.
From the time of Lindley Murray on, the rule of the
grammarian and the lexicographer came to be generally
recognized even if not always followed. Their authority
was recognized in the cultivated speech of English country
life. Mr. Allen in Jane Austen's *Northanger Abbey* objects
to Catherine Morland's use of the word *nicest*. "You had
better change it," he tells her, "or we shall be overpowered
by Johnson and Blair." Their influence penetrated even
the backwoods of America. Davy Crockett, in his *Autobiography* (1834), at least recognizes the existence of grammar, although he says, "I hadn't time to learn it, and make
no pretensions to it." "We lived in the backwoods," he
says, "and didn't profess to know much, and no doubt
used many wrong words." Although he asserts that grammar is "pretty much of nothing at last," he nevertheless
saw to it that his writings were "run over by a friend or so"
who made "some little alterations . . . in the spelling and
grammar."

If among the unlearned the authority of the grammarian
was recognized, among the learned it was all but supreme.
"Why," asks Hannah More (1745-1833), "in teaching language to youth do you sedulously infuse into his mind the
rudiments of syntax? Why in parsing is he led to refer

every word to its part of speech, to resolve every sentence
into its element, to reduce every word to its original. . . .
Why all this, but because you wish him to be grounded in
his acquirements? Why, but because you are persuaded
that a slight and slovenly and superficial and irregular way
of Instruction will never train him to excellence in anything?" L. H. Hunt, the author of *A Syntax of the English
Language* (1823?), who adopts these words for use on his
title page, elaborates further and asserts that syntax is "a
thing which marks the education of a person young or old;
without which the pretence to gentility is revolting, and
with which, a person in humble life is tolerable, if not
interesting." The change that has come over English ideals
in language is striking. One should recall the language,
only a hundred years back, of De Foe's *Compleat English
Gentleman*, that of Squire Western, and that in the letters
of the Verney and the Wentworth families.

Correctness in language was not the concern only of the
prig and the pedant. In 1823 a *Grammar of the English
Language* was produced by a man of distinctly unacademic
type, the prolific and forceful journalist, William Cobbett.
"In the immense field of knowledge," says Cobbett, "innumerable are the paths, and Grammar is the gate of entrance to them all." Cobbett's grammar, a work distinctly
practical in character, has been many times reissued down
to our own time. It is composed in the form of letters to
his son James "now arrived at the age of fourteen years."
But it is intended for wider service, "for the Use of Schools
and of Young Persons in general; but more especially for
the Use of Soldiers, Sailors, Apprentices, and Plough-boys."
Grammar is thus brought down to the popular level, for
which Cobbett assigns a patriotic reason, for as he remarks
in his Dedication to Queen Caroline, "Royalty has, in the
hour of need, no efficient supporters but The People."

An interesting feature in the development of English grammar is the way in which the grammarian of one generation adopts as subject for criticism the language of the most eminent authorities of the period preceding. In this respect Cobbett follows precedent. Little a respecter of eminence, he subjects the language even of Blair and of Blackstone to criticism. He dares to differ with Lowth in his judgment of certain constructions. Lowth's condemnation of such expressions as *It is the dews and showers that make* he dismisses as "an opinion which arose from want of a little more reflection." Letter 149 is devoted to "Specimens of False Grammar, Taken from the writings of Doctor Johnson and from those of Doctor Watts." Not only does he show little respect for earlier grammarians, but he even dares attack the King's English, for Letter 22 is devoted to "Errors and Nonsense in a King's Speech."

Giving to logic and analogy a position of authority above that of natural usage, Cobbett condemns a number of idiomatic expressions of most respectable lineage. Blair's use of *it had been better omitted* for *would have been better to omit it,* he condemns as "a sheer vulgarism, like *I had as lief be killed as enslaved,*" which, he says "ought to be *I would as lief.*" He condemns the expressions *very honest* and *extremely just* on the logical grounds that "a man cannot be more honest than another." Governed apparently by a feeling for analogy, he condemns the expression *The Noble Countess was eloped,* which exemplifies a construction still not uncommon in good use, particularly in England. "It should be *had* eloped," asserts Cobbett. Governed by the principle of analogy, he conceives an aversion for irregular verbs, and is led to support the analogically formed preterit forms: *blowed, bursted, casted, clinged, drawed, freezed, growed, meaned, slinged, splitted, springed, stinged, strided, sweeped, swimmed, swinged, throwed, thrusted, weaved, weeped.* Into such absurdities are led the clearest and most independent of thinkers when they deviate from the path of established usage into that of theory.

Shaken in one's faith in the infallibility of the grammarian by such exhibitions of arbitrary assumption of authority, one approaches the consideration of later grammarians with misgivings. Here again one meets with new assumption of power, the application of more rigid rule and lack of respect for earlier authority or for rival contemporary grammarians.

The amount of attention, however, given to the study of grammar in England and in America in the first half of the nineteenth century is a matter of great significance. The success of Lindley Murray's book, which was so great a surprise to the author, is still a subject for wonder and amazement. In the course of 11 years his larger *English Grammar* ran through 20 editions in England and twice that many in America and the *Abridgment* through 20 editions in England, 30 in America. Such success was sure to stimulate imitation and rivalry. A dozen men produced new editions or abridgments of his books, and before 1850 it has been estimated there had appeared 200 editions with a total of between 1,500,000, and 2,000,000 copies.[1] The expanding interest in the subject of grammar following Murray's work appears from statistics of grammars in America recently assembled. The number of grammars written by Americans and printed in America before 1800 is estimated at about 30, of which 18 were produced between 1790 and 1800. In the following decades the production was continuous; 14 between 1800 and 1810, 41 between 1811 and 1820, 81 between 1821 and 1830, 63 between 1831 and 1840, 66 between 1841 and 1850.[2]

[1] R. L. Lyman, *English Grammar in American Schools before 1850.*
[2] *Ibid.*

Murray's popularity in America was at its height about 1833. But he had important rivals. Of rival works the most popular, judged by circulation, were the grammars by Jeremiah Greenleaf (3d ed., 1821), Goold Brown (1823), Roswell Smith (1824) and Samuel Kirkham (1825). Of these works, all of which had wide circulation, the most popular was that of Kirkham, which passed through 94 editions between 1829 and 1851 and of which, its author boasts, 60,000 copies were sold in a year. "Since the days of Lowth," says Kirkham, "no other grammar, Murray's only excepted, has been so favorably received by the publick." The end of the half century was marked by the publication of an encyclopedic work, *The Grammar of English Grammars* (1851) by Goold Brown. In this gigantic work of more than 1100 pages Brown offers the results of a lifetime of study and observation. He displays a remarkable range of knowledge of grammatical opinions and theories, ancient and modern, and the theories derived from others he supplements by original judgments, which are supported by observations, wide in range, of the usage of English writers. The significant feature of this work is the basis adopted by the writer for his judgments. Abandoning the classical doctrine of usage the mistress of language, adopted by Priestley as the guiding principle and recognized by Murray and Noah Webster as a principal source of authority, he adopted as a guiding principle a statement by Quintilian (Lib. i, Cap. 6) that "language is established by reason, antiquity, authority, and custom." He points out that Quintilian makes reason the principal thing and asserts further that "of reason the chief ground is analogy, but sometimes etymology." With this whole-hearted adoption of reason as the principal basis for judgment in language, a principle to which Murray and Webster had given only half-hearted allegiance, Brown was in position to find fault with the language of English writers early and late. This he proceeds to do, and for the exhibition of "improprieties" and "false syntax" he selects examples from the English Bible and from classical English writers from the sixteenth century down. Most striking, in the lists of expressions that Brown in his turn subjects to criticism, is the number of examples derived from other grammatical writers. From Johnson, from Blair, from Murray, and particularly from his contemporary Kirkham, he selects modes of expression for which in his "key" he offers corrected forms.

This *Grammar of English Grammars,* admirable in the wealth of information assembled, is, at the same time, like the grammar by Cobbett, an interesting exhibition of the danger of setting theory above practice. It provides subject for ironic humor in its exhibition of a form of perversity which seems at all times to be an attribute of the genus grammarian. At the same time, historically considered, it has its significance because of the sharp distinctness in which it brings out the conflict so frequent in language between the regularity supported by reason and analogy and the anomaly in idiomatic expression based on natural usage. In this work the schoolmaster grammarian ceases to be the recorder of established practice and becomes the autocratic imposer of law.

The attention paid to the study of grammar is related both as cause and effect to a changed attitude toward the use of English. Correctness in language, which in the days of De Foe and Addison and Swift was often regarded in fashionable circles as a mark of pedantry, by the beginning of the nineteenth century had become established as a test of cultivation. "Vulgar expressions," Lord Chesterfield had said, "imply either a very low turn of mind, or low education, and low company." "A false accent, or a mistaken syllable," says Ruskin in the new century, "is enough, in the parliament of any civilized nation, to assign to a man a certain degree of inferior standing forever." To raise popular speech to the level of refinement was a process of time. In the early nineteenth century, however, a change in attitude is apparent. Cobbett's professed purpose should be held in mind. Lists of words with pronunciation differing from spelling which had been features of earlier grammars like those of Watts and Dilworth were succeeded by lists of words and expressions now labelled "vulgarisms." Survivals of earlier irregular forms of speech became marks of vulgarity in the speech of the classes made familiar by the novels of Dickens.

An interesting stage in the refinement of speech is exhibited in the *Anecdotes of the English Language* published by Samuel Pegge in 1803, which lists not only certain "heinous charges and grievous offences" such as the double comparative and double superlative and the redundant negative, which, he points out, come down from the time of Shakespeare, but some of the "little peccadillos" in words whose pronunciation is "a little deformed by the natives of London." Among these Londonisms Pegge includes the familiarly known shifting of the sounds represented by *v* and *w* as in *weal, winegar,* etc., and the pronunciations: *curous, curosity, stupendious, attackted, gownd, shay, partender* ('partner'), *argufy, kiver* ('cover') and the group of words, *daater* ('daughter'), *saace* ('sauce'), *saacer* ('saucer'), *saacy* ('saucy') which, he says, "savour rather of an affected refinement."

As remarked in an earlier chapter, in the late eighteenth century the corruptions which were bringing about a degeneration in the English language had been a matter of great concern. This concern was especially felt by the Scotch critics, who were humbly disposed to accept the idea that Scotch influence was a principal source of this corruption. In zeal for the purity of English no one surpassed James Beattie. In a letter written in 1790 [3] Beattie, speaking of the notes appended to a new edition of the *Tatler*, describes the language as "full of those new-fangled phrases and barbarous idioms that are now so much affected by those who form their style from political pamphlets and those pretended speeches in parliament that appear in newspapers. Should this jargon continue to gain ground among us, English literature will go to ruin. During the last twenty years, especially since the breaking out of the American war, it has made alarming progress. . . . If I live to execute what I propose on the writings and genius of Addison, I shall at least enter my protest against the practice; and by exhibiting a copious specimen of the new phraseology, endeavor to make my reader set his heart against it."

The task that Beattie had proposed for himself was carried out in part by an anonymous writer in 1826 in a book entitled *The Vulgarities of Speech Corrected*. This work, composed, it is to be noted, "for the use of those who are unacquainted with grammar," is really a book of speech etiquette, aiming to provide "elegant expressions for provincial and vulgar English, Scots, and Irish."

In his remarks on pronunciation the author refers to the different modes still prevailing among good speakers: the varying manner of placing the accent in *miscellany* and *revenue,* the two ways of pronouncing *wind*. He alludes to the practice among the "vulgar-genteel" of pronouncing *whole* and *above* with the vowel sound of *who,* evidently a survival of a mode of pronunciation which the evidence of Wharton's grammar (1655) indicates as prevalent in the seventeenth century. He speaks of the double pronunciation

---

[3] Quoted by T. R. Lounsbury, *The Standard of Usage,* p. 33.

of *gold* and *Rome* (*o* or *oo*) among the "best speakers," but expresses a preference for the *o* sound.

He offers interesting information regarding a growing tendency to reverse the natural order and to make the spoken language conform to the written. As instances of "vulgar book-speaking" he cites the pronunciation *buzziness* and *buzzy* instead of *bizness* and *bizzy* and of *suggar* instead of *shoogar*. He condemns the growing practice of "sounding the silent letters" in *could, would, should, castle, hustle*. A "vulgar" mode of pronunciation he indicates by the spellings, *apostle, bankruptcy*, etc., of which the "correct sound" is represented by *apossle, bankrupcy*, etc.

He condemns the "contraction or rather mispronunciation of *ing* as *in*" which, he says, is "extremely common in all parts of the empire," and the mistakes with initial *h* and with initial *v* and *w*, which he says are not confined to London "but may be met with in every part of England." He comments on the sounding of a final *r* at the close of words ending in *a* or *o*, as in *idearr, mammarr, paparr, winderr, fellerr, hollerr, Elizer, Mariar, yeller, larr* ('law'), *arr* ('awe'), *jarr* ('jaw'), which he says is to be heard "in most parts of England, but most particularly in London, and along the South and East coasts." He speaks of the silent *r* in the London pronunciation of *pul* ('pearl'), *wuld* ('world'), *ghell* or *gul* ('girl'), *cawt* ('cart'), *cawd* ('card'), in which he holds that the *r* should be "sounded, though but slightly." His comment on the pronunciation of *a* is significant and confirmatory of conclusions reached regarding pronunciation of the eighteenth century. Among the vulgarisms of London he lists the "sounding of *a* long as in *far* for *a* short as in *man*" in such pronunciations as *chawnce, dawnce, pawrt, bawnkeet, awfter, glawss*, etc.

In the pronunciation of the words beginning with *c* or *g* this writer revolts somewhat from the authority of Walker.

He lists as "vulgar" such pronunciations as *kyar* ('car'), *kyarat* ('carat'), *kyarrot* ('carrot'), *ghyarden* ('garden'), *reghyard* ('regard'); on the other hand, with the "short sounds of *a* after *c* or *g*," the case is different. Words such as *captain, cannot, candle, cant,* and *garret, garrison, gallop, gambler,* he asserts, are correctly pronounced as *kyaptain,* etc., and *ghyarret,* etc.

Most definite and most decided, however, are the directions of this writer regarding the pronunciation of words with "long u." In words such as *suit, suicide, superfluous,* etc., the "correct sound of the *u* . . . is precisely the same as in *you*." "To a correct ear," the sounding of long *u* like *oo,* instead of *you,* in words such as *duty, produce, due, dew, Kew, steward, lieu, Luke, lunar, music, new,* etc., "appears extremely offensive and vulgar."

In the pronunciation of the early nineteenth century there were evidently many cross currents. There was difficulty in adjusting a correct mode of pronunciation with a correct mode of writing, and there resulted variance in opinion and variation in use. That speech in its progress toward a uniform standard of correctness lagged behind the language of writing and of formal discourse appears from the remarks of this writer. "Most women," he asserts, "and all ordinary people in general, speak in defiance of all grammar." "Nothing," he says, "is more common, nor more offensive than such . . . expressions as *more greater, most beautifulest, more prettier, most commonest*." He condemns the current use of the double negative and of expressions such as *chiefest, the very first, the very best, them* for *these* or *those,* and such locutions as *who do you lodge with?* and *it is him* or *it is me you mean.* Such evidence offers interesting suggestion of the nature of popular speech before the influence of Murray and his fellow grammarians had had its full effect. This writer recommends the avoidance of the contracted forms: *isn't, wa'nt, wer'n't, won't,* etc. But these forms, he asserts, "from being more universally used, are not so vulgar as *a'n't.*" The discrimination made is a strange one, and the singling out of this one particular form for special stigma affords an illustration of the way individual forms and expressions may become branded and associated with vulgarity.

An interesting change that was in progress appears in this writer's remarks on the pronunciation of foreign names. "Gottingen" [*sic*], he says, "when pronounced as it is spelled, is well understood in Britain." This older pronunciation Gottingen still survives in a street name in Halifax, Nova Scotia. "But," this writer continues, "if a pedant were to pronounce it Yettingen in the German fashion, it would be quite unintelligible to the mere English scholar. . . . The name of the celebrated Goethe, is also pronounced by pedants, vain of their German scholarship, as if it were written with a French *u* Gutté, and sometimes Ghetté, both of which are unintelligible to the English scholar. . . . Calais also is pedantically called *Calay,* Lyons is called *Leeong,* the late king of France is called Louee . . . and the present king Sharl, instead of Charles." The habit of trying to reproduce the foreign sounds in foreign names seems to have been new at the time of this book. The earlier anglicized pronunciation of *Dieppe, Calais, Rheims,* etc., appears from earlier works that have been quoted in the present volume. The attitude of our anonymous writer of a century ago is much like that of the scholars promoting the present-day Society for Pure English.

But the greatest interest in this book lies in the comments on words and forms of expression in his mind associated with vulgarity. The use of oaths is out of fashion. Swearing, our author asserts, is a "pernicious habit, which is at present extremely rare among the well-educated classes, and is only to be heard from the profane lips of some hoary disciple of the fashions of the last age. . . . The only oath which I can recollect of lately meeting with, in circles that have any pretension to fashion, is *by Jove!*" The bluff manner of the Elizabethan Age belongs to the past. The Restoration license in speech has been superseded. The Victorian Age is near at hand.

Somewhat more venial are the "Vulgar Bye-Words and Exclamations." One will recall Swift and his notebook collecting the bromidic expressions in the "Polite Conversation" of the early eighteenth century. To such expressions our anonymous writer of a century later devotes about thirty pages of his book. Among the expressions listed appear: *He has caught a Tartar; It stands to reason; To raise the wind,* 'procure money'; *To box Harry,* 'to shift for money'; *To sow wild oats; Not by any chance; Mum is the word; All my eye and Betty Martin; Figs and Fiddlesticks.* Some of these are attributed to dialectal or colonial influence: *I guess* and *I calculate* are called American; *That is great* and *Bother me!* or *Botheration!* are called Irish; and *Sorrow tak me* is labelled as Scotch.

Vulgar proverbs and vulgar comparisons, such as *As proud as Lucifer,* are exhibited in long lists followed by lists of learned, pedantic, and professional vulgarities. Among professional vulgarities he lists the "mercantile phrases": *Ditto to that, per, via, sundries, a pretty piece of goods, a concern, a good spec, minus, a pretty article.* Among legal phrases he lists: *subject matter, rejoinder, rebut, moot point, the said man, set-off, put the case, party, parcel* (for 'portion'). To military influence he assigns the words: *quarters* and *muster.* The Chesterfieldian refinement of speech which Johnson had undertaken in gingerly fashion, is here undertaken in a confident manner. Many of the expressions, it is of interest to note, appear in the lists of proscribed expressions in the books of later purists and in the style sheets of later publishers.

Most interesting from the point of view of today is the discussion of the "slang vulgarities" of a hundred years ago. One must, of course, bear in mind that the word *slang* in the eighteenth century had a meaning different from that of today and in the early nineteenth century was only beginning to take its present meaning. If one will bear this difference in mind, and will not make the mistake of accepting all the expressions quoted as of fresh coinage, one may learn from the book under consideration many interesting details of the colloquial speech of a century ago.

"It is but very recently," remarks this author, "that the peculiar language of vagabonds, pick-pockets, swindlers, professed boxers, and horse jockies, has obtained a partial currency among some of the middle, and even of the upper, ranks of society; and in consequence of this, a few of the terms and expressions which are known under the various names of slang, cant, or flash language, have been introduced into common discourse." As examples he cites words such as *bore* and *rum one.* "If," he continues, "I should be asked what I mean by slang, I would answer . . . that it is chiefly what was originally invented, and is still used, like the cipher of diplomatists, for the purposes of secrecy, and and as a means of eluding officers." This form of language, he continues, "is subject to continual change, yet the greater part of it has remained unchanged for centuries." Words used in the plays of Beaumont and Fletcher and of Ben Jonson, he asserts, are still to be heard in St. Giles's and at the Fives Court. As instances he cites the words: *prig,* 'to steal'; *fib,* 'to beat'; *prancers,* 'horses'; *duds; cove;* et al.

As causes of diffusion of this mode of speech, this writer mentions the extensive circulation of newspaper reports of boxing matches, memoirs of pick-pockets, such as those of Harry Vaux, and police-office reports. As examples he cites the words: *do*, 'cheat'; *done*, 'ruined'; *row*, (University of Cambridge language); *blow up*, 'scold'; *heavy wet*, 'porter'; *jacky* or *blue rain*, 'gin'; *knowledge box*, 'head'; *daylights* or *peepers*, 'eyes'; *grinders* and *ivories*, 'teeth'; *listeners*, 'ears'; *natives*, 'a sort of oysters,' a name applied to Londoners, hence the expression, "astonish the natives."

There follows a long list of words and locutions, some of which, the author remarks, have become reputable later. The list occupies ten pages. Some of the more interesting examples coming first in the alphabetical list, are: *against the grain; all agog; back out; saved his bacon; badgered into it; a baker's dozen; bilk*, 'cheat'; *Billingsgate; in black and white; to look blank*, 'disappointed'; *blarney; a blind*, 'deception'; *to bolt; done brown; kick the bucket; cut capers;* etc. Obviously to exclude all locutions of this kind would be to bring the language to a purely bookish standard.

This English account of the vulgarisms at the end of the first quarter of the nineteenth century, strange to say, does not offer a list of Americanisms. But Scotch vulgarisms received attention. Boswell's admonition to his countrymen not to attempt an English pronunciation is echoed with the warning that one making such an attempt is "almost certain of going into ludicrous affectation," and a list of forms classed as "Vulgar Scotch" is provided, including: *almost never; by-gone; curt, curtly, curtness*, 'brief,' etc.; *close the door*, 'shut the door'; *head* or *foot* of a table, 'upper' or 'lower' end; *poorly*, 'in ill health'; *huckster*, 'chandler'; *it makes great odds*, 'difference'; *a queer man*, 'comical' or 'humorous'; *simply impossible*, 'quite impossible'; he will *some day* repent, 'one day'; *yard*, 'garden.' The author evidently draws from earlier lists of

Scotticisms by Beattie and Campbell and Elphinston, and, like his Scotch predecessors, he is not always correct in his assignment of expressions to Scotch origin. The list, however, suggests the provincial source of many locutions later generally adopted in English, and particularly, in American use.

The spirit of purism was evidently actively alive in the early nineteenth century. The sense of a classical perfection to be striven for survived from the eighteenth century. The language must not only be made more regular, but it must be protected from the corrupting influences that were felt to be on all sides. Vulgarisms were to be avoided and new words, if they were to be tolerated, must conform not only to analogy but to good taste. Most zealous in the cause of purism was Walter Savage Landor, who regretted that Bishop Lowth and Horne Tooke, who were separated by political enmity, might not have joined forces in the defense of the mother tongue in order "to stop innovations and to diminish the anomalies of our language." Landor objects to the word *execute* used for 'put to death' because this meaning is not directly to be derived from the Latin original. He appears to be entirely unaware that *execute* in the sense objected to had been in standard English use from the fifteenth century on. His objection proved as unavailing as has been the later more valid objection to the new formation, *electrocute*. He objects to the redundancy of the words *good* or *bad* attached to *orthography,* of which the etymological meaning is obviously 'correct writing.' On similar grounds he condemns *examine into* and *under the circumstances.* In other instances, as in his judgments concerning words such as *horse-laugh, gossamer, island* and *whites,* he betrays ignorance of the etymology upon which his criticism is supposed to be based.

Landor had a special abhorrence of hybrid words. "It

disturbs me," he writes, "to find, in Southey, . . . the word *rewrite.* I had thought it, and *reread,* the spawn infecting a muddier and shallower water. Properly *re* should precede none but words of Latin origin, though there are a few exceptions of some date and authority." Truly the mother tongue is a breeder of prejudices. The example of Landor may be taken as a lesson in the dangers of incompetence in passing judgment on forms of language. To the work of Lounsbury, from whom most of the cited illustrations have been borrowed, the reader is referred for an eloquent account of Landor and his "devil of derivation."

The puristic spirit which Landor exemplifies in so unadmirable a fashion, was widely prevalent in his day. Macaulay in a letter (May 28, 1831) records that Lady Holland objected to certain words. Macaulay appends his own objection to *talented, influential,* and *gentlemanly.* "I never could break Sheridan," he says, "of saying 'gentlemanly' though he allowed it was wrong." Many of the words coming into use in this period, such as *reliable, environment, lengthy,* had to run the gauntlet of criticism, and a number of them, unable entirely to outgrow the stamp of impropriety with which they were branded at this time, have continued to appear among the proscribed expressions listed in the style sheets of later publishing houses.

The objection attached to certain words was also raised against certain phrases and constructions. One should recall the storm of controversy regarding the progressive passive form of the verb. This new form, of which the phrase *being built* is usually taken as the typical example, had begun to creep into use in the eighteenth century. It is now so thoroughly established and so familiar that it is not easy to conceive of the feeling of an earlier time when it grated on the nerves of the purist like a neologism. That the sensitive ear was keenly alive to the novelty appears from the parenthetic phrase in De Quincey's remark, "not done, not even (according to modern purism) *being done,*" in which De Quincey by the word *purism* means 'exactness.' Macaulay studiously avoids the expression. It finds its way, however, into the writings of Southey, Lamb, Coleridge and even of Landor. It has been condemned by the American philologian George P. Marsh as "corruption in language" and objected to by many others but particularly by Richard Grant White, who devotes to the subject a whole chapter of his book, *Words and their Uses*. "The full absurdity of this phrase," he says, "the essence of its nonsense, seems not hitherto to have been pointed out." It is "a new phrase which has nothing of force or of accuracy in its favor." It is not "consistent with reason" and not "conformed to the normal development of the language." It is "a monstrosity, the illogical, confusing, inaccurate, unidiomatic character of which I have, at some length, but yet imperfectly, set forth." "In fact, it means nothing, and is the most incongruous combination of words that ever attained respectable usage in any civilized language." The very vehemence of the language betrays the writer's sense of weakness in his position. In the heated controversy over this expression between White and Fitzedward Hall, the wealth of epithets applied by White prevailed little against the array of facts from English usage and the analogical support brought forward by his opponent. The language of White is quoted here in illustration of the extremes in unreasonableness that may be reached by one assuming an individual authority in the public domain of language.

Somewhat similar to the history of the *is being built* construction in the nineteenth century is that of the phrases, *had rather* and *had better*. These last expressions, however, unlike the disputed passive construction, were not objected to as new creations, since both had by the eighteenth century been long in use. The origin of these expressions has been traced in an earlier chapter. In the eighteenth century the apparent anomaly of *have rather* caught the attention of Samuel Johnson, who pronounced it "a barbarous expression" and said it was better to say *will rather*. Johnson's objections were echoed by Sheridan and Lowth, and in the nineteenth century were sounded anew by Landor and a number of later writers. It is interesting to note that, in spite of objections, *had rather* has retained in later usage an equal place with its somewhat older competitor, *would rather*, preferred by Johnson and the purists who followed him.

The combination *had better* had a similar experience. Aversion to the anomalous in language led to the introduction of a rival form, *would better*, mistakenly assumed to be the correct expansion of the contracted forms, *I'd better*, *he'd better*, etc. This neologism won the support of Landor and was adopted by Browning in later years due to the magisterial authority of his friend.[4] The new form, however, has not had wide adoption. The present writer has noted the use of *had better* by such eminent writers as Hazlitt, Jane Austen, Kipling, Hawthorne, Henry James, Quiller-Couch, Lady Gregory, Conrad, Brander Matthews, Dickens, Wilde, Saintsbury, Barrie, Shaw, Holmes, and Samuel Butler. On the other hand he has met with the artificial form *would better* in the use of no recent British writer of reputation and in the use of only a small minority of American writers.[5]

Another "danger" sign on the route to good English was set up in the first part of the nineteenth century and now bears the inscription "split infinitive." The earliest objection to this construction cited by Fitzedward Hall [6] is from

[4] Lounsbury, *op. cit.*, pp. 150-1.
[5] *Cf. American Speech*, I, 15, 16.
[6] *American Journal of Philology*, III, 17-24.

Mr. Richard Taylor, who in 1840 complained that "Some writers of the present day have a disagreeable affectation of putting an adverb between *to* and the infinitive." Dean Alford refers to this practice as "entirely unknown to English speakers and writers," and the attitude of the purist toward this expression has been generally one of hostility. The striking label "split infinitive" which, succeeding an earlier "cleft infinitive," has been attached to the form of expression, on the one hand begs the question by an assumption that *to* is an integral part of the infinitive, on the other hand has had the effect of singling out the expression for special attention. Whereas faulty forms of construction unlabelled may pass unnoticed, this construction by its label catches the eye and, although popularly regarded as a peccadillo, is felt to be a typical feature of careless writing. A recent writer, Cosmo Hamilton, speaks of his task as editor of "going over a mass of proof to watch for split infinitives and the small inaccuracies."

This much discussed construction is not, as often supposed, a modernism in English. Instances of its use have been pointed out from the fourteenth century down. Its use, however, has not been frequent until modern times. Recent observation by the present writer of the usage of English writers before the nineteenth century has brought to light a surprisingly small number of instances. In comparatively recent times instances have been cited from the most fastidious of writers, from Samuel Johnson, Macaulay, Matthew Arnold, Henry James. These instances, however, indicate not habitual, but occasional, use by these writers. More remarkable is the infrequency of its use by the very writers who are its most outspoken champions. In the history of the language the objection to the construction is of significance mainly as one more instance of the efforts of the purist type of critic to bring the language to a **fixity** in form, an effort in this case made more than usually effective through the force of the epithet.

English purism voiced by men like Cheke in the sixteenth century, developing under the influence of the critical taste of the Augustan Age, and formulated in the dictionaries and grammars and rhetorics of the later eighteenth century, was evidently a powerful force in the nineteenth century. It was a conservative force. In the avoidance of threatened "corruption" of a language assumed to have reached a classic perfection, bookish authority ranked above current use. Browning is said to have "enlarged his vocabulary by the diligent study of Johnson." A Victorian attitude is that of Cardinal Newman. In language as in religion Newman ardently favored guarding what the past has bequeathed. "When a language has been cultivated," he says, "and so far as it has been generally perfected, an existing want has been supplied, and there is no need of further workmen." The ideal of a classical perfection attained, thus voiced in the nineteenth century, had been generally prevalent in the preceding century. An extreme instance of the adoption of a definite classical model appears in the case of Fox, who in his history announced the purpose to use no words not to be found in Dryden. The English writings which provided the basis for the authority in Johnson's *Dictionary*, as has been pointed out, were limited in range, and yet the American scholar, Witherspoon,[7] in 1784 accepts Johnson as a final authority on the assumption that in his *Dictionary* Johnson had "collected every word, good and bad, that was ever used by any English writer." Deviation in the use of words from the path made by predecessors and marked by the lexicographer was a departure from classical perfection.

The observance of all the laws laid down by grammarians

[7] *Works,* IV, p. 472.

and the avoidance of all the expressions branded by the purists, would have left little chance for growth in the language. The Sanskrit language was thus put in a strait-jacket, but Sanskrit became a dead language. Latin also, brought to strict Ciceronian form by the lacing processes of the sixteenth century, ceased to be a living language. The English language resisted this treatment. Signs of revolt had appeared at an early date. Listen to the words of the writer who in the opinion of Johnson "wrote like an angel" even if he did speak "like poor Poll." "Rules," says Goldsmith,[8] "will never make either a work or a discourse eloquent. . . . Examine a writer of genius on the most beautiful parts of his work, and he will always assure you that such passages are generally those that have given him the least trouble. . . . A good preacher should adopt no model, write no sermons, study no periods; let him but understand his subject, the language he speaks, and be convinced of the truth he delivers." One should recall in this connection the judgment of Noah Webster (1789), already cited, on the style of Gibbon. Goldsmith's opinion of the efforts of the purists may be inferred from another of his remarks. In his essay on *The Present State of Polite Learning,* he says that "by the power of one monosyllable our critics have almost got the victory over humour amongst us. Does the poet paint the absurdities of the vulgar, he is *low;* does he exaggerate the features of folly to render it thoroughly ridiculous, he is then *very low.*"

A like opinion has in an earlier chapter been cited from Fielding. Somewhat similar in its defense of the natural as opposed to the artificial was the opinion expressed by Colman [9]: "Every language, more especially the English, has its idioms, which we should not register, with gram-

[8] *Of Eloquence,* 1759.
[9] *The Gentleman,* No. 3.

marians and lexicographers, among its irregularities, but with poets and orators, number among its beauties." The feeling of Noah Webster was much the same. He refers, it will be recalled, to a "singular stiffness" in the conversation of men academically trained, an artificiality which, he boasts, "after ten years of study" he has been able in great part to unlearn. In England also a century ago youth resisted artificial rule. Always rebellious, in language youth broke out of bounds. The priggish author of *Vulgarities Corrected* speaks with regret of the "unintelligible jargon affected by those youths whose money and influence enable them to take the lead at Harrow and Eton, as well as at Oxford and Cambridge."

In the early nineteenth century there are apparent, as in the time of Caxton, in the time of Shakespeare, in the time of Dryden, in the time of Swift, two opposing forces contending for the control of the language. The alignment of the forces was but little changed. On the one side were aligned men like Goldsmith and Colman contending for free play of the natural tendencies in the language. These forces were supported by the vivacious spirit of youth, eternally irrepressible. On the other side were aligned the forces contending for a classical regularity in grammatical forms and for a decorous propriety in the use of words.

The conflict between these forces is an eternal one, and fortunately so. Progress in language, as in political government, has been a product of living energies checked by conservative control. In this conflict at the stage reached in the early nineteenth century, the Romantic movement had a share. Wordsworth, it will be recalled, in his Preface to the *Lyrical Ballads* (1798), announced his purpose "as far as possible to adopt the very language of man." In carrying out this purpose he abandoned the conventional modes of expression, "what is usually called poetic diction."

Coleridge, to be sure, objected that the "real language of men" is not the exclusive property, as Wordsworth assumed, of the rustic. A reaction, however, from eighteenth-century artificiality was a product of the movement.

The restriction of the English vocabulary which was promoted by the classicizing tendencies of the eighteenth century was appreciably loosened by the spirit which produced the Romantic movement. One should recall the eighteenth-century judgment of Milton's language, expressed by the phrase "quaint uncouthness." From this spirit of dislike to liberties taken with words and to the use of older words there was a reaction. There came a new estimate of the value of earlier writers. The poetry of Spenser came once more to be prized. The vogue for Spenser appears from the remark concerning the statesman Chatham, made by his sister, that he "knew nothing accurately except Spenser's *Faery Queen*." With the renewed vogue for Spenser came a new estimate of his language, which from the time of Ben Jonson on had been generally subject to criticism and regarded as not of the kind to imitate. The result of the changed attitude was a restoration of many abandoned words of the kind kept alive by the archaicizing manner chosen by Spenser. The range for models of English expression was extended back. The influence on Keats of Chapman's translation of Homer we know from that poet's eloquent words. Through Chapman and other Elizabethans Keats was led to an appreciation of the Elizabethan language and to the adoption of an Elizabethan freedom in the use of older words and of new compound forms. Southey was something of a rebel in language. He shows little respect for the authority of Johnson. In a letter to William Taylor (1803 or 1804) he protests against the use of words "which are so foreign as not to be even in Johnson's farrago of a dictionary." And yet Southey permits himself many word coinages, to such an extent in fact that Coleridge, in phrase reminiscent of that applied to Spenser's language by Ben Jonson, refers to Southey's English as "no English at all." In some of his writings, as Fitzedward Hall has pointed out, Southey indulges in an extravagance of expression worthy of Rabelais or of that Elizabethan forger of words, Thomas Nashe. In *The Doctor* appear word contributions such as *agathokakological, cacodemonize, dendanthropology, gelastics, kittenship, magnisonant, critickin* and scores of others. Even the dignity of the *Quarterly Review* endures in contributions from Southey words such as *abolishment, critickaster, donivorous, diabolocracy, humgig, frizzgig, evangelizationeer.*[10] Obviously the language was not entirely sterilized by the antiseptic methods of eighteenth-century classicism.

One should recall in this connection the liberties taken with English by Carlyle. This native of Scotland in his earliest writings was as subject to discipline in English as his eighteenth-century countrymen had been. But early in his literary career he threw off the trammels and, joining a German manner of expression to German ideas, developed the idiosyncrasies for which was required the new word *Carlylese.* The revolt of Charles Lamb from the prevailing formal correctness of his time appears in his exclamation, "This damn'd unmasculine canting age!" One of the elements in the charm of his writings is the quaintness of manner produced by the adoption of words and turns of expression from his beloved writers of the seventeenth century. De Quincey in his essay on rhetoric complains that "since Dr. Johnson's time the freshness of the idiomatic style has been too frequently abandoned for the lifeless mechanism of a style purely bookish and mechanical." Lacking a learned grammar, he protests, "we have allowed

[10] For longer list see Fitzedward Hall, *Modern English,* pp. 21, 22.

the blundering attempt of an imbecile stranger [evidently Lindley Murray] to supersede the learned (however imperfect) works of our own Wallis, Lowth, &c." The "drooping idiomatic freshness of our diction" and the "tumid and tumultuary structure of our sentences" he attributes to the "striving toward the professional language of books," a tendency which he attributes to the influence of the newspapers. In illustration of the prevailing tendency in everyday speech he cites the words: *category, predicament, individuality, procrastination, anteriorly* and *speaking diplomatically,* which he heard from the lips of the mistress of a lodging house.

The search for a form of English not spoiled by bookish bombast led De Quincey, not like his contemporary, Wordsworth, to the speech of the rustic, but to the natural speech of women and children. "The idiom of our language, the mother tongue," he asserts, "survives only amongst our women and children; not, Heaven knows, among our women who write books—they are often painfully conspicuous for all that disfigures authorship; but amongst well-educated women not professionally given to literature. . . . Would you desire at this day to read our noble language in all its native beauty, picturesque from idiomatic propriety, racy in its phraseology, delicate yet sinewy in its composition—steal the mail-bags, and break open all the letters in female handwriting."

These acute observations, written in genial vein, perhaps expressed only a half truth. Like the paradoxical utterances of a later day, however, they not only startle one to attention but offer interesting suggestion regarding the stage reached in the cultivation of the language. They indicate a decided lift in the general level of cultivation. Women, whose backwardness in spelling and in other features of correct language had been the subject of patronizing and facetious remarks for centuries, are elevated by De Quincey to the first rank among speakers of English.

De Quincey makes one other remark of real significance in the subject of present concern. "The language of high life," he asserts, "has always tended to simplicity and the vernacular ideal, recoiling from every mode of bookishness." Let us test the truth of this statement by a few glances at the speech of cultivated English society in the country life of England in the early nineteenth century. For this purpose we may safely turn to the writings of Jane Austen, in which one may find a realistic portrayal of the manners, and supposedly of the speech, of the time. In *Mansfield Park,* written between 1811 and 1814, the reader is introduced into two households, the Price home at Portsmouth, "the abode of noise, disorder, and impropriety," and Mansfield Park, where all was "elegance, propriety, regularity, harmony." A difference in the manner of speech of the two households is to be expected. This difference is not exaggerated into caricature, but such expressions as—*Whereabouts does the Thrush lay at Spithead? She lays close to the Endymion*—betray the social class of the Price family. With this uncultivated form of speech we are not at present concerned but with the speech of the cultivated society of Mansfield Park. Here we find a language governed less by the grammarian than by social custom and native idiom. The distinctions between *shall* and *will, should* and *would* are fastidiously made. But there survive many of the irregular forms of expression familiar in eighteenth-century cultivated use but not conforming to the rules of the grammarian. There is lack of concord between indefinite pronouns and the following pronoun or verb form: "*nobody* put *themselves* out of *their* way," "*each* had *their* favorite." "I would have *everybody* marry if *they* can," "while *each* of the Miss Bartrams *were* meditating," "*everybody* likes to go *their* own way," "*everybody* who shuts *their* eyes while *they* look . . . *feels* the comfort of." *Who* is used for *whom*: "*who* should I look to . . . but the children," "*Who* have they got to meet us?" The phrase *it is me* is used: "Depend upon it, *it is me*," "*It is me*, Baddely, you mean." Concord between subject and predicate is not always maintained. "Miss B—'s attention and opinion *was* evidently his chief aim." An expression disapproved of by the grammarian appears in: "used to *these sort of* hours," "engaged in *these sort of* hopes." Other irregularities are to be met with in considerable numbers: the redundant negative, "*not* so bad with you *neither*"; the redundant conjunction, "*but, however,* speaking from my own observation," "*But, however,* I soon found"; the use of the superlative (of two); "*the youngest* Miss Bartram," "the *youngest* and the *eldest*" (of the two daughters). There are frequent verb forms later superseded: *leant,* for 'leaned'; *bid,* for 'bade'; *broke,* for 'broken'; *drank,* for 'drunk'; *ate,* for 'eaten.' Another feature worthy of attention is the frequent use of the words *allow, apt, confess, furnish, anxious* in ways objected to by some later rhetoricians and of the widely disapproved forms: *aggravation,* for 'irritation'; *parties,* for 'persons,' and *demean,* for 'lower.'

The citations here given are from a single one of Miss Austen's novels. Her other works afford abundant further illustration of the form of language, controlled by social usage rather than by book rule, that prevailed in England a century ago. They also serve to illustrate a stage in the continuous stream of cultivated colloquial English and help to make clear the irregularities, the absence of bookishness, persisting in the cultivated colloquial speech of England at the present time.

The writings of Sir Walter Scott afford further illustration of the grammatical irregularities still persisting in the

English of the early nineteenth century. A comparison of the language in a modern edition of one of Scott's works and that in the original edition, and an observation of the changes which modern editors have seen fit to make in order to bring Scott's language into conformity with the standard of today, will provide a surprise to many not alive to the changing nature of the language. In some ways, perhaps, Scott's writings are not entirely representative. More than other great writers Scott depended on his printer for the external form of his writings. This dependence appears not only in the punctuation of his writings but in features of more fundamental importance. His careless willingness to accept suggestions in stylistic matters from his publisher, Ballantyne, appears from one of his marginal notes on his proof-sheets, in which, referring to a disputed construction, Scott writes: "As it must be decided, I have e'en tossed up half a crown and the luck is yours." Then, too, many features of Scott's language are to be attributed to his attempt to create the atmosphere of different periods in his historical novels by the use of modes of expression peculiar to particular periods. The evidence of his language, therefore, needs to be interpreted with caution. With all allowance, however, for the influence of Scott's printers and for Scott's purpose to use language historically appropriate, in the first editions of his writings may be found evidence of a language less regulated, or differently regulated, than the cultivated English of today.

In *The Fortunes of Nigel* (1st ed.) one finds older forms of spelling such as *chuse, controul, shew, sate* ('sat'), *centinel, gipsey, expence, smoaking, mattin, similies, anti-room,* etc., and older forms of the strong verbs, such as *sunk* (for 'sank'), *run* ('ran'), *spoke* ('spoken'), *drunk* ('drank'), *eat* ('eaten'). One finds words in older uses or uses since condemned, such as: *unrespective,* 'disrespectful'; *successive,*

Sir Walter Scott (1771-1832): a page of the manuscript of *Kenilworth*.

'succeeding'; *amongst; betwixt; the whilst; annunciation,* 'announcement'; *curious* ('painstaking') accuracy, *opined; implicit* obedience. One meets with an occasional redundant negative: "we should *not* want gold . . . *neither"; "*I am *not* such a fool as that *neither"; "never* the worse gentleman for that *neither.*" Very striking are some of the uses of plural verbs with collective nouns, such as: "to the public, who *have"; "the world *are* disposed to be"; "The world *say* you will"; "The world *say* true"; "The Club . . . *are* turned fastidious." Logical rather than grammatical concord appears in the expression, "the company and conversation *was* agreeable." Perhaps to Scott's purpose to give an Elizabethan quality to his language are to be attributed some of his peculiar uses of prepositions: "little thought *on"; "the age is so poor *of* genius"; "hope I have not affended you *for* my little joke"; "*At* a word" ('in brief') ; "to partake her dainties"; "Nigel was not long *of* experiencing"; "attempt *of* serving"; "asked some questions *at* the warder"; "in comparison *of* you."

Coming down one generation later, in the novels of Charles Reade[11] one finds evidence that the language is even yet not finally fixed in its constructions or in its vocabulary. One meets with constructions for which the grammarian's label is solecism: *"He don't hinder you to sell yours"; "everybody was on deck amusing themselves as they could"; "That is no excuse for him beating you"; "between each brilliant event"; "Ah, it is her you love"; "Who but he . . . admired?"; "lay in wait; mutual friend."* One meets also with coined words such as: *common-senseadox, disclamatory, facticide, funky, peachify, picnician, maniform, melancholiac, senectude, cephalomant.* The rule of the grammarian and the lexicographer evidently still has its limits.

11 Hall, *Ibid.,* pp. 25-26.

What is to be the eventual outcome of the two opposing tendencies, on the one hand the desire for logical control and regularity, on the other hand the resistance of natural usage to fetters? The issue is to this day undecided. Development in England and in America has been somewhat divergent. In both countries a greater regularity has been brought about in the forms of verbs. In syntax, however, the idiomatic forms of expression, products of earlier conditions, particularly in England, have stubbornly resisted the shackles of logical and analogical control. "The English distrust of logic," says Dean Inge, "is a deep-seated characteristic of the natural character. . . . Our legal system is built up of precedents, not on any general principles." "I hate the very sound of abstractions," said Burke. Conservative England, therefore, with its pounds, shillings, and pence, its miles, yards, and feet, its pounds and ounces, standing apart from other European nations with their measurements of value, of distance, and of weight brought into a regularity based on a decimal system, might be expected to cling to traditional forms of expression such as *had better, had rather, try and,* as well as to violations of grammatical concord in expression which had become fixed through custom.

An attitude characteristically English is that taken by Dean Alford in his *Queen's English.* This work expressed an English feeling toward language already prevalent and at the same time helped to give a fixity to this feeling. That it expressed a prevalent view and that it exerted a lasting influence may be inferred from the scores of editions that have been called for between the original date of publication and the present time. "Most of the grammars and rules, and application of rules," says Dean Alford, "are in reality not contributions towards its purity, but main instruments of its deterioration." The object of his book, he announces, is "not so much to enquire in each case what is according to strict rule and analogy, as to point out what is the usage of our spoken language." "Neither grammar nor rule governs the idiom of the people," he asserts. His object is to explain "not the grammarian's English, nor the Dictionary-writer's English, but the Queen's English." This expounder of Victorian English proceeds to pass judgment on forms of expression. *Those kind of things,* he asserts, is "now almost become idiomatic and commonly found in the talk of us all." *I had rather be,* he maintains, is "completely sanctioned by usage." *It is me,* in like manner, he defends as "an expression which every one uses. Grammarians (of the smaller order) protest; schoolmasters (of the lower kind) prohibit and chastise; but English men, women, and children go on saying it, and will go on saying it as long as the English language is spoken." Certain other disputed constructions, however, he does not defend. Regarding *different to,* which one of his correspondents had stigmatized as "very common of late," he remarks, "I was not aware of it," and adds, "of course, such a combination is entirely against all reason and analogy." This expression, which has the authority of a considerable number of English writers down to the present day, evidently was not current in the social circles in which this Churchman moved. The "split infinitive" also, which, unlike the expressions defended, is not so much an idiomatic form handed down by tradition, as an optional form which in the nineteenth century was gaining in frequency of use, Dean Alford condemns with the comment: "But surely this is a practice entirely unknown to English speakers and writers."

This popular and influential English critic based his authority definitely on the classical doctrine of "Usage, the mistress of language." Usage, however, is not only varying and unstable but within a given period is lacking in uniformity. Hence the Dean's judgments did not stand undisputed. Full of human as well as grammatical interest is the rejoinder entitled *The Dean's English* written by George W. Moon. There is no space here to quote the spicy comments on the Dean's judgments and on the Dean's own forms of expression, but the two works in conjunction afford an entertaining and instructive exhibition of the fallibility of human judgment and of the impossibility of reducing to dogma the usage which reflects not only changing fashions but varying individuality.

While the actual usage in living English speech proved not subject to definitive formulation by Alford, the attempts on the part of the grammarian to establish a uniformity based on absolute principles proved equally ineffective. In the later decades of the nineteenth century the teaching of formal English grammar in English schools lost ground. A school inspector in England in 1894 reported that "English Grammar has disappeared in all but a few schools, to the joy of children and teacher." [12]   The effect of this abandonment of the study of grammar, as might be expected, has been variously judged. J. E. Barton declares that "the official discouragement of formal grammar has sacrificed absolute accuracy in the old grammatical sense." On the other hand, Dr. P. B. Ballard maintains that "during the last fifteen years English composition, both written and oral, has steadily improved in the elementary school, and this improvement has taken place concomitantly with a declining attention to grammar and an increasing attention to literature." [13]

Let us now examine the facts of actual English usage and see how the opposing tendencies that have been discussed are reflected in the practice of English writers and the colloquial use recorded in English fiction. First let us look

[12] *Report of the Newbolt Commission*, p. 51.
[13] *Ibid.*, p. 279.

at the use of collective nouns. There is greater importance attached to grammatical concord in American speech than in British. Occasionally, in emancipated American use, a subject with plural meaning, though singular in grammatical form, is followed by plural form, verb or pronoun. For example:

Hay's unruly team *were* less fidgety.
>(Henry Adams, *The Education of Henry Adams*, p. 393.)
The party *were* too intimate for reserve.   (*Ibid.*, p. 443.)
We believe that mankind would get along better than *they* do
>now if . . .   (Charles W. Eliot's *Unitarian Creed*.)
No man or woman who has really . . . can hesitate to give
>to the very limit of what *they* have.
>(Woodrow Wilson, New York Address, September 27, 1918.)
. . . the bacteriology class *were* nervous.
>(Sinclair Lewis, *Arrowsmith*, p. 33.)

With these relatively infrequent instances in American use may be compared the prevalent practice in British use represented by the following citations:

. . . the world *are* disposed to be . . .
>(Walter Scott, *The Fortunes of Nigel*, 1st ed., Introd.)
The world *say* you will.   (*Ibid.*)
The court *is* hurrying to *their* seats.
>(Thomas De Quincey, *Joan of Arc*.)
All the world *are* . . . (Jane Austen, *Pride and Prejudice*.)
the whole party *were* welcomed . . .
>(Jane Austen, *Mansfield Park*, Everyman ed., p. 69.)
The audience *are* careless.
>(Leonard Merrick, *Whispers about Women*, p. 15.)
the Oxford University Press *has* adopted . . . in *their* small
>edition . . .   (Robert Bridges, S. P. E., II, p. 31, note.)
The Committee *are* grateful.   (S. P. E., III, p. 20.)
The public *are* disposed to attend.   (*Ibid.*, back cover.)

The audience *are* desperately anxious.

> (Stephen Leacock, *Over the Footlights,* p. 60.)

The audience *haven't* seen her yet.   (*Ibid.,* p. 61.)

This latter group of facts *are* the subject of . . .

> (H. C. Wyld, *Historical Study of Mother Tongue,* p. 11.)

I understand the United States government *are* considering.

> (Arthur Ponsonby, Speech in Parliament.)

his class *have* gone to *their* homes.

> (Lord Dunsany, *Don Rodriguez,* p. 70.)

In the use of pronouns following words or word combinations with collective meaning, British use often gives a shock to an American's grammatical nerves. *"Their,"* says Richard Grant White, "is very commonly misused with reference to a singular noun." [14]   "A misuse of the word *every,*" he says in another place,[15] "is worth remark,—the using it in a plural sense, which is very common. Thus: 'Every person rose and took their leave.' " The kinds of "misuse" here condemned in American use, in British use are established not only by long tradition but by current practice. The awkward necessity so often met with in American speech of using the double pronoun, "his or her," is obviated by the "misuse" of *their:*

every man went to *their* lodging.

> (Berners, Translation of Froissart, VI, p. 379.)

Every servant in *their* maysters lyverey.   (*Ibid.,* p. 382.)

every one prepared *themselves.*

> (Pettie, *Petite Pallace,* ed. Gollancz, p. 18.)

nobody put *themselves* out of the way.

> (Jane Austen, *Mansfield Park,* p. 10.)

each had *their* favourite . . .   (*Ibid.,* p. 33.)

have everybody marry if *they* can.   (*Ibid.,* p. 35.)

---

[14] *Every-Day English,* p. 415.
[15] *Ibid.,* p. 421.

not one in a hundred . . . who is not taken in when *they* marry. (*Ibid.*, p. 37.)

every horse had been groomed with as much rigour as if *they* belonged to a private gentleman.

(Thomas De Quincey, *English Mail Coach.*)

. . . the majority of mankind . . . quite consistent with *their* being . . . (Matthew Arnold, *Literature and Science.*)

his great concern being to make every one at *their* ease.

(Cardinal Newman, *Knowledge and Religious Duty.*)

everybody made good use of *their* liberty.

(Gilbert Cannan, translation of *Jean Christophe,* I, p. 452.)

everybody . . . had made up *their* minds.

(*Ibid.*, XI, p. 452.)

everyone in London will be talking . . . won't *they?*

(Anne Douglas Sedgwick, *Adrienne Toner*, p. 173.)

anyone may thank you, too, mayn't *they?* (*Ibid.*, p. 297.)

no one is ever safe . . . unless *they* always remember.

(*Ibid.*, p. 304.)

teach anyone how to arrange *their* lives.

(Sheila Kaye-Smith, *The House of Alard*, p. 289.)

each generation of people begins by thinking *they've* got it.

(Rose Macaulay, *Told by an Idiot*, p. 39.)

I cut no one, except when I'm afraid of being bored by *them.*

(*Ibid.*, p. 165.)

everybody has to take *their* chance.

(James Stephens, *The Crock of Gold*, p. 198.)

everyone of those *belong* to the Middle Ages.

(George Moore, *Hail and Farewell*, II.)

everyone always puts *their* boots on in the kitchen.

(E. S. Wilkinson, *Blackwood's, Living Age*, February 8, 1919.)

everybody ought to look where *they* are going.

(Frank Swinnerton, *Nocturne*, p. 15.)

I have never known any one myself who achieved style in *their* first piece of work.

(Lord Dunsany, *Literary Review*, January 23, 1921.)

Every one's to relieve *themselves.*

(Rose Macaulay, *Potterism,* p. 137.)

Every one's got to decide for *themselves.*   (*Ibid.,* p. 214.)

. . . each person stretched backwards covering *themselves.*

(James Stephens, *The Demi-Gods,* p. 163.)

. . . but every body must act exactly as *they* are able to act.

(*Ibid.,* p. 301.)

. . . everyone . . . *were* pleased.

(Samuel Butler, *The Way of All Flesh,* p. 173.)

Everyone in this age sought . . . justification of *their* own
activities.   (A. E., *The Interpreters,* p. 70.)

If he fought anybody he'd kill *them.*

(Margaret Kennedy, *The Constant Nymph,* p. 42.)

look at a person as if he saw . . . everything that had ever
happened to *them.*   (*Ibid.,* p. 45.)

It happens to everybody, God help *them.*   (*Ibid.,* p. 71.)

Another British idiom that grates on the ear of the
American grammatically trained is the one represented by
the phrase "those kind of things." This expression, which
is defended by Dean Alford, has the support of long tradition and of frequent use in present-day English:

those kind of rimes.   (George Gascoigne, *Instructions,* p. 38.)

Those kind of objections.

(Sir Philip Sidney, *Defense of Poesie.*)

These kynde of caterpillers.

(Thomas Harman, *A Caveat for Common Cursetours,* p. 48.)

these kind of thoughts.

(John Dryden, *Dramatic Poesie,* Dedication.)

these kind of schemes.

(Jane Austen, *Pride and Prejudice,* Everyman ed., p. 53.)

these sort of things.   (*Ibid.,* p. 101.)

these sort of hopes.   (*Mansfield Park,* p. 269.)

. . . these sort of critical verdicts . . .

(William Hazlitt, *On Patronage and Puffery*.)

Those sort of ideas in his head and that sort of life with his wife.   (A. S. M. Hutcinson, *If Winter Comes*, p. 324.)
start telling you those sort of things?

(H. G. Granville-Barker, transl. of *Anatol*.)

The distinction between *who* and *whom* American schooling aims to maintain.   British avoidance of the artificiality often resulting from strict adherence to grammatical rule appears in the natural and idiomatic use exemplified in the following citations:

but *who* should I see there but . . .

(*Spectator*, No. 266 (Steele).)

Asked *who* he called a fool.

(Smollett, *Roderick Random*, p. 98.)

and *who* are those peaches designed for?

(Charles Lamb, *Rosamond Gray*, Chap. iv.)

who should I look to . . . but the children. . . .

(Jane Austen, *Mansfield Park*, p. 11.)

It depends altogether on *who* I get.

(May Sinclair, *Mr. Waddington of Wyck*, p. 23.)

But *who* am I to marry?

(Sheila Kaye-Smith, *The End of the House of Alard*, p. 18.)

And *who* will we fight?

(Anne Douglas Sedgwick, *Adrienne Toner*, p. 203.)

who with?   (A. A. Milne, *The Camberley Triangle*, p. 147.)

who to?   (Rose Macaulay, *Told by an Idiot*, p. 18.)

who are you talking about?

(James Stephens, *The Crock of Gold*, p. 190.)

Who else could he have asked?

(Joseph Conrad, *Chance*, p. 252.)

William, *who* are you living with?

(L. Housman, *Angels and Ministers*, p. 111.)

Who are we writing to?

(S. Gwynn, Title of article in *The Irish Statesman*.)

Know *who* one is writing to.   (Text of same article.)

... for *whom,* and to *whom* does one write? (*Ibid.*)
... *who* has he come for?
(George Meredith, *The Ordeal of Richard Feverel,* Chap. xxv.)
who is he coming to kill? (W. B. Yeats, *On Baile's Strand.*)
Who on earth did you stay with?
(Margaret Kennedy, *The Constant Nymph,* p. 38.)
I can't think *who* this is from. (*Ibid.,* p. 202.)
By the way, *who* are they likely to send down to examine us?
(Rudyard Kipling, *Debits and Credits,* p. 240.)

The conflict between artificial correctness and natural idiom is nowhere more sharply defined than in the struggle for supremacy between *It is I* and *It is me.* The stages in the history of this expression have been traced from the Old English *ic hit eom,* through the Middle English *hit am I,* to the sixteenth-century *it is I,* and the debated form, *it is me,* which appeared not much later as a rival form. Here again natural, idiomatic use finds support from the British. Dean Alford's comment has been quoted. The following citations will show how strongly intrenched is *It is me* in English colloquial use:

It is not *me* you are in love with.
(*Spectator,* No. 290 (Steele).)
depend upon it, it is *me.* . . . It is *me,* Baddeley.
(Jane Austen, *Mansfield Park,* p. 269.)
It's *me.* (Joseph Conrad, *To-morrow,* p. 247.)
The last person he recognized was *me.*
(Sheila Kaye-Smith, *The End of the House of Alard,*
p. 324.)
Then it must be *me.*
(Anne Douglas Sedgwick, *Adrienne Toner,* p. 330.)
picture to myself that it's not *me.*
(Stephen Leacock, *Over the Footlights,* p. 68.)
If it had been *me.* (May Sinclair, *The Tree of Heaven,* p. 26.)
That's not *me.*
(A. S. M. Hutchinson, *If Winter Comes,* p. 328.)

It's not my body . . . It's *me*.

> (St. John Ervine, *Changing Winds*, p. 507.)

We followed . . . Tarlyon first, then *me*, then. . . .

> (Michael Arlen, *These Charming People*, p. 118.)

He would very much rather it had not been *me*.

> (Michael Arlen, *The Green Hat*, p. 190.)

It is *me*, isn't it?   (A. A. Milne, *Mr. Pim Passes By*, p. 109.)

. . . she thought it must be *me*.   And it was *me*.

> (May Sinclair, *Mr. Waddington of Wyck*, p. 14.)

Yes, my dear, it's *me*.

> (L. Housman, *Angels and Ministers*, p. 111.)

Then it's going to be *me*.   (*Ibid.*, p. 128.)

You thought it was *me*.   (Rose Macaulay, *Potterism*, p. 181.)

Yes, it's *me*.

> (Margaret Kennedy, *The Constant Nymph*, p. 197.)

In the case of the other personal pronouns following the verb *to be*, the grammarian is in stronger position.   But the attitude of H. G. Wells is particularly worthy of note:

"That's *him*" [italics], said Ann Veronica, in sound idiomatic
    English.   (H. G. Wells, *Ann Veronica*, Chap. vi.)

This radical attitude finds some support in the usage of other British writers:

It was *him* that Horace Walpole called . . .

> (J. W. Croker in edition of Boswell's *Life of Samuel
>   Johnson;* cited by Macaulay as a solecism.)

No, it's not *him*.

> (Margaret Kennedy, *The Constant Nymph*, p. 9.)

He thought that if it wasn't *him*. . . .   (*Ibid.*, p. 137.)

This isn't *us* talking at all.

> (A. S. M. Hutchinson, *This Freedom*, p. 27.)

It was just *her*—I suppose the great Whatsisname would say, "It was just *She*," but then that isn't what I mean.

> (A. A. Milne, *The Romantic Age*, p. 210.)

he knew that the hand . . . was not *him*.

> (James Stephens, *The Crock of Gold*, p. 219.)

If I were *her*.

> (J. Middleton Murry, *The Things We Are*, p. 259.)

A most conspicuous instance of British defiance of grammatical correctness appears in the occasional "misuse" of the forms of the verb *lie* and *lay*. The confusion in the forms of these verbs is always at hand in the colloquial speech of both countries. According to Dean Alford, it is particularly prevalent among Eton men. Hence, perhaps, a certain degree of prestige. The expression "there let him lay" which appeared in Byron's *Childe Harold,* canto 4, became the subject of a long controversy beginning in correspondence to the *Times* in 1873 and continuing intermittently down to 1922. Byron's defense, a weak one, has recently been brought to light. In the proof sheets, Gifford, the editor, had written, "I have a doubt about lay." Byron's note in comment was, "So have I, but the post, and *Indolence* and *Idleness ! ! !*" One would be interested to hear from the authors concerned a defense of the following cited passages:

And you were quite alone and very weak; Yea, *laid* a dying . . .   (William Morris, *Defence of Guinevere.*)
. . . manuscripts which had long *laid* hidden . . .
(Lytton Strachey, *Books and Characters,* p. 84.)
from where I *laid* hidden in the woods.
(Fiona Macleod, *Deirdre,* p. 27.)
and found it in a man *laying* there with foam upon his lips.
(George Moore, *The Brook Kerith,* p. 38.)
Then Ali, tired out . . ., *laid* down in the shade of the canoe.
(Joseph Conrad, *Almayer's Folly,* Concord edition, p. 187.)

It is doubtful if from American writers there could be produced such an exhibition of defiance of rule. It must be borne in mind how few Americans, even Americans prominent in public life, in earlier generations were reared in centers of culture or in circles where a cultivated manner of speech was prevalent. American cultivation in language, consequently, has in the past taken the direction of a correctness gained from schools or from the imitation of literary models. It may safely be asserted, for instance, that in correctness Washington Irving surpassed eighteenth-century English models such as Addison and Goldsmith. Then, too, in America the disposition to set up an absolute rule of reason has been particularly strong. One should recall Noah Webster's emphasis on analogy as a guiding principle in language and the exaltation by Goold Brown of reason to the place of supreme authority. From the substitution of abstract principle in place of concrete example there results frequently a loss in the naturalness and ease of manner that belongs to purely idiomatic expression.

That American language, however, was entirely the loser from this enforced substitution is not to be admitted without debate. The phrase "muddling through" which has often of late been applied to English methods of achieving success, applies to a certain extent to irregular methods which have determined the character of English speech. Is there not gain to be derived from the adoption of more logical methods? In its industrial methods England has been conservative. Through the system of master and apprentice, older methods of operation have been preserved. In America the very lack of men trained through apprenticeship has in many instances led to the return to experimentation and the application of pure theory, leading not infrequently to improvements in method. In the speech of Americans unversed in the elegance of expression gained through social apprenticeship, likewise, may not experiments in modes of expression and the application of theoretical principles be expected to lead to improvement in expression? In the matter of spelling the case is clear. Even the few simplified forms of spelling introduced by Noah Webster have proved themselves of value. A more thorough

revision of spelling, most American language students believe, would result in notable gain. In pronunciation, in
syntax, and in the use of words, the English language remains a product of "muddling through." There are some
who hold that in language there is room for the application of new methods, less realistic, more idealistic in nature,
if language like other elements of life is to advance toward
the goal of perfection.

Some such ideal was in the mind of Noah Webster.
Goold Brown also in his exaltation of reason to the throne
in the realm of language was governed by a like idea. As
more or less representative of the prevalent American attitude a generation later than Goold Brown, may be taken
the writings of Richard Grant White. These works, now
nearly a half century old, are still widely read, as appears
from new editions which continue to appear. White not
only has done much to form American opinion, but his
books have owed their popularity not alone to their
pungency of style, but also to the fact that they expressed
American views already prevalent. Americans then, as today, in the lack of training in good English from social
experience, welcomed positive directions, and these they
found in the dogmatic, often perverse, assertions of White.

As a motto for his title page White adopted the Latin
words, *Ratio imperatrix supra grammaticam,* and in his
first book, *Words and their Uses,* published in 1871, he
expands this idea in detail. English he holds to be a "grammarless tongue," but, differing from Alford, he contends that
the "authority of eminent writers conforming to or forming
the usage of their day, . . . does not completely justify or
establish a use of words inconsistent with reason, or out
of the direction of the normal growth of the language. . . .
There is a higher law than usage." He asks if long-established usage may make that correct which will not bear the

tests of reason and analogy and gives the reply: "Observation justifies the answer that it does not."

Unfortunately White used reason mainly as a base from which to launch his own private views, often whims and prejudices. A lawyer by training, he too often undertook the defense of weak cases. He was endowed with a sensitiveness for refinement in expression, and by his liveliness of manner he creates an interest not always to be found in grammatical discussions. In fact, his mode of discussion is that usually associated with political debate. To use the words of his opponent, Fitzedward Hall, his fighting spirit was that of the "black flag and no quarter." He was after all an amateur as a linguist. The thinness of his knowledge of the history of the language is covered by a positive and dogmatic manner. One amusing instance must be cited illustrating how the defense of a weak position sometimes led him into positive error. He is attempting to justify the expression *the sun sets.* To condemn this expression firmly established by usage would, he realized, be pedantry. But in the search for more logical grounds than mere usage on which to justify the expression, he is led to the grotesque explanation of *set* in this phrase as due to the use as a verb of a noun which he imagines to be derived from the Old English *setl* meaning 'seat.' The contrast, however, between White, the American, and Dean Alford, the Englishman, is more apparent than real. Upon fundamental principles quite contradictory, that of reason in the one case, that of natural usage in the other, were based decisions which in reality represented little more than arbitrary opinion. The decisions, however, of these self-constituted authorities, were accepted by a great mass of docile readers looking only for a leader, and became the source of widely diffused prejudices on questions of language.

Much more trustworthy as a leader was Fitzedward Hall,

whose standards of judgment are today generally accepted. Instead of setting himself up as an autocratic authority, Hall derived his authority from the will of the governed. In a number of books and articles he presented the results of long and patient observation of the facts of actual usage. The polemic tone of his writings combined with the lack of popular appeal in the assemblage of dry facts with which he supported his judgments, deprived Hall's works of immediate popularity and of the popular influence exerted by his amateurish rivals and opponents. The soundness, however, of Hall's methods has been generally recognized by the expert, and his work was a stimulus to that monumental undertaking, the Oxford Dictionary, which after the labor of nearly half a century has just been completed. In this work are at last assembled English words from the earliest times, their different meanings and the dates associated with their earliest use with the different meanings. Upon the solid foundation of facts thus assembled, may be based judgments that must supersede those of men who, since the sixteenth century, have been able to offer only the results of individual observation and individual opinion.

CHAPTER XXI

REVOLT

THE end of the nineteenth century brought not a climax in development, but a change in direction in the forces governing the language. The phrase *fin de siècle* current in the final decade applied not to a summation of earlier tendencies, but to an abandonment of earlier ideals. A recent English novelist speaks of one of his women characters as "so well-bred that she never practiced what you would call deportment." [1] This characterization applies to the new age which began at the end of the nineteenth century. Victorian decorum and propriety passed out of fashion. In conduct there was an abandonment of older standards of propriety; in language, which is a phase of conduct, the absolute rules lost their authority. Formal grammar lost its dominancy in school instruction. A mode of expression formed by rule came in great part to be superseded by a mode of expression formed by imitation of admired models or created from the varied situations of actual life.

Those of the older generation today will recall the changes which they felt going on in the later years of the last century, the ground slipping from under their feet. They will recall Stevenson with his adoption of a thrilling form of narrative that had before been associated with vulgar taste or with a taste only slyly indulged in. They will recall his "continual seeking after slight novelty" in expression, a novelty which he secured by the occasional use of older words and expressions brought to life or of expressive words

[1] Michael Arlen, *The Green Hat.*

and phrases drawn from his native Scotch dialect. They will recall the new color to expression given by Maurice Hewlett through his adoption of medievalisms. They will recall the fresh wave of impressions and of expressions introduced by Kipling. They will recall all this and much more. The change in modes is now so complete as to be realized only through memory. Members of the younger generation can hardly realize the sensations that accompanied the transition in modes of thought and conduct and language.

The nineteenth century was an age of repression, of restriction in language. The remarkable progress in science and general knowledge had required a vast expansion in the English vocabulary. This expansion, however, had been a guarded one. The purist was ever at hand to challenge a new word. The very phrase "word coinage" suggested a counterfeiting operation. The words challenged by the critic and grammarian found their way into lists of proscribed expressions such as those made by Bryant for the *Evening Post,* by Dana for the *Sun,* by Gilder for the *Century Magazine.* The dictionary was felt to be the source from which to derive new modes of expression. One should recall some of the names such as *thesaurus,* meaning 'treasure,' *alvearie,* meaning 'bee-hive,' applied in the sixteenth century to the collections of words which served as dictionaries. The honey of language Browning sought in a later form of alvearie, the eighteenth-century dictionary of Johnson. With the conception of the dictionary as a repository of all English words, which, it will be recalled, was President Witherspoon's conception of Johnson's *Dictionary,* should be contrasted the modern conception of a dictionary requiring a large staff of editors to record the new words to be included in new editions. The two supplementary volumes of the *Century Dictionary,* which had to be added to the six original volumes after a period of only seventeen years, afford indication of the rapidly expanding English vocabulary.

Indeed the rapid expansion of the English vocabulary in modern times is comparable to that following the Renaissance. The "hard words" in the earlier period derived from classical sources and the "terms of art" originating with the birth of new science and the creation of new forms of art have their parallel in the new technical terms that have to be reckoned with by publishers of modern dictionaries. In each case the expansion in vocabulary has been in response to an expansion in knowledge, and expansion in knowledge in the present age in many ways has surpassed that of the sixteenth century. The geographical explorations of the sixteenth century did not yield more new knowledge than is yielded by the intimate acquaintance with foreign lands gained through commercial penetration or governmental protectorates. But modern exploration has also penetrated regions hitherto unexplored. The new knowledge of the North Pole cannot be compared in importance with the new knowledge derived from the exploration of the inner recesses of the mind, of the structural secrets of the material world, and of the hidden sources of natural energy. A graduate of the college of a generation ago almost needs to repeat his undergraduate course in order to keep pace with the progress made even in elementary science. Then, too, as in the earlier period, the achievements of pure science are being applied in practical use. Now as then the new ideas are applied in new physical activities, and they are certain now as then to lead to new conceptions of social relations and even of divine purpose.

For a new world a language brought to completeness and to classical perfection for the uses of another mode of life is obviously inadequate. The structure of the language, to be sure, seems to be fixed with a fair degree of permanency. Its constructions will now bear their load of expression without the added props of Latin grammar which have served so long. The progressive passive form of the verb has been newly evolved in the last two centuries and the increasing use of the "split infinitive," which some are disposed to regard as an actual gain, seems to have its origin in an increased service demanded of the infinitive construction in modern English. Such new features, however, are exceptional. The language appears to be cast in permanent form. But for the expression of changing conceptions of life, there is constant need of renewal in word and phrase. In this respect the language is proceeding as in the past. There is occasional sheer creation of new elements of expression. Generally, however, the older elements are woven into new combinations. New automatic devices for saving human labor are named by hundreds of new word compounds making use of the old classical prefix *auto-*. The bringing of the distant into closer communication has required scores of new words making use of the Greek element *tele-*. The modern age is perhaps not so fertile in abstract conceptions. Hence a diminishing production of words once so much in vogue ending in *-osity* and *-ation*. But newly adopted processes have called into frequent use the suffix *-ize,* and new shades of belief have called for many words in *-ist* and *-ism*. More painful to contemplate are the words ever increasing in number with the all too familiar ending *-itis*.

A feature of modern literature that has its origin in the use of scientific observation as a source of knowledge is the dominance of naturalism. A more intimate knowledge of nature and of life has made the illusions of romance all too apparent. In an age of disillusionment it has become regrettably more and more difficult to bring oneself under the spell of narratives which represent not what things are but what one would like them to be. At the same time a new form of romance is being revealed in a clearer realization of the wonder of things as they are, revealed by scientific knowledge. The effect on language has been to call into service words and phrases expressive of stark realism. The veiled forms of expression which served when one was unwilling to look facts in the face have been succeeded by naked expressions exhibiting reality. For the new uses it has been necessary to bring into service words that had formerly been consigned to the rubbish heap, or words belonging to occupations in which the bare facts of life needed to be faced, or intimate words restricted to the privacies of life. Naturalism, with the close-up view of life that it demands, has thus called into new service the more coarse and brutal elements of the language.

The latent powers of the language have been called upon in recent years for new services. Efforts have been made, independent of the ordinary processes of reasoning, more directly to externalize the flow of human consciousness. In passages in the writings of James Joyce this is attempted by means of a breathless flow of words independent of grammatical analysis or the use of punctuation or of capital letters by which this analysis is indicated. In even more radical attempts to convey, not facts and situations, but human reaction to external stimuli, the language has been even further strained from the conventional and the normal. In the works of a group of expressionistic writers, for the most part expatriates settled in Paris, words are employed for associational effects and in varied rhythmical combinations are made to externalize surging emotions. Such efforts, experimental in nature and abnormal in their general tendency, cannot be said to have had appreciable effect on the general character of the language. Among other writers of the younger generation quickened senses turned to a renewal of fresh observation have led to fresh imagery, an abandonment of forms of expression become blunted and dull in favor of more biting word and phrase.

In a word we are living in an age of revolt. Besides the defined programs of schools in literary expression that have been mentioned there is a general stirring of new life, a tumultuous ill-defined movement, chaotic in great part, but seeking a new interpretation of life and a freshened mode of expression. The movement is international. In French critical writings one reads of "breaking their servitude to words" and of "putting a liberty cap on the dictionary." [2] In search of a parallel one is led once more back to the Elizabethans, to the period before the varying efforts to improve the language had combined in a common endeavor to bring English to a state of classical perfection. The need of a freshened medium led in Ireland to an astonishing discovery of the euphony and expressiveness of word and phrase in the Irish form of English hitherto associated with contempt and ridicule. In England the same sense of need led to a demonstration by Masefield, Blunden, and others of rich sources of neglected expression in the English provincial dialects.

Most significant of all, probably, for the future of the language was the discovery by America of its own resources in language. This subject, which provides an interesting sequel to the colonial beginning of American speech, needs to be considered more in detail. American assertion of independence in language, it will be recalled, had closely followed the American Revolution. Lowell, also, it will be recalled, in witty verses, had exposed to ridicule the colonial spirit persisting in American literature. The ideas supported by Lowell in theory if not in practice, found more

[2] C. M. Cowley, *Saturday Review of Literature,* May 7, 1927.

consistent support in Walt Whitman. In regard to his own poetry, Whitman said: "It is an attempt to give the spirit, the body and the man, new words, new potentialities of speech—an American, a cosmopolitan (for the best of America is the best cosmopolitanism) range of self-expression." He then adds, in a prophetic strain: "The Americans are going to be the most fluent and melodious-voiced people in the world—and the most perfect users of words. The new times, the new people, the new vistas need a new tongue according—yes, and what is more they will have a new tongue." [3]

The spirit of cultural independence, however, was not easily kindled. Americans continued to be engrossed in the physical exploitation of a new land. Culture they continued willing to take at second-hand. Their natural accent they kept with little attempt at regulation. The written form of language they learned by book and rule. Spelling which was made a main test of culture they learned from spelling books. Up to 1865 the circulation of Webster's spelling book alone was about 42,000,000, and even in the later years of the century the popularity of this "old Blue-Back" was well maintained. In the one year, 1866, the sale was 1,596,000 copies, and in the quarter century, 1876-1900, its circulation was 11,500,000. The moral earnestness which at one time dominated American life appears in the disposition to apply the distinction of right and wrong, not only to conduct, but to language, and the laws of right and wrong in language were found in spelling-book and grammar and dictionary. Authority in language was looked for, not in American colloquial practice, but in British use or, more frequently, in grammatical rule. The natural order of things was inverted. The living colloquial idiom which should determine the written form, was itself

[3] H. L. Mencken, *The American Language*, p. 10.

governed, as far as it was governed at all, by the artificial forms of literary use.

"Lowell and Walt Whitman," says Mr. Mencken, "were the first men of letters, properly so called, to give specific assent to the great changes that were firmly fixed in the national speech during the half century between the War of 1812 and the Civil War." These ideas, however, were slow in taking root, or at least were slow in bearing fruit. The false gods of American letters were not easily overthrown. From west of the Alleghanies came W. D. Howells to succeed Lowell as editor of America's most prominent literary magazine. From his post as editor of the *Atlantic Monthly* and later from the "Editor's Study" of *Harper's Magazine,* his influence was a dominant one. In the words of Mark Twain, he was "the recognized critical Court of Last Resort in this country." In critical theory belonging to the naturalistic school, in his novels he pictured in naturalistic fashion at least the pleasanter aspects of American life. From the shadier sides of American life, however, his optimistic nature held him aloof. In language he might be called a parlor naturalist. In the "Editor's Study" of *Harper's Magazine* in 1886 he quotes with approval the words of Alphonse Daudet regarding Turgenev and the Russian language. "What a luxury it must be to have a great big untrodden barbaric language to wade into! We poor fellows who work in the language of an old civilization, we may sit and chisel our little verbal felicities only to find in the end that it is a borrowed jewel we are polishing." "We," adds Howells, "have only to leave our studies . . . and go into the shops and fields to find the 'spacious times' again." And yet so strong was the spirit of conservatism absorbed by this son of the Middle West and strengthened by his New England associations, that he does not wade deeply in the "big untrodden barbaric language" of America.

Only in gingerly way does he commend the slangy forms of language circulating in American speech. "One need not invite slang into the company of its betters, though perhaps slang has been dropping its *s* and becoming language ever since the world began, and is certainly sometimes delightful and forcible beyond the reach of the dictionary."

In actual practice Howells' language is characterized by refinement of taste, susceptible, however, to the flavor of racy idiom. He is governed by a conformity to cultivated practice, itself in turn based on literary use. English literary use, therefore, forms the ultimate language background of this Ohioan exposed to New England culture. "My own greater bookishness" he mentions in speaking of himself in relation to Mark Twain. How well-rooted in Howells were the principles of correctness in speech is shown by his cultivated distinction between *shall* and *will*, *should* and *would*. This distinction, sacred in New England culture, though by no means universally prevalent in general American use, is usually followed even in the speech of Silas Lapham, whose language is in other respects contrasted with that of the cultivated Bostonians.

That Howells was alive to the artificial qualities of cultivated American speech he makes sufficiently clear. "A civilization comes through literature now, especially in our country," says Bromfield Corey, a representative of Boston culture, to his son Tom, and then continues: "A Greek got his civilization by talking and looking, and in some measure a Parisian may still do it. But we, who live remote from history and monuments, we must read or we must barbarise. Once we were softened if not polished, by religion; but I suspect that the pulpit counts for much less now in civilising." That, too, Howells looked with envy on the cultivated colloquial idiom of England, we know from his own words. "If one has moved in good English society, one has no need to ask how a word is pronounced far less to go to the dictionary; one pronounces it as one has always heard it pronounced. The sense of this gives the American a sort of despair. . . ."

An artificial refinement derived from cultivated New England practice, itself having its background in the literature of England, is then a distinguishing feature of the language of Howells. By it he was held from carrying into practice his theories of naturalism as far as language is concerned.

Different from that of Howells, yet in some respects like it, was the literary career of Henry James. In his later writings, influenced by his efforts at dramatic composition, James sought a colloquial basis. For this, however, like Howells, he did not trust to American idiom. For colloquial idiom with the distinction which represented his ideal, he crossed the Atlantic to England.

By such influences American literature was long prevented from the use of its own wealth of native expression. In reading, Americans were entertained and instructed by English books or by American books made after an English pattern. In schools they were trained in ideals and in style by popular reading books which made universally familiar the conventional manner of literary expression.

But with the Atlantic seaboard settled in its habits and drilled in European manners of expression, there still remained the frontier in the West. On the western front the English speaking pioneer absorbed many words, as has already been pointed out, from Indians and from earlier French and Spanish settlers. The full revelation of the potentialities of American colloquial idiom had to come from the West. "The West," says Howells, "when it began to put itself into literature, could do so without the sense, or the apparent sense, of any older or politer world outside of it; whereas the East was always looking fearfully over its shoulders at Europe." But the man on the frontier does not content himself with the borrowing of words from foreign lingo. Confronted with new facts and new situations, he needs new words. Removed from the influence of books and schools, he has to contrive words of his own. The *prospector* for gold, after he has found *grubstake,* or financial support, loads his effects on a *burro,* or as he often calls him, a *jack.* He *pans* or *winnows* for *nuggets* or breaks up rock for *showings* of ore. If he finds *pay dirt,* he *stakes* his claim. Perhaps he comes into conflict with a *claim jumper.* Such rude ore has *panned out* into many a precious phrase.

The cattle ranch and the lumber camp yield similar stores of fresh minted words and phrases. In general the native of the American West, where a road is still called a *trail,* where to *carry* is still to *pack,* where wife and babies may be referred to as wife and *outfit,* enjoys the advantage of a form of language with fresh and living associations, a crude manner of speech but one capable of yielding gems of polished expression.

The American frontier in recent times is rapidly being brought within definite bounds. Order and method and sophistication are reaching the extreme bounds of our American civilization. But the spirit of earlier freedom still lives in word creations of earlier times, such as *cowcatcher* and *stump speaker* and *blizzard* and *beehive,* and *bluff* and *bogus* and *boost,* in *clear out* and *cloudburst* and *cold snap,* in *hayseed,* in *joy-ride,* in *backbone* (for courage), in *whole souled* and *make good.*

The rich language material of the mining life of the West was brought into service by an eastern writer, Bret Harte. Through his writings many a picturesque word and phrase was made familiar, not only to the Atlantic seaboard

of America, but to Europe. A rich vein of expression yielded
literary ore for world use. Bret Harte, however, was re-
absorbed in the eastern civilization from which he sprang.
The real spirit of the West reached American literature in
the writings of Mark Twain. Of him W. D. Howells said
that his "great charm is his absolute freedom in a region
where most of us are fettered and shackled by immemorial
convention. . . . Of all the literary men I have known he
was the most unliterary in his make and manner . . . his
manner was as entirely his own as if no one had ever written before." And yet Mark Twain in his writings had to
submit to discipline. When the American had won his
freedom in language from foreign domination, he came
under the rod of the schoolmaster. Mark Twain's proof-
sheets, Howells informs us, "came back a veritable 'mush
of concession.' " Howells himself cut out much of the
profanity from Mark Twain's contributions to the *Atlantic*.
It would be interesting to know how many solecisms were
eliminated.

With Mark Twain, however, may be said to come to an
end the period of colonialism in American language. Since
his time there has been an increasing freedom from the
inhibitions that oppressed earlier American writers and a
development of freedom and natural ease in the use of the
native idiom. An earlier solemnity in literary manner, the
result of studied imitation of the speech of our elders in
culture, has been in considerable part succeeded by a national youthful gayety. Formal rule as a guide has been
superseded by natural use. The contrast appears in the old
and the new attitude toward the debated phrase, *it is me.*
The older attitude appears in the story of an earlier college
generation. A number of students in the midst of revelry
were disturbed by a knock at the door. "Who's there?"
called out one of the revellers. "It's me, Professor Smith,"

was the response. "You're a liar," returned the student, "Professor Smith doesn't use that kind of English." The attitude of today appears in a distinction made by a recent writer of the younger generation to whom we are indebted for a revelation of the manners of modern youth. F. Scott Fitzgerald represents a sophisticated character as saying: "It is me, who tries . . . " and then in the same passage, represents a valet as saying, "it's I, sir." [4] In earlier days to be "a writer" meant to possess a command of correct expression that was exceptional. To write correctly is today supposedly an ability that belongs to anyone who pretends to cultivation. A violinist on the vaudeville stage, besides displaying a command over his instrument, feels it necessary to pass his bow behind his back or toss it in the air in time to the music drawn from the strings. The modern journalistic writer, like the vaudeville artist, often feels it necessary to display his tricks of style. With a conventional correctness, once in itself an accomplishment, must be joined a display of acrobatic flourish. One must be able not only to play a theme but to play with it.

We are thus introduced to the presence of American slang. There is a prevalent belief that slang is a distinctively American product. This idea is obviously false. French slang, or *argot*, is perhaps even richer than American slang. Earlier English had its slang, although bearing a different name. The Elizabethan period of English had its "pedlar's French" or "fustian" or "gibbridge." The Restoration period had its fashionable cant so much objected to by Swift. The "flash language" and "canting terms" in this period and in the eighteenth century following are frequently alluded to and were collected in dictionaries. Their use in polite society arose in great part from a revolt from gentility in manners. The language of the underworld pro-

[4] F. Scott Fitzgerald, *The Beautiful and Damned*, p. 51.

vided words facetiously adopted by the fashionable world, many of which, such as *fun* and *queer* and *banter* and *bluff* and *fib* and *sham* and *humbug,* eventually made their way into dignified use. But there is a distinctive quality in American slang. Whatever it may have been in the past, it is not now "the dishwater from the washings of English dandyism." [5] A democratic unwillingness to recognize a superior, which interferes with subjection to military discipline, appears in an unwillingness to submit to discipline in language. There is a revolt from the conventional, a striving after the odd rather than the usual. In speech as in music the graceful and the beautiful yield to the grotesque. For the expression of this American spirit the frontier life of the woodsman provided much unrefined word material. From industrial occupations, from the less reputable amusements of the gaming table, the race track, and the prize ring, and from life on the stage came more word material which expressed a revolt from decorum and propriety.

In recent years, a change is appearing in the spirit of American slang. Instead of being the crude creation of the illiterate, or chance-tossed gems of speech, the products of a momentary sense of the incongruous, slang expressions are coming more and more to be products of conscious invention. The need for variety of expression in the daily reports of the sporting writer has been a stimulating cause. But the striving for variety and for the qualities of ironic humor and the grotesque has become general. The college student strives for distinctive qualities in his speech as well as in his dress. It is said that committees are created in college fraternities to provide the needed supplies of new "collegiate" expression. The creation of slang has become an organized effort.

What is to be the direction taken by the English language

---

[5] Oliver Wendell Holmes, *The Autocrat of the Breakfast Table,* p. 247.

of the future? How much of the crude ore in the speech of the American frontier is to be refined into pure English for general use? How many flashy gems of slang origin are to find a permanent setting in the speech of tomorrow? Who can say?

At the beginning of the nineteenth century Wordsworth led a revolt from the conventional "poetic diction" of his predecessors and turned to the language "really used by men." A century later American poets with even greater courage are turning to the natural speech of the frontiersman and of the industrial proletariat. Words such as *bunkshooter, con men, dockwalluper, honky tonk, floozies, yen, cahoots, leatherneck, mazuma, slimpsy, flooey, sbyzch,* when assembled by themselves, as they are in the Introduction provided for the English edition of Carl Sandburg's *Collected Poems,* create an impression beyond the grotesque, that of utter rawness. The value of such words may be mainly for local color, nevertheless by means of them woven into the texture of his verse the poet has been able to exhibit the inner qualities, some of the real beauty, in a life superficially ugly. By the use of similar forms of expression brought into new rhythms Vachel Lindsay has succeeded in reuniting poetry with music. The verse is not that of the Elizabethan lyric because the music is not the same. Its tones and rhythms are not those of the sixteenth-century virginals or the lute but those of the twentieth-century saxophone and drum.

To prose expression in America new energy and vigor have been given by the adoption of more brutal forms of speech. The princely stock of the language has been renewed by the infusion of peasant blood.[6] In the new prose manner Mr. Mencken has been a leader. Abandoning the nerveless niceties that have become a part of literary tradition, he

[6] See article by J. W. Beach, *American Speech,* I, 299-307.

adopts the cruder elements of popular speech. Instead of drawing the sword he puts on the gloves or even uses his bare fists and is able on occasion to deliver the punch. The new manner appears in a recent popular book on an economic theme written by a professor at Harvard, who brings up the heavy artillery of language in words and phrases such as *highly iniquitous, crowning infamy, skulduggery, devilish ingenuity, honey-fugling, malversation, notorious obfuscation, kaleidoscopic transmogrification.* The effect is super-Rooseveltian. The greater immediacy in the popular form of speech has been revealed in even more radical fashion by America's most popular evangelist, who has demonstrated a new moving power in bible narratives when translated into the language of slang. The throng-swaying power in such translations comes not alone from the shock of incongruity that startles the hearer into attention, but from the nakedness of the meaning in the colloquial version.

The danger of extremes in American modernity has not lacked attention. The purist spirit so long dominant in American literature is by no means extinct. One of its spokesmen, Paul Elmer More, sees in American speech a tendency like that which debased pure Greek to "Hellenistic Greek." Is English, he asks, to be permitted to become not English but 'Englistic'? More concrete is the demonstration of danger recently offered in a zestful editorial of the *New York Times* (July 16, 1927). If Chaucer's language may be paraphrased into modern English, the same, it is demonstrated, may be done with the language of later poets. Shakespeare's "Out, out, brief candle. Life's but a walking shadow," paraphrased in American expression becomes, "Turn off the bulb. Life's but a wornout flivver." Shakespeare's "A poor player that struts and frets his hour upon the stage" becomes "A trouper who hamfats his turn upon the stage." In the same way memorable lines from Longfellow in modern American colloquial jingles become:

It was the Fokker Hesperus
That took the air that day.
And its skipper had brought him a Broadway cutie
To neck with on the way.

One in search of further illustration of the dual modes of expression and of the humorous effect created by the substitution of one for the other may find a rich abundance in the facetious productions of American undergraduate publications. Translation becomes travesty; paraphrase becomes parody. The light manner of colloquial speech obviously will not bear the weight of a serious message. A flippancy quite in keeping with the intimacies of colloquial use is not in keeping with a manner adapted to a world audience for which literary composition is intended.

That bolshevistic experimentation in speech may not yield valuable results it would not be safe to say. A modern English writer, who has herself exhibited rare power in creative expression within the bounds of the older tradition, nevertheless shows a keen sensitiveness to the value in the new art and the new tradition in the making in America today. "That both are in process of birth," she writes,[7] "the language itself gives us proof. For the Americans are doing what the Elizabethans did—they are coining new words. They are instinctively making the language adapt itself to their needs. In England, save for the impetus given by the war, the word-coining power has lapsed; our writers vary the metres of their poetry, remodel the rhythms of prose, but one may search English fiction in vain for a single new word. It is significant that when we

[7] Virginia Woolf, *Saturday Review of Literature*, August 1, 1925.

want to freshen our speech we borrow from America—poppycock, rambunctious, flipflop, booster, good mixer—all the expressive ugly vigorous slang which creeps into use among us first in talk, later in writing, comes from across the Atlantic. Nor does it need much foresight to predict that when words are being made, a literature will be made out of them."

The English attitude, however, toward the freshening influences in language has been on the whole characteristically conservative. Traditional modes of expression serve the needs of a mode of life that is traditional. Mr. Masefield, as already remarked, has given fresh color to literary expression by the adoption of words from the provincial dialects of England, but in doing so he avoids harshness of combination and blends old and new into harmony. American slang on the whole remains a foreign language to the Englishman. American plays such as *Is Zat So?* and American novels such as *Babbitt* have had to be provided with glossaries in order to be intelligible in England. John Galsworthy in his recent novel *The Silver Spoon* makes a naturalistic use of colloquial idiom. He exhibits the rich element of native slang in the colloquial speech of England. He also introduces in accurate use the American creations, *stunt* and the *limit,* which seem to have been assimilated into English colloquial use, and in the speech of an American he introduces the Americanism *put him wise* with the precise American meaning. In other instances, however, he shows that American slang is to him a foreign language. He uses *fallen for* as synonymous for 'fallen in love with' and he distorts *the gift of gab* into *the gift of the gab*.

Amusing mistakes of this kind appear in H. G. Wells and other recent English novelists and even in the Glossary provided for the English edition of *Babbitt*. From this interesting word-list one learns that a *dumb-bell* is a 'silent fool,' that *Heck* is 'familiar for Hecuba, a New England deity,' that a *hoodlum* is a 'crank,' that a *hop* is 'a Freshman's College dancing club,' that a *Hunky* is a 'Hun,' that *lounge-lizards* are 'men hanging about hotels for dancing and flirting,' that *pep* is 'galvanized human energy,' that a *precinct* is a 'ward,' that to be *rambunctious* is to be 'cantankerous,' that a *saphead* is 'one having water on the brain,' that a *yeggman* is a 'hooligan,' that a *nut* is a 'madman.' Such instances of English misunderstanding afford definite evidence of a widening gap between the colloquial languages of the two countries, and this gap is held open by the zeal shown on both sides of the Atlantic to preserve the purity of the native idiom. Edith Wharton, for instance, has recently been taken to task by a reviewer for her use in an American novel of the Anglicisms: *cinema,* for 'movie'; *bonnet* (of a motor car) ; and *the pointsman at the shunting station.*

There are of course language radicals in England as elsewhere. But a point of view which is on the whole typically English has recently been set forth by the English novelist, Frank Swinnerton.[8] Mr. Swinnerton apologetically reminds American readers that "while the English readily adopt American slang in colloquial speech, they do not very quickly absorb into their written language any slang whatever." "This leads some Americans," he continues, "ignorant of the fact that there is a racy English slang, which is similarly excluded from written English, to suppose that the English have a prejudice against American phrases as such. Not at all, what they feel is that written English is on the whole Standard English; and that written English differs from spoken English as well as from any other form of English."

What is to be the future relation between the English

[8] *Harper's Magazine,* January, 1927.

of England and that of America? The question is the most important one to be answered regarding the future of the language. On both sides of the Atlantic great concern is felt. Many Englishmen view with concern changes transforming the language which is a product of English life, which is stamped with English character and which continues to reflect English modes of thought. English become a world language could not continue to serve as precisely as now the needs of expression peculiarly English. On the other hand Americans demand a form of speech directly responsive to American life. Mr. Mencken, the champion of an independent American language, has many followers whose numbers are increased through the influence of a portentously growing spirit of American nationalism. It is evident that distinctive features, distinctive attitudes of mind in the two countries, must find expression in distinct forms of language. On the other hand, beneath these surface distinctions there lies in England and in America a common stock of traditions, a common basis of character and custom and ideal, held together by a common literary heritage, for which a common form of language may be made to serve in the future as it has served in the past. Let us hope that a modern pride in prosperity may not, as in the Scriptural past, lead to a confusion of tongues, the greatest possible source of international discord.

CHAPTER XXII

MODERN SPELLING AND PRONUNCIATION

THE signs of life appearing in the use of words are convincing evidence that the English language has not yet reached a classical perfection. The stage of permanent fixity seems to be most nearly reached in the matter of spelling. There are, to be sure, minor differences between the spelling of England and that of America. Spellings such as *tyre, gaol, cyder, kerb, waggon, honour, shew, storey, jewellery, pyjamas* are usually signs of British writing or British printing. There still remain, also, a considerable number of words which in either country may be spelled in more than one way. The large standard dictionaries offer many pages with parallel columns of words with variant spellings. There has been reached, however, a uniformity in spelling so nearly complete as to approach an absolute standard. Conformity to this standard has come to be the most definite test of cultivation in language.

In earlier days, of course, the situation was different. One should recall the nature of Elizabethan spelling as it appeared in the writings of Queen Elizabeth herself. In the eighteenth century a note written by Pope is transcribed by Boswell "with minute exactness, that the peculiar mode of writing, and imperfect spelling of that celebrated poet, may be exhibited to the curious in literature." Will Honeycomb preferred to spell like a gentleman rather than like a pedant. Today the spelling of the gentleman and the pedant are the same. In popular opinion a misspelled word is the greatest sin in language. Misspelling is regarded as evidence of business incompetence, of social inferiority.

There is, of course, in the nature of English spelling little to merit this feeling of its sacredness. As has appeared in preceding pages, English spelling is in great part the production of the printer. The approximate uniformity in spelling gradually reached by printers in the seventeenth and early eighteenth centuries became the basis for the spelling registered in Johnson's *Dictionary*, and this spelling with minor modifications, such as the dropping of the final -*k* in words such as *music*(*k*), *physic*(*k*), has remained fixed. The changes which have taken place in English pronunciation have been little reflected in the conservative written forms. Hence the distance that has often come to separate the written from the spoken form, a distance sometimes closed in modern times by reversing the natural order of things and making the pronunciation conform to the spelling, a procedure, it will be recalled, that was recommended by Samuel Johnson. The other great languages of modern times have at one time or another been subjected to reform in spelling. In the French Academy dictionary, for instance, published in 1762, there are new spellings for about five thousand words, about twenty-eight per cent of all the words in the dictionary. It was about the same time that the task of registering English spelling fell to the hands of conservative Samuel Johnson. Spelling formed under such conditions may deserve the veneration that belongs to the antique, but unphonetic, irregular, and illogical as it is, modern English spelling does not merit the name *orthography* which is made up of two Greek words meaning 'correct writing.'

Attempts to improve English spelling have been by no means lacking. As early as the thirteenth century the writer, Orm, attempted through the use of double consonants to give an exact indication of pronunciation. In the sixteenth century many English words of Latin derivation were brought into conformity with Latin originals, a process, however, attended with many mistakes which have been perpetuated in later English. In the sixteenth, seventeenth, and eighteenth centuries plans were brought forward for bringing conformity between spelling and pronunciation. Benjamin Franklin even went so far as to have cast types of letters to be used in a phonetic system of printing, and tried to induce his younger contemporary, Noah Webster, to carry his plan through. Webster in his earlier years favored, and personally used, many reformed spellings. Overruled, however, in most cases by the conservative sentiment of his generation, in his great dictionary published in 1828, he introduced a relatively small number of modified spellings.

In the last quarter of the nineteenth century, following the remarkable expansion and rectification of philological ideas that the century had produced, came an attempt on the part of the learned to bring about spelling reform. The attempt had the effect of stirring up deep prejudices and provoking endless argument but produced only slight results. The shortened spellings *program* and *catalog* which no longer look as strange as they once did, may be cited as evidence of the trivial results achieved by great efforts. In the last decade of the century began an organized movement which still persists. The organizers of the movement wisely abandoned the phrase "reformed spelling" which had become associated with deep prejudices and adopted in its place the phrase "simplified spelling." The movement began with much promise. It had support from men eminent in various forms of activity, not only eminent professional scholars, but men of varied activities and professions such as Henry Holt, Mark Twain, Andrew Carnegie, and Theodore Roosevelt. It published an admirable series of pamphlets setting forth the aims of the movement and the arguments for simplified spelling. It was supported by an affiliated organization in England and had ample financial support.

The theoretical arguments were strong. Through simplified spelling the language would be better adapted for use as an international language. There would be economic gain, an annual saving in the United States alone estimated about 1900 at $40,000,000. There would be an enormous economy in the energies of the school child in the period most active in the acquisition of knowledge, an economy estimated at two and a half years in school life. There would be substituted a logical training in place of a training conducive to the formation of irregular and illogical habits of thought. Opposed to the change in spelling is the argument that there would result an increased confusion on account of the increase in the number of homophones in English. That is to say, the many words in English indistinguishable to the ear would become indistinguishable to the eye as well. There were also many arguments based on sentiment for what is traditional. But strongest of all in obstructing the movement was the force of inertia. Too much trouble was required to learn a new system of spelling to replace one already laboriously acquired after years of effort. The strength of the opposing sentiment and the deep-seated nature of existing prejudices were strikingly exhibited when Theodore Roosevelt, popular idol though he was, ventured to violate the sanctity of traditional spelling. In 1906 Roosevelt, then President, directed the Public Printer to make use of the "three hundred words" favored by the Simplified Spelling Board in the Government publications of the Executive Departments. The popular storm that followed is memorable. Editorial writers gave free rein to satire, and cartoonists gave full play to ridicule.

The revelation of the deep-seated veneration for a system of spelling logically indefensible was illuminating and startling.

The movement for improved spelling has been interesting in many ways. It has revealed not only an unreasoning popular sentiment but a form of perversity on the part of the theorists. Strange to observe is the lack of consistency displayed. The scholars most active in support of irregular grammatical forms derived from tradition have generally been most radical in favoring the abandonment of traditional modes of spelling. On the other hand among those most active in supporting the traditional spelling have been men of the schoolmaster type who have supported grammatically regular forms of expression which have tended to supplant traditional idioms. In matters of language logical consistency has always been a rare quality, virtue perhaps it should not be called.

The need for improved English spelling still exists. Any movement, however, to bring it about should be guided by light derived from the earlier history of the language. It should be held in mind that English spelling in the past was in large measure determined by the practice of printers. The spelling in Milton's first editions, for example, was not that of Milton but that of Milton's printers. Shakespeare's own spelling it is impossible to determine with certainty, but his works are now read in editions the spelling of which may be seen in gradual evolution in the four Folio editions of the seventeenth century. To the printer, therefore, one should turn in modern times if one will find the force able to disaccustom people to the illogical forms now in use and to accustom them to forms more near the ideal in giving visible form to the language. Popular sentiment and individual opinion can avail little unless they serve to convince the printer that a change in spelling on the printed page would meet with popular approval and would be profitable.

To turn from the subject of spelling to that of pronunciation is to turn from dead forms of language to living speech itself. Bernard Shaw has wittily estimated the number of spoken dialects in Great Britain as more than 40,000,000; in other words each individual has his own peculiar mode of pronunciation. Sir James Murray writes of being "present at a meeting of a learned society, where, in the course of a discussion, he heard the word *gaseous* systematically pronounced in six different ways by as many eminent physicists." The simple word *girl* has recently been recorded as pronounced in ways indicated by the spellings: *gal, göl, goil, geöl, gyurl, gurrul, girrel, gurl.* Is it possible to bring such varying pronunciation to anything like uniformity?

The experience of lexicographers down to the present time gives little ground for optimism. In the eighteenth century, it will be recalled, the spellings registered by Johnson won general acceptance, but in the matter of pronunciation no such harmonious result was achieved. Wise Scotchmen resignedly accepted the impracticability of acquiring the English accent, as they have continued to do down to our day. Sheridan and Walker and their rival orthoëpists failed to reach agreement in their recommendations regarding pronunciation and were able only to set up disputing claims to authority. From then to the present day pronunciation has been the subject of widest variance in opinion and of most violent prejudices. Modern dictionaries, unable to establish undisputed authority, adopt the method of recording varying modes of pronouncing. In their pages will be found hundreds of words that may be pronounced in more than one way. The Webster dictionaries from the start have maintained the practice of indicating the recommendations of other lexicographers by means of a section in the Introduction with parallel lists of variant pronunciations. The Standard Dictionary seeks a broader basis for its recommended pronunciations, a basis found in the judgment of a large Advisory Board composed of men representing most widely varied activities. The lack of uniformity in American pronunciation appears from the large section in the Appendix in which are recorded the varying judgments on pronunciation among members of this representative council.

A principal source of the confusion regarding English pronunciation is the English traditional spelling. The sounds in individual words in the course of centuries have undergone profound change; the spelling has remained relatively fixed. As a consequence in modern English the spelling has ceased to be a reliable guide to the pronunciation. There has been, to be sure, from early times a tendency to make the pronunciation of words conform to the spelling. The written form has again and again laid a dead hand on a living word. This tendency, already existing, naturally gained in force after the introduction of printing which through the multiplication of books made words increasingly familiar to the eye. An impression of this influence on pronunciation may be gained by an examination of the seventeenth- and eighteenth-century lists of words with pronunciation differing from their spelling and noting the changes that have since taken place in such words as *apothecary, anemone, apron, atheist, awkward, dictionary, mastiff, jaundice, nurse, saffron, vault, verdict, etc., etc.* In the cultivated speech of today an earlier traditional pronunciation still survives in words such as *iron, asthma, colonel, cupboard, wristband, scent, liquor.* More frequently, however, the written form in modern times has come to govern the spoken word. Even in simple words such as *yes* and *yet*, the traditional pronunciation, *yis* and *yit*, still surviving at the end of the eighteenth century, has been abandoned in favor of a pronunciation conforming to the spelling.

In the colonial isolation of America many of the older modes of pronunciation survive, as has already been pointed out, in the speech of the rural New Englander and the Southern mountaineer. In the social isolation also of the illiterate in London the older modes of pronunciation persist. The conservative pronunciation of such well-known London characters as Sam Weller and Mrs. Gamp has recently been made the subject of an interesting article.[1] Mrs. Gamp, one is told, "talked like an early Georgian duchess and Sam Weller like a town 'blood.'" Lady Wentworth in the early eighteenth century calls her son "dearest creetur"; Sairey Gamp speaks of the "torters of the imposition." Both Lady Wentworth and Mrs. Gamp had "lodgins." *Nuss* ('nurse') and *ojus* ('odious') and *sparrowgrass* and *cowcumber,* vulgarisms which are heard from the lips of Mrs. Gamp in the nineteenth century, are pronunciations supported by the authority of eighteenth-century orthoëpists.

The older modes of pronunciation independent of spelling are most strikingly persistent in proper names. Place names in England in older days, when they were familiar to the ear but not to the eye, were strangely distorted in pronunciation. The significant syllable was projected through the lips and the rest of the word swallowed. Some of the earlier pronunciations like those of *London, St. Albans, Holborn, Bristol* which have already been cited in the present volume, have been later superseded. English fidelity to her traditions, however, appears in the pronunciation of names such as *Harwich, Greenwich, Okehampton.*

In America, where cultivated language has unfortunately

[1] Ernest Weekley, *Cornhill Magazine,* 1922.

too often had to be learned from reading rather than from social contact, the influence of the printed form on the pronunciation has been greater than in England. The influence of spelling appears in the distinctively American pronunciation of such words as *trait* and *schedule* and *lieutenant* and in American struggles with the pronunciation of the word *literature*. It appears most strikingly in American pronunciation of adopted English names such as *Harwich, Chatham, Westmoreland,* and *Lancaster,* which in local American use are generally pronounced as spelled. The same influence, however, is to be observed in Great Britain. The Scotch name Auchinleck continues to some extent to be pronounced 'Affleck,' but the present writer was informed by the custodians of the famous Manuscript in the Advocate's Library at Edinburgh that pronunciation according to the spelling was the more usual. Even the traditional pronunciation of 'Sisiter' (for Cirencester) dear to the hearts of Americans learning English ways, Professor Wyld informs us, in local English use is being superseded by a spelling-pronunciation.

That English pronunciation, however, is ever to be brought into complete conformity with English spelling is inconceivable. In the first place traditional English spelling is too irregular ever to serve as a general guide to English sounds. Suppose one were to give a uniform pronunciation to the letters *ough* in the combination of words, *Though* he *brought* a *bough* large *enough* to put *through* the *trough.* The resulting jargon would be as absurd in sound as in sense. To attempt to make the spelling fit the sound Samuel Johnson believed would be to measure by a shadow. To reverse the process and reduce the elusive sounds of speech to a fixity would be equally inconceivable.

The sounds of speech must continue in the future to be governed as in the past by social custom. The judgment of the eighteenth century appears in the words of Lord Chesterfield: "A man of fashion takes great care to speak very correctly and grammatically, and to pronounce properly—that is, according to the use of the best companies." The same standard in speech persists today. To pronounce a word according to spelling is not necessarily "good English." The contrary is often the case as appears from a remark appearing in a recent English novel [2]: "What sort of people are the Herberts? Is Mrs. Herbert a lady?" is asked. To which is given the significant reply, "She is the sort of person who pronounces the 't' in 'often.'" Similar evidence is offered by the lexicographer, Henry Bradley: "I remember," he writes, "hearing a highly intelligent working class orator repeatedly pronounce the word *suggest* as 'sug-jest.' . . . Many people, though hardly among those who are commonly reckoned good speakers, pronounce *forehead* as it is written." "This practice," he believes, "is especially common among imperfectly educated people who are ambitious of speaking correctly."

But the speech in "the use of the best companies" is subject to change. It belongs to the realm of fashion, and fashion like fortune is fickle. New fashions in speech are adopted like new fashions in dress. Demoded language garments, as has been seen, fall to the use of the Yankee rustic or the London Cockney. From the capricious rule of fashion the practical-minded Yankee, Noah Webster, revolted. "I shall make one general effort," he declares, "to deliver literature and my countrymen from the errors that fashion and ignorance are palming upon Englishmen." Newer modes of pronunciation which in England had superseded older ones surviving in America, Webster regarded as corruptions, products of affectation. Hence his hostility to forms of speech introduced in America by English actors.

[2] Thomas Fowler, *The Faringdons,* cited by Oertel.

He refers with scorn to the "strolling party of players, who, educated in the school of corruption, have no profession, but to make people laugh, and who, dependent on opinion for subsistence, must conform to caprice, at the expense of every principle of propriety." James Fenimore Cooper, of similar opinion, declares that in English speech "fashion is even more imperious than the laws of the schools." [3] He says contemptuously [4] that "it may be enough for an Englishman that an innovation in language is supported by the pretty lips of such and such a belle of quality and high degree; but the American sees too many pretty lips at home to be very submissive to any foreign dictation of this sort." To fashionable affectations in the English speech of today even British critics have recently turned their attention. Arnold Bennett has made some interesting comments on the "grave errors of pronunciation rife in the West End." For example he cites "the horrible interpolated *r* between two vowels." "Thus," he says, "many actors will pass from the cradle to the grave and never say correctly 'soda-and-milk.' They will always say 'soda-rand-milk.'" The cultivated speech of Oxford, the affected "Oxford voice," also comes in for criticism from John Galsworthy who asserts that "some of those who employ an affected Oxford accent are more to blame for the corruption of that language than those who are born into an uneducated Cockney speech."

But the most outspoken criticism of modern fashionable English comes from St. John Ervine. He joins Galsworthy in criticism of the "abominable Oxford voice," the speech of the people of Oxford "who are steadily debasing the coins of the English speech with their emasculated voices." He criticizes the pronunciation in the liturgy of the church

[3] *Notions*, p. 161.
[4] *Ibid*, p. 168.

and ridicules a manner of speech strikingly reminiscent of that satirized by Swift. He denies uniformity even in the speech of the royal family. The King and the Queen, he declares, pronounce their *r's*. The Prince of Wales, on the other hand, does not pronounce them. The Prince of Wales, he asserts, "has a marked cockney voice and says 'howpe' when he means 'hope.' " Mr. Ervine's criticism is directed against the use and the non-use of *r*. Oxford men, he asserts, "cannot ask you to dinner, they ask you to 'dinnah.' They do not come to a lecture, they come to a 'lectchah.' The King and the Queen, on the other hand," he asserts, "overstress the *r ;* in their pronounciation 'raw eggs' would be 'rawr reggs.' "

The fashionable vowel pronunciation in words such as *five* (the diphthong *ay + ee*), Mr. Ervine represents by the spellings: *fave o'clock, refaned, polate,* etc. The manner of pronunciation referred to seems to be a survival of the "mincing manner" referred to by earlier speech critics already cited, and seems to originate, like the English pronunciation of long *o* in *no* as *eh + oh* and of *ou* in about as *eh + oo*, in a disposition to throw the sound to the front of the mouth. Such sounds lack the resonance of full-throated sounds. They are so lacking in carrying power that Mr. Ervine asserts "people who go to the theatre instead of taking opera glasses with them, take ear trumpets."

English speech, however, with all its extravagant features, with all its affectations, is a well-groomed speech. It is produced by a cultivated voice. The English accent is cherished with pride by a cultivated Englishman. It is a mark of caste. The "funny accents in those great places overseas" is the subject of a soliloquy of Soames in Galsworthy's *The Silver Spoon*. There were funny accents in England, too, but in the school at Slough where Soames had been trained, "the accent had been all right." "If it wasn't," he muses, "a boy got lammed."

American boys in school do not get "lammed" for faults in pronunciation. For mistakes in spelling no mercy is shown; but in pronunciation the only features that receive attention are the position of the accent and the length of the vowel sound in the word. These features form customarily the sole tests of correctness in American pronunciation. In other respects American oral speech runs wild. The dictionaries with their lack of precise indication regarding qualities of sound, rather than observation of the niceties of speech in the use of cultivated associates, have been in preceding generations the sole guides for most Americans seeking "correct" pronunciation. There have been a few American communities where the niceties of oral speech have been prized. This test of social caste appears in *The Autocrat of the Breakfast Table* in which one reads that "a movement or a phrase often tells you all you want to know about a person." In the training of the majority of Americans prominent today, however, such tests have not existed. Under such circumstances one can readily understand why an American like Howells should look with envy at the cultivated society of England, where "one has no need to ask how a word is pronounced, far less to go to the dictionary; one pronounces it as one has always heard it pronounced." One is also able to understand the position reached by Richard Grant White in his second book, *Every-Day English* (1880) in which he reaches the conclusion regarding pronunciation that "just in so far as it deviates from the language of the most cultivated society in England it fails to be English." The feudal homage paid to English manner of speech, by Howells and White, most Americans are unwilling to pay. Correction offered to the pronunciation of the individual is a matter of extreme delicacy and is likely to be resented. There survives regarding the quality of sounds the feeling so much in evidence in the sixteenth and seventeenth centuries that the mother tongue is a product of nature not subject to artificial regulation. Improved modes of speech taught in school are regarded as breeders of affectation and are resented by pupils and by parents.

There is much to be said in favor of this spirit of independence. Good writing conveys not only subject matter but the quality of style, and oral speech must express not only thought but personality. But there may be offensive qualities in personality. There are certainly qualities that may be learned through study and through imitation of the admirable. Even that most personal element in speech, the quality of the tone, may be regulated to advantage.

Fortunately both in England and in America much progress is being made of late in the regulation of this last element in English to be regulated. In England the "accent," the mark of social caste, subject to changing fashions and leading to affectation, is being abandoned in favor of a mode of speech based on more sound foundation. Phonetic analysis of the finer qualities of speech sound has made sources of difference more easily appreciable and has made more easy the selection of what is to be admired. Phonetic symbols for the indication of shades of sound are making it possible to convey on the printed pages information regarding the elements in pronunciation. In this way is provided a means for a cultivation of speech that is more general, through which is being created a more uniform type of cultivated pronunciation often referred to as Public School English.

In America progress in this direction has been more slow. There is to be reckoned with the American resistance to discipline, the fear of affectation in anything which has not been hitherto customary in speech and which, therefore, is felt to be not natural. The new generations in America, however, are being reared under conditions quite different from earlier ones. Modes of urban life are creating new forms of social refinement, and manner of speech is gradually coming to be more looked upon as a sign of cultivation. The schools more slowly are reckoning with new conditions but may be counted on in the near future to give proper prominence to the regulation of the least regulated feature of American speech.

At the present time, particularly in America, there is a disposition to assume the existence of an absolute standard in language. In pronunciation, as in grammar, there is assumed to be a manner that is *right* and a manner that is *wrong*. There is a prevalent demand for books and for periodicals that undertake to discriminate what is *right* from what is *wrong*. Such tests, of course, do not exist, as cannot fail to be seen by anyone who has followed the course of the development of standard English. There is, however, a good English and a bad English, and good English is the kind that is supported by the use of cultivated people. Language, one must not forget, is a conventional sign, and the more generally it is used, the clearer its intelligibility. But complete uniformity does not exist in language. The variations which exist in syntax and in the use of words are more conspicuous in pronunciation. *Municipal* with the accent on the second syllable is the prevalent pronunciation in the United States, but can one say that it is the only "right" pronunciation when one hears the word accented on the third syllable in the speech of an Englishman of prominence and cultivation speaking on a political subject? The word *doctrinal* in American use is stressed on the first syllable, but can one call this the only "right" mode of pronunciation when one hears the word pronounced with accent on the second syllable by an authority on doctrine as eminent as the Bishop of Oxford? In the same way is an American justified in saying that the "right" pronunciation of *evolution* is with a short *e* when the Advisory Committee of the British Broadcasting Company recommends the sound of long *e?*

Absolute standardization has not been reached by the English language. The differing modes of pronunciation used by two successive American Presidents, Wilson and Harding, were made the subject of an interesting communication to the American press on the occasion of President Harding's inauguration. In these days, however, when change and progress are making such rapid strides, one is justified in looking into the future. The amazing achievements in broadcasting speech by radio messages excite dreams regarding the future of the language and of a time when all English-speaking peoples may be controlled by a single standard. With remarkable foresight the British Broadcasting Company has taken this eventuality into account and has formed an Advisory Committee of six experts to regulate the speech of British Broadcasters. The kind of men composing this committee has real significance. The aim evidently is not through the far-reaching influence of the sound waves to propagate a local, insular manner of speech. The men composing the committee are six in number. Of these one is Scotch, two are Welsh, one is Irish, and one is American by birth. The form of speech to be propagated, therefore, cannot be the mother tongue in the literal sense of the phrase, but must be a form of standard English such as would be learned by men of foreign birth resident in England.

The immense possible influence of the radio in the future excites one's imagination. In the earlier days of the Elizabethans and the Augustans the standard of good English was cultivated by men in direct social contact. The speech cultivated in courtly society or coffee-house gatherings became adopted as a general manner. In the twentieth century English-speaking men in countries as distant as America and India and China and Australia are only infrequently brought into direct social contact other than with their immediate neighbors and are therefore held to a common standard only through the language of books. In isolated American communities in the past perhaps the only person to represent the standard cultivated mode of speech has been the local preacher whose manner of speech has served as the standard of correctness for the community. Through the instrumentality of the radio something like the older condition is established. From centers of culture the spoken language is to be *heard* over the English-speaking world. An American writer has recently made some interesting predictions based on the analogy of dress. In earlier days in frontier American communities anyone dressed in conventional urban garb was labelled a "dude." Today the dress of the former "dude" has become universal and consequently the "dude" as a class has ceased to exist. In a similar way in provincial communities today the cultivated urban mode of speech is regarded as priggish and affected. The writer from whom this analogy is derived dreams of a time when the speech of the broadcaster from centers of culture will diffuse a form of well-dressed speech.

The influences favoring standardization of speech have gained greatly in strength. That the language will profit thereby can hardly be open to question. Efficiency in industrial enterprises has been greatly increased through standardization. Efficiency in speech may be increased by the same means. Speech is a medium for the conveyance of meaning. Words and sounds and grammatical forms that are uniform, and, therefore, have precisely the same meaning to speaker and to hearer, will obviously convey a message with less resistance to be overcome. They will form a more efficient medium of communication. But efficiency is not all of life. The most precious elements in human existence are those associated with individuality and personality. These qualities find expression in language in a subtle and indefinable quality to which is usually given the name style. Language that lacks the personal elements that create the quality of style has lost its most precious human quality. May we have uniformity in language, but may the English language never be deprived of the freedom which has in the past made possible the revelation of personal charm, which has expressed the national characteristics of the English people, and which of late is being made to express the spirit of the young American nation.

APPENDIX I

THE NEAR RELATIONS OF ENGLISH

The English language did not originate on the soil of Great Britain. It was brought to Great Britain in the fifth century A.D. by the Angles and Saxons and Jutes, the Teutonic ancestors of the English. The closeness of the relation of early English to the kindred Teutonic languages on the Continent of Europe will appear from a comparison of early versions of the Lord's Prayer.

I. Old High German (Tatian) Version. Ninth Century

Fater unser thu thar bist in himile, si giheilagot thin namo, queme thin rihhi, si thin uuillo, so her in himile ist, so si her in erdu, unsar brot tagalihhaz gib uns hiutu, inti furlaz uns unsara sculdi, so uuir furlazemes unsaren sculdigon, inti ni gileitest unsih in costunga, uzouh arlosi unsih fon ubile.

(Sievers edition, Paderborn, 1872.)

II. Gothic Version. Fourth Century

Atta unsar þu in iminam, weinai namo þein, qimai þiudinassus þeins, wairþai wilja þeins swe in himina jah ana airþai. Hlaif unsarana, þana sinteinan, gif uns himma daga, jah aflet uns þatei skulans sijaima swaswe weis afletam þaim skulam unsaraim, jah ni briggais uns in fraistubnjai, ak lausei uns af þamma ubilin, unte þeina ist þiudangardi jah mahts jah wulpus in aiwins. *Amen.*

577

III. Icelandic Version.   Sixteenth Century

Faðir vor, sa þu ert a himnum, Helgist nafn þitt, Til komi
þitt riki, Verði þinn vili, svo a jörðu sem a himni, Gef oss i dag
vort dagligt brauð, og fyrirlat oss vorar skuldir, svo sem ver
fyrirlatum vorum skuldu-nautum, og inn leið oss eigi i freistni,
Heldr frelsa þu oss af illu; þviat þitt er rikit mattr og dyrð um
alldir allda. *Amen.*

(Translation of Lawman Odd Gotskalkson, printed in the Vigfusson
and Powell *Icelandic Reader.*)

IV. Old English Version.   Tenth Century

Fæder ure þu þe eart on heofonum, si þin nama gehalgod.
Tobecumue þin rice.   Gewurþe ðin willa on eorðan swa swa
on heofonum.   Urne gedæghwamlican hlaf syle us to dæg.
And forgyf us urne gyltas, swa swa we forgyfað urum gylten-
dume.   Anhd ne gelæd þu us on costnunge, ac alys us of yfele.
Soþlice.

(West Saxon Gospel of St. Matthew, ed. by J. W. Bright.)

V. Modern Welsh Version

The following version of the Lord's Prayer in the language of the modern Welsh, the lineal descendants of the ancient Britons, will serve to illustrate the difference between
the Teutonic languages on the one hand and the language
of the conquered Britons on the other.

Ein Tad, yr hwn wyt yn y nefoedd, santeiddier dy enw.
Deled dy deyrnas.   Gwneler dy ewyllys, megis yn y nef,
felly ar y ddaear hefyd.
Dyro i ni heddyw ein bara beunyddiol.

A maddeu i ni ein dyledion, fel y maddeuwn ninnau i'n dyledwyr.

Ac nac arwain ni i brofedigaeth; eithr gwared ni rhag drwg. Canys eiddot ti yw y deyrnas, a'r nerth, a'r gogoniant, yn oes oesoedd. *Amen.*

APPENDIX II

The languages closely related to English form the Teutonic group of languages. But this Teutonic group is itself descended from a larger group known as the Indo-European family. Languages of the Indo-European family are distinguished from other languages by their inflectional system and by a common stock of cognate words. The English language is, therefore, distantly related to other Indo-European languages, since it has with them a common ancestry.

The relationship of English to other Indo-European languages appears in the list of cognate words opposite. The relationship between the Indo-European languages is made more apparent by the lists of corresponding words from the non-Indo-European languages, Arabic, Turkish, and Hungarian.

RELATIONSHIP OF ENGLISH TO OTHER INDO-EUROPEAN LANGUAGES

English	two	three	seven	thou	me	mother	brother	daughter
Dutch	twee	drie	zeven	thu	mij	moeder	broeder	dochter
Icelandic	tvö	thriu	siö	du	mik	modhir	brodhir	dottir
High German	zwei	drei	sieben	thu	mich	mutter	bruder	tochter
Gothic	twa	thri	sibun	tu	mik		brothar	dauhtar
Lithuanian ...	du	tri	septyni	tü	manen	moter	brolis	dukter
Slavonic	dwa	tri	sedmi	tu	man	mater	brat	dochy
Celtic	dau	tri	secht	tu	me	mathair	brathair	dear (?)
Latin	duo	tres	septem	tu	me	mater	frater	
Greek	düo	treis	hepta	sü	me	meter	phrater	thugater
Persian	dwa	thri	hapta	tum	me	matar		
Sanskrit	dwa	tri	sapta	twam	me	matar	bhratar	duhitar
Arabic	ithn	thalath	sab'	anta	ana	umm	akh	bint
Turkish	iki	üch	yedi	sen	ben	ana	kardash	kiz
Hungarian ...	ket	harom	het	te	engem	anya	fiver	leany

(Whitney, *Language and the Study of Language*, p. 196.)

INDEX

Academy, 278, 279, 280, 321, 322, 326, 375

Adams, John Q., 487

Adams, Joseph Q., 150 n., 155 n., 156 n., 158 n., 214 n.

Addison, Thomas, 317-20

Agreement, 196-8, 527-31

Alden, R. M., 420 n.

Aldus, Manutius, 418

Alexander, H., 462 n.

Alford, Dean, 524-6, 537

Alliterative verse and prose, 11, 12, 20, 52, 53, 66, 116

American and British usage, 527 ff.

Americanisms, 479

Analogy, 81, 497

Apostrophe, 197

Arber, Edward, 137 n.

Arbuthnot, John, 358

Archaic and obsolete words, 65, 122, 135, 145, 305-6, 413-5

Aristotle, 120, 121

Arlen, Michael, 539 n.

Arthur and Merlin, 6

Ascham, Roger, 98, 99, 117 ff.

Austen, Jane, 495, 520-1

Babbitt, Glossary, 556-7

Bacon, Francis, 216, 283

Bailey, N., 252, 361-2

Baker, Robert, 400-1

Baldwin, Charles S., 79 n., 80 n., 81 n., 82 n., 83 n.

Bale, John, 133

Ballads, 164

Baret, J., 225

Barrow, James, 422, 423

Baskerville, C. R., 99 n.

Bayley, Anselm, 384, 431-2

Beach, J. W., 553 n.

Beard, C. A. (and M. R.), 490 n.

Beattie, James, 405, 406, 414, 502

Behn, Mrs. Aphra, 277-8, 466

Bellum Grammaticale, 330-1

Bennett, Arnold, 569

Bentley, Richard, 307, 337, 386 n.

Berdan, J. M., 45 n., 48 n., 55 n., 60 n., 61 n.

Berners, Lord, 167, 206

Beverley, R., 463 n., 464

Bible translations, 89, 110 ff., 118, 123, 256-7

Blackburn, F. A., 202 n.

Blair, Hugh, 391-2, 406

Blount, Thomas, 247-8, 251, 265, 313

Boke of Curtesye, 25, 41-2

Borrowed words, 30-2, 36, 104-5, 119, 169, 470-1

Bradley, Henry, 105 n., 214 n., 260 n.

"Bravery," 140, 143

Brightland, John (Grammar), 325 ff., 332

Brinsley, John, 128, 288
British Broadcasting Company, 574
Bronsson, J. J., 124 n.
Brown, Goold, 499-500
Bryan, W. F., 406 n.
Bryant, W. C., 492
Buchanan, James, 380 ff., 433
Bullokar, John, 251
Bullokar, Wm., 191, 229
"Busteous" style, 52-3
Butler, Charles, 160, 220
Butler, Samuel, 261-2, 465

Cambridge, 86, 119, 121, 123, 128
Campbell, Archibald, 371
Campbell, George, 391, 406 ff.
Capitals, 424, 427
Carew, R., 150
Cases, 194-5, 531-3
Castelain, 216 n.
Cawdrey, R., 177, 250
Caxton, Wm., 26, 40, 56 ff.
Chamberlin, F., 109 n., 136 n.
Channing, W. E., 489
Chaucer, 17 ff., 72, 122
Cheke, John, 108, 117 ff.
Chesterfield, Lord, 357, 360, 365, 371-3, 411-2, 568
Church, 223
Cicero, 21-2, 45, 94-5, 125-6, 128, 130, 142, 160
Clark, D. L., 45 n., 47 n., 114 n.
Classical learning, 110-1, 127, 175-6, 213 ff.
Cobbett, William, 496-7
Cockeram, H., 251
Coined words, 413
Coles, E., 252
Colet, John, 90-1, 93, 115

Collins, A. S., 357 n.
Colloquial English, 70 ff., 267
Colman, George, 515-6
Compound words, 145-6, 183
Congreve, William, 429
Connectives, 78
Connoisseur, The, 359
Cook, Albert S., 95 n., 149 n.
Cooper, Charles, 235
Cooper, J. Fenimore, 467, 475-6, 479, 488, 491-2, 569
Coote, Edmund, 231
Coote, Chas., 388-9
Courtly tendencies, 135 ff., 152-7
Cowley, C. M., 544 n.
Cox, Leonard, 128-9
Craigie, W. A., 473 n.
Crockett, Davy, 495
Croft, H. H. S., 99 n.
Croll, M. W., 141 n., 153 n., 217 n.

Daines, Simeon, 220, 421, 452
De Foe, Daniel, 290, 310, 337-8
De Quincey, Thomas, 518-20
Dialects, 2, 3, 10-3, 15 ff., 36, 67, 73-4, 76, 83, 152, 167-8, 186-7, 460 ff.
Dickens, Charles, 424
Dictionaries, 249 ff., 361-2, 433 ff.
Dilworth (Guide), 332-3, 348-50
Double comparatives, 80, 193
Double negatives, 192-3
Dryden, John, 19, 20, 220, 266 ff., 274-5
Duncan, C. S., 281 n., 282 n., 283 n.
Duns Scotus, 89, 125

Durham, W. H., 297 n.
Dyce, Alex., 47 n.
Dyche, Thomas, 332-3

Edward I, 6
Elizabeth, Queen, 136, 171, 173, 204-5, 208
Eloquence, 46, 115, 125, 142
Elphinston, James, 405, 434, 436
Elstob, Elizabeth, 331
Elyot, Sir Thomas, 60, 61, 99 ff., 249
Erasmus, D., 89 ff., 115
Ervine, St. John, 569-70
Etherege, G. W., 309
Euphuism, 140 ff.
"Excellence" of English, 149-50

"False Syntax," 382-3
Fell, John, 390-1
Fenner, D., 129
Fielding, Henry, 389-90, 410, 411
Figures, 44-5, 132, 161-2
Fisher, John, 86, 114-5
Fitzgerald, F. Scott, 551
"Flat" adverbs, 193
Foreign models, 20, 21
France, Anatole, 114
Franklin, Benjamin, 426-7, 434, 478, 482
Franz, W., 183 n., 185 n., 194 n., 200 n., 201 n., 202 n., 203 n., 210 n.
Fraunce, A., 129, 217
Freeman, E., 280 n.
French, 4, 5, 8, 20, 31, 64, 221-3, 272-4, 407

Fries, C. C., 389 n., 420 n.
Frontier, 468-9, 548-9

Galsworthy, John, 556, 570
Gardner, Bishop, 114, 117
Garland, John of, 22, 26-7, 44-5
Garnett, J. M., 142 n.
Gascoigne, George, 144-5
Sir Gawain and the Green Knight, 12
Gignoux, John, 429, 430
Gill, Alexander, 233, 246, 422
Gloucester, Robert of, 4
Goldsmith, Oliver, 389, 410, 515
Good usage, 265
Gower, John, 8, 18, 38, 40-1
Gr., P. (Grammatica), 230
Grandgent, C. H., 451, 462 n.
Graves, F. P., 94 n.
Greene, Robert, 155-6
Greenwood, James, 327-8
Grocyn, William, 89
Grosart, A., 147 n.
Grose, Captain, 408
Guevara, 142

Had rather (had better), 200, 511-2
Hall, Fitzedward, 512, 518 n., 523 n., 537-8
"Hard words," 107-8, 170 ff.
Harman, 106
Harris, James, 384 ff.
Harrison, William, 133
Hart, John, 191
Harte, Bret, 549-50
Harvey, Gabriel, 134, 137, 147-8, 205, 225

Havens, R. D., 414 n.
Hawes, Stephen, 41, 43, 47
Henry VIII, 136
Henryson, Robert, 39, 40
Hewes, Io., 232
Heywood, Thomas, 214
Hickes, G., 331
Higden, Ralph, 5, 7
Hitchcock, Elsie, 50 n., 71 n.
Hoby, Sir Thomas, 118, 137
Holmes, E., 261 n.
Holmes, O. W., 552 n.
Hoole, 289
Hotten, J. C., 408 n.
Howells, W. D., 546-8, 571
Hughes, John, 309
Humanism, 52-3, 55, 86 *ff.*
Hunt, Leigh, 455, 458-9
Hunt, L. H., 496

Inflections, 33 *ff.*, 78 *ff.*, 224
"Ink-horn terms," 108, 121-2,
   169 *ff.*
Intensives, 183-4
Irving, Washington, 490-1
"Italianated" English, 122

James I of Scotland, 39
Jespersen, Otto, 76 n., 210 n.,
   211, 220 n., 452, 454 n., 455 n.
Jests, 130
Jewel, Bishop, 133
John of Gaunt, 8, 9
Johnson, Samuel, 352, 364 *ff.*,
   428-9, 432, 448, 560
Johnston, William, 433, 434
Jones, Hugh, 477
Jones, John, 449
Jonson, Ben, 145, 158, 201, 216,
   234, 248, 266 *ff.*

Joyce, James, 543
Junius, F., 368

K., J. (*Dictionary*), 361
Kelso, Ruth, 136 n.
Kemble, John P., 458-9
Kenrick, William, 431, 432,
   435-6
King, Humphrey, 220
"King's English," The, 226
K(irke), E(dward), 145
Kirkham, Samuel, 499
Krapp, G. P., 129 n., 132 n.,
   133 n., 134 n., 136 n., 149 n.,
   216 n., 283 n., 452, 455 n.,
   465, 475 n.

Landor, W. S., 509-10
Lane, A., 291 *ff.*
Latimer, Hugh, 115-6
Latin, 5, 6, 32, 43, 49, 55, 78,
   92, 100, 101-4, 105-6, 109,
   114, 172-3, 218 *ff.*, 232-3, 260-
   1, 355, 383
Leach, A. F., 43 n., 44 n., 91 n.,
   92 n.
Lee, S. L., 167 n.
Leland, John, 133
Lily, Wm., 89, 90, 92, 219
Linacre, Thomas, 89, 90
Logic in grammar, 293
Lollard writers, 15
London, 16-18, 83, 152, 340 *ff.*,
   501
Lounsbury, Thomas R., 438 n.,
   502 n., 512 n.
Low, Samuel, 480
"Low" words, 372
Lowell, J. R., 461, 462, 493-4
Lowth, Robert, 377 *ff.*, 422

Luckombe, P., 418, 419
Lydgate, John, 38, 39, 40, 46-7, 71
Lyly, John, 96, 137, 140 ff., 153, 199, 217
Lyman, R. L., 476 n., 478 n., 498 n.

Maar, H. G. de, 415 n.
Macaulay, Thomas B., 510
Machyn, Henry, 106, 206 ff.
Mair, G. H., 131 n.
Malapropisms, 107-9
Malone, Kemp, 429 n.
Malory, Sir Thomas, 79 ff.
Mannyng, Robert, of Brunne, 2, 5
Many Advantages of a Good Language, The, 358, 363-4
Marston, J., 214 n.
Masefield, John, 544, 556
Mattaire, Michael, 328-9
Matthew of Westminster, 6
Mencken, H. L., 492 n., 545 n., 546, 553-4, 558
Meres, Francis, 156
Middleton, T., 220
Miege, Guy, 242-3
Milton, John, 244 ff., 258-9, 260-1, 307 ff., 418
Monboddo, Lord, 383, 405
Monroe, B. S., 279 n.
Moore, J. L., 215 n., 225 n., 248 n., 257 n., 265 n., 318 n.
More, Hannah, 495
More, P. E., 554
More, Sir Thomas, 88 ff., 113
More, Sir Thomas (the play), 208
Morte Arthur, 12
Mulcaster, Richard, 149, 179-80, 223-5

Murray, Lindley, 381, 393 ff., 416, 421, 450, 498

Nares, Robert, 376, 436
Nashe, Thomas, 134, 146-8, 205
Native words, 73, 113, 181
Naturalism, 542-3
New Learning, 53, 68, 87 ff., 128
Newbolt Commission, 526 n.
Newfangled words, 215, 216
Newman, Cardinal, 514

Observations upon the English Language, 401-4
Occleve, Thomas, 17, 38-9
Oertel, H., 568 n.
Oliphant, T. L. K., 65 n., 73 n., 114 n.
Onions, C. T., 187 n.
Orbellis, Nicolaus de, 125
Ovid, 159-60
Oxford, 15, 89, 124-5

Palsgrave, John, 97
Parliament, 7, 18
Passive constructions, 511
Paston Letters, 72-4
Peacham, Henry, 129, 132, 218
Pearl, 12, 13
Pecock, Reginald, 49-51, 71
Pegge, Samuel, 501
Pettie, George, 144, 149
Phillips, Edward, 249, 251
Phonetics, 572
Pickering, John, 489-90
Piers Plowman, 13, 14, 51
Pilgrim's Progress, 257

Piozzi, Mrs. H., 409, 410, 411
Poe, Edgar A., 491
Pope, Alexander, 218, 303
Possessives, 243-4
Preaching, 114-6
Prepositions, 184-5
Priestley, Joseph, 379 ff., 390 ff.
Printing, 56 ff., 61-2, 243, 419, 424
Prodigal Son, The, 107
Profanity, 214-5, 505-6
Progressive forms, 200
Pronouns, 77, 82, 193-4
Pronunciation, 37, 75-6, 205 ff., 209-1, 348-50, 374-5, 441 ff., 451 ff., 456, 458
Propriety, 371-2
Prose, 24-6, 31-2, 49, 64
Publication, 139, 356-7
Puns, 177, 268, 300
Purists, 110 ff, 118 ff., 134, 144, 400 ff., 540
Puritans, 261, 264
Puttenham, George (*Arte of Poesie*), 131, 144, 152, 170

Quintilian, 125-6, 129-30

Radio, 574-5
Rainold, Richard, 129
Raleigh, Sir Walter, 157, 168
Ramus, Peter, 94, 126-8, 222
Rastell, John, 99
Ray, John, 287
Reade, Charles, 523
Reason in language, 535
Restoration of English, 7 ff.
Rhetoric, 21 ff., 45 ff., 121, 124 ff., 126-129, 132, 151-154

Robertson, Joseph, 423
Rollin, M., 379
Routh, E. M. G., 86 n., 115 n.
Rowe, Nicholas, 302
Royal Society, 282

Saintsbury, G. W., 273 n.
Sandburg, Carl, 553
Schemes, 132, 140-2
Schick, Josef, 71 n., 85 n.
Schoolmasters, 155, 159, 190, 213 ff.
Schools, 18, 43-45, 91 ff., 124-5, 154, 289 ff., 473 ff.
Science, 280-4, 541-2
Scotch poets, 39-40
Scott, Walter, 418, 521-3
Scotticisms, 405, 508
Scribes, 71-2
Selden, John, 247
Shakespeare, William, 98, 108, 151 ff., 166 ff., 235 ff., 270-1, 301 ff., 419-20
Sharp, Granville, 429, 430
Shepherd, H. E., 337 n.
Sheridan, Thomas, 351 ff., 376, 434-8
Sherry, Richard, 129
Sidney, Sir Philip, 143, 149, 224-5
Skeat, Walter W., 72 n.
Skelton, John, 25-6, 40-1, 47, 52 ff., 85, 90
Skinner, S., 368
Slang (and cant), 122, 252, 301, 372, 408 ff., 507-8, 551-2
Smetham, Thomas, 430, 431
Smith, Adam, 405
Smith, C. Alphonso, 196 n., 236 n.
Smith, Logan P., 32 n., 104 n., 298 n.

Smith, Sir Thomas, 117 *ff.*, 191
Spectator, 312 *ff.*
Spelling, 119-20, 171, 191-2, 206 *ff.*, 228-9, 368, 448-50, 560-3, 565-7
Spencer, H., 271 n.
Spenser, Edmund, 17, 41, 42, 144-5, 168, 248, 415, 517-8
Spiller, R. E., 488 n.
Society for Pure English, 323
Southey, Robert, 517-8
Split infinitive, 203, 512-3
Stackhouse, Thomas, 423
Standard English, 3, 4
Steel, David, 423
Strachey, J. St. Loe, 311 n.
Style, levels of, 26-29, 129-30, 161, 176, 187-8
Surrey, Earl of, 84-5, 166
Swift, Jonathan, 312 *ff.*, 336, 353
Swinnerton, F., 557

Talæus (Talon), 125-7, 160
Tatler, 313 *ff.*
Taylor, Richard, 513
Technical words, 366-7
Terms, literary, 104
Thaler, A., 258 n.
Theobald, L., 303
Tibino, Nicolo, 45
Tilley, M. P., 214 n., 264 n.
Tooke, Horne, 385
Tranlacing, 134
Translations, 63, 158
"Translations" of meaning, 182
Trevisa, John de, 2, 7, 10-11, 15, 51, 64-5
Tropes, 22, 132, 178
Twain, Mark, 550
Tyler, M. C., 461 n., 474 n., 475 n.

Tyler, Royall, 479, 481
Tyndale, William, 111, 113-4, 118

Universal grammar, 385-6
Upland, Jack, 51
Usage, tests, 407 *ff.*
Usk, Thomas of, 9, 38-9

Van Dam, B. A. P., 236 n., 462 n.
Van der Gaaf, W., 200 n.
Vaugelas, 416
Verbs and verb forms, 78-9, 82, 199-203, 534
Verney papers, 255-6, 448
Vinsauf, Geoffrey de, 22-3
Vives, Juan L., 93, 99-100
Vocabulary, 186
Vodoz, J., 231 n., 244 n., 247 n.
Vulgarities, correction of speech, 562 *ff.*
Vulgarities of Speech, 455

Walker, John, 376, 436 *ff.*
Waller, Edmund, 320
Wallis, John, 245, 284-5
Warburton, William, 304-5, 363
Ward, John, 384
Ward, William, 381, 384, 387-8
Warton, Thomas, 93 n., 115 n.
Watson, Foster, 93 n., 96 n., 97 n., 139 n., 218 n., 255 n., 257 n., 288 n., 289 n., 323 n.
Watts, Isaac, 332, 341
Webster, Noah, 421, 470-2, 478, 482 *ff.*, 545, 568
Weekley, Ernest, 566 n.

Welsted, Leonard, 297, 414

Wendell, B., 493 n.

Weston, Jessie L., 2 n.

Wharton, Edith, 557

Wharton, J., 237, 242

White, Richard Grant, 400, 511, 536-7, 571

Whitman, Walt, 545

Wilkins, John, 285

William of Palerne, 6

Wilson, Sir Thomas, 42, 106, 107, 108, 117 *ff.*, 129 *ff.*, 160, 165, 173

Wilson, V., 254 n.

Witherspoon, John, 478-9, 514

Women, 138, 253-5, 311, 355-6, 519

Woolf, Virginia, 555 n.

Worcester, Joseph, 490

Words objected to, 400 *ff.*

Wyatt, Sir Thomas, 58-60

Wyclif, John, 15, 49, 110

Wyld, H. C., 76 n, 168 n., 206 n., 208 n., 256 n., 448 n., 449 n., 456 n., 457 n., 464 n.

CATALOGUE OF DOVER BOOKS

Language Books and Records

GERMAN: HOW TO SPEAK AND WRITE IT. AN INFORMAL CONVERSATIONAL METHOD FOR SELF STUDY, Joseph Rosenberg. Eminently useful for self study because of concentration on elementary stages of learning. Also provides teachers with remarkable variety of aids: 28 full- and double-page sketches with pertinent items numbered and identified in German and English; German proverbs, jokes; grammar, idiom studies; extensive practice exercises. The most interesting introduction to German available, full of amusing illustrations, photographs of cities and landmarks in German-speaking cities, cultural information subtly woven into conversational material. Includes summary of grammar, guide to letter writing, study guide to German literature by Dr. Richard Friedenthal. Index. 400 illustrations. 384pp. 5⅜ x 8½.
T271 Paperbound **$2.00**

FRENCH: HOW TO SPEAK AND WRITE IT. AN INFORMAL CONVERSATIONAL METHOD FOR SELF STUDY, Joseph Lemaitre. Even the absolute beginner can acquire a solid foundation for further study from this delightful elementary course. Photographs, sketches and drawings, sparkling colloquial conversations on a wide variety of topics (including French culture and custom), French sayings and quips, are some of aids used to demonstrate rather than merely describe the language. Thorough yet surprisingly entertaining approach, excellent for teaching and for self study. Comprehensive analysis of pronunciation, practice exercises and appendices of verb tables, additional vocabulary, other useful material. Index. Appendix. 400 illustrations. 416pp. 5⅜ x 8½.
T268 Paperbound **$2.00**

DICTIONARY OF SPOKEN SPANISH, Spanish-English, English-Spanish. Compiled from spoken Spanish, emphasizing idiom and colloquial usage in both Castilian and Latin-American. More than 16,000 entries containing over 25,000 idioms—the largest list of idiomatic constructions ever published. Complete sentences given, indexed under single words—grammar in immediately useable form, for travellers, businessmen, students, etc. 25 page introduction provides rapid survey of sounds, grammar, syntax, with full consideration of irregular verbs. Especially apt in modern treatment of phrases and structure. 17 page glossary gives translations of geographical names, money values, numbers, national holidays, important street signs, useful expressions of high frequency, plus unique 7 page glossary of Spanish and Spanish-American foods and dishes. Originally published as War Department Technical Manual TM 30-900. iv + 513pp. 5⅜ x 8.
T495 Paperbound **$1.75**

SPEAK MY LANGUAGE: SPANISH FOR YOUNG BEGINNERS, M. Ahlman, Z. Gilbert. Records provide one of the best, and most entertaining, methods of introducing a foreign language to children. Within the framework of a train trip from Portugal to Spain, an English-speaking child is introduced to Spanish by a native companion. (Adapted from a successful radio program of the N. Y. State Educational Department.) Though a continuous story, there are a dozen specific categories of expressions, including greetings, numbers, time, weather, food, clothes, family members, etc. Drill is combined with poetry and contextual use. Authentic background music is heard. An accompanying book enables a reader to follow the records, and includes a vocabulary of over 350 recorded expressions. Two 10″ 33⅓ records, total of 40 minutes. Book. 40 illustrations. 69pp. 5¼ x 10½.
T890 The set **$4.95**

AN ENGLISH-FRENCH-GERMAN-SPANISH WORD FREQUENCY DICTIONARY, H. S. Eaton. An indispensable language study aid, this is a semantic frequency list of the 6000 most frequently used words in 4 languages—24,000 words in all. The lists, based on concepts rather than words alone, and containing all modern, exact, and idiomatic vocabulary, are arranged side by side to form a unique 4-language dictionary. A simple key indicates the importance of the individual words within each language. Over 200 pages of separate indexes for each language enable you to locate individual words at a glance. Will help language teachers and students, authors of textbooks, grammars, and language tests to compare concepts in the various languages and to concentrate on basic vocabulary, avoiding uncommon and obsolete words. 2 Appendixes. xxi + 441pp. 6½ x 9¼.
T738 Paperbound **$2.75**

NEW RUSSIAN-ENGLISH AND ENGLISH-RUSSIAN DICTIONARY, M. A. O'Brien. Over 70,000 entries in the new orthography! Many idiomatic uses and colloquialisms which form the basis of actual speech. Irregular verbs, perfective and imperfective aspects, regular and irregular sound changes, and other features. One of the few dictionaries where accent changes within the conjugation of verbs and the declension of nouns are fully indicated. "One of the best," Prof. E. J. Simmons, Cornell. First names, geographical terms, bibliography, etc. 738pp. 4½ x 6¼.
T208 Paperbound **$2.00**

96 MOST USEFUL PHRASES FOR TOURISTS AND STUDENTS in English, French, Spanish, German, Italian. A handy folder you'll want to carry with you. How to say "Excuse me," "How much is it?", "Write it down, please," etc., in four foreign languages. Copies limited, no more than 1 to a customer.
FREE

Philosophy, Religion

GUIDE TO PHILOSOPHY, C. E. M. Joad. A modern classic which examines many crucial problems which man has pondered through the ages: Does free will exist? Is there plan in the universe? How do we know and validate our knowledge? Such opposed solutions as subjective idealism and realism, chance and teleology, vitalism and logical positivism, are evaluated and the contributions of the great philosophers from the Greeks to moderns like Russell, Whitehead, and others, are considered in the context of each problem. "The finest introduction," BOSTON TRANSCRIPT. Index. Classified bibliography. 592pp. 5⅜ x 8.
T297 Paperbound **$2.25**

HISTORY OF ANCIENT PHILOSOPHY, W. Windelband. One of the clearest, most accurate comprehensive surveys of Greek and Roman philosophy. Discusses ancient philosophy in general, intellectual life in Greece in the 7th and 6th centuries B.C., Thales, Anaximander, Anaximenes, Heraclitus, the Eleatics, Empedocles, Anaxagoras, Leucippus, the Pythagoreans, the Sophists, Socrates, Democritus (20 pages), Plato (50 pages), Aristotle (70 pages), the Peripatetics, Stoics, Epicureans, Sceptics, Neo-platonists, Christian Apologists, etc. 2nd German edition translated by H. E. Cushman. xv + 393pp. 5⅜ x 8. T357 Paperbound **$1.85**

ILLUSTRATIONS OF THE HISTORY OF MEDIEVAL THOUGHT AND LEARNING, R. L. Poole. Basic analysis of the thought and lives of the leading philosophers and ecclesiastics from the 8th to the 14th century—Abailard, Ockham, Wycliffe, Marsiglio of Padua, and many other great thinkers who carried the torch of Western culture and learning through the "Dark Ages": political, religious, and metaphysical views. Long a standard work for scholars and one of the best introductions to medieval thought for beginners. Index. 10 Appendices. xiii + 327pp. 5⅜ x 8. T674 Paperbound **$2.00**

PHILOSOPHY AND CIVILIZATION IN THE MIDDLE AGES, M. de Wulf. This semi-popular survey covers aspects of medieval intellectual life such as religion, philosophy, science, the arts, etc. It also covers feudalism vs. Catholicism, rise of the universities, mendicant orders, monastic centers, and similar topics. Unabridged. Bibliography. Index. viii + 320pp. 5⅜ x 8.
T284 Paperbound **$1.85**

AN INTRODUCTION TO SCHOLASTIC PHILOSOPHY, Prof. M. de Wulf. Formerly entitled SCHOLASTICISM OLD AND NEW, this volume examines the central scholastic tradition from St. Anselm, Albertus Magnus, Thomas Aquinas, up to Suarez in the 17th century. The relation of scholasticism to ancient and medieval philosophy and science in general is clear and easily followed. The second part of the book considers the modern revival of scholasticism, the Louvain position, relations with Kantianism and Positivism. Unabridged. xvi + 271pp. 5⅜ x 8.
T296 Clothbound **$3.50**
T283 Paperbound **$2.00**

A HISTORY OF MODERN PHILOSOPHY, H. Höffding. An exceptionally clear and detailed coverage of western philosophy from the Renaissance to the end of the 19th century. Major and minor men such as Pomponazzi, Bodin, Boehme, Telesius, Bruno, Copernicus, da Vinci, Kepler, Galileo, Bacon, Descartes, Hobbes, Spinoza, Leibniz, Wolff, Locke, Newton, Berkeley, Hume, Erasmus, Montesquieu, Voltaire, Diderot, Rousseau, Lessing, Kant, Herder, Fichte, Schelling, Hegel, Schopenhauer, Comte, Mill, Darwin, Spencer, Hartmann, Lange, and many others, are discussed in terms of theory of knowledge, logic, cosmology, and psychology. Index. 2 volumes, total of 1159pp. 5⅜ x 8.
T117 Vol. 1, Paperbound **$2.50**
T118 Vol. 2, Paperbound **$2.25**

ARISTOTLE, A. E. Taylor. A brilliant, searching non-technical account of Aristotle and his thought written by a foremost Platonist. It covers the life and works of Aristotle; classification of the sciences; logic; first philosophy; matter and form; causes; motion and eternity; God; physics; metaphysics; and similar topics. Bibliography. New Index compiled for this edition. 128pp. 5⅜ x 8. T280 Paperbound **$1.00**

THE SYSTEM OF THOMAS AQUINAS, M. de Wulf. Leading Neo-Thomist, one of founders of University of Louvain, gives concise exposition to central doctrines of Aquinas, as a means toward determining his value to modern philosophy, religion. Formerly "Medieval Philosophy Illustrated from the System of Thomas Aquinas." Trans. by E. Messenger. Introduction. 151pp. 5⅜ x 8. T568 Paperbound **$1.25**

LEIBNIZ, H. W. Carr. Most stimulating middle-level coverage of basic philosophical thought of Leibniz. Easily understood discussion, analysis of major works: "Theodicy," "Principles of Nature and Grace," "Monadology"; Leibniz's influence; intellectual growth; correspondence; disputes with Bayle, Malebranche, Newton; importance of his thought today, with reinterpretation in modern terminology. "Power and mastery," London Times. Bibliography. Index. 226pp. 5⅜ x 8. T624 Paperbound **$1.35**

CATALOGUE OF DOVER BOOKS

THE SENSE OF BEAUTY, G. Santayana. A revelation of the beauty of language as well as an important philosophic treatise, this work studies the "why, when, and how beauty appears, what conditions an object must fulfill to be beautiful, what elements of our nature make us sensible of beauty, and what the relation is between the constitution of the object and the excitement of our susceptibility." "It is doubtful if a better treatment of the subject has since been published," PEABODY JOURNAL. Index. ix + 275pp. 5⅜ x 8.
T238 Paperbound **$1.00**

PROBLEMS OF ETHICS, Moritz Schlick. The renowned leader of the "Vienna Circle" applies the logical positivist approach to a wide variety of ethical problems: the source and means of attaining knowledge, the formal and material characteristics of the good, moral norms and principles, absolute vs. relative values, free will and responsibility, comparative importance of pleasure and suffering as ethical values, etc. Disarmingly simple and straightforward despite complexity of subject. First English translation, authorized by author before his death, of a thirty-year old classic. Translated and with an introduction by David Rynin. Index. Foreword by Prof. George P. Adams. xxi + 209pp. 5⅜ x 8.
T946 Paperbound **$1.60**

AN INTRODUCTION TO EXISTENTIALISM, Robert G. Olson. A new and indispensable guide to one of the major thought systems of our century, the movement that is central to the thinking of some of the most creative figures of the past hundred years. Stresses Heidegger and Sartre, with careful and objective examination of the existentialist position, values—freedom of choice, individual dignity, personal love, creative effort—and answers to the eternal questions of the human condition. Scholarly, unbiased, analytic, unlike most studies of this difficult subject, Prof. Olson's book is aimed at the student of philosophy as well as at the reader with no formal training who is looking for an absorbing, accessible, and thorough introduction to the basic texts. Index. xv + 221pp. 5⅜ x 8½.
T55 Paperbound **$1.65**

SYMBOLIC LOGIC, C. I. Lewis and C. H. Langford. Since first publication in 1932, this has been among most frequently cited works on symbolic logic. Still one of the best introductions both for beginners and for mathematicians, philosophers. First part covers basic topics which easily lend themselves to beginning study. Second part is rigorous, thorough development of logistic method, examination of some of most difficult and abstract aspects of symbolic logic, including modal logic, logical paradoxes, many-valued logic, with Prof. Lewis' own contributions. 2nd revised (corrected) edition. 3 appendixes, one new to this edition. 524pp. 5⅜ x 8.
S170 Paperbound **$2.00**

WHITEHEAD'S PHILOSOPHY OF CIVILIZATION, A. H. Johnson. A leading authority on Alfred North Whitehead synthesizes the great philosopher's thought on civilization, scattered throughout various writings, into unified whole. Analysis of Whitehead's general definition of civilization, his reflections on history and influences on its development, his religion, including his analysis of Christianity, concept of solitariness as first requirement of personal religion, and so on. Other chapters cover views on minority groups, society, civil liberties, education. Also critical comments on Whitehead's philosophy. Written with general reader in mind. A perceptive introduction to important area of the thought of a leading philosopher of our century. Revised index and bibliography. xii + 211pp. 5⅜ x 8½.
T996 Paperbound **$1.50**

WHITEHEAD'S THEORY OF REALITY, A. H. Johnson. Introductory outline of Whitehead's theory of actual entities, the heart of his philosophy of reality, followed by his views on nature of God, philosophy of mind, theory of value (truth, beauty, goodness and their opposites), analyses of other philosophers, attitude toward science. A perspicacious lucid introduction by author of dissertation on Whitehead, written under the subject's supervision at Harvard. Good basic view for beginning students of philosophy and for those who are simply interested in important contemporary ideas. Revised index and bibliography. xiii + 267pp. 5⅜ x 8½.
T989 Paperbound **$2.00**

MIND AND THE WORLD-ORDER, C. I. Lewis. Building upon the work of Peirce, James, and Dewey, Professor Lewis outlines a theory of knowledge in terms of "conceptual pragmatism." Dividing truth into abstract mathematical certainty and empirical truth, the author demonstrates that the traditional understanding of the a priori must be abandoned. Detailed analyses of philosophy, metaphysics, method, the "given" in experience, knowledge of objects, nature of the a priori, experience and order, and many others. Appendices. xiv + 446pp. 5⅜ x 8.
T359 Paperbound **$2.25**

SCEPTICISM AND ANIMAL FAITH, G. Santayana. To eliminate difficulties in the traditional theory of knowledge, Santayana distinguishes between the independent existence of objects and the essence our mind attributes to them. Scepticism is thereby established as a form of belief, and animal faith is shown to be a necessary condition of knowledge. Belief, classical idealism, intuition, memory, symbols, literary psychology, and much more, discussed with unusual clarity and depth. Index. xii + 314pp. 5⅜ x 8.
T235 Clothbound **$3.50**
T236 Paperbound **$1.75**

LANGUAGE AND MYTH, E. Cassirer. Analyzing the non-rational thought processes which go to make up culture, Cassirer demonstrates that beneath both language and myth there lies a dominant unconscious "grammar" of experience whose categories and canons are not those of logical thought. His analyses of seemingly diverse phenomena such as Indian metaphysics, the Melanesian "mana," the Naturphilosophie of Schelling, modern poetry, etc., are profound without being pedantic. Introduction and translation by Susanne Langer. Index. x + 103pp. 5⅜ x 8.
T51 Paperbound **$1.25**

CATALOGUE OF DOVER BOOKS

AN ESSAY CONCERNING HUMAN UNDERSTANDING, John Locke. Edited by A. C. Fraser. Unabridged reprinting of definitive edition; only complete edition of "Essay" in print. Marginal analyses of almost every paragraph; hundreds of footnotes; authoritative 140-page biographical, critical, historical prolegomena. Indexes. 1170pp. 5⅜ x 8.
T530 Vol. 1 (Books 1, 2) Paperbound **$2.50**
T531 Vol. 2 (Books 3, 4) Paperbound **$2.50**
2 volume set **$5.00**

THE PHILOSOPHY OF HISTORY, G. W. F. Hegel. One of the great classics of western thought which reveals Hegel's basic principle: that history is not chance but a rational process, the realization of the Spirit of Freedom. Ranges from the oriental cultures of subjective thought to the classical subjective cultures, to the modern absolute synthesis where spiritual and secular may be reconciled. Translation and introduction by J. Sibree. Introduction by C. Hegel. Special introduction for this edition by Prof. Carl Friedrich. xxxix + 447pp. 5⅜ x 8.
T112 Paperbound **$2.25**

THE PHILOSOPHY OF HEGEL, W. T. Stace. The first detailed analysis of Hegel's thought in English, this is especially valuable since so many of Hegel's works are out of print. Dr. Stace examines Hegel's debt to Greek idealists and the 18th century and then proceeds to a careful description and analysis of Hegel's first principles, categories, reason, dialectic method, his logic, philosophy of nature and spirit, etc. Index. Special 14 x 20 chart of Hegelian system. x + 526pp. 5⅜ x 8.
T254 Paperbound **$2.75**

THE WILL TO BELIEVE and HUMAN IMMORTALITY, W. James. Two complete books bound as one. THE WILL TO BELIEVE discusses the interrelations of belief, will, and intellect in man; chance vs. determinism, free will vs. determinism, free will vs. fate, pluralism vs. monism; the philosophies of Hegel and Spencer, and more. HUMAN IMMORTALITY examines the question of survival after death and develops an unusual and powerful argument for immortality. Two prefaces. Index. Total of 429pp. 5⅜ x 8.
T291 Paperbound **$2.00**

THE WORLD AND THE INDIVIDUAL, Josiah Royce. Only major effort by an American philosopher to interpret nature of things in systematic, comprehensive manner. Royce's formulation of an absolute voluntarism remains one of the original and profound solutions to the problems involved. Part One, Four Historical Conceptions of Being, inquires into first principles, true meaning and place of individuality. Part Two, Nature, Man, and the Moral Order, is application of first principles to problems concerning religion, evil, moral order. Introduction by J. E. Smith, Yale Univ. Index. 1070pp. 5⅜ x 8.
T561 Vol. 1 Paperbound **$2.75**
T562 Vol. 2 Paperbound **$2.75**
Two volume set **$5.50**

THE PHILOSOPHICAL WRITINGS OF PEIRCE, edited by J. Buchler. This book (formerly THE PHILOSOPHY OF PEIRCE) is a carefully integrated exposition of Peirce's complete system composed of selections from his own work. Symbolic logic, scientific method, theory of signs, pragmatism, epistemology, chance, cosmology, ethics, and many other topics are treated by one of the greatest philosophers of modern times. This is the only inexpensive compilation of his key ideas. xvi + 386pp. 5⅜ x 8.
T217 Paperbound **$2.00**

EXPERIENCE AND NATURE, John Dewey. An enlarged, revised edition of the Paul Carus lectures which Dewey delivered in 1925. It covers Dewey's basic formulation of the problem of knowledge, with a full discussion of other systems, and a detailing of his own concepts of the relationship of external world, mind, and knowledge. Starts with a thorough examination of the philosophical method; examines the interrelationship of experience and nature; analyzes experience on basis of empirical naturalism, the formulation of law, role of language and social factors in knowledge; etc. Dewey's treatment of central problems in philosophy is profound but extremely easy to follow. ix + 448pp. 5⅜ x 8.
T471 Paperbound **$2.00**

THE PHILOSOPHICAL WORKS OF DESCARTES. The definitive English edition of all the major philosophical works and letters of René Descartes. All of his revolutionary insights, from his famous "Cogito ergo sum" to his detailed account of contemporary science and his astonishingly fruitful concept that all phenomena of the universe (except mind) could be reduced to clear laws by the use of mathematics. An excellent source for the thought of men like Hobbes, Arnauld, Gassendi, etc., who were Descarte's contemporaries. Translated by E. S. Haldane and G. Ross. Introductory notes. Index. Total of 842pp. 5⅜ x 8.
T71 Vol. 1, Paperbound **$2.00**
T72 Vol. 2, Paperbound **$2.00**

THE CHIEF WORKS OF SPINOZA. An unabridged reprint of the famous Bohn edition containing all of Spinoza's most important works: Vol. I: The Theologico-Political Treatise and the Political Treatise. Vol. II: On The Improvement of Understanding, The Ethics, Selected Letters. Profound and enduring ideas on God, the universe, pantheism, society, religion, the state, democracy, the mind, emotions, freedom and the nature of man, which influenced Goethe, Hegel, Schelling, Coleridge, Whitehead, and many others. Introduction. 2 volumes. 826pp. 5⅜ x 8.
T249 Vol. I, Paperbound **$1.75**
T250 Vol. II, Paperbound **$1.50**

THE ANALYSIS OF MATTER, Bertrand Russell. A classic which has retained its importance in understanding the relation between modern physical theory and human perception. Logical analysis of physics, prerelativity physics, causality, scientific inference, Weyl's theory, tensors, invariants and physical interpretations, periodicity, and much more is treated with Russell's usual brilliance. "Masterly piece of clear thinking and clear writing," NATION AND ATHENAEUM. "Most thorough treatment of the subject," THE NATION. Introduction. Index. 8 figures. viii + 408pp. 5⅜ x 8.　　　　　　　　　　　　　　　　　　　　S231 Paperbound **$1.95**

CONCEPTUAL THINKING (A LOGICAL INQUIRY), S. Körner. Discusses origin, use of general concepts on which language is based, and the light they shed on basic philosophical questions. Rigorously examines how different concepts are related; how they are linked to experience; problems in the field of contact between exact logical, mathematical, and scientific concepts, and the inexactness of everyday experience (studied at length). This work elaborates many new approaches to the traditional problems of philosophy—epistemology, value theories, metaphysics, aesthetics, morality. "Rare originality . . . brings a new rigour into philosophical argument," Philosophical Quarterly. New corrected second edition. Index. vii + 301pp. 5⅜ x 8.　　　　　　　　　　　　　　　　　　　　T516 Paperbound **$1.75**

INTRODUCTION TO SYMBOLIC LOGIC, S. Langer. No special knowledge of math required — probably the clearest book ever written on symbolic logic, suitable for the layman, general scientist, and philosopher. You start with simple symbols and advance to a knowledge of the Boole-Schroeder and Russell-Whitehead systems. Forms, logical structure, classes, the calculus of propositions, logic of the syllogism, etc., are all covered. "One of the clearest and simplest introductions," MATHEMATICS GAZETTE. Second enlarged, revised edition. 368pp. 5⅜ x 8.　　　　　　　　　　　　　　　　　　　　S164 Paperbound **$1.85**

LANGUAGE, TRUTH AND LOGIC, A. J. Ayer. A clear, careful analysis of the basic ideas of Logical Positivism. Building on the work of Schlick, Russell, Carnap, and the Viennese School, Mr. Ayer develops a detailed exposition of the nature of philosophy, science, and metaphysics; the Self and the World; logic and common sense, and other philosophic concepts. An aid to clarity of thought as well as the first full-length development of Logical Positivism in English. Introduction by Bertrand Russell. Index. 160pp. 5⅜ x 8.　　　　T10 Paperbound **$1.25**

ESSAYS IN EXPERIMENTAL LOGIC, J. Dewey. Based upon the theory that knowledge implies a judgment which in turn implies an inquiry, these papers consider the inquiry stage in terms of: the relationship of thought and subject matter, antecedents of thought, data and meanings. 3 papers examine Bertrand Russell's thought, while 2 others discuss pragmatism and a final essay presents a new theory of the logic of values. Index. viii + 444pp. 5⅜ x 8.
　　　　　　　　　　　　　　　　　　　　　　　　　　　　　　T73 Paperbound **$2.25**

TRAGIC SENSE OF LIFE, M. de Unamuno. The acknowledged masterpiece of one of Spain's most influential thinkers. Between the despair at the inevitable death of man and all his works and the desire for something better, Unamuno finds that "saving incertitude" that alone can console us. This dynamic appraisal of man's faith in God and in himself has been called "a masterpiece" by the ENCYCLOPAEDIA BRITANNICA. xxx + 332pp. 5⅜ x 8.
　　　　　　　　　　　　　　　　　　　　　　　　　　　　　　T257 Paperbound **$2.00**

HISTORY OF DOGMA, A. Harnack. Adolph Harnack, who died in 1930, was perhaps the greatest Church historian of all time. In this epoch-making history, which has never been surpassed in comprehensiveness and wealth of learning, he traces the development of the authoritative Christian doctrinal system from its first crystallization in the 4th century down through the Reformation, including also a brief survey of the later developments through the Infallibility decree of 1870. He reveals the enormous influence of Greek thought on the early Fathers, and discusses such topics as the Apologists, the great councils, Manichaeism, the historical position of Augustine, the medieval opposition to indulgences, the rise of Protestantism, the relations of Luther's doctrines with modern tendencies of thought, and much more. "Monumental work; still the most valuable history of dogma . . . luminous analysis of the problems . . . abounds in suggestion and stimulus and can be neglected by no one who desires to understand the history of thought in this most important field," Dutcher's Guide to Historical Literature. Translated by Neil Buchanan. Index. Unabridged reprint in 4 volumes. Vol I: Beginnings to the Gnostics and Marcion. Vol II & III: 2nd century to the 4th century Fathers. Vol IV & V: 4th century Councils to the Carlovingian Renaissance. Vol VI & VII: Period of Clugny (c. 1000) to the Reformation, and after. Total of cii + 2407pp. 5⅜ x 8.

T904 Vol I	Paperbound	**$2.50**
T905 Vol II & III	Paperbound	**$2.75**
T906 Vol IV & V	Paperbound	**$2.75**
T907 Vol VI & VII	Paperbound	**$2.75**
	The set	**$10.75**

THE GUIDE FOR THE PERPLEXED, Maimonides. One of the great philosophical works of all time and a necessity for everyone interested in the philosophy of the Middle Ages in the Jewish, Christian, and Moslem traditions. Maimonides develops a common meeting-point for the Old Testament and the Aristotelian thought which pervaded the medieval world. His ideas and methods predate such scholastics as Aquinas and Scotus and throw light on the entire problem of philosophy or science vs. religion. 2nd revised edition. Complete unabridged Friedländer translation. 55 page introduction to Maimonides's life, period, etc., with an important summary of the GUIDE. Index. lix + 414pp. 5⅜ x 8.　　　T351 Paperbound **$2.00**

Americana

THE EYES OF DISCOVERY, J. Bakeless. A vivid reconstruction of how unspoiled America appeared to the first white men. Authentic and enlightening accounts of Hudson's landing in New York, Coronado's trek through the Southwest; scores of explorers, settlers, trappers, soldiers. America's pristine flora, fauna, and Indians in every region and state in fresh and unusual new aspects. "A fascinating view of what the land was like before the first highway went through," Time. 68 contemporary illustrations, 39 newly added in this edition. Index. Bibliography. x + 500pp. 5⅜ x 8.   T761 Paperbound **$2.00**

AUDUBON AND HIS JOURNALS, J. J. Audubon. A collection of fascinating accounts of Europe and America in the early 1800's through Audubon's own eyes. Includes the Missouri River Journals —an eventful trip through America's untouched heartland, the Labrador Journals, the European Journals, the famous "Episodes", and other rare Audubon material, including the descriptive chapters from the original letterpress edition of the "Ornithological Studies", omitted in all later editions. Indispensable for ornithologists, naturalists, and all lovers of Americana and adventure. 70-page biography by Audubon's granddaughter. 38 illustrations. Index. Total of 1106pp. 5⅜ x 8.   T675 Vol I Paperbound **$2.25**
                                                                                T676 Vol II Paperbound **$2.25**
                                                                                The set **$4.50**

TRAVELS OF WILLIAM BARTRAM, edited by Mark Van Doren. The first inexpensive illustrated edition of one of the 18th century's most delightful books is an excellent source of first-hand material on American geography, anthropology, and natural history. Many descriptions of early Indian tribes are our only source of information on them prior to the infiltration of the white man. "The mind of a scientist with the soul of a poet," John Livingston Lowes. 13 original illustrations and maps. Edited with an introduction by Mark Van Doren. 448pp. 5⅜ x 8.
                                                                                T13 Paperbound **$2.00**

GARRETS AND PRETENDERS: A HISTORY OF BOHEMIANISM IN AMERICA, A. Parry. The colorful and fantastic history of American Bohemianism from Poe to Kerouac. This is the only complete record of hoboes, cranks, starving poets, and suicides. Here are Pfaff, Whitman, Crane, Bierce, Pound, and many others. New chapters by the author and by H. T. Moore bring this thorough and well-documented history down to the Beatniks. "An excellent account," N. Y. Times. Scores of cartoons, drawings, and caricatures. Bibliography. Index. xxviii + 421pp. 5⅝ x 8⅜.   T708 Paperbound **$1.95**

THE EXPLORATION OF THE COLORADO RIVER AND ITS CANYONS, J. W. Powell. The thrilling first-hand account of the expedition that filled in the last white space on the map of the United States. Rapids, famine, hostile Indians, and mutiny are among the perils encountered as the unknown Colorado Valley reveals its secrets. This is the only uncut version of Major Powell's classic of exploration that has been printed in the last 60 years. Includes later reflections and subsequent expedition. 250 illustrations, new map. 400pp. 5⅝ x 8⅜.
                                                                                T94 Paperbound **$2.25**

THE JOURNAL OF HENRY D. THOREAU, Edited by Bradford Torrey and Francis H. Allen. Henry Thoreau is not only one of the most important figures in American literature and social thought; his voluminous journals (from which his books emerged as selections and crystallizations) constitute both the longest, most sensitive record of personal internal development and a most penetrating description of a historical moment in American culture. This present set, which was first issued in fourteen volumes, contains Thoreau's entire journals from 1837 to 1862, with the exception of the lost years which were found only recently. We are reissuing it, complete and unabridged, with a new introduction by Walter Harding, Secretary of the Thoreau Society. Fourteen volumes reissued in two volumes. Foreword by Henry Seidel Canby. Total of 1888pp. 8⅜ x 12¼.   T312-3 Two volume set, Clothbound **$20.00**

GAMES AND SONGS OF AMERICAN CHILDREN, collected by William Wells Newell. A remarkable collection of 190 games with songs that accompany many of them; cross references to show similarities, differences among them; variations; musical notation for 38 songs. Textual discussions show relations with folk-drama and other aspects of folk tradition. Grouped into categories for ready comparative study: Love-games, histories, playing at work, human life, bird and beast, mythology, guessing-games, etc. New introduction covers relations of songs and dances to timeless heritage of folklore, biographical sketch of Newell, other pertinent data. A good source of inspiration for those in charge of groups of children and a valuable reference for anthropologists, sociologists, psychiatrists. Introduction by Carl Withers. New indexes of first lines, games. 5⅜ x 8½. xii + 242pp.   T354 Paperbound **$1.75**

GARDNER'S PHOTOGRAPHIC SKETCH BOOK OF THE CIVIL WAR, Alexander Gardner. The first published collection of Civil War photographs, by one of the two or three most famous photographers of the era, outstandingly reproduced from the original positives. Scenes of crucial battles: Appomattox, Manassas, Mechanicsville, Bull Run, Yorktown, Fredericksburg, etc. Gettysburg immediately after retirement of forces. Battle ruins at Richmond, Petersburg, Gaines'Mill. Prisons, arsenals, a slave pen, fortifications, headquarters, pontoon bridges, soldiers, a field hospital. A unique glimpse into the realities of one of the bloodiest wars in history, with an introductory text to each picture by Gardner himself. Until this edition, there were only five known copies in libraries, and fewer in private hands, one of which sold at auction in 1952 for $425. Introduction by E. F. Bleiler. 100 full page 7 x 10 photographs (original size). 224pp. 8½ x 10¾. T476 Clothbound **$6.00**

A BIBLIOGRAPHY OF NORTH AMERICAN FOLKLORE AND FOLKSONG, Charles Haywood, Ph.D. The only book that brings together bibliographical information on so wide a range of folklore material. Lists practically everything published about American folksongs, ballads, dances, folk beliefs and practices, popular music, tales, similar material—more than 35,000 titles of books, articles, periodicals, monographs, music publications, phonograph records. Each entry complete with author, title, date and place of publication, arranger and performer of particular examples of folk music, many with Dr. Haywood's valuable criticism, evaluation. Volume I, "The American People," is complete listing of general and regional studies, titles of tales and songs of Negro and non-English speaking groups and where to find them, Occupational Bibliography including sections listing sources of information, folk material on cowboys, riverboat men, 49ers, American characters like Mike Fink, Frankie and Johnnie, John Henry, many more. Volume II, "The American Indian," tells where to find information on dances, myths, songs, ritual of more than 250 tribes in U.S., Canada. A monumental product of 10 years' labor, carefully classified for easy use. "All students of this subject . . . will find themselves in debt to Professor Haywood," Stith Thompson, in American Anthropologist. ". . . a most useful and excellent work," Duncan Emrich, Chief Folklore Section, Library of Congress, in "Notes." Corrected, enlarged republication of 1951 edition. New Preface. New index of composers, arrangers, performers. General index of more than 15,000 items. Two volumes. Total of 1301pp. 6⅛ x 9¼. T797-798 Clothbound **$12.50**

INCIDENTS OF TRAVEL IN YUCATAN, John L. Stephens. One of first white men to penetrate interior of Yucatan tells the thrilling story of his discoveries of 44 cities, remains of once-powerful Maya civilization. Compelling text combines narrative power with historical significance as it takes you through heat, dust, storms of Yucatan; native festivals with brutal bull fights; great ruined temples atop man-made mounds. Countless idols, sculptures, tombs, examples of Mayan taste for rich ornamentation, from gateways to personal trinkets, accurately illustrated, discussed in text. Will appeal to those interested in ancient civilizations, and those who like stories of exploration, discovery, adventure. Republication of last (1843) edition. 124 illustrations by English artist, F. Catherwood. Appendix on Mayan architecture, chronology. Two volume set. Total of xxviii + 927pp.

Vol I T926 Paperbound **$2.00**
Vol II T927 Paperbound **$2.00**
The set **$4.00**

A GENIUS IN THE FAMILY, Hiram Percy Maxim. Sir Hiram Stevens Maxim was known to the public as the inventive genius who created the Maxim gun, automatic sprinkler, and a heavier-than-air plane that got off the ground in 1894. Here, his son reminisces—this is by no means a formal biography—about the exciting and often downright scandalous private life of his brilliant, eccentric father. A warm and winning portrait of a prankish, mischievous, impious personality, a genuine character. The style is fresh and direct, the effect is unadulterated pleasure. "A book of charm and lasting humor . . . belongs on the 'must read' list of all fathers," New York Times. "A truly gorgeous affair," New Statesman and Nation. 17 illustrations, 16 specially for this edition. viii + 108pp. 5⅜ x 8½. T948 Paperbound **$1.00**

HORSELESS CARRIAGE DAYS, Hiram P. Maxim. The best account of an important technological revolution by one of its leading figures. The delightful and rewarding story of the author's experiments with the exact combustibility of gasoline, stopping and starting mechanisms, carriage design, and engines. Captures remarkably well the flavor of an age of scoffers and rival inventors not above sabotage; of noisy, uncontrollable gasoline vehicles and incredible mobile steam kettles. ". . . historic information and light humor are combined to furnish highly entertaining reading," New York Times. 56 photographs, 12 specially for this edition. xi + 175pp. 5⅜ x 8½. T964 Paperbound **$1.35**

BODY, BOOTS AND BRITCHES: FOLKTALES, BALLADS AND SPEECH FROM COUNTRY NEW YORK, Harold W. Thompson. A unique collection, discussion of songs, stories, anecdotes, proverbs handed down orally from Scotch-Irish grandfathers, German nurse-maids, Negro workmen, gathered from all over Upper New York State. Tall tales by and about lumbermen and pirates, canalers and injun-fighters, tragic and comic ballads, scores of sayings and proverbs all tied together by an informative, delightful narrative by former president of New York Historical Society. ". . . a sparkling homespun tapestry that every lover of Americana will want to have around the house," Carl Carmer, New York Times. Republication of 1939 edition. 20 line-drawings. Index. Appendix (Sources of material, bibliography). 530pp. 5⅜ x 8½. T411 Paperbound **$2.25**

Art, History of Art, Antiques, Graphic Arts, Handcrafts

ART STUDENTS' ANATOMY, E. J. Farris. Outstanding art anatomy that uses chiefly living objects for its illustrations. 71 photos of undraped men, women, children are accompanied by carefully labeled matching sketches to illustrate the skeletal system, articulations and movements, bony landmarks, the muscular system, skin, fasciae, fat, etc. 9 x-ray photos show movement of joints. Undraped models are shown in such actions as serving in tennis, drawing a bow in archery, playing football, dancing, preparing to spring and to dive. Also discussed and illustrated are proportions, age and sex differences, the anatomy of the smile, etc. 8 plates by the great early 18th century anatomic illustrator Siegfried Albinus are also included. Glossary. 158 figures, 7 in color. x + 159pp. 5⅝ x 8⅜.   T744 Paperbound **$1.50**

AN ATLAS OF ANATOMY FOR ARTISTS, F Schider. A new 3rd edition of this standard text enlarged by 52 new illustrations of hands, anatomical studies by Cloquet, and expressive life studies of the body by Barcsay. 189 clear, detailed plates offer you precise information of impeccable accuracy. 29 plates show all aspects of the skeleton, with closeups of special areas, while 54 full-page plates, mostly in two colors, give human musculature as seen from four different points of view, with cutaways for important portions of the body. 14 full-page plates provide photographs of hand forms, eyelids, female breasts, and indicate the location of muscles upon models. 59 additional plates show how great artists of the past utilized human anatomy. They reproduce sketches and finished work by such artists as Michelangelo, Leonardo da Vinci, Goya, and 15 others. This is a lifetime reference work which will be one of the most important books in any artist's library. "The standard reference tool," AMERICAN LIBRARY ASSOCiATION. "Excellent," AMERICAN ARTIST. Third enlarged edition. 189 plates, 647 illustrations. xxvi + 192pp. 7⅞ x 10⅝.   T241 Clothbound **$6.00**

AN ATLAS OF ANIMAL ANATOMY FOR ARTISTS, W. Ellenberger, H. Baum, H. Dittrich. The largest, richest animal anatomy for artists available in English. 99 detailed anatomical plates of such animals as the horse, dog, cat, lion, deer, seal, kangaroo, flying squirrel, cow, bull, goat, monkey, hare, and bat. Surface features are clearly indicated, while progressive beneath-the-skin pictures show musculature, tendons, and bone structure. Rest and action are exhibited in terms of musculature and skeletal structure and detailed cross-sections are given for heads and important features. The animals chosen are representative of specific families so that a study of these anatomies will provide knowledge of hundreds of related species. "Highly recommended as one of the very few books on the subject worthy of being used as an authoritative guide," DESIGN. "Gives a fundamental knowledge," AMERICAN ARTIST. Second revised, enlarged edition with new plates from Cuvier, Stubbs, etc. 288 illustrations. 153pp. 11⅜ x 9.   T82 Clothbound **$6.00**

THE HUMAN FIGURE IN MOTION, Eadweard Muybridge. The largest selection in print of Muybridge's famous high-speed action photos of the human figure in motion. 4789 photographs illustrate 162 different actions: men, women, children—mostly undraped—are shown walking, running, carrying various objects, sitting, lying down, climbing, throwing, arising, and performing over 150 other actions. Some actions are shown in as many as 150 photographs each. All in all there are more than 500 action strips in this enormous volume, series shots taken at shutter speeds of as high as 1/6000th of a second! These are not posed shots, but true stopped motion. They show bone and muscle in situations that the human eye is not fast enough to capture. Earlier, smaller editions of these prints have brought $40 and more on the out-of-print market. "A must for artists," ART IN FOCUS. "An unparalleled dictionary of action for all artists," AMERICAN ARTIST. 390 full-page plates, with 4789 photographs. Printed on heavy glossy stock. Reinforced binding with headbands. xxi + 390pp. 7⅞ x 10⅝.
T204 Clothbound **$10.00**

ANIMALS IN MOTION, Eadweard Muybridge. This is the largest collection of animal action photos in print. 34 different animals (horses, mules, oxen, goats, camels, pigs, cats, guanacos, lions, gnus, deer, monkeys, eagles—and 21 others) in 132 characteristic actions. The horse alone is shown in more than 40 different actions. All 3919 photographs are taken in series at speeds up to 1/6000th of a second. The secrets of leg action, spinal patterns, head movements, strains and contortions shown nowhere else are captured. You will see exactly how a lion sets his foot down; how an elephant's knees are like a human's—and how they differ; the position of a kangaroo's legs in mid-leap; how an ostrich's head bobs; details of the flight of birds—and thousands of facets of motion only the fastest cameras can catch. Photographed from domestic animals and animals in the Philadelphia zoo, it contains neither semiposed artificial shots nor distorted telephoto shots taken under adverse conditions. Artists, biologists, decorators, cartoonists, will find this book indispensable for understanding animals in motion. "A really marvelous series of plates," NATURE (London). "The dry plate's most spectacular early use was by Eadweard Muybridge," LIFE. 3919 photographs; 380 full pages of plates. 440pp. Printed on heavy glossy paper. Deluxe binding with headbands. 7⅞ x 10⅝.   T203 Clothbound **$10.00**

ART ANATOMY, William Rimmer, M.D. Often called one of America's foremost contributions to art instruction, a work of art in its own right. More than 700 line drawings by the author, first-rate anatomist and dissector as well as artist, with a non-technical anatomical text. Impeccably accurate drawings of muscles, skeletal structure, surface features, other aspects of males and females, children, adults and aged persons show not only form, size, insertion and articulation but personality and emotion as reflected by physical features usually ignored in modern anatomical works. Complete unabridged reproduction of 1876 edition slightly rearranged. Introduction by Robert Hutchinson. 722 illustrations. xiii + 153pp. 7¾ x 10¾.
T908 Paperbound **$2.00**

ANIMAL DRAWING: ANATOMY AND ACTION FOR ARTISTS, C. R. Knight. The author and illustrator of this work was "the most distinguished painter of animal life." This extensive course in animal drawing discusses musculature, bone structure, animal psychology, movements, habits, habitats. Innumerable tips on proportions, light and shadow play, coloring, hair formation, feather arrangement, scales, how animals lie down, animal expressions, etc., from great apes to birds. Pointers on avoiding gracelessness in horses, deer; on introducing proper power and bulk to heavier animals; on giving proper grace and subtle expression to members of the cat family. Originally titled "Animal Anatomy and Psychology for the Artist and Layman." Over 123 illustrations. 149pp. 8¼ x 10½.
T426 Paperbound **$2.00**

DESIGN FOR ARTISTS AND CRAFTSMEN, L. Wolchonok. The most thorough course ever prepared on the creation of art motifs and designs. It teaches you to create your own designs out of things around you — from geometric patterns, plants, birds, animals, humans, landscapes, and man-made objects. It leads you step by step through the creation of more than 1300 designs, and shows you how to create design that is fresh, well-founded, and original. Mr. Wolchonok, whose text is used by scores of art schools, shows you how the same idea can be developed into many different forms, ranging from near representationalism to the most advanced forms of abstraction. The material in this book is entirely new, and combines full awareness of traditional design with the work of such men as Miro, Léger, Picasso, Moore, and others. 113 detailed exercises, with instruction hints, diagrams, and details to enable you to apply Wolchonok's methods to your own work. "A great contribution to the field of design and crafts," N. Y. SOCIETY OF CRAFTSMEN. More than 1300 illustrations. xv + 207pp. 7⅞ x 10¾.
T274 Clothbound **$4.95**

HAWTHORNE ON PAINTING. A vivid recreation, from students' notes, of instruction by Charles W. Hawthorne, given for over 31 years at his famous Cape Cod School of Art. Divided into sections on the outdoor model, still life, landscape, the indoor model, and water color, each section begins with a concise essay, followed by epigrammatic comments on color, form, seeing, etc. Not a formal course, but comments of a great teacher-painter on specific student works, which will solve problems in your own painting and understanding of art. "An excellent introduction for laymen and students alike," Time. Introduction. 100pp. 5⅜ x 8.
T653 Paperbound **$1.00**

THE ENJOYMENT AND USE OF COLOR, Walter Sargent. This book explains fascinating relations among colors, between colors in nature and art; describes experiments that you can perform to understand these relations more thoroughly; points out hundreds of little known facts about color values, intensities, effects of high and low illumination, complementary colors, color harmonies. Practical hints for painters, references to techniques of masters, questions at chapter ends for self-testing all make this a valuable book for artists, professional and amateur, and for general readers interested in world of color. Republication of 1923 edition. 35 illustrations, 6 full-page plates. New color frontispiece. Index. xii + 274pp. 5⅜ x 8.
T944 Paperbound **$2.25**

DECORATIVE ALPHABETS AND INITIALS, ed. by Alexander Nesbitt. No payment, no permission needed to reproduce any one of these 3924 different letters, covering 1000 years. Crisp, clear letters all in line, from Anglo-Saxon mss., Luebeck Cathedral, 15th century Augsburg; the work of Dürer, Holbein, Cresci, Beardsley, Rossing Wadsworth, John Moylin, etc. Every imaginable style. 91 complete alphabets. 123 full-page plates. 192pp. 7¾ x 10¾.
T544 Paperbound **$2.25**

THREE CLASSICS OF ITALIAN CALLIGRAPHY, edited by Oscar Ogg. Here, combined in a single volume, are complete reproductions of three famous calligraphic works written by the greatest writing masters of the Renaissance: Arrighi's OPERINA and IL MODO, Tagliente's LO PRESENTE LIBRO, and Palatino's LIBRO NUOVO. These books present more than 200 complete alphabets and thousands of lettered specimens. The basic hand is Papal Chancery, but scores of other alphabets are also given: European and Asiatic local alphabets, foliated and art alphabets, scrolls, cartouches, borders, etc. Text is in Italian. Introduction. 245 plates. x + 272pp. 6⅛ x 9¼.
T212 Paperbound **$2.75**

CALLIGRAPHY, J. G. Schwandner. One of the legendary books in the graphic arts, copies of which brought $500 each on the rare book market, now reprinted for the first time in over 200 years. A beautiful plate book of graceful calligraphy, and an inexhaustible source of first-rate material copyright-free, for artists, and directors, craftsmen, commercial artists, etc. More than 300 ornamental initials forming 12 complete alphabets, over 150 ornate frames and panels, over 200 flourishes, over 75 calligraphic pictures including a temple, cherubs, cocks, dodos, stags, chamois, foliated lions, greyhounds, etc. Thousand of calligraphic elements to be used for suggestions of quality, sophistication, antiquity, and sheer beauty. Historical introduction. 158 full-page plates. 368pp. 9 x 13.
T475 Clothbound **$10.00**

CATALOGUE OF DOVER BOOKS

THE HISTORY AND TECHNIQUE OF LETTERING, A. Nesbitt. The only thorough inexpensive history of letter forms from the point of view of the artist. Mr. Nesbitt covers every major development in lettering from the ancient Egyptians to the present and illustrates each development with a complete alphabet. Such masters as Baskerville, Bell, Bodoni, Caslon, Koch, Kilian, Morris, Garamont, Jenson, and dozens of others are analyzed in terms of artistry and historical development. The author also presents a 65-page practical course in lettering, besides the full historical text. 89 complete alphabets; 165 additional lettered specimens. xvii + 300pp. 5⅜ x 8.   T427 Paperbound **$2.00**

FOOT-HIGH LETTERS: A GUIDE TO LETTERING (A PRACTICAL SYLLABUS FOR TEACHERS), M. Price. A complete alphabet of Classic Roman letters, each a foot high, each on a separate 16 x 22 plate—perfect for use in lettering classes. In addition to an accompanying description, each plate also contains 9 two-inch-high forms of letter in various type faces, such as "Caslon," "Empire," "Onyx," and "Neuland," illustrating the many possible derivations from the standard classical forms. One plate contains 21 additional forms of the letter A. The fully illustrated 16-page syllabus by Mr. Price, formerly of the Pratt Institute and the Rhode Island School of Design, contains dozens of useful suggestions for student and teacher alike. An indispensable teaching aid. Extensively revised. 16-page syllabus and 30 plates in slip cover, 16 x 22.   T239 Clothbound **$6.00**

THE STYLES OF ORNAMENT, Alexander Speltz. Largest collection of ornaments in print— 3765 illustrations of prehistoric, Lombard, Gothic, Frank, Romanesque, Mohammedan, Renaissance, Polish, Swiss, Rococo, Sheraton, Empire, U. S. Colonial, etc., ornament. Gargoyles, dragons, columns, necklaces, urns, friezes, furniture, buildings, keyholes, tapestries, fantastic animals, armor, religious objects, much more, all in line. Reproduce any one free. Index. Bibliography. 400 plates. 656pp. 5⅝ x 8⅜.   T557 Paperbound **$3.00**

HANDBOOK OF DESIGNS AND DEVICES, C. P. Hornung. This unique book is indispensable to the designer, commercial artist, and hobbyist. It is not a textbook but a working collection of 1836 basic designs and variations, carefully reproduced, which may be used without permission. Variations of circle, line, band, triangle, square, cross, diamond, swastika, pentagon, octagon, hexagon, star, scroll, interlacement, shields, etc. Supplementary notes on the background and symbolism of the figures. "A necessity to every designer who would be original without having to labor heavily," ARTIST AND ADVERTISER. 204 plates. 240pp. 5⅜ x 8.
T125 Paperbound **$2.00**

THE UNIVERSAL PENMAN, George Bickham. This beautiful book, which first appeared in 1743, is the largest collection of calligraphic specimens, flourishes, alphabets, and calligraphic illustrations ever published. 212 full-page plates are drawn from the work of such 18th century masters of English roundhand as Dove, Champion, Bland, and 20 others. They contain 22 complete alphabets, over 2,000 flourishes, and 122 illustrations, each drawn with a stylistic grace impossible to describe. This book is invaluable to anyone interested in the beauties of calligraphy, or to any artist, hobbyist, or craftsman who wishes to use the very best ornamental handwriting and flourishes for decorative purposes. Commercial artists, advertising artists, have found it unexcelled as a source of material suggesting quality. "An essential part of any art library, and a book of permanent value," AMERICAN ARTIST. 212 plates. 224pp. 9 x 13¾.   T20 Clothbound **$10.00**

1800 WOODCUTS BY THOMAS BEWICK AND HIS SCHOOL. Prepared by Dover's editorial staff, this is the largest collection of woodcuts by Bewick and his school ever compiled. Contains the complete engravings from all his major works and a wide range of illustrations from lesser-known collections, all photographed from clear copies of the original books and reproduced in line. Carefully and conveniently organized into sections on Nature (animals and birds, scenery and landscapes, plants, insects, etc.), People (love and courtship, social life, school and domestic scenes, misfortunes, costumes, etc.), Business and Trade, and illustrations from primers, fairytales, spelling books, frontispieces, borders, fables and allegories, etc. In addition to technical proficiency and simple beauty, Bewick's work is remarkable as a mode of pictorial symbolism, reflecting rustic tranquility, an atmosphere of rest, simplicity, idyllic contentment. A delight for the eye, an inexhaustible source of illustrative material for art studios, commercial artists, advertising agencies. Individual illustrations (up to 10 for any one use) are copyright free. Classified index. Bibliography and sources. Introduction by Robert Hutchinson. 1800 woodcuts. xiv + 247pp. 9 x 12.
T766 Clothbound **$10.00**

A HANDBOOK OF EARLY ADVERTISING ART, C. P. Hornung. The largest collection of copyright-free early advertising art ever compiled. Vol. I contains some 2,000 illustrations of agricultural devices, animals, old automobiles, birds, buildings, Christmas decorations (with 7 Santa Clauses by Nast), allegorical figures, farm engines, horses and vehicles, Indians, portraits, sailing ships, trains, sports, trade cuts — and 30 other categories! Vol. II, devoted to typography, has over 4000 specimens: 600 different Roman, Gothic, Barnum, Old English faces; 630 ornamental type faces; 1115 initials, hundreds of scrolls, flourishes, etc. This third edition is enlarged by 78 additional plates containing all new material. "A remarkable collection," PRINTERS' INK. "A rich contribution to the history of American design," GRAPHIS. Volume I, Pictorial. Over 2000 illustrations. xiv + 242pp. 9 x 12.   T122 Clothbound **$10.00**
Volume II, Typographical. Over 4000 specimens. vii + 312pp. 9 x 12. T123 Clothbound **$10.00**
Two volume set, T121 Clothbound, only   **$18.50**

CATALOGUE OF DOVER BOOKS

DESIGN MOTIFS OF ANCIENT MEXICO, J. Enciso. This unique collection of pre-Columbian stamps for textiles and pottery contains 766 superb designs from Aztec, Olmec, Totonac, Maya, and Toltec origins. Plumed serpents, calendrical elements, wind gods, animals, flowers, demons, dancers, monsters, abstract ornament, and other designs. More than 90% of these illustrations are completely unobtainable elsewhere. Use this work to bring new barbaric beauty into your crafts or drawing. Originally $17.50. Printed in three colors. 766 illustrations, thousands of motifs. 192pp. 7⅞ x 10¾. **T84 Paperbound $1.85**

DECORATIVE ART OF THE SOUTHWEST INDIANS, D. S. Sides. A magnificent album of authentic designs (both pre- and post-Conquest) from the pottery, textiles, and basketry of the Navaho, Hopi, Mohave, Santo Domingo, and over 20 other Southwestern groups. Designs include birds, clouds, butterflies, quadrupeds, geometric forms, etc. A valuable book for folklorists, and a treasury for artists, designers, advertisers, and craftsmen, who may use without payment or permission any of the vigorous, colorful, and strongly rhythmic designs. Aesthetic and archeological notes. 50 plates. Bibliography of over 50 items. xviii + 101pp. 5⅝ x 8⅜. **T139 Paperbound $1.00**

PAINTING IN THE FAR EAST, Laurence Binyon. Excellent introduction by one of greatest authorities on subject studies 1500 years of oriental art (China, Japan; also Tibet, Persia), over 250 painters. Examines works, schools, influence of Wu Tao-tzu, Kanaoka, Toba Sojo, Masanobu, Okio, etc.; early traditions; Kamakura epoch; the Great Decorators; T'ang Dynasty; Matabei, beginnings of genre; Japanese woodcut, color print; much more, all chronological, in cultural context. 42 photos. Bibliography. 317pp. 6 x 9¼. **T520 Paperbound $2.25**

ON THE LAWS OF JAPANESE PAINTING, H. Bowie. This unusual book, based on 9 years of profound study-experience in the Late Kano art of Japan, remains the most authentic guide in English to the spirit and technique of Japanese painting. A wealth of interesting and useful data on control of the brush; practise exercises; manufacture of ink, brushes, colors; the use of various lines and dots to express moods. It is the best possible substitute for a series of lessons from a great oriental master. 66 plates with 220 illustrations. Index. xv + 177pp. 6⅛ x 9¼. **T30 Paperbound $2.00**

THE MATERIALS AND TECHNIQUES OF MEDIEVAL PAINTING, D. V. Thompson. Based on years of study of medieval manuscripts and laboratory analysis of medieval paintings, this book discusses carriers and grounds, binding media, pigments, metals used in painting, etc. Considers relative merits of painting al fresco and al secco, the procession of coloring materials, burnishing, and many other matters. Preface by Bernard Berenson. Index. 239pp. 5⅜ x 8. **T327 Paperbound $1.85**

THE CRAFTSMAN'S HANDBOOK, Cennino Cennini. This is considered the finest English translation of IL LIBRO DELL' ARTE, a 15th century Florentine introduction to art technique. It is both fascinating reading and a wonderful mirror of another culture for artists, art students, historians, social scientists, or anyone interested in details of life some 500 years ago. While it is not an exact recipe book, it gives directions for such matters as tinting papers, gilding stone, preparation of various hues of black, and many other useful but nearly forgotten facets of the painter's art. As a human document reflecting the ideas of a practising medieval artist it is particularly important. 4 illustrations. xxvii + 142pp. D. V. Thompson translator. 6⅛ x 9¼. **T54 Paperbound $1.35**

VASARI ON TECHNIQUE, G. Vasari. Pupil of Michelangelo and outstanding biographer of the Renaissance artists, Vasari also wrote this priceless treatise on the technical methods of the painters, architects, and sculptors of his day. This is the only English translation of this practical, informative, and highly readable work. Scholars, artists, and general readers will welcome these authentic discussions of marble statues, bronze casting, fresco painting, oil painting, engraving, stained glass, rustic fountains and grottoes, etc. Introduction and notes by G. B. Brown. Index. 18 plates, 11 figures. xxiv + 328pp. 5⅜ x 8. **T717 Paperbound $2.25**

METHODS AND MATERIALS OF PAINTING OF THE GREAT SCHOOLS AND MASTERS, C. L. Eastlake. A vast, complete, and authentic reconstruction of the secret techniques of the masters of painting, collected from hundreds of forgotten manuscripts by the eminent President of the British Royal Academy: Greek, Roman, and medieval techniques; fresco and tempera; varnishes and encaustics; the secrets of Leonardo, Van Eyck, Raphael, and many others. Art historians, students, teachers, critics, and laymen will gain new insights into the creation of the great masterpieces; while artists and craftsmen will have a treasury of valuable techniques. Index. Two volume set. Total of 1025pp. 5⅜ x 8. **T718 Paperbound $2.25**
T719 Paperbound $2.25
The set $4.50

BYZANTINE ART AND ARCHAEOLOGY, O. M. Dalton. Still the most thorough work in English— both in breadth and in depth—on the astounding multiplicity of Byzantine art forms throughout Europe, North Africa, and Western Asia from the 4th to the 15th century. Analyzes hundreds of individual pieces from over 160 public and private museums, libraries, and collections all over the world. Full treatment of Byzantine sculpture, painting, mosaic, jewelry, textiles, etc., including historical development, symbolism, and aesthetics. Chapters on iconography and ornament. Indispensable for study of Christian symbolism and medieval art. 457 illustrations, many full-page. Bibliography of over 2500 references. 4 Indexes. xx + 727pp. 6⅛ x 9¼. **T776 Clothbound $8.50**

METALWORK AND ENAMELLING, H. Maryon. This is probably the best book ever written on the subject. Prepared by Herbert Maryon, F.S.A., of the British Museum, it tells everything necessary for home manufacture of jewelry, rings, ear pendants, bowls, and dozens of other objects. Clearly written chapters provide precise information on such topics as materials, tools, soldering, filigree, setting stones, raising patterns, spinning metal, repoussé work, hinges and joints, metal inlaying, damascening, overlaying, niello, Japanese alloys, enamelling, cloisonné, painted enamels, casting, polishing, coloring, assaying, and dozens of other techniques. This is the next best thing to apprenticeship to a master metalworker. 363 photographs and figures. 374pp. 5½ x 8½. T183 Clothbound **$8.50**

SILK SCREEN TECHNIQUES, J. I. Biegeleisen, Max A. Cohn. A complete-to-the-last-detail copiously illustrated home course in this fast growing modern art form. Full directions for building silk screen out of inexpensive materials; explanations of five basic methods of stencil preparation—paper, blockout, tusche, film, photographic—and effects possible: light and shade, washes, dry brush, oil paint type impastos, gouaches, pastels. Detailed coverage of multicolor printing, illustrated by proofs showing the stages of a 4 color print. Special section on common difficulties. 149 illustrations, 8 in color. Sources of supply. xiv + 187pp. 6⅛ x 9¼. T433 Paperbound **$1.75**

A HANDBOOK OF WEAVES, G. H. Oelsner. Now back in print! Probably the most complete book of weaves ever printed, fully explained, differentiated, and illustrated. Includes plain weaves; irregular, double-stitched, and filling satins; derivative, basket, and rib weaves; steep, undulating, broken, offset, corkscrew, interlocking, herringbone, and fancy twills; honeycomb, lace, and crepe weaves; tricot, matelassé, and montagnac weaves; and much more. Translated and revised by S. S. Dale, with supplement on the analysis of weaves and fabrics. 1875 illustrations. vii + 402pp. 6 x 9¼. T209 Clothbound **$5.00**

BASIC BOOKBINDING, A. W. Lewis. Enables the beginner and the expert to apply the latest and most simplified techniques to rebinding old favorites and binding new paperback books. Complete lists of all necessary materials and guides to the selection of proper tools, paper, glue, boards, cloth, leather, or sheepskin covering fabrics, lettering inks and pigments, etc. You are shown how to collate a book, sew it, back it, trim it, make boards and attach them in easy step-by-step stages. Author's preface. 261 illustrations with appendix. Index. xi + 144pp. 5⅜ x 8. T169 Paperbound **$1.45**

BASKETRY, F. J. Christopher. Basic introductions cover selection of materials, use and care of tools, equipment. Easy-to-follow instructions for preparation of oval, oblong trays, lidded baskets, rush mats, tumbler holders, bicycle baskets, waste paper baskets, many other useful, beautiful articles made of coiled and woven reed, willow, rushes, raffia. Special sections present in clear, simple language and numerous illustrations all the how-to information you could need: linings, skein wire, varieties of stitching, simplified construction of handles, dying processes. For beginner and skilled craftsman alike. Edited by Majorie O'Shaugnessy. Bibliography. Sources of supply. Index. 112 illustrations. 108pp. 5 x 7¼. T903 Paperbound $1.00

THE ART OF ETCHING, E. S. Lumsden. Everything you need to know to do etching yourself. First two sections devoted to technique of etching and engraving, covering such essentials as relative merits of zinc and copper, cleaning and grounding plates, gravers, acids, arrangement of etching-room, methods of biting, types of inks and oils, mounting, stretching and framing, preserving and restoring plates, size and color of printing papers, much more. A review of the history of the art includes separate chapters on Dürer and Lucas van Leyden, Rembrandt and Van Dyck, Goya, Meryon, Haden and Whistler, British masters of nineteenth century, modern etchers. Final section is a collection of prints by contemporary etchers with comments by the artists. Professional etchers and engravers will find this a highly useful source of examples. Beginners and teachers, students of art and printing will find it a valuable tool. Index. 208 illustrations. 384pp. 5⅜ x 8. T49 Paperbound **$2.50**

WHITTLING AND WOODCARVING, E. J. Tangerman. What to make and how to make it for even a moderately handy beginner. One of the few works that bridge gap between whittling and serious carving. History of the art, background information on selection and use of woods, grips, types of strokes and cuts, handling of tools and chapters on rustic work, flat toys and windmills, puzzles, chains, ships in bottle, nested spheres, fans, more than 100 useful, entertaining objects. Second half covers carving proper: woodcuts, low relief, sculpture in the round, lettering, inlay and marquetry, indoor and outdoor decorations, pierced designs, much more. Final chapter describes finishing, care of tools. Sixth edition. Index. 464 illustrations. x + 239pp. 5½ x 8⅛. T965 Paperbound **$1.75**

THE PRACTICE OF TEMPERA PAINTING, Daniel V. Thompson, Jr. A careful exposition of all aspects of tempera painting, including sections on many possible modern uses, propensities of various woods, choice of material for panel, making and applying the gesso, pigments and brushes, technique of the actual painting, gilding and so on—everything one need know to try a hand at this proven but neglected art. The author is unquestionably the world's leading authority on tempera methods and processes and his treatment is based on exhaustive study of manuscript material. Drawings and diagrams increase clarity of text. No one interested in tempera painting can afford to be without this book. Appendix, "Tempera Practice in Yale Art School," by Lewis E. York. 85 illustrations by York; 4 full-page plates. ix x 149pp. 5⅜ x 8½. T343 Paperbound **$1.50**

SHAKER FURNITURE, E. D. Andrews and F. Andrews. The most illuminating study on what many scholars consider the best examples of functional furniture ever made. Includes the history of the sect and the development of Shaker style. The 48 magnificent plates show tables, chairs, cupboards, chests, boxes, desks, beds, woodenware, and much more, and are accompanied by detailed commentary. For all antique collectors and dealers, designers and decorators, historians and folklorists. "Distinguished in scholarship, in pictorial illumination, and in all the essentials of fine book making," Antiques. 3 Appendixes. Bibliography. Index. 192pp. 7⅞ x 10¾. **T679 Paperbound $2.00**

JAPANESE HOMES AND THEIR SURROUNDINGS, E. S. Morse. Every aspect of the purely traditional Japanese home, from general plan and major structural features to ceremonial and traditional appointments—tatami, hibachi, shoji, tokonoma, etc. The most exhaustive discussion in English, this book is equally honored for its strikingly modern conception of architecture. First published in 1886, before the contamination of the Japanese traditions, it preserves the authentic features of an ideal of construction that is steadily gaining devotees in the Western world. 307 illustrations by the author. Index. Glossary. xxxvi + 372pp. 5⅝ x 8⅜. **T746 Paperbound $2.25**

COLONIAL LIGHTING, Arthur H. Hayward. The largest selection of antique lamps ever illustrated anywhere, from rush light-holders of earliest settlers to 1880's—with main emphasis on Colonial era. Primitive attempts at illumination ("Betty" lamps, variations of open wick design, candle molds, reflectors, etc.), whale oil lamps, painted and japanned hand lamps, Sandwich glass candlesticks, astral lamps, Bennington ware and chandeliers of wood, iron, pewter, brass, crystal, bronze and silver. Hundreds of illustrations, loads of information on colonial life, customs, habits, place of acquisition of lamps illustrated. A unique, thoroughgoing survey of an interesting aspect of Americana. Enlarged (1962) edition. New Introduction by James R. Marsh. Supplement "Colonial Chandeliers," photographs with descriptive notes. 169 illustrations, 647 lamps. xxxi + 312pp. 5⅝ x 8¼. **T975 Paperbound $2.00**

CHINESE HOUSEHOLD FURNITURE, George N. Kates. The first book-length study of authentic Chinese domestic furniture in Western language. Summarises practically everything known about Chinese furniture in pure state, uninfluenced by West. History of style, unusual woods used, craftsmanship, principles of design, specific forms like wardrobes, chests and boxes, beds, chairs, tables, stools, cupboards and other pieces. Based on author's own investigation into scanty Chinese historical sources and surviving pieces in private collections and museums. Will reveal a new dimension of simple, beautiful work to all interior decorators, furniture designers, craftsmen. 123 illustrations; 112 photographs. Bibliography. xiii + 205pp. 5¼ x 7¾. **T958 Paperbound $1.50**

ART AND THE SOCIAL ORDER, Professor D. W. Gotshalk, University of Illinois. One of the most profound and most influential studies of aesthetics written in our generation, this work is unusual in considering art from the relational point of view, as a transaction consisting of creation-object-apprehension. Discussing material from the fine arts, literature, music, and related disciplines, it analyzes the aesthetic experience, fine art, the creative process, art materials, form, expression, function, art criticism, art and social life and living. Graceful and fluent in expression, it requires no previous background in aesthetics and will be read with considerable enjoyment by anyone interested in the theory of art. "Clear, interesting, the soundest and most penetrating work in recent years," C. J. Ducasse, Brown University. New preface by Professor Gotshalk. xvi + 248pp. 5⅝ x 8½. **T294 Paperbound $1.65**

FOUNDATIONS OF MODERN ART, A. Ozenfant. An illuminating discussion by a great artist of the interrelationship of all forms of human creativity, from painting to science, writing to religion. The creative process is explored in all facets of art, from paleolithic cave painting to modern French painting and architecture, and the great universals of art are isolated. Expressing its countless insights in aphorisms accompanied by carefully selected illustrations, this book is itself an embodiment in prose of the creative process. Enlarged by 4 new chapters. 226 illustrations. 368pp. 6⅛ x 9¼. **T215 Paperbound $2.00**

VITRUVIUS: TEN BOOKS ON ARCHITECTURE. Book by 1st century Roman architect, engineer, is oldest, most influential work on architecture in existence; for hundreds of years his specific instructions were followed all over the world, by such men as Bramante, Michelangelo, Palladio, etc., and are reflected in major buildings. He describes classic principles of symmetry, harmony; design of treasury, prison, etc.; methods of durability; much more. He wrote in a fascinating manner, and often digressed to give interesting sidelights, making this volume appealing reading even to the non-professional. Standard English translation, by Prof. M. H. Morgan, Harvard U. Index. 6 illus. 334pp. 5⅜ x 8. **T645 Paperbound $2.00**

THE BROWN DECADES, Lewis Mumford. In this now classic study of the arts in America, Lewis Mumford resurrects the "buried renaissance" of the post-Civil War period. He demonstrates that it contained the seeds of a new integrity and power and documents his study with detailed accounts of the founding of modern architecture in the work of Sullivan, Richardson, Root, Roebling; landscape development of Marsh, Olmstead, and Eliot; the graphic arts of Homer, Eakins, and Ryder. 2nd revised enlarged edition. Bibliography. 12 illustrations. Index. xiv + 266pp. 5⅜ x 8. **T200 Paperbound $1.75**

THE AUTOBIOGRAPHY OF AN IDEA, Louis Sullivan. The pioneer architect whom Frank Lloyd Wright called "the master" reveals an acute sensitivity to social forces and values in this passionately honest account. He records the crystallization of his opinions and theories, the growth of his organic theory of architecture that still influences American designers and architects, contemporary ideas, etc. This volume contains the first appearance of 34 full-page plates of his finest architecture. Unabridged reissue of 1924 edition. New introduction by R. M. Line. Index. xiv + 335pp. 5⅜ x 8. T281 Paperbound **$2.00**

THE DRAWINGS OF HEINRICH KLEY. The first uncut republication of both of Kley's devastating sketchbooks, which first appeared in pre-World War I Germany. One of the greatest cartoonists and social satirists of modern times, his exuberant and iconoclastic fantasy and his extraordinary technique place him in the great tradition of Bosch, Breughel, and Goya, while his subject matter has all the immediacy and tension of our century. 200 drawings. viii + 128pp. 7¾ x 10¾. T24 Paperbound **$1.85**

MORE DRAWINGS BY HEINRICH KLEY. All the sketches from Leut' Und Viecher (1912) and Sammel-Album (1923) not included in the previous Dover edition of Drawings. More of the bizarre, mercilessly iconoclastic sketches that shocked and amused on their original publication. Nothing was too sacred, no one too eminent for satirization by this imaginative, individual and accomplished master cartoonist. A total of 158 illustrations. Iv + 104pp. 7¾ x 10¾. T41 Paperbound **$1.85**

PINE FURNITURE OF EARLY NEW ENGLAND, R. H. Kettell. A rich understanding of one of America's most original folk arts that collectors of antiques, interior decorators, craftsmen, woodworkers, and everyone interested in American history and art will find fascinating and immensely useful. 413 illustrations of more than 300 chairs, benches, racks, beds, cupboards, mirrors, shelves, tables, and other furniture will show all the simple beauty and character of early New England furniture. 55 detailed drawings carefully analyze outstanding pieces. "With its rich store of illustrations, this book emphasizes the individuality and varied design of early American pine furniture. It should be welcomed," ANTIQUES. 413 illustrations and 55 working drawings. 475. 8 x 10¾. T145 Clothbound **$10.00**

THE HUMAN FIGURE, J. H. Vanderpoel. Every important artistic element of the human figure is pointed out in minutely detailed word descriptions in this classic text and illustrated as well in 430 pencil and charcoal drawings. Thus the text of this book directs your attention to all the characteristic features and subtle differences of the male and female (adults, children, and aged persons), as though a master artist were telling you what to look for at each stage. 2nd edition, revised and enlarged by George Bridgman. Foreword. 430 illustrations. 143pp. 6⅛ x 9¼. T432 Paperbound **$1.50**

LETTERING AND ALPHABETS, J. A. Cavanagh. This unabridged reissue of LETTERING offers a full discussion, analysis, illustration of 89 basic hand lettering styles — styles derived from Caslons, Bodonis, Garamonds, Gothic, Black Letter, Oriental, and many others. Upper and lower cases, numerals and common signs pictured. Hundreds of technical hints on make-up, construction, artistic validity, strokes, pens, brushes, white areas, etc. May be reproduced without permission! 89 complete alphabets; 72 lettered specimens. 121pp. 9¾ x 8. T53 Paperbound **$1.35**

STICKS AND STONES, Lewis Mumford. A survey of the forces that have conditioned American architecture and altered its forms. The author discusses the medieval tradition in early New England villages; the Renaissance influence which developed with the rise of the merchant class; the classical influence of Jefferson's time; the "Mechanicsvilles" of Poe's generation; the Brown Decades; the philosophy of the Imperial facade; and finally the modern machine age. "A truly remarkable book," SAT. REV. OF LITERATURE. 2nd revised edition. 21 illustrations. xvii + 228pp. 5⅜ x 8. T202 Paperbound **$1.75**

THE STANDARD BOOK OF QUILT MAKING AND COLLECTING, Marguerite Ickis. A complete easy-to-follow guide with all the information you need to make beautiful, useful quilts. How to plan, design, cut, sew, appliqué, avoid sewing problems, use rag bag, make borders, tuft, every other aspect. Over 100 traditional quilts shown, including over 40 full-size patterns. At-home hobby for fun, profit. Index. 483 illus. 1 color plate. 287pp. 6¾ x 9½. T582 Paperbound **$2.00**

THE BOOK OF SIGNS, Rudolf Koch. Formerly $20 to $25 on the out-of-print market, now only $1.00 in this unabridged new edition! 493 symbols from ancient manuscripts, medieval cathedrals, coins, catacombs, pottery, etc. Crosses, monograms of Roman emperors, astrological, chemical, botanical, runes, housemarks, and 7 other categories. Invaluable for handicraft workers, illustrators, scholars, etc., this material may be reproduced without permission. 493 illustrations by Fritz Kredel. 104pp. 6½ x 9¼. T162 Paperbound **$1.00**

PRIMITIVE ART, Franz Boas. This authoritative and exhaustive work by a great American anthropologist covers the entire gamut of primitive art. Pottery, leatherwork, metal work, stone work, wood, basketry, are treated in detail. Theories of primitive art, historical depth in art history, technical virtuosity, unconscious levels of patterning, symbolism, styles, literature, music, dance, etc. A must book for the interested layman, the anthropologist, artist, handicrafter (hundreds of unusual motifs), and the historian. Over 900 illustrations (50 ceramic vessels, 12 totem poles, etc.). 376pp. 5⅜ x 8. T25 Paperbound **$2.00**

Trubner Colloquial Manuals

These unusual books are members of the famous Trubner series of colloquial manuals. They have been written to provide adults with a sound colloquial knowledge of a foreign language, and are suited for either class use or self-study. Each book is a complete course in itself, with progressive, easy to follow lessons. Phonetics, grammar, and syntax are covered, while hundreds of phrases and idioms, reading texts, exercises, and vocabulary are included. These books are unusual in being neither skimpy nor overdetailed in grammatical matters, and in presenting up-to-date, colloquial, and practical phrase material. Bilingual presentation is stressed, to make thorough self-study easier for the reader.

COLLOQUIAL HINDUSTANI, A. H. Harley, formerly Nizam's Reader in Urdu, U. of London. 30 pages on phonetics and scripts (devanagari & Arabic-Persian) are followed by 29 lessons, including material on English and Arabic-Persian influences. Key to all exercises. Vocabulary. 5 x 7½. 147pp. Clothbound **$1.75**

COLLOQUIAL PERSIAN, L. P. Elwell-Sutton. Best introduction to modern Persian, with 90 page grammatical section followed by conversations, 35-page vocabulary. 139pp.
Clothbound **$2.25**

COLLOQUIAL ARABIC, DeLacy O'Leary. Foremost Islamic scholar covers language of Egypt, Syria, Palestine, & Northern Arabia. Extremely clear coverage of complex Arabic verbs & noun plurals; also cultural aspects of language. Vocabulary. xviii + 192pp. 5 x 7½.
Clothbound **$2.50**

COLLOQUIAL GERMAN, P. F. Doring. Intensive thorough coverage of grammar in easily-followed form. Excellent for brush-up, with hundreds of colloquial phrases. 34 pages of bilingual texts. 224pp. 5 x 7½. Clothbound **$2.00**

COLLOQUIAL SPANISH, W. R. Patterson. Castilian grammar and colloquial language, loaded with bilingual phrases and colloquialisms. Excellent for review or self-study. 164pp. 5 x 7½.
Clothbound **$2.00**

COLLOQUIAL FRENCH, W. R. Patterson. 16th revision of this extremely popular manual. Grammar explained with model clarity, and hundreds of useful expressions and phrases; exercises, reading texts, etc. Appendixes of new and useful words and phrases. 223pp. 5 x 7½.
Clothbound **$2.00**

COLLOQUIAL CZECH, J. Schwarz, former headmaster of Lingua Institute, Prague. Full easily followed coverage of grammar, hundreds of immediately useable phrases, texts. Perhaps the best Czech grammar in print. "An absolutely successful textbook," JOURNAL OF CZECHO-SLOVAK FORCES IN GREAT BRITAIN. 252pp. 5 x 7½. Clothbound **$3.00**

COLLOQUIAL RUMANIAN, G. Nandris, Professor of University of London. Extremely thorough coverage of phonetics, grammar, syntax; also included 70-page reader, and 70-page vocabulary. Probably the best grammar for this increasingly important language. 340pp. 5 x 7½.
Clothbound **$2.75**

COLLOQUIAL ITALIAN, A. L. Hayward. Excellent self-study course in grammar, vocabulary, idioms, and reading. Easy progressive lessons will give a good working knowledge of Italian in the shortest possible time. 5 x 7½. Clothbound **$1.75**

COLLOQUIAL TURKISH, Yusuf Mardin. Very clear, thorough introduction to leading cultural and economic language of Near East. Begins with pronunciation and statement of vowel harmony, then 36 lessons present grammar, graded vocabulary, useful phrases, dialogues, reading, exercises. Key to exercises at rear. Turkish-English vocabulary. All in Roman alphabet. x + 288pp. 4¾ x 7¼. Clothbound **$4.00**

DUTCH-ENGLISH AND ENGLISH-DUTCH DICTIONARY, F. G. Renier. For travel, literary, scientific or business Dutch, you will find this the most convenient, practical and comprehensive dictionary on the market. More than 60,000 entries, shades of meaning, colloquialisms, idioms, compounds and technical terms. Dutch and English strong and irregular verbs. This is the only dictionary in its size and price range that indicates the gender of nouns. New orthography. xvii + 571pp. 5½ x 6¼. T224 Clothbound **$2.75**

LEARN DUTCH, F. G. Renier. This book is the most satisfactory and most easily used grammar of modern Dutch. The student is gradually led from simple lessons in pronunciation, through translation from and into Dutch, and finally to a mastery of spoken and written Dutch. Grammatical principles are clearly explained while a useful, practical vocabulary is introduced in easy exercises and readings. It is used and recommended by the Fulbright Committee in the Netherlands. Phonetic appendices. Over 1200 exercises; Dutch-English, English-Dutch vocabularies. 181pp. 4¼ x 7¼. T441 Clothbound **$2.25**